CRITICAL ESSAYS ON JOHN KEATS

DE ALMEIDA, HERMIONE 1950-

Critical Essays on
John Keats

Critical Essays on
John Keats

Hermione de Almeida

G.K. Hall & Co.
An Imprint of Simon & Schuster Macmillan
NEW YORK

Prentice Hall International
ɔNDON · MEXICO CITY · NEW DELHI · SINGAPORE · SYDNEY · TORONTO

G.K. Hall & Co.
An Imprint of Simon & Schuster Macmillan
1633 Broadway
New York, New York 10019

Library of Congress Cataloging-in-Publication Data

De Almeida, Hermione, 1950–
    Critical essays on John Keats / Hermione de Almeida.
        p. cm.—(Critical essays on British literature)
    Includes bibliographical references.
    ISBN 0–8161–8851–3
    1. Keats, John, 1795–1821—Criticism and interpretation.
I. Title. II. Series.
PR4837.D38 1990
821′.7—dc20   89–71719
                                                           CIP

This publication is printed on permanent durable acid-free paper
MANUFACTURED IN THE UNITED STATES OF AMERICA

CRITICAL ESSAYS ON BRITISH LITERATURE

The Critical Essays on British Literature series provides a variety of approaches to both the classical writers of Britain and Ireland, and the best contemporary authors. Formats of the volumes in the series vary with the thematic designs of individual editors, and with the amount and nature of existing reviews, criticism, and scholarship. In general, the series represents the best in published criticism, augmented, where appropriate, by original essays written by recognized authorities. It is hoped that each volume will be unique in developing a new overall perspective on its particular subject.

Hermione de Almeida's collection consists of seventeen essays dating from 1965, with seven published during the last decade and seven more original studies written specifically for this volume. Together they represent a cross-section of the best in current American and British critical opinion on Keats.

Most of de Almeida's selections deal with larger aspects of Keats's poetry, philosophy, and source material. Several original essays present new historical evidence of major influences on the poet's works and include details of the social and gender biases of Keats's contemporaries that influenced the poet's early reception. The volume presents an original, informed overview of the state of the research and critical work being done today.

ZACK BOWEN

University of Miami

To George, Sr., and Billie Gilpin

CONTENTS

INTRODUCTION: Intellectual Keats   1
      Hermione de Almeida

"That Last Infirmity of Noble Mind": Keats and the
    Idea of Fame   11
      Aileen Ward

On Looking into Keats's Voyagers   28
      Carl Woodring

The "Epistle to John Hamilton Reynolds"   36
      Stuart M. Sperry

Endymion: "Pretty Paganism" and "Purgatory Blind"   47
      John Barnard

Keats and the Problem of Romance   68
      Robert Kern

Reading Keats's Plots   88
      Jack Stillinger

"Keats" [from *Inescapable Romance*]   103
      Patricia A. Parker

Keats the Humanist   129
      John Clubbe and Ernest J. Lovell, Jr.

Keats's Chemical Composition   143
      Donald C. Goellnicht

Keats and Blushing   157
      Christopher Ricks

The Silent Work of Imagination   183
      Leon Waldoff

Keats and Byron   206
      Beth Lau

"Keats" [from *Hazlitt: The Mind of a Critic*]   222
      David Bromwich

The Politics of Greek Religion   261
   Robert M. Ryan
Romantic Evolution: Fresh Perfection and Ebbing
  Process in Keats   279
   Hermione de Almeida
Noumenal Inferences: Keats as Metaphysician   292
   Alan Grob
Feminizing Keats   317
   Susan J. Wolfson

INDEX   357

INTRODUCTION

Intellectual Keats

"I think I shall be among the English Poets after my death," Keats writes to his brother, George, in October 1818. His comment, made in the wake of the reviewers' charged and hostile reception of *Endymion*, and after he had himself remarked that there was "no greater Sin after the 7 deadly than to flatter oneself into an idea of being a great Poet," was a modest statement of fact.[1] Literary history has more than justified this claim by the youngest and last-born Romantic poet whose productive poetic life spanned just three years between his twenty-first and twenty-fourth birthdays. Eminent among English poets and exemplary to poets since, Keats's "posthumous existence" among us (to borrow the dying poet's phrase for his last months) has endured since his death. The past three decades alone have produced three biographies of Keats, by Aileen Ward and Walter Jackson Bate in 1963, and Robert Gittings in 1968; three scholarly editions of the poetry, by Miriam Allott (1970), John Barnard (1973), and Jack Stillinger (1978); and at least three distinct generations of Keats scholars, from Bate to Stuart Sperry to Leon Waldoff in America, from John Bayley to Christopher Ricks to Barnard in England. All these are fair testament both to our commitment to Keats's interests and to his contemporaneity with our concerns. Students in search of the long and substantial tradition of scholarship on Keats need look no further than to Stillinger's engaging and thoroughly reliable bibliographical essay in Frank Jordan's *The English Romantic Poets: A Review of Research and Criticism* (1985), an essay commendable for its cheerful brevity—he reviews 595 books and articles in fifty-two pages; supplementary annual bibliographies can be found in the *Keats-Shelley Journal* and in the *MLA International Bibliography*.[2]

It may seem surprising that my selection of essays should propose to assert the intellectual life and philosophical tenor and currency of Keats. But in fact—and notwithstanding the best efforts of serious scholars such as those cited above—the poet must repeatedly be rescued from some of his "friends." These would include those contemporaries of Keats who alternately maligned the verse for po-

1

litical reasons and canonized the poet for emotional reasons; those nineteenth-century admirers who adopted Keats because of the poignant circumstances of his life as a sickly pet lamb for a sentimental Victorian farce; those late Victorian and early twentieth-century critics who found in the very accessibility of his verse sufficient image of a poet of little education and luxurious sensation; those Modernist, "aesthetic" critics who have appropriated the Victorians' judgment of Keats as a sensual poet who did not need to think and made of it an excuse for reading the poetry out of its context and in ignorance of what the poet knew; and those contemporary critics whose restrictive new history would liberate Keatsian criticism by containing the poet within his "Cockney" or "working-class" milieu so as to show how the biases of history (his, ours, theirs) are never sprung.[3]

Like the other great Romantic poets—and perhaps with greater urgency because of his firsthand knowledge of the charity hospital— Keats believed that the poet had to function out of an informed commitment to the welfare of the human community. His aspirations as a poet combined with his aspirations as a physician, and his scientific and practical knowledge of human nature learned in the wards and lecture-theaters of Guy's Hospital joined and enhanced those philosophical ideas on the function of art that he was to acquire as a poet. "Nothing is finer for the purposes of great productions, than a very gradual ripening of the intellectual powers," he told his brother in January 1818, and, in April 1818, he wrote to a friend that his "cavalier days" and idle versifying since leaving his surgeon's dressership at Guy's "are gone by": "I find that I can have no enjoyment in the World but continual drinking of Knowledge. . . . I have been hovering for some time between an exquisite sense of the luxurious and a love for Philosophy . . . [but, now,] I shall turn all my soul to the latter" the better to "follow Solomon's direction of 'get Wisdom—get understanding'." Committed from the start to "the idea of doing some good for the world," he saw this "ambition" of his intellect as something that could be fulfilled through a comprehending sympathy with human distress—in medicine, and in poetry as medicine: in "Sleep and Poetry" he had defined poetry as "a friend / To sooth the cares, and lift the thoughts of man" (255–56), and in *The Fall of Hyperion* he was to conceive of the poet in terms of a physician's duty to serve suffering "Humanity," "sure[ly] a poet is a sage; / A humanist, physician to all men" (1:189–90).[4] Licensed to practice general medicine by the Society of Apothecaries in 1816, aware in early 1818 that by his own estimate he was not yet a philosopher and poet ("but my flag is not unfurl'd . . . and to philosophise / I dare not yet," he wrote in the verse-epistle to Reynolds), Keats the poet between 1818 and 1820 came to see himself, ever increasingly, as a philosopher and humanist precisely because of the poetic ambitions and humanitarian aspirations of his intellect. When we read his poetry we must do likewise.

Students of Keats in the early 1960s were well served by two major collections of essays edited by Kenneth Muir (1959) and Walter Jackson Bate (1964); since that time, and with the possible exception of a casebook on the narrative poems and a brief and eclectic volume in the Chelsea House series, there have been no general collections of essays on Keats.[5] My edition is therefore cast as a collection of recently published work and studies-in-progress on Keats. Seven of the essays, by Jack Stillinger, Donald C. Goellnicht, Beth Lau, Robert M. Ryan, Alan Grob, Susan J. Wolfson, and myself, were written specifically for this volume, and I am grateful to these authors for their commitment to the collection. Seven more, by Aileen Ward, John Barnard, Robert Kern, Patricia A. Parker, John Clubbe and Ernest J. Lovell, Jr., Leon Waldoff, and David Bromwich, were published within the last ten years. In addition, I have included three essays, by Carl Woodring, Stuart M. Sperry, and Christopher Ricks, that are representative of important work done on Keats between 1965 and 1978; I regret that I could not include more essays from this period. In my selection for this volume I have deliberately eschewed "readings" of individual poems for general discussions of the poet; students in search of commentary on specific poems will nevertheless find it in the main text of several essays—early, short poems in Woodring and Sperry; *Endymion* in Barnard; the narrative poems in Kern, Stillinger, and Parker; the *Hyperion* fragments in Ryan and de Almeida; the odes in Bromwich and Grob.

Scholars are accustomed to measuring Keats, whether in his increasing manifestations of talent or in his growing maturity of mind, against the poet's own estimate of what he had accomplished within the terms of his declared purpose and according to a timetable of months, not years. Ward's essay on Keats and the idea of fame begins this collection with a discussion of the poet's largely unselfish vision of poetic greatness. She proposes Keats as one of the last heirs of the Renaissance idea of fame as altruistic goodness and nobility of mind and sees an "ethical imagination" and a concept of sympathetic genius operating behind Keats's resolve to be among the English poets.

When real genius is present, according to Romantic thinkers, it always manifests its existence early. Two early poems of Keats, the sonnet to Chapman's Homer and the impromptu verse-epistle to Reynolds, testify to the truth of this notion, for they exemplify the sudden manifestation of immense talent in a very young poet even as they provide an unusual glimpse of the quick maturation of his mind. Woodring's essay on the first of these poems mines the recesses of the sonnet for clues to Keats's wide range of reading and the intellectual ferment of the poet's mind during its composition; he shows how exploration becomes exultant discovery *in* the sonnet but also *for* the poet and *for* the reader of the poem, and he marks the kinship of all discoveries whether actual or imaginary. In the process of showing us how Keats read, wrote, and imagined in the sonnet on Chapman's Homer, Woodring also tells us how we might read, imagine, and, perhaps, write. Sperry's "The 'Epistle to John Hamilton Reynolds,' " a much favored chapter from his *Keats the Poet* (1973), discusses the generation of associative images in Keats's verse-epistle. By considering how these images are spawned simultaneously by Keats's re-creative viewing of a painting by Claude Lorrain called *The Enchanted Castle*, the poet's creative depression following the completion of *Endymion*, and his overweening need as a physician to use his imaginative verse to comfort an unhappy and sick friend, Sperry's essay tells us much about the ways in which Keats's mind operated *through* periods of creative darkness. The two early poems (and the two critics' inquiry into their origins) provide us with alternating perspectives of the "innumerable compositions" and "re-perceptions" that take place "between the intellect and its thousand materials" in a youthful and committed Romantic poet's mind.[6]

Barnard's discussion of the paganism and purgatory of *Endymion* continues my symposium on the intellectual Keats. He describes Keats's long and diffuse epic as a poem-in-process that places humanity and human love at its center and uses its portrayal of erotic emotions to remind us that all knowledge of beauty is tied to, and therefore binds us to, the earth. Barnard's thesis that *Endymion* is not a conventional romance but one driven by underlying and very real subversions is an important tonic to a sluggish critical tradition that has consistently underestimated the conceptual message and therefore the accomplishment of Keats's first long poem. Morris Dickstein's fine chapter in *Keats and His Poetry: A Study in Development* (1971) on the intellectual crisis and poetic change that took place in Keats between the completion of *Endymion* and the start of *Hyperion* (December 1817–September 1818) belongs here but, unfortunately, could not be included. The overarching subject of the poems of this period is what Keats called "the thinking principle," and Dickstein's perceptive reading focuses on those "pains of consciousness" felt and portrayed in verses like "In drear-nighted December," the sonnet on *King Lear*, and the lines inspired by the "cold beauty" of Robert Burns's country. Certainly, in these poems of the "change that has taken place in my intellect lately" (as Keats said in January 1818),[7] the poet confronts the difficulties of being a poet of romance and heir to Spenser in the drear-nighted days of a British winter; the poems born of such a winter of the mind, when the creative imagination resides in the disintegrated and frozen suspension of a "purgatory blind," allow us to evaluate the high personal cost to the artistic consciousness of the art that Keats would create so as to better minister to and integrate other human psyches.

"[Byron] describes what he sees—I describe what I imagine—Mine is the hardest task," Keats said in 1819.[8] Romance and the problems of writing romance in the era following the Battle of Waterloo are the subjects of the next three essays in the collection. The unforgivable truth of Stillinger's famous essay, "The Hoodwinking of Madeline: Skepticism in *The Eve of St. Agnes*" (1961), serves as a subtext for each of these three essays on Keats's narrative stance. Kern sees the poet of *The Eve of St. Agnes* as struggling with, instead of repudiating, romance, and he describes how Keats's manipulation of history, time, and the reader reveals tragic lessons learned from Shakespeare's art in *King Lear*. Parker's excerpted chapter on the poetics of Keats's verse-romances presents a larger view of the tradition since Spenser; she declares Keats to be at a turning point in the history of poetry, and her discussion of *The Fall of Hyperion* marks the ways in which his ambivalence in writing romance represents the historical schism in worldviews between the Renaissance and the Romantic era. Stillinger's "Reading Keats's Plots" is cast as a modest assay of the ways in which we might teach Keats's verse-narratives now that we have been fully apprised of their poet's skepticism; his essay is, in fact, an insightful and suggestive piece on genre traditions, our assumptions about what constitutes fiction or the protagonist of a fiction, and on our interpretive tendency to ignore what lies at surfaces before our eyes.

No student of Keats is well served if he or she does not have some firsthand encounter with the poet's letters. Clubbe and Lovell's wholesome assessment of Keats's accomplishment as a humanist describes the "unusual gentleness of Keats's strength of mind" through a substantial and sensitive evocation of the letters; they mark the humanistic underpinnings of the poet's "aesthetic" statements on "negative capability" and "disinterestedness of Mind," and extend both Ward's earlier discussion of the meaning of humanity in Keats and Lionel Trilling's 1955 definition of the poet's "geniality" of spirit.[9]

Keats, of course, learned much about serving humanity and about the pains of human existence during his clinical year at Guy's Hospital and, before that, in the Edmonton practice of the surgeon to whom he was apprenticed for five years. The three essays on chemistry, embarrassment, and the silent imagination that follow Clubbe and Lovell's contribution are all diverse attempts to explain aspects of Keats's actual and imaginative medicine. Goellnicht calls upon his considerable knowledge of medical—and specifically chemical—courses that the poet took at the Borough Hospitals' Medical School to address the meaning of composition for Keats. Ricks, in a whimsical chapter called "Keats and Blushing," uses early psychology texts and the literary practice of portraying embarrassment begun by Milton to describe what he calls Keats's "intimate" knowledge of "a physiology of the mind." Issues of blushing, Ricks says, can tell us a great deal not only about color, image, and sensations of the body in Keats's poetry, but also about the poet's personal diffidence and generous attunement to the feelings of others, what he meant when he described a "neutral intellect" of "no Identity" as ideal for a poet, and the larger meaning of self-consciousness in Romantic art. Waldoff's chapter, "The Silent Work of Imagination," is an intelligent and summary essay on the imagination and its workings as these must be understood by all students of Keats. His discussion of the unconscious dimension in imaginative and cognitive activity uses contemporary psychologies of the subconscious (and Freud's paper on "Mourning and Melancholia") to make original statements about Romantic creativity and the transformative power of Keats's particular kind of creative thinking.

Keats's creative response to contemporary ideas and issues (and personalities like Byron) as these reached him through his association with Leigh Hunt, Reynolds, William Hazlitt, and members of the London scientific community, forms the subject of the next four essays in the collection. Lau's "Keats and Byron" uses the poems and letters to make clear Keats's growing distinction from Byron: his attempts to fashion himself against Byron's popular image, his suspicion of Byron's aesthetic stance and counter-definition of the unegotistical "chamelion Poet," and his very real disagreement with Byron on the Romantic poet's intellectual status and philosophical needs. Bromwich's intelligent essay on Keats, from his intellectual biography of Hazlitt, addresses not only Hazlitt's influence on Keats and their parallel conceptions of artistic sympathy, but also the poet's extension of Hazlitt's ideas. Bromwich speculates, furthermore, on a possible symbiotic relationship between the two creative minds that are his subject. Ryan, in "The Politics of Greek Religion," also invokes real ideas to rescue Keats's intellectual life from "aesthetic" and "theoretical" suppositions of thoughtless poetry; he explains the central role of Greek mythology in Keats's philosophy in terms of religious politics in 1818–1819 and traces the humanitarian vision of *The Fall of Hyperion* to a conscious blending of Reynolds's Christianity with Thomas Paine's "austere radical faith." My essay, "Romantic Evolution: Fresh Perfection and Ebbing Process in Keats," places the poet squarely within the Romantic debate on life that was sparked by the public quarrel between John Abernethy and William Lawrence over the Hunterian "principle of life" (the quarrel began in 1814 and continued through the years of Keats's attendance at Guy's). I find evidence in poems like the "Ode to a Nightingale" and the *Hyperion* fragments of Keats's full knowledge and deliberate evocation of ideas on life and extinction from the new science of evolution that alternately terrified and exhilarated Romantic intellectuals during his lifetime.

"I by no means rank poetry or poets high in the scale of intellect," Byron opined in 1813.[10] This was not Keats's opinion, nor was it true of Keats. From the evidence presented by Bromwich, Ryan, and myself, if not from the cumulative stance of the rest of the essays in this collection, we can be certain that Keats could hold his own ground intellectually among the best contemporary minds and within the larger ferment of ideas in his age and that he was a philosopher by his own high requirements of himself. Two final essays, on Keats as metaphysician and on the critical tradition that has "feminized" the poet, complete this volume; they reiterate the continuing need to rescue the poet from too zealous critics and serve as important additions to our consideration of the poet's real ideas. Grob protests the rout of the metaphysical critics by the school of Stillinger; he sees a parallel advance in Keats's skeptical questionings and metaphysical speculations and uses Kant's perspective and tangible occasions of the nightingale's song, the Grecian urn's silent presence, and the poet's laugh, to assert the noumenal and visionary in Keats. Grob's commitment to the truth of his subject convinces even as it has the salutary effect of reminding us that Earl Wasserman was a great scholar and far above the fray (and fuzzy thinking) of his disciples. Wolfson's energetic essay, meanwhile, confronts all those critics—Victorians or modern recidivists—who would gender or ungender Keats according to their own biases of gender; her discussion of the "permeable boundary between masculine and feminine" that animates both the poet's sensibility and the reception of it by his readers is a significant counterperspective on a long and otherwise varied critical tradition.

Noumenal realms, happiness, embarrassment, melancholy, politics, religion, gender, laughter, skepticism, paganism, Christianity, evolution, immortality, misperceptions of sentiment, geography, medicine, astronomy, navigation, practical chemistry, blushing psychology, Kant, Hazlitt, Byron, Freud, John Hunter, the extinction of beauty, the irremissibility of pain, skeptical Moderns, foolishly fond Victorians, disassociated contemporary critics, and gendering readers of all hues— any survey of the subjects in this collection of essays will attest to the vigor and range of Keats's intellectual life and the vitality of his existence as a subject for intelligent dialogue. "[The] Minds of Mortals are so different and bent on such diverse Journeys that it may at first appear impossible for any common taste and fellowship to exist between two or three under these suppositions—It is however quite the contrary. . . . Man should not dispute or assert but whisper results to his neighbour, and thus by every germ of Spirit sucking the Sap from mould ethereal every human might become great, and Humanity instead of being a wide heath of Furze and Briars with here and there a remote Oak or Pine, would become a grand democracy of Forest Trees."[11] In an age of warring and self-destructive ideologies when it is considered unfashionable to speak of serving humanity, suspect to speak of democracy, embarrassing to place human love at the center of one's artistic inquiry, foolish to hold to a Renaissance ideal of character, and ridiculous to wish to be a philosopher and humanist when meaning has been dismantled, deconstructed, and banished from the earth, Keats has nevertheless survived by doing all these things. He has kept his humanizing place among the greatest English poets, and his values and ideas still confront us and endure with the best of his critics.

HERMIONE DE ALMEIDA

University of Miami

Notes

1. *The Letters of John Keats*, ed. Hyder Edward Rollins, 2 vols. (Cambridge, Mass.: Harvard University Press, 1958), 1:394, 143. See also 1:374, on the poet's belief that he is his own best critic: "My own domestic criticism has given me pain without comparison beyond what Blackwood or the [Edinburgh] Quarterly could possibly inflict. and also when I feel I am right, no external praise can give me such a glow as my own solitary reperception & ratification of what is fine."

2. *The English Romantics: A Review of Research and Criticism*, ed. Frank Jordan, 4th ed. (New York: Modern Language Association, 1985), 666–718; *Keats-Shelley Journal* (New York: Keats-Shelley Association of America, 1984–); *MLA International Bibliography of Books and Articles on the Modern Languages and Literatures* (New York: Modern Language Association, 1984–).

3. Many of these views (from 1816 through 1863) can be found in excerpt form in G. M. Matthews, *Keats: The Critical Heritage* (New York: Barnes and Noble, 1971); the Victorian perspective on Keats lingers at least through the period that produced Amy Lowell's excessively fond 1925 biography; I find the Modernist "aesthetic" readers of Keats, as well as the quasi-Marxist critics who would position Keats within his purported class origins and circumscribe his "plainspoken" poetry in the accents of liberation, to be the logical albeit unacknowledged progeny of the Victorian misperceptions of the poet.

4. *Letters*, 1:214, 271; see also 1:167, 387. I quote from Jack Stillinger's edition of the verse, *The Poems of John Keats* (Cambridge: Harvard University Press, 1978).

5. *John Keats: A Reassessment*, ed. Kenneth Muir (Liverpool: Liverpool University Press, 1959); *Keats: A Collection of Critical Essays*, ed. Walter Jackson Bate (New Jersey: Prentice Hall, 1964). I refer to John Spencer Hill's casebook, *Keats: The Narrative Poems* (London: Macmillan, 1983) and Harold Bloom's *John Keats* (New York: Chelsea House, 1985).

6. *Letters*, 1:264–65, 374.

7. *Letters*, 1:214.

8. *Letters*, 2:200.

9. Lionel Trilling, "The Poet as Hero: Keats in His Letters," in *The Opposing Self* (New York: Viking, 1955), 3–49.

10. *Byron's Letters and Journals*, ed. Leslie A. Marchand, 12 vols. (Cambridge: Harvard University Press, 1974–1982), 3:179.

11. *Letters*, 1:232.

"That Last Infirmity of Noble Mind": Keats and the Idea of Fame

Aileen Ward[*]

In October 1818 Keats wrote to Richard Woodhouse in some embarrassment to retract a rash statement he had made the month before, at the time the first blast against *Endymion* had appeared in *Blackwood's*. After thanking Woodhouse for his kind letter in response to the recent *Quarterly* attack, Keats reassured him that he had no real intention of giving up poetry, as he had announced in a despondent moment in September, then added, "The faint conception I have of poems to come brings the blood frequently into my forehead." Thanks to Christopher Ricks, we have become alert to all the fine shades of embarrassment in Keats's work—blushing and glowing and burning, warming and mantling and reddening. This admission to Woodhouse is a special case, however—an example not of blushing but of flushing, not with embarrassment but with honorable aspiration.[1] The embarrassment is rather on our side. We blush for Keats at the naïve confessions of ambition strewn through his early poems and letters—his artless longing for "posterity's award," "the laurel wreath on high suspended, / That is to crown our name when life is ended," or his fantasied quest for "Wings to find out an immortality." We catch an obsessive note in his recurrent mention of the pantheon of poets to which he aspires—"the laurell'd peers" he imagined looking down on him from the clouds of sunset. To Henry Stephens, his medical-school roommate in 1815–1816, Keats let it be known that poetry was "the only thing worthy the attention of superior minds"; poets were "the greatest men in the world," he informed Stephens, and to rank among them was "the chief object of his ambition." His "thirst for glory" became so extreme at this time that he reportedly told his brothers that if he did not succeed he would kill himself.[2] Even after the publication of his first volume of poems,

[*] Reprinted by permission of New York University Press from *The Evidence of the Imagination: Studies of Interactions Between Life and Art in English Romantic Literature*, edited by Donald H. Reiman, Michael C. Jaye, and Betty T. Bennett. ©1978 by New York University.

11

when success came to seem within his grasp, his ambition was not yet slaked. "How great a thing it is[to be a Poet]," he exclaimed to Hunt as he began writing *Endymion*, "how great things are to be gained by it,—What a thing to be in the mouth of Fame!" Somehow we feel these remarks must be explained away—perhaps as the brashness common to upwardly mobile young men of talent, or as the overassertions of unselfconfident adolescence, or, in more Keatsian terms, as the expressions of a very young man who will soon have the fine point taken off his soul. We prefer to recall his modesty, his realism, his irony: the Keats who, on hearing that he was to be invited to a literary party to celebrate Shakespeare's birthday, remarked "Shakespeare would stare to see me there"; the Keats who once suggested that his friends honor his memory by drinking a dozen of claret upon his tomb.

If young writers today think about being among the English poets after their death, they do not talk about it, much less write poems about it. Indeed the word "greatness" seems to have disappeared from the critical vocabulary in the last fifty years, ever since Eliot stated that the critic's proper task is "not to assign rank, but to discriminate quality." Yet our discomfort with the idea of greatness— to say nothing of the notion of immortality—may be a sign of loss as much as of gain: the dimming of that "habitual vision of greatness" which, Whitehead once said, is essential to education, perhaps even to civilization itself. Keats's unabashed resolve to "be among the greatest" may seem less of an embarrassment when viewed in the context of certain cultural assumptions with which we have lost touch. In his own time, or certainly within the century preceding it, such striving for fame would not be regarded ironically or defensively, as today, but as the necessary concomitant to any real achievement. The desire for the esteem of one's contemporaries, or what is now termed "approbativeness," was viewed by the Enlightenment as the driving force behind culture, even though rooted in human pride rather than reason. As Pope put it, "Virtue's ends from vanity can raise, / Which seeks no int'rest, no reward but praise."[3] From La Rochefoucauld, with his anatomizing of *l'amour propre* and *la gloire*, through Mandeville with his view of pride as the origin of virtue, to Immanuel Kant, who saw the desire for esteem as the instrument of man's moral evolution, the pursuit of individual glory was justified as socially valuable.[4] Indeed it was widely held in the later seventeenth and the eighteenth century that approbativeness was the only motive in social conduct—"ingeniously implanted in man by his Creator as a substitute for Reason and Virtue, which he does not possess," according to Sir Richard Blackmore, and thus "necessary for the good order of society and the progress of mankind."[5] The idea then modulated into the nineteenth-century novel with Stendhal and Balzac and their myth of the young man winning his way up the ladder of worldly power, to fade in our time into the debased lingo of "making it."

Throughout the eighteenth century, of course, this view of human motivation had its opponents, and the countervailing ideal of disinterestedness found one of its last and staunchest supporters in Keats's mentor William Hazlitt. With Hazlitt, if not before, the possibility of disinterested action became linked with the imagination as its ethical goal, thereby transforming the imagination from one of the faculties into "the great instrument of moral good," as Shelley described it in *The Defence of Poetry*. In his *Treatise on Morals* Shelley attempted to rescue the pursuit of glory from its supposed root in pride and to claim it for the cause of the disinterested imagination. Citing the examples of three legendary heroes of Roman history who endured torture and death for their city's sake, he insisted that even if they had sought posthumous fame they were not moved by considerations of "private interest": some of the greatest heroes, he pointed out, "have even defied infamy for the sake of good." "There is a great error in the world with respect to the selfishness of fame," Shelley continued. "It is certainly possible that a person should seek distinction as a medium of personal gratification. But the love of fame is frequently no more than a desire that the feelings of others should confirm, illustrate, and sympathize with our own. In this respect it is allied with all that draws us out of ourselves. It is the 'last infirmity of noble minds.' "[6]

The phrase from *Lycidas* leads us back to the point just before the notion of fame became embroiled in the controversy over the necessary interestedness of all human action. Milton, for all his humanistic faith in man's ethical nature, gave only qualified approval to the approbative impulse: "Fame is the spur that the clear spirit doth raise / That last infirmity of noble mind / To scorn delights, and live laborious days." When the desire for praise is uprooted from the "mortal soil" of this world and translated to "fame in heaven," it is fully justified; but in this life it remains a kind of honorable weakness. Yet in viewing it as an infirmity of the noble mind in particular, Milton looks back to an earlier tradition which more readily ascribed virtue to worldly fame, the Renaissance concept of the glory to which the poet may aspire: an idea derived from the Horatian assurance that the society whose values the poet proclaims will reward him with a fame more lasting than that of other men. Horace's boast that the greatest heroes of a nation are dependent on the poet to transmit their renown is a theme on which the Elizabethan poets were to play countless variations. In Shakespeare's Sonnets, for instance, it swells from the reassurance to his beloved that his beauty will never die—"So long as men can breathe, or eyes can see, / So long lives this, and this gives life to thee"—to the proud assertion *(Exegi monumentum aere perennis)* of his own immortality: "Not marble, nor the gilded monuments / Of princes, shall outlive this powerful rhyme." But this vision of poetic greatness includes more than the self-assurances of triumphant artistry: it rises to the belief, perhaps more Christian than classical,[7] but even more remote to us today, that the great poet is such not by his special skill or insight alone but by nobility of character as well. As Milton stated in the *Apology for Smectymnuus,* the man who hopes to write well of "laudable things" ought "himself to be a true poem." By this definition the great poet has a triple responsibility—not only to delight and to instruct but also to persuade, to move men to wise and noble action not merely by presenting just examples of characters for imitation but by manifesting justice in his own character, by being himself (as Milton said) "a pattern of the best and honorablest things."

For almost any young poet this view of greatness must raise it—as Keats wrote to Hunt in the spring of 1817—"monstrously beyond [his] seeming power of attainment": and poetry since Milton has been one long descent from such a level of aspiration. W. J. Bate has shown how acutely, among writers of his own time, Keats was aware of the burden of the past. Yet we might also recall that Keats—who seems from his letters to have done weight lifting as a form of exercise ("using dumb bells on a rainy day")—once described his study of philosophy as "trying myself at lifting mental weights." If the example of the past was a burden, it was also a challenge, and Keats may be counted fortunate as one of the last heirs of the Renaissance idea of greatness. From the start of his career, Keats veered back and forth between a sense of humility before true greatness—"a cowering under the wings of the great poets," as he once put it, or "awe at [his] own strange pretense" in daring to follow in their footsteps—and a confident squaring up to the example they set him. The writing of the four thousand lines of *Endymion* was one such test—"Did our great Poets ever write short Pieces?"—which he counted on to take him a certain number of paces "towards the Temple of Fame." At first his steps were "all uncertain": "The high Idea I have of poetical fame," he wrote to George Keats, "makes me think I see it towering too high above me." Yet the anxiety he felt at the start of this endeavor was not only generated by his attempt to measure himself against the greatest models but also partly assuaged by them. On the day he finally began writing *Endymion* he opened his copy of Spenser and found a good omen in the first lines his eyes lighted on:

> "The noble Heart that harbors vertuous thought,
>   And is with Child of glorious great intent,

Can never rest, until it forth have brought
Th' eternal Brood of Glory excellent—''

A few weeks later, his work had gone well enough that he let himself fancy Shakespeare as a good genius presiding over him, and he started a confident letter to Haydon telling him of his progress by invoking Shakespeare's own defense of "the pursuit of Honor":

Let Fame, which all hunt after in their Lives,
Live register'd upon our brazen tombs,
And so grace us in the disgrace of death:
When spite of cormorant devouring time
The endeavor of this present breath may buy
That Honor which shall bate his Scythe's keen edge
And make us heirs of all eternity.

Yet in setting "honor" as his "prime object" Keats was not engaging in a kind of Homeric *aristeia* or struggle to be first in the race. Rather he hoped only to "be among the greatest," "among the English poets": and from the start his longing for recognition was joined with a characteristically generous acknowledgment of the achievement of others. "The genius-loving heart" of the Epistle "To George Felton Mathew" spoke of the pleasures of their "brotherhood in song" and invoked their favorite poets in a spirit of "reverence." The memory of great men, Keats remarked several years later, is the only thing to which he will humble himself—along with "the Eternal Being [and] the Principle of Beauty." Throughout his early poems Keats's boyish hero-worship echoes in the recurrent roll calls of "great spirits," not only poets but political figures—from Brutus and Alfred to Kosciusko, from Homer to Wordsworth and Leigh Hunt. He prophesies the victory of Hunt's "immortal spirit" over the "wretched crew" of his jailers in the unsullied fame which he will enjoy long after their deaths. In a letter to Haydon of May 1817 he wrote that the thought of his friend's fame "will be a chief Pleasure to me all my life." Indeed fame is such a certain good to Keats at this stage that he will not begrudge it even to a man whose politics he deplores, the Duke of Wellington: "A Man ought to have the Fame he deserves." But even more characteristic is the twist he gives to the idea of fame in his first sonnet to Haydon of November 1816. The "glorious affection for the cause / Of stedfast genius" shown by the "unnumber'd souls" breathing out "their still applause" for Haydon bespeaks a "highmindedness" in the public which Keats himself applauds. Bestowing fame is thus seen as benefiting those who give it as well as those who receive it.

This easy confidence that a man not only should but indeed will have "the Fame he deserves" must have been somewhat shaken by the faint praise his *Poems* received in the spring and summer of 1817.

It was seriously jarred that autumn with the opening of *Blackwood's* campaign against the Cockney Poets, which threatened to lampoon Keats through his association with Hunt months after he had withdrawn from that discipleship. For the first time Keats became aware of the force of literary politics intervening in the ideal relationship between poet and audience in which he had previously trusted. Still more depressing was the onset of Tom's illness that winter, bearing with it the possibility of his own. As it suddenly appeared that the ambitious program he had announced in "Sleep and Poetry" might be cut short years before he fulfilled it, his dreams of fame sank "to nothingness." In such a mood, he told Bailey, he would "refuse a petrarcal coronation": and as Tom grew worse the very thought of fame began to seem "a crime." But it was his dissatisfaction with *Endymion* while revising it in the spring of 1818, and his anxiety over the treatment it seemed likely to receive from the Tory critics, that finally extinguished his hope for immediate recognition. Now the public came to seem "an Enemy": a "thousand jabberers about Pictures and Books" loomed up between him and the readers he had sought, the men "who look with a zealous eye to the honour of English literature." This mingled attitude of bitterness and scorn for "that most vulgar of all crowds, the literary" was to intensify in the months ahead, at times driving him into "a qui bono temper" when there seemed no point to "writing poems and hanging them up to be flyblown on the Reviewshambles," at other times stirring up a "Pride and Obstinacy" with which he felt he could "refuse the poisonous suffrage of a public" even while it was in his power to win it. "Just as much as I am hu[m]bled by the genius above my grasp," he wrote his publisher John Taylor in August 1819, "am I exalted and look with hate and contempt upon the literary world."

Some such disillusionment awaits every young writer, of course. Yet it is striking to note the loss of the sense of a literary community, in which the serious writer could identify more or less readily with his contemporary audience, in the forty or fifty years since Johnson had expressed his willingness to concur with the common reader and defer to the general suffrage. Keats's feeling of hate and contempt for the literary world, conjoined with his respect for his imagined readers, is a curious echo of Wordsworth's distinction between the Public and the People at the end of his 1815 *Essay Supplementary to the Preface* (which Keats undoubtedly had read). With the hostile reception of his own work at the back of his mind, Wordsworth assailed the local and transitory acclamation and "factitious influence" of the Public, which cries up the extravagant and superficial, in contrast to "that Vox Populi which the Deity inspires," the more lasting judgment of the People, through whose wisdom alone great poetry survives.[8] The *Essay* may also have opened Keats's eyes to the fact that both Shakespeare and Milton found far fewer readers in the seventeenth century than a score of far lesser poets. It soon became clear to Keats, once he surmounted his disappointment with *Endymion*, not only that fame in his own time was not the inevitable reward of the great poet but that it could be an irrelevance or worse—"a cloying treacle on the wings of independence." Partly this was the result of his growing independence and maturity of judgment: "Praise or blame," he wrote to Hessey after the worst of the reviews of *Endymion* had appeared, "has but a momentary effect on the man whose love of beauty in the abstract makes him a severe critic on his own works." And in some part this insight may have been sharpened by the experience of his pilgrimage to Burns's birthplace in the summer of 1818, where he was appalled by the cant and "flummery" commemorating a poet who had been miserably undervalued in his lifetime. "O smile among the shades," he exclaimed in his sonnet to Burns, "for this is fame!"

But the dissociation of the ideas of fame and greatness must also be related to Keats's ongoing effort to define the true nature of genius, a project to which he was apparently impelled by his first disillusionment with Haydon in the autumn of 1817. Keats had already sensed the factitiousness of Leigh Hunt's claim to poetic stature— perhaps as a result of Hunt's unfortunate insistence one evening that spring that they actually crown each other with laurel "after the fashion of the elder Bards" and write sonnets on their sensations. "There is no greater Sin after the 7 deadly," Keats wrote Haydon afterward, "than to flatter oneself into the idea of being a great Poet." But it was his growing insight into Haydon's own egotism that precipitated the distinction he made in November 1817 between Men of Genius, who "are great as certain ethereal Chemicals operating on the Mass of neutral intellect—[but] have not any individuality, any determined Character," and Men of Power, who "have a proper self." This distinction—an interesting anticipation of Hazlitt's characterization of Shakespeare in his *Lectures on the English Poets*—was to generate Keats's contrast between Shakespeare and Coleridge on which he based his definition of Negative Capability in December 1817; it was then to be elaborated in his later description to Woodhouse of the poetical character ("that sort of which, if I am any thing, I am a Member") as "every thing and nothing," having "no character," "no self" of its own, but "continually infor[ming] and filling some other Body"—in contrast to "the wordsworthian or egotistical sublime, which is a thing per se and stands alone." Wordsworth as well as Haydon, Keats had discovered in the interim, was given to displays of power, imposing his "proper self" not only on his audience but on his creations, "bullying" his reader and "peacocking" over his speculations till he had stamped them with his own image "in a false coinage." But true poetry—Shakespeare's Sonnets, for instance—is "unobtrusive" in its greatness: it enters the reader's soul and startles it "not with itself but with its subject," as the true poet analogously disappears into the creatures of his imagination. Hazlitt's description of Shakespeare in his February 1818 lecture as "nothing in himself, but . . . all that others partly were, or could become" touched a chord that echoed in Keats's letters for months afterward; he must also have been struck by Hazlitt's statement, in the same lecture, that Shakespeare "had no love of fame." Thus the "humility and capability of submission," the ability to "annul self" in order to take part in the existence of others which Keats was beginning to identify as the source of his own poetic strength, was increasingly linked in his mind with the abjuration of fame. His valediction was announced in two sonnets "On Fame" in April 1819, where he describes Fame as a wayward girl to be repaid "scorn for scorn," or as a ripe plum fingering its own misty bloom; a temptation to the poet to "rob his fair name of its maidenhood" or, still worse, to "spoil his salvation for a fierce miscreed."

So Keats came to realize that to aim at immediate recognition from the public was to lose all chance "to be among the greatest," and that the true poet must learn to endure uncertainty and neglect, even ridicule, in his lifetime. The vision of the "godlike hardship" of great art that had overcome him on first seeing the Elgin Marbles in March 1817 grew in his mind from the "turmoil and anxiety" that must accompany any great plan brought to its conclusion—as he learned in working on *Endymion*—to "the dark passages" which the great poet must explore as the price of his insight into the human condition. So his view of Shakespeare—as always his touchstone— changed gradually from the poet living in gusto, delighting equally in Iago and Imogen, to the "miserable and mighty Poet of the human Heart," who had been "trampled aside into the bye paths of life and seen the festerings of Society." "The english have produced the finest writers in the world," he explained to Mary-Ann Jeffery[9] in June 1819, because "the English world has ill-treated them during their lives and foster'd them after their deaths." Some such understanding of the cost of ultimate recognition—as well as the calm assurance that *Hyperion*, which he had recently begun, would win it—was in his mind in October 1818 when he dismissed the *Quarterly*'s devastating review of *Endymion* as "a mere matter of the moment" and added, "I think I shall be among the English Poets after my death."

This relinquishment of immediate fame for ultimate immortality may appear to be the final transformation of Keats's early ambition, one that links him firmly with those "heirs of all eternity" who had given him heart at the outset of his career. Keats held to the hope of writing a work that would make his friends proud of his memory and (in Fanny Brawne's words) "rescue his name from the obloquy heaped upon it," till the last despairing months of his illness.[10] Still this longing for ultimate renown betrays the approbative impulse. It is at best the secular equivalent of Milton's "fame in heaven," analogous to the secular scheme of salvation through soul-making: not a vindication of his work by the ultimate Critic, but admission into the ranks of "the laurell'd peers" Keats had dreamed of at the start of his career. Although "the living pleasures of the bard" he envisaged in the Epistle "To My Brother George" had proved an illusion, his faith in "posterity's award" sustained him till almost the end. Yet at the same time there are hints scattered through his poems and letters of 1818 and 1819 that Keats was working toward a more profound conception of poetic greatness uniquely his own, one going beyond both Shakespeare and Milton, transcending personal glory in the quest of disinterested achievement. This is not to imply that he reached any final "resting place and seeming sure point" in his thinking on the subject, a clear-cut synthesis of previous antinomies. With his distrust of "consequitive reasoning," his belief that the mind should be a thoroughfare for all ideas, Keats resists being boxed into a neat dialectical progression. Nevertheless, we can trace in his speculations on the nature of greatness a gradual shift of attention away from the poet himself to the poem, or to society at large, or (in a crucial narrowing of focus) to the reader.

Keats's first reaction to the *Quarterly*'s attack on *Endymion* was to withdraw—like Shakespeare's snail shrinking back "into his shelly cave with pain"—into a kind of aesthetic isolation, in which the creation of the poem itself becomes the sole locus of value. This state of "solitary indifference to applause even from the finest spirits" was the most constructive defense he could mount against criticism: in this state, as he wrote Woodhouse in October 1818, he felt assured he would continue to write "from the mere yearning and fondness I have for the Beautiful even if my night's labours should be burnt every morning and no eye ever shine upon them." Such total self-sufficiency strikes a new (and, as it turned out, temporary) note in Keats's poetic, though dedication to the principle of beauty is of course a recurrent theme. The previous summer, his first response to the English Lakes had been a resolve that now more than ever his writing would endeavor "to add a mite to that mass of beauty which is harvested from these grand materials, by the finest spirits, and put into etherial existence for the relish of one's fellows." A similar sense of fellowship with his audience in the self-justifying creation of beauty appears in the ode "To Maia," composed the previous month, in which in effect he put behind him the disappointment and apprehension with which he had sent *Endymion* off to the press. Those Greek bards who died content, "Leaving great verse unto a little clan," would, he hoped, teach him their contentment to be "Rich in the simple worship of a day." But in the autumn of 1818, as his imagined audience narrowed from "few ears" to "no eyes," he found a sublimity in solitude itself: as his imagination strengthened, he wrote George, he felt he lived "not in this world alone but in a thousand worlds." Or, as he put it to Reynolds in August 1819, "The Soul is a world of itself and has enough to do in its own home." Yet the idea of "great verse" as an end in itself, of beauty as a self-sufficient good, raised an almost immediate doubt of its own validity in Keats's mind. This ranged from the mild scepticism he expressed to Bailey in March 1818 of thinking poetry "a mere Jack a lanthern to amuse whoever may chance to be struck with its brilliance," to his scathing self-indictment in a letter to Haydon a year and a half later: "I have done nothing—except for the amusement of a few people who refine upon their feelings till anything in the ununderstandable way will go down with them." The all-consuming dedication to poetry of the previous extraordinarily productive summer—"Poetry is all I care for, all I live for"—came to seem "an idle-minded, vicious way of life" in the fall of 1819.

It is not simply that what Lionel Trilling once described as the "genial" side of Keats's nature could not long be satisfied with such solitude, however creative. There was a deeper demand to be met, one reaching to the bedrock of Keats's character: the need to be of service to others, if not through art then through action of some kind. This pervasive impulse appears as early as his Epistle "To My Brother George," in which he suggests that by renouncing his "mad ambition" in poetry—presumably to continue in his medical career— he would be "Happier, and dearer to society." A year and a half later, at the height of his admiration for Haydon and Wordsworth, Keats could condemn it as a kind of vanity in himself to speak of works of genius as "the first things in the world." Rather, he insisted, the "probity and disinterestedness" with which he still credited his friend Bailey held "the tip top of any spiritual honors"—just as, in the summer of 1819, he qualified his extravagant admiration for *Paradise Lost* by stating that fine writing took second place to fine doing as "the top thing in the world." Pushed to the choice, he wished to be praised "not for verses, but for conduct." Part of his dissatisfaction with *Endymion* in the spring of 1818, we can surmise, sprang from the reawakening of the motive toward disinterested service to others in nursing Tom through the early stages of his illness. It is at this point that the theme of what Keats repeatedly called "ambition" begins to be sounded in his work: an ambition very different from his earlier preoccupation with literary fame. "I find there is no worthy pursuit but the idea of doing some good for the world," he wrote Taylor, a statement echoed the following autumn in his letter to Woodhouse: "I am ambitious of doing the world some good." This ambition was never clearly defined except as an alternative to poetry: sometimes it seems to have been writing on philosophical or political topics—"the road lies through application study and thought"; sometimes, it appears, serving actively in the continuing struggle for freedom after Waterloo. Keats remarked jokingly to Reynolds in the spring of 1818 that he would "jump down Aetna for any great Public good"; more soberly he spoke to Bailey of "placing my ultimate in the glory of dying for a great human purpose."

We catch the note here of Keats's earlier acclamation of the martyrs for human freedom such as Sidney, Russell, and Vane; but the exemplar he had clearly in mind at this time was Milton—"an active friend to Man all his Life"—who for over a year was to replace Shakespeare as his chief model for emulation. Keats had already begun his close study of *Paradise Lost* in preparation for *Hyperion*, and was apparently reading Milton's "delectable prose," as he iron-ically described it to James Rice—impelled, perhaps, by Hazlitt's quotation in his February lecture of a long and eloquent passage from *The Reason of Church Government*. Milton's ambition to prove himself "anything worth to [his] country" finds an echo in Keats's mention, in the summer of 1818, of "the glory of making by any means a country happier." Certainly there is a strong sense of iden-tification with Milton in one of the notes Keats penned into his copy of *Paradise Lost* at about this time: that Milton would have been content in cultivating his "exquisite passion for poetical Luxury . . . if he could, so doing, have preserved his self-respect and feel of duty performed." In the performance of that duty Milton had interrupted his career in poetry to serve as Cromwell's Latin Secretary—perhaps an example of what Keats had in mind when he remarked, in com-paring Milton and Wordsworth, that "a mighty providence subdues the mightiest minds to the service of the time being." And perhaps the thought of Milton was also in Keats's mind when in September 1819 he announced his own intention of giving up poetry to "write on the liberal side of the question." This project soon proved abortive, yet it was not uncharacteristic: Keats had evidently entertained at least a passing thought some months before of joining Lord Cochrane's expedition to South America to fight for Chilean independence.[11] It is also characteristic that Keats could see the temptation to vanity in such heroics. "There are many Madmen," he remarked in his October 1818 journal to George, "who would like to be beheaded on tower Hill merely for the sake of eclat, . . . but there are none prepared to suffer in obscurity for their Country." The quest of a truly dis-interested "human purpose" remained elusive—"the work of maturer years," as he described it to Woodhouse at this time: in the interval he would "assay to reach to as high a summit in Poetry as the nerve bestowed upon me will suffer." The most enviable happiness, he thought, would be to fuse these impulses, "the yearning Passion I have for the beautiful, connected and made one with the ambition of my intellect."

This was also the need to bring into focus his two conceptions of the raison d'être of poetry, to work out in his mind what "great human purpose" could be served by the poet in his specific function— not so much as a man speaking to men within their shared social context, in "the service of the time being," but more particularly as poet speaking to reader across boundaries of time and space. Milton had been an active friend to man all his life, Keats wrote to Rice, but also "since his death": *Paradise Lost* might stand as the supreme example of what Keats called "the Benefit done by great Works to the 'Spirit and pulse of good' by their mere passive existence." Not a great name, then, but an enduring influence is what the poet should hope to achieve. The nature of the good to be done through "great Works" is suggested by the animizing imagery in which Keats speaks not only of the poet but of the poem, the work of art, as "a friend to man"—one "to soothe the cares and lift the thoughts of man," as he put it in "Sleep and Poetry." The poem is thus no mere artifact, "a thing of beauty," but possesses a kind of human identity, is indeed a "soul" which the dead poet leaves behind on earth. This idea of the poem as a living and speaking presence articulates the possibility of that "direct communication of spirit" which is the closest Keats could come to a belief in "immortality of some nature or other." So, after Tom's death, he suggested to George in America that they each read a passage of Shakespeare every Sunday at ten o'clock and thus "be as near each other as blind bodies can be in the same room." In the ode on "the double immortality of poets" which he wrote at this time, Keats declares that the poets' "earth-born souls still speak / To mortals of their little week," and thus may "teach us every day / Wisdom though fled far away." Even the silent form of the Grecian urn, by a more complicated process of stirring up questions within the viewer and "teasing" him into an answer, can "say" a message "to the spirit."

Yet Keats was rightly distrustful of poetry "with a palpable design upon us," which "if we do not agree, seems to put its hand in its breeches pocket": and the manner in which the poem teaches was crucial. In "Sleep and Poetry" he resolved not to "insult" the spirit of his reader by telling him "what he sees from native merit." Just as "Man should not dispute or assert but whisper results to his neighbor," the poem with a similar trust and tact should provide a series of "ethereal finger-pointings" for the reader by which he may be led to create within his own mind the imaginative experience which the poem is in essence. As Keats wrote Taylor in February

1818, poetry "should strike the Reader as a wording of his own highest thoughts, and appear almost a Remembrance." Poetry is thus no one-way process running from poet to reader but a transaction, in which the poet in Socratic fashion calls forth some poetic potential within the reader himself. We may count Keats fortunate, among other things, in the progressive schooling he received: at least the Clarkes' most famous pupil took with him an idea of education as a drawing out of knowledge, not a flogging in. "Many have original Minds who do not think it," he wrote Reynolds in his beautiful letter of 19 February 1818; and poetry should foster this originality in the manner suggested by his image of an old man and a child talking together as they walked, with "the old Man led on his Path, and the child left thinking." The metaphorical density of Keats's letters, which often requires as much imaginative activity on the reader's part as that of his poems, may be viewed as another expression of the requirement that the reader collaborate in the poetic process: so Keats concluded another letter to Reynolds, "If you think for five minutes after having read this you will find it a long letter." Thus the reader of the great poet who seeks to "understand [him] to his depths," as Keats did Shakespeare, will in a kind of reflexive action enter into the soul of the poet and be rewarded with a sense of communion with him, as Keats was with Shakespeare his Presider.

The "self-annulling" character of the poet as teacher, or of poetry which startles the reader "not with itself but with its subject," is implicit in the catalytic image of his earlier definition of Men of Genius as "certain ethereal Chemicals operating on the Mass of neutral intellect": in this view the poet transforms his audience while remaining invisible, "nothing in himself" as Hazlitt said. The nature of this transformation is suggested more clearly, however, in another strain of imagery recurrent in Keats's writing, in which he speaks of the poet not as remaining catalytically unchanged in the process but as ingested and assimilated by his readers as they draw nourishment from his work. In an early sonnet he himself describes his favorite poets as "the food / Of my delighted fancy," and in April 1818 he wrote Reynolds of his longing "to feast upon old Homer as we have upon Shakespeare, and as I have lately upon Milton." That this ingestive imagery was no dead metaphor appears from the sonnet on "The Human Seasons" (first version), where in the summer of his intellect man is said to ". . . chew the honied cud of fair spring thoughts / Till, in his Soul dissolv'd, they come to be / Part of himself." This ruminative process which is the essence of ideal reading is described at length in the February 19th letter to Reynolds. "A certain Page of full Poesy or distilled Prose" becomes the starting post for the reader's own voyage of conception; like the spider filling the air "with a beautiful circuiting," the reader "spins from his own inwards his own airy Citadel" of thought, tipping his web on a "few points" of the page before him. This "dissolving" of the poem in the imagination of the reader is no irreverence to the writer, Keats insists, but rather a demonstration of that "Benefit done by great Works . . . by their mere passive existence": for thus "by every germ of Spirit sucking the Sap from mould ethereal every human might become great, and Humanity instead of being a wide heath of Furse and Briars with here and there a remote Oak or Pine, would become a grand democracy of Forest Trees." In this dazzling fusion of images of spiritual nutrition and spiritual politics Keats suggests the vitally reciprocal relationship not only between the poet and his reader, but also between the poet and the tradition he is nourished by and helps in turn to create. The ideal community of the mind is a great ecosystem in which each organism lends vitality to all the others and eventually to the soil from which they all spring. And in the democratic emphasis of this image Keats strikes out his most characteristic definition of great poetry: by liberating the imaginative capacity in every man it acts to make every human great, making him as it were "more of an artist."

This definition, framed in a rare moment of creative calm and self-possession in February 1818, seems to have weathered the vicissitudes of uncertainty and self-dissatisfaction of the following year and a half to emerge as a dominant motive in Keats's last work. *The Fall of Hyperion* explores, among other things, the nature of the imaginative community between the poet and the ordinary man. For this theme to emerge, however, something was required to bridge the abyss which had opened up between Keats and his imagined readers in the latter part of 1818, some recovery of his earlier faith in his audience—not in the Public but in the countervailing force of the People, or what Keats had called his "fellows." The events of the summer and fall of 1819—the Manchester Massacre and Henry Hunt's triumphal entry into London in September, which Keats witnessed—seem to have effected this change. Writing to George in mid-September about "the present struggle in England of the people" against Government repression, he stated, "This is no contest between whig and tory—but between right and wrong." Evidently it was this resurgence of political concern that precipitated Keats's brief resolve to "write on the liberal side of the question"; more than this, the sight of thirty thousand people lining the London streets to welcome Henry Hunt revived his earlier idea of the "unnumber'd souls" ennobled by their applause of great art. "I am certain any thing really fine will in these days be felt," Keats wrote to Haydon a few weeks later. "I have no doubt that if I had written Othello I should have been cheered by as good a Mob as Hunt." In such a mood of renewed faith in the people he began recasting his epic of *Hyperion* as a dream-vision.[12]

The central theme of the new version is the transformation of the poet from mere dreamer to a "sage" and "humanist"—like "the human friend Philosopher." "Humanize" (II.2) may be taken as a key term for the poet's development from dreamy self-absorption to full awareness of "the giant agony of the world," in which he may join those "slaves to poor humanity" who "labour for mortal good." While the first version showed the youthful Apollo transformed into a god of poetry by a sudden access of divine power, *The Fall of Hyperion* portrays a much more protracted process, one that links the poet with his fellow mortals in all the pain and uncertainty of human growth. The induction, however ambiguous it may be on the precise status, ethical or metaphysical, of dreams, asserts unequivocally the universality of the dreaming faculty, of the gift of imagination itself. The visionary capacity is shared by "every man whose soul is not a clod"; the fully humanized poet, though set apart from other men by his gift of language, achieves the stature of greatness as the result not of a unique identity or special insight but of his ability to share "the miseries of the world," to take part in all other human existence. The manner in which this imaginative participation may work "for mortal good" is suggested by the climactic definition of the poet as "physician to all men." Bearing the freight of all Keats's early dedication to a medical career and the never-quite-resolved guilt he felt at giving it up, this image conveys the selfless concern of the being who has learned to confront human suffering in its fullest extent and, moved but not disabled by it, act somehow to ease it. This quality of interested disinterestedness is most memorably imaged in the gaze of Moneta, Keats's symbol of the superhuman consciousness that could sustain, as the merely mortal poet could not, the awareness of human history as the totality of human pain. Looking down from immense perspectives of time on the human drama, her "planetary eyes" (unblinking as a star's) filled with tears, Moneta provides an image of seeing "as a god sees" to the poet striving for insight into the human condition. To see in this fashion is not only to achieve a kind of immortality of the imagination in this life, as the poet moves beyond the limits of his own time and place into "a thousand worlds," but also to live on after death as an embodiment of the racial memory, the teller of those truths which other men sense without being able to speak them but will not willingly let die. It is significant that the act by which the dreamer-poet of *The Fall of Hyperion* is transported from the isolated garden of sensuous delight to the august Temple of Saturn with all its wreckage of human history, is a pledge which he drinks to "all the mortals of the world, / And all the dead whose names are in our lips": "that full draught," he tells us, was "parent of my theme." By recognizing his kinship with every man who has ever lived on earth, great or forgotten, by learning to share each man's dreams and help him confront his anguish, the poet is at last "fitted for verses fit to live" and becomes a sage and humanist, a friend to man.

So Keats conveys his final idea of great poetry as encompassing the awareness of all past experience standing behind and giving meaning to the present, and of all living beings in their struggle to make their souls within this world of painful circumstance. It was an insight that took on meaning only as Keats himself developed and the boundaries of his own imaginative experience widened. But not only did his growing apprehension of human experience transform his own poetry and his insight into the nature of poetry itself; his developing notion of greatness in poetry and what it demanded of the poet shaped his own selfhood. Few things are more characteristic of Keats than his attempt to sum up the meaning of his life in the face of the blank future that confronted him at the beginning of his last illness in February 1820. "I must make myself as good a Philosopher as possible," he wrote Fanny Brawne. " 'If I should die,' said I to myself, 'I have left no immortal work behind me—nothing to make my friends proud of my memory—but I have lov'd the principle of beauty in all things, and if I had had time I would have made myself remember'd.' Thoughts like these," he added, "came very feebly whilst I was in health and every pulse beat for you— now you divide with this (may *I* say it?) 'last infirmity of noble minds' all my reflections." It is a touching parenthesis, that "May *I* say it?" The thought of the great name which he had struggled to win and finally (as he now believed) had failed to attain, returned with the remembrance of Milton and his struggle in *Lycidas* to surmount the temptation of worldly fame. The irony with which Milton had admitted to "that last infirmity" spurred Keats to his last and finest *aristeia*, in which he disclaimed comparison with Milton's greatness even as he vied with him in self-annulling irony. It is a nobility of mind such as Keats believed the great poet could teach, and a final proof—if we need one—of the double immortality of poets.

Notes

1. Ricks mentions this passage on page 162 of *Keats and Embarrassment* (Oxford: Clarendon Press, 1974) as a manifestation of "creativity," an example of the connection Keats sensed between physiological and artistic creation—a connection made explicit by William Howitt in his remark (in 1847) on Keats's "vivid orgasm of the intellect" (in *Keats: The Critical Heritage*, ed. G. M. Matthews [New York: Barnes & Noble, 1971], p. 311; quoted by Ricks, p. 160). But the tone of the statement to Woodhouse

is more aggressive and emulative than erotic—like "the burning and the strife" which left Keats's forehead "hot and flushed" on seeing a lock of Milton's hair.

2. *The Diary of Benjamin Robert Haydon,* ed. Willard Bissell Pope (Cambridge: Harvard University Press, 1960), II, 107. The phrase "athirst for glory" occurs in the sonnet on "The Floure and the Leafe," 1. 11.

3. *Essay on Man,* II, 245-46.

4. See A. O. Lovejoy, *Reflections on Human Nature* (Baltimore: Johns Hopkins University Press, 1961), Lecture IV: "Approbativeness as the Universal, Distinctive, and Dominant Passion of Man."

5. *An Essay upon False Vertue* (Dublin, 1716), p. 22; quoted by Lovejoy, p. 164.

6. *The Complete Works of Percy Bysshe Shelley,* ed. Roger Ingpen and Walter E. Peck (London: Ernest Benn, 1926-1930), VII, 76.

7. It originates, however, in Plato (*Republic,* iii. 400) and was echoed by Strabo: cf. M. H. Abrams, *The Mirror and the Lamp* (New York: Oxford University Press, 1958), p. 229.

8. *Poetical Works,* ed. Thomas Hutchinson, rev. Ernest de Selincourt (London: Oxford University Press, 1936), p. 953. Cf. also Hazlitt's remarks in his lecture "On the Living Poets" (which Keats heard on 3 March 1818): "Fame is the recompense not of the living, but of the dead. . . . Those minds which are the most entitled to expect it, can best put up with the postponement of their claims to lasting fame" (*Works,* ed. A. R. Waller and Arnold Glover [London: J. M. Dent, 1906], V, 143-144.

9. So Robert Gittings corrects the identification of the recipient of Keats's letter of 9 June 1819 in his edition of *Letters of John Keats* (London: Oxford University Press, 1970), p. 402, n. 5.

10. As Donald Reiman has suggested, it is both ironic and touching that the work which, more than any other, was to keep Keats's name alive for the first quarter-century after his death was Shelley's *Adonais,* and that this tribute was based on an idea of the poet's immortality very close to Keats's. This is not just a matter of verbal coincidence, such as Shelley's description of Keats's fame as "a light unto eternity" (st. 1) echoing the phrase "a light unto posterity" in Keats's letter to Hunt of May 1817. Shelley's conception of "the thorny road" which the poet must tread "through toil and hate, to Fame's serene abode" (st. 5) and, still more, of the eclipse of the poet's reputation by lesser lights during his lifetime, to be followed by his emergence among "the immortal stars" after his death (st. 29,44), is strikingly similar to Keats's insight into the cost of true achievement and of the difference between immediate and ultimate recognition.

11. Cf. the cryptic statement by an anonymous correspondent ("Y") in *The Morning Chronicle* of 27 July 1821 that Keats once intended to go to South America and "write a Poem on Liberty" (quoted by M. B. Forman, ed., *The Letters of John Keats* [London: Oxford University Press, 1952], p. 488 n.); also Keats's own remark in a letter to Dilke that he had two choices before him—"South America or Surgeon to an Indiaman" *(loc. cit.).* The date of Keats's letter is uncertain: Forman assigns it to May 1820, while Rollins less convincingly conjectures June 1819 (*The Letters of John Keats,* ed. H. E. Rollins [Cambridge: Harvard University Press, 1958], II, 114). The correspondent in *The Morning Chronicle* has been identified by Leonidas M. Jones as Keats's school friend Edward Holmes, and the conversation which Holmes records in his letter dated early in September 1820, when Holmes paid a visit to Keats just before he left for Italy ("Edward Holmes and Keats," *Keats-Shelley Journal,* 23 [1974], 119-128). Jones prints "Y's" letter in full and discusses it in detail; he dismisses the reference to South America, however, as "a sort of conventional daydream of adventurous escape" out of *Robinson Crusoe,* concocted by Keats to amuse his old school friend (p. 122). But contemporary readers of *The Morning Chronicle* would immediately

connect the reference to South America and the cause of freedom with the daring and successful naval campaign in the Chilean War of Independence organized and led by Lord Cochrane from 1818 to 1821. On Thomas Cochrane, tenth Earl of Dundonald—a hero of the Napoleonic War, radical M. P. from Westminster, later commander of the Brazilian and the Greek fleets in their Wars of Independence, and leader of the movement for reforming the British Navy—see *Dictionary of National Biography*. By 1821 Cochrane's name had become a byword for courageous and decisive action—as in Byron's remark in a letter to John Murray castigating Bowles for abusing Hobhouse: "I will cut him out, as Cochrane did the Esmeralda" (*Letters and Journals of Lord Byron*, ed. R.E. Prothero [London: John Murray, 1922], V, 299). The *Esmeralda* was a Spanish frigate destroyed by Cochrane in a raid on Callao on 5 November 1820.

12. Leonidas M. Jones has recently challenged the traditional dating of *The Fall of Hyperion*, assigning the first 326 lines to September and October of 1818 ("The Dating of the Two *Hyperions*," *Studies in Bibliography*, 30 [1977], 120–135). There is not room here to reply to Professor Jones's article, which I hope to do in another place. I am still convinced that a careful examination of all the evidence will assign *The Fall of Hyperion* neither to the fall of 1818 nor to the summer of 1819 (as in the three recent biographies of Bate, Bush, and Gittings), but to September through November or December 1819 (as Brown indicated: cf. *The Keats Circle*, ed. H. E. Rollins [Cambridge: Harvard University Press, 1948], II, 72) and that the *Hyperion* which Keats told Reynolds he had given up on 21 September 1819 (the same day he wrote Woodhouse quoting with evident satisfaction three passages from *The Fall* as though they were new), was in fact the first *Hyperion*. See my *John Keats: The Making of a Poet* (New York: The Viking Press, 1963), p. 433, n. 3 and p. 434, n. 15 for a summary of the evidence on this question; also pp. 313–314, 325–328, 338–341. To the reasons there given for this dating might be added the well-known fact of Keats's "unsteady & vagarish disposition"—"a creature of fits and starts," as Hessey called him (Edmund Blunden, *Keats's Publisher: A Memoir of John Taylor* [London: Jonathan Cape, 1936], p. 56). Keats may have silently changed his mind a few weeks later about giving up *Hyperion* (if in this remark he meant to indicate the revised version), just as he silently abandoned the journalism project. The record of the letters, we need constantly to remind ourselves, is incomplete.

On Looking into Keats's Voyagers

Carl Woodring[*]

Few readers, if any, will doubt that the finest of Keats's sonnets in the Petrarchan form is "On First Looking into Chapman's Homer." Among extollers of this early work, praise has usually been given to the clarity and grace of the division between octave and sestet. After the precursory theme of exploration in the first eight lines there follows "as naturally as the Leaves to a tree," in the last six lines, the congruent theme of discovery. On the value of this division and its harmonious resolution, critics have generally agreed. But it has not been established that the horizontal division has a counterpart

[*] Reprinted from *Keats-Shelley Journal* 14 (1965): 15–22. Reprinted by permission of the Keats-Shelley Association of America, Inc.

of equal clarity in the vertical division between the professed subject (the "tenor") and the instrument of expression (the "vehicle"). Students of the poem continue to identify the "many western islands" as the isles of Greece. Because this identification cannot result when the structure of the poem is understood, the following paragraphs are presented as an attempt to describe explicitly the vertical division between the announced subject of voyaging among books and its primary metaphor of voyaging in the Atlantic. Such a description leads to other discoveries about the poem.

The vehicle of exploration in the western hemisphere is not delayed until the last four lines bring in their confusion of Cortez with Balboa. Even as it opens, the sonnet follows those who followed Columbus:

> Much have I travell'd in the realms of gold,
> And many goodly states and kingdoms seen;
> Round many western islands have I been
> Which °°°°° in fealty to °°°°° hold.

Except for the two words withheld, *bards* and *Apollo*, the language denotes travel westward after 1492. The persona half-assumed—more precisely, the persona metaphorically imagined—is a seaman who has gone on voyages of exploration in the New World. He has sailed extensively in such areas as the Western Islands (that is, the Azores), the West Indies, and whatever other islands a layman may believe to exist at some distance from England on a voyage to the Americas. Readers need not ultimately confine the "goodly states and kingdoms" to the Atlantic: the procedure of the sonnet is to confine the experience of the speaker, ultimately, in no way at all. We begin and end, nonetheless, in the New World. The fourth line is prepared for only by the title and by an ambiguous phrase in the first line, "the realms of gold." From the title we immediately take these realms as in one sense regions occupied by poets of golden tongue. According to the tenor, he who addresses us has read much good literature, including, say, many fine sonnets, short lyrics, modest pieces. Tenor and vehicle are here distinct. The alchemy of metaphoric fusion is reserved for the fourth line, "Which bards in fealty to Apollo hold." Now we apply from the vehicle the sense that viceroys or governors hold the islands in fealty to their European monarchs. And we have had time to ponder the definite article in "*the* realms of gold."

We know that the last four lines of the sonnet involve a fusion of memories, probably from *The History of America* by William Robertson, which was available to Keats at Clarke's school in Enfield. Robertson not only describes the two episodes most obviously fused, Balboa's advance to the peak in Darien, where "he beheld the South Sea stretching in endless prospect below him," and the surprise of

Cortes and his men when they looked from the mountains of Chalco toward "the vast plain of Mexico," but he describes similarly Ferdinand Pizarro's stirring first view of an Inca Palace.[1] Although Cortes is one of the major figures in Robertson's two volumes, as Balboa is not, it was Pizarro whom Keats named when Robertson excited him again in 1819.[2] Illness, says Robertson, kept Cortes from Darien, but Pizarro was there with Balboa. It was probably through Pizarro that Keats slipped from Balboa to Cortez. To the wild surmises of these three before sudden prospects, we could add as easily Alonzo de Molina's exhilaration upon viewing simultaneously both Atlantic and Pacific, as narrated in a work owned by Keats, *Les Incas*, by J. F. Marmontel.[3] We should, in fact, in pursuit of the realms of gold, take Robertson's history as a symptom rather than as a source. Keats might have been in trouble metrically had he known only Robertson's spelling *Cortes* or Marmontel's *Cortès*. Fortunately *Cortez*, the spelling in every contemporary version of Keats's sonnet, appears in such works as the then-popular William Russell, *The History of America from Its Discovery by Columbus to the Conclusion of the Late War, 1778*.

A larger issue is involved than the spelling of a name. To Marmontel the Spaniards were adventurers who murdered noble nonsavages. Although less acidly than Marmontel, Robertson also describes the Spanish conquest as a noxious combination of fanaticism and greed for gold. Why did Keats show no such revulsion? The chief part of the answer lies, not in distinctions made by Robertson between the plundering Spanish and the colonizing English, but in a sliding gradation that unites the two. In a posthumous volume that Keats could have seen (it was included in editions of the history after 1796), Robertson introduced an account of English exploration by reminding his readers that the exploits of Columbus had filled all Europe with admiration: "But in England it did something more; it excited a vehement desire of emulating the glory of Spain, and of aiming to obtain some share in those advantages which were expected in this new field opened to national activity." Elizabeth's charter to Sir Humphrey Gilbert, paraphrased by Robertson, shows what advantages were expected: "She ordains, that all the lands granted to Gilbert shall hold of the crown of England by homage, on payment of the fifth part of the gold or silver ore found there."[4] *An Account of the European Settlements in America*, by William and Edmund Burke, after promising in a chapter-heading to tell *"What caused the spirit of discovery,"* immediately fulfills its promise: "What animated these adventurers, at the same time that it fixes a stain upon all their characters and designs, is that insatiable thirst of gold, which ever appeared uppermost in all their actions." Even English colonization, the Burkes sorrowfully admit, grew by chance out of such thirst:

"Virginia was constructed out of the wrecks of an armament destined on a golden adventure, which first tempted us to America."[5] The chief distinction, then, is this: although the English also sought El Dorado, that they might hold it in homage to their Virgin Queen, the conquistadors actually discovered and held realms of gold in fealty to Spanish monarchs. Keats involves his love of adventurous Englishmen in the "Chapman's Homer" sonnet, but his theme required novel adventure beyond emulation, excitement added to courage, and exploration ending in discovery.

It took no close, dull study of history and travel to discover the gilded portion of his theme. The golden age of English literature is filled with a hunger for gold. We need not sail repetitiously on the faery seas where Drake, Frobisher, Hawkins, and Gilbert sought the realms of gold. We need not linger over poems addressed by one adventurer to another, as when Francis Drake praises voyaging, in a tribute to Gilbert, as "The path to Fame, the proof of zeale, and way to purchase golde."[6] Nor need we go to *Tamburlaine* or related plays, even though the lust for empire and gold depicted by Marlowe would satisfy the Keats who wrote to Bailey: "The Sward is richer for the tread of a real, nervous, english foot."[7] We can rest on one stanza of the richest of "goodly states" frequented by Keats, *The Faerie Queene*, where Spenser praises the warlike Amazons as prologue to chiding the English for the mildness of their rivalry with Spain:

> Joy on those warlike women, which so long
> Can from all men so rich a kingdome hold;
> And shame on you, O men, which boast your strong
> And valiant hearts, in thoughts lesse hard and bold,
> Yet quaile in conquest of that land of gold.
> But this to you, O Britons, most pertaines,
> To whom the right hereof it selfe hath sold;
> The which for sparing litle cost or paines,
> Loose so immortall glory, and so endlesse gaines.
>
> (IV.xi.22)

William Russell, in his "Advertisement" to *The History of America*, brings this cry up to 1778: "The gold and silver of the Western World alone can enable us to purchase the precious commodities of the East" (I, iii). Compared with Spenser, Russell seems a petty accountant, but Keats gives us the principle to apply: "Though a quarrel in the streets is a thing to be hated, the energies displayed in it are fine; the commonest Man shows a grace in his quarrel."[8]

Not until we have first fixed the realms of gold and the western islands within the rivalry of Spanish and Elizabethan voyagers can we move freely through the aura of connotations, where Frobisher is united with Homer in Apollo's "western halls of gold" (as Keats calls the realms of sunglow and poetry in the "Ode to Apollo" of 1815). In this aura, to be sure, the realm of gold symbolizes Homer's Greece, which in turn suggests the richness and freedom of man's hope. Fairness to the historian Robertson, as an influence on Keats, requires the admission that he bridged the space, in his own way, between Spanish greed and "poetic" dreams. As incredible as it seemed to him that Ponce de Leon sought the fountain of youth in Florida, he described the vision before Cortes and his men at Chalco as non-commercial: "the scene so far exceeded their imagination, that some believed the fanciful descriptions of romance were realized, and that its enchanted palaces and gilded domes were presented to their sight; others could hardly persuade themselves that this wonderful spectacle was any thing more than a dream" (I, 198, II, 50).

Almost as often as they report success or failure in the search for gold, the historians tell whether or not their adventurers made good their vows of fealty. In the tenor of the sonnet, the word *fealty* represents the idea of bardic inspiration—technically, and perhaps designedly, counter to Keats's belief that "That which is creative must create itself."[9] In the metaphor of voyaging, fealty is central, for feudal loyalty had its last flowering in the conquest of the New World. Robertson laid great stress on Spanish claims to acquisition through the power vested in a particular sovereign by the Pope. Joseph Warren Beach has noted the significance for Keats's sonnet of Robertson's language describing Cortes' insistence that Montezuma make a "profession of fealty and homage" to the king of Castile.[10] In the last quarter of the eighteenth century, histories of America emphasized the distinction betwen title in right of the crown and subsequent commerical monopoly. If merchants could be said to own or control the colonized land, then influence in the New World would pass irrevocably from Britain to France.[11] George Chalmers, in a suppressed work of 1780, gave the text of such English documents as Henry VII's license of 1496 to the Cabots, to "possess and occupy . . . as our vassals" any "town, city, castle, island, or continent, by them newly discovered," and the oath administered in Virginia "that the queen's highness is the only supreme governor of this realm."[12] Every historian of the New World cited similar documents of fealty.

In the second quatrain, where the strict references of the "one wide expanse" are the American continents and the two epics of Homer, fealty becomes unnecessary, because the creative has created itself: "Oft of one wide expanse had I been told / That deep-brow'd Homer rul'd as his demesne." Praise could not go higher. The *Oxford English Dictionary* defines *demesne* as "land possessed and held by the owner himself and not held of him by any subordinate tenant." Keats's Homer is a king among poets. He is a Montezuma unconquered and unreached. Deep-browed (originally "low-brow'd"), he owes no fealty, for he can say with the Apollo of *Hyperion* (III, 113): "Knowledge enormous makes a God of me." In the sonnet to Homer, not published in Keats's lifetime, the imagery is of the ocean; the tribute comes as from one who longs "To visit dolphin-coral in deep seas." This lesser poem encourages our tendency, as naturalized denizens of the sonnet on Chapman's Homer, to associate the "wide expanse" not only with epic and continent but also with the Pacific and the blue sky.

The speaker has reached, we must remember, only the English Homer of Chapman: "Yet never did I breathe its pure serene / Till I heard Chapman speak out loud and bold." Three early versions give us a greatly inferior seventh line: "Yet could I never judge what Men could mean." Amy Lowell put the proper interpretation bluntly: "Hitherto Pope had been all he knew of Homer."[13] Given both versions of the line, we must ask whether the much-traveled poet supposes himself now to have reached the "wide expanse," or whether he has only heard a returned ambassador, the bold-voiced Chapman, make him feel that he was there. Robertson tells how Ferdinand and Isabella had their admiral and viceroy Columbus to court, "that from his own mouth they might receive a full detail of his extraordinary services and discoveries." Columbus, no Elizabethan, "delivered it with a gravity and composure . . . and with that modest simplicity which characterises men of superior minds." On a later page Robertson attributes the stream of adventurers after Columbus to "the magnificent descriptions he gave of the regions which he had visited."[14] Illustrated editions of the various histories, plentiful after 1800, almost unfailingly gave prominence to some one of the many available engravings of Columbus either describing the glorious new lands to Ferdinand and Isabella or presenting American products to them in evidence. In the posthumous volume Robertson describes a similar presentation by Raleigh's first emissaries to Virginia: "Amadas and Barlow returned to England with two of the natives, and gave such splendid descriptions of the beauty of the country, the fertility of the soil, and the mildness of the climate, that Elizabeth . . . bestowed on it the name of Virginia; as a memorial that this happy discovery had been made under a virgin queen."[15] Again, in Marmontel's *Incas*, Pizarro proclaims to the young emperor at Seville: "They have boasted to you of the riches of America; now let me tell you that they know nothing of the riches. The islands whose discovery has created glory for Columbus, the kingdom whose conquest has made Cortez so famous, are nothing in comparison with the country I have discovered and now render to you in homage."[16] Marmontel next has Pizarro re-create in words the Incas' mountain-chain of gold.

If we can take Pizarro's re-creation as something like the way Chapman speaks out loud and bold, so that Chapman can be welcomed as an enthusiast who bears a continent on his tongue, then the sonnet concerns writing almost as directly as it concerns reading. Through Chapman's translation I am as good as there; it is as if I were a Hellene listening to Homer, as if I had stood *there* silent with a wild surmise. The "wide expanse" now takes on the further dimension of Homer's matter. Through the power of the creative imagination to provide us with vicarious experience, it is not only as if I were reading Homer in Greek; it is as if I were landing in Ithaca with Odysseus. The speaker of the sonnet is a reader of poetry; he assumes a persona from the far Atlantic. But he has also a third aspect as a reader of travel books and histories. The historians, aided by the poetry he has devoured, have enabled him without traveling to feel the near-identity between discovery in reading and discovery in travel. Keats himself has been able to make the tenor (on reading) and the vehicle (on traveling) from distinct experiences each accessible to him only through his imagination as a reader. In turn he conveys to others, far beyond the ability of explorers or historians to convey it, the excitement of geographical exploration and discovery.

One final excursion remains. The sestet begins with the sonnet's single departure from the metaphor of travel. Even here, in lines nine and ten, the periphrastic designation of an astronomer includes secondarily a navigator at sea: "Then felt I like some watcher of the skies / When a new planet swims into his ken." Unlike stringently cerebral poems, the sonnet returns to its chief vertical member, the metaphor of travel, by a casual extension of the simile of sky-watching: "Or like stout Cortez." Then felt I like an astronomer, or like Cortez—or Balboa, or somebody like that. However uncerebral, the casual step downward to simile has removed the "I," the reader of Homer, and left to epitomize the theme only the geographical discoverer. Meanwhile, the brief expedition among the stars has accomplished its purpose. The theme of exploration and discovery has burst its initial limits. Because the couplet on astronomy departs boldly from the strict equation of reading and travel, the sonnet does not merely say that reading is like landing is like using a telescope. The sonnet demonstrates, even while we explore its workings, that the discovery of every new world, large or small, actual or imaginary, of matter or of spirit, can be wondrous, and all discoveries wondrously akin. Vehicle and tenor interchange and coalesce in a root experience, discovery of land and sky from the sea and of sea and sky from the land, all "one wide expanse" of the mind's encompassment. The work uncovers in its progress an aspect of the self—the self as discoverer.

Both by what it says and by what or how it is, the sonnet suggests several ways of making discoveries in poetry. "Columbus's discovery of the New World," says Robertson, "was the effort of an active genius, enlightened by science, guided by experience, and acting upon a regular plan, executed with no less courage than perseverance." Robertson mentions, but makes little of, Columbus' perseverance in the hope of finding a passage to the East near the Gulf of Darien. As for the world Columbus did find, Alvarez Cabral in 1500 might have found it anyway, says Robertson, by "fortunate accident."[17] There is discovery by plan, discovery by active search for something else, and discovery by sheer chance. Keats's astronomer keeps watch night after night for the remotely expected novelty that could be recognized by none save him of strenuous and educated eye. Keats's Cortez may suffer from displaced identity, but he knew what to look for. Despite Homer's reputation, however, Chapman came to Keats as a sudden, glorious, unmitigated surprise. The recesses of the sonnet that resulted can be discovered in at least as many ways.

Notes

1. Robertson (2nd ed., London, 1778), I, 204, II, 50, 156.

2. *The Letters of John Keats*, ed. Hyder E. Rollins (Cambridge, Mass., 1958), II, 100. Richard Garnett called attention to the collocation of Pizarro's name, and not Balboa's, with contemplating "from a sudden promontory, the distant, vast Pacific" in a note attached by Wordsworth to *The Excursion*, III, 931.—See *The Poems of John Keats*, ed. E. de Sélincourt (7th ed., London, 1951), p. 565.

3. (Paris, 1777), I, 144: "De montagne en montagne, on s'éleve, on parvient jusqu'au sommet qui les domine, & d'où la vue, au loin, s'étend vers l'un & l'autre bord, sur l'immense abyme des eaux. De là se découvrent à la fois, d'un côté l'océan du nord, de l'autre la mer Pacifique, dont la surface, dans le lontain, s'unit avec l'azur du ciel. 'Compagnons, leur dit Molina, saluons cette mer, cette terre inconnue, où nous allons porter la gloire de nos armes.' " A footnote at I, 149, confesses it unlikely that both oceans could be seen from any one spot on the isthmus. The several separately printed editions with the same imprint differ in pagination but for this passage differ otherwise only in spelling and mechanics. On Keats's possession of Marmontel, see *The Keats Circle*, ed. Hyder E. Rollins (Cambridge, Mass., 1948), I, 259, II, 164.

4. *The History of America* (9th ed., London, 1800), IV, 135, 160.

5. (6th ed., London, 1777), I, 46–49.

6. *The Voyages and Colonising Enterprises of Sir Humphrey Gilbert*, ed. David B. Quinn (Hakluyt Society, Ser. 2, Nos. 83–84), II (1940), 438. For the full Tudor context, see Franklin T. McCann, *English Discovery of America to 1585* (New York, 1952).

7. *Letters*, I, 242. Keats is here employing a recurrent argument of Robertson's.

8. *Letters*, II, 80.

9. *Letters*, I, 374.

10. "Keats's Realms of Gold," *PMLA*, XLIX (1934), 246–257. See Robertson, II, 67, and compare I, 93, 204, 444–446, II, 26, 79, 135, 143, 158, 353. The word *fealty* appears five times in *The Fairie Queene*, always of the *act* of swearing fealty.

11. The strongest statement I have seen declares France "a powerful State, whose Opposition of Interest makes her a natural Enemy, and whose military and commercial Knowledge makes her formidable as well in Peace as in War."—Introduction to Thomas

Jefferys, *The Natural and Civil History of the French Dominions in North and South America* (London, 1760).

12. *Political Annals of the Present United Colonies. . .* , pp. 7–8, 25, 40.

13. *John Keats* (Boston, 1925), I, 178.

14. Robertson (1778), I, 108–109, 148. These passages are reprinted in William Winterbotham, *An Historical, Geographical, Commercial, and Philosophical View of the American United States . . .* (4 vols., London, 1795), I, 37, 61–62.

15. (1800), IV, 163–164. Robertson cites Hakluyt, III, 246.

16. II, 208–209 (but see note 3 above): "On vous a vanté les richesses de l'Amérique; & moi, je vous annonce qu'on ne les connoît pas. Les îsles dont la découverte a fait la gloire de Colomb, le Royaume dont la conquête a rendu Cortès si fameux, ne sont rien en comparaison des pays que j'ai découverts, & dont je viens vous faire hommage."

17. (1778), I, 151–152, 162, 166–167.

The "Epistle to John Hamilton Reynolds"

Stuart M. Sperry[*]

The period immediately following the revision of *Endymion* for the press was one of dislocation poetically. Keats was relieved to have the major task completed and out of the way, leaving him once more free for new endeavors. At the same time, beyond a sense of general dissatisfaction with the work, he was left with the pressing intellectual and aesthetic questions it had raised which he knew he would have to face in order to make progress. The best evidence of this unsettled state of things is his verse epistle to John Hamilton Reynolds. The verses make up the greater part of a letter he sent his friend on March 25, 1818, about a month before *Endymion* went to press, and recount the effects of a powerful and strangely moving depression he has been suffering. In the past there has been considerable reluctance to view the poem as much more than the reflection of a passing mood.[1] For one thing it is an occasional piece that begins as a playful attempt to provide some humorous distraction for Reynolds, who was ill at the time, starting off with a jocularity Keats is only briefly able to maintain. The poem as a whole seems strangely disjointed and even, at times, incoherent, especially when compared with the poet's more polished work. Indeed it is somewhat unfair, as Bate reminds us, that these hasty and impromptu verses Keats never intended to meet the public eye have been printed alongside his other poetic work "and then approached with formal expectations that are wildly irrelevant."[2] Yet it is precisely the kind of disturbance

[*] Reprinted from *Keats the Poet.* ©1973 by Princeton University Press. Excerpt, 117–31, reprinted with permission of Princeton University Press.

they succeed in revealing that tells us a great deal about Keats and that, in the study of his development, makes the poem of greater interest than the new romance in which he sought refuge—the longer, more finished, but languid *Isabella*. The "Epistle to Reynolds" goes far toward explaining the sense of mist and darkness, the feeling of the "burden of the Mystery," that was beginning to oppress him while forcing him, at the same time, to extend his vision into the "dark Passages" that were opening on all sides.

In many respects the lines to Reynolds mark a return to the manner of the earlier verse epistles and the longer pieces of the 1817 volume. The poem begins with the very situation that had in the past proved so fruitful for composition: a sleepless evening passed amid a flow of images and associations. One recalls, for example, the origin of "Sleep and Poetry" in a sleepless night spent "upon a couch at ease" (353) in Hunt's study. Once again there is the device Keats had used so often in the past of working into the poem by elaborating a chain of images and associations that he hoped might lead on to a major theme. Again we find the poet ready to spin "that wonted thread / Of shapes, and shadows, and remembrances" (2–3) into the woof of poetry. Yet the opening of the lines to Reynolds reads almost like a caricature of Keats's earlier technique, for the images that now come forward are all perversely incongruous or anachronistic:

> Things all disjointed come from north and south,—
> Two witch's eyes above a cherub's mouth,
> Voltaire with casque and shield and habergeon,
> And Alexander with his nightcap on;
> Old Socrates a-tying his cravat,
> And Hazlitt playing with Miss Edgeworth's cat.
>
> (5–10)

The passage seems at first only a bit of admirable fooling intended for Reynolds's diversion until Keats's tone darkens and we realize that what he is describing is a more serious and unaccountable disruption of the usual associative processes of composition. There are few, he proceeds to lament, whose reveries and dreams are not sometimes spoiled by "hellish" apparitions. It is not merely that the images themselves are ludicrously inconsistent with each other; but they neither suggest nor lead on to anything more. They are, in fact, totally inconsistent with that ideal process that, by way of contrast, he proceeds to describe in terms of

> flowers bursting out with lusty pride,
> And young Æolian harps personified;
> Some, Titian colours touch'd into real life,—
>
> (17–19)

that flowering of art into the fullness of reality that is the end of all
aesthetic creation. It is this criterion of "aliveness," of higher verisimilitude, that Keats has most in view and that suddenly prompts
him, by way of providing an example, to "touch into life" the scene
of pagan sacrifice so remarkably prefigurative of stanza four of the
"Ode on a Grecian Urn," a scene full of flashing light, color, movement, and music caught in a moment of ceremony and communal
worship:

> The sacrifice goes on; the pontiff knife
> Gleams in the sun, the milk-white heifer lows,
> The pipes go shrilly, the libation flows:
> A white sail shows above the green-head cliff,
> Moves round the point, and throws her anchor stiff;
> The mariners join hymn with those on land.
>
> (20–25)

As various commentators have pointed out, there is no painting
known by Titian that contains a scene similar to the one Keats
describes; and it is commonly assumed that, through some slip of
memory, he confused with the Venetian the work of another painter,
perhaps the *Sacrifice to Apollo* of Claude Lorrain, whose *Enchanted
Castle* Keats is shortly to recall at length.[3] Most probably Keats's
description draws upon a general recollection of a number of different
prints and canvases. Yet the mention of Hazlitt a few lines earlier
strongly suggests there is a deeper logic at work in his allusion to
Titian within this particular context and that he had in view, at the
same time, central differences between the two painters. In his essay
"On Gusto" in *The Round Table,* a collection with which Keats was
familiar, Hazlitt had praised Titian for the very ability the poet is
attempting to depict. Hazlitt had written of Titian's power to "interpret one sense by another" so as to bring to "the look and texture
of flesh" the sense of "feeling in itself,"[4] the power, in short, to
bring a scene or a face "swelling into reality" (to use Keats's phrase)
by endowing the elements of nature with an intensity of human
passion and feeling. A few months earlier, in the Negative Capability
letter written near the very end of 1817, Keats had, as we have seen,
defined this ability with specific reference to the work of a painter
quite different from either Titian or Claude—Benjamin West. Familiar
as it may be, the passage must be quoted in full:

> I spent Friday evening with Wells & went the next morning to see
> *Death on the Pale horse.* It is a wonderful picture, when West's age
> is considered; But there is nothing to be intense upon; no women
> one feels mad to kiss; no face swelling into reality. the excellence
> of every Art is its intensity, capable of making all disagreeables
> evaporate, from their being in close relationship with Beauty &

Truth—Examine King Lear & you will find this examplified throughout; but in this picture we have unpleasantness without any momentous depth of speculation excited, in which to bury its repulsiveness. (I, 192; Keats's italics)

As Bate has shown, Keats's conception of "intensity" owes a great
deal to Hazlitt's "gusto,"[5] although one must add that the two are
far from identical. Indeed the "Epistle to Reynolds" represents Keats's
working through in a far deeper way some of the notions that had
first been suggested to him by the older critic and his own consideration of West's painting.

Keats's method in the lines to Reynolds is progression by way
of contrasts and oppositions. He turns from Titian and the idealized
scene of ritual he has just touched into life to a particular painting
that has come to mind, the work of a quite different master—Claude
Lorrain. The imaginative scene he has created, in its relation to the
two painters, has slowly crystallized the major preoccupation of his
poem: the degree of idealization—both in a good and bad sense—
that art can achieve in its transcendence of actuality. The theme, of
course, is one intimately connected with his growing interest in the
sublime, both as a general and long-established ideal of art and in
its relation to his own more particular sense of the process of aesthetic
sublimation by which the materials of art are purged of "disagreeables," fused in imagination, and "put into etherial existence for the
relish of one's fellows"(I, 301). It is natural, then, that he should
turn to one of the great neoclassic exemplars of the sublime, not of
those aspects associated with scenes of terror and destruction (the
conditions he is to touch on at the end) but rather with peace,
security, happiness, and a sense of repose.[6] The painting, *The Enchanted Castle,* is one that best epitomizes "the grand quiescence of
Claude." Yet Keats's attitude toward the aspect of sublimity, however
attractive, that Claude represents is, as we shall see, hardly one of
unqualified admiration. Here again our best guide for tracing the
chain of association that leads Keats from Titian to Claude and *The
Enchanted Castle* is Hazlitt who, in his essay "On Gusto," turns from
praising the earlier painter to a more detailed analysis of the peculiar
charm of the later:

> Claude's landscapes, perfect as they are, want gusto. This is not
> easy to explain. They are perfect abstractions of the visible images
> of things. . . . He saw the atmosphere, but he did not feel it. He
> painted the trunk of a tree or a rock in the foreground as smooth—
> with as complete an abstraction of the gross, tangible impression,
> as any other part of the picture. His trees are perfectly beautiful,
> but quite immovable; they have a look of enchantment. In short,
> his landscapes are unequalled imitations of nature, *released from
> its subjection to the elements,* as if all objects were become a

delightful fairy vision, and the eye had *rarefied and refined away the other senses.* (IV, 79; my italics)

Turning to Keats's long description for Reynolds of the exact impression he holds of Claude's painting, one can see that it is this very quality of enchantment, of abstraction from gross reality, that he singles out as most characteristic. Whereas, however, Hazlitt sees the effect Claude achieves by his mastery as serene and charming, Keats represents the mood as partly frozen, unnatural, even perverse. Claude's trees, which Hazlitt describes as "perfectly beautiful, but quite immovable" with "a look of enchantment," for Keats seem held under a harsh, restraining spell so that they "shake / From some old magic like Urganda's sword" (28–29). Hazlitt had written that Claude's landscapes "are perfect abstractions of the visible images of things. . . . He saw the atmosphere, but he did not feel it." Keats's impression of *The Enchanted Castle,* on the other hand, while once again following the general tenor of Hazlitt's remarks, is more ambivalent and complex:

> You know it well enough, where it doth seem
> A mossy place, a Merlin's Hall, a dream;
> You know the clear lake, and the little isles,
> The mountains blue, and cold near neighbour rills,
> All which elsewhere are but half animate;
> There do they look alive to love and hate,
> To smiles and frowns; they seem a lifted mound
> Above some giant, pulsing underground.
>
> (33–40)

At first glance the painting seems perfectly dreamlike in its self-containment and abstraction. Yet this unifying mood is not everywhere maintained. Parts of the landscape seem unnaturally, even morbidly, alive with feeling. The image of some giant pulsing underground in particular creates a sense of titanic forces of upheaval ready at any moment to break into open eruption to destroy the surface placidity. The mood of sublimity the painting creates, in other words, only imperfectly transcends a vast underlying disorder it can only partly repress or conceal.

Other aspects peculiar to Keats's view of *The Enchanted Castle* can be best defined by briefly returning to Hazlitt's remarks. For example, Hazlitt marvels at Claude's ability to transform the elements of nature into "a delightful fairy vision." So Keats develops the idea of enchantment, but with a quite different emphasis:

> The doors all look as if they oped themselves,
> The windows as if latched by fays and elves,
> And from them comes a silver flash of light,
> As from the westward of a summer's night;

Or like a beauteous woman's large blue eyes
Gone mad thro' olden songs and poesies.

(49–54)

The note of elvish mischief seems incongruous with the larger theme
of calm and sublimity, while the flashing eyes of the woman, like the
Abyssinian maid's vision of "flashing eyes" and "floating hair" in
Coleridge's "Kubla Khan" (a poem that, in its preoccupation with
the balance art struggles to achieve between energy and control,
resembles Keats's) introduces a hint of danger and madness. Even
the "sweet music" that issues from the castle to greet the "golden
galley all in silken trim" (56) as it serenely approaches its port for
some reason brings fear to the herdsman who hears it. Hints of dark
magic in its more bizarre aspects also color Keats's description of
the castle itself. He had noted, of course, that the castle in Claude's
painting is very much a conglomerate affair, combining, as Colvin
points out,[7] ancient Roman features with medieval battlements and
later Palladian elements in the manner of many old structures that
have been built onto through the centuries. Though somewhat fanciful, the fusion of styles is not inharmonious in Claude's painting
but creates an effect that is calm, mysterious, and imposing. Keats's
imaginary account of its architects and history, however, reduces the
structure to the level of the macabre and fantastic:

Part of the building was a chosen See,
Builty by a banish'd Santon of Chaldee;
The other part, two thousand years from him,
Was built by Cuthbert de Saint Aldebrim;
Then there's a little wing, far from the sun,
Built by a Lapland witch turn'd maudlin nun;
And many other juts of aged stone
Founded with many a mason-devil's groan.

(41–48)

The same sense of anachronism that characterized the train of disjointed images passing before Keats's eyes at the very outset of the
poem in all their ludicrous incongruity now extends itself to his
awareness of Claude's painting. There is the same failure of the
associative process, now visualized as an aspect of the painting itself,
to achieve a harmonious and unified effect.

Critics have at this point generally accepted the failure as Keats's
own, an instance of the moodiness and morbidity of which he openly
complains to Reynolds at the end. The disordered state of imagination
he has described to his friend at the outset has now obtruded itself
upon his appreciation of the painting and perversely distorted the
values of Claude's landscape.[8] Yet the implications of the poem go
a good deal beyond this. Keats obviously recognizes that the creations

of art necessarily depend for their success upon a large degree of sympathy and responsiveness. As the poem goes on to make clear, however, the ability to respond can be impaired not merely by a captious state of mind but by a condition of awareness that, in its fullness or complexity, exceeds the powers of any particular work of art to harmonize or satisfy. More specifically, in its effort to expel all "disagreeables," to "swell into reality" and idealize a particular aspect of beauty or truth, the work of art can fatally remove itself from that wealth of human knowledge and experience that provides the substratum of all aesthetic apprehension. As in his remarks some months earlier on West's *Death on the Pale Horse*, what preoccupies Keats in his reflections on *The Enchanted Castle* is a failure in the attempt to achieve the sublime.[9] Yet the problem he now returns to is one he had barely touched on earlier, a problem related to his whole conception of "intensity." The failure as he had analyzed it in West's painting was a lack of anything "to be intense upon," a dearth of material for the imagination to "swell into reality." The problem that confronts him now, however, is a deeper one, for it has to do with the very nature of "intensity" itself: its continual tendency to refine away too much that is fundamental to our general awareness of life, its drift into one-sidedness and subjectivity. Such, at least, is the larger aspect of the problem that, turning away from his immediate consideration of Claude's painting, Keats seeks to sum up for Reynolds in what is the most abstract and in many ways difficult section of his poem:

> O that our dreamings all, of sleep or wake,
> Would all their colours from the sunset take:
> From something of material sublime,
> Rather than shadow our own soul's day-time
> In the dark void of night. For in the world
> We jostle
>
> (67–72)

A key phrase (a consciously ironic one) for elucidating Keats's meaning is "material sublime," expressing as it does the desire of the imagination to possess at once the best of both worlds, the ethereal and the concrete. Here again perhaps our best gloss on the passage as a whole is provided by some general remarks of Hazlitt's on the nature of painting, written, though they were, after the poet's death:

> A fine gallery of pictures is a sort of illustration of Berkeley's Theory of Matter and Spirit. It is like a palace of thought—another universe, built of air, of shadows, of colours. Every thing seems "palpable to feeling as to sight." Substances turn to shadows by the painter's archchemic touch; shadows harden into substances. "The eye is made the fool of the other senses, or else worth all the rest." The

material is in some sense embodied in the immaterial, or, at least, we see all things in a sort of intellectual mirror. The world of art is an enchanting deception. (x, 19)

Once again the dissimilarity-in-similarity between Keats's lines and Hazlitt's remarks is revealing. What for Hazlitt is an ideal translation of the material into the spiritual is the very aspect of the creative process most troubling to Keats. We long in our reveries, whether those of mere dreaming or those that engross us in our contemplation of the world of art, for the colors of the sunset—some substantial element of the real world that lies outside. Yet instead of such colors we must remain content with fleeting, doubtful moments of inner illumination that fade away into shadows and uncertainty. Hazlitt recognizes and accepts an element of illusion as a part of aesthetic creation: "The world of art is an enchanting deception" tinted into reality by the painter's "arch-chemic touch." Yet it is clear that Keats is unwilling to accept the easy logic of such an equation and that what Hazlitt delights in as enchantment can assume for him the horror of a subjective *enfer*.

For a moment he draws back from some of the metaphysical questions he customarily sought to avoid confronting head-on, then plunges a little further into the problem:

> but my flag is not unfurl'd
> On the admiral-staff,—and to philosophise
> I dare not yet! Oh, never will the prize,
> High reason, and the lore of good and ill,
> Be my award! Things cannot to the will
> Be settled, but they tease us out of thought;
> Or is it that imagination brought
> Beyond its proper bound, yet still confin'd,
> Lost in a sort of Purgatory blind,
> Cannot refer to any standard law
> Of either earth or heaven? It is a flaw
> In happiness, to see beyond our bourn,—
> It forces us in summer skies to mourn,
> It spoils the singing of the nightingale.
>
> (72–85)

In his remarks a few months earlier prompted by his consideration of West's *Death on the Pale Horse* he had gone on to postulate as an ideal for the artist the state of Negative Capability, that is "when man is capable of being in uncertainties, Mysteries, doubts, without any irritable reaching after fact & reason." More particularly, he had imagined that the great work of art would, like *Lear*, achieve what West's painting had failed to accomplish, that it would bury all "unpleasantness," all "repulsiveness," all disagreeable and insistent questioning, by engrossing the imagination in a "momentous depth of speculation" (I, 192–93). However it is precisely the failure of this stratagem that now forms the burden of his complaint to Reynolds. Resisting the lure of speculation, the will remains unappeasable in its desire for certainty. Moreover Keats has come to realize that the state of speculation itself can be as vexing in its irresolution as it can be momentous in its implications. The phrase "tease us out of thought," which he was to use again within a subtly different context in the "Ode on a Grecian Urn," here suggests the tantalizing ability of the speculative life to raise, only to defer answering, our final questions. Seen in a different light, that very immunity of the imagination to ordinary kinds of interrogation that had in the past seemed of positive value might suggest corresponding limitations and defects. The "Penetralium of mystery," rich with suggestiveness and undiscovered meaning, could become the poet's "Purgatory blind." The latter phrase, apt like so many of his personal coinages, sums up the dilemma he seeks to convey. Though liberated, the poetic imagination can relate itself to no single "standard law" of either earth or heaven, the material world or the sublime. Lacking the ability to reconcile the two domains, it must experience them as a "hateful siege of contraries"[10] that together spoil whatever consolations either taken singly might afford. Thus we can mourn at the beauty of summer skies or at the singing of the nightingale. The poet is trapped in limbo, somewhere between the uncertain heaven figured by the visionary imagination and the real hell of actual existence when stripped of all romantic possibilities.

It is, of course, to the hell life becomes when viewed in an uncompromisingly realistic and antiromantic light that Keats turns in the final section of the poem. The Darwinian vision of life as an unrelenting struggle for survival waged throughout nature is terrifying and quite unlike anything in his earlier verse. The scene as it unfolds, however, does not stand in isolation but relates itself organically to earlier sections of the poem. The setting in the early evening by the seaside briefly recalls in its pastoral tranquility the mood of Claude's painting. Once again, however, Keats's eye probes beneath the surface to discern signs of sacrifice, oppression, and underlying disorder— not the bloodless and beautifully ceremonial picture of sacrifice that had earlier come alive in his imagination but one of nature "red in tooth and claw." The sublimity and refinement of the painter's ideal world are sensed in contrast to the naked brutality of primeval nature, and the two contexts for conceiving reality develop between them uneasy reverberations in a way now familiar to us as the prevailing method of the poem.

With its abrupt shifts and changes of perspective the "Epistle to Reynolds" reveals an undeniable instability and lack of central focus. The poem may compress only the transitory fantasies of a single evening, but the dislocation it exposes is too fundamental to be written off, as some critics would have it, as a passing case of bad nerves. Although at the very end Keats berates those "horrid moods! / Moods of one's mind" (105–106), the work is much more than a mere poem of mood. The strange distortion of Claude's scene of elysian quiet and the brief, terrifying glimpse of nature reduced to universal rapacity are both, in different ways, troubling and even perverse, but it is not sufficient to dismiss them as unaccountable aberrations from Keats's usual poetic mode, instances of that "horrid Morbidity of Temperament" (I, 142) of which he from time to time complained. There is a logic to the poem's apparent disorder, and if such scenes can justly be described as "morbid," they are so in such a way as to counterbalance and explain each other. If at the end Keats appears more naturalist than poet and sees "Too *far* into the sea" (94), it is in part because he has earlier sensed the treacherous tendency of art to encourage us "to see beyond our bourn" (83) in the opposite extreme. There is a principle of compensation at work by which the imagination struggles to rectify itself and discover a proper balance. The charge of morbidity is unjust if only because the poem itself provides the grounds for understanding how depression and unevenness of vision are to some degree unavoidable to those who struggle to reconcile a full and sympathetic participation in the world of art with a knowledge of the actuality that lies outside. As in Wordsworth's mature reappraisal of the relationship art holds to reality in his "Elegiac Stanzas" on Sir George Beaumont's painting of Peele Castle, a poem that in theme and method must have been in the back of Keats's mind,[11] the true subject is not the vagaries of an errant imagination but the way in which our whole approach to art is radically altered by a change in our perspective on the reality it mirrors. If Keats emphasizes the element of subjectivity in our awareness, he does so with an understanding of the various ways in which, during the centuries spanning Titian, Claude, and his contemporary West, a spontaneous sublimity of style has become increasingly difficult to achieve. His lament is not purely personal but in part historical and cultural.[12]

The deeper questions that lie behind the "Epistle to Reynolds" are philosophic and more particularly aesthetic and reveal how much, during the months following the completion of *Endymion*, Keats had come to question some of his earlier poetic assumptions, especially those concerning the nature of the poetic process. The point now most at issue is his deepening sense of the nature of "intensity" and the role it plays in the creation of art. The central question, to put it simply, is what and how does art "intensify"? Does the imagination, in fact, concentrate and sublime a material and substantial beauty? Or does it rather, in purging away "disagreeables"—all that is discordant or repulsive—distill a vision that, for any complex intelligence, must remain hopelessly tenuous and unreal? Is art a heightening and enrichment, or is it rather an abstraction and evasion, of reality? The chain of associations leading Keats, partly in company with Hazlitt, from Titian, Claude, and the sublime in painting to the terrors of brute nature reveals the degree to which such questions had become of vital concern. It reveals, too, a state of irresolution it would not be too much to call a period of crisis.[13] Although it cannot claim to rank among his major productions, the "Epistle to Reynolds" illuminates more clearly than any other single work the major problems with which Keats wrestled in passing from *Endymion* to his first attempt at *Hyperion*.

Notes

1. Criticism of the poem has been, relatively speaking, small. I have found especially useful Albert Gérard's "Romance and Reality: Continuity and Growth in Keats's View of Art," *Keats-Shelley Journal*, XI (1962), 17–29, incorporated as a part of ch. 10 of his *English Romantic Poetry*; Walter Evert's discussion in *Aesthetic and Myth in the Poetry of Keats* (Princeton, 1964), pp. 194–211; and Mary Visick's " 'Tease us out of thought': Keats's 'Epistle to Reynolds' and the Odes," *Keats-Shelley Journal*, XV (1966), 87–98. My discussion is in varying ways indebted to all these as well as to Bate.

2. *John Keats* (Cambridge, Mass., 1963), p. 307.

3. See Sir Sidney Colvin, *John Keats* (London, 1920), p. 264, whom most commentators have followed. The *Sacrifice to Apollo*, however, does not depict the mariners who join the hymn; and most recently James Dickie (*Bulletin of the John Rylands Library*, LII [1969], 96–114) and Alan Osler (*TLS*, April 16, 1971) have suggested Keats was remembering as well other specific paintings by Titian or Claude. In *Keats and the Mirror of Art* (Oxford, 1967), Ian Jack takes the scene the poet describes as a composite and thinks "it is certainly most unlikely that Keats is here describing any particular painting" (p. 221).

4. *The Complete Works of William Hazlitt*, ed. P. P. Howe (London, 1930), IV, 77. References to this edition are hereafter included within the text of this chapter.

5. *John Keats*, p. 244.

6. See the contrast drawn between Salvator and Claude in "The Sublime in Painting," ch. 9 of Samuel Monk's *The Sublime* (New York, 1935).

7. *John Keats*, p. 264.

8. See, e.g., Evert, *Aesthetic and Myth*, pp. 200–201.

9. Bate points out (*John Keats*, p. 243) that West's painting had been praised as a successful effort at the sublime.

10. See Keats's use of this phrase from *Paradise Lost*, ix.121f., in a letter some months later (*Letters*, I, 369).

11. So Claude Finney has argued in *The Evolution of Keats's Poetry* (Cambridge, Mass., 1936), I, 391.

12. There is no need to elaborate here a point developed throughout Bate's biography and again by Harold Bloom in "Keats and the Embarrassments of Poetic

Tradition," in *From Sensibility to Romanticism: Essays Presented to Frederick A. Pottle*, ed., F. W. Hilles and Harold Bloom (New York, 1965).

13. See Evert's discussion, noted above, and p. 212.

Endymion: "Pretty Paganism" and "Purgatory Blind"

John Barnard[*]

Endymion: A Poetic Romance (1818), started shortly after the publication of Keats's first volume, is a "dream of poetry," of youth and of love, yeasty, ardent and diffuse. Almost before its completion Keats dismissed his pastoral as an adolescent failure, though he also knew that its 4,000 lines of poetry had been essential to his development as a poet. Looking back on its composition, he wrote to his publisher, "In Endymion, I leaped headlong into the Sea, and thereby have become better acquainted with the Soundings, the quicksands, & the rocks, than if I had stayed upon the green shore, and piped a silly pipe, and took tea & comfortable advice" (*Letters*, i, 374). As this suggests, *Endymion* is more a poem in process than a considered whole. Keats takes up again the story of the love of the moon-goddess, Diana, for the shepherd-prince, Endymion, with which he had concluded "I Stood Tip-toe."

Endymion is a Romantic quest-poem portraying the poet's search for true imaginative powers. Its structure follows the progressive tests and initiation-rites through which the hero proves himself. Most of Endymion's confusions in the poem arise from Diana's decision to visit the poet-prince first in the form of an unknown goddess, and later in guise of an Indian Maid. In love with all three, Endymion's bewildered and divided feelings are resolved by the long-delayed discovery that all three are one. The poem concludes with the immortalisation of Endymion and his marriage to Diana.

Endymion's plot is an argument for the essential interconnectedness of human love and the truth of ideal beauty. If Endymion longs for his goddess, Diana pursues her union with an earthly lover with equal determination. The poem's broad outline is clear enough. In Book I, the hero is set apart from his Latmian subjects by the "cankering venom" (I. 396) caused by his dream of a heavenly goddess, which threatens his worship of the moon (Diana), and has left him dissatisfied with reality. Endymion is the alienated modern poet bearing the cost of consciousness. To attain his dream of ideal love, Endymion is initiated first into the mysteries of the heavens

[*] Reprinted from *John Keats*. ©1987 by Cambridge University Press. Reprinted with the permission of Cambridge University Press.

(Book I), then into those of the earth (Book II) and those of the sea (Book III). In the final book, he is returned to earth. The appearance of the Indian Maid, with whom Endymion instantly falls in love, forces him to choose between actual human love and his dreams. His choice of human love is, ironically, the last test in his progress to godhead.

Endymion also shows its hero progressively learning to sympathise with the sufferings of other lovers, as the stories of Alpheus and Arethusa (II. 932–1017) and of Glaucus (III. 187–1015) are meant to show. In addition to knowledge of the universe, empathy with human pain, and a final commitment to earthly life, are essential to Endymion's simultaneous assumption of poethood and godhead. However, interpretations of the allegory are so various[1] that, for most readers, *Endymion* offers the sort of pleasure which Keats attributed to the long poem: "Do not the Lovers of Poetry like to have a little Region to wander in where they may pick and choose, and in which the images are so numerous that many are forgotten and found new in a second Reading: which may be food for a Week's stroll in the Summer?" (*Letters*, i. 170). *Endymion* 's "poetic romance" is the first sustained example of Keats's style and highly personal use of mythology, artificial and yet true to feeling. Both John Bayley and Christoper Ricks reject the common judgement (Keats's own) on *Endymion*'s immaturity: "the central Keats is the rich poet of *Endymion* and 'The Eve of St. Agnes' rather than the sombre mature poet (strained and against the grain) of, say, *The Fall of Hyperion.* Keats's art at its best risks vulgarity: 'It turns what might appear mean and embarrassing into what is rich and *disconcerting.'* "[2]

The rejection here of *The Fall of Hyperion* seems to me mistaken and the case for *Endymion* over-stated, but the up-ending of conventional judgement is salutary. At issue is the verbal excesses which have embarrassed earlier and later critics, yet *Endymion* is most alive when real feelings invest its mythological figures with disconcerting vitality. Both Ricks and Bayley cite the description of Niobe:

> Perhaps, the trembling knee
> And frantic gape of lonely Niobe—
> Poor, lonely Niobe!—when her lovely young
> Were dead and gone, and her caressing tongue
> Lay a lost thing upon her paly lip,
> And very, very deadliness did nip
> Her motherly cheeks.
>
> (I. 337–43)

Bayley points to the potency of "gape," and says, "This is the real anguish of the human heart. . . . The contrast between *caressing,* with its firm sexual meaning, and the terrible disregard for itself of this face in torment, would be almost too painful were it not that the intensity of the image 'causes all disagreeables to evaporate.' "[3] In extreme grief, the human face becomes inhumanly distorted, wholly unconscious of how it might appear to others.[4] The threat which "gape" poses to poetic decorum reflects the undecorous nature of grief. While the lines allow the reader to feel the physical and emotional intensity of Niobe's grief, they respect its otherness. There is no prying into or savouring of Niobe's grief: it is registered through feeling and sensation but with objectivity.

John Hamilton Reynolds was alone among contemporary critics in recognising the lack of Romantic "egotism" in *Endymion*'s treatment of natural scenes—"You do not see him, when you see her [Nature]."[5] As in "To Autumn," while humanising the natural world, Keats celebrates its non-human life. In the "Hymn to Pan" he writes,

> O thou, to whom
> Broad-leaved fig trees even now foredoom
> Their ripen'd fruitage; yellow-girted bees
> Their golden honeycombs; our village leas
> Their fairest-blossomed beans and poppied corn
> (I. 251–5)

The closed fullness of natural "completions" (line 260), of living things fulfilling their functions with the yearly cycle, is mediated directly to the reader.

Keats's sense of the differing life of other ways of being gives vitality to his recreation of mythological figures, as in his description of Cybele:

> alone—alone—
> In sombre chariot; dark foldings thrown
> About her majesty, and front death-pale,
> With turrets crowned. Four maned lions hale
> The sluggish wheels; solemn their toothed maws,
> Their surly eyes brow-hidden, heavy paws
> Uplifted drowsily, and nervy tails
> Cowering their tawny brushes.
> (II. 640–7)

On other occasions, his gods take on the scale and grandeur he saw in sculpture and mythological paintings: "Like old Deucalion mountained o'er the flood, / Or blind Orion hungry for the morn" (II. 197–8).

The first part of Book I offers sustained passages recreating *Endymion*'s lost pagan world. The early morning gathering of the forest population round Pan's altar (lines 89–231) and the ensuing stanzaic hymn to Pan (lines 232–306) evoke the simplicity and physical beauty of the pagan world with an animist sense of awe. The pastoral world created has a physical actuality touched by a sense of poignancy at its irrevocable loss. Keats's source is not Greek literature itself, but an amalgamation from second-hand sources. Similarly eclectic and similarly successful are the descriptions of the triumphal progress of Bacchus (IV. 193–272) and that of Circe's route (III. 490–537).

The extreme harshness with which Keats rejected his romance ("every error denoting a feverish attempt, rather than a deed accomplished") was in direct proportion to his fervent belief in the importance and fragility of the world which *Endymion* attempted to recall. "I hope I have not in too late a day touched the beautiful mythology of Greece, and dulled its brightness."[6] The endeavour to recreate "the beautiful mythology of Greece" lies at the centre of any understanding of what Keats was trying to do in *Endymion*. Although the poem attempts too many things at once, its themes and argument call for attention as much as its style.

Wordsworth's dismissal of the Homeric hymn to Pan as "a Very pretty piece of Paganism"[7] attacked Keats's ambitious venture precisely at the point which caused the young poet most anxiety—the fear that *Endymion*'s failure desecrated the grand simplicity and beauty of the Greek world, reducing it to mere decoration. For both Keats and Wordsworth, the poem's paganism was an important matter. The painter, Benjamin Haydon, ascribed Wordsworth's reaction to the fact that his "puling Christian feelings were annoyed."[8]

Endymion is a serious effort to imagine the "natural theology" of its "Greek" world. Keats shared Hunt's dislike of institutionalised Christianity, parsons, and the Christian belief in man's innate corruption, but, as an unassertive agnostic, held well short of Shelley's avowed atheism. Sympathising with Benjamin Bailey, who had been disappointed in his hopes of a curacy, Keats told his Anglican friend that there were two sources of consolation for the troubles of this world, those "of Religion and [those of] undepraved Sensations. of the Beautiful. the poetical in all things."[9] For Keats, Joseph Severn reported, the essence of the Greek spirit was "the Religion of the Beautiful, the Religion of Joy, as he used to call it."[10] *Endymion*'s opening lines, beginning "A thing of beauty is a joy for ever," assert that the "sweet dreams" of art, "Some shape of beauty" can move away "the pall / From our dark spirits" (I. 1–13).

The danger that a modern poet's reworking of Greek myth might lead only to insipid prettification was, as some of Hunt's poetry showed, real enough. But the Hellenic revival of these years could cut deeper. *Endymion*'s "religion" and its ideas on the nature and origin of myths are best understood when Keats's response to mythological paintings is taken in conjunction with contemporary accounts of the origins of Greek mythology. Keats owned a copy of William Godwin's *The Pantheon: or Ancient History of the Gods of*

Greece and Rome . . . (1806), a book aimed at the young reader and published under the name of "Edward Baldwin." Godwin writes:

> The most important senses of the human body are seeing and hearing
> . . . it is a delightful thing to take a walk in fields, and look at
> the skies and trees and the corn-fields and the waving grass, to
> observe the mountains and the lakes and the rivers and the seas,
> to smell the new-mown hay, to inhale the fresh and balmy breeze,
> and to hear the wild warblings of the birds: but a man does not
> enjoy these in their most perfect degree, till his imagination becomes
> a little visionary; the human mind does not have a landscape without
> life and without a soul: we are delighted to talk to the objects
> around us, and to feel as if they understood and sympathised with
> us: we create, by the power of fancy, a human form and a human
> voice in those scenes, which to a man of literal understanding may
> appear dead and lifeless.[11]

Hence, according to Godwin, Greek religion "gave animation and life to all existence: it had its Naiads, Gods of the rivers, its Tritons and Nereids, Gods of the seas, its Satyrs, Fauns and Dryads, Gods of the woods and trees, and its Boreas, Euros, Auster and Zephyr, Gods of the winds."[12] If this admiration for the simplicity and the sensuousness of the ancient Greek world is linked to the way in which Keats and his immediate circle looked at painters' representations of mythological episodes, the kind of effects he was aiming at in *Endymion* becomes clearer. Mythological paintings made the vitality of Greek myth live again for the modern viewer. In looking at a painting, Hazlitt wrote, "We are abstracted to another sphere: we breathe empyrean air; we enter into the minds of Raphael, of Titian, of Poussin, of the Caracci, and look at nature with their eyes; we live in time past, and seem identified with the permanent form of things. . . . Here is the mind's true home. The contemplation of truth and beauty is the proper object for which we were created, which calls forth the most intense desires of the soul, and of which it never tires."[13] The "permanent form of things" are perceived not through a Wordsworthian meditation upon nature, but through the "abstractions" of an art work. *Endymion's* mythological figures and inset stories are vehicles for Keats's exploration of beauty and truth, and an attempt to recreate, as Poussin and Titian had in painting, the "beautiful mythology" the Greeks had drawn from nature. For Keats there were dangers in the analogy between poetry and painting. Kenneth Burke has said that "the form of thought in Keats is mystical, in terms of an *eternal present.* "[14] The "eternal present" of a painting's arrested time is hard to imitate in poetry, particularly in a narrative poem. To take one from many examples, the Bower of Adonis episode (II. 387–427), which draws on Poussin's *Echo and Narcissus,* [15] comes close to halting the story's progress. The pull between narrative and

Keats's predilection for static "pictures" is an important cause of the reader's difficulties in following *Endymion*. Nevertheless, the way in which Keats and Hazlitt saw Poussin, Claude, Titian, and Raphael points to the nobility of conception which underlies the romance. The "mind's true home" is not in the imperfections of contemporary society, but in "another sphere" in which the soul can contemplate truth and beauty. Mythological paintings demonstrate how a modern recreation of ancient stories can seem to create an alternative timeless world.

Endymion is less an act of historical imagination (though it is that), than an imaginative vision of the past which implicitly offers a principle in answer to contemporary despair and despondency. It may, indeed, be in part a reply to the apparent pessimism of Shelley's *Alastor, or the Spirit of Solitude* (1816).[16] Since the "gloom" of the second generation Romantics was fuelled by a shared anger at the political and social repression of the times coupled with their knowledge of the failure of the French Revolution, *Endymion*'s mythological "Greece" proposes an alternative to the dominant values and beliefs represented by the repressive policies of Castlereagh and Sidmouth, and the narrow puritanical values of the Society for the Propagation of Christian Knowledge. The shrill and obscure attack upon the "baaing vanities" of bishops, kings, and emperors at the beginning of Book III (lines 1–22) was intended by Keats not just as an attack upon reactionary regimes in general, but as a specific attack upon "the present Ministry."[17] *Endymion* is a rejection of the unheroic and oppressive values of the rulers of Regency Britain.

What is placed against their tyranny, however, is not a political answer, but an assertion of the primacy of other values. While *Endymion* is not explicitly anti-Christian (and was extravagantly admired by a dedicated Christian like Haydon), the whole drift of the poem is to place humanity and human love at its centre. The animist worship of Pan in Book I, the belief in a "Great Maker," and the shepherd-king's ascent to godhead, imagine a pattern of belief which ignores the doctrines of the Trinity and Original Sin in favour of a theistic natural religion. It is a religion which believes in an after-life and the immortality of the individual human soul, and which regards human love, both in its physical and spiritual manifestations, as generative and self-transcending. A passage towards the end of the poem denies the virtues of self-denial and chastity. It occurs after Endymion has chosen the Indian Maid in preference to his dream. He is then told that there is a ban upon their love: Endymion plans to take up his kingly duties, but dedicates himself to the solitary life of a hermit, worshipping Diana. Unaware that he has just succeeded in his ultimate trial, Endymion breaks out bitterly against his enforced solitude:

> "And by old Rhadamanthus' tongue of doom,
> This *dusk religion, pomp of solitude,*
> And the Promethean clay by thief endued,
> By old Saturnus' forelock, by his head
> Shook with eternal palsy, I did wed
> Myself to *things of light* from infancy;
> And thus to be cast out, thus lorn to die,
> Is sure enough to make a mortal man
> Grow impious."
>
> (IV. 953–61; my italics)

The impiety is justified. Self-denial, chastity and gloom are unnecessary since the Maid and Diana are one. Love and fulfilment are the natural order. Endymion's dedication to "things of light" triumphs over the "dusk religion" of solitary worship. The classical allusions, although obscure, probably identify the "dusk religion" with Christianity's suspicion of sensual love, and the stigma cast on human sexuality by the story of Adam and Eve.[18] The poem's conclusion, then, "proves" the truth of Endymion's discovery in Book I—"this earthly love has power to make / Men's being mortal, immortal" (lines 843–4). Although subversive of conventional belief, *Endymion* is not an argument for free love.

Its conclusion circles back to and explains the opening invocation. The claim, "A thing of beauty is a joy for ever," does not advocate a life-denying aestheticism. Rather, the knowledge of beauty "binds" us to the earth:

> Therefore, on every morrow, are we wreathing
> A flowery band to bind us to the earth,
> Spite of despondence, of the inhuman dearth
> Of noble natures, of the gloomy days,
> Of all the unhealthy and o'er-darkened ways
> Make for our searching: yes, in spite of all,
> Some shape of beauty moves away the pall
> From our dark spirits. Such the *sun*, the *moon*,
> *Trees* old, and young . . .
> And such too is the grandeur of the dooms
> We have imagined for the *mighty dead;*
> All *lovely tales* that we have heard or read—
> An endless fountain of immortal drink,
> Pouring unto us from the heaven's brink.
>
> (I. 6–24: my italics)

We are bound to earth, despite its evils and shortcomings, by the human imagination's "searching" of the natural world, its memory of the "mighty dead," and its access to earlier poetry. Throughout *Endymion*, Keats sees the role of the poet in the same terms as he had in "I Stood Tip-toe." The truths contained in the natural world remain immanent until an individual human imagination makes them apprehensible through poetry. Once created, the story is given its "universal freedom," and its truths are available to later readers (II. 829–41). It is the insistence upon the necessity of human intervention which makes Keats's "Platonism" highly idiosyncratic. Refusing the normal Platonic ascent from sensual to ideal love, *Endymion* says that the ideal is only apprehended through individual sensual experience, and through a commitment to the actual. But the individual imagination's discovery of divine truth from the materials of the world comes very close to claiming that man creates his own immortality. The point is made explicitly, if briefly, in Book I. When human beings combine and "interknit" with love, says Endymion, "Life's self is nourished by its proper pith, / And we are nurtured like a pelican brood" (lines 814–5). This is not the usual position taken in *Endymion*, which normally says that human imaginings are drawn from an eternal source, but the lines stress that the imagination be grounded upon human actuality. *Endymion*'s overall pattern is an optimistic one. The re-imagining of an ancient Greek myth leads to the creation of a modern myth, pointing the way to the possible fulfilment of humanity's potential, a potential denied by the dominant political and religious beliefs of the day.

Keats's use of Greek mythology for these purposes was not unusual. From the Enlightenment onwards sceptical thinkers from Voltaire to Hume had used pre-Christian mythology to question Christianity's claims to unique truth. As Marilyn Butler points out, in the second decade of the nineteenth century Greek mythology provided writers like Hunt, Peacock, Hazlitt, Keats, and Shelley, with an important occasion for dissent (whether liberal, deist, radical, or atheist) from prevailing orthodoxies.[19] Keats, like Hazlitt, saw the Greek world as one which attested to the pre-eminence of Art and "Beauty." *Endymion* adds to that a metaphoric equation between human love and poetry. The four books of *Endymion* are a prolonged speculative attempt to establish an equivalence between sexual love and poetry's ability to link the mortal and immortal spheres.

The poem's allegory wishes to force this analogy into an identity, hence the insistently physical depiction of heavenly loving throughout the poem, which risks both obscurity and ridicule. However, the questions forced upon him in the course of composition were, from autumn 1817 onwards, increasingly taken up in the letters. There his "speculations" are more easily understood. Keats's important letter on the nature of the imagination, written to Bailey on 22 November 1817, outlines the intended centre of *Endymion*. He is replying to Bailey's "momentary start [i.e., fears about] the authenticity of the Imagination": "I am certain of nothing but of the holiness of the Heart's affections and the truth of Imagination—What the imagination

seizes as Beauty must be truth—whether it existed before or not—
for I have the same Idea of all our Passions as of Love they are all
in their sublime, creative of essential Beauty" (*Letters*, i. 184). Keats
continues his letter to Bailey by referring him to passages in *Endymion*:

> In a Word, you may know my favorite Speculation by my first Book
> and the little song ["O Sorrow," IV. 146–81] I sent in my last
> [letter]—which is a representation from the fancy of the probable
> mode of operating in these Matters—The Imagination may be com-
> pared to Adam's dream—he awoke and found it truth. I am the
> more zealous in this affair, because I have never yet been able to
> perceive how any thing can be known for truth by consequitive
> reasoning—and yet it must be—Can it be that even the greatest
> Philosopher ever arrived at his goal without putting aside numerous
> objections. (*ibid.*, i. 184–5)

This is not a simple assertion that imaginative truth is superior to
rational thinking. Keats makes two related points. Consequitive thinking alone cannot reach truth: in order to formulate a new concept,
even the philosopher (and by implication the scientist), has to make
an imaginative leap, ignoring apparently contradictory evidence. Secondly, a truth is not properly *known* until it is imaginatively com-
prehended. In both cases, the imagination creates truth. "The Imagination may be compared to Adam's dream—he awoke and found it
truth."

This is a realisation central to Keats's own poetry, but goes beyond
it. However, the "speculation" which immediately follows this passage
puts forward a less satisfactory belief explored by *Endymion*. The
problem is caused by Keats's sceptical humanism, a humanism which
nevertheless wishes to believe in the immortality of the individual
soul: "O for a Life of Sensations rather than of Thoughts! It is 'a
Vision in the form of Youth' a Shadow of reality to come—and this
consideration has further conv[i]nced me . . . that we shall enjoy
ourselves here after by having what we called happiness on Earth
repeated in a finer tone and so repeated—And yet such a fate can
only befall those who delight in sensation rather than hunger as you
do after Truth" (*Letters*, i. 185). *Endymion* believes that the imagination, working on sensation and intense human passion, prefigures
a transcendent world hereafter, a world of etherealised human happiness. Keats tried to explain his belief to Bailey by asking him to
remember "being surprised with an old Melody—in a delicious place—
by a delicious voice . . . at the time it first operated on your soul—
do you not remember forming to you[r] self the singer's face more
beautiful than [written "that"] it was possible and yet with the
elevation of the Moment you did not think so—even then you were

mounted on the Wings of Imagination so high—that the Prototype must be here after—that delicious face you will see—what a time!" (*ibid.*).

This heady mixture of Platonic idealism and youthful longing means that *Endymion*'s "Vision in the form of Youth" and its reality to come are persistently imagined in terms of "delicious faces" and of human love "repeated in a finer tone." When Diana, the moon-goddess, describes their future life in heaven to Endymion, her mortal lover, poetry and sexuality are inextricably mingled:

> Now a soft kiss—
> Ay, by that kiss, I vow an endless bliss,
> An immortality of passion's thine.
> Ere long I will exalt thee to the shine
> Of heaven ambrosial . . .
> And I will tell thee stories of the sky,
> And breathe thee whispers of its minstrelsy.
> My happy love will overwing all bounds!
> O let me melt into thee; let the sounds
> Of our close voices marry at their birth;
> Let us entwine hoveringly—O dearth
> Of human words! roughness of mortal speech!
> Lispings empyrean will I sometime teach
> Thine honeyed tongue—lute-breathings, which I gasp
> To have thee understand
>   (II. 806–21)

"What a time!" Tenor and vehicle are confusingly related. Is the lover's embrace a kind of heavenly poetry, or the heavenly embrace meant as a metaphor of poetry's and the imagination's powers to transcend the physical? In *Endymion* the answer is, quite simply, both.

Keats's version of neo-Platonic love no doubt owes much to his early reading of Spenser, but the literalness of his equation of divine and earthly love is informed more by adolescent fantasy than by any apprehension of Heavenly Love. Endymion begins the exchange with Diana:

> O known Unknown! from whom my being sips
> Such darling essence, wherefore may I not
> Be ever in these arms? in this sweet spot
> Pillow my chin for ever? ever press
> These toying hands and kiss their smooth excess?
>   (II. 739–43)

His speech ends in over-excited metaphor:

> "Enchantress! tell me by this soft embrace,
> By the most soft completion of thy face,

> Those lips, O slippery blisses, twinkling eyes
> And by these tenderest, milky sovereignties—
> These tenderest—and by the nectar-wine,
> The passion—
>
> (II. 756–61)

Keats's difficulties in describing women's breasts reaches an apotheosis here,[20] and the coy phrasing of these lines invites mockery. But there is also a kind of innocence, springing from Keats's idealism. The long account in Book I of the "Pleasure Thermometer" (lines 777–842) explains *Endymion*'s metaphoric linkage between immortal poetic imaginings and physical love. It is a passage whose composition Keats felt to be "a regular stepping of the Imagination towards a Truth,"[21] and begins with an apparently Platonic assertion:

> Wherein lies happiness? In that which becks
> Our ready minds to fellowship divine,
> A fellowship with essence; till we shine,
> Full alchemized, and free of space. Behold
> The clear religion of heaven!

The scale climbs from the physical enjoyment of nature, to our apprehension of poetic tales in natural settings and the pleasures of music and poetry, to "love and friendship," culminating in "love" which "interknits" our souls "so wingedly": indeed, human love may be more than the "mere commingling of passionate breath"—

> but who, of men, can tell
> That flowers would bloom, or that green fruit would swell
> To melting pulp, that fish would have bright mail,
> The earth its dower of river, wood, and vale,
> The meadows runnels, runnels pebble-stones,
> The seed its harvest, or the lute its tones,
> Tones ravishment, or ravishment its sweet,
> If human souls did never kiss and greet?
>
> (I. 835–42)

Benjamin Bailey was right to fear that *Endymion*'s imaginative stepping towards truth came close to endorsing "that abominable principle of Shelley's—that *Sensual Love* is the principle of *things*."[22] Keats does not go that far: instead he invents a sensual Platonism in which human love and poetry are linked manifestations of the same power which both give access to immortal truth.

The resultant balance between physical and ideal love is unstable. Uncertainty about the relationship between human and immortal worlds is as much a result of the intrusion of Keats's own erotic fantasies as the weak control over his allegorical narrative. For instance, the story of Alpheus, the river-god, and the nymph Arethusa, is meant to demonstrate that by the end of Book II Endymion has taken on the powers of the original poets who invented Graeco-Roman myths. The episode (II. 914–1017) is a copy-book example of natural beauty providing the ancient poets with the source of "lovely tales." Endymion hears the sound of two gushing springs, and invents the story of the love of Arethusa and Alpheus which cannot be consummated because Arethusa is one of Diana's huntresses, and therefore bound to chastity. Not only does Endymion invent the story, but having done so appeals to Diana to allow their love to be assuaged, thus demonstrating the true poet's necessary sympathy with suffering. But Keats's telling of the story separates off from the allegory, becoming an "aesthetically" distanced fantasy of an imagined sexual encounter. Arethusa is prevented from bathing in Alpheus' waters a second time: he regrets being deprived of the opportunity

> to run
> In amorous rillets down her shrinking form!
> To linger on her lily shoulders, warm
> Between her kissing breasts, and every charm
> Touch raptured!—See how painfully I flow!
>   (II. 944–8)

(In the draft version Alpheus kisses "raptur'd—even to her milky toes.") It is no surprise that when Cupid is apostrophised as god of love, the etherial "essences" of "fellowship divine" turn out to be directly physical: "O sweetest essence! sweetest of all minions! / God of warm pulses, and dishevelled hair, / And panting bosoms bare!" (III. 983–5). The earthly and ideal realms have changed places. It requires a sympathetic reader to see what Keats's allegory is trying to say in the Alpheus and Arethusa story.

Other reactions were possible. The reviewer in *The British Critic* assaulted *Endymion*'s sexual impurity: "not all the flimsy veil of words in which he would involve immoral images, can atone for their impurity; and we will not disgust our readers by retailing to them the artifices of vicious refinement, by which, under the semblance of 'slippery blisses, twinkling eyes, soft completion of faces, and smooth excess of hands,' he would palm upon the unsuspicious and the innocent imaginations better adapted to the stews."[23] *The British Critic* isolates the cause of Byron's violent revulsion to "Johnny Keats's p[i]ss a bed poetry."[24] In part this is a clash of sensibilities—Byron's sang froid when dealing with Don Juan's escapades is the antithesis of Keats's intense identification with the young lovers in *The Eve of St Agnes*. Byron's objections went beyond *Endymion*. In 1820 he wrote to his publisher, Murray, "such writing is a sort of mental masturbation—Keats is always f[ri]gg[in]g his *Imagination*. I don't mean he is *indecent* [Byron would have been less disturbed if Keats had been], but viciously soliciting his own ideas into a state."[25]

Byron's objections to Keats were also partly animated by class antagonism. G. M. Matthews shrewdly observes:

> This sort of socio-sexual revulsion is an oddly persistent feature of Keats criticism. . . . Its origin seems to lie in the disturbance created by a deep response to Keats's poetic sensuality in conflict with a strong urge towards sexual apartheid. At any rate, Byron's astonishing outbursts . . . must have had some such components. That is, it was more or less accepted—since Crabbe and Wordsworth had insisted on it—that the domestic emotions of the lower classes were a fit subject for poetry; but that a poet of the lower classes should play with *erotic* emotions was insufferable, unless these were expressed in a straightforward peasant dialect, as with Burns or Clare.[26]

If class was one cause of the anger directed at Keats's "Cockney" temerity in portraying erotic emotions, another, and more powerful cause was that Keats's approving depiction of sexuality cut through the conventional belief that ladies had, in the words of *The British Critic*, "unsuspicious and innocent imaginations." While Keats's own attitude to women was frequently ambivalent, *Endymion* assumes that women as well as men have strong sexual drives. Arethusa "burns" as a result of bathing in Alpheus' waters:

> But ever since I heedlessly did lave
> In thy deceitful stream, a panting glow
> Grew strong within me: wherefore serve me so,
> And call it love?
>
> (II. 969–72)

And throughout the pastoral it is the women who seduce the men.

From a twentieth-century viewpoint Keats may seem frequently guilty of an adolescent failure of taste. The poem now looks naive rather than shocking. However, the schizophrenic reaction to *Endymion* when it was published in 1818 ("a dream of poetry," "better adapted to the stews"), does raise the question of what Keats and his publishers thought they were presenting to the public. Taylor worked very closely on the manuscript of *Endymion*, suggesting verbal changes and seeing it through the press on Keats's behalf: there is no sign at this stage that the man, later so exercised over the impropriety of the revised version of *The Eve of St. Agnes*, saw the narrative as anything other than "a dream of poetry" or that he doubted Keats's genius. Similarly, Keats writing to his young sister Fanny told her the story of his poem, remarking, "I dare say [you] have read this and all the other beautiful Tales which have come down from the ancient times of that beautiful Greece. If you have not let me know and I will tell you more at large of others quite as delightful" (*Letters*, i. 154).

The violence of *The British Critic* stems precisely from a fear that the Ovidian stories, taken too literally, were not at all suitable for young ladies. Yet while the readers in the later twentieth century cannot avoid reading *Endymion* as a series of often barely disguised erotic fantasies, it was not only Keats's publisher who read the poem as an idealistic romance. Richard Woodhouse was particularly pleased to tell Keats in December 1818 that his own copy had been borrowed by Mary Frogley and then read and admired by Jane and Maria Porter "of romance celebrity"—Jane Porter, author of *The Scottish Chief* and other works, thought the poem showed "true Parnassian fire" (*Letters*, ii. 9–10).[27]

The response of readers like these indicates that "romance" created a *cordon sanitaire* which allowed the expression and enjoyment of feelings and emotions which could not be consciously admitted. Sexual doings among the Greek gods were "pretty" fictions, suitable for young ladies.[28] Keats's reaction to Woodhouse's offer to introduce him to the Misses Porter was quizzical: "I must needs feel flattered by making an impression on a set of Ladies—I should be content to do so in meretricious romance verse if they alone and not Men were to judge" (*Letters*, i. 412). "Meretricious romance verse" is the kind of anodyne romance which offered the pleasure of mildly titillating fantasy to an unreflecting audience. Keats may have felt that, in the end, *Endymion* had achieved no more than this, but he had hoped for readers willing to pay serious attention to the poem's substantial themes. That Taylor and Woodhouse failed to perceive the underlying subversiveness of *Endymion* is not surprising: Keats's subject matter resembles that of conventional romance (for example, Mrs. Tighe's *Psyche* (1805)),[29] and its rambling allegory is sufficiently oblique to obscure its real argument. The similarity between Keats's poetry and the flaccid romances of the day was close enough for some readers to confuse one with the other.

Endymion does not succeed in establishing a properly meaningful relation between the "etherial" and mundane. It does, however, show Keats already struggling with his major preoccupations. Throughout the poem there is a latent, sometimes open, fissure between "the power to dream deliciously" (II. 708) and the actualities of "dull mortality's harsh net" (III. 907). "Beauty" is found within a dream, or even in a dream within a dream which ends abruptly in the sleep of unconsciousness (I. 553–709). But the promise that "solitary thinkings" which dodge "Conception to the very bourne of heaven" will leaven "this dull and clodded earth" giving it "a touch etherial—a new birth" (I. 293–8) proves elusive, and may be only a dream. "There never lived a mortal man, who bent / His appetite beyond his natural sphere, / But starved and died" (IV. 646–8). Throughout *Endymion* there is a persistent movement towards associating the moment of fulfilment not just with unconsciousness but with death: "we might embrace and die: voluptuous thought!" (IV. 759). The Indian Maid's pursuit of pleasure and beauty leads to sorrow—

> Come then, Sorrow!
> Sweetest Sorrow!
> Like an own babe I nurse thee on my breast:
> I thought to leave thee
> And deceive thee,
> But now of all the world I love thee best.
>   (IV. 279–84)

There is also a sinister aspect of love. As a whole, the Glaucus episode (III. 187–1017) symbolises the role of the poet, whose suffering and vision brings comfort to humanity, forecasting the subject of Keats's two poems on Hyperion, but his tale begins ominously. Glaucus is seduced by the enchantress Circe, but the promised "long love-dream" (III. 440) turns to nightmare: he is the victim of the "arbitrary queen of sense" (III. 459). Circe's rout of tormented animal shapes, who wish to "be delivered from this cumbrous flesh, . . . this gross, detestable, filthy mesh" (III. 551–2), are clearly images of revulsion in the aftermath of sexual gratification. Circe is the principle of female sexuality as destroyer, and this passage (III. 417–614) an expression of the tensions which lie behind "La Belle Dame sans Merci" and *Lamia*.

The initial optimism of *Endymion*'s combination of "humanistic hedonism"[30] and aching idealism comes close to being denied by powerful undercurrents in the poem—the ambiguity of the hero's dreams and visions, his recurrent despondency and long withdrawal from kingly duties, and the threat of the real, all question the efficacy of the religion of beauty.

Keats's maturing views on poetry and the imagination could not be contained by *Endymion*, but were worked out in the "speculations" of the letters. "Speculation," containing the Latin sense of spying out as well as the usual abstract meaning, is Keats's own word for his exploratory forays. Their truth then is provisional: they represent a hypothesis with no claim to ultimate or exclusive truth. Indeed, "eve[r]y point of thought is the centre of an intellectual world" and—"almost any Man may like the Spider spin from his own inwards his own airy Citadel—the points of leaves and twigs on which the Spider begins her work are few and she fills the Air with a beautiful circuiting" (*Letters*, i. 231–2). In both his speculations and his poetry Keats's mode is essentially exploratory and tentative. He wrote to Bailey in March 1818, "I must once for all tell you I have not one Idea of the truth of any of my speculations," and went so far as to say, "I am sometimes so very sceptical as to think Poetry itself a mere Jack a lanthern to amuse whoever may chance to be struck with its brilliance" (*Letters*, i. 242). It is precisely the ability to hold contrary truths together in creative tension which Keats saw as the essential quality which goes "to form a Man of Achievement especially in Literature & which Shakespeare posessed so enormously—I mean *Negative Capability*, that is when man is capable of being in uncertainties, Mysteries, doubts, without any irritable reaching after fact & reason—Coleridge, for instance, would let go by a fine isolated verisimilitude caught from the Penetralium of mystery, from being incapable of remaining content with half knowledge" (*Letters*, i. 193–4). Keats's famous remark, made in December 1817 while finishing *Endymion*, is at the heart of his own achievement. The ambitions of poetry and its claims to a supra-rational and intuitive order of truth, were themselves at risk. With his suspicion that poetry may be no more than a "Jack a lanthern," Keats entertains a peculiarly modern fear that the secrecy and inviolability of the products of the imagination may offer false consolation, may be, in the end, illusory. Even *Endymion*, committed as it is to affirming the superior truth of poetry, is firmly framed as a fiction. The motto chosen for the poem, "The stretched metre of an antique song," is taken from Shakespeare's Sonnet XVII which ironically foresees a time when the real feeling expressed in his poem will be mocked as a mere poetic fantasy. Placed at the head of the poem, the quotation questions whether *Endymion*'s "stretching" of the classical tale to over 4,000 lines is nothing more than a "poet's rage." The poem's fictiveness is further emphasised by the picture which Keats gives of himself, in the country and far from "the city's din," beginning to write the poem we are reading, and proposing the timetable for its composition (I. 34–62). Poetry for Keats is in the end fictive, and its assertions perhaps overweeningly arrogant.

An extreme faith in the power of poetry and the imagination is set against an awareness that when measured against our knowledge in time, poetry is *a* truth, but possibly a severely limited one or even one which is finally untrue. That ambiguity is evident throughout Keats's work. It appears in the provisional note of the aspiring early poetry and in the confusions of *Endymion*, though its clearest expression is to be found in the mature work—the odes, *Lamia* and *The Fall of Hyperion*—where it has become an explicit rather than a potential concern.

What ties these speculations, and Keats's poetry, to common experience, is the insistence on truth to "sensation." The desire "for a Life of Sensations rather than of Thoughts" most obviously relates to a recurrent wish to lose the self in being. "Sensation," however, is more than self-indulgence. It is central to a belief in the veracity of concrete experience. At one extreme it is quite literally the information of our senses. As Keats was to write in April 1819, "suppose a rose to have sensation, it blooms on a beautiful morning it enjoys itself—but there comes a cold wind, a hot sun—it can not escape it, it cannot destroy its annoyances" (*Letters*, ii. 101). This gives the basis for the characteristic tactile, visual and auditory effects in the poetry, and the preference for metaphors of fullness, of a selfhood bursting with its own identity. Sensation then is linked with Keatsian empathy. Being taken up into sensation, into something deeply other to the self, takes Keats a long way from simple sense experience. For him, sensations are internal as well as external. "My sensations are sometimes deadened for weeks together," or again, writing to Reynolds, "I was to give you a history of [my] sensations, and day-night mares" (*Letters*, ii. 146). Keats imagined in sensory terms: the imaginative experience therefore started from direct experience, but its meaning went beyond mere day-dreaming. It was in fact a kind of thinking through images. The crux was that the truth once apprehended was seen to be true. Like Adam's dream it is self-authenticating. Thus the "Ode to a Nightingale" both tells one truth (that poetry reaches back and overcomes time), and poses against it a counter-truth (that this is only a fiction): it fleetingly attains a stance which can accommodate contradictory orders of experience. But the poem must start in the experience of actually hearing a bird, and end in a truthfulness to the poet's literal experience—the sense of loss as the bird flies off. It is at once a day-dream and a "day-night mare."

Negative capability, with dependence on sensation and empathic projection, defines a Romantic polarity opposed to the practice of Wordsworth and Coleridge. All Romantic artists shared the problem of relating the subjective and the objective. As John Bayley says, "the premises on which any romantic poem is written are an acute consciousness of the isolated creating self on the one hand, and of a world unrelated, and possibly indifferent and hostile, on the other; and the wish somehow to achieve a harmonious synthesis of the two."[31] Coleridge's response to this problem was analytic and metaphysical, marked by a fascination with his own mental and creative processes. Keats, who believed that the poet's ego should go out into the thing perceived, thought Coleridge, like Wordsworth, guilty of forcing himself upon both the material and the reader, and of allowing the self to obtrude upon the impersonality of great poetry. As Keats was to insist, there is profound difference between his own genius and that of Wordsworth:

> As to the poetical Character itself, (I mean that sort of which, if I
> am any thing, I am a Member; that sort distinguished from the

wordsworthian or egotistical sublime; which is a thing per se and
stands alone) it is not itself—it has no self—it is every thing and
nothing—It has no character—it enjoys light and shade; it lives in
gusto, be it foul or fair, high or low, rich or poor, mean or elevated—
It has as much delight in conceiving an Iago as an Imogen. What
shocks the virtuous philosop[h]er, delights the cameleon Poet. (Letters, i. 386–7)

The difficulty of reconciling the amoral creativity of the "cameleon
Poet" with the demands of truth was in some part answered by the
notion of "intensity" which Keats puts forward in a letter to his
brothers written on 20 December 1817: "the excellence of every
Art is its intensity, capable of making all disagreeables evaporate,
from their being in close relationship with Beauty & Truth—Examine
King Lear & you will find this examplified throughout; but in [Ben-
jamin West's painting, *Death on the Pale Horse*] we have unpleasantness without any momentous depth of speculation excited, in which
to bury its repulsiveness" (*Letters*, i. 192).

Preparing *Endymion* for the press in January 1818, Keats knew
that his speculations would take him far beyond the bounds of his
pastoral romance—"I think a little change has taken place in my
intellect lately" (*Letters*, i. 214). Although that "little change" had
mapped out an alternative to Coleridgean introspection and Wordsworth's "egotistical sublime," it offered Keats little immediate help.

The disjointed verse letter which he wrote to J. H. Reynolds in
March 1818 reveals a crisis in Keats's thinking. Beginning in a jocose
manner, it plays off the grotesque and incoherent wanderings of the
fancy in nightmares and daydreams against the beauty to be enjoyed
in poetry and painting, before abruptly turning to a vision of nature's
alien destructiveness:

> I saw
> Too far into the sea, where every maw
> The greater on the less feeds evermore.—
> But I saw too distinct into the core
> Of an eternal fierce destruction . . .
> Still do I that fierce destruction see—
> The shark at savage prey, the hawk at pounce,
> The gentle robin, like a pard or ounce,
> Ravening a worm.
>   (lines 93–105)

The self-consuming violence of the natural world shocks the
imagination which has perceived it by seeing "Too far into the sea":
consciousness of that violence destroys normal human satisfactions:

> is it that imagination brought
> Beyond its proper bound, yet still confined,

> Lost in a sort of purgatory blind,
> Cannot refer to any standard law
> Of either earth or heaven? It is a flaw
> In happiness to see beyond our bourne—
> It forces us in summer skies to mourn;
> It spoils the singing of the nightingale.
>
> (lines 78–85)

Imagination sees beyond the mortal but cannot attain the full perspective of "heaven's Law." Its "purgatory blind" is created by the imagination's ability to conceive the essential violence of natural destruction without being able to understand it. The intensity of art and the imagination cannot make disagreeables evaporate: instead, the awareness it brings may prove disabling and destructive.

Keats's impasse here signals the intellectual and aesthetic crisis he underwent between the autumn and winter of 1818. "Beauty" was an insufficient answer to suffering and pain. The danger was that the etherealising imagination took too little cognisance of ordinary life. John Wilson, writing in 1819, argued that the decline of poetic drama after the seventeenth century came about because the imagination no longer "submitted to life": "The whole character of our life and literature seems to us to show in our cultivated classes a disposition of imagination to separate itself from real life, and to go over into works of art." The lyric nature of "the great overflow of poetry in this age may be in part from this cause."[32] Keats could perceive this limitation clearly enough in the work of Hunt: his difficulty was to find a way beyond it.

Notes

1. These range from an allegory grounded on Renaissance neo-Platonism (C. L. Finney, *The Evolution of Keats's Poetry*, Cambridge, Mass., 1936, i. 291–319) to the denial that it is an allegory at all (E. C. Pettet, *On the Poetry of John Keats*, Cambridge, 1957, pp. 127–29). For a brisk account of the varieties of readings, and an account of some of the reasons for the variety, see Jack Stillinger, "On the Interpretation of *Endymion:* The Comedian as Letter E," *The Hoodwinking of Madeline* (Urbana, Chicago, London, 1971), pp. 14–30. See also, Walter H. Evert, *Aesthetic and Myth in the Poetry of Keats* (Princeton, 1965), pp. 88–176, and Morris Dickstein, *Keats and his Poetry: A Study in Development* (Chicago and London, 1971), pp. 53–129. None of these is wholly satisfactory, though most agree that it *is* an allegory.

2. Christopher Ricks, *Keats and Embarrassment* (Oxford, 1974), pp. 7–8, quoting from John Bayley's "Keats and Reality" (1962), rptd, rev., and expanded as "Uses in Poetry," Chapter II, *The Uses of Division: Unity and Disharmony in Literature* (1976), p. 115. This revision includes a reply to Ricks.

3. Bayley, *ibid.*, p. 124.

4. Ricks, *Keats*, p. 9.

5. *The Alfred*, 6 Oct. 1818. Rptd *The Young Romantics and Critical Opinion 1807–1824*, ed. Theodore Redpath (1973), p. 479.

6. *John Keats: The Complete Poems*, ed. John Barnard (Harmondsworth, 2nd edn, 1976), p. 505.

7. *The Keats Circle: Letters and Papers 1816–1879*, ed. Hyder E. Rollins (Cambridge, Mass., 1958), ii. 144.

8. *Ibid.*

9. *Letters*, i. 179 (Nov. 1817).

10. *The Life and Letters of Joseph Severn*, ed. William Sharp (New York, 1892), p. 29.

11. *The Pantheon: or Ancient History of the Gods* . . . (1806), pp. 6–7.

12. *Ibid.*, p. 6.

13. "Mr. Angerstein's Collection," *Sketches of the Principal Picture Galleries in England* (1824), *The Complete Works of William Hazlitt*, ed. P. P. Howe (1930–34), x. 7–8.

14. *A Grammar of Motives and a Grammar of Rhetoric* (Cleveland and New York, 1962), p. 449.

15. On the influence of the visual arts, see Ian Jack, *Keats and the Mirror of Art* (Oxford, 1967): for this identification of the source in Poussin, see p. 157. Further, see *Keats-Shelley Memorial Bulletin*, xxxiii (1982), 12–16.

16. See W. J. Bate, *John Keats* (Cambridge, Mass., 1963), p. 177; Miriam Allott, "Keats's *Endymion* and Shelley's *Alastor*"; *Literature of the Romantic Period*, ed. R. T. Davies and B. G. Beatty (Liverpool, 1976), pp. 151–70; and Walter H. Evert, *Aesthetic and Myth in the Poetry of Keats* (Princeton, 1965), pp. 113–15n.

17. In her edition of *The Poems of John Keats* (1970), p. 206, Miriam Allott cites Woodhouse's note in his own copy of *Endymion*: "K. said, with great simplicity, 'It will easily be seen what I think of the present Ministers by the beginning of the 3d Book [II. 1–22].' " Keats's blithe belief in the passage's transparency is unwarranted. Miriam Allott notes that reactionary regimes had gained strength since the restoration of the monarchy in France (1814) and the Congress of Vienna (1814–15). She also records the similarity between these lines and Hunt's articles in *The Examiner* in August 1817. The "empurpled vests" (line 11) of the clergy echoes Hunt's mockery of the French clergy for their recent acceptance of the "Roman purple" of Cardinal's hats, while the reference to "trumpets . . . and sudden cannon" (lines 17–18) is likely to refer to the peace celebrations in London which followed Napoleon's abdication and culminated on 1 August 1814. Further, though Allott does not make the point, the "idiot blink" (line 6) seems to refer to the mad George III, and the following lines to his ministers' (the "Fire-branded foxes" of line 7) destruction of the hopes raised by the Peace, and to their disastrous refusal to allay distress caused by poor harvests. The act passed in 1815 prohibited the import of foreign corn until wheat had reached famine prices:

> O torturing fact!—
> Who, through an idiot blink, will see unpacked
> Fire-branded foxes to sear up and singe
> Our gold and ripe-eared hopes.

18. This passage is even more obscure than Book III's attack on the Ministry. Rhadamanthus, one of the judges of the underworld whose function, says Lemprière, was "obliging the dead to confess their crimes, and in punishing them for their offences," is set against the Golden Age of the overthrown Saturn and its innocent sexuality. The puzzling reference to Prometheus seems to invert the conventional meaning. Lemprière

says, "Prometheus made the first man and woman that ever were upon the earth, with clay, which he animated with fire which he had stolen from heaven." Keats sees the "dusk religion" as based on a theft, and "Promethean clay" suggests that the god has visited his own lonely suffering onto humanity. Coming at a strategic point as the poem ends, the identification of the "dusk religion" with contemporary middle class attitudes would support the whole poem's argument for light and freedom.

19. See *Romantics, Rebels, and Reactionaries; English Literature and Its Background 1760–1830* (Oxford, 1981), 130–31, 134–7, and "Myth and Myth-making in the Shelley Circle," *English Literary History*, xlix (1982), 50–72.

20. If the testimony of Walter Cooper Dendy is to be believed, and it seems unlikely in the extreme that he would have invented it, Keats scribbled out the beginning of a "Spenserian" romance while listening to Astley Cooper lecture at St Thomas's hospital: it ends, "The authore was goynge onne withouten discrybynge yᵉ ladye's breste, whenne lo, a genyus appearyd—'Cuthberte,' sayeth he, 'an thou canst not descrybe yᵉ ladye's brest, and fynde a simile thereunto, I forbyde thee to proceede in thy romaunt.' Thys, I kenned fulle weele, far surpassyd my feble powers, and forthwythe I was fayn to droppe my quille" (*The Philosophy of Mystery* (1841), p. 99, rptd in *The Poetical Works and Other Writings of John Keats*, ed. H. Buxton Forman, rev. M. Buxton Forman, New York, 1939, v. 322).

21. *Letters*, i. 218.

22. *Keats Circle*, ed. Rollins, i. 34–5.

23. Quoted Tim Chilcott, *A Publisher and His Circle: The Life and Work of John Taylor, Keats's Publisher* (1972), p. 34.

24. Cited Ricks, *Keats*, p. 78.

25. *Ibid.*, p. 85.

26. *Keats: The Critical Heritage*, ed. G. M. Matthews (1971), p. 35.

27. See also *Letters*, i. 410, 412.

28. See, for instance, the long-running series of letters describing "A New System of Mythology by "Clermont" in *The Ladies' Monthly Museum; or, Polite Repository of Amusement and Instruction: being an assemblage of whatever can tend to please the fancy, interest the mind, or exalt the character of the British Fair. Improved Series*, vi–vii (1817–18), *passim*. The story of Endymion is told as follows: "[Diana's] adventure with Endymion will, perhaps, account for this relaxation from her usual severity [i.e., waiving her law of chastity in favour of the nymph Egeria]; under the names of Luna and Phoebe, she was Goddess of the Moon; and the scandalous chronicles of Olympus inform us, that the handsome, young Endymion was favoured with a visit from her every night in a cave on Mount Latmos. This young Prince, who was a descendant of Jupiter, was admitted into Olympus, but having behaved disrespectfully to Juno, he was condemned to perpetual sleep. Fifty daughters and one son were said to be the offspring of this amour" (vii. 14).

29. The young Keats enjoyed Mrs Tighe's poetry: E. V. Weller, *Keats and Mary Tighe* (New York, 1928) wholly over-estimates her influence. Her poem reached a fifth edition in *Psyche, with Other Poems* (1816).

30. Harold Bloom, *The Visionary Company: A Reading of English Romantic Poetry* (New York, 1961; rptd New York, 1963), p. 396.

31. *The Romantic Survival* (1957), pp. 9–10.

32. "A Few Words on Shakespeare" (1819), *Works* (Edinburgh, 1847), vii. 430 (quoted by Bate, *John Keats*, pp. 365–6n).

Keats and the
Problem of Romance
Robert Kern[*]

Despite the efforts of recent criticism to establish Keats as "the Romantic poet most likely to survive in the modern world,"[1] to see him, that is, as more or less free of illusions about the capacities of the visionary imagination and as a participant in our own skepticism and doubt about the possibilities of romance—understood as a kind or quality of experience rather than strictly as a literary genre[2]—it is Keats himself, at crucial points throughout his career, who raises these possibilities and refuses to let go of them entirely even after they are exposed as deceptive. The classic instance of such refusal occurs at the end of the "Ode to a Nightingale," after the poet has been tolled back to his "sole self," and the possibility of his having joined the bird in its own unreflective and undying world has been rejected as a trick of the fancy. Here he can still raise the question of the status of his experience: "Was it a vision, or a waking dream? / Fled is that music:—Do I wake or sleep?" (79–80).[3] The point is that something in Keats still longs for vision, for transcendent experience beyond the "sole self," and in ending the poem on a question he seems to be delicately insisting on the ambiguous nature of his experience and on his own ambivalence, though some of his modern critics have been all too eager to decide the issue for him and to steer the poem toward an almost doctrinal statement about the inadequacy of the imagination.

Jack Stillinger, for example, in several influential essays, has been arguing for some time now that the repudiation of romance and of the reality of visionary experience is the central theme of Keats's poetic development. Taking as evidence a number of statements from the letters, the epistle to Reynolds, and the sonnet "On Sitting Down to Read King Lear Once Again," Stillinger contends that during the winter of 1817–18 Keats decisively changed his mind about the authenticity of the visionary imagination and began to regard romance with an increasingly skeptical eye, particularly while copying out Endymion for the printer. In accordance with these changes of attitude, Keats became, in the terms of Stillinger's often ingenious argument, a kind of saboteur against the romantic elements in his poetry, so that the proper context for his work after the Lear sonnet, from the beginning of 1818 on, is an anti-romantic one. Thus, the final phase of Keats's development, as Stillinger sees it, starts with the "wormy circumstance" of Isabella, proceeds to The Eve of St.

[*] Reprinted from Philological Quarterly 58 (1979): 171–91. ©1979 by The University of Iowa. Reprinted with permission.

Agnes regarded, somewhat cynically, as the "hoodwinking" of Madeline, and ends up with what he calls "the anti-romances and ultimately skeptical lyrics of 1819." Intending to save Keats from a naive romanticism, Stillinger puts forward a view of his work that all but declares him to be our contemporary.[4]

What I want to suggest, however, is that rather than a repudiation of romance, Keats's poetry constitutes a continuing struggle with it that becomes the very condition of his work. Least visible in the early poems, which are important precisely because they virtually establish for Keats the notion of poetry *as* romance, this struggle reaches its climax in the great odes, which are simultaneously romantic and anti-romantic, texts which register the force both of desire and of knowledge. Though Stillinger argues that it is only in his liberation from romance that Keats's work reaches its greatest authenticity and value, it seems to me that the notion of such a liberation is finally incompatible not only with Keats's development, which is not quite the steady movement from the poetry of dream to the poetry of actuality that standard accounts propose, but with the actual texture of his work, especially of the odes, which are dramatizations of conflict far more than they are statements of settled philosophical position. To insist that after writing the *Lear* sonnet "Keats never again wholeheartedly embraces the *idea* of romance"[5] is seriously to oversimplify that idea, as well as to miss the strong sense in which the idea of romance continues to inform the idea of poetry itself for Keats. The nature of his work suggests that he can function as a poet only so long as he recognizes and acts upon the impulses toward romance within his own sensibility, impulses that urge him toward the autonomy of pure imagination even as they are countered by an opposing "sense of real things" ("Sleep and Poetry," 157). The dilemma that romance becomes for Keats does not lie in the question of whether or not to reject it but in the question of how to make it more inclusive, how to establish a greater continuity between the beauty of romance and the harsh truths of reality.

In this sense, change or development for Keats can be defined most accurately not as a movement away from romance but as an increasing self-consciousness about its presence in his work and in his sensibility. The problem that romance poses—escapism, solipsism, avoidance of what is most commonly regarded as empirically (and, in Keats, tragically) real—is never, strictly speaking, solved, at least not in the sense that Keats ever manages to reconcile his romantic desires for transcendence with his awareness of the realities of history and the human condition. But that problem does move more and more to the center of his poetic thought, becoming, in effect, his chief subject. As Howard Felperin points out in his suggestive study of Shakespearean romance, one of the ways in which serious writers have always dealt with the problem of romantic truancy has been by incorporating it into their work, by acknowledging, within the text, the differences between desire and reality. Shakespeare, Felperin observes, avoids escapism in his last plays by making them about escapism, by including an anti-romantic dimension against which the romantic possibilities of character, action, and setting are tested.[6] Keats, perhaps, does not go so far in this direction as Shakespeare, though a self-conscious romance like *The Eve of St. Agnes,* as I shall try to show, is ultimately controlled by a narrator who fully indulges his characters' romantic desires while withholding his own commitment from them and finally separates himself and his readers from the poem's romance world. Keats's development, then, leads him not toward a rejection of romance but toward a critical awareness of its claims that, in *The Eve of St. Agnes* at least, is balanced against a more unqualified expression of romantic desire—an expression that proceeds from the poem's characters rather than from the poet himself.

Keats's earliest work, on the other hand, is most remarkable precisely for its unguarded and perhaps naive willingness to embrace a definition of poetry as romance in an exclusive and oversimplified way, a definition that merely exacerbates the otherwise inescapable differences between poetry and life. In his early work, it is often argued, Keats is overwhelmed by his very desire to write, as well as frustrated by his "sense of not yet having written great verse."[7] But if the early work is largely a "poetry about trying to write poetry."[8] then it is easy to see why, in that work, poetry should take on qualities of remoteness and otherness for Keats. Poetry exists in some other place, at some other time, or depends upon a condition of mind or soul, or even physical circumstances, that he has not yet managed to achieve. Keenly aware of all he has not done, Keats continually looks forward to a future productivity, and such long poems as "I Stood Tiptoe" and "Sleep and Poetry" are energized and propelled by a kind of dialectical shuttling back and forth between hopes for a future poetic plentitude and despair about a present emptiness or inability, which Keats sometimes projects onto his historical and cultural situation.[9]

The present, in fact, is precisely what Keats is trying to avoid in these early poems—even if, in doing so, he is merely being unusually and naively open about an aspect of literary experience that more sophisticated writers work hard to disguise: the fundamentally romantic nature of all literature, which means in some measure that literature is always the representation of absence. As several recent students of romance have suggested, of all imaginative modes romance is the most basic and inclusive, the poetic act inherently and unavoidably constituting a world elsewhere.[10] If all literature is fundamentally romantic, however, for the early Keats romance is the only literary possibility, the journey into a world elsewhere providing the one enabling mechanism by which the act of writing can take place. When the present is noticed at all, as in the "Epistle to George Felton Mathew" (1815), it is barely and vaguely characterized as a time of "cares" and "contradictions," an undefined set of circumstances seen as inimical to poetic creativity. Keats is able to write only when he can imagine some alternative to his present circumstances, and this alternative inevitably takes the form of an escapist fantasy involving an idealized nature whose sources lie not in experience but in literature, especially literature in a pastoral or mythological mode:

> Too partial friend! fain would I follow thee
> Past each horizon of fine poesy;
> Fain would I echo back each pleasant note
> As o'er Sicilian seas, clear anthems float
> 'Mong the light skimming gondolas far parted,
> Just when the sun his farewell beam has darted:
> But 'tis impossible; far different cares
> Beckon me sternly from soft "Lydian airs,"
> And hold my faculties so long in thrall,
> That I am oft in doubt whether at all
> I shall again see Phoebus in the morning;
> Or flush'd Aurora in the roseate dawning!
> Or a white Naiad in a rippling stream;
> Or a rapt seraph in a moonlight beam . . .
> But might I now each passing moment give
> To the coy muse, with me she would not live
> In this dark city, nor would condescend
> 'Mid contradictions her delights to lend.
> Should e'er the fine-eyed maid to me be kind,
> Ah! surely it must be whene'er I find
> Some flowery spot, sequester'd, wild, romantic,
> That often must have seen a poet frantic;
> Where oaks, that erst the Druid knew, are growing.
> And flowers, the glory of one day, are blowing
>   (11–40)

Here, in the midst of "cares" (presumably his duties as a medical student) that sternly beckon the poet away from poetic activity, the very context of doubt about whether he can ever again participate in such activity becomes the occasion for cataloguing the absent visions, the mythological figures and idealized natural props that constitute "poesy" for Keats. The "dark city," an allusion familiar from Wordsworth and Coleridge, is already a romantic cliché for him, a force hostile to poetry that receives no further explanation or analysis. What is most surprising, though, is that the doubt that controls the overall tone of the passage is never clarified or pursued, never examined as a concrete situation. Rather than deal with the sources of his difficulties, Keats prefers to imagine circumstances that simply displace them. In a typically escapist gesture, he turns from "this dark city" (where he cannot write) to "some flowery spot" (where he can), from the actual and present to the imagined and remote, and allows the latter to expand and fill his mind. By the end of the passage, he has arrived, in imagination, at the heart of the romantic forest, a place free of contradictions where both erotic and poetic pleasures await him. Only here, it is not yet a place to move through (as it will become in the *Lear* sonnet) but one still to appreciate and linger in—a permanent place, apparently immune to time, that nevertheless accommodates natural process and, if not actual or public history, then at least a separate history of native myth and poetic frenzy. As such, it is a perfect emblem for Keats's early conception of poetry, defined as or associated with a time or place or condition that is essentially distinct from the here and now of the poet's ongoing life. It is also inseparable from his notion of romance, which, in the early poems, as Morris Dickstein has noted, inevitably involves the motif of the bower—"the enclosed, sheltered nook, the place of nestling green."[11]

Keats's absorption in such "places" or "spots," his idealized yearning for the *locus amoenus* in which poetic activity becomes possible and is closely identified with erotic activity, suggest the extent to which he is enthralled, even victimized, by romantic escapism in his early work. As Dickstein shrewdly observes, Keats is aware that such bowers represent a kind of innocent sexuality and self-annihilating pleasure which are ultimately inimical to moral growth; but he indulges his desires for them anyway, prompted by an irresistible longing for a peaceful merging with a perfected nature far from any actuality, and lured by the promise of self-transcendence that such merging holds out.[12]

At this stage of his development, then, Keats is writing in a naively romantic style that results, once he has left the real world behind and is freely ranging over the landscape of his purely imagined world, in a seemingly self-generating text—self-generating, and potentially infinite in structure, because it is the expression of a boundless desire that encounters few, if any, obstacles from reality in its pursuit of a locus of sheer absence. As he pauses briefly in the midst of cataloguing the delights of rambling through the woods in "I Stood Tiptoe," for example, the speaker asks "What next?" (107), a question that is only the most explicit manifestation of the imaginative energy of this style, its restlessness and freedom from the constraints of the actual. In terms of imagery from the "Ode to Psyche," it might be described as the transcription of thoughtless wandering in a forest, and it will remain intact throughout most of Keats's early poetry. But it will also continue to appear in important ways in the later work. The fact that Keats will call both the style and its assumptions into question in the *Lear* sonnet will not prevent their revival and revision in a variety of later contexts, including the "Ode to Psyche" and *The Fall of Hyperion*. The real importance of the *Lear* sonnet lies not in what critics all too easily assume to be its outright rejection of romance but in the way it consciously focuses on romance as a problem, offering an intensified reenactment of earlier moments of self-criticism, a renewal in stronger and broader terms of that sense of impatience or dissatisfaction with his own work that occasionally comes to the surface even in the early poems. At one point in "Sleep and Poetry," for instance, Keats doubts his ability to give up the "pure fountains" (101) and "shady places" (105) of pastoral seclusion so that he might move on to the vision of "a nobler life . . . the agonies, the strife / Of human hearts" (123–25). Yet, in a way that directly anticipates the sonnet, he speaks in terms of an obligation or duty to do so: "And can I ever bid these joys farewell? / Yes, I *must* pass them" (122–23; my italics). In the sonnet, however, the status of romantic pleasure itself is no longer an unqualified one, and the difficulty of passing on to loftier levels of poetic experience is all the greater, given the austere and specific example of *King Lear* that Keats invokes as an alternative to romance. About to read Shakespeare's tragedy, he suddenly becomes aware of the limitations of all he has done in poetry.

A key text in Keats's artistic development and a crucial one for understanding his notion of romance, the *Lear* sonnet describes one dispute and dramatizes another. The first is the "fierce dispute / Betwixt damnation and impassion'd clay" that he finds in Shakespeare's tragedy, and the second is his own dispute with romance, or at least those aspects of romance—its luxurious serenity, its remoteness from the here and now, and the irrelevance of its "melodizing" in the context of more compelling realities—that he seems to find problematic in his own work:

> O golden tongued Romance, with serene lute!
>   Fair plumed Siren, Queen of far-away!
>   Leave melodizing on this wintry day,
> Shut up thine olden pages, and be mute:
> Adieu! for, once again, the fierce dispute
>   Betwixt damnation and impassion'd clay
>   Must I burn through; once more humbly assay
> The bitter-sweet of this Shakespearian fruit:
> Chief Poet! and ye clouds of Albion,
>   Begetters of our deep eternal theme!
> When through the old oak forest I am gone,

> Let me not wander in a barren dream,
> But, when I am consumed in the fire
> Give me new phoenix wings to fly at my desire.

It seems clear, to begin with, that Keats is viewing romance not simply as a literary genre but as a category of experience or a mode of perception—one whose limitations, moreover, are immediately exposed by the mere thought of reading *King Lear*. As a kind of experience, or as a way of viewing it, romance is made to seem suddenly narrow and inadequate, quite incommensurate with the demands and scope of tragedy. But even as a dismissal of romance, the sonnet begins with a series of courtly, if not hyperbolic, gestures that acknowledge the continuing power of romance over Keats, a power that he was to confront again and again in his subsequent work, and dismiss again and again, in such forms as the "Cold Pastoral" of the Grecian Urn and the "deceiving elf" of the Nightingale. From this point of view, the sonnet's farewell to romance is seriously qualified and perhaps only temporary.[13] Like Wallace Stevens after him, Keats seems to find romance incongruous with the reality of winter's "plain sense of things," but there is no reason to assume that he will not return to it and reopen its "olden pages" on a day other than the poem's "wintry" one.

That this is the case is suggested by more than just a decorous correspondence between the seasons and poetic styles. Written in January, 1818, while he was revising *Endymion,* the sonnet is frequently viewed as Keats's most serious attempt, thus far in his career, to shake himself free from the seductions of romance, to break his addiction to a mode and an outlook once prized but now regarded, from the perspective of *King Lear,* as enervating and ultimately self-deluding, despite its continuing attractions. To the relief of the devotees of the reality principle among his critics, Keats seems at last to be growing up. Yet this anti-romantic mood, if that is what it was, does not seem to have lasted, given the fact that Keats was to insist a short time later on calling *Endymion* "A Poetic Romance." And in a poem written just a few days after the *Lear* sonnet, he expresses his fears about not living long enough to fulfill his poetic ambitions, which still include tracing the shadows of "high romance."[14] In the light of such developments, perhaps the most that can be said is that for the moment of the sonnet's composition Keats seems to have experienced a genuine self-recognition, a sudden critical insight into the meaning of his own poetic allegiances. But this in itself falls short of any decisive or final rejection of romance.

What seems to be most dismaying to Keats "on this wintry day" is the distance of romance, and thus of much of his own work, from the harsher realities of human experience, a distance that creates, in turn, his sense of alienation from the "deep eternal theme" of English poetic tradition. Focused entirely on the sweetness of a remote music, romance neglects the bitter immediacy of the human condition in its tragic phase, a whole dimension of experience whose absence can apparently turn poetry into a "barren dream." To this extent, the poem reverses the early Keats's typical impulse to flee the cares and contradictions of the present. Poetry is now to be located not in the serene luxury of some distant bower but in the very heart of the human struggle. Yet Keats embraces this new definition with less enthusiasm than we might expect from someone newly liberated from the trivial fantasies of romantic idyll. He approaches *King Lear* with humility, but also with some dread, and seems concerned with its "fierce dispute" less as a new poetic possibility than as an area of experience which he has been unable to accommodate in his own work and which, he fears, may simply be beyond his powers. This accounts for the tone of appeal in the sestet and, indeed, for the fact that the poem's overall emphasis falls much more on Keats's sense of inadequacy than on his dedication to a new kind of poetry, which in any case remains somewhat vague. The heaviness of tone in the poem's middle section indicates Keats's attitude most clearly. There is no excited rush toward Shakespeare's play and its "fierce dispute," but rather a certain reluctance, as though Keats were approaching them out of a sense of moral obligation or resolve more than relief ("*Must* I burn through"). He is aware of tragedy's differences from romance, certainly, but also of its greater difficulties, and he returns to them as if compelled to do so, bound by a sense of duty not only to a larger view of experience but to those "Begetters of our deep eternal theme" who stand as both threatening and saving figures in the poem, reminding Keats that poetry must deal with more than just the harmonies of summer. In fact, it is precisely as a poet of summer who is trying to learn to be a poet of winter and ultimately a poet of all seasons that Keats comes to *King Lear* again to begin with. As Morris Dickstein points out, in all the poems of this period (the winter of 1817–18), winter represents "not only the absence of the 'passed joy' of summer, but also a winter of the spirit, which is making poetry impossible for Keats."[15] In turning to a poetry that is more appropriate to wintry days than romance (which in Northrop Frye's system is "the mythos of summer"), Keats is trying to insure his continuity or even survival as a poet during seasons that are utterly unresponsive to romantic desire.

Keats's quarrel with romance, though less "fierce," certainly, than the dispute that Shakespeare describes, is thus an ambivalent one—more ambivalent, and perhaps more in the nature of a lover's quarrel, than most readers of the poem have tended to acknowledge. Critics who read it as the poet's final farewell to his youthful infatuation with the realms of "Flora, and old Pan" ("Sleep and Poetry," 102) seem to be taking their cue from the poem's apparent dichotomy between tragedy and romance, forgetting the extent to which Keats continued to value romance and assuming that these categories represent fundamental extremes, as well as moral opposites, in literature and in life, rather than poetic constructs that both originate in acts of imagination. Following Keats himself, they reduce romance to its simplest terms and argue that his growing skepticism toward the imagination leads him away from such romance toward a poetry of the actual. But it is important to recognize, first, that the sonnet avoids any thoroughgoing moral distinctions between tragedy and romance, and, second, that implicit in any skepticism toward the imagination is not merely a distaste for its more unbridled forms, such as romance, but a distrust of all aesthetic representation, a radical awareness of the ultimate incompatibility between the artificial, patterned constructs of verse and the unorganized flux of experience. In these terms, Keats could not give up romance without giving up poetry and imaginative activity altogether, though this is the point to which he seems to bring himself at the ends of the two greatest odes, where the primary strategy is precisely to bring the romantic dream into collision with more immediate experience.

What the sonnet implies, then, is less the necessity of leaving romance, which may be only temporary, than the difficulties of taking on a more inclusive form than Keats's own version of romance has thus far proved to be. If anything is to be rejected, it is not the poetry of dream but the dream that has become barren. Thus Keats's difficulties are not simply those of confronting tragic experience, nor even of moving from romance to some higher form, whether it be tragic or epic, but of broadening his whole poetic orientation, moving toward a greater inclusiveness, establishing the reality, as it were, of the dream—all of which demands, essentially, his entire remaking as a poet. For it to continue in a naively romantic mode, as he now sees, is to "wander in a barren dream," then the only way to participate authentically in English poetic tradition and do justice to its "deep eternal theme" is to go through the fire of such experience as *King Lear* encompasses and emerge from it poetically renewed. Consumption by the fire is a certainty, and there is no guarantee of emerging from it successfully, but the risk of destruction for the sake of such a possibility nevertheless seems preferable to the "barren dream."

In expressing a dilemma that will become an almost obsessive concern for the later Keats, the sonnet really points to what might be considered the fundamental problem of romance, namely, how does the serious writer reconcile his ideal or in any case unreal representations with his own and the reader's sense of reality?[16] In more Keatsian terms, this becomes a question of poetic value: what is the value of a poetry that pursues beauty at the expense of truth, or that foregoes any function—such as the humanitarian or the epistemological—beyond the aesthetic? Unlike his several generations of critics, for whom he was at first an esthete intent upon the magic and charm of the world inside the poem and later on a skeptic in increasingly demystified pursuit of the actual, Keats himself seems to have chosen the precise route of attempted reconciliation, persisting with various forms of romance while seeking out the ground on which an accommodation between the imagined and the real might be achieved. At the end of the sonnet, he prays for his rebirth as a poet on some higher level of being or understanding, one on which desire can be actualized, the contraries resolved. Yet this prayer in itself, with its evocation of the miraculous phoenix, is romantic, and the problem that inspired it will continue to haunt him, more or less urgently, in his subsequent work.

In refusing any longer to avoid a tragic reality, at any rate, Keats realized that he is running the risk of being consumed by it; and while this may mean failure through inability, it could also mean the end of poetry altogether, its collapse in the face of a reality with which it is completely discontinuous. In this view of it, the dichotomy in the poem is not between tragedy and romance but between poetry and reality, and such a formulation of its dilemma suggests, again, a radical definition of all poetry as romance, as a world elsewhere that can never be harmonized with any real world. Bringing his discussion of romance poetics into the context of the Romantic period, Howard Felperin points to the paradox that "it is only when literature realizes its full autonomy in creating a world apart, and the poet claims his full authority as a creator in his own right, that the value of his quest becomes wholly problematic."[17] To my mind, the full force of this paradox can be felt not so much in Keats's early and demonstrably escapist work but throughout his career and perhaps never so strongly as in the "Ode to Psyche," when the speaker makes his grand and daringly solipsistic assertion, "I see, and sing, by my own eyes inspired," and then proceeds, in a passage of utterly transparent internalization, to describe the exclusive and self-sufficient "fane" that he will build for Psyche in "some untrodden region of my mind." This is not to suggest, of course, that Keats breaks all ties with empirical reality, though he comes closer here to doing just that than anywhere else in his later work. But neither is the opposite true— that he simply exchanges his subjective imagination (even if he could) for an exclusive reliance on empirical event as his poetic source. What the poetry *does* seem to depend on is the continuing possibility, as one element within it, of the creation of a world apart, along with a continual probing of the validity of that possibility. And to this extent, romance, however qualified or revised, persists.

Far from banishing romance from his work, therefore, Keats will learn how to make poetry out of his increasing sense of misgiving about its claims, and the best, certainly the least troubled, example might well be *The Eve of St. Agnes,* a poem which focuses attention on the romantic theme of wish-fulfillment both in its plot and in the mind of its reader.[18] Written in January and February of 1819, a full year after the *Lear* sonnet, the poem, to be sure, is romantic in several ways, from its *Romeo and Juliet*-like plot and Gothic trappings, to its use of the Spenserian stanza, to the rich concreteness of its style and imagery. But the important difference from the early work lies in the quality of its narration, specifically in the altered relation between the poet and his material. Of course, Keats here is writing a romance proper, and not simply luxuriating in the generalized romantic mode of his early work. But this specificity of genre is significant in itself, suggesting a new alertness to the possibilities of artistic control. No longer the seduced victim of his own romantic longings, Keats's narrator here is a practiced and self-conscious manipulator of romantic conventions. He has learned to use romance rather than be used by it; yet the purpose of his newly ironic posture is not to expose romance as an empty deception but to arrive at, and steer the reader toward, a deeper understanding of the processes of fiction and the dynamics of wish-fulfillment, dynamics that involve the reader as much as the characters within the fiction. The result is an inclusive poetry of dream that forestalls barrenness by maintaining a critical perspective on itself, acknowledging its status as dream and in this way directing the reader to issues beyond those of romantic plot alone. Ultimately, then, Keats's achievement in the poem is to be measured not simply by his new mastery of objective narrative or playful irony but by his understanding and control of reader expectations, which include both the demand for some continuity between romance and reality and, equally, the satisfaction of desires for the near-miraculous solutions to reality's problems that romance typically provides. Since to read the poem at all is to be drawn into its world—a process that is further enabled by Keats's positive and expert use of romantic conventions—we respond with some degree of sympathy to its characters' motives and desires. At the same time, by being continually reminded of the fictive nature of the poem's romance world, we are prevented from responding naively, with all disbelief suspended; and the poem's narrator, through the same habit of pointing to the unreality of romance, avoids the escapism inherent in the very mode he is using. We are given a dream, but one whose "truth" is established by the critical scrutiny to which its author subjects not only several forms of dreaming within the poem but eventually the poem itself.

The emphasis at the beginning seems to fall on the realism of the narrative. The magical implications of the St. Agnes legend are bypassed in favor of some straightforward, omniscient scene-setting. With the very first line—"St. Agnes' Eve—Ah, bitter chill it was!"— the narrator assumes the story-teller's traditional posture, suggesting not only that he knows everything about the story but that he has direct experience of its events. He is not merely narrating but re- membering, thus seeming to claim a more than fictional status for his narration. The naturalistic details of the cold owl and the hare "trembling through the frozen grass" continue this stress on the actuality of the poem's unfolding world, and are naturalistic in the further sense that they establish a logical relationship between the bitter cold of the night and the suffering of the animals. But when he turns his attention to the beadsman, whose numb fingers do not prevent him from telling his rosary and who says his prayers with "frosted breath," the narrator apprises us of a break in this naturalistic logic and of a difference between the direct awareness of reality with which he begins his story and the ability of characters within that reality to distort or displace it through the use of subjective imagi- nation. Such is the power of this imagination that it can virtually disrupt and reverse natural process, as when Madeline, in the grip of her vision, is compared to a rose that shuts and becomes a bud again. But the purpose of the poem's opening stanzas, in part, seems to be to provide a realistic norm by which such distortions and displacements can be judged, and the narrator, in the course of his tale, will return to it from time to time. In the case of the beadsman, the ability to alter or ignore reality is shown to be an inability, a failure of nerve, a turning away from possibilities and feelings to which he is vulnerable but which he has long repressed. Thus he is "Flatter'd to tears" by music as he flees from it, and "his weak spirit fails" to imagine, or even notice, how the sculptured forms of knights and ladies in the chapel "seem to freeze." Exposed as a sublimating escapism, the beadsman's otherworldly spirituality almost completely suspends his awareness of his actual environment, and he is left by the narrator in his circumscribed world of self-imposed penance.

Yet such criticism is not the result of an entirely realistic per- spective on the part of the narrator. If his awareness, in its extension to living things in an actual, physical world, is simply more lively and inclusive than the beadsman's, it is also more romantic precisely in its capacity to imagine the "suffering" of sculptured, inanimate forms. Thus it is not imagination that is being criticized, in the sense of romantic tendencies to exceed the realm of strict, empirical fact, but an essentially negative and exclusive form of imagination, one that turns away from the real rather than toward it, as exemplified by the beadsman's barren dream of reaching heaven "without a death." Instead of narrowly demonstrating their opposition, the poem seems to celebrate the possibilities of alliance between the imagination and reality, and herein lies one aspect of its authentic complexity.

With the introduction of Madeline into the narrative, the same sort of distinction between an escapist imagination and one that grounds itself in the real is maintained and extended further—complicated now, however, by the narrator's sudden refusal to endorse the reality of the poem's primary level of action, the very reality that the beadsman, in his harsh self-repression, has just been shown to avoid. As opposed to the realistic clarity of image in the poem's opening stanzas, we are given the dazzling blur of "the argent revelry," a whirl of conventional romantic color and synecdochic detail that, together with a metaphor of insubstantiality, seems to call into question the reality of the very action that is being described:

> At length burst in the argent revelry,
> With plume, tiara, and all rich array,
> Numerous as shadows haunting fairly
> The brain, new stuff'd, in youth, with triumphs gay
> Of old romance. These let us wish away,
> And turn, sole-thoughted, to one Lady there,
> Whose heart had brooded, all that wintry day,
> On love, and wing'd St. Agnes' saintly care,
> As she had heard old dames full many times declare.
> (37–45)

We see a plume here, a tiara there, but no clear, emergent whole of which these are parts, as though the narrator were not only insisting on the conventionality of such scenes and props in romance—thus releasing himself from the obligation of more detailed description—but even, with the shadow metaphor, deliberately pointing to their uncertain ontological status. In a sense, of course, what is being presented, in a kind of proleptic description, is Madeline's dimming perception of external reality. We see not so much what she sees as how she sees it, at a moment when external reality is far less vivid to her than the "visions of delight" that she hopes to achieve through her observance of the ceremonies of St. Agnes' Eve. It is both understandable and ironic, then, that she should turn away, as she does in the ensuing stanzas, from "the argent revelry . . . Numerous as shadows"—understandable because the external scene means less and less to her as her visionary hopes increase, and ironic because in turning from that scene to her own fancies she is merely exchanging one unreality for another.

In this way the narrator complicates the distinction between what is real and what is imagined in the poem, emphasizing the artificiality of its primary level of action by introducing language and imagery that are curiously opaque and self-consciously literary in the opening lines of the stanza. In this way, too, he qualifies the mimetic transparency of the poem's beginning and modifies our response to Madeline's rejection of the action taking place around her. We are not witnessing a simple conflict between imagination and reality in an otherwise realistic setting but a complex one between (for the moment) two different sets of imagined shadows in a context that is itself shifting and uncertain. Clearly we can no longer regard the narrator as firmly committed to any single perspective on the world of the poem, no longer see him as taking a consistently realistic stand against imaginative excess, for example, or even going beyond conflict to a position calling for some sort of final reconciliation between imagination and reality. His perspective, instead, takes on a kind of plasticity, a tendency to shift from one point to another along an axis formed by varying combinations of fact and fancy, and this is precisely what holds the poem before us as a fiction, as a continual, steadily self-conscious play of conventions and perspectives, as opposed to the sustained illusion of a sequence of events authorized by some "reality" or consistent point of view anterior to their presentation. The poem, that is to say, is a performance whose reality lies in our experience of the narrator's shifting attitudes toward material that is largely traditional and familiar.

This aspect of *The Eve of St. Agnes* is most clearly illustrated by the narrator's treatment of Porphyro, who is arguably the most sympathetic and the most "realistic" figure in the romance, the one who apparently embodies the narrator's own valued tendency to pay homage to the real in the very act of obeying the promptings of strong desire. Yet even he is immune neither to the poem's irony nor to the narrator's sliding perspective. When we first see him, Porphyro has come across the moors "with heart on fire / For Madeline." He is a likely candidate at this point for the same sort of realistic criticism that has been levelled against the ungrounded dreaming of the beadsman and of Madeline herself, except for the fact that the object of his desire has a more certain existence and he actively pursues it. At first, however, there is something almost blatantly unearthly and idealized about the quality of Porphyro's longing for Madeline. Despite his active nature and the "realism" of his motives, he is a conventionalized Romeo, and the narrator's language both registers this quality and treats it with an undermining amusement:

> Beside the portal doors,
> Buttress'd from moonlight, stands he, and implores

> All saints to give him sight of Madeline,
> But for one moment in the tedious hours,
> That he might gaze and worship all unseen;
> Perchance speak, kneel, touch, kiss—in sooth such things
> have been.
>
> (76–81)

Porphyro's readiness simply to "gaze and worship all unseen" threatens to turn him into a passive, indulgent dreamer, not unlike the beadsman and Madeline, content with a passion that has been sublimated into a form of religious worship. And though this is immediately qualified by his equal readiness to pursue his passion and act on his desire, this side of Porphyro's personality is also dramatized in the breathless terms of ironic melodrama: "He ventures in: let no buzz'd whisper tell: / All eyes be muffled, or a hundred swords / Will storm his heart, Love's fev'rous citadel" (82–84).

Porphyro is simultaneously the serious hero of the poem, the main vehicle for its thrust toward the discovery of continuity between the imagined and the real, and a conventional figure within its self-consciously fictive framework, subject to a variety of local ironies and to the narrator's overall awareness of the improbabilities that subtend the whole enterprise of romance. He succeeds more by luck and coincidence, the "happy chances" of romantic plot, than by any action that he consciously undertakes, though it is important to recognize also that he *does* take action in order to realize his goals. Coming to the stronghold of his enemies in pursuit of Madeline at all is an act of chivalric courage for Porphyro, as well as a demonstration of faith in the possibility of transforming desire into reality— an enactment, as Earl Wasserman argues, of the Keatsian conviction about "the truth of Imagination."[19] Yet, through rhetorical overstatement and the easy fulfillment of the expectations that the narrative sets up, we are continually reminded of the conventionally romantic nature of the plot, of the fact that much of it conforms to general eighteenth-century usage for the term "romantic," which meant precisely "something that could happen in a romance."[20] A convenient, if complex, example is the magical way in which the very bolts and chains and doors of the oppressive castle, seemingly endowed with a life of their own, cooperate in the lovers' escape at the end.[21] As Stuart Sperry remarks in his fine reading of The Eve of St. Agnes, the poem "achieves its magic, but only in such a way as to dramatize the particular tensions that oppose it."[22] These tensions begin to emerge most critically in the final section of the poem, when all at once the romance reaches its successful conclusion and the narrator seems to become curiously reluctant to confirm its success.

After Porphyro manages to rescue Madeline from the enthrallment of her dream, the poem's "Solution sweet," by which he, in fact, melts into that dream, represents a compromise between what are actually competing romances or conceptions of romance within the poem as a whole. It is, of course, the narrator who suggests that this compromise, a successful blend of passive dreaming and active questing, has taken place. But it is also the narrator who calls our attention to its realistic context, the reality of darkness and storm which surrounds the lovers in their moment of fulfillment and which is deliberately counterpointed against Porphyro's sense of triumph:"'Tis dark: quick pattereth the flaw-blown sleet: / 'This is no dream, my bride, my Madeline!' / 'Tis dark: the iced gusts still rave and beat" (325–27). Porphyro's assertion here that he and Madeline are done with dreaming at last is ironic, at the very least, in the sense that the reality into which they have awakened—the raging storm—represents dangers that ought to qualify any headlong optimism. It is Madeline, to be sure, who becomes the more realistic of the two at this point, upset initially by her fear that Porphyro may have played her false, and then, though reassured by his declaration of love and fidelity, still "beset with fears" as they begin to make their escape. But in a poem that has so consistently confused or destabilized the categories of the real and the imagined, Porphyro's assertion seems calculated to create several waves of irony, reminding us that the ontological status of the poem's entire action is in question and that the storm, neither more nor less "real" than any of its other elements, is certainly a part of the poem's romantic machinery.

Most ironic of all, though, is the fact that Porphyro is only just beginning to dream, interpreting the situation in the most conventionally romantic terms. He is, he tells Madeline, as though he were taking on her own earlier perspective, "A famish'd pilgrim,—saved by miracle," and the storm raging outside is "an elfin-storm from faery land, / Of haggard seeming, but a boon indeed" (339; 343–44). Both characterizations are deeply informed by that most romantic of all plot formulas, all's well that ends well, and it is precisely as the hero of such a plot that Porphyro now sees himself. The possibility that he is being cheated by fancy, however, by some barren dreaming of his own, is left open by the narrator's lack of comment, the fact that he neither affirms nor denies Porphyro's sense of triumph. Certainly the narrator takes the poem somewhat beyond the point of simply ending well, and his conclusion is more problematic than romantically satisfying. Instead of being told that the lovers lived happily ever after, we are given terms which are inconclusive at best and which hold the possibility of any ultimate success in permanent suspension. Indeed, in its final stanzas the lovers are ushered, like gliding phantoms, not only out of the castle but outside the temporal limits of the poem itself, whose very dramatic immediacy is now exposed as fictive, an imaginative projection. The narrative of Madeline and Porphyro simply breaks off with the bare but remarkable comment: "And they are gone: ay, ages long ago / These lovers fled away into the storm" (370–71). With so slight a gesture, the narrator breaks the spell of his poem as a dramatically immediate series of events, distancing us, in this final shift of perspective, from his characters in a way that must qualify our concern about their immediate welfare. At the same time, all the poem's play with perspective and the ontological status of its events seems to darken here into a distinct sense of loss, loss of the lovers to the depths of time and mortal experience. In fact, they are lost and saved. On the one hand, united at last, they are successful in making their escape from an oppressive environment that constitutes the chief threat to their love. But on the other, the narrator qualifies their success by displacing them from the poem's temporal foreground into an ancient past, a gesture that suddenly places the whole story in a context of history and mortality and thus acknowledges limits to the power of desire, the ultimate subjection of Madeline and Porphyro to the constraints of human time.

Had Keats been content with traditional romance as a genre, such a gesture would have hardly been necessary. Yet his refusal to remain within the limits of the genre suggests not a cynicism toward romance or even a dissatisfaction with it so much as an awareness of its limitations and a desire to extend that awareness to the reader. The lovers' success at the end is circumscribed by the narrator's muted understanding that it is the kind of success possible only in fiction, in a world elsewhere, and this is communicated to us by his sudden denial of the poem's dramatic immediacy and by the resulting temporal and even ontological gap that opens, at the beginning of the last stanza, to separate us, finally this time, from the lovers and their world. The critical debate about the poem's conclusion, with its variety of interpretations ranging all the way from visionary transcendence to tragedy, is one consequence of the narrator's muteness at the end, his refusal to follow the lovers beyond the point of their escape; and this refusal leaves a void that interpretation rushes in to fill. But it also leads outside the dramatic framework of the poem to a recognition of romance as an ordering of things that is different and essentially unreachable from the one we inhabit with the poem's narrator.[23]

Keatsian romance persists, then, but not without a coexistent awareness of its limitations, which here takes the form of the narrator's insistence that romance is *only* romance, a beautiful fiction. Most important, though, is the fact that Keats has learned the secret of serious romance, which is to say the techniques of successful fiction. In this sense, his choice of *King Lear* as a model, during the crisis with romance recorded in the *Lear* sonnet, was not a far-fetched one, at least not if we regard it, *contra* Keats himself, as a model of technique rather than one of subject-matter, and accept a characterization of Shakespearean tragedy in general and *King Lear* in particular as a sort of deliberate romance *manqué*, a kind of drama that uses romance to establish and reinforce its essentially tragic effect. As Howard Felperin puts it, in plays like *Hamlet* and *Lear* "Shakespeare invokes conventions of romance . . . in order to repudiate them, to expose their inadequacy or outmodedness within the world of tragic experience and thereby bring home the essential quality of that experience." In *Lear* especially, says Felperin, Shakespeare "raises romantic expectations only to defeat them with tragic actualities. The play is full of false dawns."[24]

On the one hand, of course, it is ironic that Keats should have chosen this play—so abundant in romance elements—as the opposite of romance. But on the other, it is the way in which Shakespeare uses these elements—Cordelia's return to the action, for example, or her almost magical revival of Lear, or Edmund's last-minute reformation—ultimately denying what they promise, that is relevant to Keats's methods in *The Eve of St. Agnes.* While I would not want to argue that the poem is a tragedy or that its reversals are as drastic as those in *Lear*, I do want to suggest that Keats or his narrator works similarly to Shakespeare in manipulating reader expectations—in this case by allowing romantic hopes to be fulfilled and simultaneously forcing upon us the recognition that such fulfillment is possible only in the radically fictive world of romance. Keats, we might say, raises romantic expectations not to defeat them but to fulfill them *and* call them into question with the knowledge that they *are* romantic. It is the persistence of that romance world in Keats, however, with all the questioning and doubt to which it is subjected, that accounts for his development from a victim of romance to a serious romancer to a poet, finally, of tragic knowledge.[25]

Notes

1. Jack Stillinger, "The Hoodwinking of Madeline: Skepticism in *The Eve of St. Agnes, SP*, 58 (1961), 555. Along with seven other essays on Keats, this one is conveniently reprinted (as its center piece) in Stillinger's book, *The Hoodwinking of Madeline and Other Essays on Keats's Poems* (U. of Illinois Press, 1971). Further references to Stillinger's essential and representative work on Keats as an increasingly anti-romantic skeptic will be to this book.

2. In her useful, brief study, *The Romance* (London: Methuen, 1970), Gillian Beer points out that there is a distinction "between 'the romance' and 'romance' as an element in literature," and speaks of "a shift from form to quality" in the history of the genre (p. 4). Without, I hope, unduly overriding legitimate differences between romance and visionary or transcendent experience, I want to use the term in a way that emphasizes not only romantic *quality* but the fact that, for a poet like Keats, it

is precisely the possibilities of vision and transcendence that romance, in a variety of forms, holds out. Speaking very broadly, romance might even be defined for Keats by what he calls the "pure serene" of Chapman's Homer, where again the emphasis is on the quality of experience rather than the attributes or imperatives of a specific genre. For a fuller discussion of the Romantics' inevitable association of romance with imaginative experience, see Beer, *The Romance*, pp. 59–64.

3. All quotations from Keats's poems are from *The Poetical Works of John Keats*, ed. H. W. Garrod, 2nd ed. (Oxford: Clarendon Press, 1958).

4. See *The Hoodwinking of Madeline*, pp. 31–45. Though my quotations in this paragraph come entirely from the essay "Keats and Romance," it presents the basic argument about Keats's development which informs all of the essays in Stillinger's book.

5. *The Hoodwinking of Madeline*, p. 33.

6. *Shakespearean Romance* (Princeton U. Press, 1972), pp. 50; 53–4.

7. Morris Dickstein, *Keats and His Poetry* (U. of Chicago Press, 1971), p. 27.

8. W. J. Bate, *John Keats* (Harvard U. Press, 1963), p. 70.

9. Here I have in mind Keats's attack on Augustan neo-classicism and its persistence in the poetry of his own time. See II. 162–206 of "Sleep and Poetry."

10. See Beer, *The Romance*, p. 5, and Felperin, *Shakespearean Romance*, pp. 7–8.

11. *Keats and His Poetry*, p. 30. Dickstein's discussion of the bower motif in his chapter on "The World of the Early Poems" (pp. 36–52) is extremely valuable. For a different approach to this image in Keats, see Mario D'Avanzo, *Keats's Metaphors for the Poetic Imagination* (Duke U. Press, 1967), pp. 164–72.

12. *Keats and His Poetry*, p. 35.

13. In "The Material Sublime: Keats and *Isabella*," *Studies in Romanticism*, 13 (1974), 299–311, Louise Z. Smith suggests that romance in the *Lear* sonnet "is not dismissed; it is only temporarily 'mute' " (301).

14. In a letter to his publishers (21 March 1818), Keats asks that his subtitle be kept—"for a romance is a fine thing notwithstanding the circulating Libraries" (I, 253). I am quoting here from *The Letters of John Keats, 1814–1821)*, ed. H. E. Rollins, 2 vols. (Harvard U. Press, 1958). The sonnet, "When I have fears that I may cease to be," in which the phrase "high romance" appears, was written by 31 January 1818, when Keats copied it into a letter to Reynolds (I, 222). The *Lear* sonnet had been written nine days before, on the 22nd. For the dating of both poems, see Jack Stillinger, *The Texts of Keats's Poems* (Harvard U. Press, 1974), p. 161.

15. *Keats and His Poetry*, p. 133.

16. In *Shakespearean Romance*, Howard Felperin addresses himself to this problem in similar terms (pp. 49–50) and refers to two other formulations of it, Harry Berger's in the context of Renaissance idealism and poetics, and Northrop Frye's Freudian formulation in *Anatomy of Criticism*.

17. *Shakespearean Romance*, pp. 44–45.

18. In *Keats the Poet* (Princeton U. Press, 1973), pp. 198–220, Stuart Sperry deals perceptively with *The Eve of St. Agnes* as "a romance of wish-fulfillment," and, by keeping the poem's self-conscious conventionality in view, manages to steer a middle course between Stillinger's skeptical view of it and Earl Wasserman's overly idealized and metaphysical account in *The Finer Tone* (The Johns Hopkins U. Press, 1953), pp. 97–137. I see my own treatment of the poem as a contribution to the developing tradition of responses to it that emphasize the central role of the narrator. Besides Sperry, see R. H. Fogle, "A Reading of Keats's *Eve of St. Agnes*," *College English*, 6

(1945), 325–28; Marian Cusac, "Keats as Enchanter: An Organizing Principle of *The Eve of St. Agnes*," *Keats-Shelley Journal*, 17 (1968), 113–19; Michael Ragussis, "Narrative Structure and the Problem of the Divided Reader in *The Eve of St. Agnes*," *ELH*, 42 (1975), 378–94; and William C. Stephenson, "The Performing Narrator in Keats's Poetry," *Keats-Shelley Journal*, 26 (1977), 51–71.

19. See *The Finer Tone*, pp. 102–12.

20. *The Romance*, p. 59, Gillian Beer goes on to point out, however, that "The writers who emerged towards the end of the eighteenth century . . . perceived that 'what happens in a romance' is not simply unreal or artificial" (p. 59). It is in the tension between these two attitudes that the expressive quality of *The Eve of St. Agnes* is perhaps best located.

21. Wasserman's account of the poem, despite his tendency to idealize it, reaches its high point in his consideration of such details as these in its concluding stanzas, with their shift from the active to the passive voice and their intermingling of tenses. See *The Finer Tone*, pp. 123–25.

22. *Keats the Poet*, p. 205.

23. Wasserman is precisely right in his observation that the lovers "steal away from our mode of existence" (p. 123), which, in my reading of the poem, points to a distinction implicit in the text between aesthetic or fictive and existential modes of being. But the blindness of his insight shows up, I think, in the exuberant and unqualified idealism of his argument, which overrides the distinction by implying that the lovers are freed from temporality in a wholly positive way, released into a privileged and transcendent visionary realm "outside the context of time" (p. 124) to become "the selfless spirit of a man forever captured in the dimensionless mystery beyond our mortal vision" (p. 125). Much closer to the narrator's tone in its balance of attitudes is R. H. Fogle's remark that the first two lines of the final stanza draw "a line of demarcation between art and life in its raw and unselective actuality" (p. 328). See also Arthur Carr's excellent article, "John Keats' Other 'Urn,' " *The University of Kansas City Review*, 20 (1954), 237–42, in which he argues that the poem, exposed as an "aesthetic object" by the poet's withdrawal from it at the end, differs from life in degree rather than in kind. As a "medievalized romance," itself archaic, the poem, like life, is subject to a process of fading or transience. This process, however, is governed not by the ordinary time of human existence but by the "slow time" of art, the "slow time" that fosters the Grecian Urn. Finally, for a view of the poem as a tragedy—one which, however, seems to exaggerate its elements of "sinister magic" and "hostile supernatural powers"—see Herbert G. Wright, "Has Keats's *Eve of St. Agnes* a Tragic Ending?" *MLR*, 40 (1945), 90–94.

24. *Shakespearean Romance*, pp. 102; 117–18.

25. I am grateful to my colleagues, John L. Mahoney and Andrew Von Hendy, and to the editors of *Philological Quarterly*, particularly Gerald L. Bruns and William Kupersmith, who all read an earlier version of this essay and made valuable suggestions as to how I might improve it.

Reading Keats's Plots
Jack Stillinger[*]

A multitude of causes unknown to former times have combined to produce, in the minds of students, teachers, scholars, and English department administrators, a sharp and theoretically unjustifiable distinction between poetry and other forms of fiction. "Fiction" has come to mean exclusively prose fiction, and journals with titles like *Modern Fiction Studies* and *Studies in Short Fiction* are universally understood as having to do with novels and short stories. In principle, no one should object to the proposition that *Paradise Lost, Don Juan,* and *The Ring and the Book* (for example) are long fictions, or that "The Sick Rose," "La Belle Dame sans Merci," and "Peter Quince at the Clavier" are short fictions. But in practice, as everyone knows, poems are almost always read, taught, and written about in ways markedly different from those used in the study of prose fiction.

In the last decade or so nearly all the genuine advances in practical criticism—most especially the advances that have increased our understanding of the *art* of literary art—have been made in connection with the novel and the short story. Thanks to Seymour Chatman and Gérard Genette (to name two of the most helpful recent contributors to our understanding),[1] readers and critics who study the novel nowadays routinely consider such things as the scope of the subject matter and the scale of detail with which it is treated; the basic structure of the plot and the way events are ordered and emphasized; how many plots there are and, if there are several, how the plots are related to one another; who the major characters are; who is the protagonist, who the antagonist, and how the various lesser characters relate to these principals and how they function in other ways in the work; how the characters are presented and characterized; the various kinds of point of view; the presence of a real or an implied narrator; the presence of a real or an implied reader or listener or spectator or "narratee"; the function and importance of the setting of the work; the function and importance of time (or levels of time), along with considerations of tense, duration, and frequency of repetition; the style or styles of the discourse.

But genre traditions, definitions, and expectations—in other ways so helpful in sharpening our perceptions and appreciation—have tended to set poetry apart from these considerations. Readers and critics of poetry, even at this late date in the history of practical criticism, are still primarily concerned with idea, theme, and "phi-

[*] The introductory paragraphs and the sections on *The Eve of St. Agnes, Lamia,* and "Ode on a Grecian Urn" are reprinted from "The Plots of Romantic Poetry," *College Literature* 12 (1985): 97–105, 108–112; the essay as a whole was written specifically for this volume and is published here for the first time by permission of the author.

losophy," seeking in effect to replace the literary work in process (what it *is*, what it *does*) with interpretive conversion, paraphrase, or translation (what it *means*). For much of the poetry of the last two centuries there is a decided mismatch between what the poets themselves thought they were doing and what teachers and critics (and as a consequence readers) have been extracting and describing. Wallace Stevens is just one of many writers who have commented on this kind of critical reductionism: "ideas are not bad in a poem," he says, but when "converted" into prose statement "they are a frightful bore."[2]

Poems have plots, characters, points of view, settings, and the rest just as regularly as works of prose fiction do. Here, to focus on just the first of these elements, is a short list of the commoner types of plot occurring in narrative and lyric poems of the literature that I know best, English romantic poetry. There are numerous "binary" oppositions and conflicts, with resolutions involving the triumph of one side, a merging of the two sides, or the introduction of some third term. Many of these oppositions occur in the mind, so that the events are changes of thought or feeling; in the commonest structures of this type, ignorance gives over to knowledge, delusion to awareness, loss to recompense or reconciliation. In more overtly dramatic and narrative poems we have stories of journeys, voyages, and quests. Most frequently the journey takes the form of an excursion and return—excursion into some ideal realm, followed by a changed protagonist's return to reality. There are a great many encounters: the two most common are the encounter between an imagined situation and a matter-of-fact reality (as in Wordsworth's "Resolution and Independence") and the encounter involving enchantment and unhappy awakening (as in Keats's "La Belle Dame" and *Lamia*); both kinds produce reversals representing a process of education that may be beneficial but also can sometimes be fatal.

Another type of plot involves violation and its consequence—the violation of a taboo, for example (as in *The Rime of the Ancient Mariner*), or the violation of space. In a sizable number of poems we find competition, crowding, or impingement between spatial divisions; these structures could be collected and studied together as stories of territorial dispute. Other structures depend on layers or divisions of time, most often with an attempt to combine or unify the different layers. There are a great many frame situations in romantic poems. (Shelley's "Ozymandias," for example, contains a frame within a frame within a frame: at the core there is King Ozymandias and his vanity; then there are the ancient sculptor's depiction of Ozymandias' character, the modern traveler who has come upon the remains of the sculptor's monument, and most immediately the first-person narrator who has learned of these things from the traveler. If we add Shelley the creator of the poem to the list, we have four or five levels of narration in a text only fourteen lines long.) Some of the structures are quite elaborate, as in the warp-and-woof complexity of satisfaction and dismay that makes up the texture of Wordsworth's "Tintern Abbey" or the double helical structure of turn and counterturn that has been described in Coleridge's "The Eolian Harp."[3]

There is considerable usefulness in paying more attention to the plots of poems, the structures that organize the materials of whatever stories we have at hand. One generally workable method of analyzing plot is to identify a beginning state of equilibrium, then a major event or series of events representing disturbance of this initial harmony, and then a progress toward resolution in some way related to the initial state. Another (similarly ancient) approach to plot is one that identifies first of all a protagonist, then some goal or desire associated with the protagonist, then some obstacle that stands in the way of what the protagonist wants, and finally the outcome—what in fact happens—whether comic, tragic, or ironic. When one identifies a protagonist, sees what the protagonist wants, sees what stands in the way, and then follows the events through to a closure, one is, or could be, centrally involved in the dynamics of a literary work. With poetry as with prose fiction, it is frequently in just such dynamics that the main interest and pleasure reside—not in paraphrasable "meaning" but in story elements as they are shaped and presented in the plot.

As a practical teaching device, there are immediate advantages in the use of both of these simple methods of analysis. Imagine a classroom situation in which one takes the Wedding-Guest (rather than the Mariner) as the protagonist of *The Rime of the Ancient Mariner*. What does the Wedding-Guest want? Obviously he wants to get to the wedding. What stands in the way? What stands in the way is a bearded old man who grabs him by the arm, fixes him with a glittering eye, and says, "There was a ship"! This might seem a silly way to begin analyzing so major a work as *The Ancient Mariner*, but it does, for purposes of discussion, immediately call attention to the dramatic frame provided by the encounter and interaction of Wedding-Guest and Mariner, and to the wedding background of the Mariner's tale and, when it is followed out to the end, the artistically significant fact that the Wedding-Guest never does get to the wedding but instead turns "from the bridegroom's door." For another example, try taking Dorothy Wordsworth (rather than her brother William, or the "speaker") as the protagonist of "Tintern Abbey." What does sister Dorothy want? Perhaps she'd like to say a few words. What stands in the way? In this case it is her brother, who talks nonstop for 159 lines. This example may seem even sillier than the preceding, but again it has the practical result of calling attention to the dramatic situation of the poem, the presence of a silent auditor, and the fact that the speaker does go on at considerable length (a circumstance noted at the time by Keats, Hazlitt, and several thousand other contemporaries).

But these may be considered mainly gimmicks to initiate discussion. I should like to give five examples in which narrative analysis of poetic plots may clarify some disputed matters of interpretation. Sometimes such analysis serves to illuminate what is going on in a work, and sometimes, I should emphasize, it is more useful in showing what is *not* going on. In this latter situation, narrative analysis may point the way toward relocating the center of interest. The first three of my examples are of this sort, examples in which narrative analysis shows up discrepancies between what actually happens in a text and what the critics typically describe as happening, with the suggestion that we may be going out of our way to overlook the most effective elements of the work we want to understand. The results should apply equally to interpretation and teaching.

THE EVE OF ST. AGNES

Until a couple of decades ago, *The Eve of St. Agnes* was usually read as a romantic love story, a Romeo and Juliet affair with a happy ending. Keats's young lover Porphyro enters a hostile castle, rescues his beloved Madeline, and takes her away to be his bride. More recently, critics have noticed that some of Porphyro's actions do not fit very well with his purported character as romantic hero. Early on in the poem he proposes a "stratagem" that shocks Madeline's old nurse Angela, and then he threatens to rouse Madeline's kinsmen— in effect threatens to get himself killed—if Angela refuses to aid him. Next comes the unfolding of the stratagem: Porphyro has himself taken to a hiding-place in Madeline's bedchamber whence he can spy on her as she undresses. Subsequently, after she goes to bed and he determines that she is fast asleep, he climbs into her bed and, while she is still asleep (or in some sort of dreaming state in which she is unaware of what is actually happening), he has his way with her.[4] Madeline, awakening to find a real Porphyro in her bed, is astonished and dismayed. Pretty clearly this is bad behavior on Porphyro's part, and it is connected in the poem with various images of witchcraft, sorcery, Peeping Tomism, seduction, and even rape.

But Madeline is also doing some things that go against the idea of pure romance. She is totally engrossed in pursuing a superstitious ritual known as "fasting St. Agnes' Fast," according to which, by following certain practices, she hopes to see her future husband in a dream, make love with him, and awaken still a virgin. The ritual is viewed by Angela as a foolish amusement; Porphyro sees it as the perfect occasion for the working of his stratagem; the narrator takes a scornful attitude, calling the ritual an old wives' tale and a whim and describing Madeline as hoodwinked with faery fancy, metaphorically both blind and dead. We now have a Romeo and Juliet story in which the Romeo character is Peeping Tom and cowardly seducer and the Juliet character is shown to be renouncing life in favor of a foolish and empty ritual. And this story is framed by a series of images of freezing cold and death: the opening stanzas describe the bitter chill of St. Agnes' Eve and the suffering of animals and humans and even the "sculptur'd dead" in the Beadsman's chapel connected to Madeline's castle; the closing stanzas describe an icy storm, nightmares, and the deaths of both Angela and the Beadsman. At face value, there are many things wrong in this poem, and critics have not been successful in straightening them all out.[5]

In this example, narrative analysis might begin with an attempt to determine who in fact is the protagonist of the story. Madeline is the first major character introduced, as the narration turns "sole-thoughted" to her in the fifth stanza; and then Porphyro enters the poem in the ninth stanza with all the fanfare of a stock romantic hero: "Meantime, across the moors, / Had come young Porphyro, with heart on fire / For Madeline." One or the other of these principals ought to be the protagonist, but because of some basic resemblances between Keats's poem and the Romeo and Juliet story, readers have sometimes taken the protagonist to be the two characters together, a pair of young lovers facing the oppositions of hostile kinsfolk, an icy storm, and a perilous journey back to Porphyro's home across the moors.

What narrative analysis produces (if I may condense a lengthy account into a few sentences) is a structure of two quests, each with its own protagonist, that through much of the poem are in direct opposition to one another. The initial quest is a spiritual one, Madeline's for her St. Agnes' Eve dream and the idealized (and innocent) union with her future husband. The second, countering quest is a physical one, Porphyro's for sight of and then sexual possession of Madeline's person not in any dream but in physical reality. Both characters desire union, but union in the different worlds of dream and actuality.[6] If we impose values from other poems that Keats wrote about the same time, Porphyro's world of actuality is the one with superior claims; but then Madeline is the more sympathetic character: after the first third of the poem, in which Keats makes much of her self-delusion in pursuing her ritual, the emphasis is increasingly on her role as victim of a stratagem, and at the same time Porphyro's actions are almost irreversibly damaging to his status as romantic hero.

At the end of the poem Porphyro calls Madeline his bride and says he has a home for her across the moors, and they "glide, like phantoms" out of the castle and disappear into the icy storm. The last lines describing them are: "And they are gone: ay, ages long ago / These lovers fled away into the storm." For some (romantically minded) readers, everything is concluded satisfactorily: Porphyro and Madeline are married and live happily ever after. For other readers, these final lines have an ominous ring to them: the lovers "fled away into the storm" and have not been heard from since.

Narrative analysis ultimately shows the inadequacy of any simple reading or interpretation of the poem that is based primarily on the plot. The plot is a messy one, with self-destructive tendencies at almost every turn. Now what, one may ask, is the use of a method of analysis that serves to point up flaws and inconsistencies in the plot? The answer is not too difficult: when we have a poem that (in Horace's and Dr. Johnson's terms) has outlived its century, has attained seemingly permanent status as one of the most often read and admired works in English, *and* has a seriously flawed plot, then we must look elsewhere for the principal causes of our enjoyment. Nowadays, in my own teaching of the poem, I am interested not so much in Porphyro's stratagem and the hoodwinking of Madeline as I am in the numerous distancing elements that *may* make the story romantically acceptable after all. I have my students focus on Keats's style, on the effects achieved by the use of an archaic (and archaizing) metrical form, on the color imagery (which employs mainly shades of red and blue and combinations of the two colors such as purple, rose, and amethyst), on the numerous animals, birds, and insects in the poem, and more generally on the pictorial and painterly qualities of the description. I show photographic slides of medieval tapestries, stained glass, and illuminated manuscripts (all of which are also preponderantly red and blue and are full of animals and birds). Keats himself used the terms "colouring" and "drapery" in the most suggestive of his own critical comments on the poem.[7] Narrative analysis of his plot might serve to get us more involved in these elements of "colouring" and "drapery," which I have come to think are the most important sources of the poem's pleasurable effects.

LAMIA

A good second example is Keats's last complete narrative poem, *Lamia*, a work of 708 lines based on a brief story in Burton's *Anatomy of Melancholy* about a young man named Lycius who fell in love with what Burton describes as "a phantasm in the habit of a fair gentlewoman." Lycius "tarried with her a while to his great content, and at last married her," but then at the wedding feast found out that his bride was in reality "a serpent, a lamia," whereupon, as Burton

says, "she, plate, house, and all that was in it, vanished in an instant."
In Keats's retelling, the shock of this awful discovery and loss is so
great that Lycius falls dead on the spot.

Here we have, or appear to have, a story of mortal enchantment
followed by abrupt awakening to reality. The poem is frequently read
as allegory, and certain passages might seem to support an allegorical
interpretation: there are several references to dreaming and to the
differences between gods and mortals; we are told that the dreams
of gods are "Real," with the implication that the dreams of mortals
are, by contrast, false or unreliable; mortal lovers grow pale, while
gods who are in love with goddesses do not; there is a significant
paragraph about the inseparability of pleasure and pain in human life
and about Lycius's mistaken belief that Lamia will separate out the
pleasure for him; there is a memorable passage toward the end about
"cold philosophy" putting all charms to flight and even destroying
a rainbow. But critics have not been able to discover an allegorical
interpretation (or any other) that accords with the various elements
of story, character, and tone.

What narrative analysis may offer here is an explanation of why
the critics have not been successful. When we examine the work to
see who is the protagonist—trying out both Lycius and Lamia, the
two main characters—we find that there are in fact two different
stories in the poem, one of which has to do with the enchantment
of Lycius and the other of which has to do with the exposure of
Lamia. In the first story, which occupies the last two-thirds of part
1, we are shown Lamia's transformation from serpent to a woman's
form and given some clues to her real character: she is associated
with demons; she has "elfin blood" running "in madness"; she goes
through convulsions and foams at the mouth, and the foam causes
the grass to wither and die; her permanent state is an abstraction of
"pain and ugliness." The story then proceeds with the first encounter
between Lycius and Lamia in her womanly form; Lycius is instantly
smitten, and they withdraw from the world to live together in "a
place unknown." There are various hints that Lycius is acting under
a magic spell; he is "shut up in mysteries" and his mind is "wrapp'd
like his mantle" when he first meets Lamia; he falls into a swoon,
and when Lamia arouses him with a kiss he is described as wakening
"from one trance . . . Into another"; his life is said to be "tangled
in her mesh." Lycius is clearly the protagonist of this first story, and
Lamia—as evil and deceitful enchantress—is here the antagonist.

In part 2, however, we have quite a different story. Lycius's
human nature comes to the fore, and as an expression of both ar-
rogance and vanity he insists on showing off his bride at a wedding
feast. The feast is held, and among the many guests comes, uninvited,
Lycius's old tutor, the clear-eyed realist Apollonius. Apollonius ex-

poses Lamia as a serpent, Lamia vanishes, and Lycius dies. In this second story it is primarily Lamia, now a beautiful woman become tragic figure, who has our sympathy. She is the protagonist, while first Lycius and then Apollonius are the antagonists.

I think it is this shift in the center of protagonism—as victim and victimizer exchange roles in the two parts—that has caused critics trouble in their attempts to interpret the poem as a whole. As a matter of biographical fact, there was a six-week interval between the time that Keats completed part 1 and the time that he began part 2, during which he wrote four acts of *Otho the Great* and parts of *The Fall of Hyperion* and *King Stephen*. Possibly he lost track of his narrative intentions, or changed them, during this interruption in the composition. Possibly he became confused about his narrative point of view. This is a once-upon-a-time story in which a discernible narrator gets increasingly excited by the story he is telling—to the point where, toward the end, he berates Lycius as a madman, hands out "spear-grass and the spiteful thistle" to Apollonius, and utters some extravagant and unconvincing statements about the bad effects of "cold philosophy." Perhaps Keats was experimenting with a new kind of narrative voice and the experiment did not work.

In any case, he wrote the poem initially as an attempt to gain popularity and make money, and he hoped to do this by arousing his readers' senses. "I am certain," he says in a letter to his brother and sister-in-law, "there is that sort of fire in [*Lamia*] which must take hold of people in some way—give them either pleasant or unpleasant sensation. What they want is a sensation of some sort."[8] In this, it turns out (at least in the long run), he pretty well succeeded. The critics continue to have trouble in interpreting, but the readers continue to get "sensation"—for example, in this short passage near the end, when Lamia is rendered powerless by Apollonius's steady gaze, Lycius cries out in anguish, and the noise of the wedding feast dies down to silence:

> "Lamia!" he cried—and no soft-toned reply.
> The many heard, and the loud revelry
> Grew hush; the stately music no more breathes;
> The myrtle sicken'd in a thousand wreaths.
> By faint degrees, voice, lute, and pleasure ceased;
> A deadly silence step by step increased,
> Until it seem'd a horrid presence there,
> And not a man but felt the terror in his hair.

"LA BELLE DAME SANS MERCI"

In *The Eve of St. Agnes* and *Lamia*, regardless of our problems with "meaning," we at least know what the characters are saying and doing. The antecedent details of the two stories are cloudy and the surviving characters' futures are entirely speculative (do Madeline and Porphyro even survive? where does Lamia vanish to?), but the unfolding action of the stories is fairly clear. In "La Belle Dame," by contrast, there is little clarity about anything. The characters and events are undoubtedly symbolic, much more so than in the two longer narratives, and the symbolism has always seemed to demand interpretation. But we never learn for sure what ails the knight; his own explanation at the end ("And this is why . . .") merely intensifies the confusion. In this poem, Keats gets considerable effects from what he leaves out.

One significant element of structure is the questioner, who speaks the first three stanzas and then presumably stays around to hear the knight's reply, which fills the remaining nine stanzas. Ostensibly the questioner's purpose is to ask, "what can ail thee?" But along with his questions, he gives us details of the knight's condition ("alone," "loitering," "haggard," "woe-begone," with a deathly complexion pictured in terms of a lily, "anguish moist and fever dew," and a withering rose); characterizes the landscape (withered sedge, absence of birds, absence of song); and says something about the time of year, mentioning the squirrel's granary and completion of the harvest. The questioner also, of course, provides the occasion for the knight to tell what happened to him. Perhaps most important of all, Keats's question-and-answer structure reinforces the effects of the poem's subtitle ("A Ballad"), the ballad-like stanza, and the archaizing that begins with "knight at arms" in the first line: this piece announces itself as belonging to a class of poems in which the standard materials are elemental, unexplained, and even supernatural occurrences. Naturally there will be a meeting with a mysterious lady; naturally there will be singing, strange food, lovemaking, bad dreams, and a calamitous reversal.

The wretched knight is of course the protagonist, and his goal, once he encounters her, is union with the beautiful lady. Some major problems are hinted at: he is a mortal, and she is "a fairy's child"; his "latest dream" is a nightmare warning of thralldom and death; and when he awakens, the lady has disappeared. His dream has the effect, on the knight (in the story) and on us (in reading), of turning his beloved Belle Dame into the antagonist, a merciless enchantress who will add him—perhaps already has added him—to her collection of ruined kings, princes, and warriors. "And *this* is why. . . ." He awakens alone on the cold hill's side, and the poem comes to an abrupt end.

Old-school biographical critics—the same who interpreted Lycius, Lamia, and Apollonius as Keats, Fanny Brawne, and Keats's housemate Charles Brown, principally because both Brown and Apollonius were bald!—have read "La Belle Dame" as an allegory involving Keats and Fanny Brawne (or, more abstractly, Keats and love), and also Keats and tuberculosis (Keats and death). Later writers have focused on categorical differences between the knight as mortal and la Belle Dame as nonmortal, and between the real world of the cold hill's side and the romance world of the lady's "elfin grot." La Belle Dame has even been taken to be another symbol of visionary imagination, and the knight as another of Keats's hoodwinked dreamers. But the poem itself never explains its symbolism, and every interpretation, even the old-school biographical, has to remain hypothetical. The actions are made logical solely by the poem's genre. They are just the sort of actions that happen in ballads.

"THE EVE OF ST. MARK"

Oddly "The Eve of St. Mark," a 119-line fragment that Keats abandoned before setting his plot in motion (if he ever had one), is full of narrative materials and much more readily interpreted than "La Belle Dame." As it stands, "St. Mark" is primarily description, and the center of interest is a solitary woman reading by a window. The work begins with an outdoors scene: it is a Sunday in early spring, the church bell is ringing for evening prayers, a procession of townspeople make their way to the church, and we are given various details of background sights and sounds—the cleanliness of the streets, the presence of springtime flowerings, the whispering of the people as they walk along, the shuffling of their feet on the pavement, the music of the church organ. The second and third paragraphs set the indoors scene, where Keats's protagonist, Bertha, is reading about the life of Saint Mark in an old book that is patched, torn, and decorated with pictures of stars, angels, martyrs, candlesticks, and Saint Mark's winged lion. Bertha has been reading all day long, and, although she could see the streets and square outside her window if she looked out, she instead has devoted all her attention to the elaborately decorated book. She is described as having an "aching neck and swimming eyes" and as being "dazed with saintly imageries."

Next we are returned briefly to the outdoors scene. It is now nighttime. The town has become silent except for the occasional footstep of somebody returning home, and the jackdaws that earlier were noisy have gone to rest "Pair by pair"; their resting place is the church belfry, where the former ringing of the Sabbath prayer bell is replaced by "music of the drowsy chimes" striking at intervals through the night. The remainder of the fragment presents further details of the indoors scene. Bertha lights a lamp to continue her reading, and the lamp creates a giant shadow of her body on the ceiling, on the walls, and on various furnishings of the room: chair, parrot's cage, and a firescreen decorated with "many monsters"— Siamese doves, Lima mice, birds of paradise, macaw, Indian songbird, Angora cat. Her shadow fills the room "with wildest forms and shades, / As though some ghostly queen of spades / Had come to mock behind her back." Keats adds a short passage of imitation Middle English supposedly quoted from the book Bertha is reading, and then the fragment breaks off in the middle of a line.

There is a clear running contrast between details of the outdoors scene and details indoors. The townspeople outside are a crowd, and they are engaged in a social and communal activity, going to church; they also are associated with home and family life, and even the jackdaws have retired like married couples, in pairs. Bertha by contrast is solitary and remote. The townspeople live in a commonplace actuality where time is mostly in the present. Bertha, set apart from this commonplace world, lives amid exotic surroundings, and instead of the townspeople's present time she is totally engrossed in the past, specifically in the martyrdom of Saint Mark, which happened a very long time ago. The townspeople are a plodding group; they move slowly and demurely, shuffle their feet, and whisper. The contrasting images of the indoors scene include perplexity, aching neck, swimming eyes, dazzling, glowering, wild forms, mockery, a dance of shadows— in short, a great deal of nervous, uncomfortable, even in places tortured, sensation and movement.

It would be easy to make up a story growing out of the situation that Keats has depicted: "Once upon a time there was a maiden named Bertha who lived alone near the church and spent all her time reading an old book about Saint Mark. One day. . . ." But as Keats left it, the fragment simply presents these scenes, with their contrasting atmospheres, tones, sensations, and some not very clear implications about different ways that people spend their time. Keats himself, if we can take a hint from a letter in which he copied the fragment, seems to have been mainly interested in the atmosphere and sensations he was creating. He calls it a work "quite in the spirit of Town quietude. I th[i]nk it will give you the sensation of walking about an old county Town in a coolish evening."[9]

The interpreting critics have not hesitated to discover potential antagonists. In one reading, dating back to 1946, the outdoors scene represents the "humdrum life of a provincial town in nineteenth-century England"; Bertha is a "modern" woman reading medieval legends and longing for the glories of a sainthood no longer possible. Another critic, two decades later, sees just the opposite values assigned to the contrasting situations: the townspeople and their activities are presented sympathetically, and Bertha is a person making a mistake ("by ignoring the life in the village outside her room, [she] is cheating herself of reality"). A still more recent writer, perceiving a contrast between "two modes of religious experience," thinks the fragment shows Keats responding "to religious matter by subordinating it to the process of reading about it."[10] Each of these interpretations fits a selection of the details, and each, even when in conflict with the others, usefully brings out implications that probably are somewhere in the text and certainly were at one time or another in Keats's mind. The point here, though, is that even with a fragment where there is no story as such, the sorting out of oppositions is fundamentally an exercise of narrative analysis.

"ODE ON A GRECIAN URN"

A final consideration is the use of narrative analysis in connection with the greater romantic lyric.[11] Lyric poems are generally, as one would expect, the least susceptible to narrative analysis—most obviously for the reason that, being lyrics, they are not narratives. The protagonist of Keats's "To Autumn" wants to describe and celebrate the season of autumn. What stands in the way? Virtually nothing; so he proceeds forthwith. The speaker of "Ode on Melancholy" assumes the posture of a professor lecturing on the whereabouts and nature of melancholy, but apart from experiencing a little difficulty in getting his thoughts together, this protagonist also meets no obstacle and in the received text completes his lecture in three stanzas.

But in other lyric poems—Coleridge's "Frost at Midnight," for instance, and Wordsworth's "Tintern Abbey" and "Ode: Intimations of Immortality"—there are opposing contrasts and tensions, and a progress of turns and counterturns that can be described and schematized in narrative terms. Still other lyrics have a large component of actual story. Outside the romantic period there is the handy example of Yeats's "Sailing to Byzantium": everyone would agree that this is a major lyric poem, and yet it has the form of a sea-voyage and in four stanzas tells the story of an old man who leaves his native country and sails to Byzantium, where he enrolls his soul in singing school and makes plans to sing to the emperor and the lords and ladies of the city. Keats's "Ode to a Nightingale" is similarly describable as the story of an excursion, this time with a return to something like the place where the speaker-protagonist started.

The fact that narrative analysis works more successfully with some poems than with others is itself a valuable piece of critical information. It is one way of illustrating the difference between lyrics that are essentially static in character and those that are essentially dynamic.[12] Poems like "To Autumn" and "Ode on Melancholy" have their minds made up before they begin; they are statements rather than processes, statements of thoughts already arrived at before the speakers begin speaking. Poems like "Frost at Midnight," "Tintern Abbey," "Ode: Intimations of Immortality," and "Ode to a Nightingale" are more complicated; they represent the actual processes of thinking and take their shape from the movement of the protagonist's mind, going now in one direction and now in another. Lyrics in this latter class are at least implied narratives, and often they are, like Yeats's and Keats's excursions, explicit narratives.

Keats's "Ode on a Grecian Urn" is seemingly inexhaustible as a subject of critical interpretation. In this poem, as probably in all lyric poems, we may take the first-person speaker as the principal protagonist. The antagonist here is an abstraction—time (and the attendant mutability, natural process, and death)—and what the speaker wants, as we can tell by his admiring exclamations when he contemplates the situation of the lovers, the piper, and the trees depicted on the Grecian urn, is timelessness (the absence of mutability, process, and death). But, as we learn from the opening lines, the speaker-protagonist is a person interested in history, stories, and legends, and in the course of his musings he attempts his own narrative analysis of the situations represented on the urn. Taking the urn-figures as a collective protagonist, he discovers that *their* antagonist is timelessness (just the opposite of his own), as embodied in the increasingly dismal facts that the youth will never kiss the maiden, the piper will never be able to stop playing, the trees will never lose their leaves because they are confined to a single season of the year, and, worst of all, the townspeople engaged in a procession toward some green altar are stopped forever midway between their destination and the town they have left empty, silent, and desolate behind them. The result is a complete reversal of terms and values, so that what was life before is now seen as a kind of death; what was death before becomes the only mode of life, and the speaker's former enemy, time, now becomes his ally.

The story of the urn-figures and the encompassing story of the speaker-protagonist contemplating them are further encompassed in a frame situation in which the speaker functions as a character who asks a great many questions and for a while gets no answers. "What leaf-fring'd legend haunts about thy shape," he inquires, entering into his narrative analysis. He wants to know whether the urn-figures are men or gods, what they are doing, and where these activities are taking place. There are eight questions in a series in the first stanza, and then three more in the fourth stanza about the people in the procession, the altar that is their destination, and the town whence they have come; and to none of these does the speaker get an answer, the urn remaining silent until, at the very end, something or somebody pronounces the famous answer to all questions, " 'Beauty is truth, truth beauty,'—that is all / Ye know on earth, and all ye need to know." It has never been definitively decided who is supposed to be speaking these lines and to whom. But in structural terms, as a massive, all-purpose answer following a series of unanswered questions, it *sounds* like a satisfactory resolution of everything hitherto left unsettled in the poem, even if we don't in fact know exactly what the resolution is. It was not until seventy-six years after Keats's death that a critic first called attention to the absence of literal meaning in the equation of beauty and truth.[13]

Narrative analysis of this sort can assist the teaching and understanding of poems of other periods besides the romantic and other literatures besides English. It can serve perhaps most usefully to counter our tendency to convert art into statement. All of us—critics, teachers, students alike—enter too quickly and too directly into interpretation, searching for hidden meanings without sufficiently taking in what is available on the surface. Interpretation might well be redefined as *improvement of reading*, with a more unashamed focus on surface meaning, which is, after all, where the art primarily resides.[14] Narrative analysis does have practical advantages toward this end. Unlike some other methods, it does not reduce or oversimplify the works it is used to describe. Instead, it shows up the complexity of works that are genuinely complex and in many cases serves to clarify the causes or sources of complexity. It does seem an efficient method of seeing things as they are, which is a good way at least to begin an understanding of what one is studying. As M. H. Abrams points out at the end of an essay on five ways of reading "Lycidas", a "necessary . . . condition for a competent reader of poetry remains what it has always been—a keen eye for the obvious."[15]

Notes

1. Seymour Chatman, *Story and Discourse: Narrative Structure in Fiction and Film* (Ithaca: Cornell University Press, 1978), and Gérard Genette, *Narrative Discourse: An Essay in Method* (Ithaca: Cornell University Press, 1980).

2. *Letters of Wallace Stevens*, ed. Holly Stevens (New York: Alfred A. Knopf, 1966), 250.

3. See M. H. Abrams, "Coleridge's 'A Light in Sound': Science, Metascience, and Poetic Imagination" (1972), reprinted most recently in Abrams's *The Correspondent Breeze: Essays on English Romanticism* (New York: W. W. Norton, 1984), 158–91.

4. The phrase is of course absurd, but there is no polite term for sexual intercourse taking place when one of the partners is asleep or comatose (and "partners" in this note is similarly inaccurate).

5. Space limitations preclude the usual summarizing of critical positions for this and the other main examples below, four of which (all but "The Eve of St. Mark") are among the most frequently discussed poems of the romantic period. For an up-

to-date survey, see my chapter on Keats in *The English Romantic Poets: A Review of Research and Criticism,* ed. Frank Jordan, 4th ed. (New York: MLA, 1985), 665–718.

6. This statement might seem inconsistent with Keats's highly circumspect line 320, both in the original text that was printed ("Into her dream he melted") and in the revised version surviving in transcripts by Richard Woodhouse and George Keats ("With her wild dream he mingled"). But most of the other details of 289–333 (text and variants alike) enforce the idea that Porphyro and Madeline continue in two different states until he awakens her with "This is no dream" in 326.

7. In a letter to John Taylor, 17 November 1819; *The Letters of John Keats,* ed. Hyder E. Rollins (Cambridge: Harvard University Press, 1958), 2:234.

8. 18 September 1819; *Letters,* 2:189.

9. To George and Georgiana Keats, 20 September 1819; *Letters,* 2:201.

10. Walter E. Houghton, "The Meaning of Keats's *Eve of St. Mark,*" *ELH* 13 (1946): 64–78; Jack Stillinger, "The Meaning of 'Poor Cheated Soul' in Keats's *The Eve of Saint Mark*" (1968), reprinted in *The Hoodwinking of Madeline and Other Essays on Keats's Poems* (Urbana: University of Illinois Press, 1971), 94–98; David Luke, "*The Eve of Saint Mark:* Keats's 'ghostly Queen of Spades' and the Textual Superstition," *Studies in Romanticism* 9 (1970): 161–75.

11. The two most helpful essays on the structure of the romantic lyric, written about the same time but independently of one another, are Irene H. Chayes, "Rhetoric as Drama: An Approach to the Romantic Ode," *PMLA* 79 (1964): 67–79, and M. H. Abrams, "Structure and Style in the Greater Romantic Lyric" (1965), reprinted in *The Correspondent Breeze,* 76–108.

12. See Robert Langbaum, *The Poetry of Experience* (New York: Random House, 1957), 53.

13. See Harvey T. Lyon, *Keats' Well-Read Urn: An Introduction to Literary Method* (New York: Henry Holt, 1958), 48–50.

14. A practicing structuralist might argue that plot (as I have been discussing it here) lies *beneath* the surface. But students can be taught to identify protagonists, aims, and obstacles in a matter of seconds (sometimes more rapidly than their theme-oriented teacher); these things must, therefore, be relatively visible when such speedy analysis is possible. For a non-narrative example of what I mean by focusing on surface meaning, consider lines 211–13 of *The Eve of St. Agnes,* where the "panes of quaint device" in the casement in Madeline's bedchamber are described as "Innumerable of stains and splendid dyes, / As are the tiger-moth's deep-damask'd wings." Most American students have never seen a tiger moth and without a dictionary do not know the color signified by "damask" (or even that "deep-damask'd" refers to a color). The lines are, at first glance, virtually unintelligible. But the meaning is still plainly "surface"; all one has to do is show the class a picture of a tiger moth.

15. "Five Types of *Lycidas,*" in *Milton's "Lycidas": The Tradition and the Poem,* ed. C. A. Patrides (New York: Holt, Rinehart and Winston, 1961), 231.

"Keats"
[from *Inescapable Romance*]   Patricia A. Parker°

> For Poesy alone can tell her dreams.
> With the fine spell of words alone can save
> Imagination from the sable charm
> And dumb enchantment.
> —*The Fall of Hyperion*

FAIRY LANDS FORLORN

In *The Burden of the Past and the English Poet*, W. Jackson Bate argues that we cannot arbitrarily separate the English Romantics from the century which preceded them, however striking the differences which make Romanticism a genuine literary epoch.[1] We may begin with this warning in turning to Keats, for the question of his relation to romance demands not only an historical preface but also one which includes the century he himself saw as a "schism"[2] in the history of poetry. "Romance" underwent a sea-change in the period between Spenser and the English Romantic poet who was most clearly his descendant, and a look at this history may provide the necessary counterpart to the view of Keats we have inherited from a more simply formal criticism, the kind of textual study to which his Great Odes so marvelously lend themselves and which ensured his continued popularity during a period when the other Romantics had fallen into eclipse.

Keats himself suggests the outlines of this history in his own allusions to earlier romance. His "Ode on Indolence" takes as its motto "They toil not, neither do they spin"—the invitation of Spenser's Phaedria to take no thought for the morrow—and the letter in which he explains the genesis of the Ode links it to the popular eighteenth-century imitation of Spenser, James Thomson's *Castle of Indolence*.[3] Both the Spenserian echo and the self-conscious reference to Thomson's poem suggest a context for the intervening progress of romance and its ambivalences. In Book II of *The Faerie Queene*, Phaedria's appeal is an invitation to swerve from the onward movement of the quest, to withdraw from the world of fruitless toil, and to imitate the careless ease of the lilies of the field. Her appeal to "present pleasures" (vi. 17) echoes Christ's words to men all too anxious about the morrow, but it conceals a darker temptation. The "indolence" of her island on the Idle Lake is closer to the crippling

° Excerpted from "Keats" in *Inescapable Romance: Studies in the Poetics of a Mode* by Patricia A. Parker. © 1979 by Princeton University Press. Excerpts, 159–218, reprinted with permission of Princeton University Press.

impotence of accidia and the repose it offers is not a recreation but an end to all movement, a permanent escape. Guyon resists this temptation to resign his responsibilities to a world of "care" and exposes Phaedria's appeal to Scripture as the fraud it is. But the fact that, in the very next canto, he himself echoes her argument in his answer to Mammon's insistence upon getting and spending (vii. 14–15) suggests that there is an ambivalence within repose itself, that the alternative to the world of Mammon may be at once a refusal to accept its anxious questing and the potential vortex of an enervating sloth.

Thomson's Spenserian imitation provides a crucial stepping-stone to Keats because it extends this dark temptation to the pleasures of romance itself, and its refuge from the world of Mammon. The charms offered by "Indolence," the poem's "Archimage," are tinged with suggestions of romance, of "gay Castles in the Clouds that pass, / For ever flushing round a Summer-Sky" (I. vi. 3–4), and the "alas" of Thomson's motto reveals that something larger is at stake, in the forsaking of this realm, than a mere farewell to the individual sin of sloth. Romance, like indolence, is simultaneously a refuge from the waking world and a dangerous evasion, a form increasingly suspect in an enlightened age. Thomson is both a Spenserian and a man of the Enlightenment, and the complexities of his farewell to the Castle's "Soul-dissolving" charms (I. xxxix) reveal at once a desire to banish a potentially seductive illusion and a melancholy sense of the impossibility of recovering the "artful Phantoms" of its "Fairy-Land" (I, xlv).

Thomson's poem illustrates a specifically historical schizophrenia. As early as 1694, Joseph Addison could write that the tales which pleased a "barb'rous age" could "charm an understanding age no more,"[4] and the view that the progress of enlightenment made their charms no longer palatable was echoed countless times in a century which associated romance increasingly with indolence and dream and opposed to all three the poetic protestantism of a more active musing. Certainly there did persist a regret that the clue to this "faery land" might be forever lost. The recovery of the "enchanted ground" recalled by Thomson and others[5] was the common concern of Percy, Hurd, and the Wartons. But this effort at revival was accompanied in even the most minor magazine poetry of the century by a sense that no real return was possible, that all that was left to an enlightened age was "A waking sense of truth too plain, / That vainly sighs to dream again."[6]

Even the attempts to recapture this past betray a divided mind. Thomas Warton defends his own "excursion into Fairy-Land," however "monstrous and unnatural these compositions may appear to this age of reason and refinement," by arguing that they not only throw light on ancient customs but "store the fancy with those sublime and alarming images, which true poetry best delights to display." Yet this identification of romance with "true poetry" does not prevent him from speaking of the "absurdities" of the romances or from contrasting the "depths of Gothic ignorance and barbarity" with the "new and more legitimate taste" established since the Renaissance.[7] Mark Akenside chooses the "Pleasures of the Imagination" over more mundane pursuits and scorns "The busy steps, the jealous eye" of those who suspect the "gay delusive spoils" of the Muse,[8] but he too asks that "Fancy" in her "fairy cell" be tempered by that "Reason" which calls the soul back to "Truth's severest test."[9] All these pronouncements reflect a curiously double view of history. Warton couches the progress of his *History of English Poetry* from "rudeness to elegance" in the familiar metaphors of darkness and light, yet he too seems haunted by the anxieties of the epigone, a fear that reason's daylight has dispelled both superstition's mist and imagination's golden haze, and expresses a nostalgia for the age when "Reason suffered a few demons still to linger . . . under the guidance of poetry."[10]

This sense that the fortunes of romance were virtually synonymous with the fortunes of poetry itself emerges perhaps nowhere more vividly than in Hazlitt's famous description of the march of enlightenment:

It cannot be concealed . . . that the progress of knowledge and refinement has a tendency to circumscribe the limits of the imagination, and to clip the wings of poetry. The province of the imagination is principally visionary, the unknown and undefined: the understanding restores things to their natural boundaries, and strips them of their fanciful pretensions. . . . It is the undefined and uncommon that gives birth and scope to the imagination; we can only fancy what we do not know. As in looking into the mazes of a tangled wood we fill them with what shapes we please, with ravenous beasts, with caverns vast, and drear enchantments, so in our ignorance of the world about us, we make gods or devils of the first object we see, and set no bounds to the wilful suggestions of our hopes and fears.[11]

That romance was a *chiaro-oscuro* border realm being crowded out by the empire of enlightenment links its attractions—and its dangers—to those of the secluded retreat, or enchanted ground, that countless eighteenth-century poems seek to rediscover. Each of the poems which invoke a power—"Contemplation," "Peace," "Solitude," "Fancy"—and ask to be led to that power's sequestered cell is in effect a brief romance, a quest for a respite from the waking world.[12] When the world of noisy care threatens to become as fatal to this retreat as the "rude Axe"[13] to the actual wooded haunt, the path the poet asks to be shown frequently tends to be synonymous with perception itself; his inability to find the enchanted bower or to remain for long within it brings not relief at the destruction of its "charm" but disappointment that "the fancy cannot cheat so well / As she is famed to do." And yet, if exclusion from this bower prompts an "adieu" as full of regret as Thomson's farewell to his Castle, there is at the same time the nagging suspicion that the poet who seeks it may be guilty of the purely negative side of what Stevens was to call "evasion," a cowardly refusal of responsibility to the world of things as they are.

"Romance" was an ambivalent mode, then, because its charms were indistinguishable from its snares. Hazlitt's famous description of the Spenserian stanza—"dissolving the soul in pleasure, or holding it captive in the chains of suspense" and "lulling the senses into a deep oblivion of the jarring noises of the world, from which we have no wish to be ever recalled"[14]—had its counterpart in the attractions and dangers of romance itself, a dream from which there was potentially no awaking and a "suspension" from which there might be no exit. Geoffrey Hartman has described Milton's "L'Allegro" and "Il Penseroso" as crucial landmarks in the purification of romance, the mind as magus summoning its own moods and wandering, literally, at will.[15] But *Paradise Lost* delivers a harsher judgment on the dangers of wandering and the post-Miltonic poems which are closest to the form of the companion poems frequently internalize the anxieties of the epic's darker moral, the possibility of wandering past a point of no return. In a crucial passage of Burton's *Anatomy of Melancholy*, a signal text for Keats, the delights of the wandering imagination turn to terror when the way back is suddenly blocked:

> So delightsome these toys are at first, they could spend days and nights without sleep, even whole years alone in such contemplations, and fantastical meditations, which are like unto dreams, and they will hardly be drawn from them, or willingly interrupt, so pleasant their vain conceits are, that they hinder their ordinary tasks or employment; these fantastical and bewitching thoughts so insinuate, possess, overcome, distract, and detain them, they cannot, I say, go about their more necessary business, stave off, or extricate themselves, but are ever musing, melancholizing, and carried along, as he (they say) that is led around about a heath with a Puck in the night, they run earnestly on in this labyrinth of anxious and solicitous melancholy meditations, and cannot well or willingly refrain, or easily leave off, winding and unwinding themselves, as so many clocks, and still pleasing their humours, *until at last the scene is turned upon a sudden,* by some bad object, and they being now habituated to such vain meditations and solitary places, can endure no company, can ruminate of nothing but harsh and distasteful subjects. (Part 1, Sect. 2, Memb. 2, Sub. 6; my italics)

This passage from the *Anatomy* is the one often simply cited as an example of the prose style known as the Senecan amble. But its theme, and the faintly Gothic suggestion of its sudden "turn," look forward to the ambulatory poetry of the century after Milton and its transformation of the Puckish delights of a fanciful wandering into the unsteady progress of a gloomy egotist among the tombs.

The ambivalences of romance and its delightful, and suspect, "error" suggest a context for the period we now call Romantic. In the course of one of his essays, John Stuart Mill pauses to consider the difference between two of his century's great figures, Jeremy Bentham and Samuel Taylor Coleridge, the man of enlightenment and the poet. The two are distinguished by what they led men to ask themselves with regard to any "ancient or received opinion."[16] Bentham, says Mill, would ask "Is it true?," Coleridge, "What is the meaning of it?" Bentham's question presupposes the possibility of an answer "yes" or "no," an axiom of logic which Aristotle termed the law of the excluded middle. Coleridge's question, on the other hand, suspends such direct answering in favor of an exploration, a dilation of the space between the logician's, or the pragmatist's, Either-Or. For Mill, this difference is a telling parable of the distance between the pragmatic and the poetical character; for the student of English Romanticism, it also provides an insight into the nature of this middle ground and its relation to the fine, if superstitious, fabling of the world of romance.

In his essay "Poetry Distinguished from Other Writing," Oliver Goldsmith singled out the history of the term "hanging" or "pendant" from Virgil to Milton as the epitome of the figurative or picture-making power of poetry, and his comments on the picturesque effect of the word "hung" in *Paradise Lost* anticipate Wordsworth's obser-vation that this was Milton's most characteristic expression.[17] Could he have taken his history forward to the Romantics, he might have included Wordsworth's own version of the Miltonic "suspension." But he might also have explored the attractions of pendency in a context more sinister. Coleridge's own description of this "suspen-sion" comes in his account of the division of labor between himself and Wordsworth in the *Lyrical Ballads;* "It was agreed that my endeavours should be directed to persons and characters supernatural or at least romantic; yet so as to transfer from our outward nature a human interest and a semblance of truth sufficient to procure for these shadows of imagination that willing suspension of disbelief for the moment, which constitutes poetic faith."[18] The familiarity of the passage obscures its menace; but the old ambivalence continues in the language of the description itself. The "willing suspension of disbelief" given to the "shadows of imagination" has as its undertone the Gothic danger of a *raptus* or rape by these shadows, and the

passage weighs heavily on its all-important qualifier, that such suspension is only "for the moment."

Northrop Frye has called Romanticism a "sentimental" form of
romance, that later re-creation of an earlier mode which Schiller
explored in his famous essay.[19] One of the implications of this change
is that re-creation involved distance as well as revival, that the
historical schism, however lamented, also offered a form of protection.
The odes of the ubiquitous Mrs. Robinson are all of a piece—a
movement from fascination with the "haunted glade" to a hasty retreat
when its charms appear to be darkening into necromancy and night,[20]
a concern with "ground" which suggests, in countless other minor
poems, a fear of transport of any kind. Keats inherits this eighteenth-
century strain as well as the Spenserian-Miltonic one. In the final
stanza of the "Ode to a Nightingale," it seems as if the speaker is
involuntarily falling out of an enchanted space ("Forlorn! The very
word is like a bell / To toll me back from thee to my sole self!"),
but the previous stanza has already distanced the speaker from the
nightingale even before it flies away, through a time scheme which
journeys back through "ancient days" and the "sad heart of Ruth"
to "fairy lands forlorn." It is difficult to avoid the conclusion that
this historical distance enters the poem less as fact than as strategy—
a means of distancing the speaker from an attraction, and a transport,
which also means his death.

Keats's relation to romance shares, from the beginning, in this
ambivalence. The verse epistle "To George Felton Mathew" begins
with a version of the quintessential eighteenth-century theme, the
desire to be led away from the sun of this world into some "flowery
spot, sequestered, wild, romantic" (37), and a fear, in the spistle "To
Charles Cowden Clarke," is that he comes too late to be admitted
through the "enchanted portals" which separate this world from that
of a more visionary company. Romance, even in the early Keats,
however, is inseparable from anxiety, and there is even here the
beginning of a sense that its attractions should be resisted in favor
of the demands of the waking world. The verse epistle "To My
Brother George" opens with the concern that he might not share
the vision of knights and "ladies fair," but it soon moves forward to
the wish that his "poetic lore" might be more than mere evasion.
And it is this desire not to be caught in a "barren dream" that
prompts his most famous farewell to romance, the sonnet "On Sitting
Down to Read King Lear Once Again."

The siren form of "golden-tongued Romance" is opposed both
to the higher genres of tragedy and epic and to the harsher world
of waking reality, and Keat's poetry and letters after Endymion signal
his intention to move beyond romance, in both directions.[21] So frequent are these pronouncements that critics have tended to see in

Keats a progression like that of "Sleep and Poetry" from the realm
of Flora and old Pan to the "nobler life" of the poems of 1819, an
application to his life and poetry of the images of progress which
abound in the *Letters*, from the speculations on the march of enlightenment between Milton and Wordsworth to the comparison of
human life to a mansion of many apartments.[22] The impression of
such straightforward movement in Keats's poetry, however, is deceptive. No purely developmental scheme will finally fit, just as the
characteristic fluidity or ambiguity of the verse makes any attempt
to wrest a coherent philosophy or definitive conclusion from Keats's
poetry inevitably doomed.[23] The farewell to romance remains an
attempt to say farewell, and reading the progress of Keats's career
is no more linear a process than reading the most complex of the
individual poems.

Keats's statements are often difficult to conscript to the scheme
of a straightforward "progress" because they look two ways at once.[24]
One of the characteristics Keats shares with Shakespeare is his dramatic showing forth of "attitudes" which it would be as misleading
to identify with Keats himself as it would be naive to speak of what
Shakespeare "says." Paul de Man has called the first *Hyperion* a poem
more Shakespearean than Miltonic, and in this sense, Keats can be
no more identified with the position of Oceanus on the march of
progress than can Shakespeare with Ulysses' speech on degree.[25]
Fixity of attitude defies everything Keats had to say on the chameleon
quality of the poetical character. The frozen statuary of the fallen
Titans in *Hyperion* is in one respect the visible and outward form of
their spiritual fixity, as if lack of motion were a necessary consequence
of any final taking of position. Critics who attempt to identify single
attitudes in the most complex of Keats's poems often fix what is
deliberately left uncertain and shifting.

Whatever else may ally Keats with the romance imagination, his
complex diction and the interplay of literary allusions are part of its
characteristic plentitude and frequently subvert the marshaling of
meaning towards a single end. The dramatic center of *The Eve of St.
Agnes* is the scene in which Porphyro watches Madeline awaken from
her dream into the reality of the banquet he has set before her. Her
awakening could be simply a poetic version of that transition from
dream to reality which Keats outlined in the famous letter to Bailey:
"The Imagination may be compared to Adam's dream—he awoke
and found it truth."[26] But the echoes which surround this event make
it difficult to determine whether this conclusion to Madeline's dream
is a repetition in a finer or a grosser tone, whether it is a progress
to fulfillment or a somewhat more complex fall. Porphyro re-creates
the substance of her dream, but he is also subtly linked to Satan
before the sleeping Eve and the villainous Iachimo before Shake-

speare's Imogen.[27] Similarly, in the "Ode on Indolence," the attempt to wrest a definitive statement from the poem is impeded by the lack of clear subordination, or straightforward linear movement, in the syntax itself. Several of its critics have read it as a celebration of the *penseroso* mood, a deliberate embracing of the bower of indolence and its calm repose. This reading does account for the poem's motto— "They toil not, neither do they spin"—and for the speaker's firm refusal to be taken in by the "voice of busy common-sense" (40) and its designation of all apparent inactivity as unproductive. The poem itself, however, undercuts the simplicity of statement. The argument may be linear and the voice imperative ("Vanish, ye Phantoms, from my idle sprite / Into the clouds, and never more return!" 59–60), but the interplay of images qualifies even the speaker's final word. The "clouds" to which he banishes these "Phantoms" at the poem's end are the very clouds in whose lids still hang the "sweet tears of May" (46), and this echo of the earlier image reintroduces the fact of process and change into the attempt to exile it. The shades of Spenser's Phaedria and Thomson's Indolence still linger in this retreat. Though the speaker is one, the poem is not univocal and reading is a more circuitous process than simple linear movement towards conclusion.[28]

The Odes are enduring because they are somehow at the heart of poetic diction, that plentitude of meaning which evades the Mammon world of stenolanguage and single referents. Ambiguity in Keats, however, is even more directly related to the question of romance's shadowy and evasive world. Keats is perhaps closest of all the English Romantics to a particularly Spenserian awareness of the doubleness of all things, but there is in this resemblance a significant difference. Through most of *The Faerie Queene,* the sense of doubleness is conveyed by a proliferation of dangerous look-alikes and "reading" is at least partly the activity of separating the counterfeit from the real, of uncovering the actual identity behind the seductive appearance. Keats borrows the romance motif of the revelation of a "lamia" from Burton, but in *Lamia* the elfin lady's real, or original, identity is left radically open to question. The contrary tendencies of the poem itself are finally not separable into a single conclusion about the poet's attitude or end. Lamia is compared both to the python killed by Apollo (II. 78–80) and to Eurydice (I. 248), and only critics who choose to privilege one of these allusions over the other can finally separate what the poem itself leaves in suspension.[29]

This complexity in a poem written as late as *Lamia* cannot but suggest that Keats's progress away from romance was far from a straightforward one. "Romance," as Keats inherited it, is no longer a strictly generic term and cannot, despite his own pronouncements, be so easily rejected. The romance embroidery of the earlier poems drops out, and Keats anticipates Yeats in the poetic enterprise of going naked. But chronology is no certain guide and the struggle continues in more subterranean forms. *Isabella* is a translation of "the gentleness of old romance" (387) into the "wormy circumstance" (385) of the Gothic, but it is not so much an "anti-romance" (as Jack Stillinger suggests)[30] as a variation of it, an indication that a form which tries to incorporate the pain of reality may become simply the *macabre*. In one sense, the attempts in Keats to awaken out of romance is analogous to his attempt to do without ritual trappings, like the superstitious stage-props of *melancholia* abandoned in the canceled stanza of the "Ode on Melancholy." Near the beginning of *The Fall of Hyperion*, there is a confused "heaping" of the vessels of the "Ode to Psyche" which may be as much the signal of a new direction as is the movement from the refuse of a Miltonic paradise. But Keats never fully gets rid of this baggage or of its ceremonial forms any more than he says a final farewell to the modes and superstitions of romance. Instead, he at once seeks freedom from the old forms and carries them forward as part of his assumption of the weight of tradition. Porphyro's "solution" to the transition between dream and reality is more efficacious than the antique ritual of the "legends old" (*Eve of St. Agnes*, 135), but it requires as elaborate a staging. And *The Fall of Hyperion* is an initiation ritual which, though ostensibly beyond the realm of romance, returns to its most elemental form— the healing of an ailing and impotent old king by a hero whose redemption is his "word."

None of these poems can be reduced to the linear frame of a "development" or the strict argumentative line of a particular thesis. The Keats we have often literally differs from himself, and it is difficult to reconcile the perspicacity of the Odes and the humanism of the *Letters* with the obsession of *Isabella* or the fetishism of "This Living Hand." Keats's is a poetry which yields some of its secrets to close reading, some to an exploration of related images, and still others to a more historical thematics. We shall therefore adopt the more characteristically romance technique of juxtaposition and association, exploring first the "negative capability" of wandering in the "Ode to a Nightingale" and *Endymion*, secondly the complex of images for this threshold state which connect *Endymion* with the impasse of the first *Hyperion*, and finally the darkening of this threshold and the drama of mutual trespass in *The Fall of Hyperion*, that fragment's second and final version. . . .

TRIAL BY BEARING

The contest or trial which is the central drama of *The Fall of Hyperion* is introduced in the opening lines as the problem of expression, or voice:

> Fanatics have their dreams, wherewith they weave
> A paradise for a sect, the savage too
> From forth the loftiest fashion of his sleep
> Guesses at Heaven; pity these have not
> Traced upon vellum or wild Indian leaf
> The shadows of melodious utterance.
> But bare of laurel they live, dream, and die;
> For Poesy alone can tell her dreams,
> With the fine spell of words alone can save
> Imagination from the sable charm
> And dumb enchantment.

The first *Hyperion* begins with the evocation of silence—the air without a "stir," the "voiceless" stream and the Naiad pressing her "cold finger closer to her lips." This very silence is part of the "dumb enchantment" confronted in the second attempt, and the insertion of the persona of the poet into the scene suggests that the essential drama is to be not the War between Olympian and Titan but the movement of these stony figures by the only possible countercharm, the poet's revivifying word.

It is this dialectic of voice and stony silence which makes the second fragment an intensification both of the drama of mutual trespass concealed within the concept of "Negative Capability" and of the submerged contest of another of the Great Odes, the anxious questing or questioning of the "Ode on a Grecian Urn." Both the romance theme of trespass and the uneasy dialectic of this "Ode" provide an illuminating prelude to the quest of the poet-pilgrim of *The Fall*, but only if the "Ode" is perceived in its essential dramatic context. Criticism has focused on the problematic content or philosophy of the ode which ends "Beauty is truth, truth beauty," and an endless debate has been generated on the meaning of the poem as statement. But Kenneth Burke pioneered a reading in which the focus is, instead, on the confrontation, or agon, of speaker and object.[31] and it is this confrontation which leads most directly into the scene of *The Fall*.

We have characterized romance as a form which both projects an end and defers its arrival. The "end" of the "Ode on a Grecian Urn" is *ut pictura poesis*, the emulation of the urn's silent form:

> Heard melodies are sweet, but those unheard
> Are sweeter; therefore, ye soft pipes, play on;
> Not to the sensual ear, but, more endeared,
> Pipe to the spirit ditties of no tone.
>
> (11–14)

The genre of the ode is *ekphrasis*, the verbal reproduction of an objet d'art, and the poem comes full circle in imitation of the urn. But there is a contrary movement as well, a movement in which silence is not a goal but a potential threat, and the poet's task is to make this stony shape speak. The condition of sculpture is, in this sense, the "end" of poetry not as intention but as potential nemesis, the fixity which Hazlitt describes in his contrast of poetry and painting.[32] Keats's ode moves, as statement, towards the finality of the "Cold pastoral" as fixed object. But the language itself provides an elaboration of that fixity, an interpretation of "shape" by "legend," and *ekphrasis* becomes not just genre but contest. The urn itself ("Thou still unravished bride of quietness," 1) is suspended between two potential ravishers—the poet who desires to make this shape reveal its "tale," and "quietness," the fate to which it is betrothed but not yet finally joined.[33] The praise of the "Silvan historian, who canst thus express / A flowery tale more sweetly than our rhyme" (3–4) looks foward to the "unheard melodies" of the second stanza; but the active questioning of the first stanza already begins to violate that silence. The crescendo building to "What wild ecstasy?" (10) suggests the anxiousness of the poet's desire to rescue the urn from quietude, and though the poem's central stanzas privilege its "unheard melodies," the anxiety returns as the dark underside of stanza IV, the sense that the chasm which separates the poet from this enigmatic object and its "little town" is unbridgeable,[34] that no historical *transitio*, or bringing forward, may be possible.

This anxiety culminates in the "silent form" and "Cold pastoral" of the final stanza. The urn appears to have the last word, refusing to yield its secrets to the poet's obstinate questing. The ode ends with a paradox—a message so uncompromising in its finality that it has given birth to endless interpretation. If the statement is the oracle of which the whole poem is the viaticum,[35] the urn's singular pronouncement remains, like all oracles, ambiguous:

> O Attic shape! Fair attitude! With brede
>   Of marble men and maidens overwrought,
> With forest branches and the trodden weed—
>   Thou, silent form, dost tease us out of thought
> As doth eternity. Cold pastoral!
>   When old age shall this generation waste,
>   Thou shalt remain, in midst of other woe
> Than ours, a friend to man, to whom thou say'st,
>   "Beauty is truth, truth beauty"—that is all
>   Ye know on earth, and all ye need to know.

The process of the poet's earlier questioning is cut short or suspended. As a monument which does not yield its full story to the questioner, it becomes, as well, admonishment or proscription: thus far wilt thou go and no farther.

Ostensibly the victory is the urn's. And yet, if poetry here cannot reach the silence of *pictura*, it also takes full advantage of the gap between word and object. The very stanza which professes to surrender so much to the enigma of plastic form virtually riots in its own ambiguities, the fortuitous element of punning in language that creates its own interlace of sounds and meanings. Language—even language which strains to the condition of silence—retains its links with the impurities of the "sensual ear" and its "heard melodies" create here an echo chamber in the mind. The dead end of a single meaning is evaded as deftly as the fixity of the urn itself. The urn may be "cold," but in this stanza, "brede" warms to "breed" and generates the more animated sense of "overwrought," just as "Attic" provides a playful, or poetic, etymology for "attitude." The language seems almost to increase its antics in the first half of the stanza as a declaration of freedom from the proscription, or inscription, at the end, the "Cold pastoral" and its final commandment.

The dialectic of stone and voice behind the questioning of the "Ode" becomes in *The Fall of Hyperion* the poet's particular burden. Keats admired Milton's genius for "stationing or statuary,"[36] and the first *Hyperion* is in this respect a highly Miltonic poem. Its opening picture of Saturn sitting "quiet as a stone" (I. 4) is joined by the description of Thea and the aged king "postured motionless, / Like natural sculpture in cathedral cavern" (86–87) and, later, of the council of fallen Titans as a "dismal cirque / Of Druid stones upon a forlorn moor" (II. 34–35). This sculptural positioning is part of what Geoffrey Hartman has called Keats's "picture envy," his fascination with "shaped and palpable gods."[37] But it is also, perhaps, one of the reasons why this fragment never gets moving. Saturn is not so much situated in the landscape as he is fixed in it, and the very language of the description ("Deep . . . / Far sunken . . . / Far . . . .") manages to suggest at once a location and a fall. The fixity of the pictorial is part of the frozen limbo from which the fragment never completely emerges. Keats's image of a new awakening was of each man whispering results to his neighbor until "Humanity instead of being a wide heath of Furse and Briars with here and there a remote Oak or Pine, would become a grand democracy of Forest Trees!"[38] But in this fragment, voice rises in isolation and subsides, and even the speeches of the great Miltonic consult remain soliloquies. In order to move these stony forms, the poet of *The Fall of Hyperion* places himself in the scene. And the ancient quest motif of the young hero whose word is to restore the ailing *senex* and bring about a renewal of a dead landscape becomes the agon of the poet struggling to find his own voice.

The romance motif of reanimation has its counterpart in that dramatic capacity Keats, following Hazlitt, called "gusto," the absence of self distinguished from "the wordsworthian or egotistical sublime":

"A Poet is the most unpoetical of any thing in existence; because he has no Identity—he is continually in for—and filling some other Body."[39] We are so accustomed to the Keatsian generosity of spirit—that "camelion" quality that "has as much delight in conceiving an Iago as an Imogen"—that we may fail to hear the overtones of menace in this dramatic "filling," a somewhat different aspect of the negative capability which informs the patience of *Endymion.* But slightly further on in the same letter, there is a passage which suggests that this absence of self has a more ominous side: "When I am in a room with People if I ever am free from speculating on creations of my own brain, then not myself goes home to myself: but the identity of every one in the room begins to to [sic] press upon me that I am in a very little time an[ni]hilated."

The letter is revealing when placed beside *The Fall of Hyperion.* The quest of the poet-persona is to animate the stony forms, but the very bodies he seeks to fill threaten, in turn, to annihilate him. In another letter written while he was at work on the first *Hyperion,* Keats celebrates the ability of the mind to wander at will, and alludes naturally to Milton's "Il Penseroso": "I feel more and more every day, as my imagination strengthens, that I do not live in this world alone but in a thousand worlds—No sooner am I alone than shapes of epic greatness are stationed around me, and serve my Spirit the office [of] which is equivalent to a king's bodyguard—then 'Tragedy, with scepter'd pall, comes sweeping by.' According to my state of mind I am with Achilles shouting in the Trenches or with Theocritus in the Vales of Sicily."[40] But the shapes of epic greatness which actually surround him in *The Fall* are not so much protective as oppressive and the free ranging of the *penseroso* mood is instead the possibility of the suspension of all movement—the Gothic nightmare of getting into a scene he cannot get out of.

If it is true, as is often remarked, that Keats swallowed Spenser as completely as Blake did Milton, this may be partly because "faerie" is of all literary landscapes the most shadowy and uncategorizable. Dante and Milton are primarily poets of clear boundaries and fixed places, so much so that the differences between them may be explained partly by a comparison of cosmologies. But romance, while it intensifies one aspect of place—its numen or mystery—also unfixes the boundaries and clear dividing lines between places, creating, paradoxically, a heightened sense of the possibility of trespass. Keats's concept of Negative Capability unfixes the boundaries of the self, and, paradoxically, makes the possibility of trespass more terrifying. Filling other bodies is part of a delightful *Einfühlung*, a wandering at will, but it also involves a trespass upon outer space which may invite, as part of a deadly compact, a violation in return.

In *The Fall,* the theme of trespass first takes its more traditional

form, the poet's sense of "unworthiness" (I. 182) to be on holy
ground—the topos of modesty which in Keats is frequently indistinguishable from a genuine sense of impotence—and is continued in
the tortuous distinctions of the dialogue with Moneta and her re-
minders of a barely tolerated intrusion:

> Therefore, that happiness be somewhat shared,
> Such things as thou art are admitted oft
> Into like gardens thou didst pass erewhile,
> And suffered in these temples
>
> (I. 177–80)

The subject of *Hyperion* is the War in Heaven just over, and the
fragment itself never recovers from this fall, though it does arrest
the fallen gods on this side of complete extinction. The whole effort
of *The Fall of Hyperion*, in contrast, is an attempt to move back to
the scenes which led to this event, now "enwombed" (I. 277) in the
brain of Moneta. The poet desires to find himself before—in both
senses—what he finds himself after, and this journey backward involves him in a succession of anterior scenes. The first step of the
dream is literally a retrograde one, a pilgrim's regress from a Miltonic
and Dantesque Eden into a Purgatory; the *katabasis* of the poet-
persona, traditionally an inescapable part of the initiation ritual, is
here a movement not only downward in space but backward in time.
No longer the *observer ab extra* of the first *Hyperion*, the poet literally
journeys back in order to bear the past forward, but the danger is
that this very journey involves a trespass upon ancestral space, that
he himself may be preempted by this past, as Apollo remained another
Titan, or another Endymion. The Romantic sublime in this second
fragment takes the form of a liminal contest: the poet who cannot
recross a threshold may become one, the purely negative counterpart
of the figure who is to be a "thoroughfare" for all thoughts; and the
imagery of sickness, though defended before Moneta as a "sickness
not ignoble" (I. 184), links the threshold state of *The Fall* once more
to that of the revised *Endymion* preface, the "space of life between."
Moneta herself is a threshold figure, a boundary between past and
present, whose aspect, Janus-like, depends partly on her function. As
"Moneta," she reflects the undertone suggestion of "doom" and
admonition in the "eternal domèd monument" (71) she guards. As
"Mnemosyne," she is the gateway from past to future, the authentic
Muse of transition: Keats addresses her as "Shade of Memory" as
soon as her veils are parted and he is admitted to the scenes hidden
within the "dark secret chambers of her skull" (278).

This journey involves a dialectic of persona and poet not unlike
that of Dante, the poet-pilgrim traveling to a destination which is at
the same time the origin of the poem. In *The Fall of Hyperion*, as

in the *Commedia*, the journey and the poem are finally inseparable because the subject is not only how the poem came to be written but how the poet himself was "born." The imagery is founded upon polarities—"parent" and "child," early and late, giant forms and "stunt bramble"—but the program of the fragment would seem to be to reverse these relationships, for the poet, finally, to father these ancestral forms as the children of his own brain. This initiation ritual involves a curious reversal, a "bearing" which moves at first not forward to birth, but rather, preposterous as it may appear, from "travail" back to conception, through the patient and purgatorial interval of labor necessary to give birth to his own "theme" (I. 46).

From early in the fragment, the sense of trespass inherent in this "travail" is linked to the problem of poetic "utterance" and to its potential termination:

> "Holy Power,"
> Cried I, approaching near the hornèd shrine,
> "What am I that should so be saved from death?
> What am I that another death come not
> To choke my utterance sacrilegious here?"
>   (I. 136–40)

Dante's poem begins in a region of unlikeness and the poet who tries to ascend directly to vision falls instead into a place "dove 'l sol tace" (*Inf.* I. 60). The ancient connection between light and sound, vision and voice, emerges again in the form of Keats's fragment. The trial moves first not forward to speech, to the "fine spell of words," but backwards to the "sable charm"—to the potential loss, or stifling, of voice—a return to infancy (*in-fans*) or speechlessness.

This movement suggests a rite of passage, as if the poet had to repeat the fall of the Titans into silence in order to in-feel, or invade, their space. But this particular negative capability involves as much risk as possibility. *Einfühlung* in Keats is a need as well as a capacity, and his preoccupation with the housing of the imagination continues a deep romance fear, that this Protean flexibility—the ability to assume identities at will—implies a more threatening absence of identity, its complete dissolution.[41] Keats's poetry is consistently preoccupied with the medium, with the particular body being filled or passed through: who but the poet of *Lamia* could give us, for better or for worse, the lines "the words she spake / Came, as through bubbling honey, for love's sake" (*Lamia* I. 64–65)? This preoccupation reaches its culmination in *The Fall* where the mouth becomes the temple or "roofèd home" (I. 229) of the tongue and the desired vision takes place inside the "globèd brain" (245) of the prophetess. But this housing, or enclosing, is itself dangerous. If Ovidian metamorphosis—frequently in Keats the motive power of poetry—is often literally the transformation of self into scene, it is also the movement which romance modulates into the paralyzing spell, the moment when the house or bower of the imagination becomes a stifling enclosure, a medium which cannot be passed through.

Both the delight and the threat of in-feeling are expressed in Keats in the different shadings of words, such as "smothering," which suggest this housing or enclosure. In the early poem "I Stood Tip-Toe," the line "The soul is lost in pleasant smotherings" (132) is meant to be as purely a matter of pleasure as the declaration in "Sleep and Poetry" that "the imagination / Into most lovely labyrinths will be gone" (265–66). But "smothering" elsewhere in Keats suggests the potential threat of suffocation, just as the "labyrinth" raises the possibility of an endless wandering. In Book IX of *Paradise Lost*, Milton's Satan undergoes a metamorphosis as a means to his end, his entry into the "Labyrinth" of the sleeping serpent (180–90). Milton carefully distinguishes medium from agent, so carefully in the tortured phrasing of "nor nocent yet" (186) as to suggest the danger of confounding means and end, a failure to perceive that the serpent's guilt is only by association, or trope.[42] Keats's notes on this passage in Milton, however, betray a horror at the possibility of being trapped within the medium itself: "Whose spirit does not ache at the smothering and confinement—the unwilling stillness—the '*waiting close*'? Whose head is not dizzy at the possible speculations of Satan in the serpent prison? No passage of poetry ever can give a greater pain of suffocation."[43] "Close" in the Miltonic context is simply an indication of proximity: Satan in his serpent body "waiting close th' approach of Morn" (*PL* IX. 191). But in Keats's reading, it conveys instead the "pain of suffocation," the danger of entering a body from which, like the "serpent prison-house" of *Lamia* (I. 203), there may be no egress.

The potential suffocation of not being able to proceed beyond a certain stage is frequently in Keats synonymous with a threatened loss of voice, the nightmare anxiety which hides behind the seemingly innocent muffling of Madeline in the ritual of *The Eve of St. Agnes*:

> No uttered syllable, or woe betide!
> But to her heart, her heart was voluble,
> Paining with eloquence her balmy side,
> As though a tongueless nightingale should swell
> Her throat in vain, and die, heart-stifled, in her dell.
> (203–7)

or manifests itself in the speechlessness of Lorenzo in *Isabella*, which virtually prefigures the "ruddy tide" of his death:

> all day
> His heart beat awfully against his side;

> And to his heart he inwardly did pray
> For power to speak; but still the ruddy tide
> Stifled his voice
>
> (41-45)

or informs, in the late "Ode to Fanny," the poet's own need for an expressive outlet or "theme":

> Physician Nature, let my spirit blood!
> Oh, ease my heart of verse and let me rest;
> Throw me upon thy tripod till the flood
> Of stifling numbers ebbs from my full breast.
> A theme, a theme! Great Nature, give a theme
> (1-5)

"Telling" in this last passage, however it might appear as poetic exaggeration or pure topos, is clearly a kind of release, an outlet in speech which rescues from the imminent threat of "stifling." In the first *Hyperion*, in a passage directly reminiscent of the Miltonic Satan's metamorphosis into a serpent, suffocation and the stifling of voice are part of a metamorphosis just barely escaped as Hyperion ends his address to the fallen Titans:

> He spake, and ceased, the while a heavier threat
> Held struggle with his throat but came not forth;
> For as in theatres of crowded men
> Hubbub increases more they call out "Hush!"
> So at Hyperion's words the phantoms pale
> Bestirred themselves, thrice horrible and cold;
> And from the mirrored level where he stood
> A mist arose, as from a scummy marsh.
> At this, through all his bulk an agony
> Crept gradual, from the feet unto the crown,
> Like a lithe serpent vast and muscular
> Making slow way, with head and neck convulsed
> From over-strainèd might. Released, he fled
> To the eastern gates
>
> (I. 251-64)

The threatened transformation here is in fact more Ovidian than Miltonic—not metamorphosis as a means to an end, but as victimization, and this passivity continues when, released from this stasis, the Titan tries to bring on the dawn. Though a "primeval God," he cannot force the "sacred seasons" ("Therefore the operations of the dawn / Stayed in their birth," 294-95), and this failure is repeated in the failure of the fragment itself to bring on a new dawn, the decisive advent of its Apollo.

In *The Fall of Hyperion,* Keats's final attempt to move beyond this "staying," the threat of suffocation or smothering becomes a disease, or dis-ease, which attacks the voice of the poet himself. The limbo of speechlessness into which the Titans have fallen is suggested through the imagery of sculptural immobility, of their fall as a kind of burial alive. The fallen Saturn is a kind of giant Laocoön ("Still fixed he sat beneath the sable trees, / Whose arms spread straggling in wild serpent forms," I. 446–47) who speaks of being "swallowed up / And buried from all godlike exercise / Of influence" (412–14). And suffocation is the image Thea uses for their present fallen state: "With such remorseless speed still come new woes / That unbelief has not a space to breathe" (366–67).

In *The Fall*, the implication is that the poet who trespasses upon this scene may share this silent, or stony, immobility. The danger is suggested as early as the "draught" which carries him from the Earthly Paradise of the opening scene to the barer landscape of Moneta's shrine:

> Upon the grass I struggled hard against
> The domineering potion; but in vain—
> The cloudy swoon came on, and down I sunk,
> Like a Silenus on an antique vase.
>
> (I. 53–56)

Suffocation and loss of voice are the first part of the poet's trial by ordeal, the dangerous interval which follows upon Moneta's challenge to mount the steps before the "gummed leaves be burnt" (I. 116) or "die" on the "marble" where he stands (108). The pilgrim who intrudes upon this shrine is almost stifled, in lines which at once recall Hyperion threatened with metamorphosis into serpent form ("through all his bulk an agony / Crept gradual") and significantly conflate two powerful Dantesque scenes—the challenge of the Medusa who turns to stone and the image for the serpentine metamorphoses ("Thus up the shrinking paper, ere it burns, / A brown tint glides, not turning yet to black")[44] of the Canto of the "Thieves":

> I heard, I looked: two senses both at once,
> So fine, so subtle, felt the tyranny
> Of that fierce threat and the hard task proposed.
> Prodigious seemed the toil; the leaves were yet
> Burning—when suddenly a palsied chill
> Struck from the pavèd level up my limbs,
> And was ascending quick to put cold grasp
> Upon those streams that pulse beside the throat.
> I shrieked; and the sharp anguish of my shriek
> Stung my own ears. I strove hard to escape
> The numbness, strove to gain the lowest step.
> Slow, heavy, deadly was my pace; the cold
> Grew stifling, suffocating, at the heart;
> And when I clasped my hands I felt them not.

One minute before death, my iced foot touched
The lowest stair; and as it touched, life seemed
To pour in at the toes. I mounted up,
As once fair Angels on a ladder flew
From the green turf to Heaven.

(I. 118–36)

The threat of immobilization is at once a threat from outside, delivered by Moneta, and a potential result of his own "staying," of the fixing of the senses upon an object which simultaneously involves the danger of being fixed by it, dwelling upon as a permanent dwelling in. Dante's contribution to the myth of the siren-Medusa was to reveal that her power derived from an initial movement of self-mystification or fixation.[45] Keats's version of this fixation and fixing is the interval in which he pauses to savor Moneta's warning upon his "senses" and is almost suffocated by a "chill" which threatens to reduce him to stone. The fixation in this passage is the logical culmination of what John Jones calls Keats's "aesthetic nominalism," the "glutting" of the senses upon a single object which connects the "one-pointed contemplation"[46] of the Odes to the fetishism of "This Living Hand" and the necrophilia of *Isabella*. Though the "Ode on Melancholy" banishes the clumsy machinery of a gothicized emotion, it does fix upon a single moment and single objects for the senses, a fixation which is at once a "glutting," a "feeding," and an "imprisoning":

Then glut thy sorrow on a morning rose,
Or on the rainbow of the salt sand-wave,
Or on the wealth of globèd peonies;
Or if thy mistress some rich anger shows,
Imprison her soft hand, and let her rave,
And feed deep, deep upon her peerless eyes.

(15–20)

The visual gluttony of the "Ode on Melancholy" joints the "drowsy hour" of the "Indolence Ode" as a swelling upon, or within, the embowered "Moment," and its dangers. Keats's admiring description of Milton's power of fixing—"he is 'sagacious of his Quarry,' he sees Beauty on the wing, pounces upon it, and gorges it to the producing his essential verse"[47]—is actually a description of the arch-Miltonic glutton, Death (*PL* x. 281), and in the crucial moment of fixation in *The Fall of Hyperion*, what might have been life to Milton is almost literally death to Keats. The Gothic terror of being imprisoned or fed upon—the extreme case of the romance enchantress *pasturando gli occhi* upon the paralyzed youth—is simply the gluttony and fixing of the "Ode on Melancholy" turned inside out: the poet yields momentarily to the tyranny of his senses and is almost "consumed."

The possibility of himself turning to cold stone on the pavement before the shrine is in one sense the simple consequence of putting himself into the poem, of becoming one of the shaped and palpable gods. In one of the versions of the myth of Atlas cited in Lemprière's *Dictionary*, the Titan is turned to stone when he is shown the head of the Medusa.[48] The poet who survives the first trial by ascending the stairs before the leaves are burnt wins, by this act, a second change or respite ("Thou hast dated on / Thy doom," I. 144–45) and turns Moneta, at once Mnemosyne and potential Medusa, into the Muse of his own singular "theme" (I. 46). As in the Medusa episode in Dante which Keats carefully underscored,[49] this confrontation is a crucial passage, the conversion of a potential impasse into a possible transition, or way through. The scene within *The Fall*, however, does not proceed to a *Paradiso*. Keats borrows from Dante the *scala* which leads to Saturn's altar and the image of Jacob's ladder for his miraculous ascent: "I mounted up, / As once fair Angels on a ladder flew / From the green turn to Heaven." But the image of Jacob's ladder which provides, in Dante, an ascent from the sphere of Saturn as "Contemplation" to the heaven of the fixed stars remains, in Keats's fragment, more within the realm of Saturn as the astrological patron of a paralyzing melancholia. Just as the first dream of the fragment awakened only into a darker dream, so the pilgrim-poet emerges from his first trial into another, that dangerous interval in which the "shapes of epic greatness" become the oppressive forms he must bear "ponderous" upon his senses. The growing within the poet of a power to "see as a god sees" (I. 302–4) suggests that of Dante's Glaucus in the opening vision of the *Paradiso*, but it is also the more sinister visionary initiation of the Glaucus of *Endymion* as he is paralyzed by Circe's spell. Dante's "transhumanization" is, in Keats's poem, first the threat of dehumanization, the burden of the shapes which threaten to unrealize him:

> Long, long these two were postured motionless,
> Like sculpture builded-up upon the grave
> Of their own power. A long awful time
> I looked upon them: still they were the same;
> The frozen God still bending to the earth,
> And the sad Goddess weeping at his feet,
> Moneta silent. Without stay or prop
> But my own weak morality, I bore
> The load of this eternal quietude,
> The unchanging gloom, and the three fixèd shapes
> Ponderous upon my senses a whole moon.
> For by my burning brain I measured sure
> Her silver seasons shedded on the night,
> And ever day by day methought I grew
> More gaunt and ghostly. Oftentimes I prayed

Intense, that death would take me from the vale
And all its burthens. Gasping with despair
Of change, hour after hour I cursed myself—
Until Old Saturn raised his faded eyes,
And looked around and saw his kingdom gone
(I. 382–401)

This passage and its crucial "bearing" are an insertion into the original version of the first *Hyperion*, as if this activity were the second fragment's decisive drama and the price for the poet of being privy to this scene were literally being able to bear it, to be the Atlas, before he can be the Apollo, of his chosen theme. Keats speaks in one letter of the creative revery of a "voyage of conception," a phrase in which if "voyage" suggests the activity of questing, "conception" retains its more passive sense, of a truth more brought to birth than captured.[50] This kind of oxymoron reappears in the "patient travail" (I. 91) of *The Fall of Hyperion*, a labor which is simultaneously active and passive. Keats cannot unperplex patience and passivity from their common root in *patior*, and the quest here, as in *Endymion*, is as much a passion as an action, something to be undergone.

The decisive trial of this fragment involves "bearing" in all of Keats's characteristic senses—a poetic *translatio* or carrying of these ancestral forms across into the present, the painful interval in which the poet must endure the weight of his vision's "eternal quietude," and the creative passivity of "travail" as a bringing to birth.[51] Even the language of the fragment—"sphered words" (I. 249), "globèd brain" (245)—is ensphered and ponderous, and the doctrine traditionally known as "accommodation" paradoxically becomes not a mediating of the burden but a part of it. Moneta, like Milton's Raphael, claims to "humanize" her sayings to the poet's ears (II. 2), but the emphasis throughout falls instead upon disproportion of size, the poet-pilgrim standing beside his "Shade of Memory" like "a stunt bramble by a solemn pine" (I. 293). The suggestion is that whatever "accommodation" is required will have to be on the side of the receiver, that part of the threat of a "dumb enchantment" is the possibility of something too large, perhaps, to be uttered, or withstood:

As near as an immortal's sphered words
Could to a mother's soften, were these last.
But yet I had a terror of her robes,
And chiefly of the veils, that from her brow
Hung pale, and curtained her in mysteries,
That made my heart too small to hold its blood.
(I. 249–54)

Moneta parts her veils, and admits the poet to his vision, but he remains, despite her guidance, unlike Dante or Milton, without certain guide, and faces the weight of this giant world with nothing but his own unaided senses:

> In melancholy realms big tears are shed,
> More sorrow like to this, and such-like woe,
> Too huge for mortal tongue, or pen of scribe
> (II. 7–9)

Even the sound carries the burden of the theme. The curse of perpetual transition in Moneta's face is joined by the perpetual transition of sound in "enwombed" / "tomb" / "doom" / "domèd" / "moan" / "Moneta" / "moon"—a movement in which it is impossible, finally, to unperplex sound from sense.

If the quest of the poet is the creation of the poem, the question at the end of the crucial interval of "bearing" in the dusk vale is finally whether the persona of the poet grows up or simply grows down by. the time the fragment breaks off. That the poem in fact does not end may assimilate it to the curse of perpetual transition, the death-in-life of Moneta's face. The interval of "bearing" and the release which follows it may seem a negative victory; the fragment breaks off soon after this passage. The Dantesque geography instills an expectation of movement, of progression beyond this Purgatory to a higher realm. But the oxymorons here—unlike those which move Dante's pilgrim through the "solacing pain" of the *Purgatorio* (XXIII. 72)—are part of the stasis. If the fragment starts out to be a "progress of poesy," there is in this sense no "progress." The first and only completed canto ends with a reference to the "antichamber of this dream" (I. 465), and the last allusion to Dante, as the sun or Hyperion is "sloping to the threshold of the west" (II. 48), suggests that the pilgrim is still on some kind of threshold, still before a journey to be completed. The poem breaks off at an even earlier point in the narrative of the Titans than the first *Hyperion.*

The statues here never really wake up, any more than they do in *Hyperion,* and yet there is a sense in which, once the burden has been endured, the real "theme" of Keats's brief romance has been realized. Milton in *Paradise Regained* focuses on the period of trial, the patient travail of the Son, and when that trial has been undergone, the essential story has, in one respect, been told. Keats echoes Milton's shorter epic in *Endymion,* which ends not with the translated Latmian and his goddess, but with Peona still wandering "in wonderment" through the "gloomy wood" (IV. 1003). *The Fall of Hyperion,* in the form in which we have it, holds out no promise of a paradise regained, but the poet who sighs for removal from the "vale / And all its burthens" (I. 397–98) is finally removed to the upper region of "clear light" (II. 49), like Guyon emerging from his trial in the underworld. To rise beyond this sphere would perhaps, in Keats's terms, be an act of poetic bad faith or, like the ending of *Endymion*, a palpable design. "Translation" in this late fragment is finally not ascension, but a more purgatorial *translatio*, the process of "bearing" in and for itself.

The *Fall of Hyperion* is not Keats's final, or even definitive, version of the suspensions of the liminal. This too in Keats reaches no single conclusion. "Bearing" itself is relieved of its burden in the beautifully extended, and graduated, threshold of the "Autumn Ode," and its refusal either to mourn the songs of Spring or to quest anxiously for presence. But the anxieties of the late poems to Fanny and the obsession of "This Living Hand" are even darker versions of the purgatory of *The Fall*, of "consumption" and suspension become so close to truth as to be literally unbearable. The unfinished fragment, with its echoes of the impasse of the first *Hyperion* and of the earlier poetry's dream and spell, does, however, enable us to glimpse what in romance Keats appears to have transformed for good. Pater's famous "moments," Tennyson's extension of romance plentitude into phantasmagoria, and the Pre-Raphaelites' identification of poetry with the exclusions of the "embowered," all in their different ways seem to point back to Keats's mediation, or "translation," of romance tradition. And his preference for the virtual and endurance of transition with no prospect of anything beyond itself provide a bridge even beyond the English context, to the hesitations of Valéry's lyrics and the uneasy "betrothal" of Mallarmé's *Un Coup de dés*. The second chance or respite granted by Moneta ("Thou hast dated on / Thy doom") recalls the space of dilation in Spenser or Milton, but without its promised dawning, or theological ground. The threshold, though a darker one than that of *Endymion*, remains Keats's characteristic, and hard-won, poetic space, neither the Miltonic Paradise nor the Wordsworthian earthly one, but the difficult interval in between.

Notes

1. *The Burden of the Past and the English Poet* (New York: Norton, 1970), p. 33.

2. "Sleep and Poetry," 181, in the passage in which Keats attacks the Augustan poets ruled by "one Boileau" (206). The edition used for this and all subsequent references to Keats's poetry is Miriam Allott, ed., *The Poems of John Keats* (London: Longman Group, 1970).

3. See Thomson, *The Castle of Indolence: An Allegorical Poem Written in Imitation of Spenser*, 2nd ed. (London, 1748), and Keats's journal-letter to the George Keatses, February–May 1819, in Hyder Rollins, ed., *The Letters of John Keats 1814–1821*, II, 78. All subsequent references are to these editions.

4. *Account of the Greatest English Poets* (1694), 17–31, quoted in Arthur Johnston, *Enchanted Ground: The Study of Medieval Romance in the Eighteenth Century* (London: Athlone Press, 1964), p. 6.

5. See, for example, Thomson's *Summer* (1744), 1573–75; Richard Steele, *Tatler*, 254; Bishop Hurd, *Letters on Chivalry and Romance* (1762); and Bishop Thomas Percy's *Reliques of Ancient English Poetry* (1765).

6. John Bidlake, "Ode Written Near a Solitary Chapel," in his *Poems* (1793). See also Southey's "To Contemplation" and its regret for the passing of Fancy's "visions gay" (67), and William Cowper's *The Task* (1785), where he dismisses the "Airy dreams" of the past as the poets' imposing "a gay delirium for a truth," but "still must envy them an age / That favor'd such a dream, in days like these / Impossible" (IV. 526–32).

7. *Observations on "The Faerie Queene,"* 2nd ed., 4 vols. (1762), III, 267–68, and I, i, quoted in René Wellek, *The Rise of English Literary History* (Chapel Hill: Univ. of North Carolina Press, 1941), p. 170. Similarly, James Beattie remarks in the final paragraph of "On Fable and Romance," *Dissertations Moral and Critical* (London, 1783), that the "usefulness of Romance-writing" is not to be estimated by his lengthy treatment of it, since "Romances are a dangerous recreation"; and Clara Reeve, though she defends the romances in the introduction to *The Progress of Romance* (1785) as "equally entitled to our attention and respect, as any works of Genius and literature," still cautions against their indiscriminate availability to "young persons."

8. "On Lyric Poetry," 91–100.

9. "Hymn to Science," 38–42.

10. See Thomas Warton, *History of English Poetry*, 3 vols. (1774–81), preface to I, and III, 496.

11. "On Poetry in General," *Lectures on the English Poets*, p. 18.

12. See, among others, Southey's "To Contemplation," Akenside's "To Sleep," "To the Muse," and "To the Evening Star," Mason's "Ode to Melancholy," in Dodsley's *Collection*, VI (1775), and Collins' "Ode to Simplicity." I am indebted to the discussion of this "sacred precinct" by Martin Price in "The Sublime Poem: Pictures and Powers," *Yale Review*, 58 (Winter 1969), 194–213.

13. The phrase is from "Il Penseroso" (136–38), but the threat to these woods—both the disappearing pastoral woods of an increasingly commercial England and the enchanting "selva" of romance—remains a constant one in a line of poets from Marvell to John Clare.

14. "On Chaucer and Spenser," *Letters on the English Poets*, p. 85.

15. "False Themes and Gentle Minds," *Beyond Formalism* (New Haven: Yale Univ. Press, 1970), p. 287.

16. "Coleridge," in M. Cohen, ed., *The Philosophy of John Stuart Mill* (New York: Random House, 1961), p. 58.

17. On Wordsworth, see Joseph Wittreich, Jr., ed., *The Romantics on Milton* (Cleveland: Case Western Reserve Univ. Press, 1970), p. 129.

18. Chapter XIV, *Biographia Literaria*, ed. George Watson (London: Dent, 1965), pp. 168–69.

19. *Anatomy of Criticism* (1957; rprt. New York: Atheneum, 1966), p. 35.

20. See especially her "Ode to the Muse" and "Ode to Melancholy."

21. "In drear-nighted December" and the sonnet to Spenser, for example, both suggest a turn from the idealizings of *Endymion* to a more wintry vision. The "Lines on Seeing a Lock of Milton's Hair" and the letter in which he dedicates himself to a more rigorous program of "study and thought" (To John Taylor, April 24, 1818, in *Letters*, I, 271) chart his movement away from the Spensarian mode of pastoral romance to the Miltonic epic design of the projected *Hyperion*. His preference for the realism of Smollett over the romance coloring of Scott, as later for the human tales of Chaucer

over the marvels of Ariosto (in, respectively, the letters to his brothers of January 5, 1818, in *Letters*, I, 200, and to Taylor of November 17, 1819, in *Letters*, II, 234) represents a virtual reversal of his earlier stance. In a letter to Bailey on January 23, 1818, a single question conveys his sense of the uselessness of romance: "*Why should Woman suffer?* . . . These things are, and he who feels how incompetent the most skyey knight errantry is to heal this bruised fairness is like a sensitive leaf on the hot hand of thought" (*Letters*, I, 209).

22. Letter to J. H. Reynolds, May 3, 1818, in *Letters*, I, 280–81.

23. The developmental frame is, in my view, a weakness in the approach of Jack Stillinger in "Keats and Romance: The 'Reality' of *Isabella*," *The Hoodwinking of Madeline and Other Essays on Keats's Poems* (Chicago: Univ. of Illinois Press, 1971), pp. 31ff, and Morris Dickstein, *Keats and His Poetry: A Study in Development* (Chicago: Univ. of Chicago Press, 1971), pp. 131ff, though the latter modifies Stillinger's "anti-romance" thesis and suggests that Keats's attempt to leave romance behind remained an attempt. Similarly, the endless debates over the ending of *The Eve of St. Agnes*, over the question of "consummation" in "La Belle Dame Sans Merci," and over the final tendency of *Lamia* seem to be the inevitable result of a poetry which looks so many ways at once.

24. See, for example, the simultaneous farewell to the old oak forests of romance and the lament for their passing in "Robin Hood."

25. Paul de Man, ed., *John Keats: Selected Poetry* (New York: Signet, 1966), p. xxv.

26. November 22, 1817, in *Letters*, I, 185.

27. The multiplicity of these allusions is suggestively interpreted by Stillinger in the famous essay "The Hoodwinking of Madeline: Skepticism in *The Eve of St. Agnes*," in *Hoodwinking*, pp. 67ff.

28. It is for this reason that I have difficulty with the more straightforward interpretations of the "mind" of the "Ode" in Harold Bloom, *The Visionary Company*, rev. ed. (Ithaca: Cornell Univ. Press, 1971), pp. 420–21, and Charles I. Patterson, *The Daemonic in the Poetry of Keats* (Urbana: Univ. of Illinois Press, 1970), pp. 158–65.

29. Paul de Man, for example, in his introduction to *Keats: Selected Poetry*, p. xxxiii, stresses the victory of the philosopher over the "serpent," while Northrop Frye, in the essay on Keats in his *Study of English Romanticism* (New York: Random House, 1968), p. 154, emphasizes the aborting of a possible passage of this "Eurydice" to the human world.

30. "Keats and Romance," *Hoodwinking*, p. 37.

31. "Symbolic Action in a Poem by Keats" (1943), reprinted in his *Perspectives by Incongruity* (Bloomington: Indiana Univ. Press, 1964), pp. 123–41.

32. "On Poetry in General," in *Letters on the English Poets*, pp. 20–21: "Painting gives the object itself; poetry what it implies. Painting embodies what a thing contains in itself; poetry suggests what exists out of it, in any manner connected with it. . . . Again, as it relates to passion, painting gives the event, poetry the progress of events: but it is during the progress, in the interval of expectation and suspense, while our hopes and fears are strained to the highest pitch of breathless agony, that the pinch of the interest lies. . . . But by the time that the picture is painted, all is over."

33. See the brilliant discussion of this aspect of the poem in Leo Spitzer, "The 'Ode on a Grecian Urn,' or Content vs. Metagrammar," in his *Essays on English and American Literature* (Princeton: Princeton Univ. Press, 1962), p. 72.

34. The audience of "tell" in lines 38–40 ("And, little town, thy streets for evermore / Will silent be; and not a soul to tell / Why thou art desolate can e'er return") is left suggestively open. Tell whom? If it is the town itself, the silence would

point to the state of suspended animation on the urn. But if the potential audience of the tale is the poet himself, the suggestion is that no voice from the past can cross the gap between then and now, the object and the questioning poet.

35. Burke, *Perspectives*, p. 134.

36. See Keats's note on *PL* VII. 420–23, in Forman, ed., *Complete Works*, III, 264.

37. See the interesting reading of the poem in his "Spectral Symbolism and Authorial Self in Keats's *Hyperion*," in *The Fate of Reading* (Chicago: Univ. of Chicago Press, 1975), pp. 57–73

38. Letter to Reynolds, February 19, 1818, in *Letters*, I, 232.

39. Letter to Woodhouse, October 27, 1818, in *Letters*, I, 387, the letter from which all citations in this paragraph are taken.

40. To George and Georgiana Keats, October 1818, in *Letters*, I, 403–4.

41. On the romance tradition of this fear, see Giamatti, "Poets and Proteus," in *Play of Double Senses: Spenser's "Faerie Queene"* (Englewood Cliffs: Prentice-Hall, 1975), p. 123.

42. Augustine, in the section on the cursing of the serpent in *De genesi ad litteram* XIX, draws the linguistic analogy in his observation that the serpent is involved in the guilt only in the same sense as we speak of the "lying pen" of the writer.

43. See Forman, III, 265.

44. *Inf.* XXV. 57–58, as it appears in the Henry Cary translation (1814) of the *Divina Commedia*, which Keats read carefully in the summer of 1818. Keats underlined the whole passage of the metamorphosis (54–59), and in particular this image, which is echoed in the burning "leaves" of *The Fall* I. 116. See Robert Gittings, *The Mask of Keats* (London: Heinemann, 1956), p. 39. It is interesting in relation to the theme of trespass that the memory should be of the canto of the "Thieves."

45. I follow John Freccero, "Medusa: The Letter and the Spirit," in *Yearbook of Italian Studies* (1972), p. 10, in associating the Medusa of *Inferno* IX with the Siren of *Purgatorio* XIX, who becomes an attractive siren only when the pilgrim gazes intently on her (10).

46. See John Jones, *Keats's Dream of Truth* (London: Chatto & Windus, 1969), p 193, and Frye, *English Romanticism*, (New York: Random House, 1968), p. 152.

47. See the letter to Bailey, November 22, 1817 (*Letters*, I, 186; "I scarcely remember counting upon any Happiness—I look not for it if it be not in the present hour—nothing startles me beyond the Moment . . ."), and the note on *PL* VII. 420–23, in Forman, III, 264.

48. See Lemprière, *Classical Dictionary*, s.v. "Atlas."

49. See Gittings, *The Mask of Keats*, pp. 5ff.

50. To Reynolds, February 19, 1818, in *Letters*, I, 231.

51. For Keats's use of "bear," see, for example, "Sleep and Poetry," 61–63, and "God of the Meridian," 17–19.

John Clubbe and
Keats the Humanist
Ernest J. Lovell, Jr.*

Of the major Romantic poets, Keats was the latest born, the earliest to die, the shortest lived, the most likeable, the most easily lovable. His mature creative life was incredibly brief—his first perfect poem, "On First Looking into Chapman's Homer," being written in October 1816, his last perfect poem, "To Autumn," slightly less than three years later, on 19 September 1819. In his letters we observe a mind functioning at its best over a period of about three years, when Keats was aged twenty-one to twenty-four years. On 3 February 1820 he suffered a violent haemorrhage of the lungs; in September, dying, he sailed for Italy. Keats wrote some of the finest letters in the language, but until his illness they are the letters of a young man. There was much that he did not have time to read or to think about. These few dates suggest the tremendous intensity with which, for a startlingly brief period, Keats thought about his art and worked to create it.

Although Keats never systematized his literary theory and the thoughts about the nature of human existence that we find scattered and evolving in his letters, much of this theory and speculation possesses a remarkable harmony or unity that derives directly from certain basic qualities of his character. Perhaps chief among these personal qualities is one easier to name in negative than in positive terms: the usual and genuine absence in him of self-assertiveness. The dogmatic tone or spirit was not his, and he disliked dogmatic men and arguments, believing that it was more blessed to listen, learn, and explore than to preach in support of a pre-selected text. Thus we find an unusual gentleness about Keat's strength of mind. Because of the basically explorative thrust of his thinking, he was reluctant to reach closed-end conclusions.

These personal qualities derive finally, it would appear, from Keats's stalwart selflessness virtually without neurotic fears or the need to feel himself loved by everyone who came his way. In his letter to George and Tom Keats of 21, 27(?) December 1817, sandwiched between his remarks contrasting Benjamin West's painting *Death on the Pale Horse* with *King Lear* and his account of Negative Capability, is a description of a dinner with Horace Smith, "his two brothers," and three other men of literary interests.[1] The letter suggests how easily Keats moved between the social world and the solitary world of literary theory. Of these six men, only Horace and

* Reprinted from *English Romanticism: The Grounds of Belief.* © 1983 by John Clubbe and the estate of Ernest J. Lovell, Jr. Reprinted by permission of Northern Illinois University Press.

James Smith, as co-authors of *Rejected Addresses* (1812) and *Horace in London* (1813), had any literary reputation. John Kingston, who was Deputy Controller of Stamps and to whom Wordsworth deferred, was also among those present. By and large, they were men of wit and fashion. But Keats felt little or no sympathetic identification with them, no admiration for them, no desire to become like them. At the age of twenty-two, he was already his own man, well acquainted with his own identity, feeling no need to impress these assembled wits of the fashionable world. It made no difference to him that his host Horace Smith, a friend of Shelley, was a highly successful satirist and stockbroker or that James Smith was reputed to be one of the wittiest of conversationalists in an age that elevated conversation to a fine art. "These men," Keats observed, "say things which make one start, without making one feel[;] they are all alike; their manners are alike; they all know fashionables; they have a mannerism in their very eating & drinking, in their mere handling a Decanter—They talked of Kean & his low company—Would I were with that company instead of yours said I to myself! I know such like acquaintance will never do for me" (KL, I, 193). Byron, who said he never drew well with literary men (except Scott and Moore), would have agreed.[2] Different as they were, both Keats and Byron (to say nothing here of the other major Romantics) were men of independent spirit.

Keats's equally Byronic reluctance to embrace some set of final conclusions and then live comfortably with it from that day forward, for better or for worse, may express itself as a kind of simple scepticism. Thus in the famous letter to Benjamin Bailey of 22 November 1817, he is "certain of nothing but" two grandly epic concepts, "the holiness of the Heart's affections and the truth of Imagination" (KL, I, 184). But four months later, on 13 March 1818, he is boldly sceptical of his own scepticism. After referring to his religious scepticism as a thing well known to Bailey, he in effect denies it—"I do not think myself more in the right than other people"—and then he qualifies his denial: "I must once for all tell you I have not one Idea of the truth of any of my speculations" (I, 242, 243). Keats was not of course a confirmed or philosophic sceptic, denying the possibility of arriving at certain kinds of knowledge; it is the questioning, questing nature of his mind that here expresses itself, his way of protecting himself against the dogmatic utterance of the assertive self. And so on 31 December 1818 as a kind of New Year's resolution, he "made up [his] Mind never to take any thing for granted—but even to examine the truth of the commonest proverbs" (II, 18).

Distrusting, like Blake, the abstracting and deductive faculty of the reason as dogmatic and self-assertive, Keats sought other methods of grasping reality: "I never can feel certain of any truth but from a clear perception of its Beauty" (31 December 1818: KL, II, 19).

Almost inevitably, William Godwin becomes the enemy. Charles Wentworth Dilke, the true opposite not the contrary of the poet of negative capability, is "a Godwin-methodist" (24 September 1819: II, 213) and elsewhere a "Godwin perfectibil[it]y Man" (14 October 1818: I, 397). He "was a Man who cannot feel he has a personal identity unless he has made up his Mind about every thing. The only means of strengthening one's intellect is to make up ones mind about nothing—to let the mind be a thoroughfare for all thoughts" (24 September 1819: II, 213). Even a preliminary consideration illustrates the fact that Keats's scepticism, his open-minded questing spirit, the natural enemy and antidote to dogmatic self-assertiveness, is linked with such important areas of his thought as religion, the nature and function of the imagination, the nature of the self, negative capability, and human reason.

Keats's concept of the chameleon poet, a concept he took over from Hazlitt, is also tied to all this.[3] Specifically, it appears in the absence in him of a strong streak of self-assertiveness, as in his distinction in *The Fall of Hyperion* between true poets and "mock lyrists, large self-worshippers / And careless hectorers in proud bad verse" (KL, I, 207–8)—perhaps a reference to Byron. "Man should not dispute or assert," Keats wrote to John Hamilton Reynolds, "but whisper results to his neighbour, and thus . . . every human might become great, and Humanity . . . would become a grand democracy" (19 February 1818: I, 232). The world, in short, would be transformed. As for himself, he stated, with his usual insight into his own being, "I shall never be a Reasoner because I care not be in the right, when retired from bickering and in a proper philosophical temper" (13 March 1818: I, 243).

Keats's distrust of the disputatious and assertive man, like Godwin or Dilke, surely explains much about his anticlericalism. As early as December 1816 he composed a sonnet "Written in Disgust of Vulgar Superstition." He found the Bishop of Lincoln to be "tyran[n]ical" and worse (3 November 1817: KL, I, 178); a parson "must be either a Knave or an Ideot" (14 February 1819: II, 63); and the "history" of Jesus, the only man Keats knew of with a completely disinterested heart, except for Socrates, was lamentably "written and revised by Men interested in the pious frauds of Religion" (19 March 1819: II, 80). This is very like Shelley, who more than once paired Jesus and Socrates. No wonder that Keats wrote of himself on 22 December 1818, "I am reckoned lax in my christian principles" (II, 14).

But in important ways he was knowledgeably Christian, as well as being a close student of the Bible like the other Romantic poets.[4] He was baptized in the Church of England, and on his deathbed his friend Joseph Severn read to him from Jeremy Taylor's *Holy Living and Holy Dying*. The headmaster of the school at Enfield, where

Keats was a student from 1803 to 1811, was John Clarke, who influenced his development and from whom he probably received religious training.[5] Keats's letter to his sister on 31 March 1819, instructing her in preparation for her confirmation, demonstrates how very knowledgeable he was of Anglican doctrine and of the Bible. In answer to just one of her questions, he refers her to twelve Biblical passages.[6] His faith in an immortal afterlife seems firm; earthly happiness will then be repeated "in a finer tone" (22 November 1817: KL, I, 185). Among "the grandeurs of immortality" will be the perfect understanding that the disembodied spirits will have of each other, existing outside space in the form of pure intelligence. On this day, 16 December 1818, he had "scarce a doubt of immortality of some nature" (II, 5, 4). But even more significant and revealing is the fact that two of his most famous letters—the Mansion of Life letter and the Vale of Soul-Making letter—are conceived in important part in Christian terms and rest upon Christian assumptions.

The earlier letter, to Reynolds of 3 May 1818, is centrally concerned with comparing the virtues of Milton and Wordsworth: the grounds are explicitly humanitarian or humanistic but implicitly they are Christian. Keats saw human life as process or growth of mind just as truly and habitually as Wordsworth or Byron. It was a movement from innocence to experience and beyond, as in Blake and as in Byron's *Don Juan*, however great the disparities among each's interpretation—and symbolic representation—of that journey. In life's "large Mansion of Many Apartments," the first is "the infant or thoughtless Chamber, in which we remain as long as we do not think." When we begin to reflect upon life we move into "the Chamber of Maiden-Thought," where "we become intoxicated with the light and the atmosphere, we see nothing but pleasant wonders, and think of delaying there for ever in delight." In that Chamber we also undergo a "sharpening" of "vision into the heart (head) and nature of Man." The experience has the effect of "convincing" our "nerves that the World is full of Misery and Heartbreak, Pain, Sickness and oppression" (KL, I, 280, 281). Eventually many doors open out of the Chamber of Maiden-Thought, "all dark—all leading to dark passages—We see not the ballance of good and evil."[7] To this point, Keats believed, Wordsworth had come when he wrote "Tintern Abbey." Because "his Genius is explorative of those dark Passages," it is "deeper" or more profound than Milton's (KL, I, 281). Keats judges Wordsworth superior because he has a greater "anxiety for Humanity" and "martyrs himself to the human heart" (I, 278–9), into which he has thought more deeply and more sympathetically than Milton, even though Milton's philosophic powers were surely as great as Wordsworth's.[8] From this Keats concluded that "a mighty providence subdues the mightiest Minds to the service of the time being" (KL, I,

282). Quite as significant in the present context is Keats's third and last Chamber of Life. Although he gave it but one isolated sentence (he says that at this time he could describe only two), it is obviously a chamber of redemption or salvation. It will be stored with the wine and bread of communion, "the wine of love—and the Bread of Friendship" (I, 283).

The great Vale of Soul-Making passage of 21 April 1819 in Keats's long journal-letter to George and Georgiana Keats explicitly deals with central Christian questions and assumptions: the "Protection of Providence" (uncertain), the nature of human nature (imperfect), the existence of evil (necessary). "Man is originally 'a poor [bare] forked creature,' " like Adam after the Fall, and "subject to the same mischances as the beasts of the forest." Even if mankind could achieve happiness, Keats argued, the approach of death would then become intolerable, and the individual "would leave this world as Eve left Paradise." "But in truth," Keats adds, "I do not at all believe in this sort of perfectibility—the nature of the world will not admit of it" (KL, II, 101). Keats, like Byron, also rejected the doctrine of Christ the Redeemer, whose rewards are to be had only in heaven.[9] At several points his tough-minded and realistic insight into the nature of human existence recalls Byron.[10] But the imperfect creature here described is obviously in need of redemption, and Keats provided his own "system of salvation" in his concept of a "World of Pains and troubles" as a "vale of Soul-making" (not a vale of tears), which neatly justifies the ways of God to man and solves the philosophic problem of evil (KL, II, 102).

Imperfect though man is, however, he comes from God, like Adam, and on 21 April 1819 Keats's concept of man's divine origin was as exalted as William Blake's or that of any other Christian. Man, for both Keats and Blake, is a fallen creature, in need of salvation. Intelligences, as distinct from the souls that will be created, are "sparks of the divinity"; they are "atoms of perception . . . in short they are God," to whom they may return (KL, II, 102). As Blake said, "All deities reside in the human breast."[11] Because God is One, these sparks of the divinity "must feel and suffer in a thousand diverse ways" in order to become unique "individual beings," that is, to become souls possessed of "the sense of Identity" (KL, II, 102, 103). Thus Keats explains the infinite variety of man and, by implication, the unique value of each. Even though Christianity remains for Keats only one of many "Schemes of Redemption," his "system of salvation," which he argues is far grander "than [that of] the chrystain religion," is essentially Christian in spirit and in its major assumptions.[12]

Keats, with his Christian background, must have found it easy to nourish the basically non-assertive, non-dogmatic nature of his personality. This background enabled him to gain new insights into poetry and the nature of "the poetical Character" (KL, I, 386). Aesthetic and ethical insights become one. Although he phrases his discussion in terms of aesthetics (or the psychology of the creative process and person), its implications, as with Blake and Shelley, are ethical. The egotistical poet—Wordsworth, for example—is both bully and self-deceived (I, 223). Such a poet, as Keats understood the matter at this time, violates the sanctity of other human personalities. Similarly, Leigh Hunt's "self delusions are very lamentable. . . . There is no greater Sin after the 7 deadly than to flatter oneself into an idea of being a great Poet" (11 May 1817: I, 143). Such literary criticism is clearly ethical in its assumptions, and self-deception or self-flattery became for Keats the worst possible sin for a poet. It became, in effect, the eighth deadly sin, the equivalent of Blake's sin of selfhood. "Complete disinterestedness of Mind" or heart, he found, had been possessed only by Socrates and Jesus, great men both, though neither left to posterity writings of his own (19 March 1819: II, 79, 80). But the major critical insight that Keats's sensitivity to egotism allowed him to achieve was his distinction between the "wordsworthian or egotistical sublime" and the "camelion Poet" of "no Identity" (27 October 1818: KL, I, 387)—or Keats himself. One feels it was inevitable that he should have perceived this, for Keats was in fact perceiving a fundamental aspect of his own being, his fearless selflessness, which would perhaps have permitted him, had he lived, to have excelled marvellously in the drama, creating a host of richly diverse characters.

Although Keats early gives evidence of his capacity for sympathetic identification with that or those outside the self, the Chameleon-Poet letter of 27 October 1818 is the first in which the phrase (verbally reminiscent of Shelley on Byron)[13] appears and thus deserves examination in detail. Significantly, the letter opens with a celebration of Richard Woodhouse's "friendliness" and goes on almost at once to define Keats's kind of poetical character in terms of selflessness, the absence of the egotistical—"it has no self" (KL, I, 386, 387). The implication is that the poet of "the wordsworthian or egotistical sublime" is confined, bound by and to itself in subject, point of view, and tone. (Note Keats's use of the lower-case "w" for Wordsworth's name, as the younger poet symbolically converts the older to his own doctrine, a "conversion" comparable to Blake's of Milton in his *Milton*). This poet is, like Shakespeare's Ajax, "a thing [i.e., a man] per se and stands alone." By contrast, the chameleon Keatsian poet is a being of immense variety and breadth, delighting in every level of existence, unconfined by puritanical or rationalistic restraints. All his imaginative creations, whether dark or bright, treacherous or wronged, Iago or Imogen, "end in speculation" for the reader and are accompanied by the ranging delight he feels in the poet of "no

Identity," "no self." This poet is the purified Blakean Milton, completely free of the sin of selfhood and escaped into or "filling some other Body." For such a poet, "it is a wretched thing to confess; but is a very fact that not one word I ever utter can be taken for granted as an opinion growing out of my identical nature—how can it, when I have no nature? Shakespeare is Keats's example *par excellence* of the poet who possesses Negative Capability. Such a poet quite literally lives not in the limited self but in other selves, where is his true home: when "in a room with People . . . then not myself goes home to myself: but the identity of every one in the room begins to [*for* so?] to press upon me that, I am in a very little time an[ni]hilated— not only among Men; it would be the same in a Nursery of children" (I, 387). Thus did Keats carry out, in the great generous depths of his being, the Blakean, Christian command: "Selfhood . . . must be put off & annihilated."[14] None of this implies that Keats suffered gladly dull or uninteresting persons, "unpleasant human identities . . . people who have no light and shade." To be in such company is "a capital punishment" (17 March 1819: KL, II, 77). He was of course selective.

The Byronic and the Shelleyan chameleon poet, each in his different way, could sometimes but not always attain this loss of the sense of identity. In his self-pitying "Stanzas Written in Dejection— December 1818, near Naples" Shelley failed. At the end of his journal kept for Augusta in September 1816 Byron recorded his own failure: nothing he had seen in his tour of the Alps had, he said, "enabled me to lose my own wretched identity in the majesty & the power and the Glory—around—above—& beneath me."[15] Keats's poet, by contrast, "is continually in for—and filling some other Body—The Sun, the Moon, the Sea and Men and Women." This is the expansionist urge to move outside the self, to unite with that which is the not-self, evident in all these poets, and of which one of Keats's great expressions is in *Endymion,* I, ll. 777–815. Such a selfless poet has a "relish of the dark side of things" as well as a "taste for the bright one." He delights in all aspects of existence, unlike the "virtuous philosop[h]er," who may be shocked within his rigidly moralistic system of thought (KL, I, 387).

The experience of self-annihilation may succeed or fail on any of several levels: the imaginative or artistically creative, the spiritual or religious, and the purely ethical. Keats could achieve it variously, sometimes as a temporary escape from a sense of unhappiness. He could not believe in any but present happiness. His sense of beauty awakened before the "setting sun," and such an experience gave a rise to his spirits. "If a Sparrow come before my Window I take part in its existince [sic] and pick about the Gravel."[16] Imaginative identification with either sunset or sparrow could lift him out of depression.

In these passages Keats describes an exercise in empathy. Experience of sorrow tests a man's resilience. "The first thing that strikes me on hea[r]ing a Misfortune having befalled another is this. 'Well it cannot be helped—he will have the pleasure of trying the resources of his spirit[']'" (KL, I, 186). This same letter also generalizes on an intellectual and abstract level about the difference between men of power, "who have a proper self," and men of genius, who are "great as certain ethereal Chemicals operating on the Mass of neutral intellect—by [for but] they have not any individuality, any determined Character" (I, 184). They function as catalysts, in other words, and will alter the very nature of the relationship between man and society. This action is performed most effectively by means of poems of epic grandeur written by a poet with a dramatic or Shakespearean genius, able to efface himself and enter into a host of dramatic characters. Such poets are the Shelleyan "unacknowledged legislators of the world." The same kind of speculation, phrased in more personal or limited terms, appears near the end of the Chameleon-Poet letter: "But even now I am perhaps not speaking from myself; but from some character in whose soul I now live" (I, 388).

The annihilation of self by means of empathy need not involve identification with living persons: the imaginative experience may begin and end with the imagination. As Keats felt the power of his imagination strengthening, he felt increasingly that he did "not live in this world alone but in a thousand worlds," *surrounded* by "shapes of epic greatness." "Then 'Tragedy, with scepter'd pall, comes sweeping by.' According to my state of mind I am with Achilles shouting in the Trenches or with Theocritus in the Vales of Sicily" or with Shakespeare's Troilus, into whom he throws his "whole being . . . and . . . melt[s] into the air" (24 October 1818: KL, I, 403–4). Here Keats speaks of himself as a kind of ideal reader interacting with the work of literature. Such interaction, he implies, should be a repetition of the poet's interaction with his own writing.

Whether as writer or reader, there is a dramatic outpouring of the self into some other being or thing, which may produce poetic results as different as the Blakean lines of "Where's the Poet?"—" 'Tis the man who with a bird, / Wren or eagle, finds his way to / All its instincts" (ll. 8–10)—and the "Ode to a Nightingale." The lesser poem is an exercise in definition: to the Keatsian poet even "the tiger's yell / Comes articulate, and presseth / On his ear like mother-tongue" (ll. 13–15). The Nightingale Ode, by contrast, is structured like the record of an exploration, ending on a question. It was written by a Shakespearean poet of Negative Capability, who "is capable of being in uncertainties, Mysteries, doubts, without any irritable reaching after fact & reason. . . . With a great poet the sense of Beauty overcomes every other consideration, or rather obliterates all consideration"—or calculation, or deliberation (21, 27[?] December 1817: KL, I, 193, 194). Dilke, with whom Keats had had a "disquisition," was again the catalyst for a new insight. The opposing terms or concepts are of interest, suggesting as they do a quite Byronic distrust of elaborate intellectual systems of thought: a fine isolated truth versus systematic fact and reason (or, put another way, "the single unique insight versus a consideration").[17] So far had Keats come by the end of 1817; as late as 24 September 1819 he could still find in Dilke the very opposite of the man of Negative Capability (KL, II, 213). Nevertheless, Keats came increasingly to reconcile such opposite or seemingly discordant pairs of elements as beauty and truth, "consequitive reasoning" and the real need for knowledge. And, paradoxically, it was Keats's talent for avoiding the "irritable reaching" after self-justification in argument that encouraged him to seek reconciliation of his contraries.

An example of such reconciliation occurs even in the letter on Negative Capability, where Shakespeare's *Lear* provides the example of "the excellence of every Art," which is "its intensity, capable of making all disagreeables evaporate, from their being in close relationship with Beauty & Truth" (KL, I, 192). To evaporate, one may recall, is to change a liquid (or a solid) into gaseous form by means of heat, to transform, in other words, the apparent nature of reality, even as Wordsworth and Coleridge had planned to do in *Lyrical Ballads*, as they divided up their labours, "by awakening the mind's attention from the lethargy or custom, and directing it to the loveliness and the wonders of the world before us."[18] The world, in short, was to be transformed in the mind by the poem and its beauty truly revealed. So it was also, Keats perceived, in *Lear*, a play not only of transformation (Lear himself) but also of revelation (Cordelia reveals her true self to Lear, Edgar to his father Gloucester) and reconciliation.[19] Unlike West's painting of *Death on the Pale Horse*, in *King Lear* the "unpleasantness," the "repulsiveness" is buried—it is dead, not alive—by the "momentous depth of speculation excited" by the play. The "disagreeables" have been transformed because of the "speculation" to produce finally an imaginative thing of "Beauty" (KL, I, 192).

Keats wrote a great deal about beauty, associated with truth not only by the Grecian Urn. When he said that he could never "feel certain of any truth but from a clear perception of its Beauty" (31 December 1818: KL, II, 19), he meant that the effect of beauty was therapeutic and ethical. "The mighty abstract Idea I have of Beauty in all things stifles the more divided and minute domestic happiness" (24 October 1818: I, 403), which is to say, as Blake expressed it, "You must leave Fathers & Mothers & Houses & Lands if they stand in the way of Art."[20] As late as February 1820, he expressed regret that he had created "no immortal work," but, he added as a kind of counterweight, "I have lov'd the principle of beauty in all things" (KL, II, 263). Such love also strengthens the spirit by making it independent or inner-oriented: "Praise or blame has but a momentary effect on the man whose love of beauty in the abstract makes him a severe critic on his own Works" (8 October 1818: I, 373). But Keats's most extended and profound exploration of beauty and associated subjects occurs in his letter of 22 November 1817 to Bailey, which expresses a good part of his aesthetics. Here we learn that it is love, 'like all the other "Passions" in their sublime form or aspect, that is "creative of essential Beauty" (I, 184), thus transforming our vision of life and revealing its true nature. Keats refers to a passage in *Endymion* (I, ll. 777–815) where love is sung and celebrated as the great creative force that activates the imagination and permits rich and "self-destroying" "enthralments."[21] These lead Endymion to his final realization that Cynthia and the Maid of Sorrow are one. The feminine characters have been reconciled—heaven and earth have been reconciled—and Endymion finally sees the truth, led to it by his imagination. As Keats explained to his publisher John Taylor, the writing of this passage toward the end of the first book of *Endymion* "was a regular stepping of the Imagination towards a Truth" (30 January 1818: KL, I, 218). Thus the creative imagination, as Keats had written Bailey on 22 November 1817, "may be compared to Adam's dream" of the creation of the beautiful Eve: "he awoke and found it truth" (I, 185). There she was, the first female universal particular, palpable and meaningful, symbol of all others to follow.

As for the Maid of Sorrow, subject of Keats's "little song" of Book IV, Endymion's relations with her extend his knowledge of all that Cynthia represents: the essential beauty, the ultimate truth or reality, includes the "human" maiden. This is the truth that the imagination first seized or recognized as Beauty. Sorrow has been transformed, as in *Lear*, and opposite or discordant qualities reconciled in union at the end.

Keats's highly speculative discussion in the letter to Bailey, which includes the exclamation "O for a Life of Sensations rather than of Thoughts" (KL, I, 185), begins with a statement on beauty, truth and imagination: "I am certain of nothing but of the holiness of the Heart's affections and the truth of Imagination—What the imagination seizes as Beauty must be truth—whether it existed before or not—for I have the same Idea of all our Passions as of Love[.] they are all in their sublime, creative of essential Beauty" (I, 184). The latter part of this statement illuminates the earlier and says essentially the same thing. Love, Keats writes, is "creative of"—it does not create—the essence of Beauty. But it is the imagination that is the precedent term, and *it* is the primarily creative power. For "what the imagination seizes as Beauty," or makes its own or apprehends as beauty, *must* exist—"whether it existed before or not." That which is newly or freshly apprehended is in fact newly created. As Blake said, "Mental Things are alone Real" or truly existent.[22] Shelley expressed the idea somewhat differently: "nothing exists except but as it is perceived."[23] The imaginative and sensual apprehension of that which is ideal— " 'a Vision in the form of Youth,' a Shadow of reality to come"—is clearly different from truth arrived at by "consequitive reasoning" (KL, I, 185). Although Keats had "never yet been able to perceive how any thing can be known for truth" by such means, he recognized that "it must be." This same letter moves on to describe "a complex Mind—one that is imaginative and at the same time careful of its fruits—who would exist partly on sensation [experience acquired through the senses] partly on thought—to whom it is necessary that years should bring the philosophic Mind" (I, 186), as in Wordsworth's Intimations Ode. The extreme, discordant elements have again been reconciled.

This is not to deny that Keats's thought has in it a strain of antirationalism, which may express itself in terms quite Wordsworthian in their wise passiveness: "let us not therefore go hurrying about . . . buzzing here and there impatiently from a knowledge of what is to be arrived at: but let us open our leaves like a flower and be passive and receptive—budding patiently under the eye of Apollo" (19 February 1818: KL, I, 232). "Diligent Indolence" may become a richly productive state of mind reconciling opposite, normally discordant qualities (I, 231). All poets wait passively for the Spirit of the muse to descend upon them, including Byron when the *"estro"* is upon him.[24] However, we may read Keats's "What the Thrush Said" in the same way that we read Wordsworth's "The Tables Turned." Neither poem asserts that every man on every day will learn more from a single impulse of a vernal wood than all the sages can teach. Keats was capable of writing on 27 February 1818 that "if Poetry comes not as naturally as the Leaves to a tree it had better not come at all" (KL, I, 238–9). Similarly, the effect of the poem upon the reader should seem to be a natural thing: "the rise, the progress, the setting of imagery should like the Sun come natural [to the reader]—shine over him and set soberly" (I, 238). One is reminded here of Shelley's great painting growing as naturally "under the power of the artist as a child in the mother's womb."[25]

Nevertheless, Keats did indeed fret after knowledge. The need to possess it became urgent for him. However, he drew a distinction between systematic, abstract reasoning, distrusting it as deeply as Blake and Byron distrusted it, and genuine knowledge. Temperamentally, all three poets were unfitted to put on the show of logic that Godwin, for example, was capable of. Keats wrote, as we have seen, that he did not wish to be a "Reasoner" because he did not care "to be in the right" (KL, I, 243). Apollonius is his fallen Urizen-figure. Keats's "Read Me a Lesson, Muse," written upon the top of Ben Nevis, measures the distance between his mind and Wordsworth's on Mount Snowdon, the elder poet finding there with magnificent certainty "the emblem of a mind / That feeds upon infinity, that broods / Over the dark abyss" (*Prelude*, XIV, ll. 70–2). Keats upon the summit of Ben Nevis wrote a symbolist poem also, but the sullen mist he found provided him with a symbol of ignorance (to be overcome), not knowledge. Dilke, whose mind ran on nothing but *Political Justice* and his son, was one of "the stubborn arguers" of the words who "never begin upon a subject they have not preresolved on" (24 September 1819: KL, II, 213). This way of proceeding allows for no progress at all, of course, and illustrates the kind of sterile, uncreative thinking that is the opposite of the insight characteristic of the poet of Negative Capability.

Such a poet or poetic thinker thirsts after knowledge, the highest form of which is knowledge of the suffering human heart. The felt need of such knowledge or understanding can be almost overwhelming in its intensity: "I find that I can have no enjoyment in the World but continual drinking of Knowledge" (24 April 1818: KL, I, 271). In the Mansion of Life letter "an extensive knowledge . . . helps . . . to ease the [Wordsworthian] Burden of the Mystery" (3 May 1818: I, 277). Wordsworth "is a Genius and superior [to] us, in so far as he can, more than we, make discoveries, and shed a light in them," that is, illuminate the "dark Passages" of human life that the older poet explored in "Tintern Abbey." In Keats's view as in Sidney's before him, England has produced "the finest writers in the world" because the English have caused them to suffer and to observe the suffering of "the festerings of Society" (9 June 1819: II, 115). Thus when "Knowledge enormous makes a God of" Apollo, it is chiefly knowledge of human suffering, of "gray legends, dire events, rebellions, / . . . agonies, / Creations and destroyings."[26] Apollo's "aching ignorance" (l. 107) before his transformation precisely parallels Keats's own state of mind when composing his sonnet "Why Did I Laugh Tonight": "it was written with no Agony but that of ignorance; with no thirst of any thing but knowledge" (19 March 1819: KL, II, 81).

Although Keats thought that poetry "should strike the Reader as a wording of his own highest thoughts, and appear almost a Remembrance" (27 February 1818: KL, I, 238), he also knew that "Memory should not be called knowledge" (I, 231). Blake called reason "the ratio of all we have already known," but insisted that it "is not the same that it shall be when we know more."[27] Knowledge, Keats wrote, is created by "original Minds" and expresses itself in the form of "a tapestry empyrean—full of Symbols for [the] spiritual eye" (19 February 1818: KL, I, 231, 232). Keats had confidence that such originality, although obscured "by Custom," is possessed by many men.

Except allegorically, and not very clearly, as Apollo dies into new life, Keats does not explain the nature of the new perception that transforms the Endymion-like youth into a god. However, despite Apollo's passivity, Keats's own theories of perception assumed a most *active* mind and imagination, very different from the pale personification of Memory, which is Mnemosyne and with whom Keats was obviously dissatisfied. With one great revisionary leap from Mnemosyne to Juno Moneta (the admonisher), Keats achieved that point where Blake began: "Imagination has nothing to do with Memory."[28] Moneta also recalls one of Blake's giant forms, and her allocution implies clearly that the poetic imagination cannot truly exist unless it is an ethical imagination, feelingly alive to the "giant agony of the world" (*The Fall of Hyperion*, I, l. 157). This ethical imagination presupposes that the poet feels empathetically with all that lives. Then "sure a poet is a sage; / A humanist, physician to all men" (I, 189–90).

NOTES

1. KL, I, pp. 191–4.

2. BLJ, [*Byron's Letters and Journals*, ed. Leslie A. Marchand, 12 vols. (Cambridge, Mass.: Harvard University Press, 1974–82)], IX, p. 30. "Detached Thought," no. 53.

3. See Hazlitt's "On Shakespeare and Milton," the third of his *Lectures on the English Poets* (1818): *Complete Works*, ed. Howe, V, p. 47.

4. In 1963 Walter Jackson Bate spoke of Keats's poetry as being "largely untouched by any direct interest in religion" (*John Keats* [Cambridge, Mass.: Harvard University Press, 1963] p. 133). Recent scholarship has argued convincingly for a lifelong interest. For a comprehensive study of this subject, see Robert M. Ryan, *Keats: The Religious Sense* (Princeton University Press, 1976). Ronald A. Sharp in *Keats, Skepticism, and the Religion of Beauty* (Athens: University of Georgia Press, 1979) focuses more on the poetry than (as had Ryan) on the life and the letters. Specifically on one poem is Gail McMurray Gibson, "Ave Madeline: Ironic Annunciation in Keats's *The Eve of St. Agnes*," *Keats-Shelley Journal*, 26 (1977) pp. 39–50.

5. Of Clarke's father, Ryan notes that he was "deeply interested and involved in the scriptural scholarship of the time" (p. 36). Enfield Academy provided Keats, "on the one hand, . . . with much of his formal grounding in Christian doctrine and his familiarity with the contents of the Bible. On the other, the liberal atmosphere of Clarke's school provided a matrix for his initial questioning of his religious heritage" (ibid., pp. 44–5).

6. KL, II, pp. 49–51. In "Keats and the Bible" Lloyd N. Jeffrey lists numerous allusions by Keats to the Bible in his poetry and letters (*Keats-Shelley Journal*, 10 [1961] pp. 59–70). Even Ryan, who finds Keats almost totally rejecting Christianity, is forced to admit, in regard to this letter, that "there is not a single indication that

the writer had any personal difficulty with the doctrines of which he was speaking" (p. 188).

7. Compare Byron: "All history and experience, and the rest, teaches us that the good and evil are pretty equally balanced in this existence, and that what is most to be desired is an easy passage out of it." Detached Thought," no. 95, in BLJ, IX, p. 45.

8. On Keats and Wordsworth, see Clarence D. Thorpe, "Wordsworth and Keats— A Study in Personal and Critical Impressions," *PMLA*, 42 (1927) pp. 1010–26. John Middleton Murry's *Keats* (1955) has a suggestive chapter on Keats and Wordsworth— and one on Keats and Blake. The best recent brief discussion is at the end of the last chapter of Jack Stillinger's *The Hoodwinking of Madeline and Other Essays on Keats's Poems* (1971).

9. See KL, I, p. 137, and Ryan's discussion in *Keats* (pp. 112–13). On Byron's Christless Christianity, see chapter 6, note 37.

10. For example, in a letter to his publisher John Murray of 24 August 1819, Byron compares himself to the Aztec chief Guatimozin, who, along with a favourite companion, was being tortured by Cortes to make them reveal the location of the royal treasure. When he saw his companion weakening, Guatimozin checked him by asking, "Am I now reposing on a bed of flowers?" See BLJ, VI, p. 216, and William Robertson, *A History of America*, 3rd edn, 3 vols (London: W. Strahan, etc., 1780) II, p. 427. Matthew Arnold observed "flint and iron" in Keats's character. See *The Complete Prose Works*, ed. R. H. Super, 11 vols (Ann Arbor: University of Michigan Press, 1960–77) IX, p. 211.

11. BPP [*Poetry and Prose of William Blake*, ed. David V. Erdman (New York: Doubleday, 1965)], p. 37.

12. KL, II, pp. 103, 102. Ryan in *Keats* provides an excellent discussion of this letter (pp. 196–209), seeing it as Keats's deliberate attempt to move beyond the Christian thinking of his day. Our reading stresses the Christian foundations upon which Keats based that attempt.

13. See discussion in chapter 6 of *English Romanticism: The Grounds of Belief*.

14. *Milton*, plate 40, l. 36, in BPP, p. 141. Much of plate 38 also insists upon the need to put off selfhood.

15. BLJ, V, p. 105.

16. KL, I, p. 186. 22 November 1817. Keats's empathetic power was of such intensity that he could see himself frying in a "Gridiron" (KL, I, p. 162) and as "a sort of ethereal Pig" (ibid., I, p. 223). He once imagined himself a "Billiard-Ball" (I, p. 147), which he conceived might "have a sense of delight from its own roundness, smoothness volubility. & the rapidity of its motion" (*The Keats Circle*, ed. Hyder Edward Rollins, 2nd edn. 2 vols [Cambridge, Mass.: Harvard University Press, 1965] I, p. 59). On another occasion Charles Cowden Clarke, who introduced Keats to Spenser's *Faerie Queene*, noted in his *Recollections of Writers* (1878) that Keats "hoisted himself up, and looked burly and dominant, as he said, 'What an image that is—"sea-shouldering whales!' " (Fontwell, Sussex: Centaur Press, 1969, p. 126).

17. We may compare Keats's unease before reason unaided to Blake's marginalia, "To Generalize is to be an Idiot [,] To Particularize is the Alone Distinction of Merit" (BPP, p. 630) and to Wordsworth's fears of the rational intellect in "Expostulation and Reply," "The Tables Turned," and "A Poet's Epitaph."

18. *Biographia*, II, p. 6.

19. The transformation of the world as it seems to exist within the individual consciousness also occurs within the context of the appearance versus reality theme in *Don Juan*.

20. In "The Laocoön," BPP, p. 272.

21. *Endymion*, ll. 799, 798. Stanley C. Russell, " 'Self-Destroying' Love in Keats" (*Keats-Shelley Journal*, 16 [Winter 1967] pp. 79–91), surveys Keats's alternating attraction and repulsion to love.

22. BPP, p. 555.

23. SP, pp. 173, 174.

24. Byron's word. See BLJ, X, p. 157, and elsewhere. We may set Byron's "For what is poesy but to create / From overfeeling good or ill" (*The Prophecy of Dante*, IV, ll. 11–12) against Wordsworth's "spontaneous overflow of powerful feelings." Each poet implied a state of previous passivity.

25. SP, p. 294.

26. *Hyperion*, III, ll. 113–16. Keats's awareness of human suffering was of course firmly grounded in his medical training. It is worth pointing out that Apollo is not only the god of music (including poetry) but also has traditional associations with medicine.

27. BPP, p. 2. Cf. *Milton*, plate 26, l. 46, and plate 29, l. 18 (ibid. pp. 123, 126).

28. BPP, p. 655.

Keats's Chemical Composition   Donald C. Goellnicht[*]

On 1 October 1815, having completed a five-year apprenticeship to the surgeon-apothecary Thomas Hammond of Edmonton, John Keats, then almost twenty years old, registered at Guy's Hospital for a twelve-month period of training. The new Apothecaries Act, which Parliament had passed in July just as Keats was completing his apprenticeship, required six months of hospital work for an apothecary's licence and twelve months for a surgeon's, so it is likely that Keats set his sights on the more ambitious title. Within a month of arriving at Guy's, Keats was appointed a dresser to the hospital,[1] the first member of his class to be honored with this highly responsible position, which amounted virtually to fulfilling the role of house doctor when on duty.[2] He continued to carry out the duties of hospital dresser until March 1817, even though on 25 July 1816 he took the examination to become a Licentiate of the Society of Apothecaries and, having passed, received his "Certificate to Practise as an Apothecary." This latter fact attests to his careful study of medicine, but perhaps also indicates the relinquishing of the ambition to become a surgeon as his poetic ambitions grew with his increasing allegiance to the Leigh Hunt circle.

[*] This essay is a revision of "Chemistry" in the author's *The Poet-Physician: Keats and Medical Science*. © 1984 by the University of Pittsburgh Press. It appears here courtesy of the author and the University of Pittsburgh Press.

The Borough Medical School that Keats entered was run by the United Hospitals of Guy's and St. Thomas's, and offered a comprehensive, progressive course of medical training. The teaching staff was generally excellent and the syllabus extensive, as follows:

> At St. Thomas's.—Anatomy and the Operations of Surgery, by Mr. Astley Cooper and Mr. Henry Cline. Principles and Practice of Surgery, by Mr. Astley Cooper.
> At Guy's.—Practice of Medicine, by Dr. Babington and Dr. Curry. Chemistry, by Dr. Babington, Dr. Marcet, and Mr. Allen. Experimental Philosophy, by Mr. Allen. Theory of Medicine, and Materia Medica, by Dr. Curry and Dr. Cholmeley. Midwifery, and Diseases of Women and Children, by Dr. Haighton. Physiology, or Laws of the Animal Oeconomy, by Dr. Haighton. Structure and Diseases of the Teeth, by Mr. Fox.[3]

As the senior partner with a famous past, St. Thomas's allotted to itself the teaching of anatomy and surgery, the only lectures for which there was great demand before the 1815 Apothecaries Act. Guy's had to be content with teaching the strictly medical subjects, which had not been popular until the act made them compulsory. Among these was chemistry; Keats's certificate states that he attended two courses of lectures on chemistry while at Guy's in 1815–16, which would have meant attendance at one course during each of the autumn and spring terms. That Keats took two courses of lectures on chemistry illustrates his conscientiousness as a medical student, for the new "Regulations for the Examination of Apothecaries" demanded only that the candidate attend "one course of Lectures on Chemistry."[4] As in almost all his endeavors, Keats prepared himself thoroughly.

The chemistry teachers were men with a great deal of experience. Babington, "a good-tempered, kindly Irishman," was "a very excellent practical teacher, who was listened to with great pleasure and advantage, as his lectures were full of experience and practical good sense."[5] A founding member of both the Geological and Hunterian Societies, and later elected a fellow of the Royal Society, Babington was primarily interested in minerals. Marcet, a native of Switzerland, was an experimental chemist of very high repute, a founding member of the Medico-Chirurgical Society, and a widely published member of the Royal Society.[6] The third lecturer, Allen, was travelling on the Continent in 1816, so is unlikely to have taught Keats.

During the latter part of the eighteenth century, chemistry had begun to emerge as a full-fledged modern science, based on empirical research. Prior to this, in the seventeenth and early eighteenth centuries, it was in a state of stagnation, as yet not truly distinct from the related fields of biology and botany, and still mired in the search for some mysterious "subtle fluid" that would explain life completely and finally: the total explanation that would provide a synthesis of light, heat, electricity, gravity, and life.[7] This onerous burden fell on such "subtle fluids" as phlogiston (an imaginary element of combustion, believed to flow in the blood), animal magnetism, electricity, and ether, all proposed at various times as the force behind everything that lives and moves and has a being. These theories of immanence were postulated on vague and loose analogies between very different life-forms, and were expressed in highly metaphorical language.

By the 1770s, however, scientists like Joseph Priestley were claiming that advances in chemistry and related fields could be made only through rigorous empirical research, and not through vague theories postulated on a grand scale. Ironically, the revolution taking place in chemical studies by the end of the eighteenth century was not due to the discovery of the total explanation of life that had been sought previously; on the contrary, it was instigated by the acknowledgment that phenomena have only limited explanations, that can be uncovered only gradually. This allowed empirical researchers to concentrate on smaller, more specialized areas of science, an approach that led to the great discoveries of Sir Humphry Davy and his student Michael Faraday in the first half of the nineteenth century. In the introductory discourse to his "Course of Lectures on Chemistry," delivered at the Royal Institution in January 1802, Davy states: "Before this time, vague ideas, superstitious notions, and inaccurate practices, were the only effects of the mind to establish the foundations of chemistry. Men either were astonished and deluded by their first inventions so as to become visionaries, . . . or they employed them as instruments for astonishing and deluding others. . . . These views of things have passed away, and a new science has gradually arisen."[8]

The retreat of imagination and analogy before the advance of reason and empiricism in the field of science did not, of course, appeal to many Romantic poets. Blake, for example, abhorred Newtonian mechanics and was still proclaiming the analogical existence of a whole world in a grain of sand. Keats's attitudes to experimental proof and analogy were more ambiguous. As a poet, he inevitably made extensive use of analogy and metaphor, speculated at length about life, and, at least initially, insisted on the primacy of the imagination in grasping truth. We might even conjecture that he turned away from medical science because of the insistence of new physicians, like Astley Cooper and John Hunter, that any understanding of life forces can only be partial and limited, and must be devoid of pure speculation. He perhaps sought in poetry an intuitive understanding of life that nineteenth-century science no longer offered.[9] Yet certain aspects of Keats's thought show him clinging to new scientific principles, especially his insistence that "nothing ever becomes real till it is experienced."[10] As he progressed in his poetic career, he increasingly grew to believe that knowledge and truth have to be gained by observation, experience, and proof, an idea that involves a return to the principles he had been taught in medicine. Even the famous concept of "negative capability," of accepting half-truths and doubts, may owe something to the scientific concept of limited explanation. His ambivalent attitude toward science—his attraction to its traditional use of analogy and his distaste for "consequitive reasoning" (Letters 1:185)—emerges in his borrowings from chemistry.

With the exception of Stuart Sperry's excellent article, "Keats and the Chemistry of Poetic Creation,"[11] to which I am greatly indebted, no study has paid much attention to Keats's knowledge of chemistry, an oversight difficult to comprehend when one recognizes that the poet's vocabulary brims with terms and metaphors whose meanings become wholly clear only within their contemporary chemical context. In particular, as Sperry has observed, Keats adopted certain chemical terms and theories to explain his ideas on the creative process of composition. It remains, of course, impossible to pronounce with any certainty whether Keats developed such analogies consciously, or whether his knowledge of chemical terminology and processes became an integral part of his intellectual equipment, used unconsciously. The fact remains, however, that Keats employs the chemical vocabulary almost exclusively during the eighteen-month period following the termination of his Guy's dressership, from May 1817 to November 1818, when his knowledge of chemistry was fresh in his mind. This essay traces those ideas as expressed in his letters and poems of this period.

Perhaps the most obvious use Keats makes of chemical concepts to illustrate imaginative creativity appears in a letter to Haydon of 8 April 1818, in which he describes the difficulties an artist must go through to create a work of beauty: "The innumerable compositions and decompositions which take place between the intellect and its thousand materials before it arrives at that trembling delicate and snail-horn perception of Beauty—I know not you many havens of intenseness—nor ever can know them" (Letters 1:264–65). As Sperry has indicated,[12] Keats here draws on the very definition of chemistry Babington and Allen give at the outset of their Syllabus for the chemistry course at Guy's: "CHEMISTRY therefore defined, The Science of the Composition and Decomposition of the heterogeneous particles of Matter: or 'that which teaches the intimate and reciprocal action of bodies upon each other.' "[13]

For Keats, the creative process, like the chemical one, involves the artist's imagination bringing various materials—natural objects and the sensations they evoke—into "Combinations and Decompositions," or what Babington and Allen later call analysis and synthesis

(*Syllabus* 1, 35), in order to form new, often purer, finer materials. This phenomenon provides a perfect metaphor for the workings of the imagination, which amalgamates diverse thoughts and feelings into a new creative unity. The process, according to Keats, involves various "havens of intenseness," or "intensity," a term which in chemistry often refers to the degree of heat necessary to cause a chemical or physical change in substances.[14]

That Keats uses "intensity" with this scientific meaning becomes clear at the end of the famous "Pleasure Thermometer" passage in book 1 of *Endymion:*

> But there are
> Richer entanglements, enthralments far
> More self-destroying, leading, by degrees,
> To the chief intensity: the crown of these
> Is made of love and friendship.
> (1:797–801)[15]

The metaphor of the thermometer, an instrument for measuring the degrees of heat and to which Keats himself draws attention in a letter to Taylor (*Letters* 1:218), serves here to describe the various levels of human emotion. As the degree of heat increases, the amount of "self" destroyed also increases—"love and friendship" being self-less—a concept that fits the chemical analogy as the intensity of heat applied determines the evaporation of impurities from the substance being heated.[16] The greater the "intensity" of heat applied, the greater will be the number of "disagreeables," or selfish propensities, evaporated off. The metaphor is clarified further when Keats employs it again at the end of 1817 in discussing Benjamin West's painting: "the excellence of every Art is its intensity, capable of making all disagreeables evaporate, from their being in close relationship with Beauty & Truth" (*Letters* 1:192). The intensity of art, like that of heat, is capable of burning off or evaporating all impure elements in a substance or a work, thus leaving it purified. Beauty and truth act as catalysts in the purification, until only the very essence of the subject being painted remains.

The process of evaporation is not the only one that Keats draws on in his attempts to formulate his understanding of imaginative creativity. He continually introduces the words "distill," "sublime," "abstract," and "digest," which, as Sperry has pointed out, are chemical terms used to describe processes similar to evaporation.[17] Babington and Allen state that "to the head of *Evaporation* may also be referred the process of *Distillation,* and *Sublimation*" (*Syllabus* 8–9). Babington also explains that "*Distillation* is only a process of Evaporation in a proper Apparatus that the Vapor may again be condensed" ("Lectures" 65); "*Sublimation* Is where the Saline substance is of a Volatile Nature we may proceed to apply Heat to it in a particular Vessel, where what is Volatile may be saved" ("Lectures" 101). To "abstract" in a chemical sense is "to separate an essence or chemical principle by distillation," whereas to "digest" is "to prepare by boiling or application of heat; to dissolve by the aid of heat and moisture" (*O.E.D.*). All these processes utilize heat (Keats's "intensity" of art) to resolve substances, usually chemical compounds, into their component parts, with the principal object of refining them and collecting the purified product.

In his letter of 27 June 1818, written to his brother Tom from the Lake District, Keats introduces these chemical terms in discussing poetry:

> What astonishes me more than any thing is the tone, the coloring, the slate, the stone, the moss, the rock-weed; or, if I may so say, the intellect, the countenance of such places. The space, the magnitude of mountains and waterfalls are well imagined before one sees them; but this countenance or intellectual tone must surpass every imagination and defy any remembrance. I shall learn poetry here and shall henceforth write more than ever, for the *abstract* endeavor of being able to add a mite to that mass of beauty which is harvested from these grand *materials*, by the *finest spirits*, and put into *etherial* existence for the relish of one's fellows. (Emphasis added.) (*Letters* 1:301)

The "abstract endeavor" Keats discusses here is not some vague aesthetic goal, but a specific desire to "abstract" or distill the "grand materials," the physical aspects of nature he sees around him, into "etherial existence," a more purified, refined state, the state of poetry. In chemistry this state is achieved using only the "finest spirits," which correspond to the most *refined* imaginations, those capable of reciprocally reading the landscape. Keats implies that the imagination itself must be distilled before it can abstract these material objects into art which exists on a higher, more *spiritual* plane.

Keats's description of this landscape in the Lake District has further significance. Previously, he had written to Haydon about the artist's "innumerable compositions and decompositions which take place between the intellect and its thousand materials before it arrives at that trembling delicate and snail-horn perception of beauty"; but here the "materials"—"the coloring, the slate, the stone, the moss"— have their own "intellect," or "intellectual tone," which "must surpass every imagination and defy any remembrance." Ironically, Keats proclaims that the very material landscape of the Lake District that inspires him to artistic endeavor needs no human intellect or imagination to refine or abstract it into a state of art; it already exists in a "finer tone," in a state of self-created pure beauty that defies improvement or completion by the imagination of the human "reader." It is a closed text, completed poetry incarnate, reality more ethereal than imagination could make it. No wonder, then, that he exclaims, "I shall learn poetry here."

The chemical terms associated with distillation appear again a few days later in a letter to George and Georgiana, this time in Keats's discussion of his prospects for marriage: "Notwithstand your Happiness and your recommendation I hope I shall never marry. Though the most beautiful Creature were waiting for me at the end of a Journey or a Walk; though the carpet were of Silk, the Curtains of the morning Clouds . . . my Happiness would not be so fine, as my Solitude is *sublime*. Then instead of what I have described, there is a *Sublimity* to welcome me home" (*Letters* 1:403). Keats boldly claims that even the most refined material possessions associated with conjugal bliss cannot compensate for the refinement, the sublimity, of his distilled moods of solitude, in which poetic creation occurs and in which he possesses not merely a few beauties, but all the distilled or abstracted beauty of the world: "The roaring of the wind is my wife and the Stars through the window pane are my Children. The mighty *abstract* Idea I have of Beauty in all things stifles the more divided and minute domestic happiness" (Emphasis added.) (*Letters* 1:403).

Keats's discussion of domestic happiness recalls his earlier letter of 11 May 1817 to Haydon, in which he describes "the Sun the Moon the Stars, the Earth and its contents as *materials* to form greater things—that is to say *ethereal* things—but here I am talking like a Madman greater things that our Creator himself made!!" (Emphasis added.) (*Letters* 1:143). Clearly, he speculates here about artistic production; Sperry claims that " 'etherealization,' or the way in which material forms are 'put into etherial existence,' is close to the heart of [Keats's] notion of poetic creativity."[18] It is important, therefore, that we comprehend exactly what Keats means by these terms, a task complicated by the fact that he himself employs them with a variety of meanings.

Often, he uses "ether" in its ancient cosmological sense of "the upper regions of space beyond the clouds; the medium filling the upper region of space, as the air fills the lower regions" (*O.E.D.*). From this definition comes the related, but less specific, meaning of "ethereal" as "light, airy, attenuated; heavenly, celestial" (*O.E.D.*). This concept, largely mythical, led to the eighteenth-century scientific speculation on "ether" as a "subtle" or "imponderable" fluid, "a substance of great elasticity and subtilty, believed to permeate the whole of planetary and stellar space" (*O.E.D.*).[19] While Keats uses "ether" and "ethereal" with these meanings at times, he also draws on a much narrower chemical definition of the terms. In his "Lectures," Babington never refers to "ether" as a subtle fluid, but rather as "the colourless, light, volatile liquid, resulting from the action of sulphuric and other acids upon alcohol" (O.E.D.); he outlines their production from the distillation of rectified spirits at some length ("Lectures" 265–68). As Priestley explains, "If spirit of wine be distilled with almost any of the acids, the produce is a liquor which has obtained the name of Aether, from its extreme lightness and volatility, being much lighter, and more volatile, than any other fluid."[20]

That Keats was aware of this chemical definition is evident in his comments to George and Georgiana about claret, where he distinguishes in detail between heavy and ethereal spirits (Letters 2:64). He seems also to have had this process in mind when discussing "the Sun the Moon the Stars, the Earth and its contents as materials to form greater things—that is to say ethereal things" and "that mass of beauty which is harvested from these grand materials, by the finest spirits, and put into etherial existence." Within the context of the chemical metaphor, Keats's "materials" are equivalent to the acids that are mixed with rectified spirits (Keats's "the finest spirits") to form ether (Keats's "ethereal things") by distillation. The "materials" correspond to physical things of beauty and the sensations they produce, which are refined by the imagination ("the finest spirits") of the author and his audience to produce poetry ("ethereal things"). The poetic process, like the chemical, involves distillation or purification; but as always, Keats's poetry remains rooted in the empirical world.

An even more blatant reference to the "ethereal" in the context of chemical reactions appears in an earlier letter, written on 22 November 1817 to Bailey and studded with clusters of chemical metaphors and analogies. Here Keats postulates that "Men of Genius are great as certain ethereal Chemicals operating on the Mass of neutral intellect—by [for but] they have not any individuality, any determined Character" (Letters 1:184). Just as acids can combine with rectified spirits to form ethers, so too ethers can react with other chemicals to form active substances. That Keats's "Men of Genius" have no "individuality," no "determined Character," suggests that they act as catalysts in the creative process of transmuting material "things" into art: they initiate the process but do not themselves enter into the combinations that constitute the finished product. As Humphry Davy states in his discussion of "ethereal matter" (Keats's "ethereal Chemicals," the imagination): "their principal effects seem rather to depend upon their communicating motion to the particles of common matter, or modifying their attractions, than to their actually entering into combination with them."[21] This catalytic role is precisely parallel to Keats's view of the genuine "poetical character": he must, with his imagination, distill materials and sensations into art, but he must not allow his own moral, religious, or philosophical beliefs to inform the poetry. Poetry must never be didactic: "We hate poetry that has a palpable design upon us" (*Letters* 1:224). Like the "ethereal Chemicals," the "Man of Genius" withholds his ego from his art; instead, as a catalyst or stimulant he remains invisible in the work itself, thus allowing maximum room for the participation of the reader in the coproduction of poetry.

Having made these statements about the poetic process, Keats goes on to tell Bailey in this letter of 22 November that a "philosophic Mind" must balance both intuitive imagination and rational knowledge: "and therefore it is necessary to your eternal Happiness that you do not only drink this old Wine of Heaven which I shall call the *redigestion* of our most *ethereal* Musings on Earth; but also increase in knowledge and know all things" (*Letters* 1:186). In chemistry, to "digest" means to bring to maturity using heat, usually by "keeping bodies for a considerable time immersed in a fluid at a higher temperature than that of the atmosphere, in order that combinations may take place that could not else have been effected."[22] Babington, in his lecture on the spirit of wine (Keats's "old Wine of Heaven"), writes: "It may be purified by repeated distillation & converted to a state of Alkohol by *digesting* it over mild & caustic vegetable Alkali in certain proportions & submitting it to further distillation which must be conducted *slowly & gradually*" ("Lectures" 264). Similarly, Keats's "ethereal [distilled, purified] Musings" must be digested and redigested, maturing passively over long periods of time in order to form the new combinations that constitute poetry. As he says elsewhere, "Nothing is finer for the purposes of great productions, than a very *gradual* ripening of the intellectual powers" (Emphasis added.) (*Letters* 1:214).

Before we leave the discussion of ethers, there remains one significant passage, dealing with "ethereal things," that needs explication. On 13 March 1818, Keats, in an unusually analytical mood, writes to Bailey:

> As Tradesmen say every thing is worth what it will fetch, so probably every mental pursuit takes its reality and worth from the ardour of the pursuer—being in itself a nothing—Ethereal thing may at least be thus real, divided under three heads—Things real—things semireal—and no things—Things real—such as existences of Sun Moon & Stars and passages of Shakspeare—Things semireal such as Love, the Clouds &c which require a greeting of the Spirit to make them wholly exist—and Nothings which are made Great and dignified by an ardent pursuit—Which by the by stamps the burgundy mark on the bottles of our Minds, insomuch as they are able

to *"consec[r]ate whate'er they look upon."* (Emphasis in original.)
(*Letters* 1:242–43)

In describing the three stages of ethereal reality, Keats is explaining the degree of imaginative input necessary, on the part of the artist and audience, to distill or refine "grand materials" into the "etherial existence" of artistic beauty. Again, the concept of distilling ethers underpins his explanation.

At the first or highest level of reality, that of the ethereal-real, we find things already really ethereal; that is, they already exist in their purest, most refined, or abstracted form and thus, like the landscape Keats saw in the Lake District, do not require any input from the imagination to distill them. "Passages of Shakspeare" belong here as, for Keats, Shakespeare's poetry was art already refined to its highest intensity. More difficult to understand is his reason for including "existences of Sun Moon & Stars" when he had earlier defined "the Sun the Moon the Stars, the Earth and its contents as materials to form greater things—that is to say ethereal things." But the operative word here is "existences"—"of Sun Moon & Stars"—which indicates that they already "wholly exist" or are in a state of "ethereal existence," presumably put there by previous artists, and so are no longer merely "grand materials." Of course, the sun, moon, and stars also exist in the classical mytho-cosmological "ether," the region above the clouds, which fits nicely with Keats's argument.

The second category, that of the ethereal-semireal, includes things that are at present only half-ethereal and so require some input from the imagination "to make them wholly [or ethereally] exist." That Keats denominates the imagination "the Spirit" points up the chemical metaphor, for it is rectified spirit that is mixed with acid to distill ether. The choice of the verb "greet" is also exact, for it implies a mutual interplay between the semireal (material-ethereal) thing and the "Spirit"; the onus is not entirely on the imagination to make the thing real. "Clouds" fit in this category because they are formed by a process of evaporation—a type of distillation without heat—and condensation; they remain between the "material" state of water and the "ethereal" state of pure vapor. And within the classical concept of ether, clouds exist at the transition point between the atmosphere and the ether, and so are semiethereal. Love also involves a mixture of material, or sensual, passion and refined emotion, and so requires a "greeting of the Spirit" to distill it into totally ethereal existence, where it becomes "disinterestedness."

The third category, that of ethereal nothings, is made up of material things that as yet have no ethereal existence and so are totally dependent on the "ardent pursuit" of the imagination to sublimate them into artistic beauty. This is obviously the most difficult process of distillation, and as Babington points out, when an acid shows reluctance to give off ether, "it may be made to afford more ether, by the addition of one third of very strong *ardent spirit*" ("Lectures" 266). Keats probably has this process in mind when he talks of the "ardent pursuit" of the "Spirit"-imagination necessary to etheralize nothings. This "ardent pursuit" of the imagination "stamps the burgundy mark on the bottles of our Minds," by which I understand Keats to mean "produces the best poetry." We have already seen him refer to poetry as the "old Wine of Heaven," a particularly appropriate symbol since wine is made by a process of distillation and fermentation over a long period of time, which accords with Keats's idea of a "gradual ripening of the intellect."

Keats uses a similar image of literature being distilled from "materials," put into "etherial existence," and then fermented in a humorous passage written on 24 March 1818 about Milton's attack on Salmasius. On learning that Milton rolled in a certain meadow before writing the attack, and that no nettles grew there afterwards, Keats states: "This accou[n]t made me very naturally suppose that the nettles and thorns *etherialized* by the Scholars rotary motion and garner'd in his head, thence flew after a new *fermentation* against the luckless Salmasius and accasioned his well known and unhappy end" (Emphasis added.)" (*Letters* 1:254). Again the harvesting metaphor is linked to the chemical concepts, the idea that the "etherealizing" of the thorns is produced by Milton's "rotary motion" probably deriving from the fact that in the production of some ethers it is necessary to shake the mixture to induce spontaneous distillation (Babington, "Lectures" 265). Keats labels the change in these thorns "a new fermentation" since the rectified spirit needed to form the ether must itself have originally been fermented. In the fashion of fermentation, the nettles were spontaneously transformed, in Milton's mind, into the words that produced what Keats calls "distilled Prose," but the distillate of nettles is a stinging spirit, as Salmasius discovered.

Finally, I wish to turn to two problematical terms in Keats criticism that can, I believe, be fruitfully interpreted using chemical definitions: "essence" and "essential." Babington's lectures on "Vegitable Inflamables"—which include spirit of wine and ethers—contain a section on "Essential Oils and Resins." The essential oils "differ only from the Resins in being thinner & containing the finer & more volatile, whilst the latter are the more coarse parts" of fluids from fragrant vegetables. The essential oils are separated from the resins "by distillation with water" in which "the finer & more volatile" oils rise, leaving the resin behind ("Lectures" 268).

This process of distilling essences from vegetables seems often to be at the back of Keats's use of the words "essence" and "essential." The first example occurs when he writes to Bailey on 22 November

1817 that "I have the same Idea of all our Passions as of Love they are all in their *sublime*, creative of *essential* Beauty—In a Word, you may know my favorite Speculation by my first Book and the little song I sent in my last" (*Letters* 1:184–85). The latter reference is to the "Song of Sorrow" in book 4 of *Endymion,* where Keats introduces the idea, later developed more fully in the "Ode on Melancholy," that sorrow and joy, like all passions, are, when "sublime" (or distilled) an essence of beauty or "essential Beauty." In this refined form all passions are unified just as essential oils, "by repeated distillation . . . are brought nearly to resemble each other" (Babington and Allen, *Syllabus* 135). Again, Keats points out that this purifying and synthesizing are carried out by the imagination, which sublimates passions into their essential beauty.

Keats also mentions his "first Book" of *Endymion* as a place where his speculations about "essential Beauty" are adumbrated. Presumably he refers to the well-known "Pleasure Thermometer" passage, which he discusses in a letter to Taylor on 30 January 1818, and which deals with the whole question of "essence":

> Wherein lies happiness? In that which becks
> Our ready minds to fellowship divine,
> A fellowship with essence; till we shine
> Full alchemiz'd, and free of space. Behold
> The clear religion of heaven!
> (1:777–81; *Letters* 1:218)

Critics have traditionally given this passage a neo-Platonic interpretation with "essence" as the Platonic Ideal,[23] or an anti-Platonic one, with " 'essence' as a synonym for 'a thing of beauty.' "[24] These critics have missed the point, emphasized by Sperry, that "the chief key to [the passage's] significance, as indicated by the word 'alchymized,' is its relation to chemical theory."[25] This becomes even more apparent in Keats's comment that the passage "set before me at once the gradations of Happiness even like a kind of Pleasure Thermometer." Just as a thermometer measures the different intensities of heat needed to produce chemical reactions, the Pleasure Thermometer demarcates the different levels of intensity of various pleasures; as the purest distillate is produced by the greatest intensity of heat, so the most intense pleasure is the purest.

As always for Keats, this creative process originates in sensations gained from physical objects. Thus, at the lower degrees of happiness are the feel of a rose leaf and the sound of music:

> Feel we these things?—that moment have we stept
> Into a sort of oneness, and our state
> Is like a floating spirit's.
> (1:795–97)

The sensations are already being distilled into the form of a rarefied "spirit," be it chemical or mythical. But they can be purified even further:

> But there are
> Richer entanglements, enthralments far
> More self-destroying, leading, by degrees,
> To the chief intensity: the crown of these
> Is made of love and friendship, and sits high
> Upon the forehead of humanity.
>
> (1:797–802)

His vocabulary here indicates that Keats is describing a process analogous to chemical distillation, in which the purest distillate is "love and friendship." He discusses in relation to pleasure what a month earlier he had described in the context of art: that "the excellence of every Art is its intensity, capable of making all disagreeables evaporate, from their being in close relationship with Beauty & Truth" (*Letters* 1:192). Within the moral context, the "disagreeables" are "self," which must be evaporated off, leaving pure "love and friendship."

But even this crown of "love and friendship" can be separated further:

> All its more ponderous and bulky worth
> Is friendship, whence there ever issues forth
> A steady splendour; but at the tip-top,
> There hangs an unseen film, an orbed drop
> Of light, and that is love.
>
> (1:803–7)

Here the separation of love and friendship is analogous to the separation of resins from essential oils. The resins, "the most coarse parts," correspond to friendship, the "more ponderous and bulky worth"; the essential oils, "the finer and more volatile" parts equated with love, are separated from them by further distillation. In this metaphorical context, the image of love as "an orbed drop of light" that "hangs by unseen film" emerges as an exact description of a drop of pure distillate condensing on the lip of a retort to drip into a beaker, as well as a depiction of the moon, Cynthia, who constitutes the essence of love for Endymion.

Keats makes similar use of chemical terminology in other passages of *Endymion*, the only major poem he wrote while his medical training was still fresh in his mind. After Endymion has met Cynthia and been deserted by her, he depicts his movement from ecstasy to melancholy by comparing volatile, light, and refined essences with turbid heavy spirits:

> Now I have tasted her sweet soul to the core
> All other depths are shallow: essences,
> Once spiritual, are like muddy lees,
> Meant but to fertilize my earthly root,
> And make my branches lift a golden fruit
> Into the bloom of heaven.
>
> (2:904–9)

The chemical metaphor shifts subtly into a botanical one, but the concept of refinement remains, with the "muddy lees" that fertilize the "earthly root" being transmuted, through upward growth, into golden, heavenly fruit of love.

These are some examples of Keats's frequent use of chemical terminology, analogy, and imagery. In discussing his understanding of chemistry in relation to his thoughts on poetry, however, I am not claiming that Keats developed a unified and coherent system of poetics based on his knowledge of chemistry, although we might speculate that his understanding of chemistry, which he gained before delving deeply into poetics, may have helped him to formulate his speculations on the working of the imagination. But he abhorred dogmatic system, so that his ideas on poetry were always fluid and developing. What I am suggesting is that, in his knowledge of chemistry, Keats found a ready-made vocabulary that assisted him in understanding and explaining many of his more difficult ideas concerning the poetic process. A grasp of these terms helps us to comprehend his ideas more clearly.

Notes

1. Evidence of Keats's appointment as dresser comes from entries in Guy's Hospital registers for 1815; see Amy Lowell, *John Keats* (London: Jonathan Cape, 1925), 1:74.

2. See S. Wilks and G. T. Bettany, *A Biographical History of Guy's Hospital* (London: Ward, Lock, Bowden, 1892), 90.

3. "Medical School of St. Thomas's and Guy's," *The London Medical and Physical Journal* 34 (1815): 259.

4. "Apothecaries' Hall," *The London Medical and Physical Journal* 34 (1815): 251.

5. John Flint South, *Memorials of John Flint South* ed. C. L. Feltoe (1884; reprint, Fontwell, England: Centaur, 1970), 58.

6. Wilks and Bettany, *Biographical History*, 200–201, 208.

7. See Philip C. Ritterbush, *Overtures to Biology: The Speculations of Eighteenth-Century Naturalists* (New Haven: Yale University Press, 1964).

8. Sir Humphry Davy, *The Collected Works of Sir Humphry Davy*, ed. John Davy, 9 vols. (London: Smith, Elder, 1839–40), 2:320–21.

9. For the best general discussion of the relationship between Romanticism and

science, see Hans Eichner, "The Rise of Modern Science and the Genesis of Romanticism," *PMLA*, 97(1982): 8–30.

10. John Keats, *The Letters of John Keats*, ed. Hyder E. Rollins, 2 vols. (Cambridge: Harvard University Press, 1958), 2:81; hereafter cited as *Letters* in the text.

11. Stuart M. Sperry, "Keats and the Chemistry of Poetic Creation," *PMLA* 85 (1970):268–77; revised and reprinted in his *Keats the Poet* (Princeton: Princeton University Press, 1973), 30–71.

12. Sperry, *Keats the Poet*, 36–37.

13. William Babington and William Allen, *A Syllabus of a Course of Chemical Lectures Read at Guy's Hospital* (London: W. Phillips, 1802), 1–2; hereafter cited as *Syllabus* in the text.

14. See Joseph Priestley, *Heads of Lectures on a Course of Experimental Philosophy, Particularly Including Chemistry* (1794; reprint, New York: Kraus Reprint, 1970), 138.

15. Quotations of Keats's poetry are from *The Poems of John Keats*, ed. Jack Stillinger (Cambridge: Harvard University Press, 1978).

16. William Babington, "Lectures on Chemistry," MS (Wills Library, Guy's Hospital, n.d.), 60; hereafter cited as "Lectures" in the text.

17. Sperry, *Keats the Poet*, 45.

18. Ibid., 35.

19. Ibid., 40. See also Sir Edmund Whittaker, *A History of the Theories of Aether and Electricity*, 2 vols., 2d ed. (London: Thomas Nelson, 1951).

20. Priestley, *Heads of Lectures*, 69.

21. Davy, *Collected Works*, 4:140.

22. William Nicholson, *The First Principles of Chemistry*, 2d ed. (London: Robinson, 1792), 34; quoted in Sperry, *Keats the Poet*, 47.

23. For example, Claude Lee Finney, *The Evolution of Keats's Poetry* (Cambridge: Harvard University Press, 1936), 1:297–99. Finney's interpretation follows those of Colvin, de Selincourt, Bridges, and Murry.

24. Newell F. Ford, *The Prefigurative Imagination of John Keats* (Hamden, Conn.: Shoe String Press, 1966), 14–15. See also E. C. Pettet, *On the Poetry of Keats* (Cambridge, England: Cambridge University Press, 1957), 126–27.

25. Sperry, *Keats the Poet*, 48.

Keats and Blushing   Christopher Ricks[*]

Thomas Burgess in 1839 began *The Physiology or Mechanism of Blushing* with a passionate determination not to be thought trivial:

> Who has not observed the beautiful and interesting phenomenon
> of Blushing? Who indeed has not had it exemplified in his own
> person, either from timidity during the modest and sensitive days
> of boyhood, or from the conscious feeling of having erred in maturer

[*] Reprinted from *Keats and Embarrassment* by Christopher Ricks by permission of Oxford University Press. © Oxford University Press 1974.

years? When we see the cheek of an individual suffused with a blush in society, immediately our sympathy is excited towards him; we feel as if we were ourselves concerned, and yet we know not why. The condition by which the emotion thus proclaimed is excited, viz., extreme sensibility, the innate modesty and timidity which are the general concomitants of youth, enlist our feelings in favour of the party, appeal to our better nature, and secure that sympathy, which we ourselves may have claimed from others on similar occasions.

There are some, perhaps, who may be inclined to smile at the subject of this Essay. But if these individuals will but reflect on the wonderful mechanism of their being; if they remember that there is not a function, even the simplest, carried on in the economy of man, which is not in the most perfect harmony with all the others, and suggest to themselves that there is a physiology of the mind as well as of the body, perhaps they may be inclined to excuse me for contemplating with wonder and admiration the beautiful illustration of one among the moral laws of nature.

No poet knew more intimately than Keats that "there is a physiology of the mind as well as of the body."

In *John Keats's Dream of Truth*, John Jones has a richly evocative account of what a blush can mean in Keats. He contrasts the false and the true:

My scorn for the goddess's notion of atoning for her sexual pleasure "by some coward blushes" [*Endymion*, II. 788] was at bottom directed against its mental emptiness; the cheapness of her shame, certainly there and offensive, is undercut by its incredibility. This sort of blushing Keats can never substantiate. But there is another sort, the sort of

> that cheek so fair and smooth;
> O let it blush so ever! let it soothe
> My madness! let it mantle rosy-warm
> With the tinge of love,
>
> [IV. 311–15]

which proves the object ripe for tasting. This blushing unmental proof, while it reaches forward to possess, has a way of respecting the object's freedom. In urging "let it mantle rosy-warm" Keats apprehends something alive on its own, self-charged, a separate and secret centre. He is appealing to the same imagined hidden source as when he asks the rose to "glow intense and warm the air." This life-fostering fancy of his spills over into the many attempts to guess admiringly not just at phases of other lives but at their latent principles; and then to transpose his conclusions into language which the snailhorn understands. Blushing joins with glowing and flushing, with smothering and stifling and obscure inner pressures, with floating and heaviness and aching and languor—a central knot of conditions which hover on the verge of namelessness, all hard worked by him and all striving to mature an account of how one feels into a revelation of what one is.[1]

As imaginative criticism (to which I am very much indebted), this is so good that some may wonder why anything more needs to be said about blushing. I believe that it needs to be taken in two other directions; Mr. Jones, though he is excellent on blushing as a sensation and as an imagining of life, makes no claim either to any consideration of blushing and embarrassment as a moral and social matter (involved in friendship and love) or to any consideration of the relationship here of Keats as a poet to Keats the man, the man whose letters are to many of us the greatest letters we have ever read.

"The Poet as Hero: Keats in His Letters":[2] Keats was a hero, as Lionel Trilling subtly and openly argued. Yet Keats's sense that difficulties must be faced and can be strengthening incorporates a humane acknowledgement that there need be nothing dishonourable about a "refuge": "I must think that difficulties nerve the Spirit of a Man—they make our Prime Objects a Refuge as well as a Passion."[3] Among the "disagreeables" (Keats's word) of life, among the difficulties which should nerve a man, was the ordinary human fact of embarrassment.

Keats wrote to his friend John Hamilton Reynolds:

My dear Reynolds.
    It is an awful while since you have heard from me—I hope I may not be punished, when I see you well, and so anxious as you always are for me, with the remembrance of my so seldom writing when you were so horribly confined—the most unhappy hours in our lives are those in which we recollect times past to our own blushing—if we are immortal that must be the Hell—[4]

Those last words are not a mere figure of speech; Keats is embarrassed and ashamed (not the same) for his neglect of Reynolds, especially given Reynolds's ill health; and again it is not only candour, but also a sense of the nature of embarrassment and its reciprocity, which makes him begin his letter by speaking openly of blushing. I cannot think of any other great writer who has thought that if Hell exists it will be an eternity of blushing.

Blushing in Hell, rather than in Purgatory, is morally complicated by the fact that a blush may be an acknowledgement of error; blushing in Heaven offers a mirror-image of the same complication. It has long been felt that we cannot imagine either the goodness or the livingness of gods and angels unless somehow we can imagine them blushing, despite the fact that the blush would have seemed to be a concomitant of the Fall. It is characteristic of Milton's courage and humanity that in insisting that sexual intercourse preceded the Fall he should also have asked us to imagine the full innocence of a prelapsarian blush: "To the Nuptial Bowre / I led her blushing like the Morn" (*Paradise Lost*, VIII. 510–11). C. S. Lewis found this blush embarrassing,[5] but the glory of it is the deep tact of Milton's wording: first, in that though "blushing like the Morn" mostly attaches to "her," the syntax is such that some tender possibility is left open that Adam too is blushing (more faintly, since the attachment of the words is fainter); second, in the felicity of the pathetic fallacy. For "blushing like the Morn," so boldly natural and commonplace a comparison (as natural and commonplace and fine as the morn itself), confers this simple naturalness upon the blush itself—the naturalness not just of the morn but of the very comparison; and the innocence of morn (there at the morn of life too) glows into the innocence of the blush. A hundred lines later we learn that what is good enough for Adam and Eve is good enough for Raphael:

> Love not the heav'nly Spirits, and how thir Love
> Express they, by looks onely, or do they mix
> Irradiance, virtual or immediate touch?
>   To whom the Angel with a smile that glow'd
> Celestial rosie red, Loves proper hue,
> Answer'd. Let it suffice thee that thou know'st
> Us happie, and without Love no happiness.
>   (VIII. 615–21)

This courts ridiculousness, but as often in Milton (and in the Wordsworth whom Milton animated) the possibility of the ridiculous is part of the amplitude of his poetry. Empson bluffly paraphrases: Adam "says in effect, 'Come now, what do you know about this? Have you got any sex?' and Milton to his eternal credit makes the angel blush."[6] I like *eternal* there; but what matters is to see that it is to the poem's credit as well as Milton's, and that the credit is a complicated one since it involves the complexities of guilt and innocence in blushing and embarrassment.

Keats nowhere imagines such full grandeur for the blush of god or angel. But his sense of the importance of blushing to our apprehension of others did not permit him to shirk this strange humanizing of the classical gods, whose superiority to humans seems less a matter of a finer spirituality than a more candid recognition of physicality.

> Ah, what a world of love was at her feet!
> So Hermes thought, and a celestial heat
> Burnt from his winged heels to either ear,
> That from a whiteness, as the lily clear,
> Blush'd into roses 'mid his golden hair,
> Fallen in jealous curls about his shoulders bare.
>   (*Lamia*, I. 21–6)

This was indebted to Raphael's blush, as the coming together of *love, celestial*, and *roses* in this blush suggests; and the best stroke—"jealous curls"—is pure Milton in the way it enforces innocence by using a word which in its ordinary contexts would insist upon guilt; like Eve's "wanton ringlets," Mercury's "jealous curls" are wonderfully pure, "clear," not jealous a bit. The largeness of mood is true to Keats, as is the winged movement by which the imagination converts the metaphor of "at her feet" to the literal wings of Mercury at his feet (literal but magical). All the variety of impulse in the lines comes finally to rest in the word "bare."

John Jones deplored the "imbecile morality"[7] of the goddess's adjuration to Endymion:

> I love thee, youth, more than I can conceive;
> And so long absence from thee doth bereave
> My soul of any rest: yet must I hence:
> Yet, can I not to starry eminence
> Uplift thee; nor for very shame can own
> Myself to thee. Ah, dearest, do not groan
> Or thou wilt force me from this secrecy,
> And I must blush in heaven. O that I
> Had done 't already; that the dreadful smiles
> At my lost brightness, my impassion'd wiles,
> Had waned from Olympus' solemn height,
> And from all serious Gods; that our delight
> Was quite forgotten, save of us alone!
> And wherefore so ashamed? 'Tis but to atone
> For endless pleasure, by some coward blushes:
>   (*Endymion*, II. 774–88)

This is not very vivid or precise, one might agree, but imbecility is too harsh an accusation, and moreover the human point is precisely that this is indeed a pother—that there is a strange and pathetic disparity between the fleeting coward blushes and the endless pleasure, between the small fear of blushing and the large sacrifices which men, and even goddesses, will make to avert that fear. Embarrassment can be an antagonist whom even love may sometimes succumb to fearing: this seems to me perceptive and seldom said. It is not only those who suffer from ereutophobia, a morbid propensity to blush or to fear blushing, who should acknowledge this. The difference is the size of the self-recognition in Keats, and this has its bearing on the odd relationship of embarrassability to empathy. The hypothesis of the social psychologist Modigliani[8] was that a person of empathy would be especially embarrassable, yet in the event the experiment contradicted the hypothesis. The weak correlation between empathy and embarrassability is an interesting finding, especially in its bearing on Keats, acute to embarrassment and probably more widely and subtly gifted with powers of empathy than any other English poet.[9] Being embarrassable is not, after all, the same as recognizing the possibility of embarrassment; the heat of Keats's empathy (his special gift for beauty and truth) is such as to evaporate this disagreeable. At the least I think it matters that empathy is of such importance both to Keats and to the student of embarrassment—as, of course, is identity. As Goffman says, "In all these settings the same fundamental thing occurs: the expressive facts at hand threaten or discredit the assumptions a participant finds he has projected about his identity."[10] Keats was especially sensitive to anything which threatened or discredited identity (his and others'), and he was especially audacious in believing that the healthy strength of a sense of identity depends paradoxically upon the risk and openness and not upon self-protection; depends upon risking the absence of identity rather than upon guarding the circumscription of one's identity:

> several things dovetailed in my mind, & at once it struck me, what quality went to form a Man of Achievement especially in Literature & which Shakespeare possessed so enormously—I mean *Negative Capability*, that is when man is capable of being in uncertainties, Mysteries, doubts, without any irritable reaching after fact & reason—
>
> A Poet is the most unpoetical of any thing in existence; because he has no Identity—
>
> That Dilke was a Man who cannot feel he has a personal identity unless he has made up his Mind about every thing.[11]

Keats's imagination is alive to embarrassment, so that a slack piece of writing will suddenly tauten in coming near his heart:

> Lo! how they murmur, laugh, and smile, and weep:
> Some with upholden hand and mouth severe;
> Some with their faces muffled to the ear
> Between their arms; some, clear in youthful bloom,
> Go glad and smilingly athwart the gloom;
> ("Sleep and Poetry," 142–6)

The embarrassed ones are beautifully seen and sympathized with: "Some with their faces muffled to the ear / Between their arms;"— the effect is at once richly expressive and richly emblematic, like an Elizabethan gesture or posture (melancholy pulling its hat down over its brows), or like the art of Massine which T. S. Eliot so admired: "The difference between the conventional gesture of the ordinary stage, which is supposed to *express* emotion, and the abstract gesture of Massine, which *symbolises* emotion, is enormous."[12] In Keats's lines, though, the expressive and the symbolic are both alive. "Their faces . . . the ear . . . their arms": the effect of acute embarrassment as a physical discomposure, dislocation, has seldom been better caught; it is there in the odd effect of the singular ("to the ear"), and in the muffled but oppressive movement through the prepositions ("with . . . to . . . between"). The difference in quality (perception and phrasing) between this line and a half and those around could hardly be greater. "Lo! how they murmur, laugh, and smile, and weep": this does nothing to earn the right to say "Lo!," since it shows and feels nothing of what it is to murmur, laugh, smile, or weep. "Some with upholden hand and mouth severe": this ventures upon prose and natural sculpture, often a true source of power in Keats but here without immediacy (upholden just how? severe as doing just what to the mouth?). Then in the following lines, the faces that are offered as seen—"clear in youthful bloom" and going "smilingly"—are not seen or felt with anything of the immediacy which is so moving in those muffled faces not to be seen. I think that John Jones is muffling one important implication of this passage—while clarifying others— when he finds it all equally valuable evidence of Keats's sense of the disconcerting and thrilling autonomy of the parts of the body: "Staring eyes, parted lips, 'upholden hand and mouth severe' situations, are already familiar because they recall the phenomenon of dispersal in which Keats's human theme of the moment—fear, anger, love—gets carried into the body's separate parts."[13]

Dr. Burgess in 1839 began the first chapter of *The Physiology or Mechanism of Blushing* with a confident relating of the public-private communication which is blushing to that which is poetry. "Blushing may be styled the poetry of the Soul!" When Burgess (p. 173) says of blushing that *"it is the lava of the heart produced by an eruption of feeling,"* we may recall Byron's saying that "poetry is the lava of the imagination whose eruption prevents an earthquake."[14]

The body's separate parts—and yet their vital interdependency, or in the words of Burgess's title ". . . the Sympathies, and the Organic Relations of Those Structures with which They Seem to Be Connected"—are the concern of the medical man, and in starting upon a medical career Keats joined the profession which has a more intimate relation with embarrassment than any other. There is no other profession which makes upon its practitioner so central and total a demand that he—or she—not be embarrassed; the embarrassed doctor or surgeon or psychiatrist would not be able to do his job (and not only because of the effect of his embarrassment upon the patient), whereas a chemist, an architect, or a librarian need only prefer not to be embarrassed. Again there is no other profession (not even the lawyer) which so combines the most intensely private and the most intensely public; this creates something of a counterpart to art such as has long made the medical profession of special interest to art (from the Victorian novels' preoccupation with the doctor,[15] through *Doctor Zhivago*, which is alive to the affinity of doctor to poet, down to Dr. Finlay). So it is not surprising that the doctor should be a special target for the ereutophobe: "She constantly visited every possible variety of physician, would undress for examination with an almost conscious pleasure (the doctor serving to relieve her guilt feelings), and repeatedly exposed herself elsewhere 'innocently' to attack, admitting that she was playing with fire."[16]

At the other extreme from the ereutophobe who yet longs to be stared at, and who plays with fire, her cheeks on fire, is the human being whose utter imperviousness to anybody's stare challenges our sense even of what it is to be human. I am thinking of a very famous and magnificent passage in Keats's letters. He wrote to Reynolds: "The short stay we made in Ireland has left few remembrances— but an old woman in a dog-kennel Sedan with a pipe in her Mouth, is what I can never forget—I wish I may be able to give you an idea of her."[17] A few days earlier he had done his best:

> On our return from Bellfast we met a Sadan—the Duchess of Dunghill—It is no laughing matter tho—Imagine the worst dog kennel you ever saw placed upon two poles from a mouldy fencing— In such a wretched thing sat a squalid old Woman squat like an ape half starved from a scarcity of Buiscuit in its passage from Madagascar to the cape,—with a pipe in her mouth and looking out with a round-eyed skinny lidded, inanity—with a sort of hor- izontal idiotic movement of her head—squab and lean she sat and puff'd out the smoke while two ragged tattered Girls carried her along—What a thing would be a history of her Life and sensations.[18]

It is a superb moment of imagination precisely because it finds itself confronted by the unimaginable: life and sensations from which even Keats's extraordinary powers of empathy are excluded. Yet his sympathy is not precluded, and his cry here—"What a thing would be a history of her Life and sensations"—is one that might have spurred Dickens in Keats's century or Beckett in ours. The impossibility of conceiving of an inner life for this extraordinary old woman is a counterpart in terms of an individual to the impossibility of conceiving of an Ireland free of misery; only half a dozen lines earlier Keats had written: "What a tremendous difficulty is the improvement of the condition of such people—I cannot conceive how a mind 'with child' of Philanthropy could gra[s]p at possibility—with me it is absolute despair." As so often in Keats, "conceive" there really does imagine bringing something towards birth; but the old woman's life and sensations are truly conceived of as inconceivable. Yet it is important to see that it is the grandeur of her ridiculousness which makes her so; "It is no laughing matter tho," because it would be inanity to laugh at someone who could not be imagined as capable of being moved to or by laughter. The grandeur of her ridiculousness is a matter of its imperviousness to any sense of the ridiculous; and though there is much more to Keats's vision of the old woman than can be harnessed to anything that has to do with embarrassment, the passage is among other things an evocation of the unembarrassable. The total imperviousness and unembarrassability of the old woman precipitate in Keats the awed humanity of a great anthropologist, another profession which cannot afford to have any time for embarrassment and which therefore needs to be all the more alert to it.

We can approach another aspect of embarrassment if we recall that one of its meanings is financial. In May and June 1817 Keats wrote twice to his publishers, Taylor and Hessey, the first time acknowledging their advance of £20 and the second time asking for a further £30. Both must be quoted in full.

> My dear Sirs,
>   I am extremely indebted to you for your liberality in the Shape of manufactu[r]ed rag value £20 and shall immediately proceed to destroy some of the Minor Heads of that spr[i]ng-headed Hydra the Dun—To conquer which the knight need have no Sword. Shield Cuirass Cuisses Herbadgeon spear Casque, Greves, Pauldrons Spurs Chevron or any other scaly commodity: but he need only take the Bank Note of Faith and Cash of Salvation, and set out against the Monster invoking the aid of no Archimago or Urganda—and finger me the Paper light as the Sybils Leaves in Virgil whereat the Fiend skulks off with his tail between his Legs. Touch him with this enchanted Paper and he whips you his head away as fast as a Snail's Horn—but then the horrid Propensity he has to put it up again has discouraged many very valliant Knights—He is such a never ending still beginning sort of a Body—like my Landlady of the Bell—I should conjecture that the very Spright that the "g[r]een sour ringlets makes hereof the Ewe not bites" had manufactured it of the dew fallen on said sour ringlets—I think I could make a nice little Alegorical Poem called "the Dun" Where we wold have the Castle of Carelessness—the Draw Bridge of Credit—Sir Novelty Fashion's expedition against the City of Taylors—&c &c——I went day by day at my Poem for a Month at the end of which time the other day I found my Brain so over-wrought that I had neither Rhyme nor reason in it—so was obliged to give up for a few days— I hope soon to be able to resume my Work—I have endeavoured to do so once or twice but to no Purpose—instead of Poetry I have a swimming in my head—And feel all the effects of a Mental Debauch—lowness of Spirits—anxiety to go on without the power to do so which does not at all tend to my ultimate Progression— However tomorrow I will begin my next Month—This Evening I go to Cantrerbury—having got tired of Margate—I was not right in my head when I came—At Cant^y I hope the Remembrance of Chaucer will set me forward like a Billiard-Ball—I am gald [glad]

to hear of M^r T's health and of the Welfare of the In-town-stayers"
and think Reynolds will like his trip—I have some idea of seeing
the Continent some time in the summer—
In repeating how sensible I am of your kindness I remain
                    Your Obedient Servt and Friend
                            John Keats—
I shall be very happy to hear any little intelligence in the literary
or friendly way when you have time to scribble.—[19]

It is, naturally enough, an embarrassed letter, as is clear from its
elaborate whimsy. But even here the movements of embarrassment
are active and effectual as well as shrinking; notice the fertility of
mind and language with which Keats spins his Spenserean allegory,
adapts his Biblical terminology, deploys his literary allusions, and
unfolds his jokes: these are all doubly to the point, since not only
do they reassure his own embarrassment they also reassure Taylor
and Hessey; the verbal vitality, the literary gifts, are such as to
reassure the publishers who in this very letter are having to be told
that "I hope soon to be able to resume my Work—I have endeavoured
to do so once or twice but to no Purpose." So it is not surprising
that this ordinary situation of embarrassment should have involved
him in so many of the preoccupations that are pure Keats: the
shrinking "Snail's Horn" which he revered from *Venus and Adonis*
and which served him again and again for his deep concerns ("that
trembling delicate and snail-horn perception of Beauty");[20] his own
writing and the mysterious baulkings of it; the way in which a
metaphor moves naturally and simply into the literal ("anxiety to go
on without the Power to do so which does not at all tend to my
ultimate Progression. . . . This Evening I go to Cantrerbury") and
then back into metaphor ("set me forward like a Billiard-Ball"—that
billiard-ball will set itself forward in another invigorating appearance
elsewhere in Keats);[21] the animating delight in Chaucer. All of these
rise naturally to Keats's pen when he is writing with a consciousness
of the embarrassing.

The other letter to Taylor and Hessey has the more embarrassing
purpose of asking and not just acknowledging. Its metaphor is an
intelligent protection against embarrassment, in being whimsical, in
being extreme, and in being itself a way of speaking which could
embarrass the maidenish.

My dear Sirs,
    I must endeavor to lose my Maidenhead with respect to money
Matters as soon as possible—and I will to—so here goes—A Couple
of Duns that I thought would be silent till the beginning, at least,
of next Month (when I am certain to be on my legs for certain
sure) have opened upon me with a cry most "untunable" never
did you hear such un "gallant chiding"

Now you must know I am not desolate but have thank God 25 good Notes in my fob—but then you know I laid them by to write with and would stand at Bay a fortnight ere they should grab me— In a Month's time I must pay—but it would relieve my Mind if I owed you instead of these Pelican duns.

I am affraid you will say I have "wound about with circumstance" when I should have asked plainly—However as I said I am a little maidenish or so—and I feel my virginity come strong upon me—the while I request the loan of a £20 and a £10—which if you would enclose to me I would acknowledge and save myself a hot forehead—I am sure you are confident in my responsibility— and in the sense [of] squareness that is always in me—

Your obliged friend
John Keats—[22]

The squareness is patent, not least in the true urging that it is in Taylor and Hessey's interests that Keats should indeed not spend on his duns, but on time for writing, the money he already has. But what is memorable and acute is the way in which the "maidenhead" figure of speech is so much more than a jocularity. (Even "these Pelican duns"—Lear's "those pelican daughters"—takes its place within the figure.) The relation of embarrassment to sexual feelings and to creativity is strongly intimated; moreover if Taylor and Hessey will send the money, he will be able to acknowledge it in writing "and save myself a hot forehead." Not only does this recognize the way in which the written word protects us against embarrassment, and the way in which this will be good for them as well as him (they will save themselves Keats's hot forehead—embarrassment is embarrassing); it recognizes too the erotic creativity of a blush. For Keats is pre-eminently the poet of the hot forehead, a forehead of conceptions and often of erotic conceptions. Yet what stabilizes and controls the maidenhead metaphor is its being subservient to a different love: "Your obliged friend" is a conclusion which has been authenticated by the literary allusion with which Keats speaks plainly of not having perhaps spoken plainly enough: "I am affraid you will say I have 'wound about with circumstance' when I should have asked plainly." For it is Antonio who urges Bassanio not to be embarrassed in his request:

> You know me well, and herein spend but time
> To wind about my love with circumstance;
> And out of doubt you do me now more wrong
> In making question of my uttermost
> Than if you had made waste of all I have . . .
> *(The Merchant of Venice*, I. i. 153–7)

"Your obliged friend": Keats preferred the embarrassment of knowing to whom he was obliged. He chafed when he received £25 from

"Mr. P. Fenbank" (probably a joking pseudonym). His reaction brought together all the proper reactions: that it would have been churlish of him to refuse it; that he could not help feeling a little galled; that he did his best to find out the donor; and that he did not know quite what he would do should he ever meet him. We should say of his reaction, "all very proper." "I tu[r]n'd over and found a £25-note— Now this appears to me all very proper—if I had refused it—I should have behaved in a very bragadochio dunderheaded manner—and yet the present galls me a little, and I do not know whether I shall not return it if I ever meet with the donor—after whom to no purpose I have written—"[23]

Haydon recorded in his diary, 7 April 1817: "Keats said to me today as we were walking along 'Byron, Scott, Southey, & Shelley think they are to lead the age, but [*the rest of the sentence, consisting probably of eight or ten words, has been erased*].' This was said with all the consciousness of Genius; his face reddened."[24] Keats's face was to matter to Haydon because the painter wished it to figure, along with Wordsworth's, in his *Christ's Entry into Jerusalem;* Keats's letter to Haydon succeeds in complimenting him without being self-complimentary by means of another of those good-humoured juxtapositions of the literal and the casually metaphorical: "I am glad you are hard at Work—'t will now soon be done—I long to see Wordsworth's as well as to have mine in: but I would rather not show my face in Town till the end of the Year—"[25]

Horace Smith, long after Keats was dead, recollected that "his manner was shy and embarrassed";[26] Keats himself had relished Smith's poem "Nehemiah Muggs," and one of the passages which he transcribed[27] was this evocation of embarrassed timorousness:

> He shudder'd & withdrew his eye
> Perk'd up his head some inches higher
> Drew his chair nearer to the fire
> And hummed as if he would have said
> Pooh! Nonsense! damme! who's afraid[28]
> Or sought by bustling up his frame
> To make his courage do the same
> Thus would some blushing trembling Elves
> Conceal their terrors from themselves
> By their own cheering wax the bolder
> And pat themselves upon the shoulder

Keats was not one to pat himself upon the shoulder—especially did he not pride himself upon his physical self, and perhaps one of the things he liked about Smith's poem was the good humour with which it used phrases like "Perk'd up his head some inches higher" and "bustling up his frame." For there can be no doubt that Keats felt very strongly about his height (5 ft. ¾ in.), and that this mattered most to him, and was an embarrassment more than superficial, because of love and desire. His poem "Had I a man's fair form" was glossed by his friend Woodhouse: "the author has an idea that the diminutiveness of his size makes him contemptible and that no woman can like a man of small stature."[29] Even to Fanny Brawne, Keats was to write: "Upon my soul I cannot say what you could like me for. I do not think myself a fright any more than I do M^r A Mr B. and M^r C— yet if I were a woman I should not like A—B. C. But enough of this—."[30] That last proper impatience with himself lets him bustle up his frame in a good spirit. Even to his friends he could not write without a tinge of bitterness, as when a word like "stunted" brings with it more of a crackle than the context can quite accommodate, in a letter to the Misses Jeffrey: "I wish you were here a little while— but lauk we havent got any female friend in the house—Tom is taken for a Madman and I being somewhat stunted am taken for nothing—."[31] Or there is the fuse of thought, in a letter to Fanny Brawne, which ignites the supplicating humbleness of his being on his knees so that it flares into his physical self-doubts:

If you should ever feel for Man at the first sight what I did for you, I am lost. Yet I should not quarrel with you, but hate myself if such a thing were to happen—only I should burst if the thing were not as fine as a Man as you are as a Woman. Perhaps I am too vehement, then fancy me on my knees, especially when I mention a part of you Letter which hurt me; you say speaking of Mr. Severn "but you must be satisfied in knowing that I admired you much more than your friend." My dear love, I cannot believe there ever was or ever could be any thing to admire in me especially as far as sight goes—I cannot be admired, I am not a thing to be admired.[32]

One of the things which make Keats's letters to his brother George and his sister-in-law Georgiana the most fully loving of all his letters is that they can accommodate with perfect good humour his jokes about his height. Partly this may be because Georgiana was at once a woman of whom he was very fond (yet not a blood-relation), and a woman whom he was altogether precluded from wooing— there is a lovely relaxation about the way in which his letters flirt with her. But mostly it is just that he loved George and Georgiana so much that embarrassment about his height was out of the question—and the right way to show this was by mock-ruefulness. I think it central to Keats's moral imagination that he should have felt as he did, not proclaiming to himself that of course it did not matter a bit that he was five foot tall, but rightly seeing that thanks to love it did not matter a bit. The perfect occasion manifesting this grateful ease is Georgiana's baby:

> I admire the exact admeasurement of my niece in your Mother's letter—O the little span long elf—I am not in the least judge of the proper weight and size of an infant. Never trouble yourselves about that: she is sure to be a fine woman—Let her have only delicate nails both on hands and feet and teeth as small as a May-fly's. who will live you his life on a square inch of oak-leaf.[33]

> I must not forget to mention that your mother show'd me the lock of hair—'t is of a very dark colour for so young a creature. When it is two feet in length I shall not stand a barley corn higher. That's not fair—one ought to go on growing as well as others—[34]

Another letter to George and Georgiana makes clear the strength of his feeling as well as the cluster of his feelings. It begins with a characteristic verbal germination from "shrunk from":

> I have not seen Mr Lewis lately for I have shrunk from going up the hill—Mr Lewis went a few morning[s] ago to town with Mrs Brawne they talked about me—and I heard that M^r L Said a thing I am not at all contented with—Says he "O, he is quite the little Poet" now this is abominable—you might as well say Buonaparte is quite the little Soldier—You see what it is to be under six foot and not a lord—There is a long fuzz to day in the examiner about a young Man who delighted a young woman with a Valentine—I think it must be Ollier's. Brown and I are thinking of passing the summer at Brussels if we do we shall go about the first day of May—We ie Brown and I sit opposite one another all day authorizing (N.B. an s instead of a z would give a different meaning) He is at present writing a Story of an old Woman who lived in a forest and to whom the Devil or one [of] his Aid de feus came one night very late and in disguise—[35]

Then into an astonishing *Zuleika Dobson*-like tale of how an old lady becomes irresistibly beautiful:

> evey one falls in love with her—from the Prince to the Blacksmith. A young gentleman on his way to the church to be married leaves his unfortunate Bride and follows this nonsuch—A whole regiment of soldiers are smitten at once and follow her—A whole convent of Monks in corpus christi procession join the Soldiers—The Mayor and Corporation follow the same road—Old and young, deaf and dumb—all but the blind are smitten and form an immense concourse of people who—what Brown will do with them I know not—The devil himself falls in love with her flies away with her to a desert place—in consequence of which she lays an infinite number of Eggs—

What is significant is the sequence which goes from "O, he is quite the little Poet," through the "young Man who delighted a young woman with a Valentine," to authorship and Brown's story of the magically irresistible beauty. For in choosing to be a poet—to be supremely a writer and reader—Keats chose a way of life which made differences of height least noticeable; and he knew too that "authorizing" had its own relationship to beauty and to love's imaginings. In bringing together his own height, Mrs. Brawne, a young man's valentine, authorship, and a fabulous tale, he is sketching a cluster of feelings which begin in embarrassment, a commonplace matter but really not a simple one.

Just as the impalpable subjective world of the creative imagination and its beauty can create its own liberation from embarrassment, so too can the palpable objective world of nature and its beauty. There is no discord or oddity in the fact that Keats's letter to his brother Tom, 27 June 1818, should bring together the mountains' height and his sense of his own height. But one needs to see the scale of Keats's response in order to see how it can accommodate this self-consciousness freed from embarrassment's self-consciousness:

We arose this morning at six, because we call it a day of rest, having to call on Wordsworth who lives only two miles hence—before breakfast we went to see the Ambleside water fall. The morning beautiful—the walk easy among the hills. We, I may say, fortunately, missed the direct path, and after wandering a little, found it out by the noise—for, mark you, it is buried in trees, in the bottom of the valley—the stream itself is interesting throughout with "mazy error over pendant shades." Milton meant a smooth river—this is buffetting all the way on a rocky bed ever various—but the waterfall itself, which I came suddenly upon, gave me a pleasant twinge. First we stood a little below the head about half way down the first fall, buried deep in trees, and saw it streaming down two more descents to the depth of near fifty feet—then we went on a jut of rock nearly level with the second fall-head, where the first fall was above us, and the third below our feet still—at the same time we saw that the water was divided by a sort of cataract island on whose other side burst out a glorious stream—then the thunder and the freshness. At the same time the different falls have as different characters; the first darting down the slate-rock like an arrow; the second spreading out like a fan—the third dashed into a mist—and the one on the other side of the rock a sort of mixture of all these. We afterwards moved away a space, and saw nearly the whole more mild, streaming silverly through the trees. What astonishes me more than any thing is the tone, the coloring, the slate, the stone, the moss, the rock-weed; or, if I may so say, the intellect, the countenance of such places. The space, the magnitude of mountains and waterfalls are well imagined before one sees them; but this countenance or intellectual tone must surpass every imagination and defy any remembrance. I shall learn poetry here and shall henceforth write more than ever, for the abstract endeavor of being able to add a mite to that mass of beauty which is harvested from these grand materials, by the finest spirits, and put into etherial existence for the relish of one's fellows. I cannot think with Hazlitt that these scenes make man appear little. I never forgot my stature so completely—I live in the eye; and my imagination, surpassed, is at rest—[36]

The strength of Keats's imagination is its peaceful accommodation; the surpassing imagination of Wordsworth, Milton, and Hazlitt can all be intimated here, not only without any quarrelling for ascendancy among themselves but also without any discrepancy between their kind of grandeur, beauty, size, and the landscape's kind. To speak of "the countenance of such places" is to lead without obtrusion into the watching person and his own height. The touching admission— "I never forgot my stature so completely"—is what authenticates the whole fine self-abnegation which contemplates and renders the landscape so livingly. Keats was alert to something importantly true about the dignity and beauty of nature: that among the sane, fortifying, and consolatory powers it has is the power to free us from embarrassment, to make embarrassment unthinkable ("I never forgot my stature so completely"). For Wordsworth, "The thought of death sits easy on the man / Who has been born and dies among the mountains" ("The Brothers"). Likewise, the thought of blushing—less grand but not trivial or self-absorbed.

If this is so, we can measure how distant we now are from the Romantics' respectful gratitude to nature by recalling what man has made of waterfalls even mightier than Keats's. I am thinking of Dan Jacobson's saddened acerb observations on the twentieth-century commercial trash that now surrounds the Niagara Falls:

But what about the falls? Oh yes, they're still there, falling away industriously, overwhelmed rather than merely profaned by what Parkman would call the pettiness of man. The smaller, American falls, one learns from the guide, have actually been switched off on more than one occasion in the past, to enable hydro-electric works to be done; and also to try to remove some of the rocks which have tumbled down the face of the falls and piled up messily in front, thus making them so much the less lofty and imposing. From the far bank, the yellow and brown skyscrapers of downtown Niagara NY appear to stand directly above the American falls; and above them again are enormous neon signs advertising the United Hotel and O'Keefe's Ale. The Canadian or Horseshoe Falls are much the more spectacular of the two. The water roars down; the spray rises high; a moving yet stationary line of pale green wavers forever on the all but closed circle of the rim, between the dark green rush of the river and the pure white of torrent. However, among the observation towers and neon signs and car parks, the Horseshoe Falls look from a distance rather like some kind of wildly inspired Pop Art joke: the waters run away incessantly down what is simply the biggest plug-hole in the world.

Standing in the throng of people on the pavement, immediately above the white uproar of the cataract, one can't help wondering, in fact, if there isn't some therapeutic or self-defensive intention in all the rubbish with which the spectacle has been surrounded. What else could one do with it? In making such a stupendous gesture Nature embarrasses us: it seems so excessive, so pointless. We are not explorers, we are not believers like Father Hennepin, we are not 19th-century romantics, we are just tourists.[37]

"Nature embarrasses us": this is a profound insight of Mr. Jacobson's, appallingly remote from Keats's gratitude for having his imagination surpassed. "I cannot think with Hazlitt that these scenes make man appear little"; but there is a littleness of humiliation which is not humility, and Hazlitt might ask: Why, if modern man does not feel humiliatedly little, does he so belittle and belitter these scenes?

That the cluster of feelings is not a chance collocation is clear from others of Keats's letters. The transitions, which are trains of feeling as much as trains of thought, in his superb letter to Bailey of 18 July 1818, knit a wonderful continuity of self-awareness: from courteous explanation; through apology and embarrassment ("made me blush"); his own work; apology and embarrassment towards women; rejoicing at others' happiness; his height; mountains; poetry—it is like a list of the things he cared most about and was most self-awarely aware of:

> My dear Bailey,
>
> The only day I have had a chance of seeing you when you were last in London I took every advantage of—some devil led you out of the way—Now I have written to Reynolds to tell me where you will be in Cumberland—so that I cannot miss you—and when I see you the first thing I shall do will be to read that about Milton and Ceres and Proserpine—for though I am not going after you to John o' Grotts it will be but poetical to say so. And here Bailey I will say a few words written in a sane and sober Mind, a very scarce thing with me, for they may hereafter save you a great deal of trouble about me, which you do not deserve, and for which I ought to be ba[s]tinadoed. I carry all matters to an extreme—so that when I have any little vexation it grows in five Minutes into a theme for Sophocles—then and in that temper if I write to any friend I have so little selfpossession that I give him matter for grieving at the very time perhaps when I am laughing at a Pun. Your last Letter made me blush for the pain I had given you—I know my own disposition so well that I am certain of writing many times hereafter in the same strain to you—now you know how far

to believe in them—you must allow for imagination—I know I shall
not be able to help it. I am sorry you are grieved at my not
continuing my visits to little Britain—yet I think I have as far as
a Man can do who has Books to read to [and] subjects to think
upon—for that reason I have been no where else except to Wentworth place so nigh at hand—moreover I have been too often in
a state of health that made me think it prudent no[t] to hazard the
night Air—Yet further I will confess to you that I cannot enjoy
Society small or numerous—I am certain that our fair friends are
glad I should come for the mere sake of my coming; but I am
certain I bring with me a Vexation they are better without—If I
can possibly at any time feel my temper coming upon me I refrain
even from a promised visit. I am certain I have not a right feeling
towards Women—at this moment I am striving to be just to them
but I cannot—Is it because they fall so far beneath my Boyish
imagination? When I was a Schoolboy I though[t] a fair Woman a
pure Goddess, my mind was a soft nest in which some one of them
slept though she knew it not—I have no right to expect more than
their reality. I thought them etherial above Men—I find then [them]
perhaps equal—great by comparison is very small—Insult may be
inflicted in more ways than by Word or action—one who is tender
of being insulted does not like to think an insult against another—
I do not like to think insults in a Lady's Company—I commit a
Crime with her which absence would have not known—Is it not
extraordinary? When among Men I have no evil thoughts, no malice,
no spleen—I feel free to speak or to be silent—I can listen and
from every one I can learn—my hands are in my pockets I am free
from all suspicion and comfortable. When I am among Women I
have evil thoughts, malice spleen—I cannot speak or be silent—I
am full of Suspicions and therefore listen to no thing—I am in a
hurry to be gone—You must be charitable and put all this perversity
to my being disappointed since Boyhood—Yet with such feelings
I am happier alone among Crowds of men, by myself or with a
friend or two—With all this trust me Bailey I have not the least
idea that Men of different feelings and inclinations are more short
sighted than myself—I never rejoiced more than at my Brother's
Marriage and shall do so at that of any of my friends—. I must
absolutely get over this—but how? The only way is to find the root
of evil, and so cure it "with backward mutters of dissevering Power"
That is a difficult thing; for an obstinate Prejudice can seldom be
produced but from a gordian complication of feelings, which must
take time to unravell and care to keep unravelled—I could say a
good deal about this but I will leave it in hopes of better and more
worthy dispositions—and also content that I am wronging no one,
for after all I do think better of Womankind than to suppose they
care whether Mister John Keats five feet hight likes them or not.
You appeared to wish to avoid any words on this subject—don't
think it a bore my dear fellow—it shall be my Amen—I should
not have consented to myself these four Months tramping in the

highlands but that I thought it would give me more experience, rub off more Prejudice, use [me] to more hardship, identify finer scenes load me with grander Mountains, and strengthen more my reach in Poetry, than would stopping at home among Books even though I should reach Homer—By this time I am comparitively a a mountaineer—I have been among wilds and Mountains too much to break out much about the[i]r Grandeur.[38]

It is his sense of the "gordian complication of feelings" which enlivens the very prose, moving from "Mister John Keats five feet hight" to "grander Mountains, and strengthen more my reach in Poetry."

Similarly, when Keats was momentarily disillusioned with landscape it was natural for him to believe that a landscape needed to be in the vicinity of love if it were to be loved. He wrote to Fanny Brawne: "I am getting a great dislike of the picturesque; and can only relish it over again by seeing you enjoy it"[39]—the sentiment is a vivid epitome of that vista, of the watcher watched, which is so crucial to Keats's poetry ("seeing you enjoy it," where "enjoy" is "enjoy seeing"). Then he needs once more his old figure of "maidenhead" (it takes up from "touch'd" and is followed by covert bawdy) in explaining to Dilke why the Isle of Wight made too small an impression upon him, and—one may think—did not abolish his smallness: "I have been so many finer walks, with a back ground of lake and mountain instedd of the sea, that I am not much touch'd with it, though I credit it for all the Surprise I should have felt if it had taken my cockney maidenhead—But I may call myself an old Stager in the picturesque, and unless it be something very large and overpowering I cannot receive any extraordinary relish."[40]

The combination in Keats of intense self-awareness and a richly co-operative creative subconscious was such as to make it natural for him to be liable to and alive to slips and leaps of the mind. These are both bred from and breed embarrassment. The intelligence of Keats's letter to James Rice, 24 November 1818, is manifest in its self-knowledge and in its lucidity; "it seems downright preintention" is a formulation effortlessly precise and poised.

My dear Rice,
    Your amende honorable, I must call "un surcroit d'amitié" for I am not at all sensible of any thing but that you were unfortunately engaged and I was unfortunately in a hurry. I completely understand your feeling in this mistake, and find in it that ballance of comfort which remains after regretting your uneasiness—I have long made up my Mind to take for granted the genuine heartedness of my friends notwithstanding any temporery ambiguousness in their behaviour or their tongues; nothing of which how[ev]er I had the least scent of this morning. I say completely understand; for I am everlastingly getting my mind into such like painful trammels—and

am even at this moment suffering under them in the case of a friend of ours. I will tell you—Two most unfortunate and paralel slips—it seems downright preintention. A friend says to me "Keats I shall go and see Severn this Week" "Ah" says I "You want him to take your Portrait" and again "Keats" says a friend "When will you come to town again" "I will" says I "let you have the Mss next week" In both these I appeard to attribute and [an] interested motive to each of my friends' questions—the first made him flush; the second made him look angry—And yet I am innocent—in both cases my Mind leapt over every interval to what I saw was per se a pleasant subject with him—You see I have no allowances to make—you see how far I am from supposing you could show me any neglect. I very much regret the long time I have been obliged to exile from you—for I have had one or two rather pleasant occasions to confer upon with you—What I have heard from George is favorable—I expect soon a Letter from the Settlement itself—

Your sincere friend
John Keats

I cannot give any good news of Tom—[41]

The humanity and moral intelligence derive partly from its simple decision of friendship: that the way to reassure the needlessly apologetic Rice is for Keats himself to apologize in absentia—and needlessly too ("And yet I am innocent")—to "a friend of ours." Rice will be released from his embarrassment by Keats's speaking of his own and of that which he innocently inflicted upon their friend—it is a beautiful instance not only of embarrassment as a binding chain-reaction but also of how the whole chain of the embarrassed can be dislinked and released by one imaginative act of sympathy. But I think that it is not only friendship which creates this release in the letter, but also Keats's sense of art. It is not a coincidence that both of Keats's slips concern art (Severn's portrait and Keats's poems), or that the fertility of mind which creates such slips should be spoken of in terms which suggest the fertility of art: "my Mind leapt over every interval to what I saw was per se a pleasant subject with him". What Keats sees is that the ordinary daily imagination is the same faculty that leaps to reach the delights of art. We must trust this faculty, as we must trust our friends, "notwithstanding any temporery ambiguousness in their behaviour or their tongues." The tact of the whole letter is supreme in its modesty, and it is a tact explicitly devoted to embarrassment; I even think that it was Keats's tact which would not let him risk any slight to Tom, to his own feelings about Tom, or to Rice's, and which therefore saw that the single poignant sentence about his dying brother, "I cannot give any good news of Tom," could not be accommodated within the letter's tone and its concerns and so must stand as a bleakly separate postscript.

A slip or leap of the tongue or of the mind is the not-consciously intended infliction of embarrassment on others, sometimes because they have just inflicted embarrassment on the speaker. But we do deliberately embarrass people, again sometimes because they have just inflicted embarrassment on us. Keats has a splendidly comic account of the comic therapy (to cure the ingratiations of charm) which one of his friends, Dilke, visited upon another, Brown.

> The Place I am speaking of, puts me in mind of a circumsta[n]ce occured lately at Dilkes—I think it very rich and dramatic and quite illustrative of the little quiet fun that he will enjoy sometimes. First I must tell you their house is at the corner of Great Smith Street, so that some of the windows look into one Street, and the back windows into another round the corner—Dilke had some old people to dinner, I know not who—but there were two old ladies among them—Brown was there—they had known him from a Child. Brown is very pleasant with old women, and on that day, it seems, behaved himself so winningly they [that] they became hand and glove together and a little complimentary. Brown was obliged to depart early. He bid them good bye and pass'd into the passage— no sooner was his back turn'd than the old women began lauding him. When Brown had reach'd the Street door and was just going, Dilke threw up the Window and call'd "Brown! Brown! They say you look younger than ever you did!" Brown went on and had just turn'd the corner into the other street when Dilke appeared at the back window crying "Brown! Brown! By God, they say you're handsome!"[42]

Brown had been embarrassingly "winning"; Dilke trumps him, and the whole story has a Chaucerian good humour and vitality, like so much else in Keats's letters. What makes it "very rich and dramatic" is the act of imagination by Dilke, which—as in art seizing a *trouvaille*—seized upon the simple fact of the house's layout in order to plague Brown twice over. The one cry would not have done; alone, it might have seemed shrill or sour; it is the preposterousness of "the *other* street" and the further cry that makes us feel that Dilke has the right to smile, and that even Brown, though he may have blushed, is unlikely to have scowled.

It has to be a finely judged thing, inflicting embarrassment (the fabliau must not get cruel). One feels in this case that both Dilke and now Keats have judged it perfectly. Although it is a pity to risk blurring the anecdote, one of the best and most delicate evocations of embarrassment that I know, I want to quote what introduces and succeeds the anecdote in Keats's letter to his brother George. For Keats comes to this "dramatic" creation of Dilke's imagination from having spoken of drama and farce, and then of that other farce which was Dilke's upbringing of his son; it is "farce"—"Dilke"—and then "window" which stirs the anecdote into life:

Reynolds has turn'd to the law. Bye the bye, he brought out a little piece at the Lyceum call'd *one, two, th[r]ee, four, by advertisement.* It met with complete success. The meaning of this odd title is explained when I tell you the principal actor is a mimic who takes off four of our best performers in the course of the farce—Our stage is loaded with mimics. I did not see the Piece being out of Town the whole time it was in progress. Dilke is entirely swallowed up in his boy: 't is really lamentable to what a pitch he carries a sort of parental mania—I had a Letter from him at Shanklin—He went on a word or two about the isle of Wight which is a bit of hobby horse of his; but he soon deviated to his boy. "I am sitting" says he "at the window expecting my Boy from School." I suppose I told you some where that he lives in Westminster, and his boy goes to the School there. where he gets beaten, and every bruise he has and I dare say deserves is very bitter to Dilke. The Place I am speaking of, puts me in mind of a circumsta[n]ce occurred lately at Dilkes—

As for what succeeds the anecdote, this thinks further about imagination, first in terms of its own attempt at description, then in praise of Robert Burton—and what Burton is imagining with such fertility is the fertile credulity of the lover:

"Brown! Brown! By God, they say you're handsome!" You see what a many words it requires to give any identity to a thing I could have told you in half a minute. I have been reading lately Burton's Anatomy of Melancholy; and I think you will be very much amused with a page I here coppy for you. I call it a Feu de joie round the batteries of Fort St Hyphen-de-Phrase on the birthday of the Digamma. The whole alphabet was drawn up in a Phalanx on the cover of an old Dictionary. Band playing "Amo, Amas &c" "Every Lover admires his Mistress, though she be very deformed of herself, ill-favored, wrinkled, pimpled, pale, red, yellow, tann'd, tallow-fac'd, have a swoln juglers platter face, or a thin, lean, chitty face, have clouds in her face, be crooked, dry, bald . . .

Or, "Brown! Brown! By God, they say you're handsome!"

The relationship of sexual attraction to embarrassment and to imagination is clearly rich in potentiality. I want now to quote Keats's extraordinary evocation of how a woman's sexual self-possession and freedom from embarrassment created in him a corresponding self-possession and freedom. He comes to this gradually. He has been declaring to George and to Georgiana his confidence that he will outdo the reviewers ("I think I shall be among the English Poets after my death"): "It does me not the least harm in Society to make me appear little and rediculous: I know when a Man is superior to me and give him all due respect—he will be the last to laugh at me and as for the rest I feel that I make an impression upon them which insures me personal respect while I am in sight whatever they may say when my back is turned—"[43] He is still thinking of such belittling and of respect a few lines later when he comes to the envy of the Reynolds sisters in the face of the sexual magnetism of their visiting cousin Jane Cox.

The Miss Reynoldses are very kind to me—but they have lately displeased me much and in this way—Now I am coming the Richardson. On my return, the first day I called they were in a sort of taking or bustle about a Cousin of theirs who having fallen out with her Grandpapa in a serious manner, was invited by M^{rs} R—to take Asylum in her house—She is an east indian and ought to be her Grandfather's Heir. At the time I called Mrs R. was in conference with her up stairs and the young Ladies were warm in her praises down stairs calling her genteel, interresting and a thousand other pretty things to which I gave no heed, not being partial to 9 days wonders—Now all is completely changed—they hate her; and from what I hear she is not without faults—of a real kind: but she has othe[r]s which are more apt to make women of inferior charms hate her. She is not a Cleopatra; but she is at least a Charmian. She has a rich eastern look; she has fine eyes and fine manners. When she comes into a room she makes an impression the same as the Beauty of a Leopardess. She is too fine and too conscious of her Self to repulse any Man who may address her—from habit she thinks that nothing *particular*. I always find myself more at ease with such a woman; the picture before me always gives me a life and animation which I cannot possibly feel with any thing inferiour—I am at such times too much occupied in admiring to be awkward or on a tremble. I forget myself entirely because I live in her. You will by this time think I am in love with her; so before I go any further I will tell you I am not—she kept me awake one Night as a tune of Mozart's might do—I speak of the thing as a passtime and an amuzement than which I can feel none deeper than a conversation with an imperial woman the very "yes" and "no" of whose Lips is to me a Banquet. I dont cry to take the moon home with me in my Pocket not [nor] do I fret to leave her behind me. I like her and her like because one has no *sensations*—what we both are is taken for granted—You will suppose I have by this had much talk with her–no such thing—there are the Miss Reynoldses on the look out—They think I dont admire her because I did not stare at her—They call her a flirt to me—What a want of knowledge? she walks across a room in such a manner that a Man is drawn towards her with a magnetic Power. This they call flirting! they do not know things. They do not know what a Woman is. I believe tho' she has faults— the same as Charmian and Cleopatra might have had—Yet she is a fine thing speaking in a worldly way: for there are two distinct tempers of mind in which we judge of things—the worldly, theatrical and pantomimical; and the unearthly, spiritual and etherial—in the former Buonaparte, Lord Byron and this Charmian hold the first

place in our Minds; in the latter John Howard, Bishop Hooker
rocking his child's cradle and you my dear Sister are the conquering
feelings. As a Man in the world I love the rich talk of a Charmian;
as an eternal Being I love the thought of you. I should like her to
ruin me, and I should like you to save me.

I have quoted this at length because I wished to show the generous
feeling both in Keats's disapproval of the envious and in the final
humour with which it is made clear that he does not fret: the humour
which says with childlike and unhurtful dexterity to his sister-in-law,
"I should like her to ruin me, and I should like you to save me."
But the centre of the passage is its release from embarrassment. "The
Beauty of a Leopardess" is that of an animal unembarrassable and
therefore unembarrassing; "too fine and too conscious of her Self"
catches the paradox of a proper self-consciousness. The wrong self-
consciousness is that which manifests itself as an unawareness of other
people's susceptibilities; far from dissolving embarrassment this pre-
cipitates it. Keats deplored this in Leigh Hunt, in a passage which
shows that the congeries of embarrassment, taste, Mozart, and "fine
things" ("Yet she is a fine thing"), was not limited to the vicinity of
Jane Cox: "He understands many a beautiful thing; but then, instead
of giving other minds credit for the same degree of perception as
he himself possesses—he begins an explanation in such a curious
manner that our taste and self-love is offended continually. Hunt does
one harm by making fine things petty and beautiful things hateful—
Through him I am indifferent to Mozart, I care not for white Busts—
and many a glorious thing when associated with him becames a
nothing—"[44]
Jane Cox is too conscious of herself to feel at all self-conscious,
and because of this she offers as it were the benign contagion of
unembarrassment. Keats forgets his self-consciousness in her company:
"I always find myself more at ease with such a woman . . . I am at
such times too much occupied in admiring to be awkward or on a
tremble. I forget myself entirely because I live in her." Once more,
"awkward" and "on a tremble" are Keats's special indication of
embarrassment. Then there is the firm, humorously spelled-out disclaimer that he is in love with her; the comparison, which had earlier
been with a "picture" is now with "a tune of Mozart's," beautiful,
delighted-in personally but not one's own, an art that frees from
embarrassment. Art is suggested too by the delicate paradox of Keats's
feelings for her: "I speak of the thing as a passtime and an amuzement
than which I can feel none deeper"—it wonderfully catches the
paradox of art's deep amusement. Clinching the whole thing, and
embodying the self-possession for which the ordinarily embarrassed
are rightly grateful to the unembarrassable, is this: "I like her and

her like because one has no *sensations*—what we both are is taken for granted." That Jane Cox and he are moved to the right kind of taking for granted is validated by the extraordinary turn of wording: "I like her and her like because . . ." For a moment one blinks and then sees it straight. For Keats has said that he is not in love with her; he has spoken of "such a woman," and he explicitly is not moved by her uniqueness. So he needs to insist that it is part of why he likes her that she so clearly is one of—what? several? a type? a kind? We have only to substitute "I like her and her sort," or "and her kind," "and her type," "and such women"—each of them too aloofly classificatory and unaffectionate—to see how much the delicacy, humour, and humanity of Keats's feelings depends upon his not using a word which could in any way slight her while nevertheless making the point which he needs to make. "I like her and her like": the perfect ease and grace of the transference from the one sense to the other are tenderly unembarrassed by the difficulty of getting the whole feeling exactly right. Keats's self-possession when it comes to animating the language is an exhilarating counterpart to her self-possession as "she walks across a room"; Keats's too is a "a magnetic Power." When we experience his wonderfully perceptive account of these difficult and delicate feelings (a hair's-breadth from infatuation or worldliness or beauty-worship), we are ourselves too much occupied in admiring to be awkward or on a tremble.

Notes

1. John Jones, *John Keats's Dream of Truth* (1969), p. 144. For the 'snailhorn,' see discussion below.

2. Introduction to *The Selected Letters of John Keats* (1951); *The Opposing Self* (1955).

3. To B. R. Haydon, 10–11 May 1817; i. 141.

4. 27 Apr. 1818; i. 273.

5. C. S. Lewis, *A Preface to Paradise Lost* (1942), pp. 118–20.

6. *Milton's God* (revised edn., 1965), p. 105. Compare pp. 106–7: "He may simply have had unexpected feelings about blushes. While at school I was made to read *Ecce Homo* by Sir John Seeley (1866), a life of Jesus which explains that, when he was confronted with the woman taken in adultery and wrote with his finger in the sand, he was merely doodling to hide his blushes; then the book makes some arch comments on his sexual innocence, as if by Barrie about Peter Pan. I thought this in such bad taste as to be positively blasphemous, which rather surprised me as I did not believe in the religion. Milton says in the poem that the rosy red of the angel is love's proper hue, so perhaps he did, in a Victorian manner, regard other people's blushes as a source of keen though blameless sexual pleasure."

7. *John Keats's Dream of Truth*, p. 139.

8. "Embarrassment and Embarrassability," *Sociometry*, xxxi (1968).

9. Bate's *John Keats* is especially illuminating on this.

10. Erving Goffman, *Interaction Ritual* (1967; 1972 edn.), pp. 107–8.

11. Respectively, to George and Tom Keats, 21, 27 (?) Dec. 1817, i. 193; to Richard Woodhouse, 27 Oct. 1818, i. 387; to George and Georgiana Keats, 24 Sept. 1819, ii. 213.

12. *The Criterion,* i (1923), 305.

13. *John Keats's Dream of Truth,* p. 159.

14. 10 Nov. 1813; *Letters and Journals,* ed. R. E. Prothero, iii. 405.

15. See Mrs. Leavis's excellent discussion of this in *Dickens the Novelist* (1970).

16. Edmund Bergler, "A New Approach to the Therapy of Erythrophobia," *Psychoanalytic Quarterly,* xiii (1944).

17. 13 July 1818; i. 326.

18. To Tom Keats, 9 July 1818; i. 321–2.

19. 16 May 1817; i. 145–7.

20. To Haydon, 8 Apr. 1818; i. 265.

21. See p. 149.

22. 10 June 1817; i. 147–8.

23. To George and Georgiana Keats, 29 (?) Dec. 1818; ii. 17.

24. *The Diary of Benjamin Robert Haydon,* ed. Willard Bissell Pope, ii (1960), 106–7.

25. 11 May 1817; i. 143.

26. Robert Gittings, *John Keats* (1968), p. 107 n.

27. To George and Tom Keats, 14(?) Feb. 1818; i. 229.

28. Hyder Rollins notes that Keats twice quotes this line in his letters (i. 214 and i. 246).

29. Woodhouse; quoted by Robert Gittings, *John Keats,* p. 58.

30. 5–6 Aug. 1819; ii. 137.

31. 4 June 1818; i. 291.

32. 25 July 1819; ii. 132–3.

33. 18 Sept. 1819; ii. 189.

34. 24 Sept. 1819; ii. 213.

35. 14 Feb. 1819; ii. 61.

36. i. 300–1.

37. *The Listener,* 25 Nov. 1971.

38. i. 340–2.

39. 16 Aug. 1819; ii. 142.

40. To C. W. Dilke, 31 July 1819; ii. 135.

41. i. 406–7.

42. To George and Georgiana Keats, 18 Sept. 1819; ii. 190.

43. 14 Oct. 1818; i. 394.

44. To George and Georgiana Keats, 17 Dec. 1818; ii. 11.

The Silent Work of Imagination   Leon Waldoff[*]

In a neglected section of the famous letter to Benjamin Bailey of 22 November 1817 in which Keats longs "to be talking about the Imagination," he attempts to describe his sense of how the imagination works:

> But as I was saying—the simple imaginative Mind may have its rewards in the repeti[ti]on of its own silent Working coming continually on the spirit with a fine suddenness—to compare great things with small—have you never by being surprised with an old Melody—in a delicious place—by a delicious voice, fe[l]t over again your very speculations and surmises at the time it first operated on your soul—do you not remember forming to you[r]self the singer's face more beautiful tha[n] it was possible and yet with the elevation of the Moment you did not think so—even then you were mounted on the Wings of Imagination so high—that the Prototype must be here after—that delicious face you will see.[1]

While Keats's primary concern in this passage is to provide support for his earlier assertion that "What the imagination seizes as Beauty must be truth—whether it existed before or not," and specifically for his "favorite Speculation" that the imagination prefigures a reality to come (I, 184), the passage is also of interest for its recognition of unconscious processes at work in the imagination. With words and phrases such as "repeti[ti]on," "its own silent Working," and "coming continually on the spirit with a fine suddenness," Keats calls attention to his sense of unknown workings in the mind. The example of an old melody serves him well. Indeed, what he says might almost be taken as a critical commentary on Wordsworth's "The Solitary Reaper," particularly because the recollection of the Maiden's song comes "Long after it was heard no more" and the poem itself is an act of memory and imagination.[2]

It is a common experience, he tells Bailey, that when surprised by an old melody we involuntarily recall speculations and surmises that accompanied or followed the first hearing. The speculations are not simply recalled, however, but "fe[l]t over again." Earlier in this letter he had said, in support of his faith in "the authenticity of the Imagination," that "our Passions . . . are all in their sublime, creative of essential Beauty" (I, 184). Now he says that in being surprised by an old melody and in recalling one's speculations on first hearing it, one forms the singer's face in the imagination as "more beautiful tha[n] it was possible," apparently under the creative influence of

[*] Reprinted from *Keats and the Silent Work of Imagination* by Leon Waldoff. © 1985 by the Board of Trustees of the University of Illinois. Reprinted by permission of the University of Illinois Press.

the passions, and by a process akin to idealization. Due to the "elevation of the Moment," however, one "[does] not think so." The experience is essentially one of an image and an emotion recollected less in tranquility than in intensity, where processes of feeling and thought are silently at work in the imagination and remain unconscious. Keats does not say that in the later act of thinking about the experience (as now, in the letter to Bailey), one becomes conscious of these processes or able to identify them. He says only that one recognizes later that in the act of remembering one was "mounted on the Wings of Imagination."

Keats never attempted to formulate his ideas on the imagination in anything like a systematic way, as some of the other Romantic writers did, but his remarks to Bailey on the silent work of imagination are far from an isolated comment. In a letter to Benjamin Robert Haydon a few months later (8 April 1818) in which he addresses basically the same question of how the imagination forms a beautiful object (like a singer's face), he says that he is aware that there are "innumerable compositions and decompositions which take place between the intellect and its thousand materials before it arrives at that trembling delicate and snail-horn perception of Beauty" (I, 265). As Sperry has shown, the words "composition," "decomposition," and "materials," along with many other of Keats's favorite words for referring to poetry or the work of imagination ("spiritual," "essential," "etherial," and so forth), all had "more or less exact meanings in the chemistry of his day,"[3] meanings that Keats became familiar with through his study of medicine.

When he employs an analogy between the laws of physical change and the processes of imagination, he does not usually call attention to the idea of unconscious workings. For example, in the letter to his brothers in December 1817 in which he advances the idea of Negative Capability (in the course of some critical remarks on Benjamin West's *Death on a Pale Horse*), he says only that "the excellence of every Art is its intensity, capable of making all disagreeables evaporate, from their being in close relationship with Beauty & Truth" (I, 192). But though no explicit distinction is drawn between conscious and unconscious processes of imagination, the analogy between the disappearance of "disagreeables" in an aesthetic experience and the invisible process of evaporation in chemistry suggests that imaginative experience is of a complexity and "intensity" involving more than purely conscious awareness.

In his remarks on the intensity of art, Keats is thinking of imagination's workings in the viewer of a painting, not in the artist at the time of conception or composition. "It is a wonderful picture, when West's age is considered," he says of *Death on a Pale Horse.* "But there is nothing to be intense upon; no women one feels mad to kiss;

no face swelling into reality. . . . in this picture we have unpleasantness without any momentous depth of speculation excited" (I,
192). But Keats ordinarily makes no distinction between the uses of
imagination in the response to art and in the creation of it. The
viewer of a painting or the reader of a poem is assumed to share,
and in large measure repeat or recreate, the experience of the artist.
"We read fine——things but never feel them to thee full until we
have gone the same steps as the Author" (I, 279). The assumption
that a reader's aesthetic experience repeats or approximates the poet's
creative experience was common to many eighteenth- and nineteenth-
century writers, as it has been to many twentieth-century critics, and
it remains an essential part of Keats's statements about and conception
of the imagination.[4] For example, after the passage cited above, on
the potential of a painting to excite "intensity" in a viewer, he goes
on to make his remarks on Negative Capability, but now in relation
to the mind and imagination of the poet, specifically Shakespeare. In
several attempts to conceptualize the imagination in this letter, Keats
indicates his awareness of mysterious workings, known only approx-
imately, and by surmise and analogy, where "disagreeables evaporate," where "the sense of Beauty . . . obliterates all consideration"
(I, 192, 194), and where processes of imagination are silent like
certain physical processes. Indeed, it is possible that his use of the
phrase "its own silent Working" in the letter to Bailey derives from
his familiarity with the way chemical processes such as evaporation,
distillation, and sublimation work. Near the end of the century Freud
would also revert to analogies with the physical sciences in order to
describe processes of mind that he argued were silently at work in
dreams. Two obvious examples from *The Interpretation of Dreams* are
"displacement" and "condensation," terms that have since been widely
used in literary criticism.

Critics have, of course, recognized that significant aspects of
Keats's thought and feeling emerge from a creative process that is
in large measure unconscious. Words and phrases like "intuition,"
"bias," "habit of mind," "tendency," and "preoccupation" are often
used to indicate some mental activity of the poet that is assumed to
have been more (or less) than purely conscious.[5] But this unconscious
dimension of imagination still needs to be conceptualized and then
integrated into a larger understanding of Keats's thought and development. From the outset, such an undertaking is burdened with
problems. One is the necessity of using metaphor (for example, the
spatial metaphor of an "area" of mind) to conceive a subject that is,
by definition, remote and partly inaccessible. A related problem is
that of finding a reliable means of distinguishing conscious from
unconscious thought, for at anything beyond a superficial level, no
easy or sharp distinction can be maintained, except, perhaps, one

that is at best a critical convenience (and at worst an illusion). Though probably few would doubt that there is an important unconscious dimension to every act of creativity, one cannot help asking if it is possible to distinguish and conceptualize conscious and unconscious processes of thought in a critically useful way. A special problem in this regard is that the only psychology to be centrally concerned with unconscious mental processes—psychoanalysis—has formulated an extremely complex theory of the nature and function of what is often called "the unconscious," one that alternately emphasizes related but quite different viewpoints.[6]

A problem of a different nature is what may be called the visual bias in the conception of imaginative experience. It is inherent in the Latin *imaginatio*, designating the faculty by which the mind forms images or pictures. The imagination is conceived as the mind's eye, and art as a mirror or a lamp. As Ernest Tuveson has pointed out, such a visual bias was an essential feature of the conception of imagination throughout the Enlightenment, even though the imagination was at the same time recognized to be associated with passion and sympathy.[7] The imagination is concerned wtih what is absent. It may reproduce what has been seen, as Wordsworth's daffodils are said to "flash upon that inward eye" ("I Wandered Lonely as a Cloud," l. 21) long after they were first seen. Or, more significantly, the imagination may produce a new vision of a hitherto invisible reality, as when Wordsworth says in "Tintern Abbey" that in the presence of Nature "We see into the life of things" (l. 49). The visual nature of the imagination is undeniably its most distinguishing feature. Yet imaginative experience is not purely visual. It is deeply implicated in other sensations and in emotion. Perhaps because of the strongly visual character of imaginative experience, however, we tend to think of it as largely willed and conscious, even while we remain aware that the Romantic poets themselves often emphasized nonvisual, emotional, and unconscious sources of creativity.[8]

In Keats criticism the general practice has been to introduce the notion of certain unconscious aspects of the poet's mind when considering his personal history, or character, or general tendencies of his imagination, but not to address explicitly the broader subject of the role of unconscious processes of mind and imagination in the poetry. Yet the undercurrents of feeling and thought giving direction to Keats's imagination comprise an important determinant not only of the general shape and content of his poetry but also of his psychological and intellectuaul development. If the attempt to discuss them invites greater risks than attend some other critical subjects, and if the prospects are from the beginning more uncertain, neither the subject nor its importance is diminished by the difficulties of approach. Keats's own recognition of the silent working of the imagination suggests the need to reconsider both his conception and our understanding of his imagination.

His conception of this dimension of the creative mind corresponds to, but is never identical with, that of Wordsworth and Hazlitt, the two most important contemporary influences on his critical thinking. Wordsworth repeatedly linked the imagination to passion and emotion. In his preface to the second edition of *Lyrical Ballads* he defined "all good poetry" as "the spontaneous overflow of powerful feelings" (*Selected Poems and Prefaces*, p. 448), and in *The Excursion*, which Keats at one time thought was one of the three things to rejoice at in the age (along with Haydon's pictures and Hazlitt's depth of taste), Wordsworth speaks of the "strong creative power / Of human passion" (I, 480–81). In *The Prelude*, which Keats could not have read but which frequently acknowledges the presence of unconscious workings in the imagination, and thereby gives expression to an important and in many respects typical view, Wordsworth says that "There is a dark / Invisible workmanship that reconciles / Discordant elements."[9] Although "invisible" is changed to "inscrutable" in the 1850 version of this passage, suggesting an increased sense of the complexity of these workings, the idea of an unconscious aspect of imagination in Wordsworth remains largely restricted to a notion of processes that are simply unknown to consciousness. Resolution and revelation come to him as if sent from some far region that is mysterious but ultimately beneficent. In his typical use of topographical imagery to characterize the mind, this area is perceived as distant and unknown rather than alien ("what beauteous pictures now / Rose . . . As from some distant region of my soul" [*Prelude*, 1805, IV.392–94], "That awful Power rose from the mind's abyss" [1850, VI.594], and so forth).

Keats's sense of unconscious workings in the imagination is closer to that of Hazlitt, who conceives of the imagination as directly linked to processes of feeling and thought in conflict with reason and consciousness. In his lecture "On Poetry in General," the first in a series entitled "Lectures on English Poets," given in January and February 1818 at the Surrey Institution in London and attended more or less regularly by Keats, Hazlitt related poetry and imagination specifically to passions, dreams, and wishes. The imagination, he said, "is that faculty which represents objects, not as they are in themselves, but as they are moulded by other thoughts and feelings, into an infinite variety of shapes and combinations of power."[10] To a large extent these shaping thoughts and feelings are controlled by wishes and passions ("We shape things according to our wishes and fancies, without poetry; but poetry is the most emphatical language that can be found for those creations of the mind 'which ecstasy is very cunning in' " [*Hamlet*, III.iv.138–39])[11] that are unconscious. In an untitled essay in the *Examiner* in 1815 on the general subject of mind and motive, Hazlitt asserted that "we are seldom masters either of our thoughts or of our actions. We are the creatures of imagination, passion, and self-will."[12] After 1815, John Kinnaird has argued, the word "imagination" for Hazlitt almost always refers to "irrational and sub-rational" feelings.[13] What is unconscious is not simply absent from consciousness; it is linked to feelings that are often in opposition to reason and consciousness, and are therefore repressed.[14]

Keats never explicitly addresses the idea of repressed feelings, though the idea that "the sense of Beauty . . . obliterates all consideration" (I, 192) is compatible with a notion of repression. He does conceive of the imagination, however, as subject to unconscious control. In this, as in his conception of the sympathetic nature of imagination and the "camelion" poet (I, 387),[15] and, indeed, as in so many other matters relating to poetry and poets, Keats's affinity with Hazlitt is profound and revealing. Like Hazlitt, he has a strong sense of how the imagination is continually challenged or disturbed by inner longings. "What a happy thing it would be," he wrote to James Rice in March 1818,

> if we could settle our thoughts, make our minds up on any matter in five Minutes and remain content—that is to build a sort of mental Cottage of feelings quiet and pleasant—to have a sort of Philosophical Back Garden, and cheerful holiday-keeping front one— but Alas! this never can be: for as the material Cottager knows there are such places as france and Italy and the Andes and the Burning Mountains—so the spiritual Cottager has knowledge of the terra semi incognita of things unearthly; and cannot for his Life, keep in the check rein. (I, 254–55)

The idea of a mental cottage, a pastoral bower, or, as in "Ode to Psyche," a fane built in some untrodden region of the mind, is always attractive to Keats, but it is usually shown to be in conflict with other aspirations. In this example some aspiration toward a partly unknown mental or spiritual region leads one away from the imaginatively constructed cottage and garden, and one "cannot for his Life, keep in the check rein."

In the metaphor of the "check rein," the imagination, though not named as such, is conceived as driven by an uncontrollable horse, or perhaps several. In mythology, we recall, it is the blow from a horse, Pegasus, that causes the fountain of Hippocrene to rise up, sacred to the muses and symbolic of poetic inspiration. In Plato's myth of the soul in the *Phaedrus* the soul is represented by a charioteer pulled by two steeds in opposing directions, one steed obedient, the other wanton, impulsive, and wayward. In Keats's poetry the imagination is frequently depicted as driven by winged steeds, what Sir

Sidney Colvin once called "the coursers of imagination."[16] In "Sleep and Poetry," for example, the longest poem in Keats's first volume, *Poems* (1817), and typical of the early verse in characterizing the imagination as manly and vigorous, the imagination is depicted as a charioteer crossing the skies, driven by "steeds with streamy manes" (l. 127). "Is there so small a range / In the present strength of manhood," Keats asks, "that the high / Imagination cannot freely fly / As she was wont of old? prepare her steeds, / Paw up against the light, and do strange deeds / Upon the clouds?" ("Sleep and Poetry," ll. 162–67). (In this instance Keats seems to forget—in mid-flight, as it were—that he has just characterized the imagination as masculine.) In a letter to Bailey written when he was nearing the end of *Endymion*, Keats used the equestrian metaphor to characterize the imaginative effort involved in finishing that long poem: "I assure you I shall be glad to dismount for a Month or two—although I'll keep as tight a reign [sic!] as possible till then" (28 October 1817; I, 172). But in the example from the letter to Rice he characterizes the imagination as driven, against its will, out of the home it has made for itself.

I have introduced these examples of equestrian imagery to suggest how Keats's awareness of an unconscious determinant at work in the creative process is often condensed in a traditional metaphor, and almost hidden. A similar figure appears—but with a different emphasis—in a well-known passage of *Biographia Literaria* where Coleridge is describing the workings of "that sympathetic and magical power to which we have exclusively appropriated the name of imagination." "This power," he says, is "first put in action by the will and understanding, and retained under their irremissive, though gentle and unnoticed controul (*laxis effertur habenis*)"; then he adds that it "reveals itself in the balance or reconciliation of opposite or discordant qualities: of sameness, with difference; of the general, with the concrete," and so forth.[17] The Latin phrase may be translated as "driven with loosened reins." Coleridge attributes a greater degree of conscious control to the direction of "this power" than Keats does, for it is said to be retained under the "irremissive" control of the "will and understanding." He hedges the issue of conscious control, however, with the word "unnoticed" and the image of "loosened reins." On other occasions he could concede that the imagination works under much less conscious control than he grants here, as in his comments on how "Kubla Khan" was composed, or in his *Notebooks*. There is "in genius itself," he wrote in his essay "On Poesy or Art," "an unconscious activity; nay, that is the genius in the man of genius."[18]

Freud, in an early characterization of the relationship between conscious and unconscious thought, wrote Wilhelm Fliess a letter in which he said that one of the chapters of *The Interpretation of Dreams* "was all written by the unconscious, on the well-known principle of Itzig, the Sunday horseman. 'Itzig, where are you going?' 'Don't ask me, ask the horse!' "[19] Freud remained fond of this analogy, using it again in *The Interpretation of Dreams,* and, over twenty years later, in *The Ego and the Id,* where, in characterizing the relationship of the ego (itself now conceived as largely unconscious) and the instinctual id, he comments wryly on the ego's illusion of control by observing that "often a rider, if he is not to be parted from his horse, is obliged to guide it where it wants to go."[20] Through all his revisions of psychoanalytic theory over a forty-year period, Freud remained convinced that the unconscious area of the mind exercised far greater influence over thought and action than did the conscious area, certainly more than the latter is willing to concede, though the question of the precise degree of control, like so many other questions raised by psychological and other theories invoking some form of determinism, remains indeterminate.

Keats's sense of the strain on conscious control may be said to lie somewhere between Coleridge's image of "loosened reins" and Freud's image of guiding the horse where it wants to go. At times he even expresses the view that control over the imagination should be relaxed. For example, in the poem "Fancy" (Keats makes no distinction between fancy and imagination), we are urged to "Break the mesh / Of the Fancy's silken leash. . . . Let the winged Fancy roam, / Pleasure never is at home" (ll. 89–94). For a better understanding of his views on the matter of control, however, we need to look at the verse epistle "Dear Reynolds," which was written in the same month that he completed the revision of *Endymion* and in a period of his life of substantial change and even crisis.[21] Although he never intended this poem for publication and began with no clearer intention than that of cheering his friend, who was ill with rheumatic fever, it has proved all the more valuable for its relatively unguarded manner, what Keats himself called its "unconnected subject, and careless verse" (*Letters,* I, 263).

In the opening lines he recounts for Reynolds the thoughts of a sleepless night, where "shapes, and shadows, and remembrances" came both to "vex and please." "Few are there," he states, "who escape these visitings" (l. 13). The catalogue of seemingly disconnected thoughts ("Old Socrates a tying his caveat; / And Hazlitt playing with Miss Edgeworth's cat"—ll. 9–10) may be a playful reenactment of the experience of the previous night along the lines of Hartley's associationism, with which Keats would have had some familiarity, both from his reading of Hazlitt's *Essay on the Principles of Human Action* (1805) and from the general current of ideas at the time.[22] But in the lines immediately following the description of

Claude's *The Enchanted Castle* his imagination takes a direction owing more to what a year earlier he had called his "horrid Morbidity of Temperament" (I, 142). When he wishes that "our dreamings all of sleep or wake / Would all their colours from the sunset take . . . Rather than shadow our own soul's daytime / In the dark void of night" (ll. 67–71), he acknowledges that the imagination—the waking dreaming—is under domination of some dark power. He recognizes that some questions cannot be resolved: "Things cannot to the will / Be settled, but they tease us out of thought" (ll. 76–77). But then he asks,

> Or is it that imagination brought
> Beyond its proper bound, yet still confined,—
> Lost in a sort of purgatory blind,
> Cannot refer to any standard law
> Of either earth or heaven?
>
> (ll. 78–82)

Here the imagination is not simply a visual power but a complex mode of thought, both "Lost" and "blind," "confined" yet detached from the regulating laws that make the world rationally comprehensible. Keats goes on to tell Reynolds that though it was "a quiet eve," and he was "at home, / And should have been most happy," he "saw / Too far into the sea; where every maw / The greater on the less feeds evermore . . . The shark at savage prey—the hawk at pounce, / The gentle robin . . . Ravening a worm" (ll. 89–105).[23] Once again imagination is driven from home, this time, however, toward a vision "Of an eternal fierce destruction" (l. 97). Keats's sense of imagination, as driven beyond its proper bound and kept at the mercy of "horrid moods, / Moods of one's mind!" (ll. 105–6), parallels Hazlitt's views and to some extent Freud's.

In the verse epistle to Reynolds, Keats acknowledges internal conflict and depression more openly than almost anywhere else in the letters or poetry, yet his moods of extreme dejection, at times called the "blue devils" (II, 168, 210), were anything but uncommon. Some of the poetry written on the Scottish tour acknowledges dark moods in which, as Keats remarks in the sonnet "On Visiting the Tomb of Burns," a "Sickly imagination" makes him "sin against" the "native skies" of Burns. In "There is a joy in footing slow across a silent plain," written at roughly the same time as the sonnet, July 1818, he recognizes that "Man feels the gentle anchor" of the human bond and "gladdens in its strength" (I. 40), but ends the poem with a "prayer" "That man may never lose his mind on mountains bleak and bare" and that he will "keep his . . . inward sight unblind" (II. 45–48). The notion of a blinded imagination suggests the degree of internal conflict that is felt.

Keats often makes an effort to overcome depression, as when he writes Haydon in January 1819, shortly after Tom's death, "yet I do not think I shall ever come to the rope or the Pistol: for after a day or two's melancholy, although I smoke more and more my own insufficiency—I see by little and little more of what is to be done" (II, 32). But the dark moods continue to return, forming part of an unceasing psychological process in which the imagination is deeply involved. He elaborates on the involvement in a letter to Charles Brown (23 September 1819) in which he attempts to explain what has been a history of "Imaginary grievances":

> Imaginary grievances have always been more my torment than real ones. You know this well. Real ones will never have any other effect upon me than to stimulate me to get out of or avoid them. This is easily accounted for. Our imaginary woes are conjured up by our passions, and are fostered by passionate feeling; our real ones come of themselves, and are opposed by an abstract exertion of mind. Real grievances are displacers of passion. The imaginary nail a man down for a sufferer, as on a cross; the real spur him up into an agent. (II, 181)

To some extent the use of the word "imaginary" here corresponds to Keats's frequent attempts in the poetry, usually as part of the conclusion of a poem, to establish a distinction between what is real and what imaginary or illusory, a distinction recalling Dr. Johnson's sense of imagination as self-deceiving, in need of disciplined restraint. The distinction is obviously important in a poem like *Lamia*. Yet in other poems where the distinction is crucial—"La Belle Dame," for example—the dream or vision has a presence that refuses to be put by. At the end of "Ode to a Nightingale," Keats is uncertain whether he has experienced a "vision real" (as he had written in an early draft) or a "waking dream." An unavoidable implication in the remark to Brown is that the "imaginary woes . . . conjured up by our passions" are real. They may well be imaginary in the sense that they seem to be only of the mind's making and cannot be attributed to outward circumstance. But the important meaning of the remark, taken as a whole, and in the context of other similar remarks in the letters on "imaginary griefs" or "ills" (cf. II, 113, 186, 210), is that in another sense they are all too real. Indeed, the effort to regard them as purely imaginary may be seen as largely defensive, made in order to avoid seeming to oneself and others to be nailed down for a sufferer.

My purpose in examining Keats's awareness of the unconscious dimension of his imagination and the immediate Romantic context of this awareness has been not to propose an interpretation of his poetry based on Hazlitt's sweeping statement that "the definition of genius is that it acts unconsciously,"[24] but to emphasize Keats's sense of an unknown and often conflicted inner control. The nature of this control over his creative life needs to be explored and defined, then conceptualized in relation to the dominant patterns of thought in his poetry and development. It represents a unique determinant of the character of his imagination, the attitude he takes toward this power of mind, and the structure and content of his poetry. His use of the word "mood" (or of the phrase "Imaginary grievances") to refer to some unknown disturbance attempts to minimize its importance and misleads us to suppose that it is only a minor, temporary aberration. The language evades the possibility that the imagination may be subject to a deeply ingrained psychological pattern that challenges the mind's image of itself as self-willed. This is not to argue that Keats's imagination was under the total domination of unconscious processes but, rather, to open up for critical exploration the intricacies of the relationship between the strongly visual character of imaginative experience and the matrix of feeling and thought giving the experience life and direction.

Consider, for example, the theme of the visionary imagination in his poetry and the question of its significance. At least as early as the writing of Book IV of *Endymion* in the autumn of 1817, and certainly no later than the revision of it in January–March 1818, Keats recognized the limitations of the visionary imagination and the consequences of failing to distinguish between dreams and reality. Yet he continued to write on this theme and to test various propositions about it for the next two years. This seeming anomaly in his intellectual development poses a number of questions. What kind of "recognition" requires repetition in poem after poem? If a recognition of the distinction between imagination and reality is a significant part of the conclusion of his major poems, what implications for interpreting them, either individually or collectively, are inherent in the repetition? What implications for our conception of Keats's psychological and intellectual development are inherent in the apparent need to repeat this recognition?

One might begin to answer these questions with the observation that the repetition indicates the persistence of a conflict between an awareness that there should be "no more of dreaming," as Endymion remarks to the Indian maiden (IV.669), and an irrepressible wish that dreams could come true. The verbs "seizes" and "must be" in the 22 November 1817 letter to Bailey (I, 184) represent Keats's insistence on the wish. The real difficulty he faced in his preoccupation with the visionary imagination was not in recognizing its limitations but in reconciling himself to them. He was all too aware that dreams don't come true, that "You cannot eat your cake and have it too" (the proverb he placed as an epigraph to the sonnet "How fever'd is the man"), and that "Things cannot to the will / Be settled" ("Dear Reynolds," ll. 76–77). But wish and will continually reasserted themselves, and one continued to form the singer's face as more beautiful than it had been. Here is a significant unconscious dimension of the visionary imagination. Something compels us to see beyond our bourn. The imagination has reasons that reason will hear nothing of. Or, to paraphrase Freud, the poet's imagination guides him in whatever direction his preoccupations decide to go.

The problem of repetition raises the further question of how a recognition or thought comes to be accepted (or rejected). Axioms in philosophy, Keats believed, "are not axioms until they are proved upon our pulses" (I, 279). Yet the process by which an axiom comes to be proved upon the pulse is far from clear. Keats naturally tends to conceive of the process very generally as "experience." "Nothing ever becomes real till it is experienced," he said. "Even a Proverb is no proverb to you till your Life has illustrated it" (II, 81). Certainly his own life was filled with experiences that could quickly transform proverbs into felt truths, and it is not surprising that after the death of Tom he wrote to the George Keatses that "the common observations of the commonest people on death are as true as their proverbs" (II, 4). Yet experience itself, he realized, is finally an internal process. The "vale of Soul-making" passage, his most ambitious attempt to theorize about the role of experience in one's development, seeks to understand how circumstances are transformed into touchstones in one's mind: "and what are touch stones?—but proovings of his hearrt?—and what are proovings of his heart but fortifiers or alterers of his nature? and what is his altered nature but his soul?" (II, 103). Not only the rhetorical flourish of the phrasing, with its use of repetition, but also the substance of the whole passage reflects Keats's sense of an internal process by which feelings and thoughts are repeated and "proven" until they converge to form an axiom felt on the pulse, altering one's nature.

The presence of a considerable degree of repetition (not only of recognition scenes but of similar characters, situations, images, problems, and themes) is, of course, not surprising. We expect repetition, and when it occurs with marked frequency we call its object a "preoccupation" or, on occasion, an "obsession." What would be surprising and unnatural would be the absence of any significant repetition. Aside from representing a natural strain of consistency and coherence, however, the repetition serves as a reminder that the poetry evolved as part of a larger process of psychological and intellectual development, a process that maintains a sense of inner continuity and identity in the midst of unrelenting change only by repeatedly singling out and reasserting what is most essential. That larger process of development is most familiar to us, outside of explicit biography, in the form of dominant themes in the poetry, representing the main currents of Keats's thought. The themes are well known: love that is unfulfilled and wasting, the pursuit of beauty, the problem of identity, the burden of the past, the visionary imagination, the quest for permanence, among others. Above all is the inescapable problem of the transient nature of everything and the whole problem of human mutability, with all the unanswerable questions it raises.

More than any other theme, however, melancholy holds a special potential to reveal the relationship of imagination to controlling undercurrents of feeling and thought. Although it runs through the poetry like a dark vein of marble, especially in the odes, where it is once announced as the central theme, it has attracted little attention. Yet one need only recall Keats's fascination with Burton's *Anatomy of Melancholy* and the prominence given to human and divine states of mourning and melancholy in *Isabella, Hyperion,* "La Belle Dame," *The Fall of Hyperion,* and of course the odes to appreciate its pervasiveness. "I strive to search wherefore I am so sad, / Until a melancholy numbs my limbs" (*Hyperion,* III. 88–89), cries the still mortal Apollo, soon to be replaced by the poet in *The Fall of Hyperion.* What Douglas Bush said long ago of the importance of melancholy in "Ode to a Nightingale" and "Ode on a Grecian Urn" may without exaggeration be extended to most of the poetry for which Keats is now remembered: "It is the very acme of melancholy that the joy he celebrates is joy in beauty that must die. Even when Keats proclaims that the song of the bird is immortal, that the sculptured lover feels an enduring love that is beyond the pains of human passion, his deepest emotions are fixed on the obverse side of his theme. . . . The author of these odes hears the still, sad music of humanity, but he tries to escape from it."[25]

Bush's allusion to "Tintern Abbey" reminds us that Keats remarked in his March 1819 journal letter to the George Keatses that he liked "half" of Wordsworth (II, 69). Since the remark was never elaborated upon, we do not know which "half" he liked or how he conceived it. Yet in his review of Reynold's parody of *Peter Bell,* written on 21 April 1819 and published that week in the *Examiner,* he contrasted "the sad embroidery of the *Excursion,*" which he so admired, with "the coarse sample[r]s of Betty Foy and Alice Fell." Certainly one reason for his admiration of Wordsworth was the older poet's concern with the "Burthen of the Mystery" (a recurrent phrase in Keats's letters) and the sadness inherent in human experience. A little more than a month after writing the review, he revealed in a letter to Mary-Ann Jeffery[26] (31 May 1819) the resonance he now felt for two lines from the Immortality Ode ("Though nothing can bring back the hour / Of splendour in the grass, of glory in the flower"—II. 177–78): "I once thought this a Melancholist's dream"

(II, 113). The deepest strains of sadness and loss in the poems by Wordsworth that Keats is known to have especially admired—"Tintern Abbey," *The Excursion*, the Immortality Ode—spoke to some corresponding sense of loss in him.[27] We know that the dark passages that he said Wordsworth had explored and that he hoped to continue to explore did lead eventually to the sovran shrine of Veil'd Melancholy.

In considering how a sense of loss or a melancholy (or "horrid") mood often pre-empts the attention of Keats's imagination and drives it from its home, or beyond its proper bound, we will have to be concerned with the possible causes of melancholy in his experience, particularly in the circumstances that shaped his early life. Crucial though the causes of melancholy are in any effort to understand the history and character of his imagination, however, they are less important to consider than the purpose of the mournful and melancholy states of mind found throughout the poetry. Although we do not ordinarily think of melancholy as having a purpose, perhaps because we tend to see it instead as a result or a symptom, it represents a form of psychological "work" that seeks to resolve a problem. In one of his most important metapsychological papers, "Mourning and Melancholia," Freud proposed in effect to view melancholia as a more complex and extended form of mourning, which, he asserted, had the aim of freeing the mind from its attachment to a person or object that is dead or lost so that it might form new attachments to other (or substitute) objects. "In what," he asked, "does the work which mourning performs consist?"

> Reality-testing has shown that the loved object no longer exists, and it proceeds to demand that all libido shall be withdrawn from its attachments to that object. This demand arouses understandable opposition—it is a matter of general observation that people never willingly abandon a libidinal position, not even, indeed, when a substitute is already beckoning to them. This opposition can be so intense that a turning away from reality takes place and a clinging to the object through the medium of a hallucinatory wishful psychosis. Normally, respect for reality gains the day. Nevertheless, its orders cannot be obeyed at once. They are carried out bit by bit, at great expense of time and cathectic energy, and in the meantime the existence of the lost object is psychically prolonged. Each single one of the memories and expectations in which the libido is bound to the object is brought up and hypercathected, and detachment of the libido is accomplished in respect of it. . . . when the work of mourning is completed the ego becomes free and uninhibited again.[28]

While he distinguished normal mourning from melancholia by its consciousness of an actual loss, by its limited duration, and by its apparent lack of ambivalence, he emphasized that because we never willingly abandon a loved object, even when directed to by reality, an effort is made in both mourning and melancholia to preserve the object and our relationship with it by a process of introjection.[29] In mourning, this process is evident in efforts to preserve various effects of the dead person and generally to recall, often with a strong mixture of idealization and affection, attitudes and characteristics as part of a deeper effort at restoration and preservation of our image of the person. The process often includes some identification, an adoption of these attitudes as part of our own behavior and identity. Even though we go on to establish new relationships with others, we never wholly abandon the relationship with the internal object. Ten years after the death of his second daughter, Sophie, as a result of influenza, Freud commented, "Although we know that after such a loss the acute state of mourning will subside, we also know we shall remain inconsolable and will never find a substitute. . . . And actually this is how it should be. It is the only way of perpetuating that love which we do not want to relinquish."[30]

Much of what Freud says about the psychology of mourning and melancholia holds important implications for any effort to understand the character and function of Keats's imagination. This is not to argue that he suffered from severe melancholia or extended periods of depression, or that the horrid moods of which he spoke at the end of the epistle to Reynolds completely dominated his imagination. On the contrary, from all that we know of his life (beyond the bare facts, what his friends said about him, what the incomparably natural letters reveal, what may be reasonably inferred from the poetry) it is clear that the elements were so mixed in him that one might truly say, using Wordsworth's definition of a poet, this was "a man . . . endowed with more lively sensibility, more enthusiasm and tenderness . . . a greater knowledge of human nature, and a more comprehensive soul, than are supposed to be common among mankind" (*Selected Poems and Prefaces*, p. 453). Few would question Lionel Trilling's use of the word "heroic" to characterize Keats's life and work.[31] If it can be applied to poets, none merits it more than Keats. Yet the word must not be allowed to obscure or minimize the struggle that justifies its use. Especially important is the need to avoid imposing neat but artificial limits on our conception of what is normative or healthy as we read the letters and poems. They are a record of great emotional and intellectual courage but also of loss and the fear of loss, extreme disappointment, and despair. Keats often felt that he was having to choose, as he once remarked, "between despair & Energy" (II, 113). The true measure of his frequently heroic choice of energy and life cannot be taken without due appreciation of the depths of despair against which the choice is made.

Freud's description of the work of mourning provides a structure or context within which the unconscious processes evident in the poetry may be seen to work with cohesion and unity of purpose in the direction they give to the imagination. The path that mourning takes, with its desire to recover the past, on the one hand, and to adapt to the unavoidable present, on the other, indicates the pattern that the unconscious processes of imagination follow in Keats's poems. Of foremost importance is Freud's emphasis on the mind's effort to maintain its relationship with a lost object through the continual creation of images of it and the striking of attitudes toward it. The effort does not necessarily represent a will to live in the past, a danger Keats depicts in characters like Isabella, who dies mourning the disappearance and death of Lorenzo, and the Knight-at-arms, whose sojourn is on a plain of melancholy. The effort may instead represent a determination to bring forward into the present what is felt to be most valuable from the past. Such a determination is evident in Keats's poetry in the attempt to establish a relationship with a figure like the fading immortal, Psyche, or with symbolic objects like the Nightingale and the Urn, which are imagined as descendants of a lost pastoral and mythological time. The mind's effort to maintain a relationship with an object felt to be lost is also evident in the structure of Keats's poetry, particularly in the repeated staging of scenes of separation, surprised encounter, and reunion. The poet's encounter with Moneta, the transformed image of Mnemosyne, goddess of memory, in *The Fall of Hyperion* might almost be taken as a psychological allegory of the imagination's fate in Keats's poetry.

Keats's return to scenes and characters inherited from mythology and his deep-browed precursors, from Homer to Shakespeare, suggests a devotion to literary tradition. Yet the persistence of his effort to establish a relationship with a figure from an idealized lost world, an effort so often represented in the aspiring mood of an apostrophe, indicates a need that cannot be fully explained either as impersonal imitation of forms from the past or as escape into the worlds conjured up by the mighty dead. At the end of the epistle to Reynolds, it is true, Keats remarked that he would "from detested moods in new romance / Take refuge" (II. 111–12), and shortly thereafter he turned to *Isabella*. Elsewhere he displays a tendency to take refuge in an imaginary world where the conditions of existence could be redefined more according to the heart's desire. Beyond this general tendency, however, the repeated staging of scenes of encounter between Keats's mortal heroes and various goddesses, naiads, and other supernatural figures, or between himself and a symbolic object, may be thought of more specifically as reencounters with an image from the depths of his own psyche, though the image is often displaced to mythology and then idealized (Cynthia), or in some other way distorted (Circe or Lamia), or disguised (the Indian maiden), or veiled (Moneta). In a sense every significant encounter, Freud would remind us, is a re-encounter, every choice a rediscovery.[32] Aileen Ward has suggested that behind the frequently veiled or mysterious faces of Keats's heroines one can discern the face of his mother, and other critics (and some psychoanalysts) have also discussed the maternal image underlying his heroines, particularly la Belle Dame sans Merci.[33] Of course, when we sit down to read *Endymion, Lamia,* or another poem, Frances Jennings Keats remains a very remote figure, as she probably seemed to Keats in the act of writing. Yet she is throughout the poetry what Cynthia is for most of *Endymion,* and what Endymion calls his moon goddess, a "known Unknown" (II. 739). In interpretation Frances Keats is less significant as a distinct identity in the life of Keats than as the vanished original of a much-transformed but still dynamic inner object with which the various heroines and scenes of encounter in the poetry continue to have a relationship requiring critical analysis.

Their recurrence indicates that a process in Keats's imagination is continually at work restoring and ultimately transforming an image of an inner object (or subliminal figure) associated with loss in order to maintain a relationship with it. Keats's life, the story of which is too well known to need retelling here, was marked by a series of losses: his infant brother Edward (when Keats was seven), his father, his grandfather, his uncle Midgley Jennings, his mother, and his grandmother, all before he had turned twenty. His brother Tom died when Keats was twenty-three. No other Romantic poet suffered the loss of so many members of his immediate family in such rapid succession or in such an early period of his life. In addition to the deaths, however, Keats had the potentially more traumatic experience of losing his mother twice: first, shortly after his father's death, when she made a hasty, ill-considered second marriage and, upon its failure, left Keats (then nearly eleven) and the other children with her mother while she went to live elsewhere, probably with a man named Abraham in another part of London; second, when she returned sick with consumption and died, Keats being then only fourteen. A significant part of Keats's mind and achievement would later be constructed on the ruins of that relationship. If it had not been for Keats's grandmother, who herself was soon to die, Keats, his two brothers, and his sister would have been left destitute and "Trooping together" as they might, as Wordsworth, the Romantic poet with whom Keats had the deepest affinity, had already characterized retrospectively the situation of himself and his brothers and sister after the death of their mother (*Prelude,* 1805, V. 256–60). In short, one does not have to probe very deep into Keats's life to discover the kind of experience that could easily account not only for the sense of loss and the acute sensitivity to transience and mutability in the poetry, but also for the preoccupation with real or potential separations and the mournful or melancholy moods they engender.

The idea that a poet could use his imagination as a means of repairing an absence or fulfilling an unsatisfied wish was set forth by Freud in his 1908 paper "Creative Writers and Day-Dreaming." "The motive forces of phantasies," he wrote, "are unsatisfied wishes, and every single phantasy is the fulfillment of a wish, a correction of unsatisfying reality."[34] Although Freud's statement represents an oversimplification of the motives and nature of the wish fulfillment to be found in art, it is nonetheless illuminating to set beside it a recollection by Keats of a boyhood daydream: "When I was a School-boy," he wrote to Bailey in July 1818, "I though[t] a fair Woman a pure Goddess, my mind was a soft nest in which some one of them slept though she knew it not" (I, 341). The daydream is especially significant because he remembered it in his adulthood. It represents a wish that would not die. The "pure Goddess" whom he held in fantasy when he was a boy was an attempt, all too understandable, to restore to himself an image of the maternal presence that had disappeared.

This earliest known effort at restoration may be thought of as the prototype of the later, more elaborate and varied attempts in the poetry. Like the daydream reported to Bailey (who was the recipient of Keats's most revealing letters concerning his attitude toward women), the effort at restoration originates in feelings of separation anxiety, which Keats would have experienced when his mother left him and her other three children to go and live with another man after her second marriage had failed, though he is not thought to have known the cause of this separation.[35] Joseph Severn recalled that "Keats used to say that his great misfortune had been that from his infancy he had no mother."[36] The experience of separation would have been most painful, of course, when she died. Edward Holmes, a fellow student at John Clarke's school, recalled of Keats many years later that "when his mother died—which was suddenly—he gave way to such impassioned & prolonged grief—(hiding himself in a nook under the master's desk) as awakened the liveliest pity & sympathy in all who saw him" (KC, II, 165). Keats does not speak directly of her in the letters, but in the one to Bailey in which he recalls the daydream he remarks, "When I am among Women I have evil thoughts, malice spleen . . . I am full of Suspicions. . . . You must be charitable and put all this perversity to my being disappointed since Boyhood. . . . I must absolutely get over this—but how? . . . That is a difficult thing; for an obstinate Prejudice can seldom be produced but from a gordian complication of feelings, which must take time to unravell and care to keep unravelled" (I, 341–42). Because this comment

about a disappointment felt since boyhood is made in the context of
a passage concerning his attitude toward women, it would be difficult
not to think that it refers in some way to his mother. As Gittings
has observed, Keats's "complete silence about her suggests some
shattering knowledge, with which, at various times in his life, he can
be seen struggling to come to terms."[37]

It must be admitted, however, that the specific nature of the
disappointment remains in the area of speculation. We do not know,
nor does it seem to make much difference for purposes of interpreting
the poetry, whether the sense of disappointment first arose as a part
of his earliest, pre-oedipal relationship with his mother, or out of
later oedipal and sibling rivalry, or because of her remarriage soon
after his father's death (perhaps reawakening an old rivalry in the
presence of the new stepfather), or because of her seeming abandonment of him and the other children when the second marriage
failed, or because of her death, or, indeed, because of some combination of all of these. What does matter is his repeated concern
throughout the poetry with scenes of separation from or encounter
with mortal heroines, goddesses, or symbolic objects associated with
loss, or with an irretrievable past, and his persistent efforts to deny,
deal with, or evade the consequences of loss by imagining situations
where it is feared or experienced and where an attitude toward it is
then developed. In one of his last letters to Charles Brown, written
aboard the *Maria Crowther* while it waited in harbor at Yarmouth
before sailing for Italy, we are given some idea of how painful the
sense of separation and loss, and how irrepressible the desire to evade
it, could be: "The thought of leaving Miss Brawne is beyond every
thing horrible—the sense of darkness coming over me—I eternally
see her figure eternally vanishing. Some of the phrases she was in
the habit of using during my last nursing at Wen[t]worth place ring
in my ears—Is there another Life? Shall I awake and find all this a
dream? There must be we cannot be created for this sort of suffering"
(30 September 1820; II, 345–46).

It is part of the larger story of Keats's psychological and intellectual development that he came to recognize the impossibility of
a permanent union, or even of an imaginary one, with a symbol of
permanence like the Urn, and to accept final separations as an inherent
part of human experience. Yet, as we have already seen, it was a
recognition that had to be achieved anew again and again, and could
never be unreservedly and finally accepted. The undying longing for
permanence had arisen in a gordian complication of feelings that
Keats did not have sufficient time to unravel and keep unraveled, if
indeed that was (or is) ever a real possibility. As aware as one might
be that fancy cannot cheat so well as she is fam'd to do, one would
always imagine the singer's face as more beautiful than it had been.

Try as one might to impose a limitation on desire, to say that this is all we know on earth and all we need to know, the ancient longing would always reassert itself. Keats's skepticism toward dreams, dreamers, and the visionary capacity of imagination would be forever in conflict with the simultaneous and persistent longing of the spiritual cottager in him who knew that he could not for his life keep in the check rein. For this reason Keats cannot really be thought to embrace or accept the limitations of this world in any final or unqualified way. The very nature of desire will not allow it. Much of the uncertainty and indeterminacy in his thought, especially as reflected in the odes and discussed by Sperry, arises from the fundamental impossibility of controlling imagination and the desire impelling it toward a finer conception of its object.

Imagination, more than any other critical issue, defines the essential quality of Keats as a Romantic poet. Its central role in his poetry and in every aspect of his life and thought, even in his representation of his doubts about it, and his repeated and irrepressible return to the quest for an affirming vision, make him a more complex adherent of the Romantic principle (or trust) that imagination can reconcile human nature to external reality than has been generally recognized. The adherence is evident in the unending quest conducted at the deepest levels of mind by the silent work of imagination, which repeatedly seeks to heal an insistent sense of loss and to deal with its more conscious complements—a penetrating awareness of the transience of human life and a concern with philosophical questions raised by that awareness. The sense of loss establishes a task for the *whole* mind of the poet. In the "vale of Soul-making" passage, we recall, Keats seems to feel that a touchstone or axiom is proved on the pulse when it fortifies or alters one's nature. By the time he had completed "Ode on Melancholy" and "To Autumn," it is widely agreed, he had changed. But how his mind was fortified or his nature altered cannot be explained without an account of the role of the unconscious dimension of imagination. Its silent work is the untold story of his achievement and development.

Notes

1. *The Letters of John Keats, 1814–1821*, ed. Hyder E. Rollins, 2 vols. (Cambridge, Mass.: Harvard University Press, 1958), I, 185. References by volume and page number are hereafter included in the text. Quotations from the poetry are from *The Poems of John Keats*, ed. Jack Stillinger (Cambridge, Mass.: Harvard University Press, 1978), with line numbers given in the text following the quotation. The most thorough discussion of the 22 Nov. 1817 letter to Bailey is still Newell Ford's in *The Prefigurative Imagination of John Keats* (Stanford, Calif.: Stanford University Press, 1951), pp. 20–38. But one should also see Stillinger's "Keats's Letter to Bailey on the Imagination" in *The Hoodwinking of Madeline and Other Essays on Keats's Poems* (Urbana: University

of Illinois Press, 1971), pp. 151–57, and Robert Ryan's "Keats and the Truth of the Imagination," *Wordsworth Circle*, 4 (1973), 259–66 (revised for *Keats: The Religious Sense* [Princeton, N.J.: Princeton University Press, 1976], pp. 129–40).

2. *William Wordsworth: Selected Poems and Prefaces*, ed. Jack Stillinger (Boston: Houghton Mifflin, 1965), p. 367, l. 32. References to Wordsworth's poetry (except for *The Prelude*) and prefaces are to this edition and are hereafter given in the text.

3. Stuart M. Sperry, *Keats the Poet* (Princeton, N.J.: Princeton University Press, 1973), p. 37. See also Coleridge's remark in *Biographia Literaria*, ed. John Shawcross, 2 vols. (London: Oxford University Press, 1907), II, 12–13, that what Sir John Davies observes of the "soul" "may with slight alteration be applied, and even more appropriately, to the poetic IMAGINATION," and particularly the analogies from chemistry in the poem by Davies that Coleridge cites, where the soul "turns / Bodies to spirit by sublimation strange" and "abstracts," "draws," and "transforms" things.

4. Wordsworth reveals his expectation that a reader will repeat the poet's experience in his 14 June 1802 letter to Sara Hutchinson when he attempts to explain his "feeling" at the time of writing "Resolution and Independence": "A person reading this Poem with feelings like mine will have been awed and controuled, expecting almost something spiritual or supernatural" (*The Letters of William and Dorothy Wordsworth, The Early Years, 1787–1805*, ed. Ernest de Selincourt, 2nd ed., rev. Chester L. Shaver [Oxford: Clarendon Press, 1967], p. 366).

5. David Perkins, for example, in his influential discussion of how Keats "tended to resolve the large, unanswerable perplexities . . . by constructing myths of process," states that the tendency was "a major bias of his imagination" (*The Quest for Permanence: The Symbolism of Wordsworth, Shelley, and Keats* [Cambridge, Mass.: Harvard University Press, 1959], p. 197). Morris Dickstein, in his study of "the problem of consciousness" in Keats's poetry, argues that Keats sought to overcome a "death wish" (or "quest for unconsciousness") that was itself largely unconscious in its regressive nature (*Keats and His Poetry: A Study in Development* [Chicago: University of Chicago Press, 1971], p. 25). Sperry, in his study of the poetic process in Keats, interprets the remarks on Negative Capability as "more than anything an attempt to justify poetry as a kind of thinking we might consider unconscious or preconscious" (p. 63), and in his discussion of individual poems he repeatedly relates the imagination's workings to wish and unconscious impulse as well as to conscious will and realization. Other critics have explored special concerns where many of the processes of the poet's thought are assumed to have been unconscious. See, for example, Northrop Frye's study of romance in *Endymion* in *A Study of English Romanticism* (New York: Random House, 1968), pp. 125–65; Harold Bloom's discussions of poetic influence on Keats in *A Map of Misreading* (New York: Oxford University Press, 1975), pp. 152–56 (on "Ode to Psyche"), and in "Keats: Romance Revised," in *Poetry and Repression* (New Haven, Conn.: Yale University Press, 1976), pp. 112–42 (on *The Fall of Hyperion)*; and Stuart Ende's *Keats and the Sublime* (New Haven, Conn.: Yale University Press, 1976). Thomas Weiskel's *The Romantic Sublime: Studies in the Structure and Psychology of Transcendence* (Baltimore: John Hopkins University Press, 1976) deserves a special word. In this difficult, original, and searching book, Weiskel employs a psychoanalytic conception of the unconscious dimension of imagination. His primary concern is with the experience of the sublime, however, and his passing remarks on Keats do not form a sustained commentary.

6. In his 1915 essay entitled "The Unconscious," Freud distinguished between three theoretical viewpoints: topographical, dynamic, and economic. See *The Standard Edition of the Complete Psychological Works of Sigmund Freud*, trans. James Strachey et al., ed. James Strachey, 24 vols. (London: Hogarth Press, 1953–66), XIV, 159–215. In my discussion of the imagination as partly unconscious, my concern will be with the dynamic view of it as comprised of conflicting and interacting contents that achieve

compromised expression in Keats's poetry, and with certain unconscious processes described by Freud in various works as part of his later concern with a structural view of the mind, by Anna Freud in *The Ego and the Mechanisms of Defense* (1936), and by others.

7. Ernest Lee Tuveson, *The Imagination as a Means of Grace: Locke and the Aesthetics of Romanticism* (Berkeley: University of California Press, 1960), pp. 96–97.

8. M. H. Abrams points out that in the early part of the nineteenth century "the notion of an unconscious element in the inventive process had already become almost a commonplace of English literary criticism," and he cites examples from Blake, Wordsworth, Hazlitt, Shelley, and Keats (*The Mirror and the Lamp: Romantic Theory and the Critical Tradition* [New York: Oxford University Press, 1953], p. 214). James Engell has recently shown that throughout the eighteenth century the concept of imagination included an awareness that imagination works on the passions, in part creating such feelings as hope, despair, and jealousy, at the same time that it included an appreciation of the fact that the passions work on imagination (*The Creative Imagination: Enlightenment to Romanticism* [Cambridge, Mass.: Harvard University Press, 1981]). But the unconscious dimension of imagination in Romantic theory and poetry remains uncharted territory.

9. *The Prelude: 1799, 1805, 1850*, ed. Jonathan Wordsworth, M. H. Abrams, and Stephen Gill (New York: W. W. Norton, 1979), 1805, I.352–54. See James A. W. Heffernan, *Wordsworth's Theory of Poetry: The Transforming Imagination* (Ithaca, N.Y.: Cornell University Press, 1969), for a discussion of processes such as abstracting and endowing. For an excellent study of the role of unconscious aspects of mind and imagination in the character and development of the poet, see Richard J. Onorato, *The Character of the Poet: Wordsworth in "The Prelude"* (Princeton, N.J.: Princeton University Press, 1971).

10. *The Complete Works of William Hazlitt*, ed. P. P. Howe, 21 vols. (London: J. M. Dent and Sons, 1930–34), V, 4–5.

11. *Ibid.*, p. 4.

12. *Ibid.*, XX, 43.

13. John Kinnaird, *William Hazlitt: Critic of Power* (New York: Columbia University Press, 1978), p. 91.

14. Hazlitt best reveals his conception of imagination as subject to domination by unconscious forces in his essay "On Dreams," where he seems to anticipate Freud's conception of repression: "We are not hypocrites in our sleep. The curb is taken off from our passions, and our imagination wanders at will. When awake, we check these rising thoughts, and fancy we have them not. In dreams, when we are off our guard, they return securely and unbidden. We may make this use of the infirmity of our sleeping metamorphosis, that we may repress any feelings of this sort that we disapprove in their incipient state, and detect, ere it be too late, an unwarrantable antipathy or fatal passion" (*Works*, XII, 23).

15. Engell has identified an earlier use of the chameleon metaphor in Zachary Mayne's *Two Dissertations Concerning Sense and the Imagination* (1728) and has suggested that perhaps Hazlitt ("or less likely Keats") had read Mayne. See Engell, pp. 146–47.

16. Sir Sidney Colvin, *John Keats* (London: Macmillan, 1918), p. 175. For a useful catalogue and discussion of Keats's images for this faculty, see Mario D'Avanzo, *Keats's Metaphors for the Poetic Imagination* (Durham, N.C.: Duke University Press, 1967).

17. *Biographia Literaria*, ed. Shawcross, II, 12.

18. *Ibid.*, p. 258.

19. *The Origins of Psycho-Analysis: Letters to Wilhelm Fliess, Drafts and Notes: 1887–1902*, trans. Eric Mosbacher and James Strachey, ed. Marie Bonaparte, Anna Freud, and Ernst Kris (New York: Basic Books, 1954), p. 258.

20. Freud, *Standard Edition*, XIX, 25.

21. For discussions of the "crisis" reflected in the poem, see Walter Evert, *Aesthetic and Myth in the Poetry of Keats* (Princeton, N.J.: Princeton University Press, 1965), pp. 194–211, and Sperry, pp. 117–31.

22. See James Ralston Caldwell, *John Keats' Fancy: The Effect on Keats of the Psychology of His Day* (Ithaca, N.Y.: Cornell University Press, 1945), for the view that Keats was influenced by associationist psychology.

23. As Evert has pointed out, the lines here have less to do with Keats's recognition of the dark, potentially tragic dimension of the human condition, though this is obviously important, and more to do with imagination itself: "In this passage . . . the attack is not upon the inadequacy of a particular conception but upon the conceptualizing imagination itself. As the poet has just said, the power of the imagination to alter the essential quality of experience destroys the experience's integrity. An incapacity to look at the periwinkle without seeing the shark at savage prey is clearly a derangement not of nature but of mind" (p. 210).

24. Hazlitt, *Works*, XII, 118.

25. Douglas Bush, *Mythology and the Romantic Tradition in English Poetry* (Cambridge, Mass.: Harvard University Press, 1937), p. 107.

26. In his edition, *Letters of John Keats* (London: Oxford University Press, 1970), Robert Gittings corrects Rollins and other editors who have spelled the surname "*Jeffrey*" and he ascribes Keats's letters as written to Mary-Ann Jeffrey rather than to Sarah (see p. 402). In my reference to these letters I follow Gittings's correction.

27. See Benjamin Bailey's comments on the poems by Wordsworth that Keats especially liked in the letter to Richard Monckton Milnes in *The Keats Circle*, ed. Hyder E. Rollins, 2 vols. (Cambridge, Mass.: Harvard University Press, 1948), II, 274–76. References by volume and page number are hereafter included in the text.

28. Freud, *Standard Edition*, XIV, 244–45.

29. For a discussion of the distinctions between "introjection," "incorporation," and "identification," see Roy Schafer, *Aspects of Internalization* (New York: International Universities Press, 1968). In considering Keats's poetry, it is useful to maintain the distinction between introjection (or, more generally, internalization, as I shall use the term), as an act of taking an object into the mind and possessing it, and identification, as a sense or experience of being like an object or an act of modeling one's behavior on that of an object. At the end of "Ode of Psyche" Keats seeks to internalize the presence of the goddess; in the middle of "Ode to a Nightingale" he feels an identification with the bird and seeks to model his consciousness on its seeming blissfulness. Schafer has recently argued that the term "internalization" should be avoided because it "refers to a fantasy, not to a process" (*A New Language for Psychoanalysis*, [New Haven, Conn.: Yale University Press, 1976], p. 177). I continue to use the term to indicate a process, however, because this remains its essential meaning in the works of psychoanalytic theory that I cite and because fantasies of internalization recur in Keats's poetry with such regularity as to indicate a more permanent characteristic of his psychic life than the word "fantasy" can suggest.

30. *Letters of Sigmund Freud, 1873–1939*, trans. Tania and James Stern, ed. Ernst L. Freud (London: Hogarth Press, 1961), p. 386.

31. Lionel Trilling, "The Poet as Hero: Keats in His Letters," in *The Opposing Self* (New York: Viking Press, 1955), pp. 3–43.

32. See Freud's essay "On Narcissism: An Introduction," *Standard Edition*, XIV, 73–102.

33. Aileen Ward, *John Keats: The Making of a Poet* (New York: Viking Press, 1963), p. 340. Ward's biography is still the centerpiece of psychoanalytic work on Keats, but other work has been done. See, for example, Harold G. McCurdy, "La Belle Dame sans Merci," *Character and Personality*, 13 (1944), 166–77; David Barron, "*Endymion:* The Quest for Beauty," *American Imago*, 20 (1963), 27–47; James W. Hamilton, "Object Loss, Dreaming, and Creativity: The Poetry of John Keats," *Psychoanalytic Study of the Child*, 24 (1969), 488–531; Stanley A. Leavy, "John Keats's Psychology of Creative Imagination," *Psychoanalytic Quarterly*, 39 (1970), 173–97; Stephen Reid, "Keats's Depressive Poetry," *Psychoanalytic Review*, 58 (1971), 395–418; and Barbara Schapiro, *The Romantic Mother: Narcissistic Patterns in Romantic Poetry* (Baltimore: Johns Hopkins University Press, 1983), pp. 33–60. For a more complete list, see Norman Kiell's *Psychoanalysis, Psychology, and Literature: A Bibliography*, 2nd ed., 2 vols. (Metuchen, N.J.: Scarecrow Press, 1982).

34. Freud, *Standard Edition*, IX, 146.

35. Robert Gittings, *John Keats* (London: Wm. Heinemann, 1968), p. 25.

36. Joseph Severn, "Incidents from My Life" (1858), quoted from Gittings, *John Keats*, p. 25.

37. Gittings, *John Keats*, p. 30.

Keats and Byron   Beth Lau[*]

One of Keats's earliest surviving poems is the December 1814 sonnet "To Lord Byron," which celebrates the "sweetly sad" strains of Byron's verse and urges the noble poet to "still tell the tale, / The enchanting tale—the tale of pleasing woe."[1] That he would compose a sonnet to Byron surely implies, as Amy Lowell says, that Keats was "fairly soaked in Byron at this period."[2] Other poems composed in 1814 and 1815 salute Spenser ("Imitation of Spenser") and Chatterton ("Oh Chatterton! how very sad thy fate"), and these poets are recognized major influences on the youthful Keats. Moreover, Henry Stephens, who roomed with the poet in 1815 and 1816, names Byron and Spenser as the two writers most "in favor" with Keats at this time. He also reports that Keats "used to go with his neck nearly bare á lá Byron."[3]

Throughout the last four years of his life, however, when he was writing the works that placed him "among the English Poets,"[4] Keats seldom mentions and less often praises Byron's poetry. Fanny Brawne told Keats's sister that "My dear Keats did not admire Lord Byrons poetry as many people do," and Joseph Severn left an account of

[*] This essay was written specifically for this volume and is published here for the first time by permission of the author.

Keats's outraged condemnation of Byron after reading the storm-at-sea episode from canto 2 of *Don Juan* while sailing to Italy.[5]

Why did Byron suffer such a decline in popularity for Keats as the latter matured? In this essay I shall explore three major areas of conflict in Keats's response to his popular contemporary that each provide some answers to this question. First, Byron seems to have been associated with aspects of Keats's adolescence against which the young man later reacted. Second, Keats suffered from professional, social, and sexual jealousy of Lord Byron. Finally, genuine aesthetic differences divided the two poets. This is not to say, however, that Keats's mature attitude toward Byron was entirely hostile. The younger poet did express some admiration for his elder contemporary's work, and he certainly followed Byron's career with interest. Furthermore, although for a variety of reasons Keats did not always or fully acknowledge them, a number of important similarities between the poets can be remarked.[6]

The chief appeal of Byron's poetry for the adolescent Keats, to judge from the latter's 1814 sonnet, was its melancholy. In "To Lord Byron," the noble poet is praised for catching "Pity['s] . . . tones" and is deemed the more beautiful for his "griefs" and "O'ershading sorrow." As both Lowell and Ward point out, when Keats wrote the sonnet he had recently lost his grandmother and suffered the breakup of his family circle, and he seems to have found solace in Byron's work for his own unhappiness.[7] Certainly, throughout his short life Keats had abundant reasons to be melancholy, and one might expect that the younger poet would have continued to identify with Byron's suffering heros and speakers.

For several reasons, however, Keats by 1817 objected to the note of gloom in Byron's verse. "Sleep and Poetry" attacks "Strange thunders" in contemporary literature, or "ugly clubs, the poets Polyphemes / Disturbing the grand sea" (231, 234–35). Poetry that "feeds upon the burrs, / And thorns of life," Keats continues, "forget[s] the great end / Of poesy, that it should be a friend / To sooth the cares, and lift the thoughts of man" (244–47). Richard Woodhouse glossed these lines as an "Allusion to Lord Byron, & his terrific style of poetry."[8] A similar passage condemning poets who disturb rather than sooth, which occurs near the end of Keats's career in *The Fall of Hyperion*, is also thought by many critics to refer to Byron. Moneta has just made her important distinction between poets and dreamers: " 'The one pours out a balm upon the world, / The other vexes it' " (1:201–2). In the lines thought to refer to Byron, the speaker then castigates, presumably for their "vexing" effect, "all mock lyrists, large self worshipers, / And careless hectorers in proud bad verse" (1:207–8). Although excessive melancholy is not specifically named in this list of poetic sins, "mock lyrists" might well be considered

to "vex" the world by dwelling on their sorrows. Certainly the
conviction that poetry ought to please and sooth rather than disturb
would have alienated Keats from Byron's gloomy, withdrawn protagonists.

Several of the new literary friends Keats began to meet in the
fall of 1816 probably influenced his reaction against Byron's melancholy strain. Although Hunt believed Keats's objections in "Sleep
and Poetry" to "Strange thunders from the potency of song" referred
to the Lake Poets rather than to Byron,[9] Hunt himself had criticized
Byron along similar lines in his 1815 edition of *The Feast of the Poets.*
In Hunt's verse-satire, Apollo takes Byron to task for his misanthropic
characters and dark view of the world and gives him the following
advice:

> you must not be always indulging this tone;
> You owe some relief to our hearts and your own;
> For poets, earth's heav'n-linking spirits, were born,
> What they can, to amend—what they can't, to adorn;
> And you hide the best proof of your office and right,
> If you make not as I do a contrast with night,
> And help to shed round you a gladness and light.[10]

Keats's appreciation of Hunt was at its peak when "Sleep and Poetry"
was composed, and the journalist's preference for cheerful, therapeutic literature is likely to have shaped Keats's pronouncement that
the "great end" of poetry is "To sooth the cares, and lift the thoughts
of man," rather than to give vent to morbid, melancholy feelings as
Byron did.

William Hazlitt, another major influence on Keats's thinking about
poetry and poets, also condemned Byron's melancholy, though his
reasons are somewhat different from Hunt's. In his last lecture "On
the English Poets," which Keats almost certainly attended, Hazlitt
characterizes Byron thus:

> Lord Byron (judging from the tone of his writings) might be thought
> to have suffered too much to be a truly great poet. . . . [He] shuts
> himself up too much in the impenetrable gloom of his own thoughts,
> and buries the natural light of things in "nook monastic." . . . He
> has more depth of passion, more force and impetuosity [than Thomas
> Moore], but the passion is always of the same unaccountable char-
> acter, at once violent and sullen, fierce and gloomy. It is not the
> passion of a mind struggling with misfortune, or the hopelessness
> of its desires, but of a mind preying upon itself, and disgusted with,
> or indifferent to all other things.[11]

According to Hazlitt, Byron's melancholy makes for bad poetry because it produces a self-centered, claustrophobic, and monotonous

effect. He also dislikes what he regards as an unmanly wallowing in grief in Byron's verse.

Of course, Keats would not have been influenced by either Hunt's or Hazlitt's opinions of Byron had they not touched chords within himself. Both the notion that poetry ought to comfort and the belief that poets ought to be "camelions" rather than "egotists" became central to Keats's own aesthetic credo. Keats apparently also shared Hazlitt's belief that a man ought to struggle against adversity rather than cultivate his sorrows, as attested by his oft-repeated insistence that he preferred "real grievances" to "imaginary" ones because "The imaginary nail a man down for a sufferer, as on a cross; the real spur him up into an agent" (*Letters* 2:181).[12] Hunt's and Hazlitt's pronouncements may be said merely to have helped Keats recognize and codify his own literary principles. Part of this process, however, involved rejecting some writers once enjoyed but later associated with immature and misguided literary tastes. James Beattie, Mary Tighe, and perhaps Byron fall into this category.[13]

There is also evidence that, for a number of Keats's literary friends, Byron and Wordsworth represented opposite styles of contemporary poetry, so that a preference for one involved a rejection of the other. In an 1831 essay, Hunt claims Byron resented the fact that Hunt seldom wrote about Byron's work, "the poetry he was fondest of being of another kind," for he considered "Mr. Wordsworth the first poet of the day."[14] It was just around the time Keats met Hunt, moreover, that the latter came to regard Wordsworth as "the first poet of the day," as changes in the three editions of *The Feast of the Poets* make clear. The first, 1811 edition ridicules Wordsworth and excludes him from Apollo's banquet; the 1814 edition is more generous, though still predominantly critical; but in the 1815 version, Wordsworth's virtues outweigh his faults, and he is not only admitted to Apollo's feast but declared "the Prince of the Bards of his Time!" In addition, Hunt's 1815 preface openly declares that successive editions of the poem reflect the author's conversion from a detractor to an admirer of Wordsworth's poetry.[15]

Leonidas Jones believes Hunt's 1814 *Feast* was instrumental in shifting John Hamilton Reynolds's attention from Byron to Wordsworth.[16] Reynolds's first book-length poem, the 1814 *Safie*, was, as Reynolds later told Milnes, "a downright imitation of Lord Byron."[17] By contrast *The Eden of the Imagination,* his second long poem, published less than a year after *Safie,* was distinctly Wordsworthian.[18] In a 9 December 1815 *Champion* essay, moreover, Reynolds unfavorably contrasts Byron to his new favorite. "It is true," he writes, "there are not in [Wordsworth], that haughty melancholy and troubled spirit which so peculiarly distinguish Lord Byron. . . . The truth is, Mr. Wordsworth describes natural feelings and natural beauties,—

his thoughts come from him, purified through the heart.—He indulges in calm reasonings and rich reflections."[19]

It is quite likely that Hunt, Reynolds, and perhaps others helped to convince Keats that Wordsworth rather than Byron was the contemporary poet he ought to emulate. We recall that in 1815 and early 1816, according to Henry Stephens, Byron was still a favorite with Keats. After meeting Hunt and Reynolds in October 1816, however, Keats criticized Byron in "Sleep and Poetry." Furthermore, if we again accept Woodhouse's authority, "Sleep and Poetry" praises Wordsworth just before it disapproves of the harsh and gloomy strain in Byron's verse. Lines 224–26, celebrating contemporary poetry "upstirr'd / From out its crystal dwelling in a lake, / By a swan's ebon bill" was identified by Woodhouse as a reference to "Wordsworth, who resides near one of the lakes in Cumberland."[20]

One last friend of Keats who is known to have expressed a preference for Wordsworth over Byron is Benjamin Bailey. In a 14 June 1824 letter to John Taylor, Bailey declares, "I prefer Wordsworth to Byron, because Wordsworth is more contemplative, and indeed in his higher flights more poetical."[21] Keats read and discussed Wordsworth with Bailey when the young poet visited Oxford in September 1817. We do not know if Bailey at that time also criticized Byron, but the possibility is suggested by the fact that, in a letter to Bailey written shortly after he returned from his visit, Keats declares, "I am quite disgusted with literary Men and will never know another except Wordsworth—no not even Byron" (*Letters* 1:169).

Clearly Keats began to develop his lifelong interest in Wordsworth around late 1816 and 1817. The fact that Byron fell out of favor at the same time may well have resulted from a view prevailing among literary men of the time that one could not like both poets, and a choice of one over the other served to define one's literary tastes. Keats, like Hunt, Reynolds, and Bailey, if forced to decide between the two, would opt for the contemplative naturalism of Wordsworth over the gloomy melodrama of Byron.

Henry Stephens's remark that in 1815 and 1816 Keats "used to go with his neck nearly bare á lá Byron," suggests another reason the younger poet may later have wished to distance himself from Byron. W. J. Bate believes that when Keats in a 27 April 1818 letter tells Reynolds "the most unhappy hours in our lives are those in which we recollect times past to our own blushing" (*Letters* 1:273), he is referring to the period in which he modeled himself after Byron.[22] Keats must have felt that his youthful, iconoclastic dress was affected and immature; that it implied he had sought to earn the title of poet through his clothes rather than through deserving compositions. In the same way he reacted violently against Leigh Hunt's crowning him with laurel in the spring of 1817. "God of the golden bow" expresses to Apollo Keats's contrition for assuming the outward mark of a great poet before he had earned a right to it, and, in a letter to his brother, Keats asserted "I put on no Laurels till I shall have finished Endymion, and I hope Apollo is [not] angered at my having made a Mockery at him at Hunt's" (*Letters* 1:170).

Eventually, too, Keats found a different poetic image more congenial than Byron's. "Lord Byron cuts a figure—but he is not figurative," Keats wrote in February 1819. By contrast, "Shakespeare led a life of Allegory; his works are the comments on it" (*Letters* 2:67). What truly makes a great poet, Keats came to believe, is not a dashing appearance and a notorious lifestyle but the extent to which he can transform his personal experience into something more lasting and universal. In addition, Keats felt that a poet ought to be a "camelion" who enters into the personalities of his characters but himself has "no identity—he [a poet] is certainly the most unpoetical of all God's Creatures" (*Letters* 1:387). This definition of the poet is a far cry from the one Byron represented: a colorful, striking personality whose life is almost more interesting and dramatic than his works, or whose works so strongly bear the stamp of his personality that they invite speculation about his private life.

Probably one of the major reasons why Keats initially was attracted to Byron was the mere fact of the latter's popularity. An adolescent literary enthusiast naturally would find his imagination captivated by the most dashing, successful young poet of his day, if only because he exemplified the fame and glory one might attain as a writer. What was an asset to Byron's image when Keats was a teenager, however, seems to have become a liability as the young man matured. The first of Keats's direct comments on Byron after the 1814 sonnet clearly sounds a note of rivalry that recurs in many subsequent remarks. Benjamin Robert Haydon records in an April 1817 diary entry, "Keats said to me today as we were walking along 'Byron, Scott, Southey, & Shelley think they are to lead the age, but [the rest of the sentence, consisting probably of eight or ten words, has been erased].' This was said with all the consciousness of Genius; his face reddened."[23] As Keats passed from a tentative novice to an ambitious practicing poet, Byron changed from a hero worshipped from afar to a threatening rival. Although Keats could look to great poets of the past as comforting and supportive "presiders" (*Letters* 1:142), he seems to have regarded living contemporaries as competitors whom he had to "trounce"—a word he uses in another letter in reference to Byron (*Letters* 2:84)—in order to make a space for himself in the literary scene.

Byron's immense popularity, moreover, marked him as a special rival. Particularly after it became apparent that *Endymion*, like Keats's first volume of poems, was not going to sell, the young poet seems to have felt keenly the other's easy success. Several critics have remarked the notes of bitterness, resentment, and jealousy in Keats's observation to his brother and sister-in-law on 14 February 1818: "I was surprised to hear from Taylor the amount of Murray the Book-sellers last sale. . . . He sold 4000 coppies of Lord Byron" (*Letters* 2:62).[24] Wolf Hirst also points out that Keats's hostile response to the shipwreck episode in canto 2 of *Don Juan* comes shortly before the young man chose for his epitaph, "Here lies One Whose Name was writ in Water."[25] Keats felt alternately challenged, threatened, and defeated by Byron's commercial and critical success, and he often responded by denigrating the man and the work that enjoyed such unprecedented popularity.

Another reason Keats may have felt particularly jealous and resentful of Byron was the fact that the successful poet was also a lord, whereas Keats himself, as *Blackwood's* reviewer John Lockhart took pains to remind him, was a "Cockney" with working-class origins. In a 20 September 1818 letter to Dilke that contains a humorous catalogue of different types of paper, Keats refers to "rich or noble poets—ut Byron" (*Letters* 1:368). More gloomily, to his brother and sister-in-law he complains of a neighbor's remark that he was "quite the little Poet": "You see what it is to be under six foot and not a lord" (*Letters* 2:61).

The latter comment suggests another source of resentment: Keats's insecurity about his short stature and appeal to women, as contrasted to Byron's celebrated beauty and sexual conquests.[26] Perhaps the fact that Fanny Brawne as a schoolgirl had been "half wild" over Byron's poetry, as she told Keats's sister,[27] increased the younger poet's jealousy of Byron's good looks and popularity with women. Ironically, Keats did not realize that Byron himself was self-conscious about his appearance as a result of his club foot.

Keats's disparaging references to Byron are not all personal in nature, however. The younger poet also genuinely objected to certain aspects of Byron's verse. (Although it is difficult to maintain a dis-tinction between the personal and the purely aesthetic in Keats's remarks. As with all of us, psychological, social, and other background considerations inform Keats's literary principles.) First, the self-re-ferential nature of Byron's poetry represented for Keats a dangerous, wrongheaded trend in contemporary literature. I have already quoted the letter in which Byron, who "cuts a figure," is contrasted unfa-vorably to Shakespeare, "who led a life of Allegory" (*Letters* 2:67). In an earlier, 3 February 1818 letter to Reynolds, Keats contrasts the selflessness of Shakespeare and other Renaissance writers to the "egotism" of the moderns. Although Wordsworth and Hunt furnish the chief examples of misguided, egotistic writers, a concluding hit at Byron in Keats's letter implicates that poet too in the modern

malady of self-absorption. "Let us have the old Poets, & robin Hood,"
Keats writes. "Your letter and its sonnets gave me more pleasure
than will the 4th Book of Childe Harold & the whole of any body's
life & opinions" (*Letters* 1:225).

Even if Keats had not referred to Byron in his attack on egotistic
modern poets, one would assume that he would have included the
noble poet in this category, for Byron more than any other writer
of the age was known for his self-centeredness and inability to create
characters unlike himself. Hazlitt, for example, who helped shape
Keats's own ideas on the importance of "disinterestedness," de-
nounced Byron's lack of this quality in his final lecture "On the
English Poets": "There is nothing less poetical than this sort of
unaccommodating selfishness. There is nothing more repulsive than
this sort of ideal absorption of all the interests of others . . . in the
ruling passion and moody abstraction of a single mind, as if it would
make itself the centre of the universe. . . . It is like a cancer, eating
into the heart of poetry."[28] In his review of *Endymion*, Reynolds
called Byron "a splendid and noble egotist" and continued: "He visits
Classical shores; roams over romantic lands . . . but no spot is
conveyed to our minds, that is not peopled by the gloomy and ghastly
feelings of one proud and solitary man. It is as if he and the world
were the only two things which the air clothed."[29] Finally, Woodhouse, explaining to Taylor Keats's definition of the poetical character,
remarked that "Ld Byron does not come up to this Character. He
can certainly conceive & describe a dark accomplished vilain in love—
& a female tender and kind who loves him. Or a sated & palled
Sensualist Misanthrope & Deist—But here his power ends."[30] For
Keats and for the friends with whom he shared his literary principles,
Byron's poetry exhibited a tendency Keats himself wished to avoid:
a subjective, personal strain absent in the great writers of the past.

It is interesting to note that, for Byron, Keats represented a
dangerous modern departure from classical poetic tradition. Just as
Keats unfavorably contrasted Byron to Shakespeare, Byron unfavorably compared Keats to Alexander Pope. Byron objected strongly to
Keats's attack in "Sleep and Poetry" on Pope, in Byron's opinion
"the Poet whom of all others a young aspirant ought to respect and
honour and study."[31] George Cheatham believes Byron's vehement
criticism of Keats largely reflects Byron's anxieties about his own
nonconformity to eighteenth-century aesthetics.[32] It could be that
when Keats condemns Byron and other contemporaries he betrays a
similar uneasiness about his own adherence to the selfless Shakespearean ideal he espoused. The author of poems such as "When I
have fears that I may cease to be" and "Ode to a Nightingale" cannot
after all be said to have entirely excluded personal elements from
his work.

Keats also is likely to have been put off by what he would have regarded as a lack of seriousness and dedication to his craft on Byron's part. In the 14 October 1818 letter in which he describes his encounter with Jane Cox or "Charmian," Keats characterizes Byron as a second-rate poet. "There are two distinct tempers of mind in which we judge of things," Keats writes, "the worldly theatrical and pantomimical; and the unearthly, spiritual and etherial—in the former Buonaparte, Lord Byron and this Charmian hold the first place in our Minds" (*Letters* 1:395). Although it may appear to celebrate the ability of a Byron or a Jane Cox to cut a striking figure, the passage ultimately denigrates Byron, for it excludes him from the "unearthly, spiritual and etherial" category, which is surely the more important one for serious poets. Especially the term "pantomimical" describing the class into which Keats places Byron suggests that the latter's verse is superficial and more popular entertainment than enduring art.

A related criticism of Byron's poetry or approach to poetry emerges from Keats's one direct comparison of himself to Byron, in an 18 September 1819 letter sent to his brother and sister-in-law: "[Lord Byron] describes what he sees—I describe what I imagine—Mine is the hardest task" (*Letters* 2:200). Keats here does touch on a major difference between himself and his older contemporary. As Jerome McGann explains, Byron did not exalt the imagination as Wordsworth, Coleridge, and Keats did. He regarded it as merely one ingredient in the creative process and analytic or critical in nature, serving to enhance understanding of the human world rather than to create an autonomous aesthetic realm.[33] Keats, who was "certain of nothing but of the holiness of the Heart's affections and the truth of Imagination" (*Letters* 1:184), perhaps regarded Byron's lack of a similar commitment to the imagination as evidence of a failure of true poetic calling.[34]

Other aspects of Byron's attitude toward poetry may have fostered this impression. Passages in Byron's letters denigrate poetry-writing as an occupation, as when Byron tells Anabella Milbanke "I by no means rank poetry or poets high in the scale of intellect," and to John Murray writes "If one's years can't be better employed than in sweating poesy—a man had better be a ditcher."[35] Although Keats could not have seen these passages, he may have learned of such sentiments through Hunt or other literary people. Certainly it was commonly known that, so long as Byron lived in England, he refused to accept payment for his best-selling works, even when he desperately needed the money, on the principle that aristocrats do not work for a living. Such a stance implies that, for a noble, poetry is a hobby rather than a lofty profession. The satiric deflation of literary fame in canto 1 of *Don Juan*, which Richard Abbey read to Keats in

September 1819 (*Letters* 2:192), may also have conveyed the message that Byron did not take his craft very seriously. For the ardent, dedicated Keats, who often spoke of poetry and poets in religious language, Byron's apparent lack of zeal must have appeared heretical.

On this subject it is once again revealing to compare Byron's attitude toward Keats. As Cheatham points out, Byron found objectionable what he regarded as the Cockney vulgarity of Keats's straining after fame and his glorification of the imagination.[36] Ultimately, this point of aesthetic conflict between Keats and Byron may originate in class differences. For the aristocratic Byron, a too conspicuous dedication to poetry was a sign of bad breeding; for the middle-class Keats, aspiration in one's chosen field was a decided virtue.

One final artistic contrast between Byron and Keats that probably prevented the latter from appreciating the former is the difference in their writing styles. Byron's poetry, especially in his dramatic works, is fast-paced and cumulative in its effect, and pausing to dwell on individual lines may actually detract from appreciation by revealing faulty diction and syntax or cliched phrases. Keats's poetry, by contrast, is dense with vivid imagery and suggestive language. Keats could not have "look[ed] upon fine Phrases like a Lover" (*Letters* 2:139) in Byron's poetry, and this fact, as much as anything else, probably explains the paucity of quotations and echoes of Byron poems in Keats's writing. The younger poet did not absorb memorable lines and images from Byron as he did from other writers more in keeping with his own artistic bent.

While we can trace a general falling off of admiration for Byron as Keats matured, the younger poet never completely rejected his older contemporary. For one thing, he kept track of Byron's career, remarking in letters the impending publication of *Childe Harold's Pilgrimage,* canto 4, and *Don Juan* and the impressive sale of the former work (*Letters* 1:237; 2:59, 62). He also asked James Hessey to procure him a copy of *Don Juan* and took the volume with him on his voyage to Italy.[37] Clearly Keats remained interested in what Byron was writing and to some extent made himself familiar with Byron's new publications as they appeared.[38]

More significantly, evidence from several sources indicates that the mature Keats retained some appreciation of Byron's poetry. In a 3 May 1818 letter to Reynolds, Keats approvingly quotes "Knowledge is Sorrow" (the line actually reads "Sorrow is knowledge") from *Manfred* (*Letters* 1:279), and Fanny Brawne reported that Keats considered *Manfred* one of Byron's best works.[39] In a 14 October 1818 letter, Keats attributes to Byron a statement that derives from Hunt's *The Story of Rimini:* "I am free from Men of Pleasure's cares / By dint of feelings far more deep than theirs" (*Letters* 1:396). Although the passage is not Byron's, Keats's comment on it—"this is

Lord Byron and is one of the finest things he has said" (*Letters* 1:396)—reveals that the younger poet did think Byron capable of "fine things," and the lines themselves indicate something of what he associated with Byron and valued in him. "Fare Thee Well" is quoted in *The Jealousies* (lines 610–11), and scholars have detected the influence of Byron's worldly, cynical style in this poem and others composed around the same period: *Lamia* and the September 1819 revisions of *The Eve of St. Agnes*. Finally, Leigh Hunt claimed that Keats "was an admirer of *Don Juan*."[40] Taken together, this information suggests some of the characteristics of Byron's verse that Keats continued or grew to appreciate.

First, the lines from *Manfred* and *Rimini* imply that Byron's melancholy and subjectivity retained some appeal for Keats. The quotation from *Manfred* occurs in a letter in which Keats reassesses his opinion of Wordsworth and Milton, now finding the modern superior to the Renaissance poet because of the former's greater concern with "the human heart" (*Letters* 1:282). Keats at this point seems to regard contemporary writers' "egotism"—their introspection and expression of personal feelings—as evidence of an advance rather than a decline in literary development.

The passage from *Manfred*—"Knowledge is Sorrow"—is related in Keats's letter to the poet's new appreciation of the value of wisdom and experience, even though they entail a loss of innocent delight. This concept Keats goes on to develop in his comparison of life to a "Mansion of Many Apartments" (*Letters* 1:280–81). Both Manfred and his creator could have illustrated for Keats the principle that all knowledge and experience are worthwhile, even when they cast one outside the pale of society and normal existence. Keats's decision around this time to spend the summer traveling through Scotland, and his concurrent assertions that he wished travel to be a regular feature of his future life (*Letters* 1:264, 268), may also owe something to Byron's example. Travel after all was for Byron one of the chief means of acquiring knowledge, and when Keats says that he hopes his summer in Scotland will "enlarge [his] vision" (*Letters* 1:268) he may well have the author of *Childe Harold's Pilgrimage* in the back of his mind.

Keats's interest in *Manfred* and the lines from *Rimini* may also reflect a strain of misanthropy and withdrawal from ordinary human life that the younger poet at times shared with Byron. For example, in the same letter in which he remarks that "another satire is expected from Byron call'd Don Giovanni," Keats tells his brother and sister-in-law, "I see very little now, and very few Persons—being almost tired of Men and things" (*Letters* 2:59). To Georgiana Keats he declares, "Upon the whole I dislike Mankind," and to Fanny Brawne, "I hate men and women more" (*Letters* 2:243, 312). In conjunction with the last statement Keats quotes *Hamlet*, which play is also mentioned two sentences before "Knowledge is Sorrow" is quoted in the 3 May 1818 letter. Certainly *Hamlet* and *Manfred* express a similar weariness with life and, along with the lines from *Rimini*, a contempt for common men and women. Although critics generally emphasize Keats's compassion for others, the poet did suffer, as he told Haydon, from "a horrid Morbidity of Temperament" (*Letters* 1:142) that could make him speak contemptuously of his fellow human beings. At such times, Byron's misanthropic heroes must have struck a sympathetic chord within him.

Another characteristic of *Manfred* Keats seems to have approved is its recognition of contrarieties in human experience. The phrase "Knowledge is Sorrow," as well as other aspects of the play, express the idea that one sort of loss brings another sort of gain and vice versa. Thus Manfred's love for his sister destroys her, but the very guilt Manfred suffers as a result sets him apart from and above other mortal and immortal beings. An acute sensitivity to the fine line dividing fulfillment and loss, pleasure and pain, sorrow and growth, has long been recognized as central to Keats's poetic vision, and the young poet may have perceived a similar awareness in *Manfred.* Paul Elledge draws a parallel between the concept of the " 'fatal embrace' which divides as it unites," featured in *Manfred*, and figures in Keats's poetry that similarly predicate "peak emotional intensity upon the nearly simultaneous loss of it."[41]

Don Juan also may have appealed to Keats for the way in which it juxtaposes opposite emotions or moods. Certainly the poem was notorious when it first appeared for its habit of "mingling up sentiment and sneering," as Richard Woodhouse phrased it when he remarked on a similar tendency in Keats's September 1819 revisions of *The Eve of St. Agnes.*[42] Hazlitt also wrote of "the oddity of the contrast between [the serious writing] and the flashy passages with which [*Don Juan*] is interlarded. From the sublime to the rediculous there is but one step. . . . A classical intoxication is followed by the splashing of soda-water, by frothy effusions of ordinary bile."[43] Keats in the summer and fall of 1819 may have imitated the ironic, deflationary style of *Don Juan* because it conveyed a vision of life he shared.

Keats apparently did not find Byron's satire wholly congenial, however. Few critics, beginning with Richard Woodhouse, have thought Byron's cynical style suited Keats's temperament and mode of expression, and readers generally are put off by the flippancy of Byronic passages in *Lamia, The Eve of St. Agnes,* and *The Jealousies.* In addition, in *The Jealousies* Byron's poetry and domestic affairs are among the objects of Keats's satire, for the ludicrous, philandering Emperor Elfinan is generally thought to have been modeled in part on Byron and his unwanted fairy fiancée Bellanaine on Anabella

Milbanke. If Keats was flattering Byron by imitating his style in the summer and fall of 1819, he seems to have wished at the same time to express his contempt for and distance from the older poet. Finally, Joseph Severn reports that Keats on board the *Maria Crowther* condemned *Don Juan* for its "paltry originality, that of being new by making solemn things gay and gay things solemn."[44] Such a statement does not reflect an appreciation of the poem's juxtaposition of opposite emotions.

Ultimately, although both Byron and Keats are fascinated by contrary elements in human experience, important differences also set them apart and help to account for Keats's ambivalence toward *Don Juan.* Byron found his most natural and successful voice in a comic mode. His satires cope with the absurdities of human nature and disappointments of life by laughing at them. Keats's vision in his greatest works, on the other hand, is tragic, and finds consolation for human suffering in the intensity of experience and the bond of compassion for others it produces. Byron's detached amusement at human folly and perversity could seem cruel to Keats as when, according to Severn, he complained that canto 2 of *Don Juan* "laugh[ed] & gloat[ed] over the most solemn & heart rending [scenes] of human misery."[45]

The only Byron work besides *Manfred* that Keats directly quotes is "Fare Thee Well," which mourns the dissolution of Byron's marriage. Elledge recently has analyzed this poem as one of many "farewell gestures" in Byron's work that in fact reveal a deep-seated ambivalence about relationships. According to Elledge, the poem laments Byron's separation from his wife and appeals for her return at the same time as it, and some of the circumstances surrounding its composition and delivery, implicitly condemn Anabella and discourage reconciliation. Elledge speculates that family problems—the frequent absences and then death of Byron's father and the swings between doting affection and rejection Byron experienced from his mother—may have caused the poet's approach-withdrawal syndrome as regards relationships.[46]

Leon Waldoff has written in similar terms of the preoccupation in Keats's poems with restoring lost objects, especially beloved women who have vanished, which desire nonetheless is combined with a profound suspicion of the woman to whom the protagonist wishes to be united.[47] Waldoff also believes Keats's family experiences—the death of Keats's father and more especially his mother's abandonment of her children and then her return only when she was dying—shaped these attitudes. A fear of abandonment and loss and consequent ambivalence about relationships may therefore be one of the characteristics Byron and Keats share. Moreover if, as Elledge suggests, the political and social disruptions of the period also lie behind Byron's and Keats's "sense of relational instability,"[48] the two poets may be said to share a common romantic characteristic.

Keats, however, does not appear to acknowledge the similarity between his own attitude toward relationships and Byron's. The passage in *The Jealousies* in which "Fare Thee Well" is quoted reflects little sympathy with Byron's point of view. Emperor Elfinan bids adieu to his fiancée before leaving her for the mortal woman he loves, and after reciting the well-known opening lines of Byron's poem, "he fell / A laughing!—snapp'd his fingers!—shame it is to tell!" (lines 611–12). The passage suggests Keats doubted "Fare Thee Well" 's sincerity and considered Byron in the wrong in the separation affair. Perhaps this is another case of Keats condemning in Byron a tendency he does not wish to acknowledge in himself, this time an ambivalence about women and relationships. Or, he may have detected in Byron's verses an instance of the noble poet's posturing and calling attention to himself, instead of expressing genuine love for his wife.

Whatever the reasons—reaction against his own youthful attitudes and behavior, jealousy, aesthetic and temperamental differences, or various defense mechanisms—Keats was reluctant to praise his famous contemporary, despite important similarities between the two poets to which a number of Keats's own remarks do point. Both suffered from melancholy, fear of abandonment, and ambivalence toward women, for which family and social disruptions may have been responsible. Both poets, too, were afflicted with a handicap—Byron's club foot and Keats's short stature—that made them insecure about their physical attractiveness. Both experienced misanthropic moods, and both were keenly aware of the contradictions and fine balance of rewards and losses in human life. Finally, both had doubts about the direction in which modern poetry was proceeding and looked for guidance to poets and literary styles of the past.

Besides these similarities already mentioned, one can add that both Keats and Byron are remembered for their letters almost as much as for their poems. Both also were committed to open-mindedness and honesty and recognized that such goals often were at odds with consistency of opinion. Keats believed "The only means of strengthening one's intellect is to make up ones mind about nothing—to let the mind be a thoroughfare for all thoughts" (*Letters* 2:213); Byron abhorred all forms of "cant" and wrote in his journal "God knows what contradictions it [the journal] may contain. If I am sincere with myself . . . every page should confute, refute, and utterly abjure its predecessor."[49] Finally, both Byron and Keats espoused liberal causes. In fact, Keats's assertion that he "would jump down AEtna for any great Public good" (*Letters* 1:267) was in essence acted out by Byron, who died in the service of Greek independence.

Perhaps had Keats lived to learn of Byron's death and outgrow some of his own insecurities, he would have softened toward his slightly older contemporary and more openly recognized the common ground between them, just as Byron retracted his harshest judgments of Keats after the latter's death. As it is, there is still something satisfying about the thought of Keats reading *Don Juan* on his voyage to Italy. One thinks of Shelley who was reading Keats's *Lamia* volume before he drowned. Despite their conflicts, the younger generation of Romantic poets did constitute a literary group or network who shared similar experiences and concerns, and whose artistic goals, styles, and self-images were shaped at least partly in response to one another's works.

Notes

1. Keats's poems are quoted from *The Poems of John Keats*, ed. Jack Stillinger (Cambridge: Harvard University Press, 1978).

2. Amy Lowell, *John Keats*, 2 vols. (Boston: Houghton Mifflin, 1925), 1:59.

3. *The Keats Circle*, ed. Hyder E. Rollins, 2d ed., 2 vols. (Cambridge: Harvard University Press, 1965), 2:209, 211.

4. *The Letters of John Keats*, ed. Hyder E. Rollins, 2 vols. (Cambridge: Harvard University Press, 1958), 1:394. All quotations of Keats's letters are from this edition and hereafter will be documented in the text.

5. *Letters of Fanny Brawne to Fanny Keats, 1820–1824*, ed. Fred Edgcumbe (New York: Oxford University Press, 1937), 84; Rollins, ed., *Keats Circle*, 2:134–35.

6. The most thorough previous analysis of Keats's attitude toward Byron is Wolf Hirst's "Lord Byron Cuts a Figure: The Keatsian View," *Byron Journal* 13 (1985): 36–51. Although I am indebted to Hirst for many ideas, cited below at appropriate points in my argument, my own essay concentrates on different reasons for Keats's resentment and appreciation of Byron from those Hirst develops.

7. Lowell, *John Keats*, 1:59; Aileen Ward, *John Keats: The Making of a Poet* (New York: Viking Press, 1963), 40.

8. Stuart M. Sperry, Jr., "Richard Woodhouse's Interleaved and Annotated Copy of Keats's *Poems* (1817)," *University of Wisconsin Literary Monographs*, no. 1 (Madison, 1967): 155.

9. Leigh Hunt, review of Keats's *Poems* (1817), *Examiner* (13 July 1817), in *Keats: The Critical Heritage*, ed. G. M. Matthews (New York: Barnes and Noble, 1971), 62.

10. Leigh Hunt, *The Feast of the Poets, with Other Pieces in Verse*, 2d ed. (London: 1815), 12.

11. *The Complete Works of William Hazlitt*, ed. P. P. Howe, 21 vols. (London: J. M. Dent and Sons, 1930–34), 5:152–53.

12. See also *Letters* 2:113, 185–86, 210, 329–30.

13. In a 31 December 1818 letter to his brother and sister-in-law, Keats writes, "Mrs. Tighe and Beattie once delighted me—now I see through them and can find nothing in them—or weakness—and yet how many they still delight!" (*Letters* 2:18).

14. "Lord Byron, Mr. Moore, and Mr. Leigh Hunt, with Original Letters *Not* in

Mr. Moore's Work," *Tatler* (14 January 1831); reprinted in *Leigh Hunt's Literary Criticism*, ed. Lawrence Huston Houtchens and Carolyn Washburn Houtchens (New York: Columbia University Press, 1956), 329.

15. Hunt, *Feast*, 18, ix.

16. Leonidas M. Jones, *The Life of John Hamilton Reynolds* (Hanover: University Press of New England, 1984), 52.

17. Rollins, ed., *Keats Circle*, 2:231.

18. See Jones (*Life*, 52) for a discussion of Wordsworthian elements in *The Eden of the Imagination*.

19. *Selected Prose of John Hamilton Reynolds*, ed. Leonidas M. Jones (Cambridge: Harvard University Press, 1966), 25.

20. Sperry, "Woodhouse's Copy of Keats's *Poems*," 155.

21. Rollins, ed., *Keats Circle*, 2:461.

22. Walter Jackson Bate, *John Keats* (1963; reprint, New York: Oxford University Press, 1966), 131–32.

23. *The Diary of Benjamin Robert Haydon*, ed. Williard Bissell Pope, 5 vols. (Cambridge: Harvard Unviersity Press, 1960–63), 2:106–7.

24. See Claude Lee Finney, *The Evolution of Keats's Poetry*, 2 vols. (1936: reprint, New York: Russell & Russell, 1963), 2:573; Ward, *John Keats*, 248; Robert Gittings, *John Keats* (Boston: Little, Brown and Co., 1968), 290.

25. Hirst, "Byron Cuts a Figure," 48.

26. Hirst remarks that the reason for Keats's ill will toward Byron "may partly lie in social and sexual jealousy" ("Byron Cuts a Figure," 48).

27. Edgcumbe, ed., *Letters of Fanny Brawne*, 84.

28. Howe, ed., *Complete Works of Hazlitt*, 5:153. See also 11:69, 71–72, 77.

29. Matthews, ed., *Keats: The Critical Heritage*, 118.

30. Rollins, ed., *Keats Circle*, 1:59–60.

31. Byron, "Observations upon 'Observations.' A Second Letter to John Murray, Esq., on the Rev. W. L. Bowles's Strictures on the Life and Writings of Pope," in *The Works of Lord Byron*, ed. Ernest Hartley Coleridge and Rowland E. Prothero, 13 vols. (London: John Murray, 1898–1904), 5:589.

32. George Cheatham, "Byron's Dislike of Keats's Poetry," *Keats-Shelley Journal* 32 (1983): 24–25. Cheatham quotes and discusses all of Byron's hostile remarks about Keats, many of which occur in the context of a defense of Pope.

33. Jerome J. McGann, *"Don Juan" in Context* (Chicago: University of Chicago Press, 1976), 156–65; see especially 160, 165.

34. Hirst, however, believes that when Keats criticizes Byron's lack of commitment to the imagination, "he merely objectifies a tendency within himself, and, in the guise of attacking Byron, attacks himself" ("Byron Cuts a Figure," 47). Hirst argues that, in poems such as "La Belle Dame sans Merci" and "Ode to a Nightingale," Keats himself expresses skepticism about the imagination's power.

35. *Byron's Letters and Journals*, ed. Leslie A. Marchand, 12 vols. (Cambridge: Harvard University Press, 1973–81), 3:179; 6:105.

36. Cheatham, "Byron's Dislike," 24.

37. Rollins, ed., *Keats Circle*, 1:91; 2:134.

38. It is not clear whether Keats read canto 4 of *Childe Harold's Pilgrimage*. Although he anticipates its publication, he never reports actually reading the work, and only one echo of canto 4 in Keats's poetry has been proposed (in *Otho the Great*

2:1:57–58. See Miriam Allott, ed., *The Poems of John Keats*, 3d impression with corrections [London: Longman, 1975], 567).

39. Edgcumbe, ed., *Letters of Fanny Brawne*, 84.

40. Hunt, "Lord Byron, Mr. Moore, and Mr. Leigh Hunt," in Houtchens and Houtchens, *Literary Criticism*, 330.

41. W. Paul Elledge, "Talented Equivocation: Byron's 'Fare Thee Well,' " *Keats-Shelley Journal* 35 (1986): 52.

42. Rollins, ed., *Keats Circle*, 1:91.

43. Hazlitt, "The Spirit of the Age," *New Monthly Magazine* (April 1824), reprinted in Howe, ed., *Complete Works of Hazlitt*, 11:75.

44. Rollins, ed., *Keats Circle*, 2:134.

45. Ibid.

46. Elledge, "Talented Equivocation," 42, 51 n.18, 55–56.

47. Leon Waldoff, *Keats and the Silent Work of Imagination* (Urbana: University of Illinois Press, 1985). Waldoff develops this thesis throughout his book, but on Keats's suspicions of women, see especially chapter 4, "Enthrallment and Skepticism: 'La Belle Dame sans Merci,' " 82–98.

48. Elledge, "Talented Equivocation," 42.

49. Marchand, ed., *Byron's Letters and Journals*, 3:233.

"Keats"   David Bromwich[*]

In making large claims for a critic better known to his contemporaries than to posterity, one faces the question whether this is a task of antiquarian history or part of the history of the present. About any such writer one wants to know who read him then, that we should read him now. With Hazlitt the answer can be simple and satisfying. He was read by a genius of the next generation, who pronounced Hazlitt's "depth of taste" one of the three things to be prized in that age—alongside Haydon's paintings and *The Excursion*—and sought his company in person, for conversation, for practical suggestions, and for theoretical counsel. In the story of Keats's development, biographers have always needed some event to advance him from the novice who took Hunt and Byron as his patterns, to the author who taught himself to admire Shakespeare and Milton and to enter the lists with Wordsworth. That event was his reading of Hazlitt; to a lesser extent, the informal meetings in which Hazlitt did not disappoint the expectations Keats had formed of him; and finally, Hazlitt's lectures on poetry at the Surrey Institution. This suggestion is not new, but the record of Hazlitt's influence is much fuller, more convincing and more subtly connected with the practice of Keats's

[*] Reprinted from *Hazlitt: The Mind of a Critic*. ©1984 by Oxford University Press, Inc. Reprinted by permission.

poetry, than anyone has yet shown.[1] The present chapter aims at an interpretation of the "Ode to a Nightingale" and "Ode on a Grecian Urn" in the light of Hazlitt's criticism. But I want first to exhibit several passages from Keats's letters, in the hope of demonstrating how his purpose and passion conspired with Hazlitt's. I need to admit at the outset that these imperfectly represent his letters as a whole: I chose the passages I thought would most plainly support my argument. Others could have served, however, with an emphasis very slightly different. Except Wordsworth, and the friends with whom he corresponded regularly, there was no contemporary who was more often in Keats's mind. The conclusion I will be working toward is this: that the odes test an idea of the imagination which Hazlitt had proposed in his lectures and critical essays; and that they afford, for power and for sympathy, a space as accommodating as that of the personal essays later collected in *Table-Talk,* which Hazlitt started writing about the same time.

In December 1814 Keats wrote an adoring sonnet "To Lord Byron," whom he then thought an incomparable poet, an expert unraveller of "The enchanting tale—the tale of pleasing woe." When one sets this poem against the letters of 1817, and considers that in the intervening months he had been studying Hazlitt, one can see what the first effect was. Keats had lacked a deep past, and this Hazlitt gave him. With it came the fear that he had arrived too late, but also the humility necessary to great work. In many instances he comes close to repeating Hazlitt's words from the *Round Table* essay "On Classical Education": "By conversing with the *mighty dead,* we imbibe sentiment with knowledge; we become strongly attached to those who can no longer either hurt or serve us, except through the influence which they exert over the mind. We feel the presence of that power which gives immortality to human thoughts and actions." Byron, though living, had never been a resource of this kind; and the tone in which Keats now praises the mighty dead is stronger and steadier, even if more deferential, than the tone in which he can praise any living poet. "I am," he writes to Haydon, "very near Agreeing with Hazlit that Shakespeare is enough for us."[2] In September 1817, three books into *Endymion,* he becomes aware of the connection between his progress as a poet and the close study of Shakespeare, and seeks a way of recording how much this has owed to Hazlitt. So he writes to a mutual friend, J. H. Reynolds: "How is Hazlitt? We were reading his [Round] Table last night—I know he thinks himself not estimated by ten People in the world—I wishe he knew he is."[3] Hazlitt's argument against egotism, which reached back to Shakespeare as a deeper source of poetic truth, seems to have calmed Keats's irritability and fortified his resolve in the pursuit of fame. It was always Hazlitt's lesson, from his abridgement of Tucker to "The Indian Jugglers," that genius works by unconscious exertions of power. Among the *Round Table* essays he had just been praising, Keats would have found the sentiment in "On Posthumous Fame": "Men of the greatest genius produce their works with too much facility (and, as it were, spontaneously) to require the love of fame as a stimulus to their exertions, or to make them deserving of the admiration of mankind as their reward. It is, indeed, one characteristic mark of the highest class of excellence to appear to come naturally from the mind of the author, without consciousness or effort." From this Keats took one of his "Axioms" of poetry, as sketched in a letter to John Taylor about revising *Endymion* for publication: "if Poetry comes not as naturally as the Leaves to a tree it had better not come at all."[4]

Two received ideas about Keats still limit both the specialist's and the common reader's understanding of his character. First, that he was a sensitive man, easily wounded, deficient perhaps in the comic sense that can delight in smart repartees or revenges; and second, that he was skeptical about the intellect, and believed an "irritable reaching after fact & reason" was typical of the analytic mind:[5] the part of him that laughed, and read books of philosophy, did not write his poetry, and to prove it he gave us *Lamia,* with the philosopher Apollonius who laughs into oblivion the thing of beauty that poetry has been vouchsafed by myth. Two comments from Keats's letters in the spring of 1818 will be of interest here. Writing to Haydon on March 21, he applauds Hazlitt's strength as a good hater— "Hazlitt has damned the bigotted and the blue–stockined how durst the man?! he is your only good damner and if ever I am damn'd— damn me if I shoul'nt like him to damn me"—and in a letter to Reynolds on April 27, he speaks of preparing "to ask Hazlitt in about a years time the best metaphysical road I can take."[6] That is, he has metaphysical ambitions like Hazlitt's own, and wants to embark on a program of reading and speculation, but will not venture to present himself at the door of so admired a preceptor until he feels sufficiently impressive.

A year later, in the winter and early spring of 1819, writing to his brother George and sister-in-law Georgiana, he copies out for their edification certain passages of Hazlitt's prose to set beside his own. One of these is a considerable stretch (five pages in a modern edition) of the "Letter to William Gifford." Hazlitt there exposed to public opprobrium the slanderers of the "Cockney school," and Keats would have seen it as an occasion of disinterested valor, at which he as a beneficiary was permitted to rejoice. In his journal-letter, even after laying down his pen for a day, Keats picks it up with no thought more pressing than to continue with Hazlitt: it is as important for George to hear from *him* as from the correspondent proper. The passage, copied out over two days, evokes Keats's comment, "The manner in which this is managed: the force and innate power with which it yeasts and works up itself—the feeling for the costume of society; is in a style of genius—He hath a demon as he himself says of Lord Byron."[7] I quoted part of this earlier as an allusion to *gusto*, but I think "yeast" is explained as well by Keats's letter to Benjamin Bailey of January 28, 1818: the "portion of good" which is all that even the best of men have, is "a kind of spiritual yeast in their frames which creates the ferment of existence—by which a Man is propell'd to act and strive and buffet with Circumstance."[8] By 1819, when the "Letter to William Gifford" was published, Hazlitt seemed to Keats almost an embodiment of the modern idea of genius.

Even more intriguing than this journal-letter is a slightly earlier one, which quotes a shorter passage of Hazlitt's. It is from the *Lectures on the English Comic Writers*, which Keats did not attend but had contrived to borrow in manuscript, probably through J. H. Reynolds. He quotes from the portrait of St. Leon—a hero of Godwin's fiction whom the lecturer rated second only to Falkland in *Caleb Williams*— and he adds his own emphasis.

> He is a limb torn off from Society. In possession of eternal youth and beauty, he can feel no love; surrounded, tantalized and tormented with riches, he can do no good. The faces of Men pass before him as in a speculum; but he is attached to them by no common tie of sympathy or suffering. He is thrown back into himself and his own thoughts. He lives in the solitude of his own breast,— without wife or child or friend or Enemy in the world. *His is the solitude of the Soul, not of woods, or trees, or mountains*—but the desert of society—the waste and oblivion of the heart. He is himself alone. His existence is purely intellectual, and is therefore intolerable to one who has felt the rapture of affection, or the anguish of woe.[9]

Breaking off, with the idea of pursuing other matters, Keats then decides "as I am about it" to continue with Hazlitt's character of Godwin. It is followed by the comment, "This appears to me quite correct," and then by a transcription of Keats's "Bards of passion"— as the earlier quotation had been directly preceded by the poem, "Ever let the Fancy roam." Here again one is struck by the way Keats manages to interleave Hazlitt's thoughts and eloquence with his own. In the whole body of his letters he gives this sort of prominence to the words of no other writer. By itself, and without the passages he later quoted from "A Letter to William Gifford," there would still be something extraordinary about this quotation, flanked on either side by a poem from Keats himself, and presented to his brother as the work of a single hand. It is as if Hazlitt's description of St. Leon and his own new poetry had appeared to

Keats, and were meant to appear to others, as a single continuous act of expression.

Hazlitt describes the solitude of one who finds "himself alone" intolerable, because his thoughts are still of society, the earth, all the common affections he has left behind. To such a figure egotism has become a *given* (however despised or regretted), and this Keats feared to be his situation as a poet. When in *The Fall of Hyperion* he set himself to endure whatever self-searchings were required to change his situation, he needed a second voice to dramatize the power of the accuser he faced, and it seems to have been his deliberate purpose to draw into the speech of the prophetess Moneta as many echoes as possible of Hazlitt's description. But the first echo is sounded by the poet himself. After his ascent to Moneta's shrine, he asks why the place of vision is deserted: "I sure should see / Other men here, but I am here alone." He is then told the strangeness of his fate:

> "Thou art a dreaming thing;
> A fever of thyself—think of the earth;
> What bliss, even in hope, is there for thee?
> What haven? Every creature hath its home;
> Every sole man hath days of joy and pain,
> Whether his labours be sublime or low—
> The pain alone; the joy alone; distinct:
> Only the dreamer venoms all his days,
> Bearing more woe than all his sins deserve."[10]

This is "the desert of society—the waste and oblivion of the heart," known to the man "thrown back into himself and his own thoughts," as Hazlitt had painted him. Keats's hope in *The Fall of Hyperion*, that something living may be salvaged from the desert, requires him to bear witness to a misery worse than his, that of the fallen Titans. What Hazlitt showed him was the interest of placing their drama within himself, and using it to open his sympathies. For he had found in writing the first *Hyperion* that as a tragic narrative, the story could not hold his attention. It touched him more nearly when he saw it as a motive for every exertion that the poet—like the Godwinian hero, always thrown back into himself—could undertake to heal the sickness of a "purely intellectual" existence. The character of St. Leon answers to the idea of himself which Keats cherished throughout his early life, as well as to the image of the artist, cast out by society to be preserved for immortality, which he bequeathed to a third and fourth generation of romantics. It is plain in his letters that this was also the way he saw Hazlitt. The discovery of a genius of criticism, isolated by genius as by politics, but possessed of a "demon" in all his trials, was for Keats the discovery of another self.

He first met Hazlitt in January 1818, and felt bold enough to
call on him by December 1818. But Hazlitt would have known about
Keats even before they met, not only from the poems Hunt showed
him but from Keats's article "On Edmund Kean as a Shakespearean
Actor," which appeared in the *Champion* of December 21, 1817,
and contained a sentence easily mistakable for one of Hazlitt's: "There
is an indescribable gusto in his voice, by which we feel that the
utterer is thinking of the past and the future, while speaking of the
instant."[11] Once they were acquainted, Hazlitt gave Keats advice
about writing for magazines and, what was far more important, noticed
him in a generous aside of his *Lectures on the English Poets*. We
know how this came about, again from the evidence of Keats's letters.
To Bailey, on January 23, 1818, Keats wrote that he would be
attending the lectures as they were first delivered. In the event he
missed some, but he certainly heard the sixth, "On Swift, Young,
Gray, Collins, etc.," which included a judgment of Chatterton: "He
did not show extraordinary powers of genius, but extraordinary pre-
cocity. Nor do I believe he would have written better, had he lived.
He knew this himself, or he would have lived." How Keats was
affected by this dismissal may be guessed from the circumstances of
his life; and he spoke of his response in the letter to George and
Tom Keats of February 21, 1818: "I hear Hazlitt's Lectures regularly—his last was on Grey Collins, Young &c. and he gave a very
fine piece of discriminating criticism of Swift, Voltaire And Rabelais—
I was very disappointed at his treatment of Chatterton—I generally
meet with many I know there."[12] He arrived at an earlier lecture,
as he told Tom and George, "just as they were coming out, when
all these pounced upon me, Hazlitt, John Hunt & son, Wells, Bewick,
all the Landseers, Bob Harris, Rox of the Burrough Aye & more."[13]
Beside the casual phrase, "I generally meet with many I know there,"
this seems to show that Keats was in the habit of conversing freely
after the lectures, with Hazlitt and his circle. Some such conversation
after the sixth lecture will account for Hazlitt's recognition of him
in the seventh.

> I am sorry that what I said in the conclusion of the last Lecture
> respecting Chatterton, should have given dissatisfaction to some
> persons, with whom I would willingly agree on all such matters.
> What I meant was less to call in question Chatterton's genius, than
> to object to the common mode of estimating its magnitude by its
> prematureness. The lists of fame are not filled with the dates of
> births or deaths; and the side mark of the age at which they were
> done, wears out in works destined for immortality. (V, 123)

Hazlitt's later appreciations of Keats are generally of two kinds.
First, he recognizes him as an independent voice, one who can

command the tones of genius and is leagued with himself against the mob of government critics and court bards. Keats's "fine fancy and powerful invention," he writes in the *Edinburgh Review* article on "The Periodical Press," "were too obvious to be treated with mere neglect; and as he had not been ushered into the world with the court stamp upon him, he was to be crushed as a warning to genius how it keeps company with honesty, and as a sure means of inoculating the ingenuous spirit and talent of the country with timely and systematic servility." Second, and in a very different key, he simply quotes Keats, as a touchstone of the original note in poetry after Wordsworth. In *The Spirit of the Age* for example, after illustrating the pedantic puerility of Gifford's *Baviad* and *Maeviad,* he quotes *The Eve of St. Agnes* for the pleasure of its "rich beauties and dim obscurities." In the essay "On Reading Old Books," he adds that "the reading of Mr. Keats's Eve of Saint Agnes lately made me regret that I was not young again." But the best homage he pays Keats is the impulse with which, to relieve an uneventful moment of his *Journey through France and Italy,* he launches into a one-line quotation from a poem then hardly five years in the world, as if everyone he cared to have as a reader would know it: "Oh for a beaker full of the warm South!" He had already published, in the essay "On Effeminacy of Character," a more stringent verdict on the poems than these gestures of loyalty seem to indicate.

> I cannot help thinking that the fault of Mr. Keats's poems was a deficiency in masculine energy of style. He had beauty, tenderness, delicacy, in an uncommon degree, but there was a want of strength and substance. His Endymion is a very delightful description of the illusions of a youthful imagination, given up to airy dreams—we have flowers, clouds, rainbows, moonlight, all sweet sounds and smells, and Oreads and Dryads flitting by—but there is nothing tangible in it, nothing marked or palpable—we have none of the hardy spirit or rigid forms of antiquity. He painted his own thoughts and character; and did not transport himself into the fabulous and heroic ages. There is a want of action, or character, and so far, of imagination. . . . We see in him the youth, without the manhood of poetry. (VIII, 254–55)

But I suspect he wrote this before looking closely at the 1820 volume, with *Hyperion* and the odes. Besides, he was saying no more than Keats himself had admitted in his Preface.

> [My Preface] is not written with the least atom of purpose to forestall criticisms of course, but from the desire I have to conciliate men who are competent to look, and who do look with a zealous eye, to the honour of English literature.
> The imagination of a boy is healthy, and the mature imagination of a man is healthy; but there is a space of life between, in which

the soul is in a ferment, the character undecided, the way of life uncertain, the ambition thick-sighted: thence proceeds mawkishness, and all the thousand bitters which those men I speak of must necessarily taste in going over the following pages.[14]

Hazlitt's failure to review *Endymion* doubtless proceeded from a reluctance to say anything that might be wounding to its author. He kept the disappointment to himself while Keats was alive; gave his reputation several lifts following one skeptical delay after his death; and saved a final estimate for the section on Keats in *Select British Poets* (1824), where as Keats's first anthologist he had a chance to exhibit once more the depth of taste for which he had earned the lasting esteem of his subject. There are three passages from *Endymion*—including the Procession and Hymn in Honour of Pan (ending with the words "But in old marbles ever beautiful"), and the Indian Lady's Song—along with one from *Hyperion*, the "Ode to a Nightingale," "Fancy," and "Robin Hood." I have said that Keats found his second self in Hazlitt, and that he showed this particularly in the insistence that his brother read his verse beside Hazlitt's prose, as examples of kindred energies. Hazlitt was the older man in this friendship, and a comparable intensity of response could not be expected from him. But he wrote about Keats and appears also to have treated him as his equal in genius. No other encounter between poet and critic has been so fortunate for literature.

This does not strike me as the sort of influence—involving the spread of doctrine—which it has usually been supposed to exemplify. Keats understood Hazlitt's ideas till they became second nature to him; but the ideas were always inseparable from the tact of expression; Hazlitt's power, in every way, was *communicated.* This may be harder for us to see, and more paradoxical for us to ask questions about, than it would have seemed to romantic authors, for we find border-crossing expeditions between poetry and prose more difficult than they did. At any rate I think Hazlitt's effect on Keats can be traced to something so minute as the pace of his movement in verse, which is not the sinuous grace of Coleridge or the lapidary deliberation of Wordsworth, but the variable speed of uncommon thoughts, hurried along as each shift of subject permits a new accession of power. Keats has, in poetry as well as prose, the "fiery laconicism" he praised in Hazlitt—a very different thing from Byron's whirlwind truculence. *Lamia* is perhaps his closest approach to a middle style, and to Hazlitt's prose: its verse is lively, swift to digress and return, and at home in all the possible roles of a narrator.

> Love in a hut, with water and a crust,
> Is—Love, forgive us!—cinders, ashes, dust;
> Love in a palace is perhaps at last

More grievous torment than a hermit's fast:—
That is a doubtful tale from faery land,
Hard for the non-elect to understand.
Had Licius liv'd to hand his story down,
He might have given the moral a fresh frown,
Or clench'd it quite: but too short was their bliss
To breed distrust and hate, that make the soft voice hiss.
Besides, there, nightly, with terrific glare,
Love, jealous grown of so complete a pair,
Hover'd and buzz'd his wings, with fearful roar,
Above the lintel of their chamber door,
And down the passage cast a glow upon the floor.[15]

Though the opening two couplets make an observant and not uncritical homage to Byron's style of worldliness, the disclaimer, "Hard for the non-elect to understand," and "He might have given the moral a fresh frown, / Or clench'd it quite," are pure Hazlitt, in their self-confidence and gusto, and freedom from self-regard. Yet Keats speaks as a moral narrator not in his poems, but in the aphorisms of his letters. These have made him, in a few sayings, the single most widely quoted authority on the program of romanticism, apart from Blake; and yet his aphorisms have the peculiarity that they are useless to those who respect less than the whole of their context. This was a quality of Hazlitt's aphorisms too, and it seems to belong more largely to the discursive genius of empiricism. Here I want only to remind the reader of four well-known observations for which Hazlitt's thought, as I have been tracing it, supplies a context even more satisfying than Keats's *Letters*.

The first, from a letter to Bailey of November 22, 1817, concerns the poet's freedom from the habitual or irritable demands of a single fixed identity, a set "character": "Men of Genius are great as certain ethereal Chemicals operating on the Mass of neutral intellect—but they have not any individuality, any determined Character. I would call the top and head of those who have a proper self Men of Power."[16] Men of Power are great because there is no telling what will strike them: Wordsworth's attraction to the lichen on the rock, Rousseau's care for the lustres of his remembered life, as epitomised by the memory "*Ah, voilà de la pervenche,*" are equally unpredictable from any individuality but theirs; whereas Byron is doubtless somewhere below the "top and head" of this class, having (only more fluently) the strange and picturesque imaginings that come to most men, when they put themselves in a strange and picturesque mood. Shakespeare on the contrary would rank highest among the "Men of Genius" whose individuality is dispersed through the invention of dramatic characters. Keats refers to nothing more than the mystery surrounding this dispersion, when he speaks of chemicals "operating on the Mass of neutral intellect": he makes no claim for the poet's detachment or impersonality.

John Middleton Murry thought the contrast between Shakespeare and Wordsworth must have been present to Keats's mind whenever he set men of genius against men of power.[17] The special importance of Shakespeare as a foil to the man of power, and as an example of how the highest genius surpasses the egotistical, appears more clearly by the proximity of the foregoing remarks to some others about Wordsworth, offered after two months of further reflection, in the letter to Reynolds of February 3, 1818.

> It may be said that we ought to read our Contemporaries. that Wordsworth &c should have their due from us. but for the sake of a few fine imaginative or domestic passages, are we to be bullied into a certain Philosophy engendered in the whims of an Egotist— Every man has his speculations, but every man does not brood and peacock over them till he makes a false coinage and deceives himself. . . . We hate poetry that has a palpable design upon us—and if we do not agree, seems to put its hands in its breeches pockets.[18]

Once again it was Hazlitt who gave Keats the polemical assurance one feels at work here. His review of *The Excursion* was the incitement without which we should hardly be reading Keats today, and this letter was written soon after the lecture "On Poetry in General."

The dramatic poet according to Hazlitt had a scope for his imaginative energies denied to the lyric poet—as the man of genius has a *range* of powers denied to the man of power. Keats is still pondering the difference in a letter to Haydon, of April 8, 1818, on the subject of heroic painting. What he can never know intimately about an artist of genius, but always believes in the existence of, are "the innumerable compositions and decompositions which take place between the intellect and its thousand materials before it arrives at that trembling delicate and snail-horn perception of Beauty," the result of much careful exploring in "your many havens of intenseness."[19] The immediate source is Hazlitt's lecture on Shakespeare, from a few weeks earlier, with its observation that in Shakespeare there is no "fixed essence of character" but "a continual composition and decomposition of its elements, a fermentation of every particle in the whole mass, by its alternate affinity and antipathy to other principles which are brought into contact with it." I have shown how Hazlitt adapted the same thought to a larger subject in the essay "On Imitation," where art "divides and decompounds objects into a thousand curious parts." The vocabulary of both Hazlitt and Keats in this instance, is pretty plainly Lockean, for Locke had spoken of the difficulty in "moral names" as peculiar to the associative process of composition and decomposition: "What need of a sign, when the thing signified is present and in view? But in moral names, that cannot be so easily and shortly done, because of the many decompositions that go to the making up the complex ideas of those modes."[20] One may see this as part of the same difficulty that interested Hazlitt and Keats, by reflecting that moral names are nothing but the signs for Hazlitt's "moral quantities," that is, for the stuff of character itself. Coleridge too had a way of employing this vocabulary, but generally with disgust, as a thing appropriate to the fallen labors of the understanding: "The leading differences," he writes in Appendix C of *The Statesman's Manual*, "between mechanic and vital philosophy may all be drawn from one point namely, that the former demanding for every mode and act of existence real or possible *visibility*, knows only of distance and nearness, composition (or rather juxtaposition) and decomposition, in short the relations of unproductive particles to each other. . . . This is the philosophy of death, and only of a dead nature can it hold good."[21] Keats, however, as much as Hazlitt, believed it was a philosophy of life. He would have expected Haydon as a painter to understand in advance that the compositions and decompositions can never confidently be numbered or classified; but in employing the phrase nevertheless he went out of his way to adopt an Enlightenment view of his experiments in poetry.

Their understanding of the mind's compositions and decompositions had broad implications for the politics of both Hazlitt and Keats. The same sympathies by which a reader of literature was taken out of his habitual self, allowed to inhabit other characters, and encouraged to revise the story of his own life by the alternate affinities and antipathies that he chose, made any system unnatural which supposed that the boundaries of self and of continuous identity were more permanent in society than in the individual mind, as it traveled from thought to thought. Only in the absence of such imposed boundaries could the man of genius and the man of power reside together in a single body. "Man," Keats tells Reynolds, in a letter of February 19, 1818, "should not dispute or assert but whisper results to his neighbour, and thus by every germ of Spirit sucking the Sap from mould ethereal every human might become great, and Humanity instead of being a wide heath of Furse and Briars with here and there a remote Oak or Pine, would become a grand democracy of Forest Trees."[22] Some days later, in the *Examiner* for March 7, 1818, Keats would have found a similar feeling in the first installment of Hazlitt's great manifesto, "What Is the People?": "— And who are you that ask the question? One of the people. And yet you would be something! Then you would not have the People nothing. For what is the people? Millions of men, like you, with hearts beating in their bosoms, blood circulating in their veins, with wants and appetites, and passions and anxious cares, and busy purposes and affections for others and a respect for themselves, and a desire for happiness, and a right to freedom, and a will to be free" (VII, 259). If the sound is fiercer than any we can imagine as native to Keats's grand democracy of forest trees, the reason is that Hazlitt was addressing those who must clamor and shout before they can be heard in whispers. But far from despising the quieter calling that Keats pursued, he was eager for its result, from the very start of a short career. The new voice was also an answering voice, and had for him the quality of a confirmation.

"ODE TO A NIGHTINGALE"

Negative capability was Keats's name for one elusive element that goes "to form a Man of Achievement especially in Literature, and which Shakespeare possessed so enormously."[23] The emphasis on Shakespeare owes much to Hazlitt's criticism; so does the unorthodox notion that art's task of selection and construction must begin with a negative sort of triumph: a purging away of the interfering self, and of all its particles of irritability. Apart from *The Round Table*, "A Letter to William Gifford," and Hazlitt's two books of lectures, he likely read the *Essay on Human Action;* and his thoughts about dramatic poetry were made keener by the *Characters of Shakespeare's Plays,* of which he praised the chapter on *King Lear* for its "hieroglyphic visioning." What he found most useful were Hazlitt's doubts about the predominance of the self in modern poetry: the egotistical, Hazlitt taught, was only one version of the sublime, and a limited one. The highest poetry makes us forget the identity of the poet in the many identities he assumes; thus Shakespeare had "only to think of any thing in order to become that thing, with all the circumstances belonging to it." He seems to us in dramatic works, as he passes from one character to another, "like the same soul successively animating different bodies."

In a letter to Richard Woodhouse of October 27, 1818, Keats adopted this idea for his own ends, and turned it against Wordsworth.

> As to the poetical Character itself, (I mean that sort of which, if I am any thing, I am a Member; that sort distinguished from the wordsworthian or egotistical sublime; which is a thing per se and stands alone) it is not itself—it has no self—it is every thing and nothing—It has no character—it enjoys light and shade; it lives in gusto, be it foul or fair, high or low, rich or poor, mean or elevated—It has as much delight in conceiving an Iago as an Imogen. What shocks the virtuous philosopher, delights the camelion Poet. It does no harm from its relish of the dark side of things any more than from its taste for the bright one; because they both end in speculation. A Poet is the most unpoetical of any thing in existence;

because he has no Identity—he is continually informing and filling some other Body.[24]

Keats here is curiously more polemical than Hazlitt. The main thing he wants the poet to avoid is any aspiration to the "wordsworthian or egotistical sublime": without the parenthesis his injunction would read, "As to the poetical character itself . . . it is not itself." Self, the "thing per se," Wordsworth (as Hazlitt described him) taking a personal interest in the universe, is the enemy whom the sentence rounds upon. Wordsworth remains himself entirely too much of the time. Yet why should Keats have made an antagonist of the poet who had created in *The Excursion* another of the "three things" he thought would survive the age? Keats too aimed to be a poet of the sublime, and perhaps that is reason enough. His sublimity, when he came to know it, would be closely related to Wordsworth's, but to invent it at all and discover the strength to pursue it, he had to believe the difference was going to be tremendous.

He hoped to attain a point of view from which sublime emotions could be his as a more than temporary privilege. At the same time he needed to be invulnerable to the charge of egotism that he had brought against Wordsworth. He was reconciled to seeing the self dominate his poetry as much as it had Wordsworth's; but unlike Wordsworth he would leave the way open to feel as someone or something else. The change has to do with dramatic situation. The narrator of a Keats ode is always on the verge of becoming not quite himself, and he makes us believe that to remain so is to widen experience. But this sounds like what English critics have sometimes called "empathy"—translating the German *Einfühlung*—and I need to say why it is closer to what Hazlitt all along had been calling "sympathy." Empathy is the process by which a mind so projects itself into its object that a transfer of qualities seems to take place. Keats, on the other hand, was looking for a capability of so heightening the imagination's response to anything that the identities of both the mind and its object would grow more vivid *as what they are*. Nor had Wordsworth failed utterly to advance this quest for an intenser sympathy. His poetry struck Keats as evidence that there was a "grand march of intellect"—even Milton "did not think into the human heart, as Wordsworth has done."[25] Yet the suspicion lingered with him that Wordsworth's poetry, though of a new kind, was not the most profound of its kind.

"To this point was Wordsworth come," Keats writes, in the letter I have just quoted: to this point, he means, and no further. For Wordsworth had remained content with what by Keats's lights was a constricting half-knowledge. He saw into his own heart only, and therefore the outward lesson of his poetry, which was the need for accommodation to the teachings of nature, made possible an inward deception. The accommodation really went the other way: nature, or a carefully selected aspect of it, was bent to the will of the poet. To a youthful admirer this could seem a betrayal of both poetry and nature, in the name of the human heart. Poetry, because Wordsworth by his choice of subjects and his limitation of tone, had contracted its scope so drastically; nature, because it now occupied the foreground of every poem, but was seen only through the distorting medium of poetry that had "a palpable design upon us." Keats's sense of disappointment is not what most readers can be expected to feel, when they read Wordsworth after Pope and Cowper, and beside Byron and Scott. But Keats had at this time a relentless narrowness of focus. He read Wordsworth after Shakespeare and beside Shakespeare.

Alison, and associationist critics generally, had argued that any object in nature could be expressive, because it had to be interpreted as an object of the mind, and would give back the mind's own expression as if from afar by awakening "trains of thought." If one takes this as a creed of individual life, and reads the associations of each mind as its signature, then associationism becomes a powerful sanction for the egotistical sublime. But if one supposes such trains of thought are interesting because they can be shared—if one concludes that the reader can be taught to recognize in them the workings of his own mind, and not encouraged to end in awe of the poet's— then associationism looks like the right intellectual groundwork for a poetry of sympathy. To the latter point Keats had come, by the time he wrote his odes: the reaction that his reading of Hazlitt fostered gives him more in common with Alison's American disciples like Bryant, than with Wordsworth after 1800. No single passage of Hazlitt's carries the force that the ideal of sympathy had to gather little by little in Keats's mind, through reading and reflection and the writing of new poems. Yet the conclusion of the essay "On Reason and Imagination"—written too late for Keats to have known it— gives an essence of the kind of understanding Keats was working toward, in his letters diffusely, and in his odes with an effect of such concentration that they make the ideal hard to name.

> Man is (so to speak) an endless and infinitely varied repetition: and if we know what one man feels, we so far know what a thousand feel in the sanctuary of their being. . . . As is our perception of this original truth, the root of our imagination, so will the force and richness of the general impression proceeding from it be. The boundary of our sympathy is a circle which enlarges itself according to its propulsion from the centre—the heart. If we are imbued with a deep sense of individual weal or woe, we shall be awe-struck at the idea of humanity in general. . . . If we understand the texture

and vital feeling, we then can fill up the outline, but we cannot supply the former from having the latter given. Moral and poetical truth is like expression in a picture—the one is not to be attained by smearing over a large canvas, nor the other by bestriding a vague topic. . . . I defy any great tragic writer to despise that nature which he understands, or that heart which he has probed, with all its rich bleeding materials of joy and sorrow. The subject may not be a source of much triumph to him, from its alternate light and shade, but it can never become one of supercilious in-difference. He must feel a strong reflex interest in it, corresponding to that which he has depicted in the characters of others. Indeed, the object and end of playing, "both at the first and now, is to hold the mirror up to nature," to enable us to feel for others as for ourselves, or to embody a distinct interest out of ourselves by the force of imagination and passion.[26] (XII, 54–55)

Hazlitt's "light and shade" necessary to a work of art—an associa-tionist trope for the whole that is implied by the coexistence of opposite parts—appear also in Keats's sketch of the poetical character, and they will reappear in his last letter: "the knowledge of contrast, feeling for light and shade, all that information (primitive sense) necessary for a poem are great enemies of the stomach."[27] As he prepared to write the "Ode to a Nightingale" in particular, he was pondering what it meant to write from a sanctuary of being, such as Hazlitt speaks of, and what course the imagination might trace from it. The "boundary of our sympathy," a "circle which enlarges itself according to its propulsion from the centre—the heart," was the region he hoped to explore in this poem.

Before discussing the poem I must add an unexpected link be-tween the act of sympathy which it presents, and the argument for disinterested action in Hazlitt's *Essay*. On March 19, 1819, in the same journal-letter that had quoted the "Letter to William Gifford," Keats told his brother that the energies displayed in any natural activity "though erroneous . . . may be fine—This is the very thing in which consists poetry; and if so it is not so fine a thing as philosophy—For the same reason that an eagle is not so fine a thing as a truth."[28] An eagle like a poem is beautiful quite apart from its moral qualities, moral truth not being understood here as a necessary condition of beauty. Yet it takes second place to a truth, as nature in our eyes takes second place to human society. The remark is partly explained by a passage earlier in the same letter which is not as well known: "I perceive how far I am from any humble standard of disinterestedness—Yet this feeling ought to be carried to its highest pitch, as there is no fear of its ever injuring society—which it would do I fear pushed to an extremity—For in wild nature the Hawk would loose his Breakfast of Robins and the Robin his of Worms—

The Lion must starve as well as the swallow."[29] Disinterestedness ought to be kept up: it is a finer thing than self-interest, and as Hazlitt had shown it seems harder to act from only because we are trained by habit to look first to ourselves. It is of our very humanity to be disinterested, as much as it is to be self-centered. But when we move from human society to nature the matter alters. The possibility of disinterested action then turns out to be a result of artificial arrangements which society brings into being. Reduced to a practice by the hawk, it would oblige him to lose his meal. The hawk and eagle are not expected to act from disinterested motives, any more than they are expected to feel sympathy. Do they in this resemble the poet?

Keats wrote his letter in an experimental mood. It took the Ode to show us that poetry is more impressive than the eagle of his comparison would allow it to be. In their freedom from care and sympathy alike, the eagle and hawk resemble only one of the singers in Keats's poem: the nightingale. Keats aims to feel as it does. Yet the difference between them remains his necessary human inheritance. Having once recognized this, one may call his expansive gesture of identification by the name of empathy or, as seems more in keeping with Keats's own vocabulary, sympathy, but in either case it will be understood that the poet carries out an imaginative action of which the bird is incapable.[30] Indeed, the poet is only a poet by virtue of this gesture. He of all men feels in this way, even if he regrets the continual renewals of feeling and, with each wave, the sharper awareness that his subject is compounded of light and shade. So, in the course of the poem, those elements of the poet's character that belong to the irritable self, and can encounter nothing without palpable design, will vanish. The sort of personality that Keats still believes in is what Hazlitt described in his *Essay*, as "nothing more than conscious individuality: it is the power of perceiving that you are and what you are from the immediate reflection of the mind on its own operations, sensations, or ideas."

If one places those words from the *Essay* beside Keats's appreciation of a certain phase of Milton's poetry, where the reader feels the "Author's consolations coming thick upon him at a time when he complains most,"[31] one will have a fair sense of the intellectual allegiances he took for granted when he wrote.

> My heart aches, and a drowsy numbness pains
>   My sense, as though of hemlock I had drunk,
> Or emptied some dull opiate to the drains
>   One minute past, and Lethe-wards had sunk:
> 'Tis not through envy of thy happy lot,
>   But being too happy in thine happiness—

> That thou, light-winged Dryad of the trees,
>   In some melodious plot
> Of beechen green, and shadows numberless,
>   Singest of summer in full-throated ease.

One recalls the aphorism from "The Indian Jugglers," that "greatness is great power, producing great effects." In the "Ode to Psyche" Keats's reader might have been conscious of the effects without feeling certain of the power: what kind it was, and from what source it claimed its authority. Even the identity of that poem's speaker is indefinite, until he comes upon Cupid and Psyche, and can assume their energy as his own.

> I wander'd in a forest thoughtlessly,
>   And, on the sudden, fainting with surprise,
> Saw two fair creatures.

From this lucky diversion he gets his chance to make a poetry filled with sensations as well as thoughts. Still he draws all his strength from what he beholds; he cannot offer the sympathy of one distinct being for another, because he hardly exists before he unveils the lovers; he himself, it may be said, is created by the act of sympathy. There is thus a quiet irony in the powerful line, "I see, and sing, by my own eyes inspir'd."

The reader who moves from this to the "Ode to a Nightingale" is startled by the presence of a feeling "I." One knows a good deal about this speaker after five lines: that he is acquainted with griefs and their numb aftermath; that envy (a twisted sympathy) is a motive he wants to rise above; that he is not quite conquered by cares, but acquires a strange vigilance from the pressure of having to contemplate them. The rest of the stanza opens an ambiguity which the rest of the poem will dramatize: "being too happy in thine happiness" may refer either to the poet or the bird; but the bird is never fully present except through the poet. Something must correspond to the "Thou," and yet it remains spectral without the "I," syntactically and grammatically tenuous. When the stanza achieves a finality of place and feeling, in "some melodious plot / Of beechen green, and shadows numberless," one feels that this could belong to the nightingale only with the spirit that inhabits it in conversation.

Keats's second stanza opens with a private joke against himself, "O, for a draught of vintage." Claret had appeared in his letters among the accessories proper to the full life of sensations. Now it is lovingly described, but with an awareness that its effect is to dull sensation, and to obscure identity. The effect can be felt especially in the Miltonic inversions of the last two lines—"That I might drink, and leave the world unseen, / And with thee fade away into the forest dim." The poet wishes to be unseen; but the world, given his present

state, will also be unseen by him. Were the assimilative logic extended
much beyond this, the second stanza would leave Keats in the situation
of the knight in "La Belle Dame sans Merci." But any such ending
is held back by a vision of ordinary suffering in a world less fortunate
than the nightingale's, the world without motion in which Keats had
nursed his brother Tom through the days just before his death. Its
mood is dictated by powers offstage—in the poem itself, by the "fade
away" that still governs from the last stanza—and the actions it
permits are all subordinate.

> Here, where men sit and hear each other groan;
>   Where palsy shakes a few, sad, last gray hairs,
>   Where youth grows pale, and spectre-thin, and dies;
>   Where but to think is to be full of sorrow
>   And leaden-eyed despairs,
>   Where Beauty cannot keep her lustrous eyes,
>   Or new Love pine at them beyond to-morrow.

Doubts of the real worth of poetry were crowding in upon Keats as
he wrote this stanza; what at worst is done out of vanity may be
judged by posterity to have been done in vain also. Is not every poet
an egotist, compared to every nurse? How is Tom's death to be
weighed in the balance with the composition of an ode?

From the burden of these questions Keats fancies for the moment
that he can be released by an act of willed elation. The interjection,
"Away! Away!" wards off the evil and, in the same breath, declares
him bound for new regions. He is helped in this escape by the
temporary artifice of a myth. Yet the language in which he presents
it—"haply the Queen-Moon is on her throne, / Cluster'd around by
all her starry Fays"—is facile in the worst style of *Endymion*. The
effect I think is deliberate: Keats had to hear these particular notes
ring false before he could be delivered back to himself. Unlike the
bird he cannot join the night's tenderness simply by doing what is
in his nature. He can join it nevertheless, by looking with different
eyes on what has surrounded him all along. This is the major transition
of the Ode, and as he enters it Keats's impression is that he is dazed,
and for the first time must move slowly.

> I cannot see what flowers are at my feet,
>   Nor what soft incense hangs upon the boughs,
> But, in embalmed darkness, guess each sweet
>   Wherewith the seasonable month endows
> The grass, the thicket, and the fruit-tree wild;
>   White hawthorn, and the pastoral eglantine;
>   Fast fading violets cover'd up in leaves;
>   And mid-May's eldest child

> The coming musk-rose, full of dewy wine,
> The murmurous haunt of flies on summer eves.

Here the poet is "cluster'd around" like the Queen-Moon: what she boded only he can fulfill humanly. As in "To Autumn," the catalogue here follows the course of a season, the early growths separable and a little plain, the late ones replete and intertwined. The effortless naturalism of the writing suggests that the hope Keats expressed in a letter to Bailey, of a kind of immortality from "having what we called happiness on Earth repeated in a finer tone and so repeated," was both sincere and pure of hermetic intent. That version of heaven was for those who delighted in sensation rather than hungered after truth. But Keats avoided the word "heaven"; he cared more for "havens of intenseness," wherever the artist might find them: his own life would arrive at a spiritual repetition from the effort of sympathy to compass ever vaster subjects. In this stanza he seems to have found the resting place from which the effort can begin.

He does not pause long. The sixth stanza will require his largest act of identification—the embrace of death—and Keats has too lively a sense of surprise, and even here too keen a love of the sheer sport of the exertion, to collect all his thoughts before us. Two associations seem to control his movement: "embalmed darkness" with its subtle shock had left the expectation that his mood would be explained, or more fully encountered; and the flower-catalogue had lightly echoed a similar description in "Lycidas," where the poet's bier was strewn with "The Musk-rose, and the well-attir'd woodbine, / With cowslips wan that hang the pensive head, / And every flower that sad embroidery wears." Keats must have discovered by these associations that he was composing an elegy after all. It remained for him to give it the shape of an elegy for himself, but without grief. The triumph of his movement from this to the next stanza is that he makes an apparently egotistical turn of the Ode coincide with its farthest stretch of imaginative sympathy.

> Darkling I listen; and, for many a time
> I have been half in love with easeful Death,
> Call'd him soft names in many a mused rhyme,
> To take into the air my quiet breath;
> Now more than ever seems it rich to die,
> To cease upon the midnight with no pain,
> While thou art pouring forth thy soul abroad
> In such an ecstasy!
> Still wouldst thou sing, and I have ears in vain—
> To thy high requiem become a sod.

With the phrase "Darkling I listen," an adjective probable only for the bird is appropriated by the poet; and it is understood that his readers will complete the exchange for themselves: "Thou wast not born for death, immortal Keats." Anti-sentimentalist critics have supposed that he was here confessing himself in love with death and, since there is something suspect in this, that he needed to shake free of the delusion before his poem was finished. Yet in calling death "easeful" he means, not "death, which is always easeful" but "one sort of death which has seemed easeful to me." This line, and all the lines that prepare for it, have an air neither of defiance nor of passive suffering and defeat. Death is in the poem, as a no longer terrifying allegorical figure, because death is where the full diapason of human identity must close. A sufficient motive for Keats's poise is the untroubled connection he makes, however hard we may find it, between death and immortality. He finds nothing strange in asking death to possess and continue his own wind of inspiration, "To take into the air my quiet breath."

The most perfect gloss I can imagine for the seventh stanza is Hazlitt's account of the dramatic strength in Shakespeare's poetry, which Keats heard him say aloud in the lecture-hall and never forgot: "The passions are in a state of projection. Years are melted down to moments, and every instant teems with fate. We know the results, we see the process." At the conclusion of another lecture, "On Thomson and Cowper," Hazlitt connected this "process" with listening, and not merely thinking and speaking: "The cuckoo, 'that wandering voice,' that comes and goes with the spring, mocks our ears with one note from youth to age; and the lap-wing, screaming around the traveler's path, repeats for ever the same sad story of Tereus and Philomel." In Keats's mind these two passages had now joined.

> Thou wast not born for death, immortal Bird!
>   No hungry generations tread thee down;
> The voice I hear this passing night was heard
>   In ancient days by emperor and clown:
> Perhaps the self-same song that found a path
>   Through the sad heart of Ruth, when, sick for home,
>   She stood in tears amid the alien corn;
>   The same that oft-times hath
>   Charm'd magic casements, opening on the foam
> Of perilous seas, in faery lands forlorn.

Listening to the "self-same song that found a path / Through the sad heart of Ruth," he projects himself in imagination into the prospect that stretched before her amid the alien corn. His success here makes anything possible, and so the casement becomes magic. Only after his venture into a human history, and by an effect best described, in the anachronistic language of the cinema, as montage, do we see the picture of Ruth give way to a kindred, equally generous but now visionary scene, opening "on the foam / Of perilous seas, in faery lands forlorn."

Keats, as J. R. Caldwell demonstrated in *John Keats's Fancy,* wrote many of his poems in a kind of trance-state, which he believed congenial to the high argument of psychological romance. This practice would free him from habitual trains of thought—he might be bad but he would not be second-hand—and it would allow his imagination the unchanneled freedom which gave a promise of enduring invention. Some unhappy poems were produced as a result, but his greatest poems, the "Ode to a Nightingale" among them, were evidently written in much the same way. What may puzzle us is not the strangeness of his practice, since later poets have made it familiar, but rather Keats's implicit reliance on an exalted idea of the unconscious. There was no source for this in the associationist writers he knew, and we seem to be left with the true but primitive explanation that he invented the beliefs he needed to carry conviction. I prefer instead to enlist Hazlitt's aid again, by quoting from his essay "On Dreams," but with the same limitation I placed on the passage from "On Reason and Imagination." In these cases unlike the lectures and *The Round Table,* we cannot suppose that he showed Keats the way to his own thoughts. "On Dreams" was written after the Ode, and its interest is that it presents a genius of comparable sympathies working through a similar course of speculations.

Nevertheless I believe the essay brings some sort of order to the apparently lawless drift of fancy that Keats encouraged in himself; and the following passage may be read as a commentary on Keats's preferred manner of composition from *Endymion* to the odes.

> The *conscious* or connecting link between our ideas, which forms them into separate groups or compares different parts and views of a subject together, seems to be that which is principally wanting in sleep; so that any idea that presents itself in this anarchy of the mind is lord of the ascendant for the moment, and is driven out by the next straggling notion that comes across it. The bundles of thought are, as it were, untied, loosened from a common centre, and drift along the stream of fancy as it happens. . . . Thus we confound one person with another, merely from some accidental coincidence, the name or the place where we have seen them, or their having been concerned with us in some particular transaction the evening before. They lose and regain their proper identity perhaps half a dozen times in this rambling way; nor are we able (though we are somewhat incredulous and surprised at these compound creations) to detect the error, from not being prepared to trace the same connected subject of thought to a number of varying

and successive ramifications, or to form the idea of a *whole*. . . .
The difference, so far then, between sleeping and waking, seems
to be that in the latter we have a greater range of conscious
recollections, a larger discourse of reason, and associate ideas in
longer trains and more as they are connected with one another in
the order of nature; whereas in the former, any two impressions,
that meet or are alike, join company, and then are parted again,
without notice, like the froth from the wave. So in madness, there
is, I should apprehend, the same tyranny of the imagination over
the judgment; that is, the mind has slipped its cable, and single
images meet, and jostle, and unite suddenly together, without any
power to arrange or compare them with others, with which they
are connected in the world of reality. There is a continual phantasmagoria: whatever shapes and colours come together are by the
heat and violence of the brain referred to external nature, without
regard to the order of time, place, or circumstance. From the same
want of continuity, we often forget our dreams so speedily: if we
cannot catch them as they are passing out at the door, we never
set eyes on them again. (XII, 20–21)

It is the conscious link between our ideas that organizes our
experience into a consistent mass, and creates in us the abstract idea
of self. We need this idea and this link if we are to be masters rather
than servants of our associated ideas, and use the power of the
imagination. Yet in sleep, or the kind of trance that slips the mind's
cable, we are at the mercy of every chance link that may happen to
connect our ideas, as they pass by each other and catch upon some
salient point. We are thus robbed of the idea of a coherent self which
seems to endow us with more than accidentally formed associations,
and from which we gain the conviction of our power as agents. The
waking imagination, no less than the judgment, requires the support
of some such conviction, and Keats in his final stanza has to exorcise
an impending tyranny of the dreaming imagination.

> Forlorn! the very word is like a bell
>   To toll me back from thee to my sole self!
> Adieu! the fancy cannot cheat so well
>   As she is fam'd to do, deceiving elf.
> Adieu! adieu! thy plaintive anthem fades
>   Past the near meadows, over the still stream,
>   Up the hill-side; and now 'tis buried deep
>   In the next valley-glades:
>   Was it a vision, or a waking dream?
>   Fled is that music:—Do I wake or sleep?

The contrast between waking and dreaming imagination, or between the "continual phantasmagoria" of sleep and the habitual
relations of the self, had been given a different shading in Book II

of *Endymion*, where the return from wandering thoughts was seen as a compelled tribute paid by fancy to the repressive self.

> There, when new wonders ceas'd to float before,
> And thoughts of self came on, how crude and sore
> The journey homeward to habitual self!
> A mad pursuing of the fog-born elf,
> Whose flitting lantern, through rude nettle-briar,
> Cheats us into a swamp, into a fire,
> Into the bosom of a hated thing.[32]

The recurrence in the Ode both of "cheat," and of the self-elf rhyme, persuades me that the old passage was still in Keats's mind, but he had set himself to revise it thoroughly. A great difference of tone separates the "habitual self" of *Endymion*—into which fancy betrays us by its excess, and is blamed for doing so—and the "sole self" of the Ode. The latter is a necessary thing, in charge of the daylight world which Keats no longer regrets, and which has its own sympathies to ask of us. It is fancy as such and not its "journey homeward," that Keats now describes as a cheat, exhibiting in this a self-possessed humor with some affection for his own errors: the "deceiving elf" only acts up to its name, but in the "fog-bound elf" of *Endymion* there had been something hellish. Keats in the Ode does not resent the obligation to reserve a space for less fanciful imaginings. As for the "sole self," it is what each of us has, in solitude, when for better or worse we do have the power to arrange and compare our ideas.

At the end of the Ode, dream images pass "out at the door," to adopt Hazlitt's words a last time. Keats himself remains fixed while the nightingale escapes "Past the near meadows, over the still stream, / Up the hill-side." The landscape has grown sober with the lucidity of daily things, and what survives the poem is a commitment to this mood as a final standard of comparison. And yet Keats is not oppressed by its demands, as he had seemed to be at the start of the poem. Out of the dream of truth in the middle stanzas has come the self-confidence of the egotist who is free of vanity because he has travelled outside himself for a time. "Do I wake or sleep"—it does not matter, because he is free to renew his journey, and to return again. The most nearly analogous emotion in literature is what one feels at certain moments of resolution in Shakespearean romance. One is made to believe that the ordinary must suffice but the ordinary too may be transfigured: as when, in *A Midsummer Night's Dream*, Helena speaks the lines that announce her contentment with what she can know but imperfectly, "And I have found Demetrius like a jewel, / Mine own and not mine own." Keats's poem ends like this not only because day follows night, but because the emotional extremes, being explored till they were exhausted, have at last left open a middle ground for the romance of realities.

One notices in rereading the Ode how deftly near the end it confirms Hazlitt's sense of the imagination's mastery over all associated impressions. Keats's use of the word "forlorn" has entered this poem at the suggestion of the same consonant group, f-l, which sounded in the phrase "faery lands." The adjective-noun pair was hopeful; the second adjective overcasts every hope: together, from the conformity of sounds alone, they exemplify the associative force of contrariety which was at work also in Keats's remarks about light and shade. By the end of the poem, however, he could afford to hear the low echo drawn out of high fancy, without contriving a miraculous escape. He is forlorn as a man untouched by irritations; his expansiveness and his skepticism here coincide. Imagination, he has seen, is the freedom to widen speculation; by making other things more vivid it contracts rather than expands the domain of self, though only for the moment; but what cannot ever be modified is the mind's liberty in forming new associations: to deny that would be, in Hazlitt's metaphor, "like supposing that you might tread on a nest of adders twined together, and provoke only one of them to sting you." Thus the narrowly sympathetic poetry of the Wordsworthian sermon and the Keatsian reverie have left room for a poetry that claims both the generosity and the privilege of a larger view. Long before this, in "Sleep and Poetry," in *Endymion*, and in sonnets dedicated to artists and art, Keats had written at the level he thought a modern could sustain. With the "Ode to a Nightingale" he had a poetry equal to what he loved.

"ODE ON A GRECIAN URN"

On this reading of the "Ode to a Nightingale," the poem has five distinct movements, the transitions being hard-won in each instance, and the constant sense of transition the necessary dramatic element in a poem that has one voice and yet means to shun the egotistical sublime. Keats begins by confessing his sickness of spirit; moves abruptly to dispel it, by his vow to "fly to thee" and join the Queen-Moon and her company, in what turns out to be a false effort of transcendence; finds nevertheless that this has led to an act of true imagination, with his embrace of death in "embalmed darkness"; by death is then reminded of the dead, and of another human sufferer of history or legend, whom the nightingale once soothed; and at last returns to life and the world of common realities, larger-spirited than the man who had begun, "My heart aches. . . ." These particulars need to be remembered because there has been a tendency among critics to read the "Ode on a Grecian Urn" as a companion poem, with a similar plot. The poems do seem to me to work together, but they were evidently written from very different impulses, and in the later poem it would be hard to trace any movement comparable to the one I have just proposed. Even the formal differences which separate them are not trivial. The urn is silent where the nightingale poured forth its song; static, where the nightingale was free to move and finally to depart from the poem. Keats might allow himself to "be intense upon" a creature he knew could not be captured. But the urn *can* perhaps be captured and somehow contained, whether by description or moralizing commentary, and Keats's effort to avoid doing so begins with his title. To address his poem "to" the urn would imply a degree of presumption about its identity; he writes merely "on" it. His tone through most of the poem, in keeping with the same downward modulation, is tentative and coaxing, and the exclamations of the "Ode to a Nightingale" are replaced by questions. The scenes depicted on the urn interest him to the point of excluding the artist who fashioned it, and this emphasis accounts for some of Keats's uneasiness about the sort of answer he wants. His ideas about the "poetical character" were by this time very clear, his ideas about the character of a poem much less so, as his abortive experiments with *Hyperion* had lately shown. The "Ode to a Nightingale" was a poem about the poet (warm, and adaptable to many identities) whereas the "Ode on a Grecian Urn" is about the poem (cold, and beyond interrogation). To Keats himself the first must have seemed an act of sympathy, and the second an act of power.

What readers most honor in the "Ode on a Grecian Urn," and are at the same time made uneasy by, is its dividedness of purpose. In spite of the task it assumes, it does not manage to exclude the warm strivings of life, or the troubled sympathies of the poet: he cannot finish the poem without trying to imprint on the urn the pathos of these things. By doing so he reduces the distance between himself and a chosen object of power, and implies that there are special dangers in our admiration for its cold remoteness and its grandeur above humanity. Since the object itself seemed to warn him of such dangers, Keats felt nothing wrong in allowing the object to instruct us concerning them, with a motto about the right use of art. Hence the inscription "Beauty is truth, truth beauty" which has perplexed much commentary on the poem. It is the third and fourth stanzas, with their scenes of "breathing human passion," that disturb commentators as not quite belonging there; but the weight of the protest falls on the concluding motto, which in retrospect seems answerable for every awkward fact. If he had written the poem without those stanzas, offering as complete stanzas 1, 2, and 5, we would regard it as a well-managed sublime poem on the order of Collins's "Ode to Evening." It would be more perfect and it would move us less. A recent critic of the Ode, Patrick Parrinder, writes that Keats "expresses the full allure of aestheticism, without quite taking the leap into vulgar commitment."[33] This is just perceptive enough to be irritating. Keats registers the allure only to reject it firmly, and to show an appreciation of art in which there is no want of keeping between art and humanity.

What did Keats feel when he saw before him an urn several centuries old? We have his testimony from one comparable occasion, the visit to the Elgin Marbles about which he wrote two sonnets in the spring of 1817. "On Seeing the Elgin Marbles for the First Time" seems to me the more conclusive in its statement of awestruck deference.

> My spirit is too weak—mortality
> Weighs heavily on me like unwilling sleep,
> And each imagined pinnacle and steep
> Of godlike hardship tells me I must die
> Like a sick eagle looking at the sky.
> Yet 'tis a gentle luxury to weep
> That I have not the cloudy winds to keep
> Fresh for the opening of the morning's eye.
> Such dim-conceived glories of the brain
> Bring round the heart an undescribable feud;
> So do these wonders a most dizzy pain,
> That mingles Grecian grandeur with the rude
> Wasting of old time—with a billowy main—
> A sun—a shadow of a magnitude.

The poem exhibits a poet's aspiration to compete with the grandeur of an art different from his, and greater by virtue of its duration. He hopes to find in himself a spirit as sublime as what he contemplates, yet the picture he gives of his failure is not sublime but pathetic, almost maudlin—"Like a sick eagle looking at the sky." Instead of the energy of mind that ought to reveal the poet's high contest with a nature informed by just such energy, he can show only "an undescribable feud," "a most dizzy pain." It looks as if, from a poem that began with the stock materials of the sublime—imagined pinnacles, cloudy winds—Keats were backing into a confession of defeat, which aims to move us by its sincerity. And yet the poem ends with impressive dignity in spite of its loss of heart. The new quality emerges from the sudden awareness of distance, in a mood so unexpected by Keats that he can approach it only by telegraphic dashes, and the reticence of the indefinite article: "a billowy main— / A sun—a shadow of a magnitude." The movement from an undescribable feud round the heart, to the acknowledgement of an alien strength, already suggests what Keats would mean in the "Ode on a Grecian Urn," when he spoke of being teased out of thought. His unhappier thoughts are of the soul's incompetence to gain these heights while the body still lives. But such thoughts come from our inability to be the contemporaries of our own greatness—which Keats, until the end of the poem, confuses with our inability to match the greatness of a past age. The last lines present the clearing away of that confusion. Nothing in the marbles themselves, Keats realizes, but rather the abyss that time has wrought between them and himself, brings the sensation of an incommensurable grandeur that he feels in looking at them. Cured of his weakness, he is able to participate in their glory at last, though it is experienced as something cold and inhuman. We may ponder this a moment longer in the light of all the elements that compose the resolution of the "Ode on a Grecian Urn." Here as in the later poem, the character of his feeling changes with the recognition that time itself creates sublimity, by robbing art of its signature and making it mysteriously natural. So old marbles can affect us "as doth eternity." Here too, mingled admiration and horror is a natural response to an object about which one can feel with a half-resentful certainty that "When old age shall this generation waste, / Thou shalt remain." Notwithstanding the strength of these associated feelings, there is no sense here that the sublime object could ever be "a friend to man."

Between the composition of this poem and the "Ode" two years later, Hazlitt had given his lecture "On Poetry in General," which we have good reason to suppose Keats read. The lecture included a comment on the relations between painting and poetry, and the remoteness of painting from human affections which only language can suggest. Raphael's cartoons are mentioned as proof of the rule, since their effect is inconceivable without our knowledge of the biblical texts; for contrast, Hazlitt calls to mind the "pure" beauty of Greek statues, and the phrase "marble to the touch" extends his criticism to the Elgin Marbles.

> Painting embodies what a thing contains in itself: poetry suggests what exists out of it, in any manner connected with it. But this last is the proper province of the imagination. Again, as it relates to passion, painting gives the event, poetry the progress of events: but it is during the progress, in the interval of expectation and suspense, while our hopes and fears are strained to the highest pitch of breathless agony, that the pinch of interest lies. . . . It is for want of some such resting place for the imagination that the Greek statues are little else than specious forms. They are marble to the touch and to the heart. They have not an informing principle within them. In their faultless excellence they appear sufficient to themselves. By their beauty they are raised above the frailties of passion or suffering. By their beauty they are deified. But they are not objects of religious faith to us, and their forms are a reproach

to common humanity. They seem to have no sympathy with us, and not to want our admiration.[34] (V 10–11)

Hazlitt concludes by regarding the marbles as instances of power rather than sympathy: they are a kind of Coriolanus among art objects. This, with an attendant sense of their cold self-sufficiency, was the conclusion Keats had reached in the last lines of his sonnet. He reaches it once more in the "Ode on a Grecian Urn," and one's suspicion that his reading of Hazlitt strengthened an earlier sentiment of his own is confirmed by the paraphrase, "All breathing human passion far above," which he makes of Hazlitt's "they are raised above the frailties of passion or suffering." The sharp "hopes and fears" that Hazlitt sees as special to poetry, "strained to the highest pitch of breathless agony," also have their answering interval in Keats, whose lovers are "For ever panting" and strained to the pitch of "A burning forehead, and a parching tongue."

In such intervals alone lies the hidden story that interests us when we look at works of art. But can an unspeaking object be relied on to tell the story unaided? Hazlitt thought not, and made his objection the more memorable by an allusion to Wordsworth's great line, "By our own spirits are we deified." As said by the poet in "Resolution and Independence," this had meant that only human sympathies give us a human immortality, in the minds of others. Yet as repeated by Hazlitt, and in its new form, "By their beauty they are deified," it bears witness to everything about the marbles that makes them gods above our humanity. Because the only religion we care for is the religion of humanity, this beauty renders them "not objects of religious faith to us." The irony of the allusion is directed against the marbles, and puts Hazlitt for the moment in accord with Wordsworth. When he came to write this Ode, Keats was searching for a more generous view of such objects, in which they would appear necessarily as a friend to the common affections. His problem was to do that in a poem which first acknowledged the coldness and strangeness of the object. He would thus be required to expand the interval in which, as Hazlitt said, "the pinch of interest lies," but without cheating, or somehow crediting the object with a pathos only language can express. Judged in these terms, the end of the Ode is a victory for art, but not for the urn; it is much closer to Hazlitt's distinction between poetic and plastic expression than Keats would have liked to come; for it shows the urn being rescued into meaning by the poet who speaks. The Ode is a marriage between the urn, plastic art, beauty, the "unravished bride of quietness"—and the poem, poetic art, truth, the master of verbal expression. At its consummation the urn is released into words, though of a sort possible only to writing or inscription, and not to oral speech. Decorum is thus preserved, but one feels that the poem's final weight of authority belongs with truth, without which beauty would remain cold to the touch as to the heart.

To test the argument beyond these preliminaries I have to quote the poem.

I

Thou still unravish'd bride of quietness,
　　Thou foster-child of silence and slow time,
Sylvan historian, who canst thus express
　　A flowery tale more sweetly than our rhyme:
What leaf-fring'd legend haunts about thy shape
　　Of deities or mortals, or of both,
　　　　In Tempe or the dales of Arcady?
　　What men or gods are these? What maidens loth?
What mad pursuit? What struggle to escape?
　　　　What pipes and timbrels? What wild ecstasy?

II

Heard melodies are sweet, but those unheard
　　Are sweeter; therefore, ye soft pipes, play on;
Not to the sensual ear, but, more endear'd,
　　Pipe to the spirit ditties of no tone:
Fair youth, beneath the trees, thou canst not leave
　　Thy song, nor ever can those trees be bare;
　　　　Bold Lover, never, never canst thou kiss,
Though winning near the goal—yet, do not grieve;
　　She cannot fade, though thou hast not thy bliss,
　　　　For ever will thou love, and she be fair!

A poem written entirely in the key of the first four lines of these stanzas—the key of temperate and paradoxical satisfaction—would be very tedious to the merely human reader. But the relation which obtains here between the first four lines and the last six will be carried through the entire poem. First, the paradox is stated, with an air of ironic calm and good cheer; but in every case a deep distress has been held back, which needs the rest of the stanza to bring out its painful character. The relation between the two parts of each stanza is this, that the thought of immortality leads to the thought of death: the transition will be most astonishing in the final stanza, where the fourth line is not set off from the fifth by an end-stop— "Thou, silent form, dost tease us out of thought / As doth eternity,"which I would paraphrase: "Your cold stillness shows us what silence all our thoughts end in, as for that matter our own deaths will show us." The not wholly agreeable surprise that Keats feels

almost electrically across the line break is registered by the exclamation mark at "Cold Pastoral!" But about this phrase I will say
more presently.

The thought which the opening lines of the first stanza hope to
suppress, is that the urn was not always an orphaned thing. It now
seems the "foster child of silence and slow time" because, though
it had its human parentage, all trace of this has disappeared. Its
silence, the absence of a signature, imparts mystery to the urn, and
that mystery by the passage of time is transformed into sublimity.
But the loss of any known author, and with it the loss of personal
pathos, trouble Keats more than calling the urn its own author, "Sylvan
Historian," would seem to imply. One has some sense of the violence
of the exclusion in the queer pun on "express": as if the figures on
the urn were straining against their condition, and pressed outward
toward articulate life, in spite of the formal constraint that forbids
them any verbal expression. The questions that follow are not a bit
complacent—not content as rhetorical questions are, to be subdued
to the silence that is their element—but rather tongue-tied, with the
stammering of children not yet sure of their right to speak. In the
last lines of the second stanza, Keats moves to reconcile the lover
to the frozen gesture in which he finds himself trapped so near the
goal. The over-insistent concern which he feels on the lover's account
is chiefly evident in his repeated denials: "canst not," "nor ever,"
and to close off the last hope, "never, never." But Keats has to add,
"do not grieve": poetry by its nature deals in "the flowing, not the
fixed," as Hazlitt put it; and if sculpture deals in the fixed, may it
not offer the consolation that its permanence is that of a paradise
without death? The unfamiliarity of this thought provokes him to
write two more stanzas confirming its beauty, and they are among
the saddest he ever wrote.

III

Ah, happy, happy boughs! that cannot shed
  Your leaves, nor ever bid the spring adieu
And, happy melodist, unwearied,
  For ever piping songs for ever new;
More happy love! more happy, happy love!
  For ever warm and still to be enjoyed,
    For ever panting and for ever young;
All breathing human passion far above,
  That leaves a heart high-sorrowful and cloy'd,
    A burning forehead, and a parching tongue.

IV

Who are these coming to the sacrifice?
To what green altar, O mysterious priest

> Lead'st thou that heifer lowing at the skies,
>   And all her silken flanks with garlands dress?
> What little town by river or sea shore,
>   Or mountain-built with peaceful citadel,
>   Is emptied of this folk, this pious morn?
> And, little town, thy streets for evermore
>   Will silent be; and not a soul to tell
>   Why thou art desolate, can e'er return.

It is Keats himself whose cries of "happy, happy" must end in a breathless panting. And it is this happiness, more cloying than any sorrow, that makes us think of "breathing human passion" with relief. The ambiguous syntax, too, appears temporarily to set breathing human passion above anything the urn can depict; even when we read the syntactical inversion correctly—"These things, being above all human passion"—we may still be struck by the logical inversion that follows; for it would have been sounder practice, if the poem really wished us to forget the burning forehead and parching tongue, to place them somewhere other than the strong rhetorical position they now occupy at the end of the stanza.

But Keats at this period of his life must have counted himself among the lovers coming to the sacrifice, and sincerity compelled him to mention their pains in close conjunction with the question about their identity which opens the next stanza. The opening four lines describing the life of the town, however, are free of personal concern. In his effort to describe it without sympathy, and bounded by the speechless decorum of the urn itself, he approaches a Byronic pleasure in the picturesque. He writes of what is sublime, not because it is a work of man, but because it is a work of man overthrown; and yet he writes as if art alone, without any communion between the creating mind and the human passions it regards, could supply the terms in which we feel enlarged by such sublimity. If the poem had ended in this style, it might be included in Ruskin's general protest against the picturesque as a heartless ideal. In the second part of this stanza, however, Keats associates the urn's choice of an empty town to depict with his own readiness to empty the poem of all that concerns the town's inhabitants. The connection is between the urn-maker's choice to free his representation of persons, and what it would be for Keats to deprive his poem of feelings: the poem he thought he should aspire to make would be in this sense desolating. Keats was incapable of arriving at such a recognition without tremendous regret; and with his regret comes pity: "And, little town, thy streets for evermore / Will silent be." This is the only sentence, of all those following his questions, that even sounds like an answer.

No soul can return, of course, except someone like Keats, a poet who does not accept the limits of the picture-making historian.

After the implicit equations have settled, of silence with apathy, and speech with pathos, the way open for the Ode as a poem was the way Keats took: to coax the urn, by compliment and salutation to conjure it into speech, and so to give it the sympathies of poetry. Yet he had to accomplish this in a manner that would reassure the urn that its condition as a silent and anonymous thing was not being violated.

V

> O Attic shape! Fair attitude! with brede
> Of marble men and maidens overwrought,
> With forest branches and the trodden weed;
>   Thou, silent form, dost tease us out of thought
> As doth eternity: Cold Pastoral!
>   When old age shall this generation waste,
>   Thou shalt remain, in midst of other woe
> Than ours, a friend to man, to whom thou say'st,
>   "Beauty is truth, truth beauty,"—that is all
>   Ye know on earth, and all ye need to know.

Of many readers who felt uncomfortable with this ending, Robert Bridges was the first to object to "Attic Shape! Fair attitude!" as an embarrassing pun.[35] Others have followed him; and yet this is the language of conjuring: it is not more forced than "Abra Cadabra." The stanza affords much other evidence of a workmanship of style the reverse of negligent. The use of "overwrought" is the loveliest single instance, where the several meanings—"elaborately worked over"; "inlaid and intertwined"; "excited to the point of forgetting one's manners"—all converge in our sense of the maker's pains, the visible signs of his labor, and the vivid intensity of men and maidens on the brink of going too far. This was the sort of idiomatic play on words, incorporating both etymology and common usage, which Keats could manage like nobody else. Wordsworth can return to and revive the power of a word's origin, while allowing us to read it in some commoner way at first, as in his use of "consecration" and "distress" in the Peele Castle elegy; Coleridge is adept at finding grotesque juxtapositions for a word's original and colloquial meanings, though he often turns out to have half-invented one of them, as in his etymology of "atonement" (at-one-ment); but Keats sometimes liberates all the suspended senses of a word, to the advantage of all, with a lack of fuss that would cause equal delight to a parliamentary orator and a coffee-house politician. The implications of this freedom for a poem that has affected to renounce speech entirely will be felt in the progress of the stanza.

The great turn occurs at "Cold Pastoral!" H. W. Garrod argued that it need imply no change of heart, because Keats's admiration for such coldness has in fact been less pronounced all along than the reader supposes.[36] Some of Hazlitt's strictures on Benjamin West are pertinent to the difficulty: in particular his objection that Death in West's painting had "not the calm, still, majestic form of Death, killing by a look,—withering by a touch. His presence does not make the still air cold." Coldness like this, a possible attribute of the sublime and also of death, would have governed Keats's understanding of the word in the context he was building; and he had prepared readers to admire the sublime chill in just the way Garrod warns them against, in a whole series of passages. One recalls especially, from "Sleep and Poetry," the immortals on display at the home of Leigh Hunt:

> Round about were hung
> The glorious features of the bards who sung
> In other ages—cold and sacred busts
> Smiled at each other. Happy he who trusts
> To clear futurity his darling fame!

In the more skeptical mood of The Fall of Hyperion, shortly after the Ode, there is the chill Keats feels on the steps of Moneta's temple, and her cold lips, and her face "deathwards progressing / To no death": monitory sensations, but assisting the poet on his quest, with a privation that starves his illusions. It may be difficult to admire but we can reasonably expect that Keats, when he describes the urn as cold, will be saying so in a tone of admiration. Yet "Cold Pastoral!" is said much more in a tone of shock, and even of rebuke. This comes partly of the memento mori that has just startled him across a line-break. Eternity does not tease us out of thought into something finer (a life of sensations) but rather out of thought and out of life.

"Tease us out of thought" therefore seems to me the real enigma. An earlier use of the phrase, from the verse epistle "To J. H. Reynolds, Esq."—"Things cannot to the will / Be settled, but they tease us out of thought"—promises much but turns out to be no solution. It asserts that the insights of art have nothing to do with acts of the will, and about this one is hardly in doubt after four stanzas of the Ode. The urn is silent; it is we alone who have thoughts, and must be teased out of them: the poem still leaves us to guess what our thought is here. Yet, for the sense of vocation which chiefly interests us, there seem to be just two alternatives: (1) We are thinking of art's superiority to life and nature, its freedom from their pains, and its satisfying permanence; (2) We are thinking of the debt art owes to life and nature, which can never be repaid, but which it can sufficiently acknowledge in an expressive moment of sympathy.

In the poem Keats set out to write—about an ancient relic sublimely above our humanity, and indifferent to our pains—we would have been teased out of the second thought, and into a point of view congenial to the first thought without being obliged to think it. But the effort to be honestly inclusive has worked into the poem so fully, and so shaken its structure with the climactic phrase "Cold pastoral!," that the teasing moves us in the opposite direction. It is the purist defense of plastic art that now seems merely abstract and speculative, a matter of thought rather than of sensation; while the communicative work of language, with all its associations, shows us how art can be "a friend to man." The urn teases us out of thought as art makes us go beyond art. Keats needed a reversal this strong and this assured to support the magnanimity that he almost hides with the ease of his qualifying syntax, when he says "Thou shalt remain, in midst of other woe / Than ours, a friend to man." In that other woe, a future poet will be looking at Keats himself as one of the figures on the urn, coming to the sacrifice, with a burning forehead and a parching tongue—and the apology for art which he in turn composes had better not be too fluent, or find too happy a retreat in the paradox of a career perpetually arrested before the goal. Nor ought it to deify as a thing of beauty what was once also a thing of pain. The poet of "other woe than ours" will be using the urn as a friend to man if he imagines Keats much as Keats in the "Ode to a Nightingale" had imagined Ruth.

"What the imagination seizes as Beauty must be truth": this, from a letter of November 1817—nine months after the Elgin Marbles sonnet, but eighteen months before the Ode and several strata earlier in the story of Keats's development—has often seemed an irresistible help in deciphering the Ode's conclusion. But even then it was only one of Keats's "favorite speculations," and on its most obvious construction I do not think the great poet will admit it: what strikes us as beautiful for the moment is not, even for the moment, the sum of all we need to know. I have given what seems to me a useful aid from Hazlitt's essay "On Imitation," in the statement that "to the genuine artist, truth, nature, beauty, are almost different names for the same thing"; but another statement by Hazlitt, from the "Letter to William Gifford" which Keats was copying out for his brother a few weeks before the Ode, seems to me an even stronger source. Replying to the objection that he was a florid writer, Hazlitt said: "As to my style, I thought little about it. I only used the word which seemed to me to signify the idea I wanted to convey, and I did not rest till I had got it. In seeking for truth, I sometimes found beauty." Here truth carries the main stress, as it must also in the poem Keats's Ode has become by its penultimate line.[37] But there is a special logic in the *sequence*, "Beauty is truth, truth beauty," which Hazlitt's writings on associationism help to explain. One needs to recall the tendency of any association to evoke its opposite: so light suggests shade; pleasure suggests pain; heat suggests cold; life suggests death. The process may always be reversed to conform to a different mood, as when Hazlitt writes in his essay "On the Fear of Death": "Perhaps the best cure for the fear of death is to reflect that life has a beginning as well as an end." If one grants the associationist premise that all our ideas are interrelated, it follows that by certain trains of thought, each of our experiences may imply every other, and that we come to know an experience not in itself but by its relation to every other.

When he imagined reading on the urn, "Beauty is truth, truth beauty," I think Keats was committing himself to the kind of sentiment that the urn, after his experience of it, might be supposed to say by inscription.[38] And yet he was doing more than that. Truth, in the associationist chain that he was exploring, meant "Everything that is the case," the sum of our experience; beauty meant the part of experience that art selects to represent the whole: but "is" still plays fast work with his purposes unless we read it discriminatingly. *Beauty implies truth, truth entails beauty.*[39] Or, to adapt Emerson's more responsive paraphrase, "There is no fact in nature which does not carry the whole sense of nature,"[40] and no fact of which our understanding is not modified by the whole sense of nature: this seems to me the expression of faith on which Keats's poem came to rest. We are asked to recognize that art excludes nothing of our experience, but finds in any part a sufficient clue to the whole, and in the whole the necessary modifications of each part. Keats thus ends by declaring that he values in art what Hazlitt valued in a "second nature." Beauty, truth, art, are to him almost different names for the same thing. Nor does the shift of a term imply any substantial dissent. Keats only refuses—as Hazlitt after "On Imitation" would generally refuse—to employ nature itself as an honorific name for the highest sort of art. He is, one may say, still surer than Hazlitt in his awareness of, and still more emphatic in communicating, the *work* art must do to make its selection.

Keats's sonnet on the Elgin Marbles came in spring 1817, Hazlitt's passage on them in "On Poetry in General" in spring 1818, and the "Ode on a Grecian Urn" in spring 1819. But the sequence is nicely progressive in something other than the dates. The sonnet had tried to find the marbles admirable precisely because they do not sympathize with us, and found the strain almost insupportable. Hazlitt replied in his criticism that one ought to search elsewhere for the effects of a human beauty and grandeur, because the marbles excluded on principle the moment of "breathless agony," the interval of suspended progress in which "the pinch of interest lies." The Ode deviated from its apparent theme to include that moment, and to consider it unstintingly, at the expense of concluding with an utterance more pertinent to English poetry, and what happens in this poem, than to the urn or Greek marbles for anything they show in themselves. The record would be incomplete without a final piece of evidence, from the same 1822 articles on the Elgin Marbles which I quoted in chapter 5. Hazlitt is more generous about them now, and I believe one thing that made him generous was Keats's poem. At all events he closes his account, as he had closed the chapter on *King Lear* several years earlier, with a set of propositions on the morality of art. There are ten of them, mostly too elementary in the assertion, and too elaborate in the justification, to add anything to the argument. But excerpts from the fifth, sixth, and tenth will certainly interest the reader who has come this far.

> Grandeur consists in connecting a number of parts into a whole, and not leaving out the parts.

> As grandeur is the principle of connexion between different parts; beauty is the principle of affinity between different forms, or their gradual conversion into each other.

> Truth is, to a certain degree, beauty and grandeur, since all things are connected, and all things modify one another in nature. (XVIII, 162–66)

If Keats's apology for art seems to apply more directly to poetry than to sculpture or ceramics, still the sympathy and power with which, in looking at an object, he widened speculation about its ground in human life, showed a way for the right use of any art. Hazlitt in this article was availing himself both of what he had taught Keats, and of what Keats had taught him in return.

More broadly, by helping Keats to revise his own idea of the imagination, Hazlitt altered the course of modern poetry. Keats opened up the romantic lyric from within, and by doing so lengthened its endurance. With *Hyperion,* mastered by an epic ideal, he had ended in disappointment, with an abrupt dismissal of his Miltonic experiment: "English ought to be kept up." All along Hazlitt had been moving him in the direction of Shakespeare, and if one looks in romantic poetry for a Shakespearean fullness, and a Shakespearean gusto in dialogue, the place to find them is nowhere in the poetic drama of the period, but in Keats's odes. For the odes have answering voices that are not merely echoes: Keats had come to a new understanding of how a writer's voice might implicate a reader's fate. When one considers his immense influence on the Victorians, and counts the long poems they wrote in any case, one may wonder whether the lyric need in fact have become their dominant mode, and whether it could have done so had he not enlarged its scope. Besides, there was another element of Keats's genius that made him attractive to his successors: he had found a place in poetry for the disagreeables. Not to be dispelled, evaporated, or reconciled, but to be named as part of truth, and belonging to a larger part. Hazlitt alone could have attached him to this faith, for though Keats might have sought it from Coleridge, there was, as Empson says in his essay on "Beauty is Truth," "remarkably little agony in Coleridge's theory of Imagination . . . whereas Keats was trying to work the disagreeables into the theory."[41] Keats's aims in poetry and Hazlitt's in criticism place both in accord with a concern for dramatic form that modern poets have been unwilling to disclaim.[42] Other forces, other personalities, of course intervened, but the periods of literary history are never as inviolable as we make them to speed our thinking, and one reason we read lyric poems today, and not epics or romances of solitary life, is that between 1815 and 1820 Hazlitt convinced a very young man born into a great age of poetry that something still remained to be done.

Notes

1. Of the many critics and scholars who have surveyed the influence of Hazlitt on Keats, I am chiefly indebted to Hyder Rollins, for his notes to Keats's *Letters* (Cambridge, Mass., 1958) W. J. Bate, *John Keats* (1963; Oxford University Press edition, New York, 1966), pp. 255–63; Caldwell, *John Keats' Fancy, pp. 172–86;* and C. D. Thorpe, *"Keats and Hazlitt," PMLA* 42 (1947), 487–502. Bate and Caldwell are particularly admirable for exhibiting Keats as part of the mind of the age. On the other hand, my record of the Keats-Hazlitt friendship may be read as an antidote to Herschel Baker, *William Hazlitt,* (Cambridge, Mass., 1962), pp. 247–51. In portraying Hazlitt as a recalcitrant party to this friendship, it seems to me that Baker makes the worst of appearances wherever possible.

2. Keats, *Letters, I,* 143.

3. Ibid, I, 166.

4. Ibid, I, 238–39.

5. Of Keats's biographers only Robert Gittings is sufficiently wary of these ideas.

6. Keats, *Letters, I,* 252, 274.

7. Ibid., II, 76.

8. Ibid., I, 210.

9. Ibid., II, 24.

10. *Fall of Hyperion,* canto I, lines 168–176, *The Poems of John Keats,* ed. Jack Stillinger (Cambridge, Mass., 1978), p. 482.

11. Printed as Appendix 5 in Keats's *Complete Poems,* ed. John Barnard (1973; 2nd Penguin edition, New York, 1977), p. 528.

12. Keats, *Letters,* I, 237.

13. Ibid, I, 214.

14. Keats, *Poems,* ed., Stillinger, pp. 102–103.

15. Part II, lines 1–15, *Poems,* pp. 463–64.

16. Keats, *Letters*, I, 184.

17. John Middleton Murry, *Keats and Shakespeare* (London, 1925), ch. 4.

18. Keats, *Letters*, I, 223–24.

19. Ibid, I, 264–65.

20. John Locke, *Essay Concerning Human Understanding*, (Oxford, 1975) IV.iv.9, p. 567.

21. Coleridge, *The Statesman's Manual*, in *Lay Sermons*, p. 89.

22. Keats, *Letters*, I, 232.

23. Ibid., I, 193.

24. Ibid., I, 386–87. I here adopt a textual change suggested by George Beaumont in *TLS*, February 27, May 1, 1930, pp. 166, 370: "informing" in place of "in for—." The word is characteristic of Keats as of Hazlitt, and it fits his sense.

25. Keats, *Letters*, I, 282.

26. A companion aphorism may be found in Hazlitt's *Characteristics:* "The pleasure derived from tragedy is to be accounted for in this way, that, by painting the extremes of human calamity, it by contrast kindles the affections, and raises the most intense imagination and desire of the contrary good" (*The Complete Works of William Hazlitt*, ed. P. P. Howe, 21 vols., IX, 209).

27. Keats, *Letters*, II, 360. In *Characteristics* Hazlitt writes: "Good and ill seem as necessary to human life as light and shade to a picture" (IX, 208). On the associative relation of contrast and its tendency to imply a whole, see J. R. Caldwell, *John Keats' Fancy*, (Ithaca, 1945).

28. Keats, *Letters*, II, 80–81.

29. Ibid., II, 79.

30. The opposite—that poet and bird intermingle as equals—has been asserted by Earl Wasserman, in *The Finer Tone* (Baltimore, 1953). Wasserman supposed an "antithesis of the two empathies, the poet's and the nightingale's" (p. 185), and argued that "the bird has entered into the essence of nature, and the poet into the essence of the bird" (p. 187). I believe on the contrary that Keats, as the poem starts, is burdened by an excess of consciousness and of susceptibility, whereas the bird possesses neither. Its song fits no known definition of empathy, and I am not aware that Keats ever wrote of "essence" quite in Wasserman's sense (the "fellowship with essence" passage of *Endymion* will not do). A nightingale that entered into the essence of nature would have to be outside it to begin with, and that was not the way Keats looked at things, as his descriptions in letters of the hawk, the eagle, the robin, and the swallow all indicate.

31. From Keats's annotations to *Paradise Lost*, in J. A. Wittreich, Jr., ed., *The Romantics on Milton* (Cleveland, 1970), p. 558.

32. Keats, *Endymion*, Book II, lines 274–280, in *Poems*, p. 140. In pointing out a connection between the two passages, I have been anticipated by M. R. Ridley, *Keats' Craftsmanship* (1933; reprinted, Lincoln, 1963), p. 231.

33. Patrick Parrinder, *Authors and Authority: A Study of English Literary Criticism and Its Relation to Culture 1750–1900* (London, 1977), p. 97.

34. The history of interpreting these comments of Hazlitt's as a clue to the "Ode on a Grecian Urn" is as follows. Ian Jack quoted the last few sentences, beginning with "the Greek statues are little more than specious forms," in *Keats and the Mirror of Art* (Oxford, 1967) and observed: "It would be curious to have the comment of Keats on this passage" (p. 72). Patrick Parrinder replied in *Authors and Authority* that "we have that comment; it is the 'Ode on a Grecian Urn,' " but said nothing further about Hazlitt; to Jack's quotation he added the beginning of the sentence Jack had

picked up in the middle: "It is for want of some such resting place for the imagination. . . ." I give the entire passage, of which the first half seems to me quite as
pertinent as the second, and propose that Hazlitt influenced not only the sentiment
of the poem, but a good deal of its dramatic movement.

35. *Collected Essays, Papers, etc. of Robert Bridges*, 10 vols. (London, 1927–1936),
III, 132.

36. H. W. Garrod, *Keats* (London, 1926), pp. 107–108.

37. As a corrective to the cant of "ironic distancing" at the end of Keats's poem,
I recommend Pratap Biswas, "Keats's Cold Pastoral," *University of Toronto Quarterly*,
47 (Winter 1977–1978), 95–111. The article, though not always tactful, seems to me
admirably clear in its formulations, and is the most emphatic argument I know for
Keats's sympathy with truth over beauty.

38. I have profited from Geoffrey Hartman's treatment of the saying as part of
the romantic tradition of nature-inscriptions, in "Wordsworth, Inscriptions, and Ro-
mantic Nature Poetry," reprinted in *Beyond Formalism* (New Haven, 1970); and from
Leo Spitzer's reading of the final lines as spoken by the urn, in "The 'Ode on a
Grecian Urn,' or Content vs. Metagrammar," reprinted in *Essays on English and
American Literature* (Princeton, 1962).

39. This paraphrase borrows from, and simplifies, William Empson's remarks on
the "A is B" family of logical assertions, to which Keats's sentence belongs. See *The
Structure of Complex Words* (Ann Arbor, paperback edition, 1967), pp. 350–74.
Empson's seems to me much the best twentieth-century commentary on the Ode, and
his summing up of Keats's feelings about the "little town" strikes the note I have
tried to sustain: "These people's homes will be left desolate because they have gone
to make a piece of art-work, and so will Keats' home because he is spending his life
on art. Beauty is both a cause of and an escape from suffering, and in either way
suffering is deeply involved in its production" (p. 370).

40. Emerson, "The Poet," in *Works*, (Boston, 1903, 12 vols.), III, 17.

41. Empson, *Structure of Complex Words*, p. 370. But I do not think Keats for
any stretch of his life was "working on the ideas of Coleridge." His references to
Coleridge—including the description of their walk about Highgate, and the phrase
from the "negative capability" letter, about letting go "by a fine isolated verisimilitude
caught from the Penetralium of mystery"—are as a rule lightly mocking in tone. The
matter is easy to check because the references are so few.

42. Of the continuity between the romantic and modern lyric, by way of Keats's
dramatic sympathies, the invention of the dramatic monologue by Browning and
Tennyson, and the modern need to balance the speaker's song with his situation, the
best account is Robert Langbaum's *The Poetry of Experience* (1957; 2nd Norton edition,
New York, 1971). His treatment of the romantic criticism of Shakespeare (ch. 5) with
its new emphasis on character, as the single most important connection between the
self-announcing lyric of the romantics and the self-defining monologue of the Victorians,
strikes me as especially subtle, and is for obvious reasons congenial to my argument
about Hazlitt. My disagreements are slight and have mainly to do with Langbaum's
tendency to make Keats in his odes stand for the same tendencies as Wordsworth in
a poem like "Resolution and Independence." To Keats, the dramatic encounter which
Wordsworth seemed concerned to record, and for which he raised high expectations
in his reader, was always being lost in the magnetic field of the egotistical narrator.
In this respect Keats thought of his own poetry as attempting nearly the opposite of
Wordsworth's.

The Politics of Greek Religion   Robert M. Ryan[*]

A post-Christian man is not a Pagan. . . . The post-Christian is
cut off from the Christian past and doubly from the Pagan past.
—C. S. LEWIS, "De Descriptione Temporum,"
in *They Asked for a Paper*

One of the more lively areas of Romantic studies in the 1980s
has been the intensified search for the politics of Keats's poetry, a
new phase in the old effort to rescue Keats from "aesthetic" readings
that have distorted interpretation and evaluation of his work. With
added stimulation from contemporary critical preoccupations (we have
investigated the politics of everything else—why not Keats?), scholars
have been scrutinizing his poems with the assiduity of government
spies, looking for evidence of the kind of radical political consciousness
that appears in his letters. Even the unpromising stubble fields of
"To Autumn" have been thoroughly beaten by the gleaners, who
have succeeded in flushing from invisible coverts such surprising
game as Godwin, Shelley, and Orator Hunt.[1] Yet despite this intense
scrutiny, the most important effect of Keats's politics on his verse
has all the while been hiding in plain sight—his choice of Greek
mythology as the subject matter of his most ambitious poems. This
crucial artistic decision is usually attributed to the loose junction of
aesthetic and religious predilections suggested in his frequently quoted
admiration for "the Greek spirit,—the Religion of the Beautiful, the
Religion of Joy."[2] Certainly there were temperamental and purely
aesthetic reasons for Keats's attraction to Greek mythology, but the
central role it assumed in his poetry and many of the artistic problems
it engendered can be accounted for convincingly, I think, in terms
of the religious politics of his time.

It was a time when religion and politics in Britain were inseparable, sometimes indistinguishable. In the confessional state established by the British Constitution, Christianity provided the principle
of social cohesion and the primary ideological rationale for submission
to authority. Since the Christian faith was officially and practically
the law of the land, any questioning of its truth, value, or inevitability
was politically subversive. Historically, revolutionary agitation in Britain had a tendency to begin on the religious front, as was the case
in the great political convulsions of the seventeenth century, and in
Keats's time the ruling class was generally more alarmed by attacks
on the state religion than on the government itself. Some of the most
celebrated political trials in the poet's day were prosecutions for
blasphemy rather than sedition, for example, those of William Hone

---

[*] This essay was written specifically for this volume and is published here for the first
time by permission of the author.

in 1817 and Richard Carlile in 1819, both of which Keats followed with close attention.[3]

Liberals less eager to risk prosecution and imprisonment had subtler ways of impugning the national faith. Prominent among the strategies devised by eighteenth-century rationalists was an ostentatious nostalgia for classical civilization in preference to the Christian culture that had supplanted it. The ancient Greeks demonstrated the possibility of creating a happy, humane, politically enlightened society without recourse to Biblical religion. While rigorous deists tended to despise polytheism as a corruption of the monotheistic religion of nature, other critics of Christianity found Greek superstition preferable to Biblical as being at least more tolerant and less vicious in its social and political effects. Probably the most celebrated enthusiast for "the elegant mythology of the Greeks" that had been so brutally extirpated by Christian fanatics was Edward Gibbon, whose *Decline and Fall of the Roman Empire* did much to foster the notion that what was lost in the decline of paganism was better than, or at least as good as, what replaced it.

In Keats's time, one of the more conspicuous champions of the superiority of Greek religion over Christian was Leigh Hunt, the man generally recognized, then and now, as Keats's most influential political mentor. But Hunt's war with established power was fought with equal vigor, and with apparently greater relish, on the religious front. I have argued elsewhere that Hunt had a profound influence on the poet's radical thinking in religion and on the version of deism that he adopted as his personal faith.[4] Hunt has also been credited with having inspired Keats's adoption of Greek myth as a characteristic poetic medium. In the course of its attack on the "Cockney School of Poetry," *Blackwood's* asserted: "From his prototype Hunt, John Keats has acquired a sort of vague idea, that the Greeks were a most tasteful people, and that no mythology can be so finely adapted for the purposes of poetry as theirs."[5] Similar credit has been given to Hunt in our own time by a friendlier and more authoritative critic, Aileen Ward.[6] And while "the Cockney Homer" (as *Blackwood's* called him) was illustrating in his own verse the adaptability of Greek myth to modern poetic purposes, he was also demonstrating its utility in the arena of religious polemic. The *Examiner* regularly used "Greek religion" as a touchstone to reveal moral and theological flaws in contemporary orthodoxy. An 1815 editorial, for example, introduced a favorite theme of Hunt's—the cheerfulness of the Greek religious spirit as contrasted with the gloom of Christianity:

> The very finest and most amiable part of our notions on [religion and morality] comes originally from [Greek] philosophers;—all the rest, the gloom, the bad passions, the favouritism, are the work of

other hands. . . . Even the absurd parts of the Greek Mythology
are less painfully absurd than those of any other; because, generally
speaking, they are on the chearful side instead of the gloomy. We
would rather have a Deity, who fell in love with the beautiful
creatures of his own making, than one, who would consign nine
hundred out of a thousand to destruction for not believing ill of
him.[7]

The theme was raised again in an editorial that Keats praised as "a
battering ram against Christianity" (Letters 1:137). Granted that all
religion is subject to abuses, Hunt wrote, pagan abuses at least tended
to be "on the pleasurable side of things". "They dealt in loves and
luxuries, in what resulted from the first laws of nature, and tended
to keep humanity alive:—the latter have dealt in angry debates, in
intolerance, in gloomy denouncements, in persecutions, in excom-
munications, in wars and massacres, in what perplexes, outrages, and
destroys humanity."[8] A more coherent formulation of this political-
religious-aesthetic critique may be found in Hunt's Foliage (1818),
specifically in his "Preface, Including Cursory Observations on Poetry
and Cheerfulness," which argues that "cheerful" creeds are more
conducive to poetry than "unattractive" gloomy ones made up of
"opinions which make humanity shudder"—like some of those recently espoused in William Wordsworth's published verse. One admirably cheerful creed is that of Greek mythology, a high opinion
of which, Hunt points out, characterizes the new generation of poets
just emerging on the scene, for example, Keats and Shelley.[9] Indeed,
such admiration of Greek myth has always been the sign of a true
poet. Shakespeare, although "not a scholar," knew by a kind of fine
poetical instinct how the Greek legends should be valued and used.
In Milton, however, "the beauty of natural and ancient taste" had
to struggle with "the Dragon Phantom Calvinism."

> Milton, when he was young and happy, wrote Grecian Mythology
> in his Lycidas and Comus. . . . In old age, there is good reason
> to suspect that he was, at any rate, not bigoted; and in the meantime,
> allusions to romance and to Greek mythology, which he never could
> prevail upon himself to give up, are the most refreshing things in
> his Paradise Lost and Regained, next to the bridal happiness of
> poor Adam and Eve. They are not merely drops in the desert;—
> they are escapes from every heart-withering horror, which Eastern
> storms and tyranny could generate together.[10]

"Eastern," we know from Keats's revision of Endymion 4:10, is a
code word for Biblical."[11] The alternatives, then, for an aspiring poet
are the cheerful Greek religion that graced the work of Shakespeare
and Milton, or the "heart-withering horrors," "the swarthy bigotries"
that nearly sank Paradise Lost and were sinking Wordsworth in a

later day. That Keats subscribed generally to Hunt's vision of the cultural struggle is suggested in his sonnet "Written in Disgust of Vulgar Superstition," with its scorn of the "gloominess" and "dreadful cares" of a Christian religion that distracts people from "Lydian airs," and its confidence that contemporary poetry will be efficacious in driving away the darkness. Keats identified himself publically with Hunt's nostalgia for the happier religion of the Greeks in the politically provocative sonnet "To Leigh Hunt, Esq." that dedicated his 1817 *Poems* to Hunt; I too, the sonnet says, miss the good old times when nymphs adorned the shrine of Flora in May, but I take consolation for the fact that now "Pan is no longer sought" in my ability to please Leigh Hunt with my poems.

It hardly needs to be said that the conception of Greek religion that Keats would have acquired from Hunt was eccentric and inadequate. With no real understanding of the actualities of religious practice in the ancient world, Hunt tended vaguely to equate the religion of Greece with its mythology, being always more interested in nymphs and dryads than in sacrifice or mystery. One cannot fault him for lacking insights since developed by modern anthropology, but even his literary knowledge of the Greek mind was limited by his depreciation of the tragedies, which seemed to him an aberration produced by an unhealthy "melancholy" undercurrent in the predominantly cheerful Greek consciousness.[12] He subscribed to the view that the Greeks of the golden age manifested in their religious consciousness some of the purity of the rational and natural religion that had been instilled by the Creator into the nascent human mind, and his comforting version of natural religion left little room for anything dark or disquieting.

This notion that Greek mythology embodied pristine religious truth would have been reinforced, ironically enough, by Keats's reading of *The Excursion*—a poem to which Hunt may have introduced him.[13] In book 4, a book that we know Keats read with special attention, the Greek mythopoeic imagination is presented, along with that of the Persians, Babylonians, and Chaldeans, as exemplary of a universal religious sense that, guided by Providence even when undisciplined by Revelation, developed correct intuitions of divinity from observation of nature. The Greeks were thankful, reverential, moral, and hopeful of immortality; in other words, they professed an approximation of the natural religion accessible to all inquiring minds. (4:925–40). Wordsworth would certainly not have considered Greek mythology an adequate substitute for Christianity, as *The Excursion* goes on to make clear, but that is the extrapolation that Keats seems to have made. When the older poet dismissed the "Hymn to Pan" as "a very pretty piece of paganism," he had probably detected the political tendency of this Greek poem by one of Leigh Hunt's disciples.

In his account of the incident, Benjamin Robert Haydon recalled that "Wordsworth's puling Christian feelings were annoyed."[14]

Keats's "Hymn" and its setting contain a good deal of evidence suggesting that Keats intended the opening of *Endymion* to illustrate the attractiveness of Greek worship as an enlightened natural religion with none of the negative features of Christianity. Here is Hunt's religion of joy in full tilt, complete with laughing children, dancing damsels, singing and fluting shepherds, and venerable elders whose relaxed speculations about the afterlife involve only "anticipated bliss" in a heavenly Elysium, with no hint of the darker underworld even of Greek tradition. The sacrifice they offer to Pan is a bloodless one of wine and sweet herbs. Keats must have known that animal sacrifice was a normal part of Greek worship (Endymion later promises to sacrifice a kid to Pan), so this initial insistence on a bloodless oblation is evidently meant to emphasize the cheerful innocence of the Pan festival, as compared with the blood sacrifices that play so large a role in biblical religion. While he was working on this section of the poem, Keats read in the *Examiner* (the "battering ram" issue of 4 May 1817) another of Hunt's editorials on the gloomy, bloodstained religion of the Christians, along with a news item concerning a German religious cult that practiced human sacrifice. Drawing a connection between "the dreadful Petzelians and their expiation by Blood" and the doctrine of the Atonement, Keats remarked: "and do Christians shudder at the same thing in a Newspaper which they attribute to their God in its most aggravated form? (*Letters* 1:137).

Keats's Latmians generally demonstrate a purer religious consciousness than one might expect to find in such a community. Pan worshippers in ancient Greece were rather peremptory in the demands they made of their god, not hesitating to beat and otherwise abuse his effigies to hasten his compliance. Keats's shepherds ask nothing of their divinity beyond his attention, as though aware that enlightened theists do not indulge in prayer of petition, which seems to expect that the sublime order of nature will be changed to meet individual needs.[15] And the Latmians are rather closer to monotheism than Greek shepherds typically ventured in the early stages of Pan worship. After being invoked in his primary character as the goat-like, playful patron of shepherds, hunters, and farmers, in the hymn's fifth stanza Pan's character suddenly becomes awesomely larger, taking on the dimensions of his later identity as the personification of universal nature, a cosmic rather than a local divinity. And Keats's shepherds begin to demonstrate a remarkable sophistication of thought and diction:

> Be still the unimaginable lodge
> For solitary thinkings; such as dodge

> Conception to the very bourne of heaven,
> Then leave the naked brain: be still the leaven,
> That spreading in this dull and clodded earth
> Gives it a touch ethereal—a new birth:
> Be still a symbol of immensity;
> A firmament reflected in a sea;
> An element filling the space between;
> An unknown—but no more.
>
> (1:293–302)

To select only one of these remarkable phrases,[16] the designation of Pan as "a symbol of immensity" suggests that some serious metaphysical thinking has been going on in Latmos. Rational religionists knew that every attempt to conceive a "concrete" corresponding to the abstract notion of deity necessarily falls short. Jupiter, Jehovah, Vishnu—all are only symbols pointing to what is essentially ineffable. Keats's philosophical shepherds acknowledge Pan as such a symbol, as useful as any to signify an immensity that cannot be captured in language. Throughout the hymn, even in the early stanzas where he is almost totally anthropomorphized, the worshippers merely guess at his nature and activity; they do not claim to know him. And they seem content that he remain unknown—indeed they prefer it—so long as he is willing to continue his beneficent ministry.

Keats's choice of Pan as tutelary deity of Latmos, although in one sense controlled by tradition,[17] is a quite appropriate one for his political purposes. The cult of Pan had been connected in a particular way with religious apologetics since the fourth century, when Christian commentators seized on Plutarch's strange account of a group of mariners hearing a disembodied voice proclaiming the death of "the great god Pan" and interpreted it as signifying the dispersal of the pagan gods and oracles by Jesus Christ. The tradition was evidently familiar in Keats's circle of acquaintance. Early in 1818 Leigh Hunt wrote to T. J. Hogg:

> I hope you paid your devotions as usual to the Religio Loci, and hung up an evergreen. If you all go on so, there will be a hope some day that old Vansittart [the Chancellor of the Exchequer] & others will be struck with a Panic Terror, and that a voice will be heard along the water saying "The great God Pan is alive again,"— upon which the villagers will leave off starving, and singing profane hymns, and fall to dancing again.[18]

Here the resurrected Pan is seen as ushering in a post-Christian age of political and economic renovation. In an ideological milieu where Pan symbolized an alternative social order to the established Christian one, Keats's Pandean festival would inevitably have had distinct political resonance.

The attempt to use classical mythology to express a modern conception of what religion ought to be (and thus to demonstrate the defects and inadequacies of Christianity) created problems as well as opportunities for Keats. One difficulty arose immediately in *Endymion*. After his introductory lesson on the characteristics of an enlightened, purified public religion, Keats had some difficulty accounting for the hero's private relationship with the moon goddess. The attraction here was mainly physical, but Keats seemed to feel that the behavior of Greek divinities ought to be metaphysically respectable, so he put into Endymion's mouth that Neoplatonic-sounding disquisition on "fellowship with essence," introducing it as a statement of "the clear religion of heaven." How this kind of "clear religion" relates to the established worship of Pan is not certain. Two years later in a marginal note to Burton's *Anatomy* Keats commented sourly on the "horrid relationship" that seemed to exist between our concepts of heavenly and sensual love, between "the abstract adoration of the deity" and "goatish winnyish lustful love."[19] The attempt in *Endymion* to Platonize a sensual relationship in an effort to make it seem more abstractly religious has confounded interpretation of the poem since it was published. Even a close friend like Benjamin Bailey, who ought to have understood Keats's intention, concluded that the poem was tainted by "that abominable principle of *Shelley's*— that *Sensual Love* is the principle of *things.*"[20]

In book 3 of the poem one can see another complication arising from Keats's apparent effort to raise Greek myth to a level of dignity qualifying it for moral competition with Christianity. Endymion's humanitarian, even Christ-like redemption of the dead lovers in the cave of Glaucus (the Christian archetype is the Harrowing of Hell) has generally struck readers as a successful invention, but a curiously inauthentic interpolation into the Greek legend. As Margaret Sherwood put it, "The old myth, which was a simple tale of love, takes on, in [Endymion's] sympathy with age, with suffering, a conception of love unknown to any ancient myth."[21] Jeffrey Baker's more thorough analysis of the conflicting Christian and Greek elements sees the resulting "mythopoeic pastiche" as the chief cause of the failure of the poem's third book.[22] Keats's evident dissatisfaction with the myth on its own terms and his attempt to introduce a humanitarian element into it may indicate the influence of another of the poet's close friends at this time, one whose views on Greek mythology conflicted dramatically with those that Keats would have been hearing from Leigh Hunt, and who saw himself as Hunt's antagonist in a struggle for Keats's salvation in an artistic as well as a religious sense.

Just at the time when Keats first became acquainted with Benjamin Robert Haydon, the painter was engaged in a long-running, heated argument with Hunt on the religious value of Greek mythology. We do not know whether Keats was a witness to the quarrels that Haydon records in his diary, but the theme and language of the painter's remarks do seem to resonate later in the poet's writings.

"Leigh Hunt says he prefers infinitely the beauties of Pagan Mythology to the gloomy repentance of the Christians," writes Haydon, neatly summarizing what we have seen to be Hunt's basic premise, and going on to dissect Hunt's religion of cheerfulness in a manner that reveals the full religious-political dimension of the debate:

> No man feels more acutely than myself the poetical beauties of the Pagan mythology. Apollo, with his fresh cheek & God like beauty, rising like a gossamer from out a laurel grove, heated with love, after having panted on the bosom of some wandering nymph, is rich, beaming, rapturous! But these are beauties fit for those who live in perpetual enjoyment of immortality, without a care or a grief or a want. But what consolation to the poor, what relief to the widow & the orphan, to the sick, or the oppressed? Could the minds of such beings turn for assistance to a thoughtless & beautiful youth, warm with love & wine, just rising from having debauched a girl? Christianity is a religion adapted to give relief to the wretched & hope to the good, and Christ having suffered is a bond of sympathy between man & his Saviour that nothing in any other religion before or after affords. . . . Is the association connected with Apollo issuing from a laurel grove in the morning freshness to be put in comparison with "give alms of thy goods" [Luke 11:41], and never turn thy face from any poor man, and then the face of the Lord shall not be turned from thee.

The political nature of the argument becomes clearer as Haydon develops the theme of Christianity's social contribution:

> When I said "the Ancients had no hospitals," Hunt said, "so much the better—prevent poverty and not encourage it." . . . Prevent poverty!—prevent crime!—take away evil—but how? Evil is in the World; it cannot be rooted out. Alleviate its consequences, give means of mental consolation to those who suffer from it. . . . [Christianity] teaches to bear those evils of an imperfect Nature, of a world which will not be altered in system to please us, but being as it is, Xtianity is sent to help us through it. Prevent poverty!—prevent illness, prevent old age or any weakness of the body; prevent vice or any of the aberrations of mind; prevent them you cannot, but alleviate them you may, and shew me before Xtianity such alleviation of misery as since its belief, such a triumph in Philosophy as the abolition of the Slave Trade![23]

Haydon's reference to hospitals was a commonplace of Christian apologetics at the time, traceable to William Paley's *Principles of*

Moral and Political Philosophy (1785). "It does not appear," Paley wrote, "that, before the times of Christianity, an infirmary, hospital, or public charity of any kind, existed in the world; whereas, most countries in Christendom have long abounded with these institutions."[24] Paley was participating in a debate on Christianity's social legacy that had been provoked by Gibbon's *Decline and Fall;* Haydon's rhetoric shows that in the intensification of this debate after the French Revolution, the pragmatic argument for Christianity had been reinforced by the activities of the Evangelicals, who were busily and conspicuously alleviating misery and illiteracy wherever their search for souls took them. Their most celebrated effort, as Haydon notes, was the successful campaign waged alongside the Quakers to abolish the British slave trade, but their work in prison and factory reform was widely admired as well.[25]

It seems curious that an argument on mythology should range so far, but if Greek religion were seriously to be presented as culturally superior to Christianity, its social utility needed to be demonstrated. The political quarrel between Christianity and its radical critics focused on the question of which group was best qualified to diagnose and treat mankind's distressed condition. Haydon's strictures on Greek myth challenged Keats to demonstrate that the pagan legends had something to offer the world besides their beauty, something to match the kind of consolation that Christianity provided for so many. Keats's immediate response can be detected in the humanitarian insertions in *Endymion*. But he met the challenge most boldly when he determined to write a Greek poem that would deliberately invite comparison with his country's great Christian epic, a poem that would compete ideologically as well as artistically with the effort of *Paradise Lost* to justify the ways of God to men. In *Hyperion*, as John Barnard has recently observed, "Milton's epic is divested of its Christianity, and recast as a pagan poem. *Hyperion* has no concept of Sin, no Christian cosmogony, and no Hell or Satan. It depicts an evolutionary struggle between lower and higher kinds of good, and is at root optimistic, with a progressive view of mankind's history."[26]

Any ideological revision of Milton's epic would have to include something corresponding to what Keats called the "hintings at good and evil in the Paradise Lost" (1:282), some explanation of the fallen condition of humanity and a prognosis concerning the possibility of restoration or redemption. And, given Haydon's critique of Greek myth, the poem would surely need to offer some consolation for human suffering. But *Hyperion*'s attitude toward the worth and meaning of suffering is oddly ambivalent. One viewpoint, expressed by the father of the Titans in a passage that expresses divine detachment from the concerns of humanity, despises suffering as literally ungodly.

> I have seen my sons most unlike Gods.
> Divine ye were created, and divine
> In sad demeanour, solemn, undisturb'd,
> Unruffled, like high Gods, ye liv'd and ruled:
> Now I behold in you fear, hope, and wrath;
> Actions of rage and passion; even as
> I see them on the mortal world beneath,
> In men who die.
>
> (1:328–35)

On the other hand, Keats apparently intended to show that his hero, Apollo, embraced the experience of suffering as a means of attaining the fullness of divinity. Although he told Haydon that he intended to treat *Hyperion* "in a more naked and grecian Manner" (*Letters* 1:207) than he had achieved in *Endymion,* it seems that he once again found it necessary to import non-Grecian elements into the poem. That suffering may be instructive and formative for human beings was a common enough theme in Greek tragedy, but except in fertility myths the Greeks were unable to see much value or logic in a god's agony, as St. Paul once complained to the Corinthians (1 Cor. 1:23). When Apollo's apotheosis is compared to the struggle of "one who should take leave / Of pale immortal death, and with a pang / As hot as death's is chill, with fierce convulse / Die into life," one is reminded inevitably of a quite different religious story. Indeed Apollo resembles at times a kind of Socinian version of Jesus, an apprentice deity who must earn or learn godhood through experience and effort. In trying to make Apollo more than a "thoughtless & beautiful youth" who offered no consolation to the wretched, Keats's tendency was to make him resemble Jesus Christ.

The situation of the Titans seems more authentically Greek in that no reward is offered for their pain and loss. Insofar as there is any consolation at all, it is embodied in the evolutionary optimism of Oceanus's theory "that first in beauty must be first in might" (2:229). This "radical (and non-Christian) rereading of human history and its possible future"[27] was another of Keats's original contributions to the myth. Considering himself part of the vanguard in a "grand march of intellect" that had left superstitions like those of Milton behind (*Letters,* 1:281–82), Keats attempted to make his poem express the forward-looking optimism that the Enlightenment had opposed to Christianity's retrospective emphasis on the Fall of Man, an anticipation of a secular redemption to be wrought in time by human effort. But there is a problem in Keats's use of a Greek myth to express a vision of the future (a problem Shelley avoided in *Prometheus Unbound* by detaching his titan's struggle from chronological time). Once Oceanus's speculation is thought of as a prophecy affecting the world of human civilization whose existence is noticed in the poem (1:273–280, 333–35), one realizes that historically the prophecy was not accomplished—nor has its major premise, that first in beauty must be first in might, apparently been an operative principle in history. One needed only to look at what the world had become in 1819. The Olympian succession, if such a thing may be said to have "taken place," was followed, as Gibbon eloquently lamented, by the triumph of superstition and brutal fanaticism. With a kind of dramatic irony, Keats's Miltonic model continually reminds the reader of the victory of Christianity over paganism, a cultural victory that Milton delighted in celebrating.

Whether or not it was loss of faith in the actualization of the poem's optimistic thesis that brought it to a halt, one notes that at the very time he abandoned *Hyperion* Keats also explicitly rejected the kind of "march of mind" ideology to which he had once subscribed. "In truth," he wrote in April 1819, "I do not at all believe in this sort of perfectability" (2:101), and he went on to elaborate the alternative vision of the human prospect and the rationale for human suffering that underlie his conception of the world as a "vale of Soul-making," an exercise in theodicy that also entailed a changed attitude toward the classical myths and their relation to Christianity:

> It is pretty generally suspected that the christian scheme has been coppied from the ancient persian and greek Philosophers. Why may they not have made this simple thing even more simple for common apprehension by introducing Mediators and Personages in the same manner as in the hethan mythology abstractions are personified— Seriously I think it probable that this System of Soul-making—may have been the Parent of all the more palpable and personal Schemes of Redemption, among the Zoroastrians the Christians and the Hindoos. For as one part of the human species must have their carved Jupiter; so another part must have the palpable and named Mediator and saviour, their Christ their Oromanes and their Vishnu (*Letters* 2:103).

Keats's disdain for the "common apprehension" that requires palpable and named divinities and his deistic equation of Christ with Jupiter suggest a significant qualification of his admiration for "the beautiful mythology of Greece" (*Poems*, 103). Given this repudiation of all "carved Jupiters," all palpable, personal deities, it does not seem coincidental that in his later "Greek" poems—the odes to Psyche and on a Grecian Urn, *Lamia*, and the revision of *Hyperion*— one notices a detachment and distancing from the world of the Greek myths, a new tendency to present such "religion" as something remote, transient, and fanciful. Psyche's lease on life is dependent on the poet's imaginative cooperation; the Greek town that worshipped on the urn's "pious morn" is now desolate; Lamia inhabits a time before the Greek gods were displaced by another species of "faery." Finally, in *The Fall of Hyperion*, the last of the Greek divinities, the "pale omega of a withered race," is found officiating at a shrine to which no one ever comes except a rare dreamer. This "Shade of Memory" is all that is left of Greek religion, whose gods, even Apollo himself, are "far flown."

The Fall of Hyperion persistently emphasizes the antiquity and strangeness of what it represents. Even Moneta's Latin name puts her Greek origin in an historical perspective, and the association of that name with Juno and Minerva, as well as with Mnemosyne, suggests that the reductive process of mythological syncretism is already at work.[28] Syncretism is also suggested by the appearance of the temple and its furnishings. Noticing that the "strange vessels and large draperies" seem to derive from the Book of Exodus, John Livingston Lowes called attention to "the merging in Keats's mind of the crowded glories of the tabernacle and its service with the majestic simplicity of the Greek, and the vastness of the Egyptian temples."[29] The dreaming poet brings to his encounter with Moneta an educated sense of history, particularly the history of religion. His allusions indicate knowledge of the Bible (both Testaments), as well as other Greek myths beside the one the Titaness recounts. References to the Caliphate and the scarlet conclave show that he knows the history of Islam and of Roman Catholicism. He has evidently read Dante's great Catholic poem and Milton's Protestant epic, and he can compare Moneta's temple with the "grey cathedrals" of his own era. This broad frame of religious reference tends to relativize Moneta's position, providing the poet with a rhetorical weapon that allows him, for instance, to celebrate his survival of the goddess's death threat with a biblical allusion whose very impropriety seems to liberate him from the stagnancy and ruin surrounding him: "I mounted up / As once fair angels on a ladder flew / From the green turf to Heaven" (1:134–36).

And the reader is always conscious—even when the dreaming poet seems not to be—that the dangerous goddess and her awesome temple are as much creations of the poet's brain as are the goddess and temple of the "Ode to Psyche." Moneta is an imposing figure, as are all the authoritarian divinities we project. She is able to induce feelings of anguished guilt in the poet for his dreamer's negligence of the world's miseries. But the reader may pose objections where the visionary cannot. By what ethic does Moneta criticize the poet's social conscience? What Greek standard of charity or compassion allows her to praise "those to whom the misery of the world are misery and will not let them rest"? "Where," asked Haydon, "were the hospitals in the ancient world?" And Haydon was not alone among Keats's friends in questioning the social conscience of the ancient

Greeks. In November 1819, the first of Hazlitt's lectures on the Age of Elizabeth insisted that modern humanitarianism derived not from classical culture but from the revolutionary teachings of Jesus Christ:

> The very idea of abstract benevolence, of the desire to do good because another wants our services, and of regarding the human race as one family, the offspring of one common parent, is hardly to be found in any other code or system. It was "to the Jews a stumbling block, and to the Greeks foolishness." The Greeks and Romans never thought of considering others, but as they were Greeks or Romans, as they were bound to them by certain positive ties, or, on the other hand, as separated from them by fiercer antipathies. Their virtues were the virtues of political machines, their vices were the vices of demons, ready to inflict or to endure pain with obdurate and remorseless inflexibility of purpose.[30]

We do not know whether Keats ever heard this argument from Hazlitt (he did not attend the lecture, but was given a report on it [*Letters* 2:230]), or whether he arrived at such conclusions on his own. At any rate he, too, had begun to realize that Greek religion was not more but less humane than the Christianity that replaced it. Moneta's sponsorship of humanitarian endeavor sounds strange coming from this sphinx-like figure who would have watched "with obdurate and remorseless inflexibility" as the poet died and rotted at her feet (1:107–17).

But if "Greek religion" has lost some of its political virtue (along with its cheerfulness), there is no sign that Keats is preferring Haydon's Christian alternative. He had firmly closed off that retreat in his "vale of Soul-making" letter, in which Christianity's offer of redemption from this "vale of tears" is dismissed as "a little circumscribed straightened notion." More than one critic has discerned a resemblance to Jesus in Moneta's face,[31] and he is probably meant to be thought of here along with other "palpable and named mediators." Ministering before a statue of a supreme divinity whose features are too high and obscure to be identified, Moneta represents all those surrogates and intermediaries that traditional religions have interposed between God and man. In another sense she represents the irrelevance of religious myths and rituals that operate in temples sequestered from the suffering world. Of the benefactors of humanity, those who "labour for mortal good," she says: "They come not here, they have no thought to come" (1:159, 165).

In presenting Moneta's temple as a shrine of dead and irrelevant religions, I think Keats may have been recalling another ruined temple that had been used in this way in a celebrated poem by a contemporary. In the induction to *The Fall of Hyperion*, one catches persistent echoes of the opening stanzas of canto 2 of Byron's *Childe Harold*—

stanzas that Keats read during the period of his youthful admiration
of the noble poet and which became controversial because of their
impudent skepticism. Byron's poem also makes the peculiar connection between a ruined temple, a desolate goddess, and the paradise
of which fanatics dream. The Byronic narrator sits in the ruined
temple of the "son of Saturn" looking at the Acropolis—"yon fane /
On high, where Pallas lingered, loth to flee / The latest relic of her
ancient reign"—and addresses the goddess:

> Ancient of days! august Athena! where,
> Where are thy men of might? thy grand in soul?
> Gone—glimmering through the dream of things that were
>
> . . . .
>
> Look on this spot—a nation's sepulchre!
> Abode of gods, whose shrines no longer burn.
> Even gods must yield—religions take their turn:
> 'Twas Jove's—'tis Mahomet's—and other creeds
> Will rise with other years, till man shall learn
> Vainly his incense soars, his victim bleeds;
> Poor child of Doubt and Death, whose hope is built on reeds.[32]

Like Byron's, Keats's ruined Greek temple also symbolizes the de-
clension of religion and the futility of all such attempts to concretize
and control the Divine.

The radicalism of this position was not merely a definitive response to Hunt's and Haydon's arguments. It was Keats's most explicit
poetic reaction to the political crisis that shook England in the autumn
of 1819. While recent examinations of Keats's politics have looked
closely at his response to the Peterloo Massacre, they have not very
carefully considered the religious dimension of that public crisis as
it affected Keats and his liberal contemporaries. At the height of the
angry national debate following Peterloo, Richard Carlile was tried
and convicted on a charge of blasphemous libel for having republished
Thomas Paine's The Age of Reason and other anti-Christian writings.
Carlile was closely associated in the public mind with Peterloo, having
attended the Manchester meeting and published eyewitness accounts
of the atrocities that became the basis of the radical version of what
took place, and for publication of which he was subjected to additional
indictments for seditious libel.[33]

Carlile's trial in October 1819 was the culmination of a legal
process that had been going on since January, one that attracted
widespread attention among liberals in England and abroad. The trial
was an event "of great moment" to Keats; he predicted that it "would
light a flame [the government] could not extinguish" (Letters 2:194).
The publisher's uncompromising, contentious skepticism polarized
public opinion, forcing his supporters into more radical religious

positions than they might otherwise have adopted for themselves. Many felt the need to make a choice between Christianity and Carlile's radical deism. For the first time, Leigh Hunt used that term to describe his own position and predicted the eventual triumph of deism as the dominant religion of England (*Examiner*, 24 October 1819, p. 675). Byron also predicted that Carlile's suffering for conscience's sake would win new proselytes to deism, comparing the publisher to Socrates, Jesus, and "all who dare to oppose the most notorious abuses of the name of God and the mind of man."[34] Shelley, in a letter intended to be a public defense of Carlile, proclaimed that the triumph of deism had already arrived: "What men of any rank in society from their talents are *not* Deists whose understandings have been unbiassed by the allurements of worldly interest? Which of our great literary characters not receiving emolument from the advocating a system of religion inseparably connected with the source of that emolument, is not a Deist?"[35] As Hunt had once divided the literary world into Christians and Greeks, Shelley now saw the division lying between salaried Christianity and the kind of radical religious skepticism championed by Carlile.

Carlile's contraband edition had given *The Age of Reason* new currency as a formulation of revolutionary deism (as distinct from the more scholarly 18th-century variety), and he attracted new attention to Paine's work by his insistence on reading the entire book into the record at his trial. What is significant for the purpose of the present study is that Paine gave forceful expression to the traditional deist critique of classical mythology in language that recalls Keats's in the "Vale of Soul-making" letter. Like Keats, Paine dismissed Christianity as only another species of mythology, another surrender to the polythestic impulse, one more corruption of pure theism by those who, whether ancient oracles or modern priests, would interpose mediators between divinity and humanity. In Paine's view, all such priestcraft plays into the hands of repressive governments.

> Every national church or religion has established itself by pretending some special mission from God, communicated to certain individuals. The Jews have their Moses; the Christians their Jesus Christ, their apostles and saints; and the Turks their Mahomet; as if the way to God was not open to every man alike. . . . It is curious to observe how the theory of what is called the Christian Church, sprung out of the tail of the heathen mythology. . . . The statue of Mary succeeded the statue of Diana of Ephesus. The deification of heroes changed into the canonization of saints. . . . The Christian theory is little else than the idolatry of the ancient mythologists, accommodated to the purposes of power and revenue; and it yet remains to reason and philosophy to abolish the amphibious fraud. . . . It has been the scheme of the Christian church, and of all the other

invented systems of religion, to hold man in ignorance of the Creator, as it is of government to hold him in ignorance of his rights. The systems of the one are as false as those of the other, and are calculated for mutual support.[36]

For Paine there could be no lasting political change without radical religious reform. That meant a repudiation of all revealed religion, all forms of faith that depended on priests and mediators who inevitably distort religion for their own purposes. The only way to combat priestcraft was a "return to the pure, unmixed, and unadulterated belief of one God, and no more." Paine made no scholarly or sentimental exceptions on behalf of classical polytheism. Ancient superstition was as pernicious as modern. If anything, "the [pagan] mythologists pretended to more revealed religion than the christians do. They had their oracles and their priests, who were supposed to receive and deliver the word of God verbally on almost all occasions."[37] A truly radical position demanded rigorous repudiation of all such distractions and props, however charming or beautiful.

Whether the parallel between Keats's thinking and Paine's is coincidental or conditioned by the political crisis of 1819, one finds in *The Fall of Hyperion* just such a determined renunciation of the old myths, even those that had been particularly dear to Keats. The beloved legend of Endymion is implicitly denied, along with the Greek mythopoeic imagination that invented it, when the poet says of Moneta's eyes

> they saw me not,
> But in blank splendour beamed like the mild moon,
> Who comforts those she sees not, who knows not
> What eyes are upward cast.
>
> (1:268–71)

And when Apollo is invited to send his "misty pestilence" to kill all fraudulent and incompetent poets (1:204–10), we are reminded for the first time in Keats's verse that the poet-healer, who had once symbolized Keats's "entire complex of aesthetic values,"[38] is also traditionally "the author of plagues and contagious diseases" and the god whom Homer describes "shooting his arrows in various directions at the defenceless sons of men."[39]

The stringent "system of soul-creation" that Keats formulated in April 1819 had left no room for palpable, personal deities, or mediators, or saviors, and the political crisis of autumn reinforced for him the necessity of rejecting all religion but the "abstract adoration of the Deity" allowed by the austere piety of Paine's radical faith. Of the essential truths of religion, Shelley had written earlier in the year, "each to itself must be the oracle." All other oracles were silent, and no resurrection of Pan to restore their voices was to be expected or desired. The priestcraft of the priestess Moneta had nothing to reveal to a poet but an old story of dying gods. As he relived the last agony of those fated divinities, the poet found that he could, if necessary, get by without their ambiguous inspiration.

> Without stay or prop
> But my own weak mortality, I bore
> The load of this eternal quietude.
> (1:389–91)

Notes

1. This new phase of political analysis was provoked in part by Jerome McGann ("Keats and the Historical Method in Literary Criticism," *MLN* 94 [1979]: 988–1032) and followed up by Morris Dickstein ("Keats and Politics," *Studies in Romanticism* 25 [1986]: 175–81), Marilyn Butler (*Romantics, Rebels and Reactionaries* [New York: Oxford University Press, 1982]), and Susan Wolfson ("Keats's *Isabella* and the 'Digressions' of 'Romance,'" *Criticism* 27 [1985]: 247–61), among others. The gleaners of "To Autumn" include Jeffrey Baker (*John Keats and Symbolism* [New York: St. Martin's Press, 1986]), David Bromwich, and William Keach; the last two participated in the stimulating forum on Keats's politics that appeared in *Studies in Romanticism* 25 (Summer 1986): 171–229.

2. William Sharp, *The Life and Letters of Joseph Severn* (New York: Scribner, 1892), 29.

3. *The Letters of John Keats*, ed. H. E. Rollins, 2 vols. (Cambridge: Harvard University Press, 1958), 1:191; 2:194. All quotations from Keats's letters will be taken from this edition and cited hereafter as *Letters* in the text.

4. Ryan, Robert M., *Keats: The Religious Sense* (Princeton: N.J.: Princeton University Press, 1976), 71–113.

5. "Cockney School of Poetry, No. 4," *Blackwood's Edinburgh Magazine* (October 1818).

6. Aileen Ward, *John Keats: The Making of a Poet* (1963: reprint, New York: Farrar, Straus and Giroux, 1986), 80–81, 423n.

7. *Examiner* (12 November 1815), 731–32.

8. *Examiner*, (4 May 1817), 274.

9. Hunt, Leigh, *Foliage; or Poems Original and Translated* (London: Ollier, 1818). Shelley, another constant reader of Gibbon, once defined Christianity as "those events and opinions which put an end to the graceful religion of the Greeks (*The Letters of Percy Bysshe Shelley*, ed. Frederick L. Jones, 2 vols. [Oxford: Clarendon Press, 1964], 2:203), and Timothy Webb has shown how "Shelley's Grecian world defines itself, in part at least, by its negative relationship to orthodox Christianity", in "Shelley and the Religion of Joy," *Studies in Romanticism* 15 (1976): 357–82. Marilyn Butler discusses some ways in which Shelley and Thomas Love Peacock employed Greek myth tactically to argue a liberated, nonascetic sexual ethic in contrast with Christianity's "false and inadequate religion of love", in "Myth and Mythmaking in the Shelley Circle," *ELH* 49 (1982): 50–72.

10. Hunt, *Foliage*, 25–26.

11. *The Poems of John Keats*, ed. Jack Stillinger (Cambridge: Harvard University

Press, 1978), 192n. All further references to Keats's verse will be to this edition and will be included in the text.

12. Hunt, *Foliage*, 35–39.

13. Robert Gittings, *John Keats* (London: Heinemann, 1968), 88, 92.

14. *The Keats Circle: Letters and Papers, 1816–1878*, ed. H. E. Rollins, 2 vols. (Cambridge: Harvard University Press, 1965), 2:144.

15. A concise statement of the standard rationalist objection to such prayer, and of the political dimension of the objection, is given by Shelley in a note to *Queen Mab* 7:135–36: "Christianity inculcates the necessity of supplicating the Deity. Prayer may be considered under two points of view—as an endeavour to change the intentions of God, or as a formal testimony of our obedience. But the former case supposes that the caprices of a limited intelligence can occasionally instruct the Creator of the world how to regulate the universe; and the latter, a certain degree of servility analogous to the loyalty demanded by earthly tyrants," (*The Complete Poetical Works of Percy Bysshe Shelley*, ed. Thomas Hutchinson [London: Oxford University Press, 1943], 822).

16. I have discussed the others in "Keats's 'Hymn to Pan': A Debt to Shaftesbury?" *Keats-Shelley Journal* 26 (1977): 31–34.

17. The goat-god was traditionally associated with a pastoral economy, and Michael Drayton's *The Man in the Moon*, which Keats seems to have read, also begins with a ceremony in honor of Pan. Drayton's ten-line introduction to his Endymion story does not describe the ritual in any detail, however, and its brevity accentuates by contrast the elaborateness of Keats's liturgy.

18. Scott, W. S., *The Athenians* (London: Golden Cockerel Press, 1943), 44.

19. *The Complete Works of John Keats*, ed. H. B. Forman, 5 vols. (1901: reprint, New York: AMS, 1970), 3:268.

20. Rollins, *The Keats Circle*, 1:35.

21. Margaret Sherwood, *Undercurrents of Influence in English Romantic Poetry* (1934; reprint, New York: AMS, 1971), 234.

22. Baker, *John Keats and Symbolism*, 75.

23. *The Diary of Benjamin Robert Haydon*, ed. Willard B. Pope, 4 vols. (Cambridge: Harvard University Press, 1961–63), 2:67–69.

24. *The Works of William Paley, D.D.*, introduction by D. S. Wayland, 8 vols. (London: George Cowie, 1837), 1:153.

25. Howse, Ernest Marshall, *Saints in Politics: The "Clapham Sect" and the Growth of Freedom* (Toronto: University of Toronto Press, 1952), 130–31.

26. Barnard, John, *John Keats* (Cambridge: Cambridge University Press, 1987), 58.

27. Ibid., 63.

28. Anne K. Mellor, "Keats's Face of Moneta," *Keats-Shelley Journal* 25 (1976): 66.

29. Lowes, John Livingston, "Moneta's Temple," *PMLA* 51 (1936):1112.

30. *Complete Works of William Hazlitt*, ed. P. P. Howe, 21 vols. (London: Dent, 1930–34), 6:184.

31. D. G. James, *The Romantic Comedy: An Essay on English Romanticism* (1948; reprint, London: Oxford University Press, 1963), 150; Stuart M. Sperry, *Keats the Poet* (Princeton: Princeton University Press, 1973), 330–31; Robert M. Ryan, "Christ and Moneta," *English Language Notes* 13 (March 1976): 190–92.

32. *Lord Byron: The Complete Poetical Works*, ed. Jerome J. McGann, 7 vols. (New York: Oxford University Press, 1980–), 2:44–45, 47.

33. Joel H. Wiener, *Radicalism and Freethought in Nineteenth-Century Britain: The Life of Richard Carlile* (Westport, Conn.: Greenwood Press, 1983), 42.

34. *Byron's "Don Juan": A Variorum Edition*, ed. T. G. Steffan, 2 vols. (Austin: University of Texas Press, 1957), 3:5.

35. *The Letters of Percy Bysshe Shelley*, 2:242.

36. Thomas Paine, *The Age of Reason*, ed. Moncure Daniel Conway (New York: G. P. Putnam's Sons, 1896), 23, 25, 191.

37. Ibid., 61n.

38. Walter Evert, *Aesthetic and Myth in the Poetry of Keats* (Princeton: Princeton University Press, 1965), 39.

39. William Godwin [Edward Baldwin, pseud.], *The Pantheon, or, Ancient History of the God of Greece and Rome* (1806; reprint, New York: Garland Press, 1984), 47.

Romantic Evolution: Fresh Perfection and Ebbing Process in Keats

Hermione de Almeida[*]

In 1795 Alexander von Humboldt published a fable on the nature of organic life in Friedrich von Schiller's journal *Die Hören*.[1] Humboldt's myth told of a mysterious painting owned by the people of Syracuse called "The Genius of Rhodes." The painting depicted a crowd of young men and women who stretched out their arms toward one another in desperate longing; between them, seeming to represent what prevented these lovers from consummating their desires, stood a genius holding a burning torch, with a butterfly on its shoulder. A pendant to this picture was found in Rhodes. Here the young people had united in ecstatic embraces, and the genius lay crushed beneath their senseless, falling bodies; the torch was extinguished, and the butterfly gone. A philosopher who examined both paintings, Humboldt concluded, found the correct interpretation. The young lovers represented the elements in an organism; their urge to submit to the laws of their chemical affinities was restrained by the vital force represented by the genius; as soon as the genius (or force) lost control over them they united in what is called putrefaction.[2]

Unlike the naive people of ancient Syracuse and Rhodes, the sentimental philosophers and physiologists of Keats's time would have had no trouble deciphering the myth of "The Genius of Rhodes." The butterfly had always been the symbol of life, from the earliest Greek notions of the *anima* or soul (Lemprière's Psyche has the wings of a butterfly, and he notes that in Greek art a butterfly flutters from

---

[*] This essay was written specifically for this volume and is published here for the first time by permission of the author.

the mouth of expiring humans)[3] to contemporary notions of psyche and will. A flaming torch had frequently symbolized the life-force, from earliest vitalistic notions of life as light to contemporary mechanistic notions of life as electricity and galvanic motion.[4] Humboldt's portrayal of life as those forces that resist putrefaction through the tension of their combined opposition was a familiar notion of life in the early nineteenth century; indeed it found unexpected support in the older belief in spontaneous generation from putrescent matter, and in contemporary observations of the connection between the phosphorescence of decaying bodies and living creatures like electric eels and fireflies. It was evoked alike by the vitalistic theorists of life who believed in a fine essence or ethereal will; by the electrochemical theorists of life who saw this essence as no more than an electromagnetic spark or chemical catalyst; and by the mechanistic theorists of life who saw both essence and electricity as nothing more than the products of motion, countermotion, and organization.

The poets of Humboldt's time, also, would have easily read in his myth and its mysterious works of art the meaning of organic life. In the nervous energy represented by Humboldt's vital force we recognize Schiller's definition of life as "nerve spirit," a subtle, mobile spirit of unknown origin that resides in live nerves and, as a perceiving or transmutative force, was the animating, illuminating link between matter and mind, world and soul.[5] In the poised, restraining figure of the Genius of Rhodes we recognize elements of Coleridge's comprehensive theory of life as "the principle of individuation" within unity; as "the manifestation of one power by opposing forces," or "the power which unites a given *all* into a *whole* that is presupposed by all its parts" as a tendency to individuate existing in parallel to a tendency to connect, which operates according to a general law of polarity and rests only in equilibrium; as a power that subsists in the union of opposing forces and consists (or manifests itself) in their strife.[6] In the attitude of Humboldt's restrained and satiated young lovers we recognize the stilled, pent-up figures of Keats's Grecian urn, their mortal antitheses, and the genius of the urn's vital supremacy and fraught emptiness of form.

In the captured motion of the frenzied figures on its surface, and in the intense, stressed quietude of its form, Keats's Grecian urn presents an image of life contained, with its contraries reconciled and energized process held at bay, and of infinite power gathered up and concentrated within a finite, hollowed space.[7] But power is power contained, the genius of vital force is the restraint of this force's natural expression, and the fair attitude of the urn endures because it is only a postured attitude of life. The urn's stasis is its perfection. As Walter Jackson Bate and critics since have noted, the Grecian urn is a measured ode to art, its figures are conceived negatively, through what they *cannot* experience, and more is denied them than is bestowed.[8] The urn, at least from the experiential perspective of breathing passion's "heart high-sorrowful" and "the ruddy strife of heart and lips,"[9] is an artifact framed against natural patterns, a cold pastoral that draws out the signs of life and empties to desolation a little town that it might "with garlands" dress its hollow form.

Humboldt's fable of the Genius of Rhodes was a myth of life, of that which resists putrefaction; its figures of vibrant and exhausted lovers stand as ironic patterns for the flowery tale of the urn whose statuary figures—far from resisting—welcome petrifaction on an Attic shape. "How get from lifeless marble life and pain?" the poet Chamisso asks of his lifeless statue.[10] In reverse, in spite of and perhaps because of its beauty, the urn's art is the art of *medusée*, the transfixing of action and the turning of life into stone. Its white figures transfixed in their happiness, even as they triumphantly resist the natural law espoused in *Hyperion,* bear a deathly connection to the frozen statues with "carved features" marbled by pain that frame the poet's aching vision of *The Fall of Hyperion.* Those "three fixed shapes," "postured motionless, / Like sculpture builded up upon the grave / Of their own power"—whose "eternal quietude" feeds reciprocal and "Ponderous" upon the poet's life-senses (1: 225, 382–93)—recall for us the "marble men and maidens overwrought" graven upon the urn's "silent form" (41–42).

Life, according to the Scots physician John Brown (*Elementa medicinae,* 1780) depended upon a principle of excitability that had to be maintained in even supply in the animated body. Too little excitement presaged loss of energy and death from debility. But too much excitability worked the body at too high a pitch; it produced a state of *overwrought intensity* (false energy) that masked imminent, deathly exhaustion.[11] The Brunonian theory of excitability (which had its source as much in Galvani's idea of animal magnetism as in Haller's notion of muscular irritability and nervous sensibility) found wide currency among both the vitalistic philosophers and the mechanistic physiologists of this time. Brunonian medicine influenced clinical practices in the London hospitals like Guy's, and Brownist elements can be found in the otherwise various theories of life postulated by Astley Cooper, William Lawrence, John Hunter, Erasmus Darwin, even Alexander von Humboldt.[12] Astley Cooper's opening lecture on physiology at Guy's Hospital proposed irritability as the manifest principle of life; the varying intensities of this irritability, he said, were a medical sign to vitality, health, disease, exhaustion, and age.[13] Keats's notes of Cooper's lectures describe the vital principle as nervous energy originating in the brain, an active power of polarized tension that manifests its intensity in the varying irritability and sympathy of parts.[14] The poet's notes on the vital principle cite specifically John Hunter's research on the *Gymnotus electricus* or electric eel. The public quarrel between John Abernethy and William Lawrence over Hunter's principle of life was at full flush during Keats's year at Guy's Hospital. Astley Cooper's teachings during the period incorporate the Brunonian theory of excitability and the Hunterian theory of the life of blood; they also include those theories of skeptical physiologists, like Lawrence, who said life was dependent on organization and was nothing more than the assemblage of all the functions,[15] that the body was a machine of tight synchronized action, and that consciousness was nothing more than a ghost in the machine. Cooper's lectures to Keats's class express a pragmatic compromise between mechanism and vitalism similar to that advanced by Erasmus Darwin in his theory of life.

Hunter said that the living principle was distinct from matter, "something superadded" to animate parts that was made manifest in their irritability, and that life could be recognized by its "power of resisting the operations of external chemical agency" so as to prevent decomposition in the bodies where it resided.[16] Hunter also said that this power, characterized by opposition and resistance, was allied with an ability to generate heat, and that the generation of heat increased in intensity in proportion to the "perfection" or life-power of the animal.[17] Buffon, Maupertuis, and Lamarck had taught that living matter in "hereditary particles" or "organic molecules" was responsible for the life of immutable species;[18] Erasmus Darwin, who learned from these men but also from Redi, Leeuwenhoek, Swammerdan, and Malpighi, said life began as microscopic animals whose generation in soil or water was nurtured by moisture and warmth. The essential living element for Darwin, in animalcules as in more complex (more perfect) creatures, was "the spirit of animation" or "sensorial power," which found its emblem in "the hieroglyphic figure of Adonis" as life "perpetually wooed or courted by organic matter," alternately passive and polarized.[19] Darwin claimed that his "spirit of animation" was distinct from prior notions of a subtle, elastic fluid or electric ether. Uncertain of its origin or nature, he was nevertheless positive that it was the energy that occasioned the attraction of organic particles, the agent of contraction of animal muscles, and the power that stimulated the "opposition of new parts" to form the embryo in more perfect forms of life.[20]

To the scientists of Keats's time—be they mechanists or vitalists—life was wrought in the interplay of opposing forces; the degree of vitality was the measure of perfection or higher form, and the varying intensities of this vitality were clues to both the condition of the individual form and the nature of variety among the species. When Coleridge sought to explain the dynamics of conscious and material life in metascientific terms, he noted that as life or the tendency to individuation progressed toward "some intenser form of reality," the degrees or intensities of life formed the various species, be these species organic or perceptual.[21] To early nineteenth-century thinkers, perfection and process were not incompatible but allied in the interest of perpetual, superseding novelty; intensity could be the measure of life, mind, and art.

Because of its "dull echo" and her "poor skill," Clymene, in *Hyperion*, casts forth her shell upon the sand at water's edge where life begins;[22] a wave fills it, as her senses are filled with enchantment, music that doth "both drown and keep alive" her ears (2:272–80). Clymene's "mouthed shell," a fossil picked from the ebbing tide, speaks volubly through its hollowness not of the empty stasis of perfection (like the Grecian urn) but of the ever-replenished progress of perfection: an ever "new blissful golden melody." Apollo's music drowns and keeps alive, its rapturous notes falling "one after one . . . Like pearl beads" (282–84) embody the "living death" of the natural law of supersession just articulated by Oceanus. "We fall by course of Nature's law, not force," Oceanus says, speaking with the voice of winds and tides of what he knows to be "eternal truth." As the Titans once found their forms to be "compact, and beautiful" and of "purer life" than Heaven and Earth, "So on our heels a fresh perfection treads, / A power more strong in beauty, born of us / And fated to excel us," much as "eagles golden-feather'd" surpass the "fair boughs" of forest trees—"for 'tis the eternal law / That first in beauty should be first in might" (2:181, 206–31).[23] Purer life, a higher degree of life-force, bodies forth, more full, in more distinct, complex, sensitive, intense forms of beauty.

The concept of evolution began as a sense of unrolling something primordially complete, but eventually came to imply something being unrolled, completed, perfected.[24] This change matched the transference from a belief in a supernatural, spontaneous creation of fixed and immutable life-forms, which was current well into the eighteenth century, to the nineteenth-century belief in the progressive mutation and development of the species through either small-scale gradual change (now termed "phyletic gradualism") or sudden episodic change by mysterious and revolutionary speciation events (now termed "punctuated equilibrium"). Goethe proposed that every living being was a complex of independent elements referable to one model or primordial "idea," and individuality was merely a metamorphic variation of an original interindividual pattern; unlike Robinet's monad (a simple unit of nature's construction material), Goethe's prototype (*Urpflanze*) was an all-inclusive form that manifested itself only in a multiplicity of individual modulations.[25] The prototype was static but, for Goethe, perfection was variable: it resided temporarily in that individual modulation that attained the fullest realization of the model. Oken's physiophilosophy sought to reverse the evolutionary pattern of contemporary zoologists: man was still the summit of nature's development but, since spirit preceded matter, the animal kingdom was merely representations in five classes (Dermatozoa, Glossozoa, Rhinozoa, Otozoa, Opthalmozoa) of man's five senses.[26] Perception, for Oken, was perfection.

When Buffon (*Histoire naturelle des animaux*, 1778) established the criterion of species, he insisted on their constancy; true species were perfect even though potent forces might occasion the variability of particular organisms.[27] The animal series represented an escalation of being to Lamarck (*Recherches sur l'organization des corps vivants*, 1802; *Histoire naturelle des animaux sans vertèbres*, 1815); life-forms were ever at work complicating and perfecting structures; the stimulus of environmental challenge, to which the organism's will responded creatively (*Philosophie zoologique*, 1809), caused lacunae and mutations within this organic drive to perfection.[28] Erasmus Darwin was the first to propose life's "birth upon the brine," or "the abysm-birth of elements" (*Endymion*, 3:28, 362).[29] Darwin rejected Buffon's notion that the embryo of each species was a complete, minute version of the adult form, and he denied that Lamarckian will or the ideal models of *Naturphilosophie* could control evolution.[30] Evolution proceeded naturally, gradually, and mindlessly, from a single living filament; it took eons to progress by natural selection from simple sea creatures to the complex perfection of human form.[31] (To the extent that Keats evokes evolutionary thought in his poetry—and we are certain of his knowledge of Darwin and Buffon only—this evocation proves to be as random as pre-Buffonian creation theory, as creatively selective as Darwin's natural selection, and as intentionally diffusive of the distinction between perceptual and organic evolution as *Naturphilosophie*.)

"Who had power / To make me desolate? whence came the strength? / How was it nurtur'd to such bursting forth," Saturn asks with the feverish and therefore false energy of waning power. He addresses both the enfeebled Titans and his sterile environment: "But cannot I create? / Cannot I form? Cannot I fashion forth / Another world, another universe . . . ?" (*Hyperion*, 1:102–104, 141–43). Old Saturn presumes that power, like matter, is indestructible and therefore recoverable; that perfection was fixed and completed in the Titans; that their fall is but a temporary contamination, not a fault in being, of their perfect order. His "realmless eyes" do not see that he and his fellows are "Scarce images of life" in "radiance faint," frenzied wills without the impetus of life-force, "lank-eared Phantoms" devolved from (ideal) divine form to pale, multiple, emotional shadows of "the mortal world beneath," "monstrous forms" of inaction and pain (1:19; 2:33; 1:304, 334, 228–30), hollow fossils of their former selves. Their environment, a "sad ruin," provides no stimulus to life or change, new parts or new worlds; it is a dull, echoing shell of granite, slate, and flint, a region of "black-weeded pools" that foster poisons and putrescence,[32] with an atmosphere far "from the healthy breath of morn," consisting of icy, opaque, and vitiated "fixed air" requiring "laborious breath" (1:2; 2:15–17, 22–23).[33] Stasis is cessation, sterility, and cold Saturn cannot create life from freezing "spaces of oblivion" (2:359), lacunae in the evolutionary escalation of being. The false energy of his aggressive question masks his debility, its hollowness contains its own answer, proof, as Oceanus says, why he must stoop.

David Hume in 1739 found the terms *"efficacy, agency, power, force, energy, necessity, connection* and *productive quality"* to be "all nearly synonymous."[34] This may well be Saturn's problem of perception. He mistakes the agency of nature's law, Necessity, for "Fate" accidentally "strangled in [his] nervous grasp" (1:105); he confuses his agitated will with productive force; he presumes the sharp lightning and simple thunder of his art (1:59–62) to be synonymous with (if not more powerful than) the subtle efficacy, energy, connection, and productive quality of Apollo's "untremendous might" (2:150–55). Locke, who connected the "idea of power" with the notion of change, alteration, and relation, considered power to be twofold: "as able to make, or able to receive any change. The one may be called *active*, and the other *passive* power."[35] Apollo asks not the aggressive "Who had power?", but "Where is power?"

> Whose hand, whose essence, what divinity
> Makes this alarum in the elements,
> While I here idle listen on the shores
> In fearless yet in aching ignorance?
> (3:103–7)

Passive, receptive Apollo does not assume power or perfection; his is a fresh perfection, a power more strong in beauty. But intensity, as the evolutionists implied and as Keats insisted, is the measure of life, sense, mind, and art.[36] Apollo's beauty is a greater vitality, a greater intensity, a sharper sensitivity (Schiller's nerve spirit), a more subtle and less brutish power of perception. Power (the genius of poetry) resides in receptive intensity; it cannot be possessed or repossessed as Saturn wills, because it is not a hypostatic entity.[37] Like perfection, power becomes process in Apollo's reign; and painful Promethean change plays necessity in the transformation of the "foreseeing god."[38]

"That which is creative must create itself—."[39] "Life's self is nourish'd by its proper pith, / And we are nurtured like a pelican brood" (*Endymion*, 1:814–15). Life is an "eternal fierce destruction," evolution, the tread of hungry generations upon one another ("Urn," 62), voracious nature (as Darwin called it) "one great Slaughter-house"[40] wherein we see "The shark at savage prey—the hawk at pounce, / The gentle robin . . . Ravening a worm" ("Dear Reynolds," 103–10). Life feeds on life (Blake said), and art, as a greater vitality, upon intensity. Milton, in pursuing his imagination to its utmost, was "sagacious of his quarry," Keats said, "he sees Beauty on the wing, pounces upon it and gorges it to the producing his essential verse."[41] In opposition to Milton's predatory pursuit and (apparently) lesser "anxiety for Humanity"[42] resides the "giant agony" "portion'd to a giant nerve" of the poet-figure in Keats's Hyperion poems (*Hyperion*, 1:175; *Fall of Hyperion*, 1:157, 189–90). "Knowledge enormous" of "agonies, / Creations and destroyings . . . / Pour into the wide hollows" of Apollo's brain (*Hyperion*, 3:113–17). Apollo's evolution into poetic deity involves the acquisition of a vital sensitivity quite distinct from the "pain of feebleness" Saturn feels (*Fall of Hyperion*, 1:429). His "intenser form of reality" expresses not brutish, rapacious life-force but subtle nervous sympathy; it implies vulnerability and ultimate, necessary exhaustion.[43] The intensity of an art that is required to see and portray life in the meagerness of "a few strips of Green on a cold hill" in Burns's country[44] presumes debility from depletion of intensity itself. Inner vision, "To see as a God sees, and take the depth of things" (*Fall of Hyperion*, 1:304–5), must make up for outer deprivation. As evolutionary theory presumes the sacrifice of generations for future organic perfections[45]—"Broad leaved fig trees . . . foredoom / Their ripen'd fruitage . . . / The chuckling linnet its five young unborn . . . pent up butterflies / Their freckled wings; yea, the fresh budding year / All its completions" (*Endymion*, 1:252–60)—the perfection of Apollo's art necessitates living death in each gush of sound, bleak Brunonian exhaustion of perceptual power from the stress of overwrought intensity.

    In the cyclic promise of evolution the scientists of the early nineteenth century saw progress and inexhaustability.[46] But for Keats—who held Milton's gormandizing brain responsible for the depleted dullness of subsequent generations—energy and matter, like perceptual power, are finite: as "the same quantity of matter" and "a certain bulk of Water was instituted at the Creation—so very likely a certain portion of intellect was spun forth into the thin Air for the Brains of Man to prey upon it. . . . [Milton's mind] like a Moon attracted Intellect to its flow—it has not ebbed yet—but has left the shore pebble all bare—."[47] The intensity of art exhausts perception, and life is the ebbing of life. Life is a "fragile dew-drop on its perilous way" ("Sleep and Poetry," 86), "a sleeping infant's breath" ("After dark vapours," 12), lovers pouring down marble steps "as easily / As hour-glass sand" (*Endymion*, 3:814–15), "Fast fading violets" ("Night-

ingale," 47), a "paly summer" won "From winter's ague" on visiting
the tomb of Burns where "All is cold beauty" (5–8). "Sweet life
leaving" ("Ah! woe is me," 17) finds final embodiment in the win-
nowed and deliberately minimal figure of Autumn, "postured motionless" in chilling recollection of the marbled figures of the Grecian
urn and the "three fixed shapes" in *The Fall of Hyperion.* The world
takes on "a quakerish look" of drab silence, and the poet, drinking
such bitter dregs, "must choose between despair & Energy—."[48]
Apollo's "fore-seeing" takes the depth and finitude of all things: he
has the ability to see both the wings of the air-sylph forming within
the skin of the caterpillar,[49] and the statuary petrification and ebbing
depletion of matter and mind; he sets free imprisoned Psyche and
unfolds her wings within a recessed temple of the mind, but he also
sees immortal Saturn's "carved features" wrinkling as he falls (*Fall
of Hyperion*, 1:225); in addition and unlike the leafless tree and frozen
brook of organic nature, he has hollowed, aching consciousness of
"The feel of not to feel it" in drear-nighted December (21). April's
spring is "chilly" with "aguish hills" of stone, and June "breathes
out life for butterflies" ("St. Mark," 5–12; "To the Ladies," 11) no
different from the poised and pent-up butterfly in Alexander von
Humboldt's intensely imaginary portrait of life.

Notes

I wish to thank the American Council of Learned Societies, the National
Humanities Center, and the National Endowment for the Humanities for fellowship
support that made possible the research for this essay and the book to which it is
related, *Romantic Medicine and John Keats* (Oxford and New York: Oxford University
Press, 1990).

1. Alexander von Humboldt, *"Die Lebenskraft oder der Rhodische Genius,"* *Die
Hören*, 1, no. 5 (1795), 90–96; reprinted in *Gesammelte Werke*, 6 vols. (Stuttgart: J.
G. Cottaschen, 1844), 6:303–7. The brothers Humboldt visited England, and had met
Wordsworth and Coleridge in Europe.

2. In his *Aphorisms on the Chemical Physiology of Plants* (1793), Humboldt defined
the vital force of the "inner" power that dissolves the bonds of chemical affinity and
prevents the free combination of the elements in organic bodies. See Alexander Gode-
von Aesch, *Natural Science in German Romanticism* (New York: Columbia University
Press, 1941), 193. Stuart Sperry, "Keats and the Chemistry of Poetic Creation," *PMLA*
85 (1970), 268–77, has already noted the importance of contemporary chemistry to
Keats's aesthetic theory.

3. J. Lemprière, "Psyche," in *Bibliotheca Classica, or, A Classical Dictionary*
(1797; reprint, New York: Samuel Campbell, William Falconer, et al, 1809). See also
J. Spence, "a Cupid fondling or burning a butterfly is just the same with them as a
Cupid caressing or tormenting the goddess Psyche, or the soul," *Polymetis* (London:
R. & J. Dodsley, 1755), 69–71.

4. Oceanus, in *Hyperion*, combines ancient and contemporary notions of phos-

phoric putrescence (spontaneous generation in slime), light, and electricity in his speech: "From Chaos and parental Darkness came / Light, the first fruits of that intestine broil, / That sullen ferment, which for wondrous ends / Was ripening in itself. The ripe hour came, / And with it Light, and Light, engendering / Upon its own producer, forthwith touch'd / The whole enormous matter into life" (2:191–97). Oceanus seems to recall Schelling's "All birth is a birth out of darkness into light: the seed must be buried in the earth and die in darkness in order that the lovelier creature of light should rise and unfold itself in the rays of the sun," (*Of Human Freedom* [1809]), trans. James Guttman [Chicago: Open Court, 1935], 35). See J. Livingston Lowes, *The Road to Xanadu* (Cambridge, Mass.: Houghton Mifflin, 1964), on putrescence, light, and the origin of shining "slimy things" in the Ancient Mariner's "rotting sea." See also Eramus Darwin, *The Botanic Garden; A Poem, in Two Parts* (London: J. Johnson, 1791), note to Part 1:182, on the phosphorescence of shells, will-o'-the-wisps, electric eels, and glowworms.

5. Friedrich von Schiller, "Philosophy of Physiology," in *Friedrich Schiller: Medicine, Psychology and Literature*, ed. K. Dewhurst and N. Reeves (Berkeley and Los Angeles, Calif.: University of California Press, 1978), 152, 155. Schiller said that this nerve spirit was neither elemental fire, nor light, nor ether but, quite distinct from world or mind, an "infinitely subtle," perceiving "transmutative force" whose disappearance creates "a rift between world and mind. Its presence illuminates, awakens, animates everything about it." Cf. Keats's "An element filling the space between; An unknown—" in *Endymion*, 1:301–2.

6. S. T. Coleridge, *Inquiring Spirit*, ed. Kathleen Coburn (Toronto: University of Toronto Press, 1979), 259; Appendix C to *Aids to Reflection*, in *The Complete Works of Samuel Taylor Coleridge*, ed. W. G. T. Shedd, 7 vols. (New York: Harper, 1863), 1:387, 391–92.

7. Erasmus Darwin's "Additional Note on the Portland Vase," *Botanic Garden*, Part 2, 321, pp. 97–100, is full of torches, butterflies, positioned figures, etc., reminiscent of Humboldt's myth. Bernard Blackstone's discussion of Darwin's Portland Vase, "silent as a consecrated urn," and the power contained within the Grecian urn's silent form, is pertinent here. See especially *The Consecrated Urn* (London: Longmans, 1959), xiii, 331–32.

8. Walter Jackson Bate, *John Keats* (Cambridge: Harvard University Press, 1963), 514.

9. *Lamia*, 1:40–41, *The Poems of John Keats*, ed. Jack Stillinger (Cambridge: Harvard University Press, 1978). All further citations refer to this edition and occur in parentheses in the text following the quotation.

10. Adalbert von Chamisso, "The Crucifixion" (Berlin, 1836), trans. A. I. du P. Coleman, *The German Classics*, ed. Frank Thilley, 20 vols. (New York: German Publication Society, 1913), 1:320–400.

11. All illness, according to the Brunonian theory of medicine, could be classified as *asthenic*, from debility, or *sthenic*, from an excess of excitement that in turn leads to debility; death resulted from "a perfect extinction of the excitement, either from a complete exhaustion or extreme abundance of excitability" (*The Elements of Medicine of John Brown*, trans. and rev. Thomas Beddoes, 2 vols. [London: J. Johnson, 1795], part 2, chap. 7, 1:266). During Keats's time, *overwrought* meant both "fashioned over the surface of an object" (like the Grecian urn), and "exhausted by overwork; worked up to too high a pitch; overexcited" (OED); the modern sense of "elaborated to excess" is not recorded before 1839.

12. Christoph Girtanner, a friend of Humboldt's and an avid Brownist, wrote an essay "On the Kantian Principle" (1796) which spoke of the vital force as the "genius

of organization" to produce a curious marriage of German idealism and radical mechanism. See Gode-von Aesch, *Natural Science in German Romanticism*, 195–96.

13. Sir Astley Cooper, *Lectures . . . on the Principles and Practice of Surgery*, ed. Frank Tyrrell (Philadelphia: Haswell, Barrington, and Haswell, 1939), 6. According to Cooper, the principle of irritability and the principle of restoration were allied: irritability was most intense in infancy, and easily incited to destruction; thereafter, the two principles were parallel in strength, until old age saw their diminishment.

14. John Keats, *Anatomical and Physiological Note Book*, ed. M. B. Forman (Oxford: Oxford University Press, 1934), MS pp. 9–10. This definition of the vital principle provides a curious angle on *Hyperion*, 1:317–20, describing "that beauteous life / Diffus'd unseen throughout external space," which we have always thought to largely echo *The Excursion*, 9:1–9, on "An *active* Principle" which "subsists / In all things. . . ."

15. William Lawrence, *Lectures on Physiology, Zoology, and the Natural History of Man, Delivered at the Royal College of Surgeons in 1817* (London: Benbow, 1822), 6–7, 52, 71. Lawrence's declaration on life, here and in his entry for Abraham Rees's *Cyclopaedia* (1819), was largely an attempt to correct his teacher John Abernethy's misinterpretation of Hunter's *Principium vitae*; it was not proof of vitalistic doctrine, he said, but accurate mechanistic theory.

16. John Hunter, "Of the Vital Principle" (1786), in *Collected Works of John Hunter*, ed. James E. Palmer (London: Longmans, 1835), 1:217, 221–23; John Abernethy, *Physiological Lectures . . . Delivered before the Royal College of Surgeons . . . 1817* (London: Longmans, 1822), 1–3. See also Abernethy, *Mr. Hunter's Opinions Respecting Life and Diseases* (London: Longmans, 1815), 26–27, 42–43.

17. John Hunter, "Experiments on Animals and Vegetables, with Respect to the Power of Producing Heat," *Philosophical Transactions* 45 (1775), 457, 452–54; see also Everett Mendelsohn's discussion, *Heat and Life: The Development of the Theory of Animal Heat* (Cambridge: Harvard University Press, 1964), 101.

18. See A. O. Lovejoy, "Buffon," in *Forerunners of Darwin: 1745–1859*, ed. Bentley Glass, Owsei Temkin, and W. L. Straus, Jr. (Baltimore: Johns Hopkins University Press, 1959); see also Jacques Roger, "The Living World," in *The Ferment of Knowledge: Studies in the Historiography of Eighteenth-Century Science*, ed. G. S. Rousseau and Roy Porter (London: Cambridge University Press, 1980), 275.

19. For Darwin's views on microscopic life, see *The Temple of Nature* (London: J. Johnson, 1803), Cantos 1:295–96, 2:49–56, 4:383–88, note to 2:47 (on Adonis as the "Emblem of Life"), and Additional Notes 1 and 8 (pp. 3–8); on the spirit of animation, see *Zoonomia; or The Laws of Organic Life* (Philadelphia: Edward Earle, 1818), 1:80–81; on the distinction of this spirit from animal magnetism, electric ethers, and elastic fluids, see *Zoonomia*, 1:46.

20. In *Zoonomia*, 1:28, Darwin implies that this sensorial power is secreted by the brain, but he goes on (here and elsewhere) to say that it is "too subtle" to be placed or confined anywhere in the animal system; on the sensorial power as agent of attraction, contraction, and opposition, see *Zoonomia*, 1:44–45 (on iron particles and animal muscles), and 1:393–428 (on embryos).

21. Coleridge, "Theory of Life," *Complete Works*, 1:290, 391–92. Coleridge was attempting to rescue life and consciousness from the deathliness of mechanism. Attempting to complete Abernethy's defense of Hunter's purported theory of life, Coleridge evoked a variety of prevailing scientific theories from Hoffmann and Stahl to Blumenbach to prove what he had come to believe concerning "Being," "Power," "Energy," and "Mind," as these were described by Schelling, Schiller, and Oken.

22. A shell filled and emptied by the waves was a near perfect image of evolution as conceived by Romantic evolutionists. See Darwin on the beginning of life in the

shallows of primeval oceans, *Temple of Nature*, 1:247–68, 295–302, 327–34; and note to 1:295.

23. Oceanus, god of the seas, does not counsel easeful sloth and hypostasis as Belial and Mammon do (Brian Wilkie's thesis, expressed in *Romantic Poets and the Epic Tradition*, (Madison: University of Wisconsin Press, 1965). Keats's remark, "The point at which Man may arrive is as far as the paralel state in inanimate nature and no further," is ample proof of this. *The Letters of John Keats*, ed. Hyder E. Rollins, 2 vols. (Cambridge: Harvard University Press, 1958), 2:100.

24. Raymond Williams, *Keywords: A Vocabulary of Culture and Society* (New York: Oxford University Press, 1976), 103. The idea of evolution was known to the Greeks and outlined definitively and variously by Bacon, Linnaeus, Buffon, Erasmus Darwin, Goethe, Lamarck, Lyell, and Herbert Spencer. See Fielding H. Garrison, *An Introduction to the History of Medicine* (1913; reprint, Philadelphia: W. B. Saunders Company, 1929), 513; Owen Barfield, *Saving the Appearances: A Study in Idolatry* (New York: Harcourt Brace, 1978), 60–61; and Bentley Glass, "Idea of Biological Species," in *Forerunners of Darwin*, 39.

25. Goethe's ideas on evolution are found in *A Preliminary Sketch to a General Introduction to Comparative Anatomy* (1795), *Formation and Transformation of Living Things* (1807), and *The Metamorphosis of Plants* (1790). See Gode-von Aesch, *Natural Science in German Romanticism*, 144–47; and also Charles Singer, *A Short History of Biology*, (Oxford: Clarendon Press, 1931), 216–17.

26. "Man, the most perfect of animals," is a recurring phrase in journals of this time, used alike by scientists and philosophers. See Lorenz Oken, *Elements of Physiophilosophy*, trans. Alfred Tulk (London: Ray Society, 1847); also Singer, *History of Biology*, 217–18. "May there not be superior beings amused with any graceful, though instinctive attitude my mind may fall into, as I am entertained with the alertness of a Stoat or the anxiety of a Deer?" asks Keats (*Letters*, 2:80). Keats's speculation is in accordance with German idealism's notion of the evolution of perception.

27. Buffon, in *Histoire naturelle* (1749–1804), cited by Lovejoy, "Buffon," in *Forerunners of Darwin*, 104, 111–12.

28. Because life and activity were one for Lamarck, the environment could not act directly on life. Instead, the organism or its will responded creatively to the shifting circumstances of the environment; characteristics thus acquired could then be inherited. See Charles C. Gillispie, "Lamarck and Darwin," in *Forerunners of Darwin*, 270–71.

29. See note 19, above.

30. Darwin, *Zoonomia*, 1:428, 509.

31. Darwin, *Zoonomia*, 1:392–96. Darwin subordinated the "life-force" or "sensorial power" to organic natural process and the environmental necessity of inorganic matter; the closest he came to allowing perception a place in the evolutionary system was when he proposed that the male parent's imagination influenced the sex and resemblance of the foetus (see his entire chapter "On Generation" in *Zoonomia*, vol. 1, esp. 412).

32. The description of the Titans' abode recalls specifically the sterility of Keats's Scottish peat-bog, "dreary, black, dank, flat and spongy" (*Letters*, 1:321). It also recalls another image of a sterile natural environment in the letters—rainy Devonshire, which has "No feel of the clouds dropping fatness; but as if the roots of the Earth were rotten cold and drench'd" (*Letters*, 1:267). The black-weeded pools also recall prevailing telluric theories of poison (and disease) from the inorganic putrescence of minerals in the bowels of the earth. See Lloyd G. Stevenson, *The Meaning of Poison* (Lawrence, Kansas: University of Kansas Press, 1959), 11, and Frank Dawson Adams, *The Birth and Development of the Geological Sciences* (Baltimore: Johns Hopkins University Press, 1938), chapter 9.

33. The Titans' claustrophobic place ("No stir of air was there," 1:2, 7) recalls for us that Thomas Beddoes, in 1793, had defined a "vitiated air" as an atmosphere turned to "fixed air" or carbon monoxide (Stevenson, *Meaning of Poison*, 9).

34. G. S. Rousseau summarizing Hume, *A Treatise of Human Nature* (London: John Noon, 1739; book 1, part 3, section 14, pp. 155–72), in *Ferment of Knowledge*, 31.

35. John Locke, *An Essay Concerning Human Understanding*, ed. Alexander Campbell Frazer, 2 vols. (New York: Dover Publications, 1959), 1:309–10.

36. Goethe's *Metamorphosis of Plants* (1790) speaks of how the glory and climax of the plant comes at the end in "the orgasm of the flower, dying into being," translated and quoted by C. C. Gillispie in *The Edge of Objectivity: An Essay in the History of Scientific Ideas* (Princeton, New Jersey: Princeton University Press, 1960), 193. This concept and its language is almost certainly related to Keats's notion of Apollo's transformation as a painful dying into life, and to the notion in other poems of life sacrificing itself.

37. Cf. Coleridge's "Life itself is not a *thing*—a self-subsistent *hypostasis*—but an *act* and *process*" ("Theory of Life," 416).

38. *Letters*, 1:207. Prometheus's name means "foreseeing."

39. *Letters*, 1:374 (on the genius of poetry).

40. Darwin, *The Temple of Nature*, Canto 4:55–66. Blackstone, *Consecrated Urn*, 148–49, sees Darwin's canto on the "warrior shark" in *Botanic Garden* as a source for the verse-letter to Reynolds. This passage on the "warring world" of rapacious sharks and whales seems a more direct source.

41. Notes to Milton's *Paradise Lost*, 7:420–23.

42. *Letters*, 1:278–79.

43. See Kenneth Muir, "The Meaning of Hyperion," in *John Keats: A Reassessment* (Liverpool: Liverpool University Press, 1969), 102–22. Apollo's more vital condition recalls Glaucus's cry in *Endymion*, "I am pierc'd and stung / With new-born life!" (3:238–39). We also recall Goethe's theory of plants which sees the flower as the climactic end, a "dying into being" (see note 36).

44. *Letters*, 1:323.

45. See Humphry Davy's musings on the immutable laws of destruction and decay, in *Consolations in Travel, or the Last Days of a Philosopher*, in *Collected Works*, ed. John Davy, 9 vols. (London: Smith, Elder and Co., 1840), 9:259–60, perhaps the most eloquent expression of this sad necessity.

46. See, for example, Coleridge's letter to Thomas Poole on the imperishability of force, in *The Letters of S. T. Coleridge*, ed. E. H. Coleridge, 2 vols. (London: Heinemann, 1895), 1:283. Keats's notion, "Our bodies every seven years are completely fresh material'd" (*Letters*, 2:208), would seem to echo the evolutionists' sense of endless cyclic renewal.

47. *Letters*, 1:255.

48. *Letters*, 2:113: "I pity you as much that it cannot last for ever, as I do myself now drinking bitters—Give yourself upto it—"; *Letters*, 1:293: "Life must be undergone. . . ."

49. Coleridge's and Fichte's image of the philosophical imagination. Fichte says philosophy is "the power that shall first set free the imprisoned Psyche and unfold her wings, so that, hovering for a moment above her former self, she may cast a glance on her abandoned slough, and then soar upwards" (J. G. Fichte, *The Vocation of Man* [1800], ed. Roderick M. Chisholm [New York: Bobbs-Merrill, 1956], 114). Coleridge

says they only acquire the philosophic imagination "who within themselves can interpret and understand the symbol, that the wings of the air-sylph are forming within the skin of the caterpillar" (*Biographia Literaria,* ed. James Engell and W. Jackson Bate, 2 vols. [Princeton, N.J.: Princeton University Press, 1983], 1:241–42).

Noumenal Inferences:
Keats as Metaphysician   Alan Grob°

In a now celebrated essay on *The Eve of St. Agnes* Jack Stillinger affixed a label to the objects of his critical ire that has plainly stuck: those responsible for the interpretations Stillinger sought to discredit should be called "metaphysical critics," he asserted, because in their misguidedness "they think Keats was a metaphysician."[1] Though the immediate purpose of Stillinger's essay was to rescue *The Eve of St. Agnes* from the then prevalent spiritualizing bowdlerizations of Porphyro's melting into Madeline's dream, to reclaim its prurience and by that its tough-mindedness, Stillinger stalked a larger quarry than a handful of misreaders of a single poem: for these critics, he said, represented "not so much an interpretation of the poem as a view of all Keats's poetry,"[2] one unfortunately held by some of the then most influential Keats critics. Since then, the rout of the metaphysical critics has been made virtually complete, and the view of Keats propounded by Stillinger has gained a seemingly universal currency. For almost everyone who now writes on Keats, he is the most decidedly modern of the Romantics, skeptical about our transcendent yearnings, accepting of and ultimately contented with the natural and the human, the finite and the actual. What were once regarded as full-fledged metaphysical concepts complete with an extensive philosophic genealogy, are now offhandedly and unphilosophically described as "vision" or, even more dismissively, just as "dream." Only in his earliest and least consequential poems, we are told, does Keats seriously claim that dreams and visions may come true or even be true. In the later and major poetry, dream and vision appear primarily as matter for the skeptical temper to hone itself on, admitted into poems only in order to be vanquished, refuted, denied.

The present essay shall certainly be an exercise in what Stillinger would consider metaphysical criticism, since I think Keats, early and late, was a metaphysician. In fact, I shall argue that as his skeptical questionings become increasingly more incisive, so, too, his metaphysical conceptions, as if reactively, become ever more finely for-

° This essay was written specifically for this volume and is published here for the first time by permission of the author.

mulated, more complex, more powerful, more profound. Indeed, it is in the poetry of 1819, and especially in "Ode to a Nightingale" that Keats is most spectacularly a metaphysician, with his conceptualizing powers and philosophic subtlety most fully realized. This is not to say that he was unaware of the powerful case for the empirical, the limiting, the skeptical, for, as we have learned from Earl Wasserman, each of the major poets of the period looked to settle "in his own way the kinds of questions raised by the British empiricists, whose heirs the Romantics were."[3] But the way in which the Romantics most often settled these questions was through metaphysics, resorting to just those kinds of unverifiable suppositions and intuitive leaps that empiricism had declared illicit. To be sure, the metaphysics of each poet appears special and private, uniquely his own, an expression of personal variables compounded out of individual and distinctive experiences, temperaments, and desires. Yet for all its private idiosyncracies, the metaphysics of any particular Romantic poet is but one manifestation of a common response to shared philosophic circumstances, a poetic metaphysics that, as careful inspection shows, "closely resemble[s] that of the German post-Kantians,"[4] because the poet's thinking was "as much the direct outgrowth of contemporary intellectual forces as Kant's or Coleridge's or Schelling's."[5] And if Keats now seems less a metaphysician than Blake or Wordsworth or Shelley, it is not that in his incipient modernity he was less prone to assert and explore transcendent possibility or felt noumenal longings any less deeply than the others, but rather that he was better able to mask abstruseness and to realize his ideational content through the sensuous medium of his poetry.

In this paper I shall reverse Keats's own procedures (aware of the risks this method entails) and try to turn axioms of philosophy proved upon our pulses back into something like an abstractly propositional formulation so that we can appreciate the extent to which Keats in his major work thought as a metaphysician. The question I would therefore suggest that is posed in "Ode to a Nightingale" and generates its metaphysical solutions is one that frequently appears at critical junctures in postempirical philosophizing to create an opening to metaphysics: how are we to account for the logically and empirically anomalous experiences which seem irreconcilable with the possibilities of knowledge as set forth by the laws of human understanding?

Probably the most impressive philosophic deployment of this strategy appears in what is surely the least Keatsian of analogues to "Ode to a Nightingale": Kant's metaphysical solution to the familiar ethical conundrum of how to derive "ought" from "is." For Kant, too, awakened from his dogmatic slumber by Hume, the legacy of British empiricism established the terms under which the problem was to be addressed. In response to Hume's devastating critique of knowledge, Kant had argued powerfully for the existence of a universally valid and reliable knowledge based on the forms and categories of the understanding. Like Locke and Hume, Kant insisted that we could have no knowledge of that which lay beyond the limits of human understanding, no knowledge that did not conform to the forms of time and space nor to those categories that give our experience of the world its substantial and predictable character: unity, reality, inherence, subsistence, and especially causality.

But if all human knowledge is governed by the categories and hence the principle of causality, so that within the mechanism of nature all is determined, what then, Kant asked in his turn to ethics, are we to make of the appeal to "ought" in our moral judgments, the obligation to perform our duty, dependent as this is on our freedom to choose? To explain how our consciousness of "ought" with its corollary of freedom can be possible in a world in which seemingly we have only the necessity of "is," Kant proposed a metaphysical dualism in which though necessity governed the phenomenal, the noumenal would be a kingdom of duty, freedom, immortality, and God. Thus that anomalous consciousness of "ought" and the freedom implied by it provided a single but saving manifestation of the noumenal realm within the boundaries of our otherwise natural existence. Obligation for Kant serves then not only as the basis for morality but also as the basis for a noumenal inference that enabled him to posit a something, a *Ding an sich,* to breach and move beyond that naturalistic impasse to which the experiential epistemology of empiricism seemed certain to lead.

In turning from Kant to Keats, I must emphasize a qualifying *mutatis mutandis* and make generous allowances for the vastness of differences. Yet I would argue that despite obvious differences in the substance of the arguments, the structure in both is much the same. That is, just as Kant asks how can a duty dependent on freedom be possible in a world in which all is determined, and then infers from the apparent presence of duty and freedom as facts known to consciousness the necessary existence of a noumenal order where duty and freedom can occur without contradiction, so, too, does Keats ask how is happiness possible in a world "Where but to think is to be full of sorrow / And leaden-eyed despairs," and then infers from the apparent presence of happiness as a datum of consciousness the necessary existence of a noumenal order where happiness can exist without contradiction.

On one matter, the origins of human knowledge, Keats and Kant obviously diverge. For Keats proposes no Copernican revolution in epistemology, no Kantian turn to the subject, no appeal to the contributions of the mind to experience in explaining how the phenomena given to the senses in perception are rendered almost immediately intelligible. The problems involved in normal perception do not much engage him, and he appears to take for granted the basic assumptions of the most rudimentary kind of sensationalist empiricism. In the letters, as Stuart Sperry has meticulously shown, Keats clearly roots his conceptions of poetry (and by implication his conception of mind) in "the nature of sensation" and "the primacy of sense experience"[6] as these notions had been developed by Locke and his followers. And when dealing with simple perception in the poetry, Keats seems a basically naive empirical realist for whom objects apprehended by consciousness in perception are, without further reflection, presumed to be identical with, or at least copies of, objects as they exist in the external world.

On one other important epistemological matter, Keats follows empiricist precepts, assuming the more complex forms of knowledge and activities of mind to be organized by and to operate in accordance with the laws of association. Associational psychology has been used by critics of Keats mainly to explain the apparent randomness in Keats's poetry, but it also provides the basis for the general development of the empirical understanding in Keats. According to that psychology, we build out of the elemental simples of sensation that come to us in perception the compound and complex ideas that constitute significant knowledge because these sensations have been organized into regular patterns by the laws of association, either because they tend to follow one another in a constantly recurring sequence, or because they appear repeatedly in a contiguous relationship, or because the appearance of one sensation recalls some other that resembles it. If sensations and ideas so bound together recur with sufficient frequency or impress themselves upon the mind with sufficient intensity, then that pattern will adhere so firmly to memory that the subsequent appearance of any one element in the pattern will necessarily call to mind the sensations and ideas previously associated with that element. What has been constantly or even strikingly conjoined before will doubtlessly be conjoined again: thus the child keeps its hand away from the fire because it remembers the pain of an earlier mishap. For the psychologically developed mind there can be no simple mental event experienced in isolation. Mental events occur instead as part of a "specious present" (to adapt to my own uses William James's famous phrase): they carry with them, even at the apparent instant of direct apprehension, a simultaneous consciousness of what had earlier been associated with such events. All mental activity is thus necessarily anticipatory, informing us even during the most rudimentary acts of perception of what awaits us when the presumably unvarying sequence of the constantly conjoined is completed.

For Keats the focus of his psychology in the poetry is the

pleasurable as viewed by an associationist, so that whenever we experience pleasure we are simultaneously conscious of that to which in the past we have always found the pleasurable conjoined. Indeed, some of the most memorable figurative renderings of that specious present shaped from the appearance of simultaneity fostered by the laws of association are those in "Ode on Melancholy" in which the expectedly sequential—pleasure and its aftermath—is compressed within the space of a single image: the description of "Joy, whose hand is ever at his lips / Bidding adieu" or the situating of the "sovereign shrine" of "Veiled Melancholy" "in the very temple of Delight." It is not just the fact of inevitable transitoriness that so troubles Keats—that the beauty we observe and the delight we feel must decline or decay and eventually fail—but that awareness of such decline or decay and failure is necessarily present to consciousness *at the very instant* we observe beauty or feel delight, undermining and undoing, robbing the pleasurable of its savor even as we begin to enjoy it.

Of course, that pervasive consciousness of the transitory adhering to the pleasurable, so fundamental to the poetry of Keats, most often has a strongly libidinal basis. So it does not surprise us that the syntactically appositional and presumably illustrative clauses that follow the disheartening generalization that in our world "but to think is to be full of sorrow / And leaden-eyed despairs" should advert, in explanation of that encompassing "sorrow," to the pangs of loss that we find necessarily conjoined to the tenderest occasions in erotic life: "Where Beauty cannot keep her lustrous eyes, / Or new love pine at them beyond tomorrow." Nor do we need our instruction to be frequently repeated in order to compel the psyche to accept the painful truth that suffering is invariably the consequence of love. Even one episode, Keats tells us in "In drear-nighted December," suffices by the strength of the pain it inflicts to etch ineradicably upon the memory the terrible lesson of the anguish that necessarily accompanies love. For the "gentle girl and boy" there can be no "sweet forgetting," no "feel of not to feel it," only unhappy memory, the anguish of consciousness physiologically translated into the body's "writhing," all because love's "specious present"—the simultaneous apprehension of pleasure and its painful aftermath—will never allow us to recall the "joy" we have known in love other than as that which has "passed."

But the pessimism of these bleak lines from "Ode to a Nightingale" should not be attributed simply to the disappointments of love or Keats's supposed adolescent heartache. In addition to "sorrow," thinking also induces an apparently redundant condition—one certainly not easily distinguishable from "sorrow"—that Keats speaks of as "despairs," an emotional state that seems to acquire its distinctive identity from the physical correlative Keats assigns to it, the bodily sensation of being "leaden-eyed." Why this heavy-lidded and irresistible drift toward the vacancy of sleep, this sense of deepening anesthetization, should be grounds for despair is perhaps best explained by an earlier occurrence of what seems the same condition serving as the vehicle in a dark and crucial simile in "On Seeing the Elgin Marbles." Contemplating this crowning remnant of "Grecian grandeur," Keats experiences not the exhilaration we might expect at the discovery of so special a moment of human accomplishment, but rather the debilitating sense of his own finitude, of aspiration inevitably thwarted by the "mortality" that "Weighs heavily on me like unwilling sleep." This associative linking of the conscious recognition of our mortality with its physical correlative, a helpless torpor that drags us unwillingly toward the very depths of sleep, if carried forward into "Ode to a Nightingale," should explain why being "leaden-eyed" carries associations that understandably evoke despair. It is as if Keats would now say that incorporated into all thinking— not just those rare moments when we come upon the most dazzling of human achievements—is a subliminal awareness of our mortality that manifests itself as depleted energy, fatigue, an involuntary drift toward sleep, and this, by extension, inevitably calls to mind the destiny that awaits us, that ultimate deprivation of the senses that is to come through the death that is extinction.

But if we find ourselves in a world that evokes only sorrow and despair, how then is happiness at all possible? Or, to carry this line of inquiry a stage further, if we were to experience what we judge unequivocally to be happiness, how can we accommodate such experience to the general bleakness we have already concluded to be the necessary order of things? From the earliest stages of his poetic career, Keats was engrossed by questions about happiness raised from what can only be called a candidly hedonistic perspective. But in his earliest reflections on the subject, he seemed to find no incompatibility between personal happiness and the general character of earthly existence. While it may be argued that the extended answer in book 1 of *Endymion* to the question "Wherein lies happiness?" directs us finally toward a state of self-transcendence in which we shall "shine / Full alchemized, and free of space," the sources of the happiness he looks for are undoubtedly found in the places and events and relationships of a worldly here and now. If happiness is our object, we can find it all about us, in the exquisite tactile sensations of folding "A rose leaf round thy finger's taperness," in the feelings raised by music's "Aeolian magic," and, above all, in friendship and in love, this last giving us happiness at its most intense and therefore most exalted, the happiness that comes to us at that point of libidinal arousal that "genders a novel sense, / At which we start and fret."

Even in the celebrated speculation of the letter to Bailey of 22 November 1817 where Keats wishfully conjectures that "we shall enjoy ourselves here after by having what we called happiness on Earth repeated in a finer tone and so repeated,"[7] he never implies by this conjecture that the grossly earthly counterpart of the happiness to be known hereafter is therefore illusory, never doubts that in this life we can "delight in sensation" and that to do so is better than "to hunger . . . after Truth."[8] Earthly happiness and its postmortal refinement are thought of as stages in a continuum, our happiness here sufficiently genuine happiness for its reoccurrence to be wished for as "spiritual repetition:"[9] that is, in a form recognizably the same though subtilized.

But within weeks, the optimism of the letter to Bailey dissolves within the general and unremitting bleakness of "In drear-nighted December," the poem that probably marks the beginnings of Keats's abandonment of his heretofore sanguine conception of our prospects for earthly happiness. The dismaying universality so poignantly conveyed by the plainly rhetorical question "were there ever any / Writh'd not of passed joy," taken together with the acute painfulness of remembrance that psychophysically registers itself on the body as "writhing," would seem effectively to foreclose any hopes that human consciousness is ever to have unalloyed happiness without countervailing pain. Instead, by means of a contradiction that obviously amounts to denial, Keats imputes happiness only to that which is without remembrance, to the "sweet forgetting" of tree and brook, to the unknowing, the insensate, the inanimate, and these at the frozen moment of their deepest unknowingness, insensateness, inanimateness. And by these tactics, denying happiness to human consciousness, ascribing it to sheer vacancy alone, to that which is without feelings, desires, and receptivity, those faculties and attributes that make happiness even imaginable, Keats brings starkly to the surface of his work the grave concern that now seems to amount virtually to conviction, the fear that happiness, in any humanly meaningful form, does not exist at all.

The odes provide Keats's most probing speculations on the metaphysics of happiness. Remnants of the earthly-spiritual continuum spoken of in the letter to Bailey remain, though connections between earth and heaven, now and hereafter, have become greatly attenuated. Whether we speak of human life lived out in a present that offers us only "The weariness, the fever, and the fret" or in a projected earthly future that shall yield those who come after us merely "other woe / Than ours," existence on earth has become radically estranged from any imagined hereafter. At first, with his account in "Ode to Psyche," of a mortal enskied into happiness, Keats may seem to have merely picked up where he left off in Endymion with its wishful metaphysics of happiness turning desire into reality. But the "happy, happy dove" of "Ode to Psyche" provides neither an instance of, nor a precedent for, that ontological transformation that seems the sole and necessary condition of any possible human happiness. The transparent falsity of even the cautiously advanced claim on which the whole edifice of belief in the poem rests, the possibility of having seen that very day "The winged Psyche with awakened eyes," taken together with an unsparing historical analysis that would reduce to anachronism and superstition the mythologies in which such tales of enskying are found, makes it only too evident that the ostensibly precipitating occasion of "Ode to Psyche," the sighting of the winged lovers, has been designed to yield not noumenal inferences but, at most, metaphors for poetry.

In many ways, "Ode on a Grecian Urn" is the most Kantian in its problematic cautiousness of all of Keats's explorations of noumenal imagining—Kantian in its skeptical insistence on the unrepresentability of the noumenal, on our powerlessness to either prove or to describe the fact and mode of its existence, and yet Kantian, too, in asserting that what can be neither proven nor described can still be so conceived that its reality remains at least an open possibility. By treating the figures pictured on the urn as both replications of ourselves and also as long-enduring representations of eternal prototypes, happy on the urn because they somehow participate in a happiness that exists only elsewhere, though perhaps hereafter, Keats, by the end of stanza 4, offers little more in the way of metaphysical explanation than the painful lesson of the Kantian antinomies: to conceive of the noumenally changeless through the empirically conditioned leads necessarily to contradiction. If we would imagine likeness to ourselves to be the most significant trait of those depicted on the urn, then they must share with us a common vulnerability to time, suffer like us the "high-sorrowful" aftermath of love, the wasting by age, the general "woe" of human decline. And if we would imagine them as inherently permanent, invulnerable to time, then they must be differently constituted in essence, in substance so unlike ourselves that all seeming resemblance is to be judged mere accident and thus irrelevant. Since no object congruent with these antinomial idealizings, that is, no object capable of containing these contradictions, can be found in our experience, it makes little sense to appropriate the figures on the urn to speculative uses. By stanza 5 they are taken for what they are, divested of their power of noumenal incitement, contemplated solely in terms of the phenomenal conditions under which they exist. But what is now privileged, spoken of as their defining attribute, is no longer their presumed resemblance to long-vanished human originals but rather that material from which they are constituted and which renders differences from ourselves most pronounced. We are no longer to abstract continuing and purposeful actions from their stationary poses, nor states of intense feeling from their fixed expressions. They are understood now in terms of a single defining attribute, as marble incapable of movement or thought, cold to the touch because devoid of life.

But what is unrepresentable need not be inconceivable. In a remarkably Kantian turn of phrase, Keats addresses the urn as "a silent form" that "dost tease us out of thought / As doth eternity." Just as Kant believed that ideas like eternity, though never comprehensible to the mere understanding (the *Verstand*), confined as that is to what can be known in terms of the categories and the forms of space and time, nonetheless can be conceived of by the speculative reason (the *Vernunft*) as "problematic" possibilities, as ideas whose "objective reality cannot indeed be proved, but also cannot be disproved,"[10] so, too, does Keats make much the same point in the final stanza, drawing on his own equivalents of the *Verstand* and the *Vernunft*, a purely empirical "thought" operating in accordance with the associative process and its laws of sorrow, and "imagination," a faculty that may search speculatively beyond the empirical. Thus, in dismissing what is embossed on the urn as mere marble, a consequence of the analysis of its representations by the understanding, Keats unexpectedly shifts focus from figure to ground, imaginatively reformulating his hopes on a new though less objectifiable basis.

Considered purely as "form," "shape," "attitude," a field on which the imagination can exercise its fertility of invention without regard for what is depicted there, the urn provides a sufficiently plausible analogue to a wholly indeterminate noumenon to justify our using the urn, like our imaginings of eternity, to take us "out of thought" and to imagine as real the hypothetically conceivable, a noumenal ground that has no empirically intelligible properties. Keats, in effect, excludes as accident all representational character from the urn as a vehicle for his noumenal imaginings; divests it of its likeness to life in his speculations; and, most especially, no longer pays heed to those pictured situations that had earlier in the poem served as vividly rendered illustrations of what we consider true happiness to be. But that does not mean that the noumenal conceived of as the object of these imaginings, while a blankness even to the mind's eye, is to be regarded as sheer otherness, the ultimate metaphysical principle a reality understood as alien and indeed inimical to ourselves. Just the mere prospect raised by the urn of the noumenal actually existing, that there is something other and, above all, truer than the woe of this world, apparently is reason enough for Keats to insist upon the hospitableness to us of the urn and, by extension, the noumenal "out of thought" it implies, to declare his faith in the likely congruence of the unknowable purposes of the noumenal with our needs, and interests, and desires.

If not an elementary primer, "a horn-book," in which our final happiness is pictured down to the last detail, the urn by virtue of what even in its abstractness it suggests, is still "a friend to man" Keats reassures us, speaking as a metaphysician, in his final assessment of the meaning of the urn. If a truly existing noumenal can be conceptually imagined, then even by virtue of its mere compatibility with human consciousness, we can reasonably conclude that such a noumenal is on our side. So in the famous last two lines of the poem, while encoding his claims in the most notoriously cryptic of propositions and transferring utterance to the presumed disinterestedness of the urn, Keats nonetheless closes with an extravagant declaration of faith, extravagant because it is educed from the most tenuous of noumenal inferences. Amidst the sorrows of this world, Keats offers us not the solaces of art, at best a momentary stay against confusion, but the absolute and unequivocal promise of metaphysics, asserting that the deepest and most encompassing of our longings and those least likely to be satisfied in this life shall ultimately, in some noumenal realm, be truly fulfilled. Somewhere, sometime—to revert to the unavoidable language of the merely empirical understanding—the desired will be the real, the real the desired. There and then we shall find, "Beauty is truth, truth beauty," while in the meantime the promise derived through these noumenal extrapolations from our imaginative excursions must here and now suffice.

But in "Ode to a Nightingale" Keats shows himself most assertively a metaphysician. For in a world so constituted that rightly understanding its laws and processes leads only to sorrow, evidences of an indisputable happiness must be read as anomalies, to be explained only by invoking laws and processes operative in a realm that must remain unknowable, apart from this unique manifestation of present happiness. What we have in this special instance of apparently genuine pleasureableness, "the happiness" of the nightingale conveyed without question by the melodiousness and "ease" of its song, is nothing less than the miracle of a metaphysical epiphany, the showing forth of the noumenal in the phenomenal. Unlike "Ode on a Grecian Urn," where the urn points to a noumenal beyond ourselves that might accord with our hopes and offer a happiness denied on earth, in "Ode to a Nightingale" the nightingale has "happiness" from the first, and even as it now sings that happiness, it participates in a condition we have always assumed dwells in realms wholly apart from us.

To understand why Keats should draw such an inference from the singing of the nightingale, we need only turn to a sonnet written just a few weeks earlier, "Why did I laugh to-night?," a poem that

in its metaphysical theorizing seems an elliptical test run for "Ode
to a Nightingale." Far more than the nightingale's song whose signified
referent is wholly conjectural, an outpouring from inner sources that
must remain hidden from us, our own laughter, when spontaneous
and heartfelt, can safely be taken to be an externalization of some
inward pleasure, the virtually pure translation from the subjective to
the objective of an event or experience that renders us happy. (That
the speaker's laugh indicates happiness rather than bitterness seems
a safe conclusion: to learn why he laughed, the poet has his "fancy"
survey the "utmost blisses" that might be encountered during the
mortal term of "this being's lease" and apparently finds all of them
wanting by comparison with the more intense bliss expressed by that
night's laughter.)

Yet the apparent experiential assurance of happiness, its certi-
fiable reality, does nothing to solve Keats's basic metaphysical dilemma
as the question that is the title of this sonnet makes abundantly clear.
If we are confined to a "here" where the "heart" must always be
"sad and alone," the familiar Keatsian locale of transience and mortality, how could there be any causal basis for a laughter that is the
external manifestation of some inwardly realized happiness? The ir-
reconcilability of these two competing facts of Keats's experience,
feelings of happiness given their tangible validation by his laughter
and an ongoing acquaintance with an empirical reality whose processes
can engender only sadness, leads Keats to posit a metaphysical dualism
in an attempt to break free of the impasse this contradiction imposes.
One element of this dualism we may think of according to the familiar
Kantian distinctions as the phenomenal, a necessarily sorrowful here
and now, and the other as the noumenal, more real, more true, a
realm where happiness shall be the fundamental condition of our
being. What has just transpired, why the speaker has laughed, can
be explained by believing that the noumenal has just burst forth into
the phenomenal, a hypothesis Keats eagerly entertains because of all
it promises. If the laugh is really a manifestation, the earthly effect
of a purely noumenal cause, to be read as evidence that a truly
noumenal exists, then we can safely infer, Keats asserts by the broadest
of leaps, that such a realm must be there for us to inhabit everlastingly
after death. Thus the pleasurable goods of earthly life, "Verse, fame,
and beauty," though "intense indeed," are, Keats maintains, less full,
less satisfying—marred as they are by transience—than the pleasure
manifested in that laugh and, of course, the far more enduring pleasures that according to the noumenal inference derived from that
laugh must still await us in the hereafter. On the basis of a single
laugh Keats proposes nothing less than a leap of faith into belief in
immortality, confident that a postmortal existence awaits us by comparison with which the goods of this life pale, that crossing over to

that hereafter we shall find "Death's intenser—Death is Life's high meed."

What I have said about Keats's laughter in "Why did I laugh tonight?" is, I believe, roughly true of the song of the nightingale as well. With the precedent of Coleridge already available to assure Keats that he hears "the merry Nightingale" and not the "most melancholy bird" that Milton, in conformity with the long-standing myth of Philomel, writes of, Keats from the first lets us know that the beauty of the song he overhears is finally only comprehensible if we understand it as the outward sign of some unalloyed inner happiness. Yet in a world "Where but to think is to be full of sorrow / And leaden-eyed despairs," a happiness so conceived cannot occur. It is an anomaly that can only be accounted for if we posit another world, a noumenal realm where a happiness like that which the nightingale's song expresses exists as a fundamental condition of being. Then, too, the nightingale's song, like the poet's laughter, seems an ideal vehicle, both as an effect of the noumenal and a representation of it, to render what is otherwise indiscernible and unconditioned. As a seemingly self-contained utterance, meaningful in itself without being tied to any conventional, synchronically related system of language, the nightingale's song readily presents itself as the unmediated sign of some pure presence, an ultimate signified that can easily be taken as the ground of all other meaning. Once again like that laughter, the nightingale's song evokes a sense of Being without attributes other than a freestanding happiness, thus mirroring our imaginings of noumenal purity, essence without accidents, that engenders a happiness both intense and enduring.

The choice of music by Keats as the basis of meditation in "Ode to a Nightingale" is crucial, as Helen Vendler has argued, but not on aesthetic grounds as she would have it: "Ode to a Nightingale" is not primarily a continuation by Keats of "his inquiries into the nature of art,"[11] nor does it further follow that "In choosing music as its artifact, the *Ode to a Nightingale* decides for beauty alone, without truth-content."[12] Neither did he choose the nightingale's song, however, for the reason those commentators with whom Vendler disagrees propose: that it "represented to Keats the music of nature, to be contrasted with human art, whether verbal or musical."[13] From the more general concerns of "Ode to a Nightingale" it would seem reasonable to conclude instead that Keats chose the song of the nightingale because it lent itself so readily to his purposes as a metaphysician. First, as we have seen, the assumption of the nightingale's happiness, an understandable conclusion given the melodiousness of its song, is just the anomaly required by Keats's metaphysical logic for him to infer the existence of the noumenal. Secondly, music itself in its meaningful immateriality, its organized indefiniteness, and its apparent unrelatedness to other items of our experience, is something within our phenomenal world—as philosophers have long recognized—which seems by its featurelessness best suited to illustrate our conception of an ultimate reality assumed to be wholly unlike any objective existence.

Of all the inferences drawn from the speaker's laugh and the nightingale's song none has proven more troubling to the critics than those that imply some form of immortality, whether the cryptic claim with which "Why did I laugh to-night?" closes, "Death is Life's high meed," or the equally astonishing and no less perplexing assertion that appears at the beginning of stanza 7 of "Ode to a Nightingale," "Thou wast not born for death, immortal Bird?" This last line, ascribing immortality to what has almost always been presumed to be a natural creature, has long remained one of the great cruxes of Keats scholarship, with the solutions proposed usually falling into two categories. One is to regard the object of Keats's address, the "immortal Bird," not as the nightingale he is then listening to but as the species generally, which might by the special reckoning of long-lastingness be credited with a kind of immortality. But this solution has often and justly been criticized for trivializing Keats's assertion, since surely one might argue that the "hungry generations" could be credited with a similar immortality, if humanity were also considered solely as a species. Alternatively critics have described the nightingale addressed in stanza 7 as purely symbolic, a practice that seems less an explanation of the nightingale's immortality (since those who would make the nightingale only a symbol rarely attempt to identify what is symbolized) than a strategy designed to spare an ostensibly humanistic Keats the embarrassments these assertions would create if taken at face value.

Yet the metaphysical logic that governs "Ode to a Nightingale" dictates just that approach. We are to take the assertion at face value, regard the "Bird" who sings at that time and in that place as literally "immortal," an individual creature that lives forever and shall never die. For one source of the conviction that there can be no happiness in a world "Where but to think is to be full of sorrow / And leaden-eyed despairs" is the fact of mortality weighing upon us like "unwilling sleep," dulling perception in a "leaden-eyed" sluggishness. In this life, we find associatively conjoined to our experiences of the world an accompanying consciousness that devalues and denies, dulling perception by insinuating within it the always disabling knowledge that we must die. In a world governed by these inexorable laws, where the fact of mortality as a constant of consciousness blunts all pleasures, any experience of happiness not only requires a noumenal source to explain it, but, more important to our present interpretive purposes, requires immortality as the enabling condition that permits happiness to exist. Keats calls the nightingale "immortal" then because only by being immortal could it possess the happiness which it seems so ecstatically to celebrate, and, conversely, if it possesses that happiness it must be immortal.

Of course, "Why did I laugh to-night?" and "Ode to a Nightingale" seem in certain significant respects dissimilar. In the former, Keats plainly warns us against mistaking a noumenally grounded state of well-being and the intimations of immortality that follow from it for a belated attempt at rehabilitating Christianity. Nowhere in "Ode to a Nightingale" are there any similarly overt Christian references; nowhere does Keats do anything like calling upon "God" or "Demon," or voices "from Heaven or from Hell" to tell us why the nightingale, contrary to all evidence from sense-experience, should sing of happiness, and then use the absence of an answer as sufficient reason to turn from the traditionally Christian to secularized formulations of the noumenal. At one point in "Ode to a Nightingale," however, Keats does appear to repudiate customary images of the unconditioned, the mythological representations of heavenly transcendence he had habitually drawn upon to articulate the metaphysics of his earlier poetry. In those poems that culminate in *Endymion*, Keats, following traditions that extend through Christianity back into antiquity, situates the ultimately real in the uppermost regions of the heavens, revealing itself in the sheer brilliance of those heavenly bodies that are themselves characteristically regarded by Keats as the material equivalents of divinities who, dwelling in the skies, participate in that reality. So looking heavenward to "the speculation of the stars" in "I Stood Tip-toe" Keats reads in the brightness of the moon "the bridal night" of Cynthia and Endymion, a hierogamy that yields nothing less than an ontological transformation of the earthly, with the "languid sick" made whole, awakening "clear-eyed" from their once "fevered sleep," and the course of true love, where pain invariably follows pleasure, is dramatically reversed so that "no lover did of anguish die."

But with a single pronouncement of indifference, a verbal shrug tantamount to dismissal, the word "haply" understood as a disengaged "perchance" introducing the observation that "the Queen-Moon is on her throne / Cluster'd around by all her starry Fays," Keats casually announces a decisive shift in the cosmology through which he expresses his conception of the noumenal. At first, we might imagine, from what we know of Keats, that it is these highly anthropomorphized heavens, presumably the site of a transcendence that furnishes the nightingale with his metaphysical superiority, to which the poet must fly on "viewless wings" if he is to achieve that transforming identity with the nightingale that would secure for him its ontological condition. But, in fact, it is downward to darkness that he is carried by the "wings of Poesy," to a rich and fertile center apparently infused with noumenal power, that embowered "here" where "there is no light," filled with the fragrance of unseen flowers and the ecstasy of the nightingale's song beckoning the poet downward still further, to the yet deeper and more enduring darkness of "easeful Death." In so explicitly calling for a shift in poetic focus away from the heavens to dark and boundaryless depths, Keats in "Ode to a Nightingale," probably more than anywhere else in his poetry, aligns himself with the most radical of romantic cosmologists, those who in their world pictures most defiantly renounce tradition. By noting and then ignoring the enthroned "Queen-Moon" and "all her starry Fays," Keats, in effect, banishes his sky-gods, perhaps not with the bold frontal assault with which Shelley and Blake banish Jupiter and Urizen, but with a casual gesture of disregard that produces a banishment no less absolute.

So radical a cosmological shift invariably suggests corresponding conceptual changes, the supplanting of transcendent by immanent theories of metaphysical explanation, the characterizing of the ultimately real, the noumenal principle, as something recessive, interiorized, perhaps infusing itself into the world of our experience but residing in itself within depths impenetrable by the senses. The cosmological and metaphysical direction of "Ode to a Nightingale" from the end of stanza 4 through stanza 7 is not simply earthward but inward; that darkened "here" to which the poet is carried "on the viewless wings of Poesy" is not a destination but a point of departure. From that "here" where he now stands, having refused to look to the heavens, the speaker of "Ode to a Nightingale," freed from transcendent illusions, may comprehend the message of the nightingale's song, infer from the happiness projected by it a noumenal that satisfies the heart's desires. But comprehension is different in kind from possession according to Keats's metaphysics. To participate truly, as the nightingale does, in a fully noumenal existence, the speaker must descend still further than the earth's surface—even when that surface is presented as the protective enclosure of the womblike bower—and seek in those yet lower depths the ontologically transforming self-dissolution that might gain him happiness but, as he acknowledges, might prove to be nothing more than annihilation, to repose in nothingness, to "become a sod."

In both "Why did I laugh to-night?" and "Ode to a Nightingale" Keats draws roughly similar metaphysical conclusions from correspondingly pleasurable utterances unexplainable by any appeal to the principles of ordinary sense experience. But in one obvious regard there is a sharp and fundamental difference between the situations of the two poems. Simply put, in "Why did I laugh to-night?" the listener who hears and understands what is implied by the utterance and he who utters it and thereby would seem to participate in that condition of being the laugh implies are one and the same. In "Ode to a Nightingale," he who overhears and from what he has heard infers the noumenal is distinct from the bird who sings and must therefore dwell in the state of existence expressed by that song. Because the laughter is his own, the listener who speaks in "Why did I laugh to-night?" has, in effect, inwardly validated the first in the poem's chain of inferences, that such laughter signifies pleasure within, an empirically anomalous happiness. And by that validation he is justified in making the next move, boldly asserting the astonishing proposition with which the poem closes: "Death is Life's high meed." Conversely, the unbreachable separation of the listener from the bird that sings in "Ode to a Nightingale" renders the meaning of that song altogether problematic. Unable to turn to his own inner being to verify his conjectures about the mood in which the nightingale sings, and certainly unable to gain direct access to the inner life of the nightingale, Keats's speaker must waver, leave undecided (in one of romanticism's great "undecidables") the question of whether the music overheard is, in fact, a song of happiness—indeed "ecstasy" as Keats at one point suggests—or the fading "plaintive anthem" of the closing stanza.

Bridging that gulf, the wish of the speaker not only to conceive of but to participate in the noumenal as the nightingale does, provides most of the action and pathos of "Ode to a Nightingale." From the first lines, we are to assume that simply through our powers of cognition we can draw noumenal inferences from what by the apparent law of things seems anomalous, from depths of pleasureableness that cannot possibly originate in or belong to a world "Where but to think is to be full of sorrow / And leaden-eyed despairs." As humans, Keats reassuringly tells us, we do have the power to know truly a happiness apparently incongruous with the empirical conditions under which we live, to apprehend its presence in another, and by that knowledge, to enjoy, if only in alloy and only for the moment, a happiness that the nightingale possesses in its full purity and enjoys forever. Knowing the nightingale to be happy, we can ourselves be happy, indeed be "too happy in thine happiness," even while we remain simultaneously conscious of the everpresent evidences of our mortality certain to cut short any experience of happiness and to undo whatever hopes we might glean from that experience.

The poem opens then with the speaker in crisis, with the conflict at its most intense between what both the external world and our internal impressions tell us about our condition and what we wish to believe about the nightingale on the basis of our imaginings. Caught between the desire to be transformed into the metaphysical state hypothesized in those imaginings and the mortal constraints that inner sense tells us must be placed upon these yearnings, the speaker of "Ode to a Nightingale" can report, at first, only the pain generated by what from experience he knows himself to be and what he infers from what he hears, telling us only how "My heart aches, and a drowsy numbness pains / My sense as though of hemlock I had drunk," as he listens to the bird's song. The aching heart is just the response we might expect to an episode in Keats when desire arising out of suprasensory intimations comes in contact with his ineradicable consciousness of human finitude. In fact, as early as "On Seeing the Elgin Marbles" similarly conflicted circumstances produce in him a similarly anguished and debilitated response. There Keats explains how the "dim-conceivèd" but surely transcendent "glories" suggested by the marbles produce in the viewer an unexpected and unintended "dizzy pain," or in language that most closely verges on the opening line of "Ode to a Nightingale," "Bring round the heart an undescribable feud," as aspiration fed by wonder at the example of godlike accomplishment finds itself thwarted by the countervailing consciousness that "tells me I must die."

Written in 1817, "On Seeing the Elgin Marbles" concludes in impasse, leaving unresolved the "undescribable feud" that troubles the speaker's heart and that serves as his final response to the metaphysically optimistic suggestions teased out by contemplation of the marbles. How much Keats in 1819 had advanced as a metaphysician is probably best borne out by his willingness to take the "undescribable feud" "round the heart" as a starting point in "Ode to a Nightingale," confident now that this conflict between opposed and apparently mutually exclusive phenomenal and noumenal data can somehow to the will be settled. He can do so, we quickly learn, because Keats has drastically reordered the ways in which he spatially projects his metaphysical concepts and, by implication, has correspondingly reordered the concepts themselves. No longer is he the grounded earthling gazing heavenward toward the seat of transcendence "Like a sick eagle looking at the sky." Instead, he has internalized his basic metaphysical principle, presenting it here not as transcendent but immanent, allowing the nightingale to be ontologically privileged not by virtue of the heights it can climb or the heavens it can reach as a bird that soars but because of the plenitude it possesses in its inner being that enables the nightingale, even when close to earth among the trees, to sing melodiously "in full-throated ease." And subsumed within the same spatial and conceptual reorderings, the speaker, too, is no longer required to undertake an impossible winged flight to undergo transformation but now needs just to turn within himself and enter the labyrinthine depths of the inner life to achieve ontological parity with the nightingale and become what he now only can imagine.

Most surprising, perhaps, is how close at hand he finds the apparent means to effect this change. The dulled awareness apprehended as always in the body which Keats will read in stanza 3 as that sense of mortality constantly conjoined to our thinking, the feeling of "leaden-eyed despairs" that "tells me I must die," is from another perspective a potentially liberating "drowsy numbness" that carries us "Lethe-wards" to that psychic center where we can cast off all that "the dull brain" throws up which "perplexes and retards," all those elements of the phenomenal understanding that estrange us from the noumenal and form impediments to ontological transformation. To become what the nightingale is, we must go "Lethe-wards," deeper into drowsiness and numbness, "dissolve, and quite forget," doing away with the empirical self as the precondition to essential change.

In this, what Keats seems to do is to take a single item of empirical data, the irreducible bodily fact experienced as torpor and diminished sensibility and, to suit his purposes, fits it alternatively within two opposed metaphysical schemes, one wholly naturalistic, the other looking beyond phenomenal existence to a noumenal ground and goal. So what is from one perspective the mark of despair inscribed upon the body, the state of being "leaden-eyed," powerless simply to raise the eyelids and attend to the variety and vivacity of the phenomenal world, is from another perspective an experience imbued with hope, a "drowsy numbness" that indicates suppression of all those activities of ordinary consciousness—perception, thought, and memory—that restrain the human imagination in its excursions toward ontologically different realms of knowledge, ontologically different modes of existence. Of course, the feeling of diminished sensibility and torpor from which both interpretations evolve is understood before all else, prior to either interpretation, as an indicator of our mortality, a something within the self that tells us we must die. The "leaden-eyed despairs" in stanza 3 (so different from "the wakeful anguish of the soul" in "Ode of Melancholy") are, as I noted earlier, a seeming reevocation of that "unwilling sleep" which Keats in "On Seeing the Elgin Marbles" draws upon as an analogue to describe how the weight of mortality actually feels. Similarly the "drowsy numbness" with which "Ode to a Nightingale" begins prompts thoughts of mortality as well, figuratively calling to our attention the likeness of these sensations not just to narcotically induced sleep and forgetfulness, but to the enduring effects produced by poisonous hemlock, the final and lasting obliteration of memory and cessation of consciousness.

Yet if both schemes end in death—seemingly the most irreducible of all brute facts—that death, too, can be interpreted in either of these two contrasting ways, assimilated to either of these two opposing metaphysical perspectives. Read naturalistically, the death the speaker longs for is sheer extinction, the end of a sensory existence that despite its meagerness is all we have. Read from the second perspective, death is easeful, indeed possibly enriching, perhaps the sole entryway to ontological transformation and thus identity with the nightingale. But with the two conceptions adhering to a single event, one may readily be displaced unexpectedly by the other in a single lapse from this precariously sustained faith in the noumenal. So it is not surprising that hopes of ontological transformation at death initially called forth by feelings of a drowsy numbness that is identical with the sensation of being "leaden-eyed" should end instead in a frightening premonition of extinction, fear of becoming "a sod."

It is this understandable apprehensiveness that death would lead only to vacancy and the cessation of being that finally short-circuits and undoes the visionary trajectory of "Ode to a Nightingale." Until the end of stanza 6, however, the poet's hope of achieving identity with the nightingale and thus real participation in the noumenal rests primarily on the logic that states that the "drowsy numbness" that releases him from the thought that is sorrow and seemingly serves as the enabling condition of noumenal knowledge must, if only intensified, conclude in a death that is, in fact, transfiguration. But one other agency, of course, effectively carries us at least part of the way toward ontological transformation: "Poesy," whose "viewless wings" transport us in a flight that defies the laws of time and space by the immediacy with which it is completed and that takes us from that site where the speaker listens at the opening, a location outside the "melodious plot" in which the nightingale sings, to that profoundly darkened but ontologically charged "here," which serves as the apparent ground of the nightingale's being but is still only a way station, even if crucial and indispensable, to full and final union with the visionary bird.

"Poesy" for Keats, especially in the poems instead of the letters, characteristically is not primarily a linguistic act or object, something made or in the making, but rather an activity directed less to aesthetic than to metaphysical ends, a means of noumenal contact or even noumenal empowerment. Thus Keats customarily ascribes to the poet a special visionary capacity; he points to Homer, for example, as one for whom "the veil was rent," and who can therefore extract the empirically anomalous from the most dispiriting of perceptions, finding through his "triple sight in blindness keen" the otherwise unknowable, the "light" that lies upon "the shores of darkness," or the "budding morrow in midnight." Keats's poet possesses the capacity to secure access to the implicitly noumenal, because he has actually acquired or been endowed with an ontologically privileged state of being that has "Poesy" as its product and expression. The tongues of the lovers in "I Stood Tip-Toe" are "loosed in Poesy," because they have been renewed and transformed, their illnesses cast off and their eyes made bright, as a consequence of the cosmic marriage, the hierogamy, between Cynthia and Endymion, an ontologically revitalizing event whose outcome may well have been, Keats speculates, that from their consummation there was "a poet born."

But the ardent apostrophe to "Poesy" in "Sleep and Poetry" is where Keats most strikingly asserts how closely he associates "Poesy" and an ontologically conceived self-transformation. Though the speaker begins his prayer by grasping "my pen," the initial and primary effect he hopes to achieve by that act is not communication with others by inscribing words on a page but the attainment of a profoundly private transport, to "feel / A glowing spendour around about my being." For the aspiring young poet of "Sleep and Poetry" to have his prayer answered is to be carried into the unknown by "the wings of poesy" and thus to enter into a process whose stages closely parallel those initiated by poetic flight in "Ode to a Nightingale." In the earlier poem, too, we find the powers of poetry drawing the young speaker toward a seemingly magic garden, toward flowery sweets, unseen, guessed at, overpowering in their exquisiteness. And again we find the sensory heightening achieved in this atmosphere not an end in itself but a sort of necessary requisite to a further and yet more intense stage, to a death viewed as potentially enriching, fulfilling, transforming. What Keats calls on "Poesy" to do in "Sleep and Poetry" has little to do with writing; "Poesy," the speaker prays, is to let him make use of its noumenal potency so that he can effect his own metaphysical self-transformation; it is to

> Yield from thy sanctuary some clear air,
> Smoothed for intoxication by the breath
> Of flowering bays, that I may die a death
> Of luxury.

And finally, of course, nowhere is the noumenal efficacy of "Poesy" more evident than in the spectacular apotheosis of Apollo that concludes *Hyperion*. There, too, we follow a movement from knowing into being as—dying into life—he can tell us how "Knowledge enormous makes a God of me."

"Poesy" in "Ode to a Nightingale" carries the speaker far even when we measure that distance ontologically; but in this poem "poesy" is not ultimately transformative: its "Knowledge enormous" does not make a God of him. For the anomalously perfect happiness that the nightingale possesses still remains elusive; even after the completion of his transport by the "wings of Poesy," desire, still hungering, is left unsatisfied. Acquired in this leap into darkness, this instantaneous flight to the ontologically promising conveyed by that "here," is a sort of ideal vantage point where, freed from distraction, one may attend fully to what yet has to be done. But as we well know, what has to be done, despite all its metaphysical temptation, proves so ominously perilous that poet and poem finally pull back from the brink of the grave and reverse themselves in the most famous of all romantic peripeties. About this journey back from the verge of dissolution and empathy and ontological transformation to egocentric isolation in the sole self I need say little; by this reversal Keats has apparently withdrawn all noumenal inferences and the assertion of happiness that prompted them.

We have thus arrived in the concluding stanza of "Ode to a Nightingale," at least in its first six lines, at what most critics of Keats are pleased to call reality, situated ourselves in circumstances governed by strict metaphysical limits, reinstated an empiricism without gaps, without potential openings to the noumenal, thereby confining ourselves, as these critics would have it, to the authentically human ground of the here and now. Yet, in truth, what Keats has done in these lines is restore us to the conditions of stanza 3 with nothing gained in the interim, so that the unremitting suffering experience teaches us to be the law of life still yields the same comfortless epistemological proposition: that "but to think is to be full of sorrow / And leaden-eyed despairs." That no real change takes place between earlier and later passages, that he essentially repeats in stanza 8 the grim summation of phenomenal existence given in stanza 3, is strikingly evident in the terms Keats chooses to represent both the inner life and the external world at the climax of the poem's despondent return. Of the multiple meanings that attach to the word "Forlorn," the speaker knows intuitively which definition applies most aptly to the human condition, recognizes that in the reference to wretchedness that semantically is one of the possibilities conveyed by that utterance we have stumbled upon the identifying attribute of the sole and substantial self. And turning from the self to the world, he again finds wretchedness everywhere, even in what he had once considered the probable exception to these general laws of universal suffering, assuming now with the same intuitiveness that even the nightingale in the innermost core of its being shares in that wretchedness, a likely truth to which its "plaintive anthem" bears signal witness.

Of course, the thoroughgoing empiricism and the utter despondency in which that reversal concludes are not actually granted the last word in "Ode to a Nightingale." As though he desired to undo the perhaps excessive orderliness according to which we have been taught to read the odes, those structural regularities of ascent and descent taking us from the real to the ideal and then back to the real again (from A to B to A' as Stillinger diagrammatically traces it in order to suggest that Keats does not propose a course of mere circularity but implies instead something learned or acquired in the process[14]), Keats chooses—though the cautionary lesson of visionary error has apparently been established—to throw all into confusion by raising in the last two lines the famous questions with which "Ode to a Nightingale" closes: "Was it a vision, or a waking dream? / Fled is that music—Do I wake or sleep?"

For some critics the careful balancing of antithetical options is reason to declare "Ode to a Nightingale" metaphysically open-ended, indeterminate, its great queries unanswered and perhaps unanswerable. For many others, however, an understandable hermeneutic predilection for conclusiveness and closure has proven irresistible; and since current tendencies virtually mandate that the later Keats, won over in maturity to naturalism, must, of necessity, decide in behalf of the empirical and real, most of those who find themselves compelled to choose regard the call to suspended judgment of the final questions no real impediment to the logical rigor of the counterturn of stanzas 7 and 8. Whether one chooses like Stillinger simply to truncate the poem and disregard its last two lines; or like Sperry to attribute them to "a busy common sense with" its "alien methodology of 'either / or' " that takes charge of the poem after the "illusion of mythic oneness is dissolved;" or like Vendler to find the balance tilted toward repudiation of the visionary by "the constitutive shape of the poem;" or like Dickstein to treat the very broaching of these questions as a last, wistful gesture of regret after the necessary exorcism has been completed; the reply to the poem's famous closing questions by these, the most influential of modern critics of Keats, is in every case, despite apparent differences, essentially the same: only in stanzas 7 and 8 has the poet truly awakened; what came before was baseless and potentially destructive, never "a vision," just "a waking dream."[15]

But before yielding to such authority and abandoning all claims that Keats at the end of the ode remained still receptive to the inducements of metaphysics, we must address two persistently perplexing matters that are not easily assimilated to the views of that consensus that now seems to prevail in the modern criticism of Keats. If the poem ends, as most agree it does, in a firm assertion of a kind of epistemological realism, the need to look clear-eyed and unblinkingly at things as they are, what then are we to make of the way in which the nightingale seems finally to be construed? The metaphysical project of "Ode to a Nightingale" proceeds, as I have indicated, from two basic starting points, what is assumed about the nightingale and what is desired by the poet. From the latter perspective we can agree that the poem's noumenal suppositions fall far short of confirmation. The turn to physical death, which, after the false start of wine and the uncompleted flight through poetry, seems the only conceivable means to achieve ontological change, has proven too intrinsically fearsome in itself and too uncertain in outcome to be voluntarily undertaken in order to prove or disprove these suppositions; and the misery that the speaker would forget in wine or "Poesy" or the even more absolute dissolution of death proves far too resistant and ineradicable to be effectively banished, so that even the ambiguity that resonates in the word "Forlorn" is sufficient to revive by the laws of association memories powerful enough to recall to him the sour awareness of the "sole" and presumably substantial "self" and return him to the wretchedness which is ostensibly the true and only reality.

But for the nightingale we are provided with no such disconfirming narrative. The claims that it is happy, then ecstatic, then immortal are in stanza 8 without reason or warning inexplicably withdrawn. To a song whose joyousness had initially aroused noumenal stirrings there is now imputed a plaintiveness that obviously befits the forlornness of that reality the sole self inhabits. Though Keatsian realists might be prone to dismiss the happiness ascribed to the nightingale as error, mere wishfulness, projection, surely the later representation of the bird's song as a "plaintive anthem" is no less a projection, and a projection, moreover, that seems to depend not on the actual state of the listener's own sensibility but on borrowings from a literary tradition that Keats knew had recently been put in question by Coleridge's insistence that attention to the direct testimony of nature must establish the falsity of that tradition.

Yet on the basis of that already beleaguered tradition, together with a faintly figurative intimation of mortality implied by speaking of the nightingale as "buried deep" at the end of his flight to "the next valley-glades," Keats seems willing to ascribe to the nightingale a conscious awareness of the all-consuming misery of earthly existence that seems essentially identical to the speaker's own. Curiously enough, as a realist or a naturalist, Keats in "Ode to a Nightingale" does not revert back to that distinction he had made only a few months earlier in "Bards of passion and of mirth" between the knowing human subject and the nightingale, at least in its earthly incarnation, as a purely instinctual creature, "a senseless, trancèd thing." Even when its speaker reaches his depths of despondency, abandoning the visionary in deference to the dictates of the real, the natural world of "Ode to a Nightingale" remains as it was at the poem's beginning, a place charged with meaning, where a nightingale's song must somehow register intentionality and be regarded as a purposeful expression of an inner knowing or being that is semantically accessible to us only through the speechless tones of a music without words. And yet listening closely, we cannot determine with any real finality whether what we hear is happy music or plaintive music, the manifest rendering of latent joy or latent misery.

Because it begins in happiness and concludes in plaintiveness, the account of the nightingale's own history may seem to be a sort of mirroring subplot that effectively reenacts and thus reinforces the speaker's own introspectively validated description of his enlightenment through disenchantment. But nothing could be farther from the truth. Apart from what the speaker's shifting moods and vacillating will would through transference wish to make of it, the nightingale's own tale as told in music has no genuine progression, no determining narrative logic, no plot that directs it toward a point of closure around which meaning would crystallize. The notes that pour from the nightingale at the poem's beginning are no different from those heard at the end. Thus we have no real reason to privilege that later assertion of plaintiveness over earlier claims of happiness in our final assessment of the state of being of the nightingale or the probable import of its song. Since answers to these final questions depend less upon the mood of the speaker than on the status of the nightingale and the meaning of its songs, suspension of judgment seems the perfect means by which noumenal inference, despite all that "thought" has to say against it, is intended to remain a viable option for explaining and understanding our present and future existence.

But there is one additional reason why after his striking reversal, after going as far as he does toward banishing the visionary for the sake of the actual, Keats turns yet one more time, giving the claims of the visionary at least a final hearing, preserving metaphysical options that we might have assumed to be already closed. Critics who insist that Keats in "Ode to a Nightingale" has implicitly answered his questions in the course of the poem and has firmly chosen the actual over the ideal, do so in large measure because they conceive him to be an incipient modern, who, renouncing transcendence, has in his modernity acquiesced in the need to make do with the real. But the real never quite suffices for these critics, and they would have the poems of 1819 provide, in the words of Stillinger "a facing-up to" the actual "that amounts, in the total view, to affirmation." Yet it is all too evident that what is acquiesced in at the end of the reversal depicted in the first eight lines of stanza 8 of "Ode to a Nightingale" contains nothing whatsoever that can be affirmed: to be a realist in this poem is to be a pessimist of the darkest hue, "Forlorn" and "full of sorrow," and for very good reason. Indeed, all that has been changed by the trajectory that carries the speaker from what Stillinger has called the point A of stanza 3 to the A' of stanza 8 is that at the end of stanza 8 the nightingale itself has joined the chorus of woe.

To find something affirmed, we must look metaphysically elsewhere, remembering once again the analogy with Kant. If there is only nature, Kant maintains, we can have only the wholly determined, so that if we are to claim duty exists we imply by that, as its necessary corollary, the existence as well of the noumenal and freedom. So, too, with Keats in "Ode to a Nightingale": if there is only nature, there is only sorrow, because every event, even the most pleasure-able—the appearance of "Beauty" or the emergence of "new Love"—is epistemologically conditioned by its associative links with transience and mortality to produce only despair and forlornness. And to complete the analogy, Keats indicates, too, that only by inferring immortality and the noumenal can we logically posit the existence of a genuine happiness. If we would have Keats a realist and naturalist, banishing dreams to write the poetry of earth, we must then be prepared to accept the consequences of that view as Keats presents them: that is, there neither is nor can be any real happiness. But we must surely concede that, in fact, Keats is willing at least to entertain the possibility that happiness exists, however elusive the happiness that momentarily does manifest itself finally proves to be. Of course, that such happiness can never be present in purely phenomenal affairs goes without saying. Only by looking to what we would like to believe is metaphysically beyond the phenomenal and yet its ground, can we even begin to speak meaningfully of an existing happiness; but to suppose such a metaphysical beyond is, as the empiricists have so successfully taught us, to embark on a course inevitably subject to question and doubt. Keats's understandable propensity was to do as we have always done, and seek that beyond in the heavens above: in gods and goddesses, for example, in whom, even as they descend, we cannot believe. But if we are really to believe in happiness, our best hopes for doing so must reside in something akin to immediate human experience, in the noumenal manifesting itself in our world as natural fact, not in the remote or rarefied but in the accessible and available, in an unexpected laugh, or, better yet, in the ravishingly enigmatic music of a nightingale's song.

Notes

1. Jack Stillinger, "The Hoodwinking of Madeline: Skepticism in *The Eve of St. Agnes*," *The Hoodwinking of Madeline and Other Essays on Keats's Poems* (Urbana: University of Illinois Press, 1971), 68.

2. Stillinger, *Hoodwinking of Madeline*, 68.

3. Earl R. Wasserman, *Shelley's Prometheus Unbound: A Critical Reading* (Baltimore: Johns Hopkins Press, 1965), 5.

4. Wasserman, *Prometheus Unbound*, 7.

5. Wasserman, *Prometheus Unbound*, 7.

6. Stuart M. Sperry, *Keats the Poet* (Princeton: Princeton University Press, 1973), 9.

7. *The Letters of John Keats, 1804–1821,* ed. Hyder Edward Rollins, 2 vols. (Cambridge: Harvard University Press, 1958), 1:185.

8. *Letters,* 1:185.

9. *Letters,* 1:185.

10. Immanuel Kant, *Critique of Pure Reason,* abr. and trans. Norman Kemp Smith (New York: Random House, 1958), 299.

11. Helen Vendler, *The Odes of John Keats* (Cambridge: Harvard University Press, 1983), 77.

12. Vendler, *Odes of John Keats,* 78.

13. Vendler, *Odes of John Keats,* 77.

14. Stillinger, "Imagination and Reality in the Odes," *Hoodwinking of Madeline,* 101.

15. See Stillinger, "Imagination and Reality in the Odes," 106–7; Sperry, *Keats the Poet,* 267; Vendler, *Odes of John Keats,* 95; Morris Dickstein, *Keats and His Poetry* (Chicago: University of Chicago Press, 1971), 220–21.

Feminizing Keats

Susan J. Wolfson[*]

1

an effeminacy of style, in some degree corresponding to effeminacy
of character
—Hazlitt on Keats

Feminist literary criticism frequently theorizes the "feminine" as the designated "other" in a system in which the position of privilege is "masculine." Less commonly elaborated are contestations of gender within that masculine center itself, especially in relation to men such as Keats, who are often spoken of as having qualities and attitudes "other" than those normatively deemed masculine. Yet a striking feature of the discourse on Keats—in both the nineteenth century and the twentieth—is the frequency with which his gender is an issue. This is not a matter of biology, of course, but of ideology. Like the systems that cast the feminine as "other," judgments about Keats appear in the language of gendered opposition and difference, in which decisions about what is not "masculine"—in Keats's case, variously "effeminate," "juvenile," or "puerile"—imply what is. Keats is an interesting figure in these constructions less because of their repetition and wide circulation (remarkable though these are) than because of the profound divisions of judgment he agitates—divisions

[*] This essay was written specifically for this volume and is published here for the first time by permission of the author.

not just in the language of gender per se, but about the interests being served in its application.

Why has Keats provoked such persistent—one is tempted to say obsessive—attention in these terms? This vocabulary responds in part to his literary practices, and for later readers, to comments in his letters about his character, poetic and existential. Both discourses reveal a sensibility fascinated with the permeable boundary between masculine and feminine. Keats's physical characteristics, moreover, perplexed this boundary: everyone who knew or wrote about him had to think through the question of gender when confronted with his manner, conduct, and appearance. Keats's situation in this discourse bears on more than the intrigue of his individual case, however, for the assessments are frequently produced in contexts that show him being treated as the signifier or symptom of a large-scale cultural concern. Judgments of Keats as "unmanly" typically coincide with worries about the feminization of men—especially men of, or under the influence of, letters; correspondingly, defenses of his manliness, though couched in no less traditional terms, often seem covertly to challenge orthodox determinations of "masculine" and "feminine." That Keats did not fit conventional figures made him a convenient focus for ideological debate; indeed, a manifold of literary style and sensibility, personal appearance, class origin, and the legend of his death made him a magnetic focus. Keats's peculiar position on the boundaries of discrimination, as we shall see, makes highly legible the systems of power, both social and psychological, that inform the language of gender and influence its uses.

In this essay, therefore, I will be concerned not only with Keats's practices as a poet, but also with how the language of gender operates in the literary and social culture in which he wrote and was reviewed. I will also be concerned, at the end, with where we now stand as critical inheritors of this problem. Keats's marginality typically tempts critical extremes: he either triggers efforts to stabilize and enforce standards of manly conduct in which he is the negative example, stigmatized as "effeminate," or "unmanly"; or he inspires attempts to broaden and make more flexible prevailing definitions, so that certain qualities, previously limited to and sometimes derided as "feminine," may be allowed to enrich and enlarge the culture's images of "manliness"—even to the point of androgyny. I intend for an historically based reading of this volatility to serve as a deep background for what we see at work in modern conceptions of Keats, ranging from the most traditional terms of differentiation to recent attempts by some feminist critics to redefine our understanding of "masculine" and "feminine." The way Keats figures into such discussions reveals the persistence of the problems he posed to the nineteenth-century discourses of gender and the legislating functions with which these were charged.

In 1822 Hazlitt published "On Effeminacy of Character," an essay which begins by declaring opposition to the cult of sensibility: "Effeminacy of character arises from a prevalence of the sensibility over the will: or it consists in a want of fortitude." As Hazlitt's blunt definition suggests, the excesses of effeminacy imply deficiency elsewhere: "instead of voluntarily embracing pain, or labour, or danger, or death," lovers of "exquisite indulgences" want "every sensation . . . wound up to the highest pitch of voluptuous refinement, every motion must be grace and elegance; they live in a luxurious, endless dream, or 'Die of a rose in aromatic pain!' " Keats appears as Hazlitt's summary example of "an effeminacy of style, in some degree corresponding to effeminacy of character . . . one that is all florid, all fine; that cloys by its sweetness, and tires by its sameness. . . . Every thought must be beautiful *per se,* every expression equally fine."[1] Though no particular text is cited, even Keats's loyal defender, Leigh Hunt, concedes the question of style: reading *Hyperion,* he regrets "something too effeminate and human in the way Apollo receives the exaltation which his wisdom is giving him. He weeps and wonders somewhat too fondly."[2] "Soon wild commotions shook him, and made flush / All the immortal fairness of his limbs," Keats writes (3:124–25), his manuscript revealing an even more feminine original:

> [Roseate and pained as a ravish'd nymph—]
> Into a hue more roseate than sweet-pain
> Gives to a ravish'd Nymph [new-r] when her warm tears
> Gush luscious with no sob.[3]

Apollo's transformation is registered in sensory effects exceeding those of an exceedingly feminine nymph; Keats's only other poetic use of *luscious,* in fact, refers to the eroticism of a nymph's "luscious lips."[4] The verse of *Hyperion* bothers Hunt not just because of its breach of decorum (gods should not act thus) but because of its breach of gender (men should not act thus)—even though his pairing of the adjectives *human* and *effeminate* is sufficiently striking to imply a tentative subtextual critique of the inhuman purchases of manliness.

2

Cockney (noun): " 'A child that sucketh long,' . . . a mother's darling; pet, minion; 'a child tenderly brought up'; hence a squeamish or effeminate fellow. . . . Sometimes applied to a squeamish, overnice, wanton, or affected woman."

"A derisive appellation for a townsman, as the type of effeminacy in contrast to the hardier inhabitants of the country".

"One born in the city of London, . . . used to connote the characteristics in which the born Londoner is supposed to be inferior to other Englishmen."
"One of the 'Cockney School.' "
(adj.): "effeminate, squeamish." Cockney School: "a nickname for a set of 19th cent. writers belonging to London, of whom Leigh Hunt was taken as the representative."

—*OED, C*:575–76

Keats "was spoilt by Cockneyfying and Surburbing," Byron decides. He also thought him spoilt by sexual immaturity: he calls him "the Mankin," and sneers at "Johnny Keats's *piss-a-bed* poetry"; its "drivelling idiotism"—"the *Onanism* of Poetry."[5] The term *cockney* implies attitudes about both, as *Blackwood's* first full attack on Keats, appearing in August 1818 as part of a series on the "Cockney School of Poetry," makes abundantly evident. The reviewer, John Lockhart, opens the case ridiculing both female and lower-class aspirations to what he clearly felt ought to remain male aristocratic pursuits: "The just celebrity of Robert Burns and Miss Baillie has had the melancholy effect of turning the heads of we know not how many farm-servants and unmarried ladies; our very foot-men compose tragedies, and there is scarcely a superannuated governess in the island that does not leave a roll of lyrics behind her in her band-box."[6] Like Byron, Lockhart also summons a puerilizing rhetoric to exclude Keats from adult male company, and by extension, from serious consideration as a poet. He is "Mr John," "good Johnny Keats," "Johnny," the author of "prurient and vulgar lines," and "Mr Keats . . . a boy of pretty abilities"—boy and class conflated in the summary advice to this "young Sangrado" to return to the apothecary shop.[7] It is telling that several decades later, George Gilfillan, who admires Keats's "elegant effeminacy" and sympathizes with his unmanning by adverse circumstance, innocently introduces his subject as "the hapless apothecary's boy"—a factual error all the more significant for its unwitting echo and testimony to the effect of *Blackwood's* mean-spirited precedent.[8]

Indeed, Lockhart's language attached itself to Keats with adhesive force. Z's letter in May 1818 to "Leigh Hunt, King of the Cockneys" names the author of a "famous Cockney Poem" in honor of Hunt as the "infatuated bardling, Mister John Keats." The lead article of the December 1819 issue joked about "Johnny Keates" (*sic*), and the appellation caught on: Byron enjoyed using it; so did Arnold, when in a mood to condescend to Keats's class origins—as J. R. MacGillivray notes, whenever a nineteenth-century writer referred to "Johnny Keats" he was signalling agreement with Lockhart.[9] *Blackwood's* was also rather proud of having refreshed the term *cockney* with all its associations of effeminacy, sexual immaturity, and social inferiority:

"The nickname we gave them, has become a regularly established word in our literature. Lord Byron, while patronizing the sect, called them by no other," it boasted in the "Preface" to the 1826 volume, which also derided Keats's poems as having "outhunted Hunt in a species of emasculated pruriency that . . . looks as if it were the product of some imaginative Eunuch's muse within the melancholy inspiration of the Haram."[10] By 1826, of course, Byron had put Don Juan in a harem, with decidedly different inspirations; although *Lord Byron* was sometimes called "unmanly" in Victorian letters, this usually meant "ungentlemanly," lamenting his immorality or indecency, not implying effeminacy. And he, like Shelley (who was more often called "effeminate"), benefitted not only from social rank but also from a reputation for womanizing.[11]

3

In poetry his was the woman's part
—Mrs. Oliphant on Keats

The feminizing of Keats in nineteenth-century letters was legible not just in terms of a default from codes of manliness, but also in the ready perception of qualities in his poetry deemed to have particular appeal to women. The publishers of his first volume advertised "Poems. By John Keatts" *(sic)* in *The British Lady's Magazine*, a journal whose masthead read, "Greatness of mind, and nobleness, thou seat in HER build loveliest."[12] And the epigraph for an article in an 1821 *Pocket Magazine* virtually handed Keats over to the feminine sphere with the prediction that "Albion's maidens . . . Will cherish thy sweet songs!," the text itself detailing the chief themes: "general tenderness . . . delicate taste and refined inclinations . . . uncontroulable and unlimited sympathy with all kinds of suffering," a "heart . . . peculiarly formed for the endearments of love and the gentle solaces of friendship." If, as Mrs. Sanderford's conduct manual put it, "Gentleness is, indeed, the talisman of woman," *Pocket* was happy to apply this badge to Keats as well, making him an honorary woman.[13] Even Gilfillan cooperated in writing Keats into the feminine sphere with a casual note about the curiously "elegant effeminacy" of mind displayed in *The Eve of St. Agnes*: "Its every line wears *couleur de rose*," he remarks warmly; "No poet ever described dress with more gust and beauty." The *Guardian*, less appreciatively, condescended to Keats's poems as no more than mere entertainments for women.[14] For better or worse, Keats continued throughout the century to be marketed to female audiences, welcomed by such publications as *The Young Lady's Book of Elegant Poetry*, *The Ladies' Companion*, and *The Girl's Second Help to Reading*, a compendium of "such passages as referred specifically to the high duties which woman is called up to perform in life"—for example, the stanzas from *Eve of St. Agnes* quoted by Gilfillan as an instance of the "poetry of dress." In May 1870, *Victoria Magazine*, noting with pleasure that literary values were being "effeminized" by women readers, published an article by a woman titled "Keats—The Daintiest of Poets," headed by the motto, "Glory and loveliness have passed away."[15]

The single most influential text, both on the reception of Keats by female readers and on judgments of his unmanliness, is the legend of his death disseminated by Shelley's *Adonais*. Moved by the stories of abuse by the reviews, Shelley thought himself Keats's vindicator, and for some he was. Charles Brown prefaced his biographical sketch with lines 370–83 of *Adonais*, which image Keats's absorption into a feminine afterlife—"He is made one with Nature: there is heard / His voice in all her music" (*KC* 2:52–53). For others, however, Shelley's extreme sentiment had different effects. The imagery of the "Preface," which eulogized Keats's genius as "not less delicate and fragile than it was beautiful . . . blighted in the bud"—and of the elegy itself—which lamented the rough handling of this "youngest, dearest . . . nursling" of the muse, "who grew, / Like a pale flower by some sad maiden cherished, / And fed with true-love tears . . . whose petals, nipped before they blew, / Died on the promise"— took root in hostile as well as friendly soil, indicating a sensibility lacking sufficient "masculine" vigor and resiliency to bear the slings and arrows of literary fortune.[16] When Byron, for one, learned from Shelley that "Young Keats . . . died lately at Rome from the consequences of breaking a blood-vessel, in paroxysms of despair at the contemptuous attack on his book in the *Quarterly*, he was incredulous: "is it *actually* true? I did not think criticism had been so killing . . . in this world of bustle and broil, and especially in the career of writing, a man should calculate upon his powers of *resistance* before he goes into the arena." Byron was one of the first, in fact, to transplant Shelley's "broken lily" into the garden of the faintly farcical with the famously flippant couplet in *Don Juan* (1823): "kill'd off by one critique . . . Poor fellow! His was an untoward fate; / 'T is strange the mind, that very fiery particle, / Should let itself be snuff'd out by an article."[17]

Byron's epitaph, "snuff'd out by an article," flourished: even when the subject was not Keats, as in *Blackwood's* review of Alexander Smith in 1854, it could be quoted with knowing effect. Over twenty years later, a critic for *Cornhill Magazine* wrote that *Adonais* could be "justified" only "On the theory that poetry and manliness are incompatible, that a poet is and ought to be a fragile being, ready to [']Die of a rose in aromatic pain[']"—quoting the same line from Pope's *Essay on Man* that Hazlitt had used to characterize effeminacy.

The *New Monthly* did not help things in Keats's own day when it compared the *Quarterly's* attacks on Lady Morgan—an Irish woman of letters and defender of the French Revolution, and subject, in the *Monthly's* words, to "one of the coarsest insults ever offered in print by man to woman"—to the same journal's "laborious attempt to torture and ruin Mr. Keats": the effect was to make Keats seem the victim of ungallant male behavior towards women deserving kinder, gentler treatment. By the middle of the century, this chapter of the Keats legend became canonical in *Chambers's Cyclopedia,* which began its entry on Keats with a long account of how savage handling by the reviews led to his final suffering.[18]

These widely circulated reports not only dominate nineteenth-century images of Keats, but also helped draw them into the orbit of a larger cultural preoccupation: the effort to secure distinctions between the genders and stabilize codes of conduct. If Mrs. Sanderford diagnosed "the female mind" as "constitutionally less stable than that of man," and Thomas Gisborne's manual cautioned that "the acute sensibility peculiar to women . . . is liable to sudden excesses" and "sometimes degenerates into weakness and pusillanimity," Keats, "pierced by the shaft" of malicious reviews, was readily translated into this feminine liability.[19] Thus Gilfillan speculates, sympathetically, that Keats's "great defect" was "want . . . of a man-like constitution," and Carlyle, with a caustic echo of Byron, remarked that Dr. Johnson "was no man to be killed by a review," while "the whole of Keats's poetry consists in a weak-eyed maudlin sensibility".[20] *Blackwood's* made the point in 1820 with a mock apology for its prior manner: "we are most heartily sorry . . . had we suspected that young author being so delicately nerved, we should have administered our reproof in a much more lenient shape and style." Hazlitt takes up this theme in his essay "On Living to One's-Self," in which he speaks of Keats as one for whom such abuse "proved too much . . . and stuck like a barbed arrow in his heart. Poor Keats! What was sport to the town, was death to him. Young, sensitive, delicate, he was like 'A bud bit by an envious worm, / Ere he could spread his sweet leaves to the air, / Or dedicate his beauty to the sun'—and unable to endure the miscreant cry and idiot laugh, withdrew to sigh his last breath in foreign climes." He is quoting Romeo's father on his lovesick son (1:1:157)—and if Romeo gets taunted in the play for being unmanned by love, the effeminacy of Keats's character receives fresh credit for Victorians reading his love letters. Swinburne, for one, sneers that "a manful kind of man or even a manly sort of boy, in his love-making or in his suffering, will not howl and snivel after such a lamentable fashion."[21]

Even sympathy for Keats, as Swinburne implies, may itself be read as unmanly. When a friend remarked to Carlyle that Milnes's

Life had "interested" him, Carlyle "retorted, 'That shows you to be a soft-horn!' "[22] This easy sarcasm in no small part reflects the way Keats had become the property of female readers. The myth of the poet who "burst a blood vessel on reading a savage attack on his 'Endymion' . . . and died in Rome as a consequence" was routinely rehearsed in women's journals, such as *The Ladies' Companion* (from which I quote), while the image of the lovely genius too refined for long life gained prestige with his female biographers: Frances Mary Owen closes her study with a stanza of *Adonais:* "He is a portion of the loveliness / Which once he made more lovely . . . bursting in its beauty and its might / From trees and beasts and men into the Heaven's light." And Dorothy Hewlett titles her 1937 biography *Adonais: a Life of John Keats.* As MacGillivray remarks, the story of Keats's frailty and unhappy end was made to order for "the popular Victorian and feminine ideal of the unhappy and beautiful youth of genius."[23] All those expressions of "poor Keats!" evoked responses conventionally deemed "feminine," activating impulses to pity, nurture, and protect. *Victoria Magazine* concludes its essay by exclaiming "What shall we say of the malicious, the utterly brutal criticism, the hand of the cloddish boy tearing the myriad-hued fragile butterfly to fragments! No words can express the loathing every honest educated Englishman must feel for the ruffian tasks which inaugurated a long career of prosperity for the two Quarterlies." Keats, the fragile butterfly, is implicitly cast as the wronged female, whose honor begs for all Englishmen's defense; in Mrs. Oliphant's account, he is unmanned as a defenseless child, a "poor young poet . . . savagely used by the censors of literature."

These motions are sympathetic, to be sure, but their effect was to credit the image of Keats as needing such intercession—one fulfilled by his most famous female biographer, Amy Lowell, who pauses to exclaim on one occasion, "Poor little shaver, so pitiably unable to cope with his first great sorrow," and on another, to vilify the reviewers as "first-class cads."[24] George Ford nearly understates the case when he reports that "For some women readers, the story of Keats's supposed extreme weakness had a sort of attraction." We find no better proof than Mrs. Oliphant's essay on Keats for her *Literary History:*

> He turned from the confusions of his own age, which he had neither strength nor inclination to fathom. . . . He was not robust enough for political strife, or to struggle as his contemporaries were doing with noisy questions about the Regent's morals or manners, or the corruptions of the state. It was so much easier and more delightful to escape into the silvery brightness. . . . poetry had become his chief object in life. Those whom life endows more abundantly with other interests may play with their inspiration, feeling towards that

divine gift as, according to Byron, men do toward a scarcely stronger passion—

> "Man's love is of man's life a thing apart,
> 'Tis woman's whole existence."

This was the case of Keats in respect to the heavenly gift. . . . In poetry his was the woman's part—

With no apologies for (and perhaps no consciousness of) untoward implication, Oliphant reverently aligns Keats with the sensibilities of a Byronic heroine.[25]

4

> I am certain I have not a right feeling toward Women. . . . an obstinate Prejudice can seldom be produced but from a gordian complication of feelings, which must take time to unravell[ed] and care to keep unravelled—I could say a good deal about this
> —Keats to Bailey, 18 July 1818

Keats's repeated figuring in nineteenth-century discussions as feminine or effeminate is not an arbitrary or willful misreading. It reflects and reinscribes, with varying degrees of ideological pressure, the ambivalence in his own writing about the difference between "masculine" and "feminine." In his effort to create a poetic identity and win acceptance as a poet, he profoundly internalizes and struggles with social and psychological attitudes about gender: at times he is sensitive to tendencies in himself susceptible to interpretation as feminine; at other times, and with more irritation, he imagines the masculine self being feminized or rendered effeminate by women exercising power and authority; and at still other times, he projects feminine figures as forces against manly self-possession and its social validator, professional maturity.

This dilemma is most clearly revealed in Keats's intense fascination with the feminine as the focus of male desire. It is significant that his famous simile for ideal poetic power is one that conflates sexual and visionary fulfillment, even as it supresses the feminine in the name of male consciousness: "The Imagination may be compared to Adam's dream—he awoke and found it truth."[26] To a degree unmatched by other male Romantic poets, Keats tends to represent ecstatic or visionary experience as an erotic encounter with a female or feminized figure; correspondingly, his deepest anxieties take shape in confrontations with power in a female form, or in separations from, losses of, or betrayals by a woman. In the early poems, various wish-fulfilling adventures of adolescent male imagination converge on sensuous nymphs and goddesses, and the larger plot of *Endymion* equates quest romance with erotic adventure. In the crucial post-*Endymion* sonnet on *King Lear*, "Romance" itself is a woman, and although her charms are antithetical to the literary tradition Keats hopes to join, it is telling that romantic love infuses the three poems for which the 1820 volume is named, *Lamia, Isabella,* and *The Eve of St. Agnes.*

Yet if the feminine represents fulfillment, it is often fugitive, elusive, or untrustworthy, and many of Keats's letters write his life as an allegory of sexual uncertainty. His sense of powerlessness in the politics of desire impels him at times to counter with defensive contempt and condescension: the "generallity of women," he writes, "appear to me as children to whom I would rather give a Sugar Plum than my time" (*KL* 1:104). Admiration is limited chiefly, sometimes exclusively, to physical attributes: when Fanny Brawne "uttered a half complaint once" that Keats seemed to love only her "Beauty" (*KL* 2:275), he protests, "I cannot conceive any beginning of such love as I have for you but Beauty. . . . so let me speak of you [sic] Beauty" (*KL* 2:127). The obverse of this aesthetic is contempt for men overpowered by the otherness of female beauty. Having tran- scribed a "fine" misogynist diatribe from *Anatomy of Melancholy* detailing all "such errors or imperfections of boddy [sic] or mind" the admiring "Lover" will overlook in his "Mistress," Keats remarks, "I would give my favou[r]ite leg to have written this as a speech in a Play: with what effect could [the right actor] pop-gun it at the pit!" (*KL* 2:191–92). This is a provocative trade: a favorite leg for the effective verbal weapon against the felt power of female physical allure.

It is revealing that the very texts that show men subjecting women to the control of the male gaze frequently involve figures of male vulnerability. When, for instance, we hear the poet of "Ode on Melancholy" urge men to treat women's anger as a rich spectacle— "if thy mistress some rich anger shows, / Emprison her soft hand, and let her rave, / And feed deep, deep upon her peerless eyes"—we may think that the poem is prescribing an aesthetic ideology that denies woman's subjectivity with willful restraint. But the real danger, it turns out, is the aesthete's self-cancelling devotion to a sensibility gendered as feminine: by the poem's close, it is "She," "Veiled Melancholy," who is serene and self-contained, and the male suitor who is appropriated and desubstantialized: "His soul shall taste the sadness of her might, / And be among her cloudy trophies hung". These figures of erotic entrapment and masculine self-dissolution are repeated in Keats's protests to Fanny Brawne: "Ask yourself my love whether you are not very cruel to have so entrammelled me, so destroyed my freedom" (*KL* 2:123).

"La Belle Dame sans Merci" is a suggestive staging of these erotic politics, succinctly encoding Keats's characteristic ambivalences in the contradictory signals of the title and playing these out in the ballad itself. There is, on the one hand, a climactic revelation of female treachery: the Knight's report that in the dream that followed lovemaking, "pale kings, and princes too, / Pale warriors" announce in concert, "La belle dame sans merci / Hath thee in thrall!"—their "starv'd lips" seeming in retrospect to prefigure his present depletion, their "horrid warning" confirmed by his present state. Yet the total account defeats univocal judgment. Keats allows certain details of the Knight's narrative to suggest that if the lady had a hidden design on him, he, too, was a wielder of designs: no sooner had he met her than he courted her with flowery bindings of his own ("I made a garland for her head, / And bracelets too, and fragrant zone"), claimed possession of her ("I set her on my pacing steed"), and, figuratively repeating these motions, translated her words into terms to satisfy his own desire: "And sure in language strange she said— / I love thee true." These intentional actions cast "La belle dame sans merci," in effect, less as the culpable betrayer of men's desire than as a figure defined by men's branding as "feminine" whatever urges their withdrawal from the duties coded in the poem's other important name: "knight at arms."[27] It is significant that the chorus who identifies the lady as "La Belle Dame sans Merci"—kings, princes, warriors, knight— are representative figures of a patriarchal order defined by quest, battle, conquest, and government, and secured by rejection of the indulgences the Knight associates with her, namely a zone of erotic luxury, sensuality, and near infantile pleasure.

The gendering of such conflict may be read in earlier poems as well, where the feminine, typically nymph or goddess, inhabits a world in isolation from, or on an arc of development prior to, adult demands: that "strength of manhood" that "must pass" such recesses of joy for "a nobler life" of "agonies" and "strife," as "Sleep and Poetry" puts it (163, 122–24), or as Keats's famous conceit of life as a Mansion of Many Apartments maps, and genders, this passage, the "grand march" that begins only as the "Chamber of Maiden Thought" dissolves (*KL* 1:281–82). Even Endymion's conflation of erotic with visionary success in Cynthia, the "completed form of all completeness" (1:606), tests certain critical perspectives: the temptation to retreat from the social demands of adult life gets projected, here and elsewhere, as entrapment by the supernatural and the feminine, while the need to punish (or at least judge) this impulse is suggested by the way Keats typically threatens the male lover with betrayal to a fatally forlorn state.[28] We see similar trouble in *Lamia*, where erotic fascination competes, in disastrous consequence, with the claims of "proper" manly life.

The tension between desire and self-sufficiency that drives all these plots, and seeks expression as sexual allegory, also appears, not surprisingly, in Keats's language for his vocation. If his "chief poet[s]" and presiders are men (Homer, Shakespeare, Milton, Wordsworth), it is significant that "Poesy" itself is frequently figured as a female "other," and one not always susceptible to petition or appropriation. Sometimes she appears as the hostile arbiter of the poet's desire, as in Moneta's challenges to the dreamer of *The Fall of Hyperion;* sometimes the politics of courtship are reversed so that the poet can vent his hostility, degrading the feminine figure that focuses his desire, or portraying her as a flirt whose attentions prove as inconstant as they are potent. These figurings are largely conventional, of course, but Keats shows himself attracted to them, and experiencing their implications, in a uniquely intense and eroticized way. We see the consequences of this investment in the language with which he surrounds Fanny Brawne, speaking of her both as a "dearest love" and a negative muse, a force against self-possession and an object of deepest suspicion. His projection of his felt powerlessness as her power is often cast, revealingly, in terms that pose her as a threat to the psychic integrity needed to write: "it seems to me that a few more moments thought of you would uncrystallize and dissolve me— I must not give way to it—but turn to my writing again—if I fail I shall die hard—O my love, your lips are growing sweet again to my fancy—I must forget them" (*KL* 2:142).[29]

Keats's ambivalent negotiations with the feminine as "other" are intensified by his uncertain evaluations of those aspects of his own sensibility that he or others represent as feminine. The issue animates his statements about his "poetical Character." His famous claim to write with "no self . . . no identity" (*KL* 1:387) implicates gender, for not only does this ideal cooperate with the advice of those arbiters of conduct such as Mrs. Sanderford, who urge women to "avoid egotism,"[30] but Keats himself is inclined to distinguish "camelion" flexibility of imagination from the character of "Men of Power," who "have a proper self" (*KL* 1:184). Indeed, the "camelion" poet may transcend male identity, having "as much delight in conceiving an Iago as an Imogen," in cogitating on Saturn as on Ops (*KL* 1:387). Even in nonpoetical delights, Keats admits his divergence from standard figures of manliness: he enjoys "a sort of temper indolent and supremely careless," a state he calls "effeminacy" (*KL* 2:78). And he speculates to a friend about the value of being passive, more "the flower than the Bee," asking, "who shall say between Man and Woman which is the most delighted?" Using standard codes of gender, Keats cogitates on the value of being the Woman: "let us open our leaves like a flower and be passive and receptive—budding patiently under the eye of Apollo and taking hints from eve[r]y noble insect that favors us with a visit" (*KL* 1:232).

Keats often finds it necessary to circumscribe this playful androgyny. If he worries that the object-oriented sympathy of "camelion" imagination may leave him, as a subjective power, "an[ni]hilated . . . among Men" (KL 1:387), we can see a desire to keep a place "among Men" even in the flower-and-bee scenario sketched above. He turns to a second analogy that redeems passivity from the suggestion of emasculation and powerlessness: "it is more noble to sit like Jove tha[n] to fly like Mercury—let us not therefore go hurrying about and collecting honey-bee like, buzzing here and there impatiently" (KL 1:232). It is the busy boy Mercury who seems less manly than the passive, serenely self-possessed Jove. This recovery of the masculine may also be read in the letter about "temper indolent": this state of "effeminacy," Keats makes certain to report, had a manly origin—he is nursing a black eye from a fight with a butcher. But even these alignments are unstable. Keats closes the meditation on Jove, confessing, "all this is a mere sophistication, however it may neighbour to any truths, to excuse my own indolence—so I will not deceive myself that Man should be equal with jove—but think himself very well off as a sort of scullion-Mercury or even a humble Bee"— implying that he identifies more with boyish busyness than with manly patience, before he abandons the issue altogether: "It is [no] matter whether I am right or wrong either one way or another" (KL 1:233).

These musings about the ambiguous boundaries between masculine and feminine are confined to friends and family. More pressing is Keats's vulnerable sense of masculinity in relation to the social world at large. He is acutely aware that his physical stature does not fill the normative figure of adult manly prowess. In the gaze of the other, especially "Womankind," he is "Mister John Keats five feet hight" (KL 1:342), "quite the little Poet" (KL 2:61), a "versifying Pet-lamb" (KL 2:116), a "pet-lamb in a sentimental farce" ("Ode on Indolence"), or "taken for nothing" at all (KL 1:291)—each a notable exception to Woolf's famous remark that women typically serve "as looking-glasses possessing the magic and delicious power of reflecting the figure of man at twice its natural size."[31] Keats's inverse fate presses in his psyche against hopes of success both as poet and lover, roles he frequently equates with or makes contingent on one another. "Had I a man's fair form, then might my sighs [a rueful pun on "size"?] . . . find thy gentle heart; so well / Would passion arm me for the enterprize: / But ah! I am no knight," he laments in a sonnet for his inaugural volume of 1817. He repeats these terms in another of its poems, "Calidore:" Sir Gondibert, "a man of elegance, and stature tall," tells his tales of "knightly deeds"—"how the strong of arm / Kept off dismay, and terror, and alarm / From lovely woman"— with "such manly ardour" that courtship seems simultaneous: "each damsel's hand" is ready for a kiss between syllables. Keats himself will sometimes affect such worldliness. To express frustrations about writing, he imagines a sexual drama that converts failure to woo the coy muse, poetry, into the cocky confidence of a suitor well versed in courtship ritual: "I know not why Poetry and I have been so distant lately I must make some advances soon or she will cut me entirely" (*KL* 2:74).

The anxiety is transparent through the wit, however, and as these figures of courtship and knightly prowess imply, Keats is sensitive to the function of class prejudice in his unmanning: "You see what it is to be under six foot and not a lord," he grumbles; "My name with the literary fashionables is vulgar—I am a weaver boy to them" (*KL* 2:61; 2:186). He counters by having certain of his poetic speakers affect the pose of the masculine aristocrat—one who, with fashionable weariness, regards the pursuit of fame as beneath him: "Fame," he writes knowingly, is a "wayward girl" who is "coy / To those who woo her with too slavish knees"; even if won, she proves to be the goddess of "a fierce miscreed," "a Gipsey . . . A Jilt" who "fever[s]" the man who would possess her (2:104–5). "I equally dislike the favour of the public with the love of a woman," Keats claims; "they are both a cloying treacle to the wings of independence" (*KL* 2:144).

These poses of masculine condescension to a femininely figured literary and erotic marketplace are fueled by Keats's hostility to women as readers and ratifiers of his petitions for acceptance.[32] He bristles at the thought of himself and his writing subject to real as well as figurative feminine favor: he "detest[s]" the prospect of "Women . . . tak[ing] a snack or Luncheon of Literary scraps" (*KL* 1:163) and, adamant about resisting their power over his own texts, he boldly claims that the erotic wit of *The Eve of St. Agnes* is not meant for them. When Richard Woodhouse, the legal and literary advisor to his publisher, worried that this poem might be "unfit for ladies" because no assurances are given about Porphyro's marriage to Madeline (he thinks Keats is affecting the manner of the under-six-foot Lord Byron, "The 'Don Juan' style of mingling up sentiment & sneering"), Keats retorted that "he does not want ladies to read his poetry: that he writes for men" (*KC* 2:163). Significantly, when Keats thinks about selling out—that is, writing for journals while he awaits honorable literary success—he imagines that to offer his talents thus ("any thing for sale") is to become a female commodity of the most reduced kind: "Yea I will traffic," he says in rueful and contemptuous solidarity with the streetwalker.[33]

5

> We cannot estimate the relation of Keats to his predecessors and successors without also estimating the state of manners, knowledge, religion, and politics in his age.
> —W. J. Courthope, "Keats' Place in English Poetry"

Despite his assertions against the feminine, Keats the poet continued to be read by Victorian critics as one whose "passive part of intellect, the powers of susceptibility and appreciation" showed that "masculine energy . . . in him either existed deficiently, or had not time for its full development."[34] Yet if de Vere's midcentury review of Milnes's *Life* (from which I quote), could speak dispassionately about male minds "in a feminine mould," by the 1880's, when Colvin's *Keats* was being reviewed, the stakes concerning gender were clearly different, registering widespread concern about the erosion of manly character and the consequences for the fate of civilization in general. The issue was acute in literary and art criticism, not only because refinement in such culture was desirable finishing for young ladies but also, and not coincidentally, because this was the culture most suspected of effeminizing men. An index of that concern is revealed by Patmore, whose review of Milnes was published the same year as Courthope's, above. Patmore divides poets, by gender, "into two distinct classes" of sensibility. Although he concedes "a border-line at which these occasionally become confused," about Keats he was certain: "In the first class, which contains all the greatest poets, with Shakespeare at their head, intellect predominates. . . . Such poets are truly spoken of as masculine. In the other class—in which Keats stands as high as any other, if not higher . . . beauty and sweetness, is the essential, the truth and power of intellect and passion the accident. These poets are, without any figure of speech, justly described as feminine." Patmore claims he is being merely analytical, not prosecutory, and insists that a "feminine" poet is "not necessarily" an "effeminate" one, but the adverb is carefully weighted, and the insinuation in his next clause is not difficult to discern: feminine poets "are separated from the first class by a distance as great as that which separates a truly manly man from a truly womanly woman."[35]

The uneasiness one senses in Patmore's gendering of Keats erupts as a cultural and political crisis in Courthope's review. Keats's "vivid intensity," he writes, reflects "certain tendencies of modern civilization—its softness, its luxury, its *ennui*," and reveals how "in the absorbing pursuit of ideal beauty, men forget [that] this kind of lotus-eating takes . . . the pith and manliness out of the national idiom."[36] Courthope's diagnosis repeats many other such, most famously, Buchanan's widely circulated tract of 1872, *The Fleshly School of Poetry*, which warned that the "male" character of the "body social" was being "threatened by the singers of the falsetto school . . . male, female, or other." That he named names, chiefly Swinburne and Rossetti, but also Keats, as a type of a "falsetto voice," suggests the increasing importance of literary criticism as one of the arenas in which social conduct was being legislated.[37] Just as nervously guarding the male body social was the *Edinburgh* which, the year before, implied, none too subtly, that Swinburne's poetic principles posed a fatal threat to "all existing order" in "art, literature, and civilisation itself." As for literature, Alfred Austin had already issued a lament in 1869 that "we have, as novelists and poets, only women or men with womanly deficiencies, steeped in the feminine temper of the times," incapable of producing literature "worthy of men." And Charles Kingsley, an apostle of "Christian manliness," noted symptoms well before that. Writing for *Fraser's* in 1853, he derided the age as "an effeminate one," evident for him in its willingness "to pardon the lewdness of the gentle and sensitive vegetarian" Shelley, while criticizing that of Byron, a "sturdy peer, proud of his bullneck and his boxing, who kept bears and bull-dogs, drilled Greek ruffians at Missolonghi, and 'had no objection to a pot of beer'; and who might, if he had reformed, have made a gallant English gentleman."[38]

It is true that in this widespread public agitation about the erosion of manliness, there were islands of tolerance for manly tears. The culture of mourning sometimes went to fetishistic extremes, and sometimes on literary occasions alone: Englishmen famously wept over the deaths of Little Nell and Paul Dombey; Francis Jeffrey, a reviewer often impatient with romantic excesses, confessed to Dickens, "I could not *reserve* my tears . . . they flowed and ebbed at your bidding," and about the death of Paul Dombey, "Oh, my dear, dear Dickens! . . . I have so cried and sobbed over it last night, and again this morning; and . . . blessed and loved you for making me." As Richard Altick points out, however, this "romantic emotionalism" was licensed only within a larger "ideal of 'manliness' according to which pain was to be concealed and grief suppressed". And within a few decades, even these indulgences were being restricted by codes of conduct, for men and boys alike, set explicitly against such "feminine" indulgences.[39]

Even in the Dombey decade, Carlyle was offering an influential set of exempla for containing the feminine in a lecture series on heroes, heroism, and the heroic. Though sometimes noting qualities conventionally deemed feminine, he always stressed the manly governance of the whole. So if he asks about Dr. Johnson, "was there ever soul more tenderly affectionate, loyally submissive to what was really higher than he?"—the sort of sentence Mrs. Ellis could write about the duties of the wives of England—he also insists on Johnson's "rugged pride of manhood and self-help," and the "nobleness and manfulness" therein evinced. These lectures, moreover, provided the larger containment of an explicitly masculine ethic and community: "Great Men, their manner of appearance in our world's business," and their place in that "divine relation" that "unites a Great Man to other men" (as the inaugural lecture puts it). When Carlyle turns to "The Hero as Poet," he further defends against any suggestion of feminizing influence (the suspicion that a poet is only a "beautiful verse-maker") with terms that endow him with "power of intellect," and reinforce that power with a vigorously phallic vocabulary. Thus, like Prophets of old, heroic Poets "have penetrated . . . into the sacred mystery of the Universe"; Dante "pierces . . . down to the heart of Being . . . seizes the very type of a thing" with "fiery emphasis and depth." That energy is also to be read in their heroic disdain for the realms with which Keats was habitually associated in Victorian letters: "unrealities,—clouds, froth . . . there was no footing for them but on firm earth."[40]

If Keats exemplifies enervated manliness in orthodox Victorian criticism, it is also true that the debates about his gender agitate and interact with ideological uncertainties in the culture at large. As G. M. Matthews remarks, Keats is frequently judged in contexts that demonstrate a "sort of socio-sexual revulsion," whose "origin seems to lie in the disturbance created by a deep response to Keats's poetic sensuality in conflict with a strong urge towards sexual apartheid."[41] Two basic reactions may be charted. One could, like Patmore and Courthope, regender Keats, alienating what he evoked to the sphere of the feminine, and using his example to degrade the feminine in men. Or one could embrace Keats as a way of challenging and enlarging socially restricted definitions of manhood. What I would like to do now is review specific and interelated features of these Victorian debates and suggest their bearing on the project to secure stable and legible codes of manly conduct.

As the tradition of *Adonais* reveals, Keats's status as a negative exemplum of manliness acquires its clearest outline and most vicious tone in remarks about his general sensibility: frailty, thy name is Keats. Courthope makes the issue explicitly one of gender: Keats shows how the "pursuit of mere Beauty of Form . . . involves a relaxation of all the nerves and fibres of manly thought, the growth of affectation, and the consequent encouragement of all the emasculating influences that produce swift deterioration and final decay."[42] He is speaking of Keats's "struggle to get absolutely free from the world of sense," but even the sensuous character of Keats's imagination provoked charges of unmanliness. If Byron's sensuality was linked to sexual adventure, and Tennyson's sensuous luxuries to the probings of adult moral intelligence, the palpable regressiveness of Keatsian luxury was seen as infantile, girlish, or at best, puerile. W. M. Rossetti, for example, complains about "affected or self-willed diction" that tends "to the namby-pamby," and Alexander Smith finds *Endymion* a telling document of Keats writing "in a style of babyish effeminacy about 'plums / Ready to melt between an infant's gums' " (2:450–51). That he does not note Keats has this sight make Endymion himself "impatient in embarrassment" (2:430) suggests the potent effect of "these and lines of a similar nauseous sweetness" (Smith again) in obscuring Keats's ambivalence about such excess.[43] Carlyle, in fact, felt able to sum Keats up with the comment that he "wanted a world of treacle," and Swinburne, adding to his case against the love letters, accused Keats of writing "some of the most vulgar and fulsome doggerel ever whimpered by a vapid and effeminate rhymster in the sickly stage of whelphood." Renewing attention to lines *Blackwood's* ridiculed in 1818—Endymion's call to Cynthia as a "known unknown *from whom his being sips such darling (!) essence*" (2:194)— Swinburne sneers, with his own italics and punctuation, that these "make one understand the source of the most offensive imputations or insinuations levelled against the writer's manhood." Arnold nearly regenders Keats in his disdain for those who "worship" him "as the poet of 'Light feet, dark violet eyes, and parted hair, / Soft dimpled hands, white neck, and creamy breast' "; he is quoting one of Keats's girl-raptured poems of 1817, but the effect of his syntax is to make these girlish attributes seem Keats's own.[44]

If contradictions are symptoms of ideological pressure, it is revealing that Keats's effeminacy could be noted in terms of deficiency as well as excess: his perceived relapse, or even willful escape, from the intellectual demands of manhood. That these strictures were defined with unequivocal consistency in conduct books from the 1790s to the 1880s made any reference to Keats's failings in this respect easy to decode in the schemes of gender: he always seemed more female than male. Alongside the famous tracts such as Ruskin's "Of Queen's Gardens" and numerous essays devoted explicitly to the characters of men and women, literary criticism was assuming a place as a species of conduct book. So when the *National Review* observed that Tennyson had the "reflective gift of the mature man," while Keats was only an "impulsive, original, and refined boy," Keats was doubly unmanned: not only by comparison to "the mature man," but by showing those "habits of frivolousness, and trifling enjoyment" about which Gisborne's manual, among others, cautioned women (who, Hannah More tells her readers, "do not so much generalize their ideas as men, nor do their minds seize a great subject with so large a grasp").[45] Patmore, an arbiter of conduct as well as poetry, cites the evidence of the former when he states that "In Keats the man had not the mastery"; because "a thing of beauty was . . . the supreme and only good he knew or cared to know," he failed to exercise "the manly virtue of the vision of truth." Hopkins at first argued the point, telling Patmore he did not see why "sensuality," though a fault, made a poet "feminine." But when he reread Keats, he had to agree about this particular conjunction: "It is impossible not to feel with weariness how his verse at every turn is abandoning itself to unmanly and enervating luxury!" His gendering could find no surer support than in Mrs. More's discrimination of male and female intellectual capacities: "the female . . . want[s] steadiness in her intellectual pursuits," while the male "will most certainly attain his object by direct pursuit, by being less exposed to the seductions of extraneous beauty."[46]

Whatever else was contested in these codes, the value of "a manly firmness and decision of character," to quote Hazlitt's essay on effeminacy, remains constant. "I like a person who knows his own mind and sticks to it; who sees at once what is to be done in given circumstances and does it," Hazlitt says at the outset. Just as constant was the perception of Keats's deficiency, in literature as in life. Half a century after Hazlitt, W. M. Rossetti remarks, in the last paragraph of his generally dispeptic biography, that in most of Keats's poems one hears "an adolescent and frequently a morbid tone, marking want of manful thew and sinew and of mental balance." Courthope finds Keats lacking the "masculine method" of representation that characterizes the great order of Homer, Aristophanes, Horace, Virgil, Dante, Milton, and Shakespeare: "All these men faced Nature in a masterful spirit, making imagination the servant of religion and reason," while Keats never approached the "masculine style required for the drama, the epic, or even for a stirring tale of sustained romantic action."[47]

That weakness was obvious to several readers in the very character of the Keatsian hero. If "masculine power of intellect," in Patmore's representation, is "the tenacity of spirit which cleaves to and assimilates the truth when it is found, and which steadfastly refuses to be blown about by every wind of doctrine and feeling," Keats could offer only negative examples. In their "pining away for love," his heroes are indistinguishable from his heroines: "They might all be of the same sex; the men are as effeminate as the women," Courthope complains, finding in this equation "that supine and feminine impressibility which Keats supposes to be the mark of the poetic character." "Physical debility," he decides, is the only excuse for this "unblushingly-avowed preference for the feminine over the masculine motive of composition"—that is, "the emotion of an ideal love-scene" over "*action* of any kind." Even Colvin concedes that "there is at all times a touch, not the wholesomest, of effeminacy and physical softness" in Keats's heroes, whom "the influence of passion" is apt to "fever and unman"—a fate that he, too, read in Keats himself: "a helpless and enslaved submission of all the faculties to love proved . . . to be a weakness of his own nature." In an age when Ruskin could separate the "characters" of men and women with the statement that "man, in his rough work in the open world, must encounter all peril and trial" by which he is "*always* hardened," Keats routinely failed the test.[48]

That failure was also discerned in the otherworldly orientation of Keats's imagination, his turn from or unsuitability for "the open world"—the sphere in which manly character visibly proves itself. If *Pocket Magazine* noted matter-of-factly in 1821 that Keats "was not bold or brave enough to encounter the struggles of life, and he shrunk instinctively from the conflict," Victorian assessments were sterner. Courthope found Keats "unaffected by the social influences of his age" and indifferent "to the actual strife of men." To Hopkins, Keats's retreat from "great causes" to live "in mythology and fairyland the life of a dreamer" betrayed, or at least held "in abeyance," the "distinctively masculine powers" of his mind and "the manly virtues" of his character. De Quincey mocked the "fantastic effeminacy" of *Endymion,* and turned Keats's "camelion" poetics against him: "As a man, and viewed in relation to social objects, Keats was nothing." Keats's most emphatic regendering in these terms issued from Louis Étienne, who found him lacking "cette *manliness* dont le premier effet est de sortir du rêve stérile et de la plainte efféminée, d'accepter ce qu'elle ne peut [pas] changer et d'en tirer le meilleur parti possible."[49] William Howitt, denying that Keats's "unworldliness was effeminacy," tried to argue for the steady growth of power, "vigour and acumen" in the poetry; but he nearly undid his case at the start by introducing Keats as one of the "resplendent messengers" of "infinite heaven," for which "neither ours nor any other history can furnish a specimen more beautiful." Oscar Wilde, of course, welcomed this ethereal character: "Into the sacred house of Beauty the true artist will admit nothing . . . harsh or disturbing, nothing about which men argue," he says of aesthetic ideology; for him, Keats, with his "unerring sense of beauty, and . . . recognition of a separate realm for the imagination," was "the pure and serene artist, the forerunner of the Pre-Raphaelite school." Such praise, obviously, did not settle the issue of Keats's gender, for the aesthetes were also accused of effeminacy. Wilde's values, along with the patently erotic meditations on Keats in his poetry (he "lifted up his hymeneal curls from out the poppy-seeded wine, / With ambrosial mouth had kissed my forehead, clasped the hand of noble love in mine") and at Keats's grave (like Guido's martyred Saint Sebastian, "a lovely brown boy, with crisp, clustering hair and red lips") only underscored existing questions.[50]

6

It has been said that his poetry was affected and effeminate. I can only say that I never encountered a more manly and simple young man

—Barry Cornwall

There is a parallel discourse in nineteenth-century assessments of Keats's manhood that concerns his physical appearance. We find defenses of his manliness so conspicuous as to raise anew the doubts they intend to settle, or descriptions informed by terms sufficiently androgynous and attitudes sufficiently ambiguous as to suggest Keats's accidental power of affecting observers of both sexes with qualities usually deemed feminine. Take the issue of his voice. Bailey recalls it as "sweet-toned . . . 'an excellent thing' in *man*, as well as 'in woman' " (he is echoing Lear on Cordelia's voice—"ever sweet and low"). Haydon remembers Keats reciting the "exquisite ode to Pan . . . in a low, half chaunting, trembling tone" and the "Ode to a Nightingale" "with a tremulous undertone . . . extremely affecting!" Milnes decides to steady that tremble in his *Life* and emphasize the low tone: his Keats has a "deep grave voice". Colvin compromises, giving Keats a voice "rich and low," adding that "when he joined in discussion it was usually with an eager but gentle animation"; for credit, he repeats Milnes in citing a friend of Keats from medical school, who reports that he "never observed the tears nor the broken voice which are indicative of extreme sensibility."[51]

The chief subject of these discussions are the visual impressions of Keats: his stature, his countenance, his facial contour, his hair, his eyes. If it is commonplace to distinguish men from women, as Gisborne's manual does, by men's "robustness of constitution" and larger corporeal frame, the various framings of Keats show a clear sensitivity to his aberrance, and corresponding attempts to picture a more manly shape.[52] Here is Hunt, for example:

> He was under the middle height; and his lower limbs were small in comparison with the upper, but neat and well-turned. His shoulders were very broad for his size. . . . Every feature was at once strongly cut, and delicately alive . . . the chin was bold, the cheeks sunken; the eyes mellow and glowing; large, dark and sensitive. At the recital of a noble action, or a beautiful thought, they would suffuse with tears, and his mouth trembled. His hair, of a brown colour, was fine, and hung in natural ringlets.

These sentences, published in 1828, recur almost verbatim in Hunt's midcentury *Autobiography*.[53] Charles Brown, eager to answer *Blackwood's* image of Keats as "effeminate," is more defensive, reporting to Milnes that Keats "was small in stature, well proportioned, compact in form, and, though thin, rather muscular;—one of many who prove that manliness is distinct from height and bulk" (*KC* 2:57–58). Milnes's *Life*, accordingly, stressed this more manly Keats and, following suit, most subsequent characterizations call attention to the broad shoulders supported by the small frame.

But overall impressions remain equivocal. Hunt's entry for Gorton's 1828 *Biographical Dictionary*, though eagerly recording how "handsome" Keats was, dwells lovingly on his "remarkably beautiful hair curling in ringlets"—making the "Keats, with young tresses and thoughts" in *The Feast of the Poets* (1832) seem virile by comparison.[54] Even Brown, without meaning to, cooperates: "whenever [Keats] spoke, or was, in any way, excited, the expression of the lips was so varied and delicate, that they might be called handsome," he reports (*KC* 2:57); his summary adjective seems cautiously to assign a male character, but not necessarily—women, too, could be called "handsome" (Keats himself says he will not "spend any time with Ladies unless they are handsome" [*KL* 2:20])—and nothing before that in Brown's sentence anticipates anything decidedly masculine. Milnes's alertness to the issue is evident in the way he surrounds his report of Keats's physical character with anecdotes about boyhood scrappiness and seeming destiny for military glory. Yet this strategy seems only to enable greater enthusiasm for impressions so contained: "His eyes, then, as ever, were large and sensitive, flashing with strong emotions or suffused with tender sympathies." Later biographers all tangle with the question of Keats's manly appearance, but scarcely normalize the anomalies. James Russell Lowell dispassionately opts for Hunt's jumble of gender signals, while W. M. Rossetti tries for a cool synthesis of contraries: "Keats had an unusually small head, covered with copious auburn-brown ringlets. . . . his lower limbs also were small beyond the due proportion for his broad-shouldered and generally alert and vigorous-looking, though by no means tall, frame. His eyes were large, blue, and sensitive: his mouth likewise was singularly sensitive, combined with a certain pugnacious look of the full under-lip." Colvin decides on a kind of androgynous compromise that verges on near contradiction: his Keats is a "small, handsome, ardent-looking youth—the stature little over five feet; the figure compact and well-turned, with the neck thrust eagerly forward, carrying a strong and shapely head set off by thickly clustering gold-brown hair; the features powerful, finished, and mobile; the mouth rich and wide, with an expression at once combative and sensitive in the extreme."[55]

As the balance of Colvin's details suggest, these portraits dwell on Keats's head and facial features: almost every account offers an elaborate discussion of the shape of his face, the size and color of his eyes (hazel? black? brown? blue?), and the quality, style, and even shade of his hair (brown? brown-gold? auburn? red? lighter than Titian red? golden red? sunset-red?)—preoccupations which themselves bespeak and perpetuate a certain kind of feminizing attention. Colvin, in fact, provides a scholarly note in his appendix to settle these questions. Along with Hunt's rhapsodies, we have Bailey recalling that Keats's "hair was beautiful—a fine brown, rather than auburn," and adding dreamily that "if you placed your hand upon his head, the silken curls felt like the rich plumage of a bird," and Mrs. Procter remembering how "it fell in rich masses on each side his face" (*KC* 2:268, 158). The eyes capture equal attention. George recalls that they "moistened, and his lip quivered at the relation of any tale of generosity or benevolence of noble daring, or at sights of loveliness or distress." Haydon even proposes a feminine analogue: Keats's "eye had an inward look, perfectly divine, like a Delphian priestess who saw visions." (And Colvin quotes them all.) Joseph Severn, remembering "the almost flame-like intensity of Keats's eager glances when he was keenly excited or interested," also thinks of a feminine figure—"they were like the hazel eyes of a wild gipsy-maid in colour"—but then supplements this problematic association with a masculine character, "a peculiarly dauntless expression, such as may be seen on the face of some seamen."[56]

The inscription of gender in these details is more explicit yet in evaluations of Keats's facial contour. An apt index is provided by Donald Parson's book on portraits of Keats, which tells us that his face was "oval, rather than square and masculine," a discrimination that calls attention to the gender at once implied and evaded by the syntactic imbalance. Mrs. Procter, on whom Parson seems to have drawn, is less coy: she says that when she first met Keats she was struck by the fact that "his face had not the squareness of a mans, but [was] more like some womens faces I have seen"—an impression Bailey corroborated when he read it in Milnes's *Life:* "It is in the character of the countenance what Coleridge would call *femineity,*" he remarks. "He bore . . . much beauty of feature and countenance. The contour of his face was not square and angular, but circular and oval," he recalls, adding authoritatively, "this is the proper shape for a poet's head."[57] Rossetti seems less fanciful when, after familiar notes about the small head, ringlets, and "feminine" contour, he insists that the total effect is "eminently virile and gallant." Although he remains bothered by the want of "manly thew and sinew" in the poems, he decides, in his biography, to give the face of their author the best sort of nineteenth-century masculine prestige: "The whole aspect of the face is not greatly unlike Byron's."[58]

The issues that occupy the verbal portraits of Keats also shape paintings and sketches of him made from life, rendered in memory, or invented by fancy. One of the most feminine (Figure 1) is the pure fancy of a woman, Mary Newton, who gave Keats an aspect that reminds some of George Eliot. Mary Newton's father, Joseph Severn, is sometimes accused of effeminizing Keats with the 1817 life portrait of the fat-faced dreamer (Figure 2). This "Keats" was widely disseminated in biographies and critical studies; an engraving of it was the frontispiece for Milnes's *Life* in 1848 and it was the image most often affixed to editions of the poetry. The closest competitor, though much less in evidence, is a portrait from the 1830s by William Hilton, later engraved for Taylor and Walton's 1840–41 edition of Keats's *Poetical Works* (Figure 3).[59] Hilton had sketched Keats in chalk in 1819 or 1820 (Figure 4), rendering small eyes and a firm chin. His portrait, which he claimed was based on memory, does not really resemble this earlier sketch so much as it marries the sterner features of Haydon's even earlier life mask of 1816 (Figure 5), to Severn's pose, and converts the latter's fastidious neckware into a more rakishly Byronic accessory—even though Severn worried that he himself had "Byronized" or "poeticized" his subject a trifle.[60] Hilton's "Keats" conveys a somewhat more manly look: the face is more elongated and less fleshy, the brow lower, the cheekbones more pronounced and jawline firmer, the mouth less full, the chin stronger, the hair less curly and fussy, the eyes proportionally smaller, less wide-spaced and doe-like, the gaze a bit less dreamy and more directed. Yet the fact that the author of "The Daintiest of Poets" felt able to recommend this portrait as a "most interesting and agreeable picture of the poet in all his boylike beauty" indicates the degree to which Hilton's leaner "Keats" was still lacking unequivocal masculine definition.[61]

The sheer intransigence of the controversy about Keats's manhood suggests the depth of its involvement with disturbances in the social and psychological construction of gender in the nineteenth century. Attempts to shore up Keats's manhood were various, but never silenced the debate. Those who took up the issue in terms of class sought to free Keats from continuing charges of vulgarity and bad breeding by idealizing his humble origins or nobly praising the fine Georgian architecture of his schoolhouse, but critics on both sides of the Atlantic lampooned the futility of such efforts.[62] More direct tacks, such as Hunt's, noted the "prematurely masculine vein" in the sonnet on Chapman's Homer, the "manly acknowledgement" of "youthful faults" in the "Preface" to *Endymion,* and Keats's "manly submission" to his final sufferings. These points were echoed by everyone else, including Milnes, who quite consciously framed his *Life* to give the "impression" of Keats's "noble nature" and "manly heart," and to make an even stronger case than Hunt's for the "manly" character of the life: he reports Keats's boyhood pugnacity and "skill in all manly exercises," and treats these as prefigurations of the way the mature Keats, "at the mention of oppression or wrong, or at any calumny against those he loved," would rise "into grave manliness at once, [seeming] like a tall man." Much more than Hunt, Milnes stresses Keats's "bodily vigour" and the anecdotes by which it is "signalised," such as his "giving a severe drubbing to a butcher, whom he saw beating a little boy, to the enthusiastic admiration of a crowd of bystanders."[63]

Milnes had an important revisionary effect on public perception, one Bailey recognized immediately when he wrote to congratulate him for having done such "justice to the genius and character, the *manliness*" of Keats: "He had a soul of noble integrity. . . . his character was, in the best sense, manly," he assures Milnes, whose argument began to take hold. Quoting the "Preface" to *Endymion* in full in its review of Milnes's *Life*, *The Times* praised the "masculine strength" of this "honest declaration" of faults. De Vere, writing for the *Edinburgh*, opined that "when the poetic mood was not on him," Keats's "heart was full of manly courage," and Masson's piece in 1865 referred three times in its opening paragraph to Keats's "pugnacity." Colvin made sure to quote Bailey's remarks to Milnes in his English Men of Letters biography—the first to follow Milnes's—and, like him, he labored to establish in the early pages the "spirit of manliness and honour" already evident in Keats's boyhood pugnacity. Arnold, though deploring the "underbred and ignoble" lack of "constraint" in the love letters, expressed admiration for the "attitude towards the public" revealed in others: it is "that of a strong man, not of a weakling avid of praise, and meant to 'be snuff'd out by an article,' " he says, with a pointed allusion to and refutation of Byron's famous caricature. Yet there is a sense that the case had to be tried repeatedly, and with uncertain results. If W. M. Rossetti's sketch of 1872 seconds Bailey's gratitude to Milnes for having dispelled "once and forever" and "to the deep satisfaction of all who value manliness as a portion of the poetic character" the fable of Keats undone by harsh reviews, the biography he writes a few years later implies that Milnes may have protested too much: "Because he thrashed a butcher-boy, or was indignant at backbiting and meanness, we are not to credit [Keats] with an unmingled fund of that toughness which distinguishes the English middle class. The English middle-class man is not habitually addicted to writing an 'Endymion,' an 'Eve of St. Agnes,' or an 'Ode to Melancholy.' "[64]

7

> If Keats had not existed, the Victorians would have had
> to invent one
>
> —George Ford

Judgments about Keats do not simply displace him into the feminine "other," but suggest, by their very forcefulness, that the otherness against which nineteenth-century manliness was striving for definition involves a "feminine" sensed within male subjectivity itself,

Figure 1. Portrait of John Keats attributed to Mary Newton.

Figure 2. First miniature portrait of John Keats by Joseph Severn, 1818 or 1819. Courtesy of the National Portrait Gallery, London.

Figure 3. Portrait of John Keats by William Hilton. Courtesy of the National Portrait Gallery, London.

Figure 4. Engraving of John Keats after Hilton's chalk drawing by Charles Wass, 1819 or 1820.

Figure 5. Life mask of John Keats by Benjamin R. Haydon, 1816. Courtesy of the Keats Museum, London, and Methuen & Co., London.

disturbingly at odds with orthodox prescriptions of sensibility and conduct. One of the strongest suggestions of this involution is the fact that some of the most vigorous charges against Keats were advanced by men who themselves were characterized in the dominant discourses as effeminate: *Blackwood's* assigned Alexander Smith to the implicitly effeminate Spasmodic School, finding only one sonnet "manly and pathetic," and the case against Swinburne was put quite directly—for example, by Étienne, who, writing in 1867 about Keats and Swinburne, noted that the latter, too, "peut manquer de virilité." To clarify, he provided a generous translation of Hazlitt's "On Effeminacy" before closing his review with the exhortation to all English poets: "Soyez virile!"[65] Browning flatly judged Swinburne "effeminate"; Buchanan accused him of "sickliness and effeminacy," and the *Edinburgh* argued that Swinburne's work is "not virile or even feminine, but epicene," not "noble in the masculine or any other sense." It is significant that a (mangled) allusion to Keats helps frame the indictment: the poetry in question, reeking of "luxurious abandonment and corrupted passion," "smell[s] of 'all the sunburnt south' "—a conflation of the lines from "Ode to a Nightingale" in which the poet longs for "a draught of vintage . . . Tasting of . . . sunburnt mirth . . . a beaker full of the warm South."[66] Patmore, too, was subjected to such judgments, his "slip-slop vulgarities" branded by *Blackwood's* with charges as bad as, if not worse than, those which had smeared Keats: "the weakest inanity ever perpetrated in rhyme by the vilest poetaster of any former generation, becomes masculine verse when contrasted with the nauseous pulings of Mr. Patmore's muse." It was a sense of Patmore as "effeminate," in fact, that provoked Leslie Stephen to define the prevailing ideology: "Every man ought to be feminine, *i.e.*, to have quick and delicate feelings; but no man ought to be effeminate, *i.e.*, to let his feelings get the better of his intellect and produce a cowardly view of life and the world."[67]

That Keats's effeminacy was prosecuted by some who themselves were subject to such public judgment suggests his status as a text on which others could read and negotiate doubts about their own manly character and sexual orientation, as well as cultural attitudes. Indeed, Keats seems to have had a particular, unacknowledged value as a kind of test case for challenging normative codes and extending accepted senses of manliness to include qualities habitually marked as feminine. Even as he was charged with effeminacy, versions of the sensibility covered by that term, as has long been recognized, appear throughout Victorian poetry, while in art, Rossetti declared "supreme perfection" to be the "point of meeting" where the beauty of man and woman "are most identical."[68] Pre-Raphaelite images of Keatsian heroines as big-boned, strong-jawed women show one effect: Rossetti himself painted a large-framed, impassive Mnemosyne; Holman Hunt gave Madeline in his *Eve of St. Agnes* a physique matching Porphyro's, and even used this frame for languishing heroines, such as Isabella in *Isabella and the Pot of Basil*. Most notably, the Victorian Christ was emerging as an androgynous ideal: Tennyson admired the "man-woman" quality suggested by "the union of tenderness and strength," a type for Hallam's "manhood fused with female grace."[69] Similar terms were appearing in discussions of Keats: Hunt always insisted Keats was "manly and gentle," Colvin finds his Keats "conspicuous alike for manly spirit and sweetness," while Henry van Dyke, resisting Patmore's labelling of Keats as a "feminine poet," asks for a better account of the quality that provokes such judgment: "extreme sensitiveness is not an exclusive mark of femininity; it is found in men as often as in women."[70]

These androgynous markings of manliness have an important precedent in Keats's sense of the heart as "the teat from which the Mind or intelligence sucks its identity" in a process of "Soul-making" (*KL* 2:102). This figure of the heart as a feminine nurturer of masculine self-realization finds a correlative in the way some of his detractors discover in Keats a source of emotional knowledge—a sympathetic voice for impulses deemed unmanly, but still registered as psychic truth. Though Courthope, for example, scorns Keats's heroes, he is stirred by some of the heroines: "the absorbing grief of Isabella . . . awakes strong sympathy in the reader," he remarks, offering his own reader the stanzas about Isabella's pathological doting over the head of her murdered lover. Keats's exploration of such emotional extremes seems to have appealed to men such as Courthope: mediated by or ascribed to a female figure, these expressions of intense feeling offered access to a range of sensation normally condemned as unmanly, indeed emasculating. Arnold, too—whose public criticism is occupied, at times preoccupied, with manly character, and who in that mode tends to find Keats wanting—is implicated in numerous ways with these aspects of Keats's sensibility, and not always in terms of difference. Although he castigates Keats to Clough in 1848 for lacking a sufficiently strong "Idea of the world in order not to be prevailed over the world's multitudinousness," as the century wears on, he confesses a private receptivity to the quarrel of the mind with itself. From Milnes's *Life*—which confirmed many of his early judgments about Keats's immaturity—he copies at some length into his notebooks the letter in which Keats pities the adversity that plagued Burns's life ("Poor unfortunate fellow!") and derives from Keats a "true" suggestion, unacceptable to Victorian codes of manly fortitude, namely, that "out of suffering, there is no dignity, no greatness; that in the most abstracted pleasure there is no lasting happiness."[71]

8

> How can the woman be thought about outside of the Masculine /
> Feminine framework, *other* than as opposed to man, without being
> subordinated to a primordial masculine model? . . . How can
> difference as such be thought out as *non-subordinate* to identity?
> In other words, how can thought break away from the logic of
> polar opposition?
>
> —Shoshana Felman (1975)

The contests about Keats's gender do not subside at the end of
the century. Some, such as J. C. Shairp, persist in seeing Keats's
paganism as "destructive of true manliness"; Arthur Symons thinks
his sensibility twisted up with "unhealthy nerves" and "something
feminine"; and Sir William Watson, finding Keats's letters "infantine
prattle and babble" compared to the "profound and powerful spirit"
of Charlotte Brontë's, exiles him to a no-man's land "neither manly
nor properly boy-like." On the other side, Leon H. Vincent claims
the "virile intellectual health" of "the real man" is to be read in
the letters, which yield a "refreshing" view of "the masculinity of
this very robust young maker"; in the same issue of *Century Magazine*,
Kenyon West gives an account of Keats's scrappiness to show how
"In character he was strong and manly." George Saintsbury's study
not only denies that Keats was "effeminate" and "unmanly," but calls
him "a captain and leader of English poetry," giving this "manly
Englishman" the best sort of patriarchal credential, that of inaugu-
rating a genealogy as "the father . . . of every English poet born
within the present century."[72]

These polemics shift in the twentieth century almost entirely to
the fields of literary biography, criticism, and scholarship, but the
terms persist. Thus in the 1930s, we hear Douglas Bush speaking of
the "masculine and classic style of the sonnet on Chapman" being
"recaptured" in *Hyperion* after the "luscious, half feminine" poetry
of *Endymion*, "I stood tip-toe," and "Sleep and Poetry." The next
decade finds Hoxie Neale Fairchild admiring "the manly Dedication"
to *Endymion*, and J. R. MacGillivray pausing in the introduction to
his *Bibliography and Reference Guide* to affirm "Keats' perfectly
masculine nature," now being discerned in "his courage and sense
of humour, his developing emotional restraint . . . far more strict
than that of Hunt or Haydon. . . . his intellectual energy." Though
he notes an early "tendency toward effeminate gushing about the
delights of 'poesy' and suburban 'leafy luxuries,' " a "frequent quasi-
elegance of phrase, and an occasional jaunty vulgarity" in the poems
of 1815–16 [we may note the steady link of class and gender], he
welcomes the "more masculine and classical influence" Charles Cow-

den Clarke brought to bear in the early autumn of 1816, revealed in particular by the sonnet on Chapman's Homer.[73]

Lionel Trilling devotes four pages of his 1951 edition of the letters to Keats's manliness, and the topic is still alive in the biographies of W. J. Bate and Aileen Ward. Bate offers the usual reports of his manly character, calling attention to an early "revelation of [Keats's] virility" in Mathew's recollections and the "virile, penetrating idiom" and "masculine strength of language" Keats discovered in Chapman's Homer. Ward, embellishing an early report in Milnes's *Life* about an uncle who was a naval officer, sets the stage for her Keats with a scenario of the threat of military invasion that hung over England in 1803: "In this time of mobilization and suspense, John Keats confronted an anxious future of his own—the traditional first trial of manhood in England. He was to be sent away to . . . the Clarke academy at Enfield," which had trained the uncle, "a lieutenant in the Marines"; "From the time of his first encounter with the world," Ward summarizes, "life was to seem a test of whatever fortitude he could bring to it." In significant ways, this is a test of gender: she congratulates Keats for overcoming the "half-effeminate idiom into which his early poetry had been lured" and achieving the "real nature as it is revealed in his letters—masculine, energetic, straight-forward."[74] Even the controversies about the portraits receive fresh notice, this time with the language of gender foregrounded. If Bailey thought Severn could have done more to capture Keats's "peculiar sweetness of expression," both Bate and Ward dismiss Severn's portrait as insufficiently manly. Ward derides its "effeminacy," calling it a "falsification" of "the lean masculine strength" shown by the life mask. And Bate, deeming it no more than a reflection of Severn's own "limp" character, credits Hilton's portrait as "much manlier and closer to the life mask." That mask, he adds, shows "the strength, resoluteness, the masculine good sense that almost everyone found so abundant in him"—for example, Mr. Procter, who reported that he had "never encountered a more manly and simple young man" than Keats.[75]

If our century reveals the endurance of nineteenth-century oppositions, it also continues the work of overcoming such binarism. Taking on the poetry that embarrasses even the advocates of Keats's manliness, Christopher Ricks describes a Keats who explores a sense of manhood capable of full indulgence in the sensual. For him, a phrase such as "slippery blisses," notoriously cited for immaturity or indecency, is not the "simple infantilism or sensation" it may seem, but a "patently audacious piece of writing" whose "unmisgiving largeness of mind" holds a liberating psychic value for the male reader. In Endymion's "swoon[ing] / Drunken from Pleasure's nipple" (2:868–69), for example, Ricks reads a "metaphor of adult love" that "enables us, with Keats's guiding, to feel a full pleasure comparable to the infant's . . . full innocence of gratification." Trilling honors a similar guide when, with a deliberate twist on Carlyle's manly ethos, he titles his essay on Keats "Poet as Hero" and proceeds to express admiration both for Keats's bold identification of "diligent indolence" "as the female principle" and his willingness to "experience its manifestation in himself without fear or resistance." Earlier than Trilling, Woolf had given this capacity a prestigious aesthetic value: naming Keats to her (all-male) canon of "androgynous" writers, she wonders "whether there are two sexes in the mind corresponding to the two sexes in the body," and "spiritually cooperating. If one is a man, still the woman part of the brain must have effect."[76]

For some feminists, Woolf's theory of androgyny offers a welcome deconstruction of the "binary oppositions of masculinity and femininity"; for others, it seems an aesthetic evasion of the unalterable political and experiential reality of gender.[77] Not coincidentally, Keats's situation in modern feminist discussion, especially when it holds to binary oppositions, is equally critical. If he represented to and evoked in some of his Victorian effeminizers capacities of response that they publicly needed to disparage as feminine, he has had the equally striking fate of representing to some recent interpreters sensibilities they want to identify descriptively as "feminine" or, more polemically, admire as "feminist." He is still, in other words, being treated as an exception to, or anomaly within, a monolithically conceived "masculine" discourse. Margaret Homans, for instance, in speculating that Keats's humble origins and poverty participate in "certain aspects of women's experience as outsiders relative to the major literary tradition . . . regardless of gender," exempts him from classification with poets of the dominant "masculine tradition," who are said to construct "the strong self from his strong language."[78] And before her, Adrienne Rich commented on the issue of Keats's sensibility in a way that includes him in the woman's tradition. In the course of a discussion about women's "so-called 'weak ego boundaries,' " she accepts help from Keats to articulate her point: responding to her suggestion that a woman's self-effacing tendency to "lose all sense of her own ego" might "be a negative way of describing the fact that women have tremendous powers of intuitive identification and sympathy with other people," her interviewer remarks, "John Keats had weak ego boundaries." Rich replies, "Negative capability. Exactly"—without noting that in Keats's formulation, this quality is exemplified in Shakespeare and identified as the property of "a Man of Achievement" (KL 1:193); perhaps she paused over the implication before adding a comment that seems to want to get around Keats's capable Man by transcending gender altogether: "Any artist has to have it to some extent." Erica Jong had invoked the same formula for her definition of "feminism":

"feminism *means* empathy. And empathy . . . is akin to the quality Keats called 'negative capability'—that unique gift for projecting oneself into other states of consciousness."[79] Albeit with a different emphasis, these readers perpetuate Victorian discriminations, for they have, in effect, regendered Keats by naming as "feminist" those capacities which they find anomalous to their ideology of the "male" character and the "masculine" tradition, rather than studied him as an opportunity to investigate the multiple and often conflicting interests that animate men's writing within patriarchal culture. Homans has since extended her interpretation of Keats to account both for his hostility to women readers and his conspicuous efforts to participate in and take advantage of certain aspects of masculinist ideology, and she is now in the process of returning Keats to the male party.[80] Her reassessment is an interesting process in itself, however, because it suggests how Keats's own sensitivity to gender articulates itself in ways sufficiently ambivalent—in sensibilities and poetic habits traditionally construed as feminine; in attitudes and modes of behavior recognizably sexist and reactive—to make him available for conscription into polemics active ever since the romantic era.

Each effort to gender Keats's sensibility repeats the problem of reconciling general values with a complex and elusive instance. Indeed debates about Keats by those concerned to evaluate themselves and their culture against qualities perceived in him reveal the fundamental instability of interpretive paradigms for this issue. For readings of Keats in the language of gender—by Keats himself, by his contemporaries, and by his critics—typically set into play conflicts and contradictions, the significance of which abides more in their persistent irresolution than in any possibility of a unified interpretation. If Keats continues to animate discussions of gender in literary and social experience, he continues, just as surely, to confuse the terms. Even as he provokes us to describe and differentiate among what is "masculine," "feminine," "effeminate," or "feminist," he confronts us with the need to complicate and redefine the judgments that underlie these categories—not only in literary history, but in our attempts to take the critical measure of that history.

Notes

I wish to thank the American Council of Learned Societies and Rutgers University for fellowships that enabled my research for this essay. I am also grateful to Paul Alpers, William Galperin, David Latiné, William Keach, Ronald Levao, Peter Manning, Barry Qualls, and Jack Stillinger for their generous advice and helpful comments.

1. William Hazlitt, "On Effeminacy of Character," Essay 9, *Table-Talk; or, Orig-*

inal Essays, 2 vols. (London: Henry Coburn, 1822), 2:204, 202–3, 215. In his preface to *Select British Poets, or New Elegant Extracts from Chaucer to the Present Time, with Critical Remarks* (1824), Keats is the only one of the six writers on whom he comments cited for wanting "manly strength and fortitude" ("A Critical List of Authors Contained in This Volume," reprinted in *The Complete Works of William Hazlitt*, ed. P. P. Howe, 21 vols. [1930–34]; reprint, New York: AMS Press, 1967, 9:233–45; I quote from 244–45).

2. Leigh Hunt, *Indicator* 2 (9 August 1820), 352.

3. Jack Stillinger, ed., *The Poems of John Keats* (Cambridge: Harvard University Press, 1978), 356. All quotations, cited by line number, follow this edition.

4. *Endymion* 2:942; I am indebted to Miriam Allott's note, *The Poems of John Keats* (New York: Norton, 1970), 440. This complaint about Apollo persists late into the century: W. J. Courthope, for example, comments that with such an "effeminate notion of Apollo, [Keats] could never have invented any kind of action which would have explained his subsequent triumph over Hyperion" (*The Liberal Movement in English Literature* ([London: John Murray, 1885], 184).

5. *Byron's Letters and Journals*, ed. Leslie A. Marchand, 12 vols. (Cambridge: Harvard University Press, 1973–82), 7:200, 8:102, 7:202, 2:217. For a very sharp study of the justice of Byron's assessment of Keats in ways that Byron himself was not prepared to appreciate, see Marjorie Levinson, *Keats's Life of Allegory: The Origins of a Style* (London: Basil Blackwell, 1988), 18–22.

6. "On the Cockney School of Poetry. No. 4," *Blackwood's Edinburgh Magazine* 3(August 1818), 519.

7. Ibid., variously, 519–24. *Blackwood's* subsequent caricature of "Mr. John Keates standing on the sea-shore at Dunbar, without a neckcloth, according to custom of Cockaigne" (vol. 6 [December 1819], 239) is fueled in part by Keats's presumption in affecting an aristocratic fashion, described by a contemporary in fact as "á lá Byron" (*The Keats Circle*, ed. Hyder E. Rollins, 2 vols. [Cambridge, Harvard University Press, 1948], 2:211; cited as *KC* hereafter with volume and page).

8. George Gilfillan, "John Keats," in *First and Second Galleries of Literary Portraits* (Edinburgh: James Hogg, 1854), 258.

9. *Blackwood's* 3(May 1818), 197, and 6(December 1819), 239: Lord Byron, *Letters and Journals*, 7:200 and 229; MacGillivray, *Keats: A Bibliography and Reference Guide with an Essay on Keats' Reputation* (Toronto: University of Toronto Press, 1949), xxii.

10. *Blackwood's* 19(January 1826), xvi and xxvi.

11. "Lord Byron is a pampered and aristocratic writer, but he is not effeminate," Hazlitt explains ("On Effeminacy," 215); Thomas Carlyle in fact found him "almost the only man" among English poets "faithfully and manfully struggling, to the end" in the cause of "spiritual manhood" ("Goethe," *Foreign Review* 3; reprinted in *Critical and Miscellaneous Essays* [London: Chapman and Hall, 1899]; reprint, New York: AMS Press, 1969, 5 vols., 1:243). The discourses on Shelley are much more divided. When G. H. Lewes said that he was *"par excellence*, the 'poet of women,' "he was referring not to effeminacy but to the ideals of feminism (with which he sympathized): "woman" as "a *partner* of your life" (*Westminster Review* 35 [April 1841], 169). But Charles Kingsley derided Shelley's nature as "utterly womanish"; it is he, rather than the wrongly cited Byron ("who amid all his fearful sins, was a man"), on whom one ought to blame the present age's "spasmodic, vague, extravagant, effeminate, school of poetry" (*Fraser's Magazine* 48 [November 1853], 572, 573, 574). For a similar discussion, see Alfred Austin, "Swinburne," *Temple Bar* (1869); reprinted in *The Poetry of the Period* (London: Richard Bentley, 1870), 95, 113; and Coventry Patmore, "What Shelley

Was," in *Principle in Art, Religio Poetae, and Other Essays* (1889; reprint, London: Duckworth, 1913), 71–72.

12. *British Lady's Magazine* 25 (1 May 1817), 262.

13. "Remarks on Keats" (J. W. Dalby), *Pocket Magazine of Classic and Polite Literature* 7 (4 April 1821), 333 and 335; Mrs. John Sanderford, *Woman, In Her Social and Domestic Character*, 7th ed. (London: Longman et al., 1842), 16.

14. Gilfillan, "John Keats," 260. For *Guardian* review, see Lewis M. Schwartz, *Keats Reviewed by His Contemporaries: A Collection of Notices for the Years 1816–1821* (Metuchen, N. J.: Scarecrow Press, 1973), 228–32.

15. *The Young Lady's Book of Elegant Poetry* (Philadelphia: Key and Biddle, 1835): "To Autumn," 314–15; *Ladies' Companion* (August 1837), 186–87, includes "Hither, Hither love," "Fame, like a wayward girl," "On a Dream," and "Tis the witching hour"; *The Girl's Second Help to Reading* (1854; see G. M. Matthews, ed., *Keats: The Critical Heritage* [New York: Barnes and Noble, 1971], 10); "The Daintiest of Poets—Keats," *Victoria Magazine* 15 (May 1870), 55–67. Mrs. Fields (Annie Adams) prints a MS page of "I stood tip-toe" concluding with the poet's exhortation to "Ye ardent marigolds!" (*A Shelf of Old Books* [New York: Charles Scribner's Sons, 1894], 43). *Endymion* was specially loved by women. *Victoria* called it "ever cherished reading for youthful pilgrims on the flowery road of poesy" (59) and evidence that Keats was "essentially a worshipper of beauty" (57); publishers offered parlor-table editions and Frances Mary Owen's critical study, framed "to make others love him" (*John Keats: A Study* [London: C. Kegan Paul, 1880], v), featured a long neo-Platonic explication. For the popularity of *Endymion*, see George H. Ford, *Keats and the Victorians: A Study of His Influence and Rise to Fame 1821–1895* (New Haven: Yale University Press, 1944), 105; for accounts of editions, see Helen E. Haworth, " 'A Thing of Beauty Is a Joy Forever?' Early Illustrated Editions of Keats's Poetry," *Harvard Library Bulletin* 21(1973): 88–103.

16. I follow *Shelley's Poetry and Prose*, ed. Donald H. Reiman and Sharon B. Powers (New York: Norton, 1977); I quote from p. 390, and stanza 6 of the poem.

17. Shelley, *Letters 1818 to 1822*, ed. Roger Ingpen, in *The Complete Works of Percy Bysshe Shelley*, ed. Roger Ingpen and Walter E. Peck, 10 vols. (New York: Charles Scribner's Sons, 1926), 10:225; Byron, *Letters and Journals*, 8:103, and *Don Juan*, Canto 11:60, *Lord Byron: The Complete Poetical Works*, ed. Jerome J. McGann, 5 vols. (Oxford: Clarendon, 1980–86, vol. 5).

18. *Blackwood's* 75(March 1854), 346; *Cornhill* 34 (1876), 558; *New Monthly* 14 (September 1820), 306; "John Keats," *Chambers's Cyclopedia of English Literature*, ed. Robt. Chambers, 2 vols. (Boston: Gould and Lincoln, 1866), 2:402–3.

19. Thomas Gisborne, *An Inquiry into the Duties of the Female Sex* (1796; 7th ed. London: T. Cadell and W. Davies, 1806), 34–35; Sanderford, *Woman*, 35.

20. Gilfillan, "John Keats," 261–62. Carlyle, "Burns," *Edinburgh Review* 48 (1828); reprinted in *Critical and Miscellaneous Essays*, 1:277.

21. *Blackwood's* 7 (September 1820), 686; Hazlitt, "On Living to One's-Self," *Table-Talk*, 1:229–30; Swinburne, "Keats," *The Complete Works of Algernon Charles Swinburne*, ed. Edmund Gosse and Thomas James Wise, 20 vols. (London: William Heinemann, 1925–27), 14:297.

22. William Allingham, *William Allingham: A Diary, 1824–1889*, ed. H. Allingham and D. Radford (1907; reprinted Middlesex, England: Penguin, 1985), 205.

23. *Ladies' Companion* (August 1837), 186; Frances Mary Owen, *John Keats*, 183; Dorothy Hewlett, *Adonais: A Life of John Keats* (London: Hurst and Blackett, 1937); J.R. MacGillivray, *Keats*, xiii.

24. "The Daintiest of Poets," 67; Margaret Oliphant, "John Keats," *The Literary*

History of England in the End of the Eighteenth and Beginning of the Nineteenth Century, 3 vols. (London: Macmillan, 1882), 3:141; Amy Lowell, *John Keats*, 2 vols. (Cambridge, Mass.: Riverside, 1925), 1:14 and 2:80.

25. Ford, *Keats and the Victorians*, 68; Oliphant, "John Keats," 137–38.

26. *The Letters of John Keats*, ed. Hyder E. Rollins, 2 vols. (Cambridge, Mass.: Harvard University Press, 1958), 1:185; cited as *KL* hereafter with volume and page.

27. Noticing that the Knight at the end of the poem joins an all-male chorus, Karen Swann asks: "Could this community, and not the ideal or even the fatal woman, be the true object of his quest?" For her negotiation of this question, see "Harassing the Muse," in *Romanticism and Feminism*, ed. Anne K. Mellor (Bloomington: Indiana University Press, 1988), 81–92, esp. 90–92.

28. See Stuart M. Sperry, *Keats the Poet* (Princeton: Princeton University Press, 1973), 101–9, and Christopher Ricks, *Keats and Embarrassment* (London: Oxford University Press, 1976), 12–14. Helen B. Ellis ("Food, Sex, Death, and the Feminine Principle in Keats's Poetry," *English Studies in Canada* 6 [1980]: 56–74) also gives a compelling discussion to the psychological implications. See esp. 56–57.

29. I study the literary consequences of Fanny's resistance to Keats's desire in "Composition and 'Unrest': The Dynamics of Form in Keats's Last Lyrics," *Keats-Shelley Journal* 34(1985): 53–82.

30. Mrs. Sanderford, *Woman*, 9.

31. Virginia Woolf, *A Room of One's Own* (1929); reprint, New York: Harcourt, Brace, 1957), 35.

32. Theoretical contexts for examining Keats in relation to women readers and an increasingly feminized literary marketplace are developed by Sonia Hofkosh ("The Writer's Ravishment: Women and the Romantic Author—The Example of Byron," in *Romanticism and Feminism*, 93–114) and Margaret Homans ("Keats and Women Readers," English Institute paper, 1986).

33. *KL* 2:178; *OED* (Oxford: Oxford University Press, 1971) lists the obsolete meaning of "prostitute" for "traffic" (*T*:229). The sense that adapting one's art for the market was entering the realm of the degraded feminine is also expressed by Dante Gabriel Rossetti: "to be an artist is just the same thing as to be a whore, as far as dependence on the whims and fancies of individuals is concerned" (*The Letters of Dante Gabriel Rossetti*, ed. Oswald Doughty and John Robert Wahl, 4 vols. [Oxford: Clarendon, 1967], 3:1175; cf. 2:849–50). See also Luce Irigaray, who argues that "Marx's analysis of commodities as the elementary form of capitalist wealth can . . . be understood as an interpretation of the status of woman in a so-called patriarchal societies" ("Le marché des femmes," *Ce Sexe qui n'est pas un* [1977]; reprinted as "Woman on the Market," *This Sex Which is Not One*, trans. Catherine Porter and Carolyn Burke [Ithaca: Cornell University Press, 1985], 169).

34. *Edinburgh Review* 90(October 1849), 428. Matthews attributes the essay to Aubrey Thomas de Vere (*Critical Heritage*, 341).

35. Patmore, "Keats," reviewing Colvin (1887); reprinted in *Principle in Art*, 61–62.

36. "Keats' Place in English Poetry," *National Review* 10(September 1887), 24.

37. Robert Buchanan, *The Fleshly School of Poetry and Other Phenomena of the Day* (London: Strahan, 1872), 5–7, 12.

38. *Edinburgh Review* 134 (July 1871), 75, 99; Austin, *Poetry of the Period*, 96, 89; Kingsley, *Fraser's* (November 1853), 571. For a study of the ethics of "Christian manliness" and of Kingsley's role in this movement, see Norman Vance, *The Sinews of the spirit: The ideal of Christian manliness in Victorian literature and religious thought* (Cambridge: Cambridge University Press, 1985).

39. Lord Cockburn, *Life of Lord Jeffrey with a Selection from his Correspondence*, 2 vols. (Edinburgh: Adam and Charles Black, 1852), 2:391 and 406; Richard D. Altick, *Victorian People and Ideas* (New York: Norton, 1973), 7. For the emergence of an antieffeminate ethos over the course of the century, see J. R. de S. Honey, *Tom Brown's Universe* (London: Millington, 1977), 209–10.

40. Carlyle, *On Heroes, Hero-Worship, and the Heroic in History* (1840–41), ed. Carl Neimeyer (Lincoln: University of Nebraska Press, 1966), 179, 1, 2, 84, 80, 92, 178.

41. Matthews, *Critical Heritage*, 35.

42. Courthope, *The Liberal Movement*, 194.

43. William Michael Rossetti, *Life of John Keats* (London: Walter Scott, 1887), 206; Smith, "John Keats," *Encyclopedia Britannica*, 8th ed. (1857), 13:56–57.

44. Allingham's *Diary*, 205. Swinburne, "Keats," *Complete Works*, 14:296–97; *Blackwood's* 3 (August 1818), 524; Matthew Arnold, "John Keats" (1880; reprinted in *Essays and Criticism, Second Series*, 1895), *The Complete Prose Works of Matthew Arnold*, ed. R. H. Super et al., 11 vols. [Ann Arbor: University of Michigan Press, 1960–77], 9:207.

45. *National Review* 9 (October 1859), 370–90; Gisborne, *Inquiry*, 34; More, *Strictures on the Modern System of Female Education*, 2 vols. (1799; reprinted as vols. 7–8, *The Works of Hannah More*, 18 vols. [London: T. Cadell and W. Davies, 1818], 2:29.

46. Patmore, "Keats," 62; *Further Letters of Gerard Manley Hopkins*, ed. Claude C. Abbott, 2d ed. (London: Oxford University Press, 1956), 381, 386; More, *Strictures*, 2:31.

47. Hazlitt, "On Effeminacy," 212, 208; W. M. Rossetti, *Life of John Keats*, 206; Courthope, "Keats' Place," 24, 16, 21.

48. Patmore, "Arthur Hugh Clough," *Principle in Art*, 88; Courthope, "Keats' Place," 14, 16; Courthope, *The Liberal Movement*, 181–82; Sidney Colvin, *Keats* (New York: Harper, 1887), 99; John Ruskin, "Of Queens' Gardens" (1865; rev. 1871); reprinted in *Sesame and Lillies* (London: Oxford University Press, 1936), 98 (his italics).

49. Courthope, *A History of English Poetry*, 6 vols. (London: Macmillan, 1910), 6:323, and *The Liberal Movement*, 193: Hopkins, *Further Letters*, 386; De Quincey, "Notes on George Gilfillan's *Gallery of Literary Portraits* (1845)," *Tait's Edinburgh Magazine*, N.S., 13 (April 1846), 252–53; Étienne, "La Poésie Paienne en Angleterre" / "Le Paganisme Poétique en Angleterre: John Keats et Algernon Charles Swinburne," *Revue des Deux Mondes* 69, part I (15 May 1867), 298.

50. Howitt, "Keats," *Homes and Haunts of the Most Eminent British Poets*, 2 vols. (London: Richard Bentley, 1847), I:425. Wilde's remarks on art are from his first lecture in New York, 1882, quoted in the *New York World*, and in turn by Walter Hamilton, *The Aesthetic Movement in England*, 3d ed. (London: Reeves & Turner, 1882), 115–16. As Ford remarks, the terms in which Wilde defines Keats's aesthetic purity were "vital to the complete acceptance of Keats's poetry" by the Pre-Raphaelistes (*Keats and the Victorians*, 115). I also quote "Glykypikros Eros," *The Writings of Oscar Wilde*, 12 vols. (New York: Doubleday, Page, 1923), 1:243–46, and "The Tomb of Keats" (1887), reprinted in *Writings*, 12:301–5.

51. Bailey, *KC* 2:274; Haydon, *The Diary of Benjamin Robert Haydon*, ed. Willard Bissell Pope, 5 vols. (Cambridge: Harvard University Press, 1960), 2:378, 318; Milnes, *Life, Letters, and Literary Remains, of John Keats*, 2 vols. (London: Edward Moxon, 1848), 1:245; Colvin, *Keats*, 47, 20. Milnes cites Keats's friend on 1:15.

52. Gisborne, *Inquiry*, 20.

53. Hunt, *Lord Byron and Some of His Contemporaries* (Philadelphia: Carey, Lea & Carey, 1828), 213.

54. *A General Biographical Dictionary*, ed. John Gorton, 3 vols. (London: Whitaker, 1828), 2:241–42 (Rollins names Hunt the author [*KC* 1:xcv]); "The Feast of the Poets," *The Poetical Works of Leigh Hunt* (London: Edward Moxon, 1832).

55. Milnes, *Life*, 1:7; Lowell, "Keats" (1854), reprinted in *The Writings of James Russell Lowell*, 11 vols. (Boston: Houghton, Mifflin, 1897), 1:241; W. M. Rossetti, "Biographical Sketch," in *Poems of John Keats* (New York: Cooperative Publication Society, 1872), xi; Colvin, *Keats*, 46.

56. George Keats, *KC* 1:325; Haydon, *Autobiography and Memoirs*, ed. Tom Taylor and Aldous Huxley, 2 vols. (New York: Harcourt Brace, 1926), 1:251; Colvin, 46, 221; Severn, quoted by William Sharp in *The Life and Letters of Joseph Severn* (New York: Charles Scribner's Sons, 1892) and cited by Donald Parson, *Portraits of Keats* (Cleveland and New York: World Publishing, 1954), 15.

57. Parson, ibid., 116; Mrs. Procter, *KC* 2:158; Milnes, *Life*, 1:103–4. For Bailey's note on Coleridge, see *KC* 2:268; Frances Mary Owen's biography also uses this term, in the main clause of a sentence beginning, "Although his face was strong and manly . . ." (8), and she incorporates Coleridge's observation "that something feminine— not *effeminate*, mind—is discoverable in the countenances of all men of Genius" (*Specimens of the Table Talk of the Late Samuel Taylor Coleridge*, 2 vols. [New York: Harper, 1835], 2:15–16).

58. Rossetti, "Biographical Sketch," xi, and *Life of John Keats*, 206, 128.

59. Between 1854 and 1908, Severn's Keats, copies by Severn and others, or versions done "after" it, appear in forty editions, while Hilton's Keats appears in few more than a dozen: see MacGillivray, *Keats*, appendices B–F (8–52). Readers can find Severn's portrait in the frontispiece of Allott's edition of the poems and a detail of Hilton's on the dustcover of Matthews' *Critical Heritage* volume.

60. Quoted by Sharp, *Severn*, 540.

61. "The Daintiest of Poets," 59.

62. For a romanticizing of Keats's lower-class origins ("of the humblest"), see Hunt, *Lord Byron*, 214. For improvements of the same, see Milnes, *Life*, 9; David Masson, "The Life and Poetry of Keats," *Macmillan's Magazine* (November, 1860); reprinted in *Wordsworth, Shelley, Keats, and Other Essays* (London: Macmillan, 1875), 145; Colvin, *Keats*, 4. For fuller discussion of the methods of Milnes's *Life*, see William Henry Marquess, *Lives of the Poet: The First Century of Keats Biography* (University Park: Pennsylvania State University Press, 1985), 37–57. For an amused reaction to efforts "to create [Keats] a gentleman by brevet," see J. R. Lowell (whose phrase this is), "Keats," 219 and 226, and Rossetti, "Sketch," vii.

63. Hunt, *Lord Byron*, 214 and *Imagination and Fancy* (London: Smith, Elder, 1844), 285–86; Gorton's *Biographical Dictionary*, 2:242; Milnes, *Life*, 1:2, 6, 73–74.

64. Bailey, *KC* 2:259, 274, (London) *Times* (19 September 1848), 3; de Vere, *Edinburgh Review* 90 (October 1849), 428; Masson, "Life and Poetry," 146; Colvin, *Keats*, 211, 6; Arnold, "John Keats," 103, 110; Rossetti, "Sketch," xi–xii, and *Life of Keats*, 206.

65. *Blackwood's* 75(March 1854), 348–49; Étienne, "La Poésie Paienne," 306, 317.

66. Browning, *Dearest Isa: Robert Browning's Letters to Isabella Blagden*, ed. Edward C. McAleer University of Texas Press, 1951), 303; Buchanan, *The Fleshly School*, 70; *Edinburgh Review* 134(July 1871), 74, 91. Ford, noting the frequency of the word *manly* in Swinburne's criticism, suggests that the antipathy to Keats was agitated not just by aristocratic disdain but also by insecurities about his own manliness

(*Keats and the Victorians,* 169). I am indebted to Thaïs Morgan's interesting paper, "Mixed Metaphor, Mixed Gender: Swinburne and the Victorian Critics" (Modern Language Association of America convention, 1986).

67. *Blackwood's* 56(September 1844), 342, 331; Frederick W. Maitland, *The Life and Letters of Leslie Stephen* (New York: G. P. Putnam's Sons, 1906), 314.

68. Quoted by Ford, *Keats and the Victorians,* 118.

69. *In Memoriam* 109:17, *The Poems of Tennyson,* ed. Christopher Ricks (London: Longmans, Green, 1969) Ricks (962) cites Hallam Lord Tennyson, *Alfred Lord Tennyson: A Memoir* 2 vols (New York: Macmillan, 1897) 1:326.

70. Hunt, *Lord Byron,* 230, and *The Autobiography of Leigh Hunt with Reminiscences of Friends and Contemporaries,* 3 vols (London: Smith, Elder, 1850) 1:211; Colvin, *Keats* 210; van Dyke, "The Influence of Keats," *Century Magazine* 50(October 1895), 911–12.

71. Courthope, *History,* 6:341–42; *The Letters of Matthew Arnold to Arthur Hugh Clough,* ed. Howard Foster Lowry (1932; reprinted, London: Oxford University Press, 1968), 97; *The Note-Books of Matthew Arnold,* ed. Howard Foster Lowry, Karl Young, and Waldo Hilary Dunn (London: Oxford University Press, 1952), 510. For a fuller study of Arnold's engagement with Keatsian sensibility and poetics, see Leon Gottfried, *Matthew Arnold and the Romantics* (Lincoln: University of Nebraska Press, 1973).

72. Shairp, *On Poetic Interpretation of Nature* (Boston: Houghton, Mifflin, 1898), 43; Symons, "John Keats," *Monthly Review* 13(October 1901), 145; Watson, "Keats and Mr. Colvin," in *Excursions in Criticism* (London: Elkins, Matthews & John Lane, 1893), 40, 44; Vincent, "A Reading of the Letters of John Keats," *Atlantic Monthly* 74(September 1894) 399–400; West, "Keats in Hampstead," *Century Magazine* 50(October 1895), 909; Saintsbury, *A History of Nineteenth-Century Literature* (1780–1895) (London: Macmillan, 1896), 89–91.

73. Bush, *Mythology and the Romantic Tradition* (1937; reprint, New York: Norton, 1963), 88; Fairchild, *Religious Trends in English Poetry,* 3 vols. (New York: Columbia University Press, 1949), 3:465; MacGillivray, *Keats,* xiii, xv. We may also note Ford's offhand remark that it is well that Dante Rosetti, reverence for Keats aside, "makes a complete break" with "many of Keats's more effeminate phrases" (*Keats and the Victorians,* 141).

74. Trilling, "Introduction," *The Selected Letters of John Keats* (New York: Farrar, Straus and Young, 1951), 21–25; Bate, *John Keats* (Cambridge: Harvard University Press, 1963), 56, 85, 112–16; Ward, *John Keats: The Making of a Poet* (New York: Viking, 1963), 1–3, 180–81.

75. Bailey, *KC* 2:269; Ward, *John Keats,* 89. Bate, *John Keats,* 113, 116.

76. Ricks, *Keats and Embarrassment,* 104–5, 89, 106; Trilling, "The Poet as Hero: Keats in His Letters," reprinted in *The Opposing Self* (New York: Viking, 1955); Woolf, *A Room of One's Own,* 107, 102. Even Patmore is willing to argue that "the spirit of the great poet has always a feminine element" ("Keats," 62).

77. I quote Toril Moi (*Sexual / Textual Politics: Feminist Literary Theory* [London and New York: Methuen, 1985], 13), who is disputing Elaine Showalter's critique of Woolf's theory of androgyny as an aesthetic ideal based on a problematic "class-oriented . . . ideal—the separation of politics and art"; as such, androgyny offered Woolf a myth of escape to "the sphere of the exile and the eunuch" that allowed her to "evade confrontation" with the political consequences of her femaleness (*A Literature of Their Own: British Women Novelists from Brontë to Lessing* [Princeton: Princeton University Press, 1977], 288, 285, 264).

78. Homans, *Women Writers and Poetic Identity* (Princeton: Princeton University Press, 1980), 240n.25, and 33.

79. Rich, "Three Conversations," in *Adrienne Rich's Poetry,* ed. Barbara Charlesworth Gelpi and Albert Gelpi (New York: Norton, 1975), 115; Jong, "Visionary Anger," *Ms.* 11 (July 1973), 31. The perpetuation of that term as a sign of feminist consciousness can be seen in Barbara Charlesworth Gelpi's describing as an act of enlightened "negative capability" Rossetti's sense of comparison between the artist and the whore ("The Feminization of D. G. Rossetti," in *The Victorian Experience: The Poets,* ed. Richard A. Levine [Ohio: Ohio University Press, 1982], 105; she uses Keats's phrase without referring to his bitter sense of identity with a prostitute—a comparison which evinces little, if any, negative capability.

80. Homans, "Keats and Women Readers," English Institute paper, 1986.

INDEX

Abbey, Richard, 214
Abernethy, John, 6, 282
Abrams, M. H., 101
Addison, Joseph, 104
"aesthetic nominalism," 121
"After dark vapours," 286
afterlife, 132
Akenside, Mark, 105
Allen, William, 144, 147–48, 154
Allott, Miriam, 1
Altick, Richard, 332
ambivalence and ambiguity, 106, 107, 109–10, 113, 114
Apothecaries Act, 143, 144
approbativeness, 12, 13
aristeia, 15, 26
Arnold, Matthew, 320, 334, 345
associationism, 190, 235, 242, 256, 295–96
Austin, Alfred, 332

Babington, William, 144, 147–48, 150, 151, 153
Bailey, Benjamin, 16, 20, 31, 50, 54, 55, 57, 61, 130, 138, 150, 151, 153, 173, 183, 189, 193, 200, 210, 225, 227, 230, 240, 267, 298, 337, 338, 339, 341, 347
Baker, Jeffrey, 267
Balzac, Honoré de, 12
Barnard, John, 1, 3, 4, 269
Bate, Walter Jackson, 1, 3, 14, 39, 210, 280, 347: *The Burden of the Past and the English Poet*, 103
Bayley, John, 1, 48, 63
Beach, Joseph Warren, 32
"bearing," 117, 123–24
Beattie, James, 209
Beaumont, Sir George, 45

beauty, principle of, 19–20, 53, 54–55, 60, 65, 77, 130, 135–39, 149, 154, 155, 183, 184, 195, 231, 256
Bentham, Jeremy, 107
biographical critics, 96–97
Biographical Dictionary, 338
Bishop of Lincoln, 131
Blackmore, Sir Richard, 12
Blackwood's, 11, 16, 212, 262, 320–21, 322, 323, 334, 337, 344
Blake, William, 115, 130, 132, 133, 134, 136, 137, 139, 141, 145, 230, 293; *Milton*, 134, 135
Borough Hospital's Medical School, 5–6, 144
British Critic, 58, 59, 60
British Ladies Magazine, The, 321
Brawne, Fanny, 19, 26, 96–97, 169, 175, 201, 206, 212, 215, 216, 326, 328
Bridges, Robert, 253
Bromwich, David, 3, 6, 7
Brontë, Charlotte, 346
Brown, Charles, 96, 177–78, 192, 200, 322, 337, 338
Brown, John and Brunonian theory of excitability, 281–82, 286
Browning, Robert, 344
Buchanan, Robert: *The Fleshly School of Poetry*, 331, 344
Buffon, Georges-Louis Leclerc, 282, 284
Burgess, Thomas: *The Physiology or Mechanism of Blushing*, 157–58, 163
Burke, Edmund and William: *An Account of the European Settlements in America*, 30–31
Burke, Kenneth, 51, 112
Burton, Robert: *Anatomy of Melancholy*, 93–94, 106–7, 178, 195, 267, 326

Bush, Douglas, 195, 346
Butler, Marilyn, 54
butterfly, 279–80, 287
Byron, George Gordon, Lord, 6, 7,
  58–59, 130, 131, 132, 133, 134,
  135, 139, 163, 206–20, 222, 230,
  275, 320, 321, 322, 323, 330, 332,
  333: *Childe Harold's Pilgrimage*, 215,
  216, 273–74; *Don Juan*, 132, 207,
  212, 214, 215, 217, 218, 220, 322,
  330; "Fare Thee Well," 218–19;
  Manfred, 215–16, 217

Caldwell, J. R.: *John Keats's Fancy*, 242
"Calidore," 329–30
Carlile, Richard, 262, 274–75
Carlyle, Thomas, 323–24, 332–33, 334,
  347, 348: "The Hero as Poet,"
  332–33
Castlereagh, Lord, 52
Century Magazine, 346
Chalmers, George, 32
Chamber's Encyclopedia, 323
"chamelion poet," 6, 64, 115, 131,
  134, 136, 188, 209, 211, 328–29
Chamisso, Adalbert von, 281
Champion, 227
Chatman, Seymour, 88
Chatterton, Thomas, 206, 227
Cheatham, George, 213, 215
chemistry, 143–56, 184–85, 230–31
Christ. *See* Christianity; Jesus
Christianity, 262–76, 305
Clarke, Charles Cowden, 108, 346–47
Clarke, John, 132
Clubbe, John, 3, 5
Cochrane, Lord, 21
Coleridge, Samuel Taylor, 63, 71, 107,
  190, 214, 253, 258, 280, 282–83,
  293, 303, 314, 339: *Biographia
  Literaria*, 189; "The Eolian Harp,"
  90; "Frost at Midnight," 99; "Kubla
  Khan," 41, 189; *Lyrical Ballads*, 107,
  137; *Notebooks*, 189; "On Poesy or
  Art," 189; *The Rime of the Ancient
  Mariner*, 89, 90; *The Statesman's
  Manual*, 232
Collins, William: "Ode to Evening,"
  246
Colvin, Sir Sidney, 41, 188–89, 331,
  335, 338, 341, 345; *Keats*, 331
"consequitive reasoning," 19, 65, 137,
  139, 146
Cooper, Astley, 145, 281, 282

Cornhill Magazine, 322
Cox, Jane, 179–81, 214
Courthope, W. J., 331, 333, 335, 336,
  345

Dante, 115, 122–24: *Commedia*,
  116–17, 272; *Paradiso*, 122;
  Purgatorio, 124
"dark city," 71–72
Darwin, Erasmus, 281, 282, 284
Davy, Sir Humphrey, 145, 150:
  "Course of Lectures on Chemistry,"
  145
de Almeida, Hermione, 3: "Romantic
  Evolution: Fresh Perfection and
  Ebbing Process in Keats," 6–7
de Man, Paul, 109
De Quincy, Thomas, 336
death, 241, 245, 250, 256, 303
deism, 275
demesne, 32–33
depression, 191–92, 197; *see also*
  melancholy; sorrow; suffering
"despairs," 297–98; *see also* depression;
  melancholy; sorrow; suffering
Dickstein, Morris, 72, 75, 313: *Keats
  and His Poetry: A Study in
  Development*, 4
"diligent indolence," 139
Dilke, Charles Wentworth, 131, 137,
  140, 175, 177–78, 212
"disagreeables," 42, 43–44, 45–46,
  137, 147, 155, 159, 162, 184, 258
"disinterestedness," 5, 13, 19, 20–21,
  25, 134, 153, 213, 236–37
distillation. *See* chemistry

Edinburgh, 331, 341, 344
Edinburgh Review, 228
"egotistical sublime," 17, 63–64,
  114–15, 134, 209, 216, 231, 233–34,
  245
Einfühlung, 115, 117, 234
ekphrasis, 112–13
Eliot, T. S., 12, 162–63
Elizabethan poets, 13
Elledge, Paul, 217, 218
Ellis, Mrs., 332
embarrassment. *See* Keats, John: and
  blushing
Emerson, Ralph Waldo, 256
empathy, 136, 161–62, 234, 237, 349
empiricism, British, 293–94, 312; *see
  also* Hume; Locke

Endymion: A Poetic Romance, 1, 3, 4, 11, 12, 13, 16, 17, 18, 19, 20, 36, 45, 47–67, 68, 74, 108, 111, 115, 116, 122, 123, 124, 135, 138, 147, 154–56, 158, 161, 189, 190, 193, 199, 211, 213, 223, 224, 229, 239, 242, 244, 265–66, 267, 269, 270, 284, 285, 286, 297, 298–99, 305, 333–34, 336, 340, 341, 346, 347
Enfield, 131–32, 347
enlightenment, 104, 105, 109
Enlightenment, 12, 186, 232, 270
"Epistle to George Felton Mathew," 15, 71–72, 108
"Epistle to John Hamilton Reynolds," 3–4, 36–47, 64–65, 68, 190–91, 194, 197, 198, 254, 263
"Epistle to My Brother George," 19, 20, 108
escapism, 69–70, 71, 72, 77, 78, 79, 80
"essence," 153–54
"etherial existence," 148–56
Étienne, Louis, 336, 344
evaporation. *See* chemistry
"evasion," 106; *see also* escapism
Eve of St. Agnes, The, 5, 48, 58, 59, 68–69, 70, 78–85, 91–93, 109–10, 111, 216, 217, 228, 292, 321–22, 330
"Eve of St. Mark, The," 97–99, 287
evolutionary theory, 7, 283–87
Examiner, 188, 195, 262
Exodus, Book of, 272

Fairchild, Hoxie Neale, 346
Fall of Hyperion, The, 2, 5, 6, 24, 25–26, 48, 62, 73, 95, 111, 111–12, 114–25, 141, 195, 198, 207, 226, 271, 272, 273–74, 276–77, 281, 286, 287, 328
"Fancy," 190, 229, 254
Faraday, Michael, 145
Felperin, Howard, 69–70, 77, 85
feminist criticism, 317–18, 348–49
fixity, 114, 281; *see also* immobility
Ford, George, 324
Fraser's, 332
French Revolution, 52
Freud, Sigmund, 189–90, 191, 194, 199: "Creative Writers and Daydreaming," 200; *The Ego and the Id*, 190; *The Interpretation of Dreams*, 185, 190; "Mourning and Melancholia," 6, 196–98
Freud, Sophie, 197
Frogley, Mary, 60
Frye, Northrup, 75, 108

Garrod, H. W., 254
Genette, Gérard, 88
genius, 3, 17
Gibbon, Edward: *Decline and Fall of the Roman Empire*, 262, 271
Gifford, William, 228
Gilfillan, George, 320, 321, 322, 323
Girl's Second Help to Reading, The, 321
Gisborne, Thomas, 323, 334, 337
Gittings, Robert, 1, 201
Godwin, William, 131, 139: *Caleb Williams*, 225; *The Pantheon: or Ancient History of the Gods of Greece and Rome*, 50–51
Goellnicht, Donald C., 3, 5
Goffman, Irving, 162
Goldsmith, Oliver: "Poetry Distinguished from Other Writing," 107
Grob, Alan, 3, 7
Guardian, 321
"gusto," Hazlitt's, 39, 114, 225, 227
Guy's Hospital, 2, 5, 143, 144, 281, 282

"Had I a man's fair form," 329
Hammond, Thomas, 143
happiness, 297–98, 301, 303, 305, 316
Hartman, Geoffrey, 106, 114
Haydon, Benjamin, 15, 17, 20, 24, 50, 148, 149, 168, 184, 192, 211, 223, 231, 232, 265, 267–70, 272, 273, 337, 339, 340, 346: *Christ's Entry into Jerusalem*, 168
Hazlitt, William, 6, 13, 18, 21, 23, 51, 105, 106, 113, 114, 131, 172, 173, 187, 191, 192–93, 222–58, 273, 322: *Characters of Shakespeare's Plays*, 233; *Essay on the Principles of Human Action*, 190–91, 233, 236, 237; "The Indian Jugglers," 224, 238; *Journey through France and Italy*, 228; *Lectures on the English Comic Writers*, 225; *Lectures on the English Poets*, 227; "Letter to William Gifford, 224–25, 233, 236, 255; "On Classical Education," 223; "On Dreams," 242;

"On Effeminacy of Character," 228, 319, 335, 344; "On the English Poets," 208–9, 213; "On the Fear of Death," 256; "On Gusto," 38, 39–40, 43; "On Imitation," 231, 255, 256; "On Living to One's-Self," 323; "On Poetry in General," 187–88, 231, 248–49, 256–57; "On Posthumous Fame," 224; "On Reading Old Books," 228; "On Reason and Imagination," 235–36, 242; "On Thomson and Cowper," 241; "The Periodical Press," 228; *Round Table*, 223, 224, 233, 242; *Select British Poets*, 229; *The Spirit of the Age*, 228; *Table-Talk*, 223; "What Is the People?," 232–33

Hessey, James, 17, 165, 166, 167, 215
Hewlett, Dorothy: *Adonais: a Life of John Keats*, 324
Hilton, William, 340
Hirst, Wolf, 212
Hogg, T. J., 266
Holmes, Edward, 200
Homans, Margaret, 348, 349
Homer, 15, 23, 29–35, 198, 310
Hone, William, 261–62
Hopkins, Gerard Manley, 334, 336
Horace, 13
"How fever'd is the man," 193–94
Howitt, William, 336
humanitarianism, 268–69, 273
Humboldt, Alexander von, 279–81, 287
Hume, David, 285, 293–94
Hunt, Henry, 24
Hunt, Holman: *Eve of St. Agnes*, 345; *Isabella and the Pot of Basil*, 345
Hunt, Leigh, 6, 12, 14, 15, 17, 50, 134, 143, 180, 208, 209, 210–11, 212, 216, 223, 254, 262–64, 266, 267, 268, 275, 319, 337–38, 345, 346: *Autobiography*, 337; *The Feast of the Poets*, 208, 209, 338; *Foliage*, 263; *The Story of Rimini*, 215–16, 217
Hunter, John and Hunterian "principle of life," 6–7, 145, 281–82
"Hymn to Pan," 49, 264–65
Hyperion, 3, 4, 7, 18, 21, 25, 33, 109, 115, 116, 123, 124, 195, 226, 228, 246, 257, 269–70, 271, 281, 283, 284–85, 286, 319, 346

"I Stood Tip-toe," 47, 53, 70, 72, 118, 305, 311
imagination, 54–57, 62, 65, 69, 76, 79, 81, 82, 106, 109, 130, 136, 138, 140, 145, 146, 147, 148, 150, 151, 152, 154, 183–202, 214, 245, 300
"Imitation of Spenser," 206
immobility, 121–23; *see also* fixity
immortality, 302–3, 304–5, 316
"In dear-nighted December," 4, 296
individuation, principle of, 280, 282–83
"intensity," 39, 42, 45–46, 64, 147, 148, 184, 218, 281, 283, 285, 286
Isabella, 68, 111, 118–19, 121, 195, 198

Jacobson, Dan, 172
Jealousies, The, 216, 217–18, 219
Jeffery, Mary-Ann, 18, 195
Jeffrey, Francis, 332
Jeffrey, the Misses, 169
Jennings, Midgely (uncle), 199
Jesus, 132, 135, 266, 270, 271, 273; *see also* Christianity
Johnson, Dr., 192, 323, 332
Jones, John: *John Keats's Dream of Truth*, 158–59, 161, 163
Jones, Leonidas, 209
Jong, Erica, 348–49
Jordan, Frank: *The English Romantic Poets: A Review of Research and Criticism*, 1

Kant, Immanual, 7, 293–95, 299–300, 315–16
katabasis, 116
Keats, Edward (brother), 199
Keats, Fanny (sister), 59
Keats, Frances Jennings (mother), 199–200, 218
Keats, George and Georgiana (brother and sister-in-law), 1, 14, 19, 20, 23, 24, 129 (George), 133, 149, 150, 169, 170, 178, 180 (Georgiana), 194, 195, 212, 214, 216, 224, 339 (George)
KEATS, JOHN: on beauty, 136–39; and blushing, 6, 11, 157–81; and Byron, 206–20; and Christianity, 6, 50–53, 131–33, 262–77; as "Cockney," 2, 16, 59, 215, 224, 262, 319–25; criticism on, 1–9, 317–49; and fame, 11–26; and gender, 7, 317–49; and Greek culture, 4, 6, 50–52, 54,

261–77, 346; and Hazlitt, 222–58; as
humanist, 5, 25, 55, 129; letters of,
5, 23, 109, 235; and medicine, 2–3,
5–6, 25, 143–56, 163, 279–87; and
metaphysics, 7, 292–316; odes of,
110, 111, 121, 202, 223, 235, 242,
257, 298; physical appearance of,
168–72, 212, 329, 337–41; on poetry
and the poet, 22–26, 53–54, 61–65,
134–41; and politics, 274–77; and
romance, 68–85, 103–25; selflessness
of, 134–46, 233–36; skepticism of,
130; solitude of, 20, 216–17; and
women, 59–61, 199–201, 212,
218–19, 325–26

WORKS: POETRY
"After dark vapours," 286
"Calidore," 329–30
Endymion: A Poetic Romance, 1, 3, 4,
   11, 12, 13, 16, 17, 18, 19, 20, 36,
   45, 47–67, 68, 74, 108, 111, 115,
   116, 122, 123, 124, 135, 138, 147,
   154–56, 158, 161, 189, 190, 193,
   199, 211, 213, 223, 224, 229, 239,
   242, 244, 265–66, 267, 269, 270,
   284, 285, 286, 297, 298–99, 305,
   333–34, 336, 340, 341, 347
"Epistle to George Felton Methew,"
   15, 71–72
"Epistle to George Hamilton
   Reynolds," 3–4, 36–47, 64–65, 68,
   190–91, 194, 197, 198, 254, 263
"Epistle to My Brother George," 19,
   20, 108
Eve of St. Agnes, The, 5, 48, 58, 59,
   68–69, 70, 78–85, 91–93, 109–10,
   111, 216, 217, 228, 292, 321–22,
   330
"Eve of St. Mark, The," 97–99, 287
Fall of Hyperion, The, 2, 5, 6, 24,
   25–26, 48, 62, 73, 95, 111,
   111–12, 114–25, 141, 195, 198,
   207, 226, 271, 272, 273–74,
   276–77, 281, 286, 287, 328
"Fancy," 190, 229, 254
"Had I a man's fair form," 329
"How fever'd is the man," 193–94
"Hymn to Pan," 49, 264–65
Hyperion, 3, 4, 7, 18, 21, 25, 33,
   109, 115, 116, 123, 124, 195, 226,
   228, 246, 257, 269–70, 271, 281,
   283, 284–85, 286, 319, 346

"I Stood Tip-toe," 47, 53, 70, 72,
   118, 305, 311
"Imitation of Spenser," 206
"In dear-nighted December," 4, 296
Isabella, 68, 111, 118–19, 121, 195,
   198
Jealousies, The, 216, 217–18, 219
King Stephen, 95
"La Belle Dame sans Merci," 61, 89,
   95–97, 192, 195, 199, 239,
   326–27
Lamia, 61, 62, 89, 93–95, 110, 117,
   118, 160, 192, 199, 216, 217, 220,
   224, 229–30, 271–72, 327
"Ode on a Grecian Urn," 7, 38, 44,
   74, 99–101, 112–14, 195, 223,
   245–58, 271, 280–81, 286, 287,
   299–301
"Ode on Indolence," 103, 110, 121,
   329
"Ode on Melancholy," 99, 111, 121,
   154, 202, 296, 309, 326
"Ode to Apollo," 31–32
"Ode to Fanny," 119
"Ode to a Nightingale," 7, 63, 68,
   74, 99, 108, 111, 136, 192, 195,
   223, 229, 233–45, 246, 255,
   286–87, 293, 296–97, 301–16,
   337, 344
"Ode to Psyche," 72–73, 77, 111,
   188, 238, 271, 272, 298–99
"Oh Chatterton! how very sad thy
   fate," 206
"On First Looking into Chapman's
   Homer," 3–4, 28–35, 129, 340,
   346, 347
"On Seeing the Elgin Marbles for the
   First Time," 247–48, 256, 287,
   297, 308–9
"On Sitting Down to Read King Lear
   Once Again," 4, 68, 69, 72, 73–76,
   84–85, 108, 326
"On Visiting the Tomb of Burns," 4,
   17, 191
Otho the Great, 95
"Read Me a Lesson, Muse," 140
"Robin Hood," 229
"Sleep and Poetry," 2, 16, 22, 37,
   69, 70, 73, 76, 109, 162, 189,
   207–8, 210, 213, 254, 311, 327
"There is a joy in footing slow across
   a silent plain," 191
"This Living Hand," 111, 121, 125

"To Autumn," 49, 99, 125, 129, 202, 240, 261, 287
"To the Ladies," 287
"To Leigh Hunt, Esq.,," 264
"To Lord Byron," 206, 207, 223
"To Maia," 19
"What the Thrush Said," 139
"Why Did I Laugh Tonight," 140, 301–3, 305, 306
"Written in Disgust of Vulgar Superstition," 131, 264

Keats, Tom (brother), 16, 22, 129, 148, 171, 192, 194, 199, 227, 339
Keats-Shelley Journal, 1
Kern, Robert, 3, 5
King, Stephen, 95
Kingsley, Charles, 332
Kingston, John, 130
Kinnaird, John, 188

"La Belle Dame sans Merci," 61, 89, 95–97, 192, 195, 199, 239, 326–27
La Rochefoucauld, de, François, 12
Ladies' Companion, The, 321, 324
Lake Poets, 208
Lamarck, Chevalier de, 282, 284
Lamia, 61, 62, 89, 93–95, 110, 117, 118, 160, 192, 199, 216, 217, 220, 224, 229–30, 271–72, 327
Lau, Beth, 3: "Keats and Byron," 6
Lawrence, William, 281, 282
Lemprière's Dictionary, 122, 279–80
letters, Keats's, 5, 23, 109, 235; see also under individual correspondents
Lewis, C. S., 160
"light and shade," 236, 245, 256
Locke, John, 231, 285, 294, 295
Lockhart, John, 212, 320
Lorrain, Claude, 52: The Enchanted Castle, 4, 38–42, 44, 191; Sacrifice to Apollo, 38
"love and friendship," 155
Lovell, Ernest J., Jr., 3, 5
Lowell, Amy, 33, 206, 324
Lowell, James Russell, 338
Lowes, John Livingston, 272
lyric poems, 99

McGann, Jerome, 214
MacGillivray, J. R., 320, 324: Bibliography and Reference Guide, 346–47

Mallarmé, Stéphane: Un Coup de dés, 125
Manchester Massacre, 24
Mandeville, Sir John, 12
"mansion of many apartments," 132, 140, 216, 327
Maria Crowther, 201, 218
Marlowe, Christopher: Tamburlaine, 31
Marmontel, J. F.: Les Incas, 30, 33
Masson, David, 341
maternal image, 199
Matthews, G. M., 59, 333
medusée, 281
melancholy, 6, 155–56, 196–202, 207, 216, 264
"Men of Genius," 17, 23, 150–51, 230
"Men of Power," 17, 230, 328
Milbanke, Anabella, 214, 217–18
Mill, John Stuart, 107
Milnes, R. M.: Life, Letters, and Literary Remains of John Keats, 323–24, 331, 337, 338, 339, 340–41, 345
Milton, John, 6, 13, 17, 19, 21, 22, 26, 108, 109, 114, 115, 125, 132, 134, 135, 153, 159, 173, 216, 222, 234, 237, 263, 270, 271, 272, 286: Apology for Smectymnuus, 14; "Il Penseroso," 106, 115; "L'Allegro," 106; Lycidas, 13, 26, 101, 240; Paradise Lost, 20, 21, 22, 106, 107, 118, 123, 159–60, 161, 263, 269; Paradise Regained, 124; The Reason of Church Government, 21
MLA International Bibliography, 1
"mock lyrists," 207–8
Modern Fiction Studies, 88
Modernist critics, 2
Moneta, 25, 116, 120–21, 122–25, 198, 272, 273, 276, 277, 328
More, Mrs., 335
mourning, 6, 196–202
Muir, Kenneth, 3
Murray, John, 214, 231

National Review, 334
natural selection. See evolutionary theory
"negative capability," 5, 17, 38, 348–49, 43, 62, 63, 111, 112–13, 115, 117, 135, 136, 140, 146, 162, 184–85
New Monthly, 323
Newton, Mary, 339
noumenal, the, 292–316

"Ode on a Grecian Urn," 7, 38, 44, 74, 99–101, 112–14, 195, 223, 245–58, 271, 280–81, 286, 287, 299–301
"Ode on Indolence," 103, 110, 121, 329
"Ode on Melancholy," 99, 111, 121, 154, 202, 296, 309, 326
"Ode to Apollo," 31–32
"Ode to Fanny," 119
"Ode to a Nightingale," 7, 63, 68, 74, 99, 108, 111, 136, 192, 195, 223, 229, 233–45, 246, 255, 286–87, 293, 296–97, 301–16, 337, 344
"Ode to Psyche," 72–73, 77, 111, 188, 238, 271, 272, 298–99
odes, Keats's, 110, 111, 121, 202, 223, 235, 242, 257, 298; see also under individual titles
"Oh Chatterton! how very sad thy fate," 206
Oliphant, Margaret, 324: Literary History, 324–25
"On Edmund Kean as a Shakespearean Actor (article by Keats), 227
"On First Looking into Chapman's Homer," 3–4, 28–35, 129, 340, 346, 347
"On Seeing the Elgin Marbles for the First Time," 247–48, 256, 287, 297, 308–9
"On Sitting Down to Read King Lear Once Again," 4, 68, 69, 72, 73–76, 84–85, 108, 326 ʼ
"On Visiting the Tomb of Burns," 4, 17, 191
Otho the Great, 95
Ovidian metamorphosis, 117–18, 119
Owen, Frances Mary,, 324
Oxford English Dictionary, 32

paganism, 4, 47–65, 264
Paine, Thomas, 6: The Age of Reason, 274–76
Paley, William: Principles of Moral and Political Philosophy, 268–69
Pan, worship of, 265–66
Parker, Patricia A., 3, 5
Parrinder, Patrick, 247
Parson, Donald, 339
Pater's "moments," 125
Patmore, Coventry, 331, 334, 344, 345
patriarchal culture, 327, 349
Pegasus, 188
Peterloo Massacre, 274

Plato: Phaedrus, 188–89
Platonism and Neoplatonism, 54, 56, 267
"pleasure thermometer," 57, 147, 154
Pocket Magazine, 321, 336
"Poesy," 310–12, 314, 328
Pope, Alexander, 12, 213: Essay on Man, 322
Porter, Misses Jane and Maria, 60: The Scottish Chief (Jane), 60
Poussin, Nicolas, 52: Echo and Narcissus, 51
Pre-Raphaelites, 125, 336, 344–45
Priestly, Joseph, 145, 150
Proctor, Mrs., 339
protagonist, 90, 92, 94
psychoanalysis, 186
"purgatory blind," 4–5, 44
putrefaction, 279–81

Quakers, 269
Quarterly, 11, 18, 19, 322, 323

Raphael, 52, 248
"Read Me a Lesson, Muse," 140
Renaissance, 13, 212
repetition, 194–95
repression, 188
Reynolds, John Hamilton, 3, 6, 23, 36–46, 49, 63, 131, 132, 159, 164, 195, 209–10, 213, 215, 223, 225, 231, 232: The Eden of the Imagination, 209; Safie, 209
Rice, James, 21, 22, 175, 188
Rich, Adrienne, 348
Ricks, Christopher, 1, 3, 6, 11, 48, 347–48
Robertson, William: The History of America, 29–30, 32, 34–35
"Robin Hood," 229
Robinson, Mrs., 108
romance, 5, 60, 68–85, 103–25
Romanticism, 103, 107
Rossetti, Dante Gabriel, 331, 344
Rossetti, W. M., 333, 335, 338, 339, 341
Rousseau, Jean-Jacques, 230
Ruskin, John, 252, 335: "Of Queen's Gardens," 334
Russell, William: The History of America from Its Discovery by Columbus to the Conclusion of the Late War, 1778, 30, 31

Ryan, Robert M., 3: "The Politics of Greek Religion," 6

St. Paul, 270
Saintsbury, George, 346
Sanderford, Mrs. John, 323, 328
Schiller, Friedrich von: *Die Hören*, 279, 280
"sensation," 62–63
separation anxiety, 200–201
Severn, Joseph, 50, 131, 200, 206, 218, 339, 340, 347
Shairp, J. C., 346
Shakespeare, William, 15, 17, 19, 21, 22, 23, 69–70, 109, 135, 136, 152, 185, 198, 212, 213, 222, 223, 230, 231, 233, 235, 241, 244, 257, 263: *Hamlet*, 85, 217; *King Lear*, 4, 5, 43, 69, 73–76, 84–85, 137; *A Midsummer Night's Dream*, 244; sonnets of, 13–14, 18, 62
Shelley, Percy Bysshe, 50, 57, 130, 131, 134, 135, 139, 220, 275, 276, 293, 321, 332: *Adonais*, 322; *Alastor, or the Spirit of Solitude*, 52; *The Defence of Poetry*, 13; "Ozymandias," 89–90; "Stanzas Written in Dejection—December 1818, near Naples," 135; *Treatise on Morals*, 13
Sherwood, Margaret, 267
Sidmouth, Lord, 52
"Sleep and Poetry," 2, 16, 22, 37, 69, 70, 73, 76, 109, 162, 189, 207–8, 210, 213, 254, 311, 327
Smith, Alexander, 322, 333, 344
Smith, Horace and James, 129–30, 168: *Horace in London*, 130; "Nehemiah Muggs (Horace)," 168; *Rejected Addresses*, 130
"smothering." *See* suffocation
Society for the Propagation of Christian Knowledge, 52
Socrates, 132, 134
"sole self," 68, 243–44, 312, 314
solitude, 20, 149, 226
"sorrow," 296–97, 300–302, 310, 316; *see also* depression; melancholy; suffering
"specious present," 295–96
"speculation," 44, 55, 61–62, 64, 136, 137, 145, 183, 245
Spenser, Edmund, 4, 5, 103, 106, 115, 125, 206: *The Faerie Queen*, 31, 103–4, 110

Sperry, Stuart, 1, 3, 82, 202, 295, 313: "Keats and the Chemistry of Poetic Creation," 146, 147, 149, 154; *Keats the Poet*, 4
Stendhal, 12
Stephen, Leslie, 344
Stephens, Henry, 11, 206, 210
Stevens, Wallace, 74, 89, 106
Stillinger, Jack, 1, 3, 7, 68–69, 111, 312–13, 315: "The Hoodwinking of Madeleine: Skepticism in *The Eve of St. Agnes*," 5, 292; "Reading Keats's Plots," 5
Studies in Short Fiction, 88
sublime, the, 38, 42, 44, 116, 147–48, 149, 154, 233, 234, 247–48, 251, 252, 254, 265
"suffering," 79–80, 140, 207, 218, 239, 269–77, 296, 299, 312; *see also* depression; melancholy; sorrow
suffocation, 118–20
"suspension," 4–5, 106, 107–8, 110, 298
Swinburne, Algernon Charles, 323, 331, 332, 334, 344
Symons, Arthur, 346
syncretism, 272

Taylor, Jeremy: *Holy Living and Holy Dying*, 131
Taylor, John, 16, 20, 22, 59, 60, 138, 154, 165, 166, 167, 212, 213, 224
Tennyson, Alfred Lord, 125, 333
"There is a joy in footing slow across a silent plain," 191
"This Living Hand," 111, 121, 125
Thomson, James: *Castle of Indolence*, 103, 104, 110
Tighe, Mary, 209: *Psyche*, 60
Times, The, 341
Titian, 38, 39, 51, 52
"To Autumn," 49, 99, 125, 129, 202, 240, 261, 287
"To the Ladies," 287
"To Leigh Hunt, Esq.," 264
"To Lord Byron," 206, 207, 223
"To Maia," 19
Trilling, Lionel, 5, 20, 347: "The Poet as Hero: Keats in His Letters," 159, 348
Tuveson, Ernest, 186

unconscious, the, 6, 60–61, 183–202, 242–45

"vale of soul-making," 132, 133, 194, 202, 271, 273, 275
van Dyke, Henry, 345
Vendler, Helen, 303, 313
Victoria Magazine, 322, 324
Victorians, 2, 7, 257, 321, 331, 333, 336, 345
Vincent, Leon H., 346
visual bias, 186

Waldoff, Leon, 1, 3, 218: "The Silent Work of Imagination," 6
Ward, Aileen, 1, 3, 199, 347
Warton, Thomas, 104–5: *History of English Poetry*, 105
Wasserman, Earl, 7, 82, 293
Waterloo, Battle of, 5, 21
Watson, Sir William, 346
Wellington, Duke of, 15
West, Benjamin: *Death on a Pale Horse*, 38–39, 42, 43–44, 64, 129, 137, 147, 184–85, 254
West, Kenyon, 346
"What the Thrush Said," 139
"Why Did I Laugh Tonight," 140, 301–3, 305, 306
Wilde, Oscar, 336
Wilson, John, 65
wish fulfillment, 200

Wolfson, Susan J., 3, 7
Woodhouse, Richard, 11, 17, 21, 60, 207, 210, 213, 217, 233, 330
Woodring, Carl, 3–4
Woolf, Virginia, 348
Wordsworth, William, 17, 21, 50, 63–64, 71, 107, 125, 132, 134, 160, 168, 172, 197, 199, 209, 210, 212, 214, 216, 222, 223, 228, 231, 233, 234, 235, 253, 263–64, 293: "Elegaic Stanzas," 45; *Essay Supplementary to the Preface*, 16–17; *The Excursion*, 187, 195, 196, 222, 231, 234, 264; "I Wandered Lonely as a Cloud," 186; *Lyrical Ballads*, 107, 137, 187; "Ode: Intimations of Immortality," 99, 100, 139, 195, 196; *Peter Bell*, 195; *The Prelude*, 140, 187, 199; "Resolution and Independence," 89, 249; "The Solitary Reaper," 183; "The Tables Turned," 139; "Tintern Abbey," 90–91, 99, 100, 132, 140, 186, 195, 196
"Written in Disgust of Vulgar Superstition," 131, 264

Yeats, William Butler: "Sailing to Byzantium," 99, 111
Young Ladies' Book of Elegant Poetry, The, 321